D1326959

SPORT IN IRELAND, 1600–1840

For Eva and James

Sport in Ireland
1600–1840

JAMES KELLY

FOUR COURTS PRESS

Set in 10.5 pt on 12.5pt MEhrhardt for
FOUR COURTS PRESS
7 Malpas Street, Dublin 8, Ireland
www.fourcourtspress.ie
and in North America for
FOUR COURTS PRESS
c/o ISBS, 920 N.E. 58th Avenue, Suite 300, Portland, OR 97213.

© James Kelly and Four Courts Press 2014

A catalogue record for this title
is available from the British Library.

ISBN 978–1–84682–493–7

All rights reserved. No part of this publication may be reproduced,
stored in or introduced into a retrieval system, or transmitted, in any
form or by any means (electronic, mechanical, photocopying, recording
or otherwise), without the prior written permission of both the
copyright owner and the publisher of this book.

BAINTE DEN STOC

WITHDRAWN FROM
DÚN LAOGHAIRE-RATHDOWN COUN
LIBRARY STOCK

Printed and bound by CPI Group (UK) Ltd, Croydon, CR0 4YY

Contents

Tables, Maps, Illustrations

Abbreviations

b.	born
BNL	*Belfast News Letter*
c.	*circa*
d.	died
DIB	*Dictionary of Irish Biography* edited by James McGuire and James Quinn (9 vols, Cambridge, 2009)
ed./eds	editor/editors
edn	edition
EHR	*English Historical Review*
FDJ	*Faulkner's Dublin Journal*
FJ	*Freeman's Journal*
FLJ	*Finn's Leinster Journal*
GEC	G.E. Cokayne, *The complete baronetage* (5 vols, Exeter, 1900–6)
IHS	*Irish Historical Studies*
JRSAI	*Journal of the Royal Society of Antiquaries of Ireland*
MS(S)	Manuscript(s)
n.d.	no date
NAI	National Archives of Ireland
new ser.	new series
NLI	National Library of Ireland
NLS	National Library of Scotland
NLW	National Library of Wales
no./nos	number/numbers
NUIG	National University of Ireland, Galway
NUIM	National University of Ireland, Maynooth
NYPL	New York Public Library
ODNB	*Oxford Dictionary of National Biography* (60 vols, Oxford, 2004)
PO	*Pue's Occurrences*
PRONI	Public Record Office of Northern Ireland
QUB	Queen's University, Belfast
rept.	reprinted
RIA	Royal Irish Academy
PRIA	*Proceedings of the Royal Irish Academy*
TCD	Trinity College, Dublin
TNA	The National Archives, Public Record Office

trans.	translation
UA	*Universal Advertiser*
UCC	University College, Cork
UCD	University College, Dublin
UJA	*Ulster Journal of Archaeology*

Preface

This study of recreational sporting activity in late early modern Ireland is necessarily incomplete. There are many reasons. The most obvious, and the most material, is evidential. Even by the spartan standards with which historians of popular behaviour in Ireland are familiar, sporting activity is poorly documented. Other than a handful of hunts, there are no identifiable minute books, and no working papers of any of the clubs, organisations, societies or individuals that populated the sporting landscape. Moreover, since there were no dedicated Irish sporting newspapers or periodicals, only a handful of ephemeral publications (pamphlets, tracts, broadsides), and a modest corpus of visual and material artefacts for the era that is the focus of this work, the task of reconstructing the culture of sport is no less elusive than the particulars of each activity. This notwithstanding, it is an undertaking worth pursuing. Pertinent evidence on a variety of sports can be located, primarily, though not exclusively, in municipal documents, in the news and (still-more frequently) the advertising columns of the press and, occasionally, in personal papers.

The challenge of historical reconstruction is not eased by the fact that because popular sports were regarded with varying degrees of antipathy by those in authority, one is obliged, more completely than is usual, to read the surviving evidence against the grain. This is not to imply that the opinion formers, the guardians of public morality, lawmakers, newspaper owners and writers of various hues who generated the contemporary record regarded all sports with equal distaste. Horse racing was an unambiguously respectable activity. It possessed a dense network of patrons drawn from the very elite of society, and it generated interest in proportion. Indicatively, it sustained a discrete, quasi-official publication – *The Racing Calendar* – which is a useful repository of basic information on courses, horses, owners and subscribers that facilitates the location of Irish racing within its broader archipelagic context. Moreover, because the growth in horse racing profited from the expansion in the public sphere, it sustained a significant presence in the press, which permits one to trace its growth and evolution as Ireland's first modern sport in some detail.

By comparison, hunting is more elusive, though it almost certainly engaged a larger number of participants and was pursued across a larger social and geographical area. A number of hunt clubs have left minute books; it features in private and official correspondence; it also possesses a useful secondary literature, yet because it was not pursued in an equivalently structured fashion as horse racing, because it was intrinsically more local, and because it did not possess (or require) comparable organisational scaffolding, it is more difficult to reconstruct. At the same time, it bears positive comparison with horse racing, because it too evolved during this era into a recognisably modern pastime, and was possessed of an even greater capacity to transcend social class. Indeed, no other sport permitted participation from such a wide social catchment, though hurling and cockfighting, which profited from the patronage of the social elite, also possessed an appeal that crossed class borders. Inevitably, this was contingent on mutable social attitudes, with the result that long-time popular sports, such as cockfighting, went into rapid, and irrevocable, decline when they fell out of favour with the respectable.

This process can be traced through the press, which is, by some margin, the primary repository of the snippets of information that must be assembled if one is to reconstruct the history of sport in late early modern Ireland. A thorough trawl has been made of this literature, though one cannot claim that all the available evidence there and elsewhere has been identified. Other investigators may prove more successful prospectors and locate new and, as yet, un-mined evidential seams. This notwithstanding, the chapters that follow demonstrate that, like civilisations, the fortunes of individual sports not only rise and fall but also vary dramatically. Indicatively, a number of recreations that were strong at the outset of the late early modern era, and others that rose to eminence during its time frame had either faded from view or were in decline by the eve of the Great Famine, which provides this book's *terminus ante quem*. Among the sports that enjoyed such chequered fortune, bull-baiting, bear-baiting, dogfighting, throwing at cocks, popular horse racing and bowling were either pursued out of existence or simply faded away because the environment was unsympathetic. Others, like football, hurling, commons, pugilism, tennis and athletics enjoyed mixed fortunes, but they have survived in variant forms into the present because they were either reinvented or profoundly modified. The nature and extent of the restructuring that was pursued in the second half of the nineteenth century varied, but it generally involved codification to accommodate to the demands of mass recreation, or (in the case of pugilism) its transformation into a (by comparison) sanitised recreational pursuit. However, some minority sports, such as long bullets (road bowling), survived virtually unchanged.

Though the manner in which cockfighting was transformed from a respectable to a disreputable activity in the space of a generation spanning the late eighteenth and early nineteenth centuries is as emblematical of the direction in which sporting activity was headed as the regularisation of horse racing, the incapacity to penetrate the thinking and to construct a secure social profile of those who engaged in the sport severely restricts what can confidently be ventured in respect of this and other pursuits. Be this as it may, it is still possible to explore the manner in which the recreational impulse was exercised. The inhabitants of late early modern Ireland may not have possessed the opportunity, the structures, the organisations, the facilities and, it can be surmised, the inclination to play sport in the all-consuming way that it is a feature of the modern era. Sport then generated few, if any, dominant personalities and household names; the gap between participation and spectating was less defined, and rules, which were seldom written down, were still protean. Yet the inclination to play sport existed in a tangible and observable form, and it is deserving of historical investigation, both because it is a revealing form of social expression and because it constitutes a distinct phase in the history of the manner in which people have, and continue, to express the recreational instinct that is as intrinsic to the definition of what it is to be human as the impulse to create and the need to work.

By comparison with England, the history of sport in Ireland is still in its infancy, and most of the work that has been completed to date has focussed either on the modern era or upon tracing the lineage of those sports that flourish in the contemporary sporting landscape. A majority of accounts are manifestly the work of admirers, though there has been a welcome movement in recent years away from the ideologically fuelled narratives in favour of evidentially driven reconstructions. The present work is explicitly in the latter category. Moreover, it is first and foremost a work of recovery. Little has been written to date on a majority of the sports addressed below, but, this notwithstanding, the footnotes and bibliography attest to the author's debt to the scholarship of others among whom Toby Barnard, Neal Garnham, Liam P. Ó Caithnia, Tony Sweeney, Kevin Whelan, Martyn Powell, Fergus D'Arcy, and Paul Rouse deserve particular mention. More broadly, it is gratifying also to acknowledge the work of Dennis Brailsford, Emma Griffin, I.M. Middleton, R.W. Malcolmson, Wray Vampling, Mike Huggins and others whose accounts of the history of recreation in Great Britain has been of great assistance in guiding my attempt to identify, to describe and to contextualise Irish sport.

In so far as this book may be said to have achieved its purpose, it is for others to judge, but I am grateful once more for aid and advice from various quarters, and for the friends, colleagues, archivists, librarians and publishers who have contributed to the emergence of the text and the identification of illustrations. First and foremost, I wish to thank Matthew Stout for his cartographic expertise, Paul Murphy for generating digital images, and Ciarán Mac Murchaidh for his helpful observations on the evolving text, and other kindnesses. I wish also to thank Juliana Adelman, David Dickson, Paul Ferguson, Diarmaid Ferriter, Neal Garnham, Sarah Gearty, Raymond Gillespie, Maire Kennedy, Eileen McDevitt, John Montague, Will Murphy, Breandán Ó Conaire, Daithí Ó Corráin, Martyn Powell, Paul Rouse, and Ruairí Ó Cuív for advice and assistance at various points in the preparation of this work. More generally, I am grateful to the owners, custodians, trustees and keepers of the manuscripts cited in this work in Armagh Public Library; Trinity College, Dublin; the National Library of Ireland; the National Library of Scotland; the National Archives (at Kew); the National Archives of Ireland; the National Library of Wales, the Public Record Office of

Northern Ireland, and the Royal Irish Academy without whom this text could not have been completed. More than any of my previous monographs this study is based upon the scrutiny of newspapers spanning several centuries; I wish to extend grateful thanks to the librarians, library assistants, book retrievers and others in the National Library of Ireland, the Cregan Library at Drumcondra, and the Department of Early Printed Books and Special Collections at Trinity College, Dublin, who made this possible. For help with respect of specific queries, inter-library loans and locating rare texts, it is a pleasurable responsibility once more to thank Molly Sheehan at Drumcondra and the staff at the National Library. I wish also to express my ongoing gratitude to my departmental colleagues, Juliana Adelman, Carla King, Daithí Ó Corráin and Matthew Stout for their fellowship, collegiality and belief in the merits of disinterested historical reconstruction. Their commitment is equalled by that of the Research Committee of St Patrick's College; this book has not required a major financial injection to bring it to completion, but the support forthcoming from the Committee has assisted with the illustration of the text, and the production of the book in a cost effective manner. In that context, and for their continuing commitment to the publication of elegant as well as high quality academic books it is my pleasure once more to thank Martin Fanning, Martin Healy, Michael Potterton, Meghan Donaldson, Anthony Tierney and Aisling Farrell of Four Courts Press.

Finally, not having done so in many years, I would like to dedicate this book to Eva and James Kelly. Their commitment to sports not practised in the early modern era encouraged me to embark on this attempt to make sense of the manner in which the impulse that comes so naturally to them was expressed in the past. It may even give them some pleasure!

Dublin, 2013

Introduction: Sport and recreation in the early modern era

Dancing was probably the most popular recreational activity in late early modern Ireland. This is the implication, certainly, of the account of the customs and manners in Arthur Young provided in his much cited tour of the country in the 1770s:

> Dancing is very general among the poor people, almost universal in every cabin. Dancing-masters of their own rank travel through the country from cabin to cabin, with a piper or blind fiddler; and the pay is six pence a quarter. It is an absolute system of education. Weddings are always celebrated with much dancing; and a Sunday rarely passed without a dance. There are very few among them that will not, after a hard day's work, gladly walk seven miles to have a dance.[1]

The passion for dancing identified by Young was not a passing fancy, moreover. In early nineteenth-century Ulster, the memoirists employed by the Ordnance Survey to report, inter alia, on 'the habits of the people' commented routinely to the same effect.[2] Drinking and dining were other favoured recreational activities. Drinking was much engaged in by the peasantry of the countryside, by labourers and artisans of the country's towns and cities, while the enthusiasm for sociable dining spawned a proliferation of dining clubs, which sustained a drinking culture among the respectable 'middling sort' and elite once the associational impulse took hold in the mid-eighteenth century.[3] Yet dancing, drinking and dining did not constitute the sum of the population's recreational pursuits, or exhaust their recreational capacities. Different social interests also pursued a diverse menu of sporting activities. These changed over time. In the sixteenth and early seventeenth centuries officials who sought to proscribe bull-baiting, bear-baiting, hurling, quoits and others diversions

---

1 *Arthur Young's tour in Ireland* ed. A.W. Hutton (2 vols, London, 1892), i, 446; see also p. 366 for similar sentiments, based on Young's observations while in county Kerry.   2 For examples from county Antrim only see Angelique Day and Patrick McWilliams (eds), *Ordnance survey memoirs of Ireland* (40 vols, Belfast, 1990–8), ii, 23, x, 5, 13, 40, xiii, 15, 33, 56–7, xvi, 86, 99, xxi, 138, xxiv, 47, 132, xxvi, 28, xxix, 94, 113, xxxii, 37, xxxv, 23, 93–4. Further references attesting to the centrality of dancing across Ulster are provided in chapter 7, footnote 140.   3 K.H. Connell, 'Illicit distillation' in idem, *Irish peasant society: four historical essays* (Oxford, 1968), pp 1–50; Elizabeth Malcolm, *'Ireland sober, Ireland free': drink and temperance in nineteenth-century Ireland* (Dublin, 1986), chapter 1; for a preliminary account of the dining club phenomenon, and an examination of one such club see James Kelly, 'The Bar Club, 1787–93: a dining club case study' in idem and M.J. Powell (eds), *Clubs and societies in eighteenth-century Ireland* (Dublin, 2010), pp 373–91.

on the grounds that they were unproductive or culturally disagreeable promoted archery, longbow, and allied activities that fostered useful and practical skills, and when the latter proved irretrievable, supported the more edifying diversions of lawn bowls and horse racing.[4] Subsequent generations of law officers, municipal officials and opinion makers adopted an equally negative attitude towards throwing at cocks and cockfighting. Indeed, only hunting, horse racing and bowling enjoyed official favour across the time period engaged with in this book, and that was not unconditional: parliament intervened twice (in 1739 and in 1790) to curb popular racing. Attempts by the state (parliament, privy council, the chief secretary's office and the judiciary) and by local authorities (Dublin Corporation, for example) to regulate sporting activity were generally pursued by officials working on their behalf or for them (sheriffs, soldiers etc.). However, these were not the only sources of opposition. As the ideology of improvement permeated discourse, and the ranks of the 'middling sort' expanded in the eighteenth century, public opinion became ever-more critical. One of the more striking testaments to this was the augmented willingness of aldermen, lords mayor and sheriffs who embraced the prevailing improving vision to respond to public calls to discourage or, simply, to interdict activities that were objectionable, but they were not alone in this ambition. Vestries, presbyteries and the emerging civil society came increasingly to share this vision as the eighteenth century progressed, and with notable impact in the case of cockfighting, which was effectively forced underground in the space of a few decades. This was a consequence of the change in attitude – effectively the transition from a preponderantly permissive aristocratic sensibility that defines the seventeenth and much of the eighteenth centuries to the more controlled middle-class disposition, which achieved moral ascendancy in the nineteenth – that defines the crucial cultural shift from the early modern to the modern that commenced in the final decades of the eighteenth century. Though the outlines of this shift are identifiable in the rising trajectory of evangelical religion, in the emergence of a more focussed conservative political ideology, in the expanding critique of such emblematical features of aristocratic identity as duelling, the appreciating opposition to sports that the respectable found uncongenial was another manifestation of the fundamental cultural and attitudinal reorientation that took place.[5] Moreover, as the societal authority of this tendency expanded in the early nineteenth century as a consequence of the increased ideological appeal of political conservatism, the penetration of the main protestant denominations (the Church of Ireland, and the Presbyterian Church) by evangelical religion, the intensification of the associational impulse that had taken root in the eighteenth century,

4 Sir John and Lady Gilbert (eds), *Calendar of ancient records of Dublin* (19 vols, Dublin, 1889–1944), iii, 20, 39–40, 123–4; M.D. O'Sullivan, *Old Galway: the history of a Norman colony in Ireland* (Cambridge, 1942), pp 441–2.   5 Joseph Liechty, 'Irish evangelicalism, Trinity College Dublin, and the mission of the Church of Ireland at the end of the eighteenth century (NUI, Maynooth, PhD, 1987); James Kelly, 'Conservative Protestant political thought in late eighteenth-century Ireland' in S.J. Connolly (ed.), *Political thought in eighteenth century Ireland* (Dublin, 2000), pp 185–220; idem, 'The emergence of the middle class and the decline of duelling' in Maria Luddy and Fintan Lane (eds), *Politics, society and the middle classes in modern Ireland* (Basingstoke, 2009), pp 89–93.

and, not least, the permeation of the (initially radical) model of popular politicisation pioneered by Daniel O'Connell and the Catholic Association and its embrace of modern nationalism, its effects were more broadly experienced.[6]

The impact of this socio-attitudinal shift on sport was slowly felt, but essentially the kingdom went from a phase, spanning the early and mid-eighteenth century, during which the critics of sport contrived with minimal impact to curb the demotic sporting impulse, to a phase spanning the late eighteenth and early nineteenth century when their opposition was pursued with tangible results. It was not that the critics of sport wanted for either the vocabulary or the arguments with which to articulate their displeasure during that earlier phase. The perception that sports such as throwing at cocks, bear-baiting and bull-baiting were cruel and 'barbarous' activities was already firmly rooted when it made its first identifiable appearance in the public sphere in the mid-eighteenth century. However, it was kept in check by the limited opportunity available to disseminate and, thereby, to promote this point of view. This may be ascribed in part to the fact that the press was compromised because it profited from the paid for insertions and advertising placed by, and on behalf of sportsmen, but it also echoed a world view that did not empathise with the arguments articulated by those who adopted what may be described as an animal welfare approach to such sports. This is not to suggest that the public at large cared little, if at all, about animal welfare; the publication of critical accounts of animal cruelty, and examples of egregious abuse, demonstrate that there was mounting visceral opposition to the mistreatment of animals in certain quarters.[7] However, the threshold of concern was high, and there is little evidence to sustain the conclusion that the Irish public at large was any more animated on this subject than its English equivalent, of which Emma Griffin has concluded that animal welfare was not decisive in galvanizing either public opinion or the authorities to pursue the abolition of controversial blood sports.[8] This is not to imply that such sentiment was entirely without impact; it was merely one of a number of factors that were routinely, and increasingly ritualistically, trotted out by those who objected to, or who entertained reservations with blood sports.

Another objection expressed was that the pursuit of sport was a waste of time and an encouragement to idleness. This perception registered most directly with those who conceived of life in primarily economic terms, since the sight of large numbers of people embarked, either as participants or as spectators, on what was

6 James Kelly, *Sir Richard Musgrave, 1746–1818, ultra-protestant ideologue* (Dublin, 2009); Desmond Bowen, *The Protestant crusade in Ireland: a study of Protestant-Catholic relations between the Act of Union and Disestablishment, 1800–70* (Dublin, 1978); Andrew Holmes, *The shaping of Ulster Presbyterian belief and practice, 1770–1840* (Oxford, 2006); Peter Brooke, *Ulster Presbyterianism: the historical perspective* (Dublin, 1987); Fergus O'Farrell, *Catholic emancipation: Daniel O'Connell and the birth of Irish democracy 1820–30* (Dublin, 1985); Angus Macintyre, *The liberator: Daniel O'Connell and the Irish party, 1830–1847* (London, 1965); Paul Bew, *Ireland: the politics of enmity, 1789–2006* (Oxford, 2007); R.V. Comerford and Jennifer Kelly (eds), *Associational culture in Ireland and abroad* (Dublin, 2010).   7 See below pp 214–18, 227–8. 8 Emma Griffin, *England's revelry: a history of popular sports and pastimes, 1660–1830* (Oxford, 2005), pp 115–40.

perceived of as an exercise in self-indulgence, was an obvious target. While no sport could, or did, escape criticism on this score, those who inveighed most passionately were more manifestly convinced of the merits of their argument when they appertained to the engagement in sport of labourers, journeymen, artisans and others who did not belong to the kingdom's social elite. Neither horse racing nor hunting were exempted from criticism on that score, not least because they fostered gambling – opposition to which intensified as the practice appreciated during the eighteenth century – but the critique was more acute the more popular the sport.[9]

Though undeniably significant, the concerns expressed that sport involved the abuse of sentient creatures, that it fostered idleness and was a cause of lost production, were exceeded by some margin by those targeted at sport as the cause, and occasion, of violence and disorder. The nature and import of this criticism varied greatly. It was, with justification, persistently and intently levelled at throwing at cocks and bull-baiting. It was invoked with less intensity with respect to pugilism, hurling, football and long bullets, but because there were few sports that were not subject to violent disorder (horse racing included), it was an objection that could be levelled with the very real prospect of hitting its target. Since criticisms of this nature were not always sincerely felt, it is apparent that their articulation functioned as a semaphore for another still more acute concern – that of access to and control of public space. It is significant, in other words, that the sports that attracted most criticism were those conducted in urban public spaces, and that the sharpest words were reserved for bull-baiting and throwing at cocks because the practitioners of these sports were committed to pursuing them on the streets and open places (commons, green, squares and fields) of major urban centres – Dublin specifically. In this respect, Ireland bears comparison with England, where, Griffin has convincingly demonstrated, the authorities pursued a sustained campaign to wrest control of urban squares and streets on behalf of the public, meaning in this instance the elite and the increasingly vocal 'middling sort', from the customary claims of labourers, journeymen and artisans to take possession of these spaces on festival days and during the relevant sporting season.[10] However, this was not the full story, since no sooner had the 'middling sort' and their aristocratic allies assumed control of the main streets, squares and commons of the villages, town and cities of the kingdom that were traditionally the locations where such sports were played, than they sought to control more distant public spaces as well. This tendency may be illustrated by reference to the response to the attempt in the late 1770s to confine bull-baiting to the Phoenix Park, but it was still more visibly in evidence in the response to prize fighting (pugilism).[11] In other words, while the contests generated by sport were conducted within a rhetor-

9 This is an exceptionally grey area. For some interesting observations, see Emma Griffin, 'Popular culture in industrializing England', *Historical Journal*, 45 (2002), pp 626–7; and for prospective pointers Mark Clapson, *A bit of a flutter: popular gambling and English society, 1823–61* (Manchester, 1992), p. 14 ff; also John Ashton, *The history of gambling in England* (London, 1898, reprint 1969). For evidence of Irish concerns, see below, pp 70, 98, 108, 197, 198–9. 10 Griffin, *England's rev-*

ical discourse that was ostensibly preoccupied with animal abuse, interpersonal violence and economic cost, the discourse masked a more fundamental ideological struggle over who had access to and who controlled public space, which was in turn a sub-set of a larger attempt by the middling sort to achieve ideological hegemony by eliminating those diversions that they disliked. They were not wholly successful in their pursuit of the latter object, but they had brought it close to realisation by the 1840s.

It might reasonably be objected that this is too schematic, and, by implication, too simplistic a reading of the social meaning of the changing pattern of sporting activity that took place during the late early modern era, since the sports that stood securely at the peak of the recreational pyramid as Victoria *Regina* embarked on her marathon reign were the long favoured recreations of the aristocracy – horse racing and hunting. The commanding social position of these two sports cannot be gainsaid, but it is also true that the aristocratic generation of the mid-nineteenth century was palpably more confined in the exercise of social influence than its forebear a century earlier. This is the implication of the ease with which it was persuaded to forsake the great traditional symbol of aristocratic prestige – the right to be guided by their own honour code, and to determine disputes by force of arms – but it is equally manifest in the unconditional manner with which it subscribed to the culture of respectability embraced by the middling sort, and the convictions it enshrined. There were too many historical, economic and political differences for these two social classes to meld into one seamless whole, but the narrowing of the attitudinal chasm that occurred in the course of the late eighteenth and early nineteenth centuries was integral to the creation of the situation that obtained at the end of the Hanoverian era when traditional sports that the aristocratic elite had once favoured but from which they were now disengaged – cockfighting and hurling, most notably – were either in terminal decline, as was the case with the former, or in distress, which was the case with the latter.

***

If, as the preceding suggests, an analysis of the playing of sport is historically noteworthy because it is revealing of the society as well as of the exercise of the ubiquitous recreational impulse in a particular location at a particular time, it is also significant that the expression of this impulse was only slightly less developed in Ireland than it was in England.[12] It is essential for that reason if we are to achieve an appreciation of the changing nature, and the changing place of sport in Ireland to identify the sports that were played, and to reconstruct their individual histories. This is not entirely straightforward. The recent efflorescence in interest in sports history has not left Ireland untouched, as a review of the

elry, chapter 2 passim. 11 Below pp 228–30, 288–308. 12 See Dennis Brailsford, *Sport and society: Elizabeth to Anne* (London, 1969); idem, *A taste for diversions: sport in Georgian England* (Cambridge, 1999), and idem, *British sport: a social history* (Cambridge, 1992) for a detailed overview.

programme of the annual conference of the Sports History Ireland society since 2005,[13] and of the pattern of publication in the area attests, but it is also revealing of the precedence given to the modern era, and still more particularly to the Gaelic Athletic Association (GAA).[14] The GAA is, by some distance, the most successful sporting organisation in Irish history, but the disproportionate focus on one body, however explicable this may be given its popularity, provides a distorting perspective on the broader history of sport in Ireland and on our capacity accurately to locate Gaelic football and hurling in their proper (national and international) historical contexts.[15] This is not the primary purpose of this work. The research of which this study is the outcome, was guided by more modest goals, which are, first, to identify the main recreational sports that were pursued in late early modern Ireland; second, to describe their main aspects and characteristics; and thirdly, to locate them in their social, political and economic contexts, and thereby to embrace sport within the expanding field of historically-informed social enquiry in Ireland. Its object in short is to excavate 'the sporting culture of Ireland' before the emergence of modern organised sport,

13 The society was launched at a conference devoted to the history of sport in Ireland, which was hosted by the Humanities Institute of Ireland at University College, Dublin, on 18 and 19 February 2005. It has held an annual conference every year since then: see *History Ireland*, 13:3 (2005), p. 10. 14 This is not the place for a review of the publications on Irish sports history, or the strengths (and weaknesses) of their approach. It can reasonably be pointed out that beginning with W.F. Mandle, *The Gaelic Athletic Association and Irish nationalist politics, 1884–1924* (London, 1987), a strand of sport history has emerged which seeks properly to locate the history of the GAA in the context of the sports revolution of the late nineteenth century and to demonstrate that its games cannot simply be defined as 'national sports', but (like virtually all sports) are constructs of existing diversions, modern organisational impulses, rules codifications and, on occasion, simply inventions. However, problems with accessing the records of the GAA have served only to ensure that scholarly inquiry has focussed disproportionately on 'politicized leisure'; as well as Mandle, cited above, and his articles listed therein, see Mike Cronin, 'Defenders of the nation? The Gaelic Athletic Association and Irish nationalist identity', *Irish Political Studies*, 11 (1996), pp 1–19; idem, 'Enshrined in blood: the naming of Gaelic Athletic Association grounds and clubs', *The Sports Historian*, 18 (1998), pp 90–104. Traditional narratives are either premised on the exceptionality of Gaelic sports, or unduly reverential: see, for example, Marcus de Búrca, *The GAA: a history* (2nd ed., Dublin, 2000); Philip Fogarty, *Tipperary's GAA story* (Thurles, 1960). Paul Rouse is in the vanguard of a more focussed cultural approach: see Rouse, 'The politics of culture and sport in Ireland: a history of the GAA ban on foreign games 1884–1971: part 1: 1884–1921', *International Journal of the History of Sport* 10 (1993), pp 330–47 and idem, Mike Cronin, William Murphy (eds), *The Gaelic Athletic Association, 1884–2009* (Dublin, 2009). For a pertinent review of the subject see Neal Garnham, 'Sport history: the cases of Britain and Ireland stated', *Journal of Sport History*, 3:2 (2004), pp 139–44. 15 The tendency is most vividly in evidence in the myriad of county and club histories, which are as likely as not to take as their point of departure Archbishop Croke's historically problematic call on Irish people in 1884 (see *United Ireland*, 27 Dec. 1884, p. 1) to focus on the promotion of their 'own grand national sports'. Instancing 'ball-playing, hurling, football kicking according to Irish rules, casting, leaping in various ways, wrestling, handy-grips, top-pegging, leap frog, rounders, tip-in-the-hat, and other favourite exercises and amusements, amongst men and boys', he sought to sustain an unjustifiably national (and, quite evidently, gender) exclusivity. Examples of the histories referred to include: Daniel Gallogly, *Cavan's football story* (Cavan, 1979); Con Short, Peter Murray and Jimmy Smyth, *Ard Mhacha 1884–1984: a century of GAA progress* (Armagh, 1985); Marcus De Búrca, David Gorry William Nolan, Jim Wren, *The Gaelic Athletic Association in Dublin* (3 vols, Dublin, 2005).

for the simple reason that it has, in the words of Neal Garnham, aroused 'little or no interest' to date.[16]

Because, to reinforce Garnham's sentiments with those of Patrick Bracken, 'little research has focussed on sporting recreations [in Ireland] before 1884', it was a challenge at first even to populate the sporting landscape.[17] This is not to imply that there was no pertinent previous work on which to draw. Indeed, having identified the sports, or 'diversions' to employ the contemporary phrase, that provide this book with its subject matter, it was gratifying to locate literature that pointed to the existence of data that might otherwise have been overlooked, or that mediated information helpful to the preparation of this work. Particular mention may be made of Tony Sweeney's compendious 'guide to the Irish turf from 1501 to 2001', for though the author's 'word essays' leave something to be desired, the tables, particularly the alphabetical listing of racecourses and their distribution by county, distilled from the (English) *Racing Calendar* from 1751, were very helpful in the generation of a geo-spatial perspective on the evolution of horse racing.[18]

By comparison with most of the sports engaged with in this study, horse racing may seem to possess a sizeable literature. However, other than Fergus Darcy's admirable history of the Turf Club, most accounts have little to offer on the period covered by this volume, and even Darcy's account of the seventeenth, eighteenth and early nineteenth-century contexts is less securely anchored than it might be.[19] Having attempted, elsewhere, to trace the histories of the organisations that promoted horse racing in the eighteenth century, it was apparent in advance that the absence of organisational and personal papers precluded the generation of a comprehensive account of the sport from the perspective either of the centre, or of the periphery.[20] These gaps, notwithstanding, it is still possible to present a more detailed reconstruction of horse racing than of any other sport in late early modern Ireland because of the availability from *c.*1710 of data on individual race meetings, which can be interrogated in a manner that permits one to trace the emergence, development and maturation of the sport. Since a majority of this information takes the form either of advertisements announcing the intention to hold a meeting at a particular location, articles spelling out the terms upon which horses were admitted to race and meetings conducted, or reports bearing the results of races that had already taken place, there are obvious limits to the clarity of the picture than can be drawn, but it is sufficient, when leavened with official documentation, biographical information and the occasional memoir, to sustain the conclusion that horse racing was the kingdom's first truly national sport. It was also the most organisationally sophisticated. The inspiration for its organisational precocity was provided by

16 Garnham, 'Sport history: the cases of Britain and Ireland stated', p. 141.   17 Patrick Bracken, '*Foreign and fantastic field sports*': *cricket in county Tipperary* (Thurles, 2004), p. 4.   18 Tony Sweeney, Annie Sweeney, Francis Hyland, *The Sweeney guide to the Irish turf from 1501 to 2001* (Dublin, 2002), pp 54–83.   19 Fergus Darcy, *Horses, lords and racing men: the Turf Club, 1790–1990* (Kildare, 1991).   20 James Kelly, 'The pastime of the elite: clubs and societies and the promotion of horse racing' in James Kelly and M.J. Powell (eds), *Clubs and societies in eighteenth-century Ireland* (Dublin, 2010), pp 409–24.

Newmarket in England, which adopted a set or 'articles' or rules in the 1660s that, it was soon recognised, increased the likelihood that races would be conducted fairly. It may be, as has been suggested, that horse racing was obliged to take this step because it was a gambling sport, and because individuals would not wager on an activity unless they were convinced it was conducted fairly.[21] This is logical, and it derives additional authority from the fact that cockfighting, another gambling sport, was also one of the first to adopt a written code of rules.

As helpful as the publication of 'articles' was to the growth of the sport, horse racing was dependent on the burgeoning press, which gave it access to the public sphere. Information was critical to the operational efficacy of most sports, but particularly those that encouraged the participation of the public. It may be (though there is insufficient comparative data upon which to arrive at a firm conclusion) that horse owners wagered more heavily on private matches than they did on scheduled races, but be that as it may, the oxygen of information was crucial to the capacity of the sport to function, and it was instrumental in elevating racing from its situation in the 1720s when it drew select audiences to the mass attraction it had become a century later. Estimates of attendance during the eighteenth century are rare because few, if any, courses were enclosed, with the result that people could come and go as they pleased. But such information as exists suggests that the trend was (not consistently) upwards, and the profile of the public drawn to the Curragh and the Maze during the eighteenth century, and a smattering of estimates for regional courses dating from the early nineteenth, is consistent with this conclusion. What is less clear is the use that was made by owners, riders and punters of the more detailed information that became available in the 1750s. Since this information largely displaced the more accessible and less arcane commercial inserts that were normative during the first half of the eighteenth century, it may plausibly be surmised that it was targeted at punters in the first instance, and that it was integral to the expansive gambling culture that can also be traced to the mid-eighteenth century. In any event, the availability of this information served not only to ensure racing dominated the 'sporting intelligence' column that a number newspapers experimented with during the last quarter of the eighteenth century, but also to underline the importance of newsprint to the emergence of sport as a popular pastime. Significantly, it was central to the transformation in the 1750s of the Curragh, and to its successful negotiation of the transition from an earlier era when horse racing was an occasional event to a later period when it was a busy sport, and, as a consequence, to its survival as the kingdom's most important racing ground.

The contribution of print to the growth of sport was not confined to racing, of course. The frequency with which the organisers of cockfights used the press to announce mains is evidence that it was critical also to the growth of cockfighting. Hurling matches in south Leinster, and certain pugilistic encounters were publicised after a comparable fashion for a time. By way of contrast, the

21 See Brailsford, *Sport and society, Elizabeth to Anne*, p. 213; idem, *A taste for diversions*, pp 169–70.

medium of print was not resorted to by those sports that either did not need publicity, or for which publicity was counterproductive. In these cases, the sport only featured in print when it was the subject of pejorative notice in the news columns. This sort of information is not unproblematic, but it can serve as a valuable index of a sport's respectability, as well as a source of information on the nature, impact and character of the activity and those who played.

Apart from the symbiotic relationship that developed between the press and some recreational sports, which was advantageous to both, print was also the means whereby more considered commentary was ushered into the public realm. Certain newspapers were prepared on occasion to allow authors the space to dilate at reasonable length on an individual sport and its social consequence. Most commentary of this ilk tended to be critical, but space was also provided in the public sphere for longer, more considered essays, not all of which were hostile, which were presented as books or pamphlets. The single most important intervention of this kind marketed in Ireland was Arthur Stringer's pioneering *The experience'd huntsman*, which was first published in Belfast in 1714. It served not only to provide pragmatic advice on the art of hunting, but also was 'alone in writing at length about the nature of fox-hunting in the early eighteenth century'.[22] The publication in Dublin a year earlier of a satirical song of English origin on the manner in which the Whigs pursued Henry Sacheverell (1674–1724), the clergyman and controversialist, suggests that the public was already *au fait* with the vocabulary of hunting (though Stringer deemed it useful to provide a full glossary).[23] Be that as it may, neither the Irish print sector nor the sports' audience was sufficiently developed to justify such publications on commercial grounds for several more decades, when, emboldened by a veritable explosion in English sports-print, Irish publishers and Irish booksellers espied a potential market. Based on the fact that the 1760 edition of Robert James' (1725–99) *The sportsman's pocket companion* was printed exclusively in London, though sold by 'most of the book sellers in Great Britain and Ireland', Irish publishers were disposed to proceed with caution at first, but the publication four years later by T. and J. Whitehouse of an Irish edition of Thomas Fairfax's *The complete sportsman*, which was targeted at the owners of fighting cocks, may be identified as a turning point.[24] Even then, publishers were disposed to proceed gingerly until the publication in 1774 by James Hoey, junior, of Henry Proctor's *The sportsman's sure guide, or gamester's vade-mecum*. Though essentially a guide to gambling, Hoey's intervention was notable because he proceeded in 1780 to publish *The sportsman's dictionary*, which offered a guide to all aspects of field; this title proved so popular that he published a new edition,

---

22 Arthur Stringer, *The experienc'd huntsman, or, a collection of observations upon the nature and chace of the stagg, buck, hare, fox, martern [sic] and otter. With ... directions concerning the breeding and entring of hounds: also the qualifications and conduct of an huntsman, and instructions to a park-keeper, all gathered from the experience of thirty years practice* (Belfast, 1714, reprinted 1780); Emma Griffin, *Blood sport: hunting in Britain since 1066* (London, 2007), p. 126. 23 *The pack of bear dogs* (Dublin, 1713); see D.W. Hayton, 'Irish tories and victims of Whig persecution: Sacheverell fever by proxy', *Parliamentary History*, 31:1 (2012), pp 80–98. 24 Robert James, *The sportsman's pocket companion:*

'with very considerable additions and improvements', in 1786, and a further edition in 1792.[25] Meanwhile the publication, in 1778, of an Irish edition of Richard Brookes' popular *The art of angling*, and other titles targeted at sportsmen was revealing of the extent to which by then 'recreation and amusement', its many naysayers notwithstanding, was acknowledged as an integral part of the life of the farmer as well as of the gentleman and the nobleman.[26]

This realisation was assisted by the fact that as well as print, sport was a beneficiary of larger social and economic developments. The improvement in the country's economic fortunes in the aftermath of the grievous crisis of 1740–1 inevitably had a positive impact, but the augmented interest in horse racing that was so striking in the 1750s was a repeat of what had happened twenty years earlier, albeit on a smaller scale, when the country extricated itself from the more enduring, if less acute, crisis of the late 1720s.[27] The latter crisis reinforced the attachment to improvement already visible in Ireland, and while it is not possible to establish an equivalent juncture with the emerging associational culture, a link between the latter and the surge in sports activity certainly existed. It is readily detectible, for example, in the tendency, manifest in horse racing and hunting, for racing and hunting enthusiasts to come together in clubs that combined sociability and the promotion of the activity to which they were devoted. It was an early, but practical demonstration of the impact of the still-embryonic civil societal impulse that was over time to become a mainstay of sporting organisation.[28]

If, as this suggests, important aspects of the sports' culture that flourished in eighteenth-century Ireland were either assisted by or can reasonably be connected to larger social phenomena that continue to resonate, this was not true of all sports. There were some, blood sports particularly – reflecting older, residual trends – that sought grimly to resist the tide of change represented by improvement, politeness and the embryonic civil society favoured by many of the elite and middling sort. However, the assault on these activities was unrelenting, though the target varied, and its philosophical basis was flawed and inconsistent. At the outset of the seventeenth century, Dublin Corporation singled out bull and bear-baiting as the two diversions it deemed most exceptional,[29] and it was evidently sufficiently rep-

being a striking likeness or portraiture of the most eminent race horses and stallions, that ever were in this kingdom ... (London, [1760]); Thomas Fairfax, *The complete sportsman: or country gentleman's recreation, containing the very best instructions under the following head, viz., of breeding and the management of game cocks* ... (Dublin, 1764). First published in London on 1758, this title was frequently reprinted between 1758 and 1766. **25** Henry Proctor, *The sportsman's sure guide, or gamester's vademecum, shewing the exact odds at horse racing ... the whole forming a complete guide to the turf, the cockpit, the card table* (Dublin, 1774); *The sportsman's dictionary, or the gentlemen's companion, for town and country, containing full and particular instructions for riding, hunting, fowling, setting fishing, racing, farriery, cocking hawking etc, with the various methods to be observed in bleeding and dieting of horses, both for the road and turf* ... (Dublin, 1780, 1786); *Hibernian Journal*, 7 Jan. 1782, 26 Dec. 1792. **26** Richard Brookes, *The art of angling ... in two parts ... illustrated* ... (Dublin, 1778); *The universal sportsman' or, nobleman, gentleman, and farmer's dictionary of recreation and amusement* ... (Dublin, [1795]). **27** James Kelly, 'Harvests and hardship: famine and scarcity in Ireland in the late 1720s', *Studia Hibernica*, 26 (1991–2), pp 65–105. **28** Kelly and Powell, 'Introduction' in idem (eds), *Clubs and societies in eighteenth-century Ireland*, pp 25–31. **29** Gilbert (ed.,), *Calendar of ancient records of*

resentative of public as well as official sentiment since bear-baiting was rarely pursued in Ireland thereafter.[30] Bull-baiting was a different story. Though long favoured, the tide of opinion turned against it in the sixteenth and seventeenth centuries with the result that it was deprived of the official sanction that had facilitated the erection of bullrings in many towns and cities in Britain as well as Ireland in the late Middle Ages and early modern era. As a consequence, bull-baiting did not have official endorsement in most locations thereafter. A number of towns, such as Carrickfergus, deviated from this norm but they were exceptional. The situation in Dublin was more complex. Unwilling to submit to the wish of official and respectable opinion that the sport should be discontinued, labouring and artisanal interests effectively reconstituted the sport into a form of bull running, which they contrived to pursue in the teeth of intensifying official resistance and public condemnation. Though much of the criticism that was directed at this sport, and at that of throwing at cocks, was devoted to demonstrating that it should be eliminated because it was vicious and cruel, the case made was partial, and flawed, because it was not extended to cockfighting until the end of the eighteenth century, and not applied at all to hunting. This is not to suggest that those who alleged that bull running, throwing at cocks and, later cockfighting, were 'barbarous' activities engaged in wilful doublethink, but rather that they were guided in their positions by a social attitude that allowed them to conclude that sports such as bull running were 'barbarous' because they were perpetrated by social groups that had not embraced the civilised values to which they, the opponents of bull-baiting, subscribed. In other words, they did not object to bull-baiting, throwing at cocks, cockfighting or any other blood sport *per se* because it involved the abuse of animals, but because it was part of the cultural world – indeed the identity – of socio-economic interests they were disposed to perceive as inferior, and which they believed should strive to conduct themselves in the manner that they (the respectable middling sort and elite) deemed apposite. Indeed, they held this conviction so strongly, and engaged with it so uncritically, they not only failed to recognise that they were inconsistent when they declined for so long to recognise that cockfighting was 'barbarous', but also hypocritical because they simply refused to apply a similar critique to respectable elite sports such as hunting. The Irish arbiters of what was acceptable were not unique in adopting this position, of course. Emma Griffin has drawn attention to the manner in which the press in Britain 'filtered out' the criticisms of hunting articulated by philosophers and clerics in the emerging 'animal protection debate', to create a situation where 'working class blood sports such as cockfighting and bull-baiting stood alone as the only form of cruelty about which the respectable citizen needed to be concerned'.[31] This was an entirely self-interested perspective, but it was sincerely held for all that, and it highlights the fact that the social value attached to a sport was a crucial factor in determining whether it flourished or declined. With the exception of hunting, and cockfighting for a time, the withdrawal by officials and opinion formers of

Dublin, iii, pp xi–ii, 20, 39–40, 123–4. **30** Below, pp 233–4. **31** Griffin, *Blood sport: hunting in Britain since 1966*, pp 143–4.

their support for blood sports ensured that most were pursued during the late early modern era in an environment that was not just unsupportive, but positively hostile. Given this context, it is remarkable not that they died out but that they survived for as long as they did.

This is true also of pugilism, which emerged in the mid-eighteenth century out of a shadowy existing tradition of fighting sports, embracing wrestling, cudgelling and rudimentary pugilism that was energised by the example of its more developed English equivalent. Pugilism was pursued in a largely disorganised manner at a popular level for several decades until it was energised by a post-Union surge in nationalist sentiment, and the exploits of a number of talented individuals, briefly to become a high-profile sport. However, even at its most popular, it was a pale imitation of its better-resourced English peer, and when it was not able to sustain the elevated profile it possessed during its regency heyday, it went into speedy decline. Indeed, it might have disappeared completely had it not been periodically energised thereafter from abroad. More importantly, the broader realisation that it was necessary on occasion for a sport to re-invent itself if it was to survive provided it with a lifeline it was to grasp in the second half of the nineteenth century. Had the marquess of Queensberry not intervened and (re)invented boxing, pugilism might possibly have gone the way of a number of animal blood sports and faded completely from view.[32] It was a fate that might also have befallen the three team sports – hurling, commons and football – which were played during the eighteenth century, but which were confined increasingly to their core heartlands from the 1780s. It is striking that hurling, which was the most high profile of the three, enjoyed its finest moments, outside of the modern era, when the patronage of the gentry of south Leinster and Munster conferred a measure of social respectability on an activity that was otherwise perceived nervously by a majority of the opinion-forming elite. Neither football nor commons was afforded even that notice. Indeed, the general lack of interest among the respectable in both ensured these sports a marginal social place during the eighteenth and early nineteenth centuries, which bode ill for their long-term survival, and they might have been displaced by another team sport – cricket – which grew rapidly in the second quarter of the nineteenth century had not the emerging force of nationalism dovetailed with the Anglo-Saxon impulse in the second half of the nineteenth century to codify sport along essentially common lines to create the great international (soccer, rugby, cricket, baseball, tennis, athletics) and national games (American football, Australian football, Gaelic football, hurling) of the modern era. The price of this process, and of entry into the modern era, was not only that sports had to change (modernise) to survive, but also that others (athletics, for example) barely visible on the horizon previously were effectively invented. Still others, many of them already in distress, either fell completely by

32 Kasia Boddy, '"Under Queensberry Rules, so to speak": some versions of a metaphor', *Sport in History*, 31:4 (2011), pp 398–422; W. Russel Gray, 'For whom the bell tolled: the decline of British prize fighting in the Victorian era', *The Journal of Popular Culture*, 21:2 (1987), pp 53–64; H.G.H.C., *Amateur Boxing Association: its history* (London, 1965).

the wayside (quoits, pitch and toss etc.) or survived as minority sports (bowls, real tennis and long bullets) in which niche they have been joined by many others devised or developed in the meantime.

The implication of the patterns identified for the early modern period sketched out above, and delineated below, is that the fortunes of individual sports are ever changing, and are, by extension and by implication, always at some point on the graph of rise and decline that is their fate. The era between the early seventeenth century and the mid-nineteenth century – the late early modern era – with which this book engages was not, of course, hermetically sealed from that which preceded, or, indeed, that which succeeded. Yet, it can justifiably be argued that it possesses its own character, in so far as it was the during the early part of this era that the country finally abandoned the medieval sports that sought to inculcate skills that must prove useful in life – whether that life was on the battlefield, at the tournament, or in the more useful grind of food acquisition. It was also different from the populist sporting world that emerged in the second half of the nineteenth century when a combination of forces – nationalism and other populist ideologies, industrialisation, mass transportation, mass communication, etc. – permitted when they did not oblige sports to organise after a different fashion in order to function and to thrive. The resulting mass sports drew in many instances on those already there, but others were forced onto the margins. It has always been thus.

During the two centuries or so with which this study engages, the fortunes of several sports rose and fell. In the early seventeenth century in Ireland, the sporting landscape was thinly populated. Moreover, a combination of sabbatarianism that was a product of the energising of religious conviction wrought by the Reformation, and cultural suspicion, borne out of the displacement of the once-dominant Old English and Gaelic Irish by the New English, meant that there was little agreement on what constituted acceptable sporting activity. The New English elite liked tennis, bowling, hunting, archery and the long bow. They viewed the recreations of the Old English (which included bull-baiting and bear-baiting) uneasily, and those of the Irish (which included hurling) suspiciously, and would have liked, had they been able, to have eliminated them root and branch. Their major sporting contribution was to introduce horse racing. But because the population shift that took place in the course of the seventeenth century, which made Ireland English/British,[33] embraced social groups that had little access to and, possibly, little interest in horse racing, they also cultivated various new sports. Inevitably, these derived from or were energised by the plenitude of sporting recreations that the island of Britain, but particularly England, sustained.[34] The resulting sporting landscape that emerged in Ireland was never as densely populated with sporting activities as that of contemporary England, but once the kingdom had negotiated the mid-seventeenth century crisis and the social, economic and political order that

33 For contrasting perspectives see Nicholas Canny, *Making Ireland British, 1580–1650* (Oxford, 2001); Jane H. Ohlmeyer, *Making Ireland English: the Irish aristocracy in the seventeenth century* (London, 2012). 34 Brailsford, *Sport and society: Elizabeth to Anne*, passim.

would endure for two centuries was in place, a distinctive sporting landscape began to form. It was an identifiably, but not exclusively, anglicised sporting milieu with horse racing at the peak of a recreational pyramid that embraced hunting, bowling and tennis, cockfighting, throwing at cocks, bull-baiting, hurling, commons, pugilism and so on as one moved down the social pyramid into the plebeian world, though the social categorisation implicit in this ordering must be applied sensitively since most sports, to at least some extent, possessed an appeal that crossed the prevailing social divides. They also partially transcended the still more crucial religious chasms that divided the population. This is most manifest in the manner in which cockfighting was pursued in Ulster and hurling was pursued in Leinster during the mid-eighteenth century, but it was a feature also of other sports.

Be that as it may, the elite was by no means equally open when it came to sporting activity. Moreover, as the dominant social interest, and the crucial arbiter of taste, it was enabled under the guise of respectability, first to marginalise and, then, effectively to repress those of which it disapproved. It was assisted in this by a nexus of impulses – religious, social and attitudinal – which came together to constitute a new sensibility, and by the willingness of the state to assume greater responsibility in the management and organisation of societal affairs. As a consequence, it became illegal in the nineteenth century not only to throw at cocks and to bait bulls, but also to maintain fighting cocks. This brought about a palpable narrowing of the sporting options available to the public without ever resolving crucial ethical issues as to how much pain it was appropriate to inflict on another animal or other human in the name of sport – in other words the crucial question of how sport and animal welfare (and in the case of boxing, human wellbeing) might be reconciled was left unanswered.

Whether these issues ever can satisfactorily be resolved is open to question. Sport, as this study attests, reflects the society in which it is played. The ascendancy of horse sport in the eighteenth century reflected the ascendancy of a horse-loving elite. The ascendancy of popular team sports today mirrors the prevailing configuration of mass identity, locally and nationally. Such identities existed in a much more protean manner in the eighteenth century, yet the existence of county cockfighting and hurling teams warns against the casual assumption that county identity in modern Ireland is a product of the GAA. Sport assumed a palpably different form in the late early modern era than it does today, but it is instructive, and salutary, to explore it because it bears witness to the historical truism that attitudes, identities and outlooks are never static, and that what is popular in the sporting realm today may not be popular tomorrow. There may, in other words, be a day, when the contemporary public obsession with team games will be no more and the great modern stadia will stand empty – like the Roman amphitheatres – as monuments of a bygone era. Be that as it may, the sporting impulse will, one may assume, mutate, and, like religion, assume a form that reflects the mood, attitude, and cultural language of the people then living, just as it did in the late early modern era in Ireland.

Horse racing

Horse racing was the most successful sport in late early modern Ireland, and the first to make the transition from an occasional, into a structured, and identifiably modern, recreational activity. It was also the only sport, other than hunting, to achieve a truly national profile. Horse racing was not pursued equally actively in every region in the country during this era, but other than Leitrim every county hosted at least one organised race meeting between 1710 and 1840. The number of racecourses operational at any given time varied greatly, but, in the Curragh, where racing commenced in the 1630s, and the Maze, which was the primary course of the Corporation of Horse Breeders in the county of Down from the 1680s, the sport had two iconic tracks, with an uninterrupted sequence of meetings from the late seventeenth century. They provided the sport with two national focal points, though this fact was arguably of less consequence for its emergence and development than the high esteem in which the horse, and specifically horse racing, was held. As a result, once the Protestant landed elite negotiated the challenge to its emerging ascendancy presented by James II and Jacobitism (1685–91), they were ideally placed to ensure that the recreational environment they occupied conformed as completely as their political, economic, ideological, material and cultural world to their vision of what was congenial.[1]

Consistent with their geographical and ethnic origins, and their sense of themselves as English, albeit the English of Ireland, the Anglophone elite aspired to pursue English games. The sporting landscape of seventeenth-century England was replete with possibilities, but neither the nascent New English ruling elite nor those members of the Old English who were still in a position of influence in the early seventeenth century when crucial decisions were taken that shaped the sporting environment for several centuries, sought to foster the full menu of English sports. Indicatively, in a series of decisions made in 1612 and 1620, the patricians of Dublin denominated a number of new and established games as 'unlawful', and urged their discontinuance.[2] The absence of any reference to

---

1 See, inter alia, T.C. Barnard, *A new anatomy of Ireland: the Irish Protestants, 1649–1770* (London, 2003); idem, *A guide to sources for the history of material culture in Ireland, 1500–2000* (Dublin, 2004); idem, *Making the grand figure: lives and possessions in Ireland, 1641–1770* (London, 2004); L.M. Cullen, *The emergence of modern Ireland, 1600–1900* (London, 1981); idem, *An economic history of Ireland since 1660* (London, 1972); David Hayton, *Ruling Ireland, 1685–1742: politics, politicians and parties* (Woodbridge, 2004); David Dickson, *Old world colony: Cork and south Munster 1630–1830* (Cork, 2005). 2 Sir John Gilbert (ed.), *Calendar of ancient records of Dublin* (19 vols, Dublin, 1889–1944), iii, 20, 40.

horse racing suggests that it did not exist in a recognisable form. However, the nobility of the horse was acknowledged as warmly in Ireland as it was in England,[3] and it may be that a proportion of the emerging elite had engaged in, or had experience of, horse racing prior to their migration to Ireland, as it was an identifiable sporting activity in Tudor England, although it was not so described prior to the seventeenth century.[4] The earliest references to racing in England date from the early sixteenth century. The establishment at Chester in 1540 of a racecourse was thus a significant milestone, and organized racing also occurred at Durham, Richmond and Beverley. There were some three-dozen courses by 1625, by which time the sport had received a royal *imprimatur* from James I (1603–25).[5] The contested, and unstable, environment of Tudor Ireland did not lend itself to such pursuits, and the environment of the early seventeenth century was hardly more favourable even though, as at Londonderry, permission to host horse racing was included in the royal patents for fairs and markets.[6] In so far as can be established, it was not until the second of the Stuart monarchs, Charles I (1625–49), was ensconced on the throne that the first intimation was given that the sport might prosper in Ireland.

The early history of horse racing in Ireland, which is the subject of this chapter, can be divided into a number of phases. The first, spanning a century from the 1630s, witnessed the emergence of horse racing as a coherent sport and its rapid expansion, from a small base, in the first quarter of the eighteenth century. With firm foundations in place, the sport developed rapidly during the three decades that span the reign of George II (1727–60), as evidenced by the number of racecourses, and the number of race meetings. This was sustained during the following thirty years, though this period witnessed some consolidation in the manner in which the sport was conducted, which was taken still further in the 1790s. Then a combination of political events, attitudinal change, organizational developments and the further streamlining of the number of meets sustained a maturing phase, extending into the nineteenth century, that ensured the sport easily negotiated the changing mood that prompted a contraction in the number of recreational activities that flourished (albeit in some instances in the teeth of strong opposition) during the eighteenth century. As a result, horse racing consolidated its place as the first modern sport pursued in Ireland during the early nineteenth century.

3 See Barnard, *Making the grand figure: lives and possessions in Ireland*, pp 226–37; Arthur MacGregor, *Animal encounters: human and animal interactions in Britain from the Norman conquest to World War One* (London, 2012), pp 75–85. 4 For evidence that the New English were well disposed to horse racing see Tony Sweeney, Annie Sweeney, Francis Hyland, *The Sweeney guide to the Irish turf from 1501 to 2001* (Dublin 2002), pp 46–7. 5 Dennis Brailsford, *Sport and society: Elizabeth to Anne* (London, 1969), pp 28–9, 110–12; MacGregor, *Animal encounters*, pp 84–5. 6 Sweeney, *The Sweeney guide*, p. 47.

EMERGENCE, *c.*1630–1730

Though the Curragh properly takes pride of place in most accounts of the origins of the sport of horse racing in Ireland, the suitability of the surface has been highlighted at the expense of the appeal of the location to the kingdom's aristocratic elite.[7] Respectability was key to the success or failure of most sports in late early modern Ireland, and the Curragh emerged early as the country's premier racecourse because it appealed to the leaders of government and society. Its attraction was manifest in April 1634 when various peers and senior officials of government were present at the Curragh to view a match involving James Butler, the twelfth earl of Ormond and Robert, first Lord Digby.[8] This is the earliest recorded horse race to have taken place in Ireland, for though it has been suggested that 'about this time too racing began at Bellewstown', and that elements of the New English of Munster were drawn to the sport, reliable contemporary corroboration is elusive.[9] Indeed, despite claims to the contrary, one cannot confidently locate the commencement of organized horse racing in Ireland in the 1630s since the strained stability of Wentworth's viceroyalty was succeeded by the war-torn 1640s, and the repression of the Commonwealth, neither of which was conducive to organized sporting activity.[10] Yet evidence of horse racing on Youghal strand in 1653, and the presence of Henry Cromwell, as a guest of the earl of Cork, at racing at Youghal in 1658 is consistent with the impression, provided elsewhere, that the ambition of the Puritans to transform society culturally as well as politically and religiously was pursued with less adamantine conviction in Ireland than in England.[11] Yet the restoration in 1660 of the Stuart monarchy changed matters, as instead of a regime that at best tolerated sport, power was now vested in a king who regarded horse racing and cockfighting as genuine pleasures, and for whom a visit to Newmarket offered an opportunity to pursue both.[12] Charles II's example certainly encouraged committed loyalists such as James Tuchet, third earl of Castlehaven (*c.*1617–84), whose horse was beaten at the Curragh in November 1662 in a typical two-horse match run for £200 a side. This was a private race run, like others of its ilk and time, according to *ad hoc*

---

7 John Welcome, *Irish horse racing: an illustrated history* (London, 1982), p. 5. 8 Welcome, *Irish horse racing*, p. 5; Sweeney, *The Sweeney guide*, p. 343. 9 Welcome, *Irish horse racing*, p. 5; Sweeney, *The Sweeney guide*, p. 47. The earliest reliable evidence for racing at Bellewstown dates from August 1726 (*Dublin Gazette*). 10 Welcome, *Irish horse racing*, p. 5; Jane H. Ohlmeyer (ed.), *Ireland from independence to occupation, 1641–1660* (Cambridge, 1994); MacGregor, *Animal encounters*, p. 85. 11 Barnard, *Making the grand figure*, p. 234; idem, *Cromwellian Ireland: English government and reform in Ireland, 1649–1660* (Oxford, 1975); idem, 'Planters and policies in Cromwellian Ireland', *Past and Present*, 61 (1973), pp 31–69; Sweeney, *The Sweeney guide*, p. 47; Brailsford, *Sport and society*, chapter 4. For a recent, broader, assessment of Puritan attitude, see Bernard Capp, *England's culture wars: Puritan reformation and its enemies in the Interregnum, 1649–1660* (Oxford, 2012). 12 Ronald Hutton, *Charles the second, king of England, Scotland, and Ireland* (Oxford, 1989), pp 232, 277–8, 378–9; Walter Gilbey, *Sport in the olden time* (reprint, Liss, Hampshire, 1975), pp 31–2; MacGregor, *Animal encounters*, p. 85.

rules.[13] There was (in so far as one can tell) no initiative in Ireland equivalent to that pursued by Charles II, which resulted in the adoption in October 1665 of a set of 'original articles' to apply at Newmarket from October 1666.[14]

Though the elaboration of a set of 'original articles for the plate run at Newmarket' provided a regulatory framework that other courses were to adopt in time, the absence of an equivalent code was secondary in Restoration Ireland to the low quality of the kingdom's depleted stock of horses. Anxious to address this deficit, Arthur Capell, the twenty-first earl of Essex, who was lord lieutenant for five years between 1672 and 1677 and a supporter of the turf, cast around for solutions.[15] One scheme, proffered by Sir William Temple, who represented county Carlow in the Restoration parliament (1661–6), urged the establishment of a joint horse fair and race meeting, to be held over a week in the belief that this would improve both the working and pedigree horse stock. Predicated on the assumption that it was feasible to alternate fair days and race days, and that the presence daily of the lord lieutenant, or his deputy, would guarantee success, Temple's ambitious scheme verged on the impractical, and it was not taken up.[16] However, his suggestion that the endowment 'out of the revenue of Ireland' of a number of plate races, in the manner of Newmarket, would stimulate the improvement of the quality of native stock, was more in keeping with the sort of incentives contemporaries favoured. Charles II endorsed the idea, and £100 sterling was assigned for a plate race to be run on the Curragh. Since this venue was already acknowledged as the recreational *beau ideal* of the Irish elite, royal favour proved decisive, and within a decade the race for the king's plate was established as one of the premier occasions on the kingdom's social calendar.[17]

The combination of Charles II's endorsement and vice-regal support was crucial to the emergence of the Curragh as the Irish equivalent of Newmarket because it provided a focus for horse owners, and to the growth of horse racing in Ireland during the final decades of the seventeenth century. Its importance was particularly manifest during the king's plate meeting. Describing one such occasion in 1683, John Skeffington (d. 1695), second Viscount Massereene, commented approvingly that the meeting had attracted 'many thousands of spectators, and more coaches and ladies than I ever saw at a horse match'.[18] Moreover, the appeal

13 Sweeney, *The Sweeney guide to the Irish turf*, p. 343; W.M. Hennessey, 'On the Curragh of Kildare', *PRIA*, 9 (1864–6), p. 353; Barnard, *Making the grand figure*, p. 228. 14 'The original articles for the plate run at Newmarket in October [1666]' can be found in John Philip Hore, *The history of Newmarket and the annals of the turf* (2 vols, London, 1886), ii, 246–9. For the revised articles used in the mid-eighteenth century see Reginald Heber, *An historical list of horse matches run, and of plates and prizes run in Great Britain and Ireland in 1751* (London, 1752), pp 1–3; see also Welcome, *Irish horse racing*, p. 5; Brailsford, *A taste for diversions*, p. 170. 15 Essex donated a plate to a meeting held in the 1670s on Sandymount strand: Fergus D'Arcy, *Horses, lords and racing men: the Turf Club, 1790–1990* (Kildare, 1991), p. 19. 16 William Temple, *Essay upon the advancement of trade in Ireland*, written to the earl of Essex, 22 July 1673 in *The works of Sir William Temple in two volumes, to which is prefixed the life and character of Sir William Temple* ...(2 vols, London, 1740), i, 118–19. 17 Welcome, *Irish horse racing*, p. 5; Barnard, *Making the grand figure*, p. 228. 18 Cited in Barnard, *Making the grand*

of racing was not restricted to the residents of county Kildare and to the Dublin-based elite, who travelled in numbers to the Curragh for such events. There was a comparable enthusiasm in Dublin, if the presence of 5,000 people at racing on Sandymount strand in 1665 is correct;[19] in Munster centred on Youghal;[20] and in Ulster, as evidenced by Sir Arthur Rawdon's (1662–95) efforts to establish a race-course at Ballynahinch, and Lord Massereene's obvious pride when victory at the Curragh in 1683 allowed him to bring the king's plate back to Antrim 'where I hope it will abide'.[21] Encouraged by the evident interest in improving the quality of blood-stock to believe that a comparable initiative would pay rich dividends, a 'Society of Horse Breeders' was formed in county Down in the 1680s. This undertaking received royal endorsement in 1686 when James II approved a patent conferring the right to hold races, and elevating the Society into a 'corporation' (the Corporation of Horse Breeders in the county of Down) with 'governors and freemen', and a 'reg-ister' in whose name notices were conveyed, via the press, to the public. In 1690, William III granted '£100 for a kings' plate to be run annually.[22]

If royal patronage was a significant factor in the emergence of organised horse racing in Ireland, vice-regal patronage was still more important. Without the earl of Essex, it is unlikely that the crucial king's plate would have been secured for the Curragh in the 1670s, or that successive lords lieutenant, and lords justice, would have honoured the course, and the occasion, with their presence. It is noteworthy, for example, that Charles, sixth marquess of Winchester, was present in his capac-ity as lord justice, in September 1697, and that Henry de Massue, earl of Galway, and 'other persons of great quality' were present in the following year.[23] These were symbolically notable occasions because they demonstrated that the course, and racing in general, had negotiated the difficult years that followed the deposition in 1688 of James II, and the accession in 1689 of William of Orange. There was no reason *per se* why this should not be the case, given William's commitment to racing, but the military defeat of the Jacobites, the marginalisation of many Catholic families, and the imposition by the victorious Protestant interest of sanc-tions on the Catholic population was not without implications for the sport. The most pertinent disabilities, since they militated massively against Catholics owning

figure, p. 228. **19** D'Arcy, *Horses, lords and racing men*, p. 19. **20** Toby Barnard, 'The political, material and mental culture of the Cork settlers' in C.G. Buttimer et al. (eds), *Cork: history and society* (Dublin, 1993), p. 90; D.W. Hayton, 'A presence in the country: the Brodricks and their "interest"', in idem, *The Anglo-Irish experience, 1680–1730: religion, identity and patriotism* (Woodbridge, 2012), p. 90. **21** Barnard, *Making the grand figure*, p. 228; D.W. Hayton, 'A ques-tion of upbringing: Thomas Prior, Sir John Rawdon, 3rd bt., and the mentality and ideology of "improvement"' in idem, *The Anglo-Irish experience, 1680–1730: religion, identity and patriotism*, p. 183, note 31. **22** Walter Harris and Charles Smith, *The ancient and present state of county Down* (Dublin, 1744), pp 35–6; R.H. Buchanan, 'Downpatrick' in *Irish historic towns atlas: volume II: Maynooth, Downpatrick, Bray, Kilkenny, Fethard, Trim* (Dublin, 2005), section no. 21; Barnard, *Making the grand figure*, pp 228–9, 428. **23** Humphrey May to William Blathwayt, 16 Sept. 1697 (NAI, Blathwayt–May correspondence, 1697–9, MS 3070); John Dunton, *Teague land, or a merry ramble (1698)*, ed. Andrew Carpenter (Dublin, 2003), p. 104.

and developing quality equine stock, were those entitling the authorities, in the event of an internal emergency, to seize 'all serviceable horses, which are in the custody of any Roman Catholics', and the allied power (given statutory status in 1695), which permitted the requisition of horses worth £5. Protestants were not entitled, the frequent claims to the contrary notwithstanding, to purchase any horse they might fancy in Catholic ownership for £5, but the promulgation (in the face of the spectre of invasion) in 1692, 1708, 1715, 1716 and 1719 of the regulation requiring Catholics to surrender 'serviceable horses' in their possession was a palpable discouragement to Catholics maintaining quality equine stock.[24] It had no visibly deleterious impact on the sport in the short term, if John Dunton's account of his visit to the Curragh in September 1698 is to be believed. Referring to the 'vast concourse of people ... from all parts of the kingdom' who were present for the race for the king's plate, he noted approvingly the expanding infrastructure, and the 'severall fine horses kept hereabouts for the race in stables built for the purpose'. More pertinently, racing at the Curragh was no longer exclusively dependent on the exchequer, or a once a year affair; 'there is another race yearely run here in March or April for a plate of 100 guineas, which are advanced by the subscriptions of severall gentlemen', Dunton recorded.[25]

By the reign of Queen Anne, there were further improvements; the main annual meeting was brought forward to July, and the card augmented by the allocation of different plates to different races on different days.[26] More significantly for the sport as a whole, in February 1704 the Corporation of Horse Breeders in the county of Down prepared a set of rules – *The articles and orders agreed upon by the Corporation of Horse-Breeders in the county of Down* – to apply to all races organised by the Corporation. Though obviously indebted to the 'original articles', now nearly forty years old, prepared at the request of Charles II at Newmarket, the elaboration, and publication, of the Down orders set the standard for Irish racing by specifying the criteria that should guide the organisation of any well-run race. Thus, they stipulated that the names, colours and marks of competing horses must be registered well in advance of a race (fourteen days), and appropriate fees paid. The penalisation of foul play was an abiding concern, and several articles were directed to its eradication. To this end, riders were required to make themselves available to be weighed after a race to ensure they did not cheat on weight, while jockeys that did not ride fairly were liable to disqualification. In addition, a number of rules applied to spectators; they were instructed not to intrude on the course, and forbidden from bringing dogs or offensive weapons to race meetings.[27]

24 MacGregor, *Animal encounters*, p. 85; James Kelly, '"Disappointing the boundless ambitions of France": Irish Protestants and the fear of invasion, 1661–1815', *Studia Hibernica*, 37 (2011), pp 41, 45, 48, 49, 53, 54, 56; idem, 'Sustaining a confessional state: the Irish parliament and Catholicism' in D.W. Hayton, James Kelly and John Bergin (eds), *The eighteenth-century composite state: representative institutions in Ireland and Europe, 1689–1800* (Basingstoke, 2010), pp 49–50, 56, 57. 25 Dunton, *Teague land*, p. 104. 26 *Dublin Gazette*, 1 July 1710. 27 *The articles and orders agreed*

Dunton's account of racing at the Curragh, and the elaboration of the Down rules, sustain the impression provided by other sources that by the beginning of the eighteenth century horse racing in Ireland was not only commonly acknowledged as a respectable recreational activity, but also as socially and economically beneficial. This is not to suggest that it was held universally in high favour. The lord chancellor, Alan Brodrick (1655–1728), was particularly censorious; he described horse racing as 'an introduction to cheating, sharping, hypocrisy and lying', but he was in a minority among his social group.[28] It is not yet possible to establish how many race meetings were run each year during the first two decades of the eighteenth century, but based on the intermittent nature of the reportage accorded the major meetings which were run annually at the Curragh and Maze by the fledgling press, it can plausibly be concluded that their number was small.[29] Yet it can also reasonably be suggested that a significant proportion of those organisers who went to the trouble of preparing and publishing 'articles', which established the criteria that governed how individual race meetings were run, who was eligible to enter, the length and number of heats, the prize money and the appointment of judges, did so on the assumption that these were not unique occasions. If this is correct, one can suggest, based on references in the contemporary press, that the number of race meetings in Ireland rose seven fold from a modest two (the Curragh and the Maze) at the turn of the century to something approaching the mid-teens by 1730 (Map 1). It cannot be concluded that all of the fourteen meetings for which there is evidence took place every year, but the overall impression is of a sport that was riding an accelerating wave of interest. This is reinforced by the preparedness of 'a vast concourse of people' to travel from Dublin to a nondescript meeting at Bray in the summer of 1720, and the state of the sport was still more positive eleven years later when it was publicly observed in one of the main newspapers of the day that 'horse racing is become a great diversion'.[30]

This comment captured the situation at a moment when the country's racing fraternity could take satisfaction from the fact that by the early 1730s the sport had enjoyed nearly two decades of expansion. Its growth was assisted by a surge in new newspaper titles, and by the preparedness of newspaper proprietors, beginning in the late 1710s, to publish articles advertising race meetings, since this enabled organisers to reach a larger audience than was previously possible. The intervention of the authorities in March 1719 with an instruction to 'all

upon by the Corporation of horse-breeders in the county of Down, the 21 day of February 1703, to be kept and observed by all persons who shall bring a horse, mare or gelding of what size so ever, to run for the great and less plates given by the said Corporation; and also by all persons who shall be present at such horse-race [Dublin, 1703/4]; Sweeney, *The Sweeney guide*, pp 47–8. The only known copy of this pamphlet of four pages is in the Beinecke Library, Yale University. **28** Cited in Hayton, 'A presence in the country: the Brodricks', p. 92, note 83. **29** Robert Munter, *The history of the newspaper in Ireland, 1685–1760* (Cambridge, 1966); *Whalley's Newsletter*, 4 Apr. 1719, 9 Apr. 1722; *Whitehall Gazette*, 5 June 1727. **30** *Whalley's Newsletter*, 2 Aug. 1720; *Dublin Intelligence*, 5 Aug. 1731.

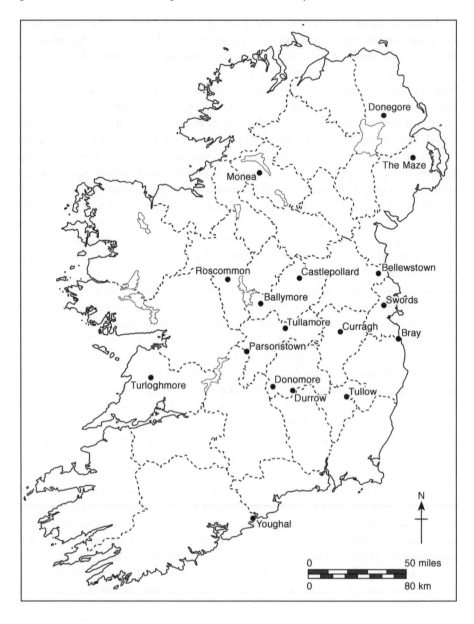

Map 1: Horse racing in Ireland, 1710–30: courses

sheriffs, justices of the peace, magistrates and other officers' to 'suppress all meetings at horse races' lest they were used to hatch, or to advance plans to endanger 'the peace of the nation, and safety of the government' in advance of a Jacobite landing, encouraged caution for a time, but within a decade the tide of sentiment had turned fundamentally.[31] It is clear, moreover, that the press followed and did not lead public opinion in this respect. The observation in Richard Dickson's *Dublin Intelligence* in 1731 that 'horse racing is become a great diversion' reflected his uncertainty as to how newspapers ought properly to respond to this trend,[32] but in this as in other aspects of public taste Dickson was in arrears of the editor of the *Dublin Journal,* George Faulkner, who replied to requests from 'several gentlemen' seeking race information, with the encouraging promise that 'if any gentleman concern'd in such races ... will send a particular account of such occurrences to the printer hereof, postage free, care shall be taken to insert them'.[33]

The increased press coverage accorded horse racing could not have taken place if landowners were not disposed, individually and collectively, to organise race meetings. A revealing early initiative of this kind, spearheaded by Clotworthy Skeffington, third Viscount Massereene (1660–1714), to provide for a plate race at Dunegore, near Antrim town, in 1710 succeeded in generating a prize fund of £135 15s. 11½d. from sixty local worthies. This was an impressive sum, though the absence of further mention of racing at this venue suggests that it did not survive the premature death of its prime mover.[34] By contrast, the two-dozen 'gentlemen of Fermanagh', headed by Ralph Gore and Sir Gustavus Hume, who agreed to subscribe a guinea a years for seven years were more cautious financially, but it is pertinent that the detailed set of 'articles for a plate to be run for every second Wednesday in May for seven years' to which they put their name included an undertaking to 'appoint' one of their number 'to be a collector and manager for the coming year'.[35] It was not necessary to be quite so ambitious in order for a meeting to get off the ground. One of the more successful early eighteenth-century meetings, at Roscommon, provided plate prizes in 1710 worth £5 and £7, and consistent with the quality of bloodstock it set out to attract, it explicitly precluded entry to horses that had run at the Curragh and at Turloghmore, county Clare.[36]

Nothing is known of the quality of the fields that were drawn to Turloghmore, but the context in which it was mentioned suggests that it

31 *Dublin Intelligence*, 31 Mar. 1719; James Kelly and Mary Ann Lyons, *The proclamations of Ireland, 1660–1820* (5 vols, Dublin, 2013), iii, no. 68. 32 Barnard, *Making the grand figure*, pp 229 247; *Dublin Intelligence*, 5 Aug. 1731; Welcome, *Irish horse racing*, p. 6. 33 *FDJ*, 29 Aug. 1732. 34 'Horse racing in Antrim in 1710', *UJA*, 2nd series, 7 (1901), p. 158. £75 of the total was subscribed by three persons – Massereene (£40), Lord Antrim (£20), and Clotworthy Skeffington (£15). 35 Barnard, *Making the grand figure*, p. 228; S.R. Lowry-Corry, *The history of two Ulster manors* (London and Dublin, 1881), pp 168–70. The absence of further reference may suggest they were no more successful in establishing a regular meeting. 36 *Dublin Intelligence*, 8 July, 17 Aug. 1710.

Map 2: Horse racing in Ireland, 1731–60: courses

attracted horses of sufficient quality to convince the organisers of the Roscommon meeting that there was a lesser niche they could colonise. There was plenty of competition for this space, however. Such was the quality of the blood-stock entered at the Curragh that the organisers of meetings at Parsonstown (King's county, 1718), Durrow (county Kilkenny, 1719), Swords (county Dublin, 1727) and Donomore (Queen's county, 1730) specified, in the words of the arti-cles advertising the meeting at Parsonstown, 'that no horse, mare or gelding that ever run for the Curra[g]h plate shall be allowed'.[37] Even the Corporation of Horse Breeders in county Down was persuaded this was a strategy worth pursu-ing; they advertised in 1727 a plate race worth £30 at the Maze course open to 'any horse, mare, or gelding that never won one hundred pounds in plate or money'.[38] This was sufficiently broadly drawn to permit entry to all but the high-est quality horses, but its invocation is a measure of the eagerness of organisers to ensure fair and competitive racecards that were open to all. The object plainly was to encourage local owners, riders and punters, while ensuring good sport. This could be a difficult balance to strike, but it is noteworthy that there was a tier of meetings below Parsonstown, Durrow, Donomore, Swords, and other locations (Ballymore (1718), Castlepollard (1729) (both county Westmeath), and Tullamore (King's county, 1730)), all of which presented plates valued at £10 or more, offering still smaller prizes.[39] The 'pair of silver spurs of forty shillings value' on offer at Tullow, county Carlow in 1718, for the best horse not exceed-ing fourteen hands, carrying 8 stone that had 'never run for above the value of five pounds' was plainly calculated to appeal to local horse owners, and this was the case also of the 'three guinea plate' reserved for smaller riding horses, known as galloways, that was scheduled for Bray commons in 1727.[40]

If the existence of these options assisted the sport to grow by allowing the owners of a variety of horse types to test the speed and endurance of their mounts against others of an equivalent capacity, the sport profited also from the efforts that were made to ensure that race meetings were well organised, and properly conducted. The key to this was the preparation, and dissemination, of a set of 'Articles' that identified the horses that were eligible, and specified the registra-tion procedure, fees and the code of behaviour to be observed on course. Though none of those that have been located dating from the early eighteenth century emulate the *ur*-text agreed at Newmarket in 1665, or in county Down in 1704, in length or detail, even the shortest conveyed key information. Take, for example, the articles promulgated in the summer of 1710 in advance of the £7 plate which was scheduled for Ranelagh Walk, Roscommon, in September. Consisting of a short introductory paragraph and three points, this was all that was required to inform prospective entrants that the race would comprise three three-mile heats

37 *PO*, 14 June 1718; *Hume's Dublin Courant*, 19 Aug. 1719; *Dublin Gazette or Weekly Courant*, 22 Apr. 1727; *FDJ*, 23 May 1730. 38 *Whitehall Gazette*, 5 June 1727. 39 *PO*, 23 Aug. 1718; *FDJ*, 13 Sept. 1729, 1 Sept. 1730; Minutes of revenue commissioners, 25 Jan. 1722 (TNA, CUST1/16 f. 53v). 40 *PO*, 19 July 1718; *Dublin Gazette*, 17 June 1727.

with a half hour interval between heats for 'rubbing' (point 1); that horses less than 14 hands would carry 7 stone, and that those that were taller would carry additional weight, to be calculated according 'to accustomed rule' (point 2). The third and final clause was more administrative; it conveyed the basic information required to enter the race.[41] By comparison, the articles published in advance of the plate meeting that was scheduled for Clonohill, Parsonstown, King's county, on 2 July 1718 were more expansive. As well as specifying the eligibility requirements, and weights to be carried (points 1 and 2), relaying that the three heats would be 'the usual four miles' (point 3), and that 'no more than half an hour will be allowed for rubbing between each heat', they also specified with whom entrants should register, and pay their entrance and other fees. In addition, it was also signalled that the 'judges', who were to be 'chosen mutually by the owners of the said horses etc, that run', would 'decide all disputes or controversies' (point 5). Since disputes were most likely to arise out of events on the course, the lengthiest point appertained to the conduct of the race:

> Every horse, etc, must carry their weight appointed through the course as usual or to have no share in the said plate, and every rider to ride fair leaving the posts on the right hand, none to jostle or cross only the two foremost horses etc, and that only the last half mile on penalty that the owners of the said horse etc shall pay the value of said plate to the owner of the horse etc. so jostled, or cross'd. Every horse must be measured the day before they run …[42]

Though the relative merits of the articles prepared in advance of the Roscommon and Parsonstown races were not the subject of public comment, the latter were so obviously superior that the more ambitious meetings from this point forward provided equivalently detailed guidance to prospective owners and jockeys. The fact that they routinely took a different form, and presented core information about eligibility, length of race, fees, registration, selection of judges and so on, in different orders and formats indicates that there was no formal template that race organisers were encouraged to follow, though the influence of the Newmarket, and the Down articles can be observed.[43] Clearly, there was agreement that 'articles' must be prepared and published well in advance of a race if the meeting was to be conducted properly, but each race organiser, including the Corporation of Horse Breeders in the county of Down, prepared and presented them in their own way.[44] This was hardly ideal, but based on those examples that have been located, it is apparent that by 1720 a set of 'articles' was commonly acknowledged as essential to the proper conduct of a race meeting.

41 *Dublin Intelligence*, 17 Aug. 1710.   42 *PO*, 14 June 1718.   43 *Hume's Dublin Courant*, 19 Aug. 1719 (Durrow); *Dublin Gazette or Weekly Courant*, 22 Apr. 1727 (Swords); *FDJ*, 23 May 1730 (Tullamore).   44 *Whitehall Gazette*, 5 June 1727.

Fig. 1 *Racing at the Curragh, c.*1730. This painting, by an unknown artist,
illustrates the way in which racing was then conducted, and the manner
in which those in a position to do so might follow the runners
(original in private possession; this image is from the photograph in
the Courtauld Institute, London; it is reproduced in John Feehan,
Cuirreach life: the Curragh of Kildare, Ireland (Dublin, 2007)).

While the obvious advantages to the public of a set of articles provided its
own justification, race organisers were also increasingly conscious from the mid-
1720s of the need to entertain. Though a single race, albeit one involving 3 or 4
heats, which was normative, could, with 'rubbing' time between heats, occupy
much of an afternoon, this was insufficient to satisfy, or fully to occupy, the gentlemen that most race meetings targeted. With this clientele in mind, the organisers of the one-day meeting at Roscommon in July 1710 promised
'buck-hunting' on the day following the races 'on the Plains of Roscommon' in
the expectation that this would appeal to prospective attendees.[45] Some twenty

45 *Dublin Intelligence*, 17 Aug. 1710.

years later, when racing occupied a more fixed space on the recreational calendar, and organisers sought to attract more than just the devotees of the turf, the
menu of options had expanded. The organisers of the meeting held 'on the race
place of Castle-pollard', on 6 October 1729, promised those who attended 'a ball
at night, and hunting in the morning'.[46] This was a palpable advance, and the
need not only to provide good racing but also evening entertainment, particularly
if women were to be attracted to racing, was widely recognised by then.
Indicatively, those present at Youghal races in September 1729 could occupy
themselves with 'plays, balls and other diversions every night', while it was made
known in advance of the three-day meeting held at Tullamore in October 1730
that 'there will be a ball every night for the entertainment of the ladies'.[47]

DEVELOPMENT, 1731–60

The surge in the number of advertisements and news reports appertaining to horse
racing dating from the early 1730s supports the conclusion that the sport had
arrived at a point by the late 1720s when it could embark on a more expansive
phase comparable to that underway in England.[48] The 'take-off' that ensued would
hardly have been possible in the absence of the recovery in economic fortunes that
followed the brush with famine in 1728–9, and the enthusiastic embrace in the
1730s of a commitment to economic improvement.[49] The expanded capacity of the
newspaper press was also important, since, like the marketing of proprietary medicine, the success of racing was contingent on its capacity to alert the public as to
its availability, and the press was the most advanced medium of mass communication available.[50] It was a two-way process of course; newspaper proprietors (like
George Faulkner), who recognised the opportunity, appealed to gentlemen to
report on recent race meetings, fully aware that the amount of free space devoted
to conveying results and news was substantially in arrear of the paid for space
allotted to the advertising of new or impending meetings.[51]

  Though the cartographic representation of the locations that either publicly
advertised their intention to host a race meeting, or that were reported to have
done so, is not an infallible guide, a comparison of the known location of race
meetings prior to 1730 (Map 1) and in the thirty years 1731–60 (Map 2) provides
a vivid visual demonstration of the fact that horse racing was the fastest-growing
sport in the kingdom in the second quarter of the eighteenth century. The most

46 *FDJ*, 13 Sept. 1729.   47 Ronayne to Grandison, 23 Sept. 1729 (PRONI, Villiers–Stuart papers,
T3131/C/5/47); *FDJ*, 1 Sept. 1730.   48 MacGregor, *Animal encounters*, p. 85.   49 James Kelly,
'Harvests and hardship: famine and scarcity in Ireland in the late 1720s', pp 65–106; Toby Barnard,
'The Dublin Society and other improving societies, 1731–85' in Kelly and Powell (eds), *Clubs and
societies in eighteenth-century Ireland*, pp 53–88.   50 James Kelly, 'Health for sale: mountebanks,
doctors, printers and the supply of medication in eighteenth-century Ireland', *PRIA* 108C (2008),
pp 75–113; Munter, *The history of the newspaper, 1685–1760*, chapter 7.   51 *FDJ*, 29 Aug. 1732.

striking statistical illustration of its appreciating appeal is provided by the fact
that the number of identifiable locations at which race meetings took place across
these two time periods climbed almost fivefold from 17 to 95.[52] The sport
expanded from its primarily Leinster heartland and an identifiable presence in 14
counties prior to 1730 to achieve near complete national penetration – 28 of the
kingdom's 32 counties – during the reign of George II. Leinster remained the
sport's core area, with 41 (43 per cent) of identifiable courses. This was almost
double the percentage (25) of Munster, which was in second place (Table 1).
Significantly, though the locations at which race meetings were held were not
evenly distributed either across the country, within provinces or within counties,
every county in Leinster and Munster hosted at least one advertised race meeting between 1731 and 1760. This was well in advance of Connaught and Ulster,
which provided the venues for 15 and 17 per cent of identified meetings. And if
one discounts one-off meetings at Drumcliff, county Sligo, in August 1732, and
at Enniskillen, county Fermanagh, a year later, the cartographic evidence suggests that organised horse racing had still not penetrated mid-Ulster and the
north-west by 1760.[53] The sport had spread from its Ulster core – counties
Antrim and Down – into Armagh and Londonderry, and from north Leinster
into county Cavan, but, private racecourses excepted,[54] it had registered little
impact elsewhere in the province. The situation was only slightly less bleak in
Connaught, where county Galway alone accounted for 60 per cent of that
province's venues (by comparison 13 per cent were in county Mayo and 20 per
cent in county Roscommon), but since Athlone, Roscommon and Castlebar each
hosted high-profile meetings the regional disparity is not as marked there as it
was in Ulster. Indeed, access to a race meeting for much of the population of
Connaught was only marginally more challenging than it was for the inhabitants
of counties Waterford, Wexford, Longford and Louth, which possessed only one
identified racecourse, though in each of these cases there were readily accessible
alternatives in bordering counties.

As these figures intimate, the 1730s and 1750s – the two decades that registered the most marked expansion – witnessed the inauguration of a host of new
racecourses. Eager to attract owners and punters, those responsible contrived as
best they could to make the most of this fact. Thus, the ambitious organisers of
a meeting at Athlone let it be known in June 1731 that the six days of racing
they planned would be run on alternate days on the two 'new courses' available
to them, one on the 'Connaught side of Athlone' at Monksland in county

---

52 Athlone is counted twice because it sustained courses on both sides of the river Shannon, one
in county Roscommon and one in county Westmeath. **53** *PO*, 22 July 1732, 17 July 1733. **54**
Information on the location of private courses is outside the range of this study, but it is sugges-
tive that Alexander Saunderson, 'a spend thrift and a gambler' established a course at Castle
Saunderson, county Cavan, and that there were courses also on the estates of the Cootes of
Cootehill, in the same county, and Dawsons of Dartrey, county Monaghan: Winifred Curtin, 'The
Saundersons of Castle Saunderson', *Breifne*, 10:39 (2003), p. 96.

Table 1: Race meetings by province and county, 1731–60							
LEINSTER		**MUNSTER**		**CONNAUGHT**		**ULSTER**	
County	*Number*	*County*	*Number*	*County*	*Number*	*County*	*Number*
Louth	1	Kerry	3	Galway	9	Antrim	6
Meath	7	Cork	7	Roscommon	3	Down	2
Longford	1	Waterford	1	Mayo	2	Armagh	3
W'meath	4	Limerick	6	Sligo	1	L'derry	1
Dublin	9	Tipperary	5	Leitrim	–	Fermanagh	1
Kildare	5	Clare	2			Cavan	3
Wicklow	3					Monaghan	–
King's County	2					Tyrone	–
Queen's County	3					Donegal	–
Kilkenny	2						
Carlow	3						
Wexford	1						
Total (%)	41 (43)		24 (25)		15 (15)		16 (17)

Source: *Faulkner's Dublin Journal*, 1731–48; *Dublin Intelligence*, 1731; *Pue's Occurrences*, 1731–59; *Dublin Gazette*, 1732–3, 1741–3, 1760; *Dublin Evening Post*, 1733–5; *Dublin Newsletter*, 1743; *Dublin Weekly Journal*, 1748; *Dublin Courant*, 1748, 1751; *Munster Journal*, 1749–51; *Universal Advertiser*, 1753–60; *Public Gazetteer*, 1759–60; *Belfast News Letter*, 1752–60; Tony Sweeney et al., *The Sweeney guide to the Irish turf from 1501 to 2001* (Dublin 2002).

Roscommon and the other on 'the Leinster side'.[55] The organisers were clearly taking a risk in bi-locating, but their ambition seemed justified as the inaugural meeting was so successful it elicited some rhapsodic forecasts that Athlone could become the most popular racing venue on the island:

> The new courses are generally approved of, and it is not doubted but their convenient situation in the centre of the kingdom, and the great accommodation of private lodgings with which the town abounds, will make the horse races of Athlone the most resorted to of any in the kingdom.[56]

David Kennedy of Belfast also harboured grand ambitions for 'the new course' on the 'county of Antrim side' of that port town but since, by his own admission, the plates he had to offer during the three-day meeting that he organised in October 1731 were 'not so valuable', caution was justified.[57] New courses at Gort and Castleblakeney (county Galway), Longford (county Longford), Minola

55 *PO*, 29 June 1731.   56 *FDJ*, 14 Aug. 1731.   57 *FDJ*, 16 Oct. 1731

(county Mayo), Ahoghill (county Antrim), Enniskillen (county Fermanagh), Tralee (county Kerry) and elsewhere, were inaugurated in the early 1730s with comparably confident expectations, which were not always realised.[58]

The reasons why courses failed to prosper varied. In some cases, it is clear that the meeting was conceived of as a unique event; one may instance Drumcliff, county Sligo, which was the location of a race meeting in 1732 whose primary purpose was to auction the pedigree horses of John Phibb, 'about 80 in number, consisting of saddle horses, breeding mares, colts and fillys'.[59] In other instances – Belfast and Enniskillen may be cited – the inability of the organiser to provide prizes of sufficient quality to attract horses and spectators suggests that these meetings were not financially viable.[60] This was not always immediately apparent. The report on the race meeting at Ahoghill in north county Antrim in 1732 was extremely positive. It observed that 'the appearance of gentlemen and ladies was so numerous, and the entertainment so good, that there have been large subscriptions made for the next year's races, where, it's hoped, gentlemen from most parts of the kingdom will partake of the diversion'. One might be excused for concluding, based on this warm endorsement, that this race meeting was set fair to become an annual event, but this is not what happened.[61] Racing at Ahoghill never took off, and it quickly disappeared from view. Even Athlone, which commenced so confidently in 1731, and aspired in 1732 to catapult itself to the forefront of Irish racing with a 'hundred pound plate', was obliged to scale back. The highest value plate competed for in 1732 was £20, and the total prize fund a disappointing £80. Local officials ensured there was a further meeting in 1733, for plates subscribed by local gentlemen, but it was held over two rather than six days, and the decision in 1734 to postpone the meeting by a week demonstrated that even this reduced card could not be guaranteed. The absence of any reference to the meeting thereafter suggests it went into prolonged hibernation until it was revived in the 1760s.[62]

If the misfortunes of Ahoghill and Athlone offer some perspective as to how difficult it was to identify the elusive formula that would guarantee success, the large number of courses that flickered still more briefly indicates just how ephemeral most courses were in practice. However, such was the level of interest that there were others prepared to take their place. Indicatively, when 'the people of the town' of Armagh contrived in 1731 to frustrate the attempt of local interests to take control of the town commons 'by making a horse-course round about them', they achieved only a temporary victory; Armagh Commons functioned as a racecourse for a time in the 1750s (Fig. 2) before it was supplanted by another location.[63] There are few examples as clear-cut as Armagh to demon-

---

58 *PO*, 21 Aug. 1731, 6 June 1732; *FDJ*, 24 Oct. 1732, 4 Sept. 1733, 20 May 1735, 7 July 1739. **59** *PO*, 22 July 1732. One may also place the race and horse auction on Beltra Strand, county Sligo, in 1768 in this category; its purpose was 'to encourage the breeding in this county [of] serviceable road horses and hack hunters': *Public Gazetteer*, 9 Aug. 1768. **60** *PO*, 17 July 1733. **61** *FDJ*, 24 Oct. 1732. **62** *PO*, 6, 24 June 1732, 17 July 1733; *FDJ*, 27 Aug. 1734. **63** *Dublin Intelligence*, 5

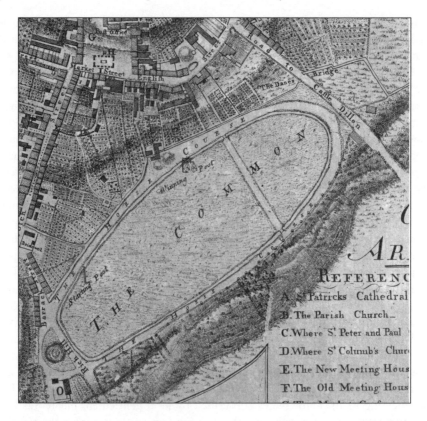

Fig. 2 Racecourse on Armagh commons, *c.*1760, from John Rocque, 'Plan of Armagh city' in *Carte topographique* (London, 1760) (by permission of the Royal Irish Academy).

strate that enthusiasm was not a sufficient foundation upon which to build a successful racecourse. More usually, it was unrealistic financial, organisational and geographical assumptions, singly or severally, that accounted for the brief lives of courses. The list is long, but one may instance Ahoghill (county Antrim), Magherafelt (county Londonderry), Kilfinane (county Limerick), Dunmanway (county Cork), Waterford (county Waterford), Rathvilly (county Carlow), Dunmore (Queen's county), Longford (county Longford), Clane and Kilcock (county Kildare), Gorey (county Wexford), and Ardrahan, Gort and Headford (county Galway) in the 1730s alone.[64] Subsequently, Castlelyons and Ovens (county Cork), Kilmallock, Loghmore (county Limerick), Dingle (county Kerry), Bailieborough (county Cavan), Ballymore-Eustace (county Kildare), Aughrim and

Aug. 1731; *BNL*, 7, 17 Aug. 1753.   **64** *FDJ*, 11 Sept. 1731, 24 Oct., 12 Dec. 1732, 4 Sept. 1733, 5 Aug. 1738, 15 July 1740; *PO*, 15, 26 June, 10, 21 Aug. 1731, 15 July 1732, 4, 8 Sept. 1733, 6, 20 Sept. 1735, 8 June 1736; *Dublin Evening Post*, 23 Aug, 1733; D.F. Fleming, 'The government and politics of provincial Ireland, 1691–1761' (Oxford University, DPhil, 2006), p. 142.

Galway (county Galway) failed in the 1740s;[65] and Carrigaline, Cork (county Cork), Cavan (county Cavan), Comber (county Down), Lurgan (county Armagh), Killarney (county Kerry), Anglesborough (county Limerick), Bagenalstown (county Carlow), Kilbeggan (county Westmeath), and Boyle (county Roscommon) did not survive the 1750s.[66] A significant proportion of these courses were, it will be noted, either attached to small settlements, or disadvantageously located in terms of the country's primary communication routes. This is not to imply that where these circumstances obtained a course was destined to fail, but simply to identify these as two obstacles that many young courses failed to overcome. Broughshane and Antrim town (both in county Antrim) were hardly more advantageously located than Ahoghill or Magherafelt, yet they operated for several decades from the 1750s.[67] Other courses inaugurated during the three decades 1731–60 that became fixtures on the landscape include Tralee (county Kerry), Mallow (county Cork), Cashel and Fethard (county Tipperary), Carlow (county Carlow), Bellewstown and Trim (county Meath) (1730s);[68] Mullingar (county Westmeath), Corofin (county Clare), Clogheen (county Tipperary), and Ballinasloe (county Galway) (1740s);[69] Rathkeale (county Limerick), Morragh (county Wicklow), and Loughrea and Tuam (county Galway) (1750s).[70] Still others, like Glenarm (county Antrim), Armagh and Richhill (county Armagh), Assollas (county Clare), Youghal (county Cork), Roscrea (county Tipperary), Finglas, Crumlin and Swords (county Dublin), Parsonstown and Tullamore (King's county), Boyerstown (county Meath), Kilcoole (county Wicklow), Castleblakeney and Eyrecourt (county Galway), and Castlebar (county Mayo) enjoyed briefer or more fitful moments in the limelight.[71] Their transience notwithstanding, their very existence was evidence of the excitement the sport generated in the middle decades of the eighteenth century.

In keeping with the pattern established during the early eighteenth century, the prime movers in the initiation of horse racing in the 1730s, 1740s and 1750s were local landowners. This was consistent with the enduring passion for horses manifested by the Irish aristocracy and gentry, but it was augmented at this time

65 *PO*, 4 Aug. 1747; *Munster Journal*, 22 May, 17 July, 24 Aug., 14 Sept. 1749; Tom Finn, 'A race ball at Dingle in 1746', *The Kerry Magazine*, 12 (2001), pp 43–4. 66 *Munster Journal*, 6 Sept. 1750; *UA*, 22 May, 21 Aug., 22 Sept., 6 Oct. 1753, 11 Apr., 7, 11 May, 2, 6 July 1754, 19 Aug., 2 Sept. 1755; *BNL*, 31 July 1753, 27 July 1756. 67 *Munster Journal*, 15 Oct. 1750 (Broughshane); *UA*, 14, 17 June 1755 (Antrim). 68 *PO*, 21 Aug. 1731, 28 Mar., 6 June, 22 July 1732, 8 July 1736, 7 Aug. 1739; *Dublin Gazette*, 11 Aug. 1733; *Dublin Evening Post*, 7 June 1735; *FDJ*, 1 Oct. 1734, 12 July 1737, 13 May, 25 Oct. 1740, 3 Sept. 1748. 69 *FDJ*, 2 Sept. 1740, 24 Mar. 1743, 6 Sept. 1748; *PO*, 5 Sept. 1741, 6 Sept. 1748; *Munster Journal*, 15 Mar. 1750, 11 Mar. 1751. 70 *UA*, 14 Aug. 1753, 17 Aug., 21 Sept., 26 Oct. 1754, 3 May, 19 June 1755. 71 *PO*, 27 Mar, 29 June, 20 Aug. 1731; 12 Aug. 1735, 25 June 1743, 13 Aug. 1745, 13 Sept. 1748; *FDJ*, 13 Apr. 1731, 6 June, 8 Aug., 9 Dec. 1732, 3 Apr., 17 July 1733, 31 May 1749, 29 June 1742, 14 May 1743, 17 Sept. 1748; *Dublin Weekly Journal*, 4 June 1748; *Munster Journal*, 5 Oct. 1749, 16 Aug. 1750; *UA*, 2 Nov. 1754. I have retained the contemporary spelling Assollas rather than adopt the present day versions – Ardsallis, or Ardsollus.

Fig. 3 Sir Edward O'Brien, 2nd baronet (1705–65) of Dromoland, MP for
county Clare, 1727–65, who was 'mad keen on horses' (reproduced from
Donough O'Brien, *History of the O'Briens* (London, 1949)).

by the perception that the development of native bloodlines dovetailed with the
common object of promoting economic growth, which was the primary legacy of
the economic crisis of the late 1720s.[72] Moreover, it was a goal that the self-interested landed elite could pursue without reservation because any improvement to
the economy must not only increase their rent rolls, but also contribute to the
generation of economic activity from which a landowner's estate village and
demesne could but benefit. An excellent illustration is provided by Hugh Massey
of Duntrileague, south county Limerick, who joined with another gentleman in
the late 1740s in organising a race meeting and other diversions (a buck-hunt and
a ball) in the hamlet of Anglesborough in an attempt to raise the profile of the
fair he had recently been permitted to hold.[73] It is unlikely, given the absence of

72 James Kelly, 'Jonathan Swift and the Irish economy in the 1720s', *Eighteenth-Century Ireland*, 6
(1991), pp 7–36; Patrick Kelly, 'The politics of political economy in mid-eighteenth-century Ireland'
in S.J. Connolly (ed.), *Political ideas in eighteenth-century Ireland* (Dublin, 2000), pp 105–29. 73
Fleming, 'Provincial Ireland', pp 141–2; *Munster Journal*, 3, 6 Sept. 1750.

subsequent reference to racing at Anglesborough, that Massey's efforts produced the dividend he anticipated, but his experience did not dissuade others. The inaugural (and only) race meeting held in the village of Minola, county Mayo, in 1735 was organised by George Browne 'explicitly for the encouragement of the new establish'd colony' of Protestant weavers.[74]

It is not always possible to identify who was the prime mover behind the establishment of a racecourse, but the proximity of a course to a local demesne or estate is a generally reliable indicator of the involvement of a local eminence, particularly when the course was some distance from a significant conurbation. Sir Edward O'Brien (1705–65) of Dromoland is a case in point. O'Brien (Fig. 3) was one of the most significant figures in racing, and a regular and competitive presence at the major plate meetings at the Curragh, yet he was also a formative influence on the sport in county Clare. He was instrumental in sustaining regular meetings at Assollas, where his stud was located, and at Corofin in the county. In 1752, he sponsored a £20 purse at the latter location explicitly 'for the encouragement of his town', and he promised, in the not unlikely event that one of his horses won any of the races, that he would give 'the money to be run for again next season'.[75] Sir Edward King (1726–97) of Boyle, who was MP for the constituency of the same name from 1749 to 1760, was another enthusiastic promoter of the sport. Having run a horse, unsuccessfully, at the high profile meeting held at Loughrea, county Galway, in August 1753, Kingsborough, which was how King was known prior to his elevation to the peerage in 1764, subscribed 100 guineas to be competed for on the new course at Boyle in 1754. Determined to create a surface 'as compleat as any in the kingdom', he spared no 'expence and pains ... in laying out the course' and employing 'great numbers of labourers ... in levelling the ground, and rendering it as compleat as possible'. He also offered larger than usual prizes, which attracted an exceptional entry for the maiden meeting of the course, which was a success. Eager to build on this achievement, Kingsborough increased the total prize money to £350 in 1755, and the main prize for the winner of the feature event to £100, but it was not sufficient. He was not assisted, to be sure, by the fact that the date of the meeting had to be changed to accommodate the spring meeting at the Curragh, but this was more a symptom than a cause, and the fact that the meeting at Boyle did not last more than a few years indicates that once Kingsborough recognised that his ambition to elevate his town into one of the country's major race meeting was unlikely to be realised, he withdrew from the sport.[76]

Kingsborough was not the only landowner to learn the hard way that horse racing was an expensive business, though this did not alter the reality that most courses required a well-connected local champion, preferably with deep pockets, if they were to last for more than a few years. It is improbable, for example, that

---

74 *FDJ*, 20 May 1735. **75** Fleming, 'Provincial Ireland', p. 142; *PO*, 10 Oct. 1752; Heber, *An historical list ... 1751*, pp 65–6. **76** *UA*, 1 Sept. 1753, 19 Feb., 2 Mar., 13, 16 Apr., 7, 11, 14 May 1754, 1, 15 Feb. 1755.

racing would have taken place at quite so many locations in county Galway if there were not others with a commitment to the sport equal to that of Colonel John Eyre of Eyrecourt.[77] Alexander, fifth earl of Antrim, was no less important in county Antrim. James Lenox Napper of Lough Crew was crucial in getting Trim races off the ground in 1733. Sir Thomas Denny did likewise in county Kerry; he provided both the ground and the inspiration that sustained Tralee races in the late 1740s, while Beauchamp Bagenal's role in making Bagenalstown races an exemplar in the promoting of Irish horses was another illustration of the decisive influence a powerful individual could bring to bear.[78]

As well as the welcome economic dividend, landowners were encouraged to support the establishment of race meetings by their fondness for the prestige their involvement with the sport conferred. The comparatively low profile assumed by the Curragh and, to a lesser extent, by the Corporation of Horse Breeders in county Down in the 1730s and 1740s, may have encouraged some outside of this circle to conclude that they could join this exclusive company, but the illusion tended not to be long lived.[79] There were insufficient quality horses, and insufficient landowners with the required resources to purchase and to maintain a stable of horses of the quality required to win major races, of which the king's plate at the Curragh was the premier prize. As a result, many courses continued to target local owners, by excluding horses that had run at the Curragh, the Maze, or elsewhere for prizes in excess of a sum guaranteed to attract local competition.[80] There were obvious practical reasons for this. Because horses had to be walked to a racecourse, which posed significant logistical demands, local horses were the obvious choice for most courses, and both subscribers, who put up the prize money, and local organisers contrived to ensure this by confining races to locally bred horses. This became common practice with time, but it was already in evidence in county Galway in the 1730s. First identified in the £20 plate race for five years olds 'bred in the county of Galway, or now … in the possession of a subscribing member' in the articles advertising the forthcoming meeting at Headford in August 1731, it was made still more explicit by the organisers of Gort races; they ordained later the same year that 'no horse, etc, belonging to any but an inhabitant of the county of Galway, or of some other county, which gives a county plate, and allows the horse etc of any inhabitant of the said county of Galway to run for the same, shall be permitted to start' for the 'county plate', which was valued at £20.[81] Two years later, in 1733, the subscription plate offered

77 Ida Gantz, *Signpost to Eyrecourt: portrait of the Eyre family* (Bath, 1975), pp 155–69; *PO*, 12 Aug. 1735.   78 *FDJ*, 4 Sept. 1733; *Munster Journal*, 26 Oct. 1749, 21 May, 16 Aug. 1750; *UA*, 2 July 1754.   79 See pp 49, 51, 58, 63.   80 See, for examples, *PO*, 27 Mar. 1731 (Youghal); ibid., 8 June 1731, 6 June 1732 (Limerick); ibid., 15 June 1731 (Headford); ibid., 29 June 1731 (Assollas); ibid., 21 Aug. 1731 (Roscommon); ibid., 14 July 1733 (Athlone); ibid., 8 Sept. 1733 (Magherafelt); *FDJ*, 13 Apr. 1731 (Parsonstown); ibid., 20 May 1735 (Minola); ibid., 15 July 1740 (Kilfinane); *Dublin Evening Post*, 28 Aug. 1733 (Gort); ibid., 7 June 1735 (Carlow). Interestingly, horses that had won at Boyle were excluded from competing at Mullingar in 1754: *UA*, 4 May 1754.   81 *PO*, 15 June, 21 Aug. 1731.

at Castleblakeney was reserved to 'hunters bred in the ... county', and to the horses of subscribers, while the restriction of the county of Galway plates, which were 'given by the high sheriff and justices of the peace', and run variously at Tuam (1733, 1754), Eyrecourt (1735), Ballinasloe (1740), and Aughrim (1747), to the horses of 'justices of the peace and freeholders', reinforced this local commitment.[82] Moreover, Galway was not alone in deeming this a legitimate tactic to encourage horse-breeding locally. The race meeting held at Trim in September 1733 reserved a £15 prize to horses 'the property of a freeholder of the county of Meath'; that at Assollas in 1735 reserved one race for horses bred in the county Clare; the races at Ballingarry, near Gorey in county Wexford, in 1738 and at Tralee, county Kerry, in 1740 did likewise, while the Corporation of Horse Breeders in county Down in 1735 confined its £20 plate race to horses, less than five years old 'bred in the counties of Antrim and Downe'.[83]

It may be that such schemes were more effective at generating interest in racing locally than in fostering economic growth. However, they mirrored, and took to its logical consequence in one sphere of activity, the disposition to favour domestic over foreign manufacture that Jonathan Swift had seminally endorsed.[84] This was put into practice by the organisers of the Parsonstown meeting in the spring of 1731 who restricted entry to Irish-bred horses. The phrase 'no English horse to run for any of the said plates' used in the 'articles' publicising the Parsonstown meeting was evidently perceived to be too blunt, as it was not echoed by other race meetings, but the sentiment struck a chord, as the three plates run for at the Tullamore course later in the year were each reserved for 'Irish bred horses'.[85] Two years later, the inaugural meeting of the course at Longford reserved a race to Irish-bred galloways.[86] The unwillingness of others to follow their example then suggests that this proved too confining in practice, but the idea persisted, and it was pursued again in the 1750s when patriot emotions again ran high. Race meetings held at Clogheen (county Tipperary), Castlebar (county Mayo) and Bagenalstown (county Carlow) reserved a race for 'Irish bred horses' aged five and six; the meetings at Boyle (county Roscommon) and Baltinglass (county Wicklow) specified Irish four-year-olds (and, in 1757, '4, 5 and 6 year' olds that never previously raced); the meeting at Corofin (county Clare), in October 1752, specified 'Irish bred galloways', and the meeting at Carrigaline (county Cork) in June 1755 simply stipulated 'Irish bred cattle'.[87]

---

82 Entry was later modified to include the 'freeholders and inhabitants' of county Galway, and other counties 'that give the like plate ... and suffer the county of Galway gentlemen to run their horses for it': see *PO*, 17 July, 8 Sept. 1733, 12 Aug. 1735, 6 Sept. 1740, 4 Aug. 1747; *FDJ*, 2 Sept. 1740. 83 Fleming, 'Provincial Ireland', p. 143; *FDJ*, 4 Sept. 1733, 5 Aug. 1738, 13 May 1740; *PO*, 22 Apr. 1735; *UA*, 26 Oct. 1754. 84 See, particularly, M.J. Powell, *The politics of consumption in eighteenth-century Ireland* (Basingstoke, 2003), chapter 6; Kelly, 'Swift and the Irish economy in the 1720s', pp 10–30. 85 *FDJ*, 13 Apr. 1731; *PO*, 21 Aug. 1731. 86 *FDJ*, 4 Sept. 1733. 87 *Munster Journal*, 15 Mar. 1750; *UA*, 10 Oct. 1752, 2 Mar., 3, 11 May, 2 July, 6 Aug. 1754, 22 Mar., 3 May, 22 July, 16 Aug. 1755, 12 June 1757.

Even the Curragh targeted Irish-bred horses in the late 1760s.[88] Evidently, the idea continued to possess appeal, and it could readily be animated at moments of political restiveness, such as the Money bill dispute, which shaped political discourse for much of the 1750s.

Besides the prestige arising from hosting a major meeting, and the intangible benefits to local sentiment that might arise if it was reported positively in the national press, a good race meeting had the capacity to generate considerable economic activity. This was bound up with the duration of the meeting, the number of horses attracted, the spending (and betting) power of the owners and spectators, the fees levied on owners, and the capacity of the locality to encourage additional spending by visitors and residents on accommodation, nutrition and entertainment. A race meeting certainly provided an opportunity to farriers, blacksmiths and the employees and owners of stables, since most race meetings required that horses entered in their races should be registered on site up to eight days before they were due to run, and that they were stabled in the locality. The articles of the inaugural meeting hosted at Limerick in 1731 illustrate the practice:

> Each horse, etc. that shall run for any of the said races, must be entered, measured and shewn before Mr Corn. Parker, and Mr John Wright, at the house of Mr Patrick O'Brien, at the *George* in the Irishtown, Limerick, 8 days before their respective days of running with their marks, and owner's names, and be kept there from the days of entrance to the days of running.[89]

Eight days was the maximum time allowed for horses to register. Six and seven days were also specified.[90] Horses could, of course, also 'enter at the post', but they did so at an additional cost; the usual requirement was that they pay 'double entrance', which in the case of the inaugural Athlone meeting in 1732 was two guineas for the £20 plate races, and a guinea for the two £10 races.[91] Entrance fees were normally of this order; they were calculated according to an implicit formula, which was based on the assumption that it was appropriate to pay 1s. entrance per £1 of prize money.[92] Thus, at Tralee later in the decade, owners were requested 'to pay, as follows, for the thirty pounds thirty shillings entrance; for the twenty pounds twenty shillings; for the fifteen pounds fifteen shillings, and for the five pounds five shillings'. A comparable scale was employed at Cashel in 1732, except it sought a moidore from owners entering a horse for the £30 plate, a guinea for the £20 race, and 'one English crown' for the race for the entrance money. The meeting at Painstown, county Carlow, employed a varia-

---

88 *UA*, 7 Feb. 1759, 12 Apr., 24 May 1760.   89 *PO*, 8 June 1731.   90 As, for example, at Athlone: *PO*, 29 June 1731; Rathvilly: *PO*, 6 June 1732; Longford: *FDJ*, 4 Sept. 1733.   91 *PO*, 24 June 1732; *FDJ*, 12 July 1737.   92 The formula 'a shilling in the pound' was employed in the published articles appertaining to the Rathkeale meeting in 1754 and the Baltinglass meeting in 1757: *UA*, 2 July 1754, 12 June 1757.

tion; it charged 30*s.* entrance to compete for its £30 prize, £1 3*s.* for the £20 purse, 18*s.* 6*d.* for the £15 purse and 11*s.* 6*d.* for the £10 prize.[93] Because many race meetings were heavily dependent on subscribers for their prize purses, the entrance fee they were charged was generally half that required of non-subscribers, though, significantly, this was generally achieved by doubling the entrance required of the latter rather than halving the fee charged the former.[94]

The preference accorded subscribers was an appropriate incentive to encourage individuals to sponsor races, but the 'entrance' was only one of the charges owners had to pay. They were also charged on the course 'for scales and straw' according to a practice that required the winning owner to pay double the fee paid by others.[95] Such charges defrayed the costs incurred in weighing and strawing horses on course. The cost of maintaining them during the six to eight days between 'the days of entrance [and] the day of running' is less readily reckonable, but it may well have amounted to a significant sum. This obviously served the beneficial purpose for the horse of ensuring it was rested and ready to run when it was scheduled to perform. But it is also apparent that the stipulation insisted upon by various organisers that horses must be 'kept in said town', or, as happened on occasion, in a designated stables on or close to the race ground was to the financial advantage of the owner of these premises, and it is no accident that tavern owners, ostlers and other interested parties in the locality did much of the registration, organisation and other tasks required to generate a successful meeting. It is not possible even to estimate how personally beneficial their involvement might have been, since the fortunes of racecourses could fluctuate wildly, but it is reasonable to assume that it was advantageous since other enterprising locals contrived to secure their share by offering 'private and separate stabling for racehorses'.[96] Obviously, the longer the meeting, and the more successful it was in attracting quality horses, in generating publicity, and in drawing a substantial concourse of spectators the more likely it was to be a money-spinner for the community in which it took place. Moreover, strategically located interests within individual communities were soon alert to the possibilities, and, building on the pattern established during the late 1720s, to take this to a different level. As a result, as well as providing assurances that 'good accommodation' was available and 'the greatest care taken to have lodgings well fitted', that a diurnal 'ordinary' was available for gentlemen and 'a dining place for the ladies', generally but not invariably in a local inn, horse racing meetings contrived to set new standards for the fare and entertainment owners and spectators alike could anticipate.[97]

93 *PO*, 22 July 1732; *FDJ*, 12 July 1737, 7 July 1739. **94** As instanced by Headford races, county Galway, where subscribers were charged an entrance of one guinea, and non-subscribers 2 guineas. **95** *PO*, 10 Aug. 1731, 20 Sept. 1735, 8 June 1736; *FDJ*, 1 Oct. 1734, 31 May 1740. **96** *PO*, 10 Aug., 24 June 1731, 8 June 1736; *FDJ*, 12 July, 9 Aug. 1737; Iris Middleton and Wray Vamplew, 'Horse racing and the Yorkshire leisure calendar in the early eighteenth century', *Northern History*, 40:2 (2003), p. 260, note 3. **97** *PO*, 28 Mar., 6 June 1732, 17 July 1733, 5 Sept. 1741, 14 May 1743, 4 July 1747, 13 Sept. 1748; *FDJ*, 15 July 1740, 19 June 1742, 24 May 1748; *Munster Journal*,

In keeping with the fact that the sport was overwhelmingly a male preserve, attention was devoted in the first instance to the provision of suitable male-oriented entertainment. Consistent with the equine focus of these occasions, many meets integrated hunting into their programme of activities. The organisers of the meeting at Limerick in July 1731 were among the first to schedule a buck-hunt on the morning of the third day of racing, but, determined not to be outdone, the ambitious organisers of the meeting at Athlone the same year not only promised 'a buck hunt each morning' but also integrated the hunt into the racing calendar on Wednesday and Friday.[98] This raised the level of expectation, which may have prompted the organisers of the meeting at Roscommon later the same summer to promise 'buck and hare hunting each morning'.[99] The Castleblakeney meeting in 1732 scheduled 'a buck hunt [and] otter hunting' on the middle day of its three-day meeting in 1732, and an otter-hunt in 1733, but the novelty of the latter must quickly have worn thin, as it was not repeated, and the necessary distraction was provided thereafter by more familiar quarry.[100] Thus, patrons were promised 'a fox hunt every second day' at Maryborough, Queen's county, on day two of the two-day meeting at Castlepollard, county Westmeath in 1733, 'each day' at Mullingar in 1741 and Richhill in 1754, and on two of the five days at Longwood, county Meath in 1743. However, buck-hunting possessed enduring appeal, and its availability, as an alternative to fox-hunting at Keeneghane, which was near Eyrescourt, in 1735, Bonnett's-rath (county Kilkenny) in 1737, Tralee in 1739, 1740, 1748, 1749 and 1750, Assollas in 1740, Carlow in 1741 and 1747, Corofin and Castleblakeney (county Galway) in 1743, and Kilmallock (county Limerick) in 1749 was an illustration of the enduring appeal of the chase to the gentlemen that were drawn to watch horse racing.[101] In the same vein, the organisers of the second Bellewstown meeting in 1754 promised 'fox-hunting and doe hunting' twice during the racing week.[102]

Novelty, and the appreciating appeal of the sport, prompted some race meetings to offer cockfighting as an additional distraction beginning in the 1740s. The decision of the organisers of a new meeting at Kilfinane, county Limerick, to offer cockfighting and buck-hunting on the afternoon of the third day of its scheduled meeting in July 1740 set a precedent that was soon emulated by Carlow and Longwood.[103] It proved a popular diversion; a 'cock-match, consisting of 20 battles, between Andrew Teally esq. and the gentlemen of Glencaney' at Antrim races in 1755 drew an unprecedented number of 'gentlemen' to that course.[104] Others followed suit, and before the 1750s were complete Trim was

14 Sept. 1749.   98 *PO*, 8, 29 June 1731.   99 *PO*, 21 Aug. 1731.   100 *PO*, 6 June 1732, 17 July 1733.   101 *FDJ*, 4, 11 Sept. 1733, 9 Aug. 1737, 7 July 1739, 13, 31 May 1740, 24 Mar. 1743, 3 Sept. 1748; *PO*, 12 Aug. 1735, 4 Sept. 1741, 25 June 1743, 4 July 1747; *Dublin Newsletter*, 15 Oct. 1743; *Munster Journal*, 24 Aug. 1749, 21 May 1750; *UA*, 2 Nov. 1754.   102 *UA*, 5 Oct. 1754.   103 *FDJ*, 15 July 1740; *PO*, 5 Sept. 1741; *Dublin Newsletter*, 15 Oct. 1743; below, pp 137, 138.   104 *UA*, 17 June 1755.

reputed for the quality of its cockfights. The county Meath course replicated the practice, long established in England, of bringing the two most structured sports together at one location.[105] The recreational imperative that guided such actions was emphasised further in 1748 when an exhibition game of hurling was included on the programme of events at the horse racing organised at Luttrellstown, county Dublin, in 1748, and at Rathkeale, county Limerick, in 1754. Even a 'rowing match between two eight oar barges' was staged for the diversion of those present at Carrigaline in 1755.[106]

If the primary purpose of the provision of hunting, cockfighting, even hurling, at horse racing was to encourage members of the gentry, first, to attend, and, second, to stay at a meeting for the full duration, the recognition that a gentry household was an even more lucrative prospect prompted a conscious effort to attract gentlemen's wives. Ladies could, and did attend the races, but the absence of appropriate viewing facilities meant that horse racing was not a comfortable spectator sport for either gender. Indeed, the fact that men rode alongside or behind the racing horses where this was practical and that no women features in the revealing contemporary image of racing provided in the painting *Race on the Curragh* (Fig. 1), which dates from the 1730s, reinforces the conclusion provided by written sources that race days were pre-eminently male occasions. It can be assumed as a result that when women went to race meetings they did so in the expectation that they would be occupied elsewhere during much of the racing week.[107] This explains why organisers, once they recognized the commercial value of a strong female presence, sought to provide entertainments women might find congenial. Beginning in the early 1730s, it became commonplace, at the end of the articles alerting the public to an impending race meeting, to advertise that there would be 'a ball and other diversions', or 'plays and assemblies for the diversion of the ladies every night'.[108] There is little or no information to indicate either the type of plays that were performed or the nature of the assemblies that were held, but it is apparent that organisers sought also to make the best of the assets they had at their doorstep. Thus, attendees at Athlone races in 1731, 1732, 1733 and 1734 were offered a menu that, as well as 'plays and assemblies', included boating, accompanied by 'choice musick, prepared for the entertainment of the ladies, on the most delightful river Shannon', 'balls and other diversions'.[109] This rich range was in keeping with the ambition of the Athlone meeting. Moreover, its very novelty helped to make the occasion a social as well as a sporting success, and to elicit a reaction that suggested some anticipated horse racing might act as a catalyst for the revolution in manners that was earnestly desired in some quarters:

105 Below p. 174; *UA*, 23 May 1758, 2 June 1759, 19 July 1760; *Dublin Gazette*, 15 July 1760. **106** *Dublin Courant*, 16 Aug. 1748; *UA*, 2 July 1754, 3 May, 21 June 1755.   **107** *Race on the Curragh*, 1730s (private collection), reproduced in A. Roger Ekirch, *Birthright: the true story that inspired* Kidnapped (London, 2012), pp 133–4.   **108** See, for example, *PO*, 8, 26, 29 June 1731. **109** *PO*, 6, 24 June 1732, 17 July 1733, 27 Aug. 1734.

It was very remarkable that such a vast concourse of gentlemen from different parts of the kingdom lived so long together without any other strife than who should entertain with the greatest politeness. The evenings were generally spent on the delightful river Shannon, which was made infinitely more so, by the company of the ladies, and the musick which always attended them on those occasions, and the nights ended in balls, where there was a greater appearance of beauty, than ever was seen in the country town before.[110]

Though their optimism for the future was misplaced, and the expenditure incurred in mounting such a programme was indicative of the overreach that contributed to the discontinuation of racing at Athlone after only four years, it did not shatter the belief in the merit of providing alternative diversions if a race meeting was to be a social as well as an economic and sporting success. Since this ambition registered strongly with the public of county towns and landlord villages, entertainments targeted at a female clientele were associated first and foremost with the races held in established urban centres such as Trim, Tralee, Headford, Fethard, Roscrea, Roscommon, Kilkenny, Tuam, Assollas, Mullingar and Carlow. It is notable that none of these locations sustained an uninterrupted sequence of race meetings, but they proved more enduring than their equivalents at Manola, Clane, Ahoghill, Castlepollard, Ardrahan and Bailieborough, which were reliant solely on the backing of the local lord of the manor, which (as in England) was often fitful, and rarely sufficient to neutralise the consequences of rural remoteness for any duration.[111]

An insight into the manner in which race meetings were conducted, and to the manner in which women, and those men who care little for horse racing, occupied themselves on those occasions is provided by a letter, written in 1746, describing one such event at Dingle, county Kerry:

We spent the last week there very pleasantly; three families ... the Ponsonbys, Hassetts, and ourselves,[112] besides straggling men. We dined in a tent that was pitched on a hill that hung over the sea. Every creature in the town assembled there by the beat of drum, at four shillings a head for the men, and one and sixpence for the ladies. I believe that one day with another there was about fifty people of us that dined in the Pavilion, for we scorned to give it so vulgar a name as a tent. It was built in the form of an octagon, tables all round and the waiters in the middle. ... Our diversions were boating, racing, and dancing. Every morning after break-

110 *FDJ*, 14 Aug. 1731.   111 *PO*, 6 June 1732, 3 Apr. 1733, 20 May, 12 Aug. 1735, 8 June 1736, 31 May, 24 June, 15 July 1740, 5 Sept. 1741, 29 June 1742, 14 July 1743, 4 July 1747; *FDJ*, 24 Oct. 1732, 4, 11 Sept. 1733, 9 Aug. 1737, 7 July 1739, 3 Sept. 1748; *Munster Journal*, 15 May 1749; Brailsford, *A taste for diversions*, pp 97–9.   112 The surname of the author of the letter is not available, so it is not possible to establish the family name.

fast, except the day of the races – for there was only one that was worth seeing – the young folk of us went boating. The old ones stayed at home and played cards ... . We generally stayed out till the hour of dinner, sat about an hour after it with the men, and then went to dress for the ball at night. ... We danced till about eleven, and then the three families went home to the Knight [of Kerry]'s house to supper, and about two we retired to our beds; and this was exactly the life we led, except one day instead of boating we went to the famous race ... I must not forget to tell you that we had a band of music from Dublin attending us constantly ...[113]

The obvious economic and other advantages to a town or village of a race meeting encouraged various municipalities and corporations to follow the example of English regional authorities and to promote horse racing in their communities.[114] The support provided by Belturbet and Youghal borough corporations in the early decades of the century has been identified, and described, by Toby Barnard.[115] Support was also forthcoming during the 1730s, when this impulse was at its strongest, at Limerick, Longford, Magherafelt, Trim, Athlone, Tralee and Kilkenny. The scale and cost of involvement varied greatly, and was not always sustained. In the early 1730s, when it was still supportive, Youghal corporation's contribution to the strand races run on the local beach consisted of three plates, total value £35, and the nomination, by the lord mayor, of judges to assist with the smooth administration of the occasion. Most municipalities opted for less direct involvement. Limerick Corporation sponsored one plate valued at £10 on the new course opened at Limerick in 1731. The corporation of the borough of Tralee provided comparable backing to the tune of £30, and that of Longford a purse of £5. The borough of Trim confined itself to the provision of practical support, while the gentlemen of the borough of Athlone did both; they assisted with the running of the race meeting in 1733 and, with the gentlemen of county Westmeath, subscribed two plate prizes, valued at £45, when that meeting encountered difficulties.[116] Impressive as this was, it was still modest when set beside the support provided by the Corporation of Kilkenny. Sustaining a commitment to the development of sporting infrastructure that was unequalled in Ireland, the Corporation allocated £400 to the purpose, and joined with a number of local eminences in 1731 in funding 'four perpetual plates to be run for twice every year in the park of Dunmore or within the liberties of the city of Kilkenny'.[117]

---

113 Tom Finn, 'A race ball at Dingle in 1746', *The Kerry Magazine*, 12 (2001), pp 43–4.   114 In 1708, York Corporation, which concluded that 'making ... a yearly horse-race ... may be of advantage and profit to the ... city', subscribed £15 towards a plate to encourage and bring about a horse race': Middleton and Vamplew, 'Horse racing and the Yorkshire leisure calendar in the early eighteenth century', p. 263.   115 Barnard, *Making the grand figure*, p. 228.   116 *PO*, 27 Mar., 8 June 1731, 17 July 1733, 27 Aug. 1734; *FDJ*, 12 Dec. 1732, 4 Sept., 1733, 7 July 1739.   117 Barnard, *Making the grand figure*, pp 228–9; Agreement to establish four plate races at Dunmore, county Kilkenny, 8 Oct. 1731 (NLI, MS 22427); 'Note', *Journal of the Royal Historical and Archaeological*

Though it may appear from these figures that racing at Kilkenny was particularly soundly grounded, the reality was that few Irish racecourses were built upon solid fiscal foundations when the sport expanded rapidly during the 1730s. Even the Curragh, which had tradition, exchequer funding, and vice-regal support on its side, was dependent on its annual grant, which in the mid-eighteenth century permitted it to run two blue-riband 100 guineas races, one for mares, the other for Irish-bred horses.[118] Moreover, based on the modest press coverage of racing at that venue during the 1730s and 1740s, it would appear that those responsible for the Curragh were slow to appreciate the importance of publicity to the success of the course.[119] They contrived in the early 1730s, by inviting commitments from subscribers to pay 'five guineas each annually, for the term of ten years, for stakes to be run for over the Curragh of Kildare', to add a subscription stakes to their racing card, but it had little visible impact.[120] While this situation remained, the Curragh might even have been displaced in the public's affections by one of the innovative and ambitious newer courses that were springing up across the country, but it had the country's most prestigious race. As a result, the owners of the best horses remained loyal, and no serious pretender emerged. The Corporation of Horse Breeders in the county of Down sustained regular meetings at the Maze, meanwhile, but it did not constitute a real rival to the Curragh. It was not assisted, certainly, by the fact that it was organisationally unwieldy. Comprising 'governors and freemen', and a 'register' in whose name notices were communicated to the public, it devoted much of its energies in the 1730s to the promotion of horse breeding, rather than racing, and its decision to hold its main annual race meeting during a fair did little to elevate its profile. The Corporation did not neglect racing. It funded three plates, which were competed for in a week-long race meeting on the Maze course near Hillsborough each summer through the thirties and forties, but they offered little more than the standard prize, and caution seemed to be the Corporation's defining characteristic at this point.[121]

In the absence of leadership from its most venerable courses and institutions, the sport of horse racing derived its inspiration from the combination of enthusiasm, self-interest and the commitment to improvement that inspired its primarily landed avatars. These qualities can be identified, for example, in the actions of the shadowy Green Cloth Club, which provided an early manifestation of the contribution that the embryonic associational culture could make to the promotion of the sport. This county Tipperary body was sufficiently well established by 1732 to sponsor an ambitious week of racing 'on the course near the city of Cashell'.[122] It remains to be established how long this body remained active, and its longer term impact (if any), but it offered one model for the future, and an

---

Association of Ireland, 4th series, 3 (1874–5), p. 154.   **118** *UA*, 23 Mar. 1756. [Investigate the grants to Curragh/Maze]   **119** Reports of racing at the Curragh were irregular: see *Dublin Evening Post*, 16 Sept. 1735; *FDJ*, 18 Sept. 1739, 4 Apr. 1741.   **120** *Dublin Gazette*, 2 Sept. 1732.   **121** *PO*, 6 June 1732; *FDJ*, 11 Sept. 1733, 20 Aug. 1734, 22 Apr. 1735, 19 Apr. 1740, 3 Sept. 1748; *Dublin Newsletter*, 9 July 1743.   **122** *PO*, 22 July 1732.

alternative to the dependence on a local landowner, or landowners, who might withdraw his support at any moment. It did not place the Cashel course on a sounder financial footing than most courses during this period, but it provides another vista onto those responsible for the promotions of the sport, and on those responsible for the multiplication of courses that hosted racing during these decades. A substantial number of these courses hosted no more than a handful of meetings, but enough survived to permit the sport to continue to grow.

It may be that the delicate equilibrium between the availability of horses and courses was not always maintained. It is noteworthy that four plates advertised to be run at Limerick in 1751 were 'put off till next year for want of a sufficient number of horses', and that a plate race at Cork two years later 'was postponed' for the same reason.[123] Since three was generally acknowledged as the minimum number of horses required to run a race, it is tempting to conclude that such postponements were indicative of deeper problems, but if so it was hardly true of Clogheen, county Tipperary, in 1753, or other established courses that had on occasion to pay a proportion of the prize money to horses that walked a course for want of competitors.[124] Moreover, there was no typical eighteenth-century racecourse life cycle. The fortunes of courses varied according to the location, organisation, financial commitment of the principals, and the appeal both of the venue and of the racing it scheduled. None of the new courses that hosted races during the second quarter of the eighteenth century became permanent fixtures on the sporting landscape, but together they provided the infrastructure that made horse racing the most vibrant, popular sport in the kingdom by the 1750s.

While the existence of a network of racecourses (Map 2) was crucial to the success of horse racing as a sport, it was also the most visible manifestation on the landscape of the attraction of the sport to the kingdom's ruling elite. Consistent with the historical description of them as the 'Protestant ascendancy', they largely subscribed to the Church of Ireland, as by law established. However, the success in the late 1740s of The Padreen Mare (the soubriquet for the mare Irish Lass), which was owned by the Catholic family of Archbold of Eadestown, county Kildare, indicated that the sport was not closed to Catholics, though the significance attached to the fact that the mare raced with a rosary beads tied to her collar indicates that the sport did not transcend the confessional prejudices that cleaved Irish society. Be that as it may, the ability of The Padreen Mare to win against the odds animated public interest in the sport in a manner that did not threaten the societal or sporting ascendancy of the primarily Protestant landed elite.[125]

---

123 Heber, *An historical list of horse matches … 1751*, p. 84; *UA*, 22 May 1753. 124 *UA*, 16 June 1753 (Clogheen); Heber, *An historical list … 1751*, p. 9 (Curragh), p. 84 (Limerick); *Public Gazetteer*, 1 May 1766, *FLJ*, 1 May 1773 (Curragh). 125 Sweeney, *The Sweeney guide*, p. 343; Con Costello, *Kildare: saints, soldiers and horses* (Naas, 1991), pp 116–18. Interestingly, the victory was deemed sufficiently significant to merit commemoration on a silver jug, in the style of William Townsend: see Sweeney, op. cit., p. 152, plate 15.

In practice, the number of individuals with stables large enough to compete at the highest level in the 1730s and 1740s was small. It included five peers – Edward, fifth earl of Drogheda (1701–58), Brabazon, first earl of Bessborough (1679–1758), Trevor, first Viscount Hillsborough (1693–1742), Alexander, fifth earl of Antrim (1713–94), and Richard, the eighth earl of Anglesey (c.1690–1761); four baronets – Sir Edward O'Brien (1705–65), Sir Laurence Parsons (1712–56), Sir Maurice Crosbie (1690–1762), and Sir Marmaduke Wyvill (c.1692–1754), the postmaster general; and a number of well-connected commoners, among whom Maurice Keating (1690–1769, of Narraghmore, county Kildare), Lucius Henry O'Brien (1731–95, of Dromoland, county Clare), Charles O'Neill (1702–69, of Shane's Castle, county Antrim), and Charles Daly (1722–68 of Callow, county Galway) were MPs, and Thomas Pigott of Dysert, Queen's county, Benjamin Bunbury (d. c.1750) of Cranovonane, county Carlow and James Dogherty (d. 1756) of Shanbally, county Tipperary, were particularly active.[126] The Curragh also attracted a smattering of English peers, such as Charles, second earl of Portmore (1700–85), who were rarely, if ever, represented at regional Irish meets. This contrasted with the keenest Irish owners – Edward O'Brien, Charles O'Neill, the earl of Antrim, Charles Daly, Sir Maurice Crosbie, and James Dogherty of Shanbally, who did not own land in his own right – who were to be found with increasing frequency at regional courses, and at the local meetings they generally sponsored close to their place of residence.[127] The superior quality of their bloodstock gave them an advantage at most local meetings, which is why they habitually either declined to enter their own horses, or surrendered whatever prize money they won. These events were targeted primarily at owners who lived within a reasonable ride of the course, which explains the number of races targeted at galloways, hunters, and horses that were either maiden or had not previously run for a purse above a stated sum, and the modest nature of the prize money (£5 was not uncommon, and sometimes prizes were provided in kind) that was often available at such courses.[128]

The different categories – national, regional, local – into which one can assign Irish racecourses was a significant factor in the ability of horse racing to penetrate virtually the whole island. Moreover, in so far as one can tell this was achieved without diluting the rules of the sport as they were defined by the 'articles ... instituted by King Charles' in 1665. Most Irish regional and local courses did not compare with Newmarket, of course, and palpably less depended on the outcome, but the readiness of owners and organisers to follow its example, and to publish, in advance, a set of 'articles' was of material significance in ensuring

126 GEC, *The complete peerage*; Sedgwick, *The history of parliament, 1715–54*, iii, 566; *FDJ*, 18 Sept. 1739, 4 Apr. 1741, 13 Sept. 1748; *Dublin Gazette*, 15 Sept. 1741, 9 Apr. 1743; *Munster Journal*, 18 Sept. 1749.   127 *FDJ*, 25 Oct. 1740, 3 Sept. 1748; *Dublin Gazette*, 29 June 1742; *PO*, 6 Sept. 1737, 6 Sept. 1748; *Munster Journal*, 10 July 1749. For Dogherty see *UA*, 27 Mar. 1756.   128 *PO*, 10 Aug. 1731 (Clane, county Kildare, £5; Donomore, Durrow, Queen's county, £5); *Munster Journal*, 24 Aug. 1749 (Kilmallock); *Munster Journal*, 14 Sept. 1749 (Castlelyons).

that racing was conducted fairly and properly. Saliently, the 'articles' issued in the 1730s and beyond went into greater specifics than those issued in the 1710s and 1720s when it came to describing the horses that were eligible, entry procedure, fees, the behaviour expected of horses on course, the outcome if there were insufficient entrants, and the responsibilities of the judges.[129] This diminished the grounds for dispute when horses were being entered and, especially, when disagreements arose on course.

Notwithstanding the regularity with which articles pronounced that 'all disputes were to be determined by the majority of the judges', the manner in which they were chosen was often haphazard. Judges, up to five in number,[130] were generally chosen daily 'in the field' often 'by the owners of the horses that run' from 'among the gentlemen in attendance' or by 'the subscribers present'. This was hardly a guarantee of impartiality, but it was certainly preferable to the variation opted for by the organisers of Gort races in 1732 and Carlow races through the 1730s and 1740s, which was that 'all disputes that may arise shall be decided by the majority of subscribers present'. The organisers of the meeting at Castleblakeney in 1743 placed an equivalent trust in the impartiality of their subscribers; they opted for the same arrangement for all races other than the 'sheriffs and justices plate', which they assigned to 'the majority of the justices then present'.[131] Flawed as it might be, it was preferable to the scheme employed at Kilkenny in 1737, which allowed 'every person running a horse, etc., to appoint his own judge', though it is not apparent what their role was since 'all disputes' that arose were to be determined by the subscribers.[132]

In so far as can be established, most disputes were resolved on the course in a timely fashion, though there were occasional exceptions. When James Dogherty's mare Miss Pepper defeated John Knox's bay mare Ajax at Castlebar in August 1754, Knox protested the outcome because, he maintained, Dogherty's horse was more than her stated four years. Obliged to prove his accuser wrong, Dogherty produced proof, with the result that Knox was obliged to accept the result at Loughrea races later the same month.[133] The requirement that owners have certificates of age and pedigree at the ready was one of the innovations instituted by the Jockey Club at the Curragh that became common currency; this diminished the opportunity to cheat on age grounds, though it was manifestly valueless when it was alleged that one horse interfered with another in the home straight.[134] Claims of crossing that were disputed were usually settled with a further heat,[135] but there were occasions when a resolution proved elusive. One such instance happened at Baltinglass in 1755 when Gorges Lowther, the MP for Ratoath, refused to cede victory to Thomas Newenham, the MP for Cork city, in the £30 plate for hunters because, he maintained, Newenham's horses was 'not

129 See, for example, the articles defining Fethard races in 1731: *PO*, 21 Aug. 1731. 130 *UA*, 2 July 1754. 131 *PO*, 15 July 1732, 5 Sept. 1741, 25 June 1743, 4 July 1747, 13 Sept. 1748; *FDJ*, 4 Sept. 1733, 3 Sept. 1748; *Dublin Evening Post*, 7 June 1735. 132 *FDJ*, 9 Aug. 1737. 133 *UA*, 10, 27 Aug. 1754. 134 *UA*, 7 Feb., 5 Aug. 1758. 135 *UA*, 27 Aug. 1757.

qualifyed according to articles'.[136] Moreover, there were practices, such as 'partnerships' when two owners colluded to determine a race to their own advantage, which course judges were powerless to detect. In an attempt to combat this practice, the organisers of the inaugural meeting at Tralee in 1740 required 'an oath to be administered to every person starting whether he is in partnership with any other', but this served only to detect those who were honourable enough to admit to deceit, and its invocation there, and elsewhere, suggested that, as the stakes rose, and horse racing became more popular, the prospect of a remunerative victory challenged the capacity of the existing system reliably to detect, and still less to prevent, collusion.[137] This encouraged exclusions such as was pursued against a shopkeeper from Rathcormack at Tralee in 1748, and belief in the merits of applying still more strict rules in order to combat 'foul play'. Indicatively, an attempt was made at Tralee, and at Castlelyons in 1749, to defeating cheating by running the meeting according to 'the articles for the king's plates in England'.[138]

If resort to 'the articles for the king's plate' at these local meetings can be perceived as an earnest of the commitment of those involved in Irish horse racing to create a sport that was free of the taint of corruption, and disposed to look outwards for guidance as to best practice, it also reflected the inescapable fact that horse racing was a costly hobby, and that the temptation to take short cuts for financial gain was stronger than any system of rules. Money was integral to the sport. It was the oil that lubricated the cogs of the complex machine that was horse racing, and the problem was that it was singularly difficult to run a racecourse, and still more so to manage a stable of racehorses, and not be out of pocket. The task might have been eased if the prize money on offer at meetings was more generous. Simply put, it was not an economic proposition to maintain a horse exclusively for the purpose of racing if the prize on offer was £20 or less, which was the case at most local and regional meets through the 1730s and 1740s. The main prize of Irish racing – the king's plate – was substantially greater, but this was on offer only once a year, and though meetings, such as Athlone and Boyle, aspired to offer better prizes and, on occasion, to equal the king's plate, this was well nigh impossible to sustain; financial realities forced the reduction in the prizes on offer at Athlone till its standard prize, £20, was fifty per cent lower than the top prize offered at Fethard and Limerick at the same time.[139]

Because it was a key consideration for owners and spectators alike, the trend was for prize money to increase over time. When a new course was established at Castlebar in 1743, the top prize was set at £40; there were, in addition, three prizes of £30 and only one £20 prize.[140] Despite this, £20 remained the norm at most regional courses for the remainder of the decade. It was the standard prize on offer at Longwood, Corofin, Castleblakeney and Galway in 1743, and Trim, Tralee, Mullingar, Eyrecourt and the Maze in 1748.[141] Smaller courses continued

136 *UA*, 16, 22 Aug. 1755. 137 *FDJ*, 13 May, 15 July 1740. 138 *FDJ*, 3 Sept. 1748; *Munster Journal*, 15 May, 14 Sept. 1749. 139 *PO*, 8, 29 June, 21 Aug. 1731, 24 June 1732, 17 July 1733. 140 *PO*, 14 May 1743. 141 *Dublin Newsletter*, 15 Oct. 1743; *PO*, 25 June 1743, 13 Sept. 1748;

to offer less. The prizes on offer at Luttrellstown and Callan in 1748, and Kilmallock and Castlelyons in 1749 were £5 and £10; final day sweepstakes were also common, and it was not unusual in the late 1740s for horses to compete for a prize of a bridle, a pair of silver spurs, or a silver mounted whip.[142]

The upward trajectory in prize-money, notwithstanding, Irish horse racing remained under-funded during the 1730s and 1740s. Some courses contrived successfully to combine sponsored plates, subscriptions and entrance money to provide prizes that attracted runners, but the short existences of many others suggests that the figures simply did not stack up. The apology offered by David Kennedy of Belfast because of the modest value of the plates he was able to offer in 1731 has already been cited;[143] the inability of Enniskillen to offer more than spurs, saddles and cash as prizes at its inaugural meeting in 1733 indicates that its finances were precarious from the outset.[144] Money, as the example of Boyle demonstrates, was not a guarantee of success, but its absence almost certainly guaranteed failure, just as certainly as the fact that the extravagant investment in horseflesh would cause financial problems for an imprudent owner. Lord Kingsborough was certainly correct therefore when he concluded that the economics of the sport obliged owners to target better-paying meets. This ensured that the trend, detectible at a minority of courses in the late 1740s, to raise the standard prize to thirty or forty pounds, was accented during the 1750s when purses of £50 became commonplace, and meetings such as Castlebar and Boyle offered top prizes that were substantially larger.[145] This had an inevitable inflationary impact. By the late 1750s, prizes of £50 were common, and could be won at Trim, Loughrea, Castlebar, Thurles, Celbridge and Rathkeale among other courses. Meanwhile, the re-energised Curragh and Corporation of Horse Breeders in county Down, with the advantage of tradition and the allure of the prestigious £100 king's plates – their number doubled in 1750 by George II – had cast off their recent slumber. They now offered more racing and larger prizes, sponsored in the case of the former by the Jockey Club, which assumed increasing responsibility (albeit in tandem with Curragh Ranger) for organising meetings at the country's premier venue following its establishment in the mid-1750s.[146] As a result, the then owners of major stables – and one may instance Edward O'Brien, Charles O'Neill, John Dillon, Marmaduke Wyvill, Thomas Burrowes, Thomas Walpole, Maurice Keating, Lord Antrim, Lord Massereene, James Dogherty, Thomas Newenham, Sir Ralph Gore (1725–1802) of Bellisle, county Fermanagh, Arthur Mervyn of Trillick, county Tyrone and John Browne

FDJ, 24 Mar. 1743, 24 May, 3, 6, 8 Sept. 1748.   **142** *Dublin Courant*, 16 Aug. 1748; *FDJ*, 3 Sept. 1748; *Munster Journal*, 15 May, 24 Aug., 14 Sept. 1749, 19 Nov. 1750.   **143** Above, pp 44, 63.   **144** *PO*, 17 July 1733.   **145** *FDJ*, 3 Sept. 1748; *UA*, 13 Apr., 11, 15 June, 2, 6, 9, 23 July 1754. In 1754, the prizes on offer at Castlebar were £120, £62, £49, £40 and £20, and in 1755 at Boyle the top prize was £100, and all other prizes £50: *UA*, 6 June 1754, 1 Feb. 1755. For the law and prize money see below, pp 95–6.   **146** *UA*, 7 Feb., 13 June, 5 Aug., 21 Oct. 1758, 2, 19 June, 24 July, 8 Sept. 1759, 5 Aug., 25 Oct. 1760; *Public Gazetteer*, 28 Apr., 24 July 1759, 11 Oct. 1760; D'Arcy, *Horses, lords and racing men*, pp 2–3; Kelly, 'The pastime of the elite', pp 417–18.

(1709–76) of Westport among their number – sent horses to a larger number of courses over a broader spatial area than was the case previously. There was still a tangible regional and local quality to the runners at many race meetings (particularly those like Ballybrittas (Queen's county), Belturbet (county Cavan)), which were unable to meet the expectation of augmented prizes,[147] but by the 1750s a larger number of owners entered a larger number of horses in the more remunerative regional meetings, though this necessitated escorting prize horses long distances, which inevitably dulled their performance.[148]

Wisdom in the racing sphere was often a hard-learned lesson. Though there was deep appreciation of the value of a fine, flat race surface, such as the Curragh, the Maze, and the Morragh, county Wicklow,[149] many Irish racecourses were little more than converted fields, which were subject to the minimum alteration to allow racing to take place, and to permit spectators to congregate. The Curragh was the most notable exception; it possessed a stand, and from 1759, a clubhouse (known as the Coffee House) in Kildare town where members of the Jockey Club congregated.[150] More usually, local purveyors of ale, wine and other gustibles set up tents and booths on race day from which they sold their wares, and it had become a sufficiently lucrative practice by the 1750s to cause a succession of courses (Trim, Bellewstown, Broughshane, Navan, Celbridge, Swords and the Curragh) to charge for the privilege of catering to the 'great appearance of company' or 'numerous and grand appearance' that the organisers sought to bring to these locations.[151]

Intervention on the scale undertaken by Lord Kingsborough at Boyle to create a bespoke running surface was unusual. Few racecourses, in other words, possessed ideal (natural or man-made) surfaces, which added to the demand on horses. Moreover, most racing was a test of stamina and endurance rather than of speed. The long-time standard race, which comprised three heats of four miles, or four heats of three miles, depending on the dimensions of the course, meant that a horse might have to rum as many as 12 miles before being declared the victor. Racing over three three-miles heats, and three two-mile heats was also pursued, at Mullingar in 1753 and Loughrea and Boyle in 1753 and 1755 respectively.[152] Though it was standard practice if a horse won the first two heats, that the third was not run, it was also accepted that a race might be pursued into a fourth or, even, fifth heat in order to establish a winner.[153] Four and five heat races were

147 *UA*, 7 Oct. 1758, 10 July 1759.　148 Based on an analysis of reported runners and owners in *UA*, 1753–9.　149 For the Morragh, which was 'noted by travellers for its fine carpet of green sod on a perfect flat, almost 12 miles together' see Survey of county Wicklow, *c*.1760 (Armagh Public Library, Lodge collection, MS KI, II, 14, f. 2).　150 D'Arcy, *Horses, lords and racing men*, pp 3–6; Welcome, *Irish horse racing*, p. 13; *Public Gazetteer*, 25 Sept. 1759; Kelly, 'The pastime of the elite', pp 420–1.　151 *UA*, 11 May, 8 June, 5, 22 Oct., 1754, 21 May 1756, 6 Aug. 1757, 21 July, 5 Aug. 1758, 5 Aug. 1760; *Public Gazetteer*, 24 May, 11, 21 Oct. 1760 (Swords); Middleton and Vamplew, 'Horse racing and the Yorkshire leisure calendar in the early eighteenth century', pp 275–6.　152 For examples of three by two-mile heats see *PO*, 14 May 1753 (Mullingar); *UA*, 21 Aug. 1753 (Loughrea); of a three by three-mile heat race, see *UA*, 15 Aug. 1753 (Loughrea); *UA*, 16 Aug. 1755 (Boyle) and *Public Gazetteer*, 29 Apr. 1766.　153 For examples of three-heat races see

unusual, and palpably less commonplace than two heat races by the 1750s, but even if the trend was in the direction of fewer heats, it was not ubiquitous, and horse racing remained a demanding sport for horse and for rider. The task was certainly not made easier by the fact that the route to be run was generally defined by nothing more than a number of strategically positioned poles, and that the penalty for failing to keep on the proper side of these poles was disqualification.[154]

Consistent with its standing as the county's leading course, the Curragh was the first location to introduce more distinct course markings. This was done initially with a line of cord, and this medium may have been persisted with until the Jockey Club assumed the responsibility of erecting a more robust barrier. Indicatively, it determined in 1760, once the Deputy Ranger had secured his perquisite, that the balance of the entrance money receipts (paid by owners) should 'be applied by the Ranger for posts, rails and repairs of the course', and that this expenditure was to be 'accounted for annually at the Club's April meeting'.[155] The result was striking. When John Murray, the publisher, visited the course in 1775 he noted approvingly that 'part of the course from the winning post is railed in for about a mile for the horses to come in, and this part of the sod is equal to a bowling green for hardness, level and verdure'.[156] The Curragh was unusual in this respect. Most courses privileged stamina rather than speed. Good breeding usually won out, but it was not invariably the case. Horses were generally ridden by jockeys, rather than by their owners, though this too was not invariable. The stipulation included in the articles for Gort races in 1733 that 'no man is to ride his own horse; the riders [are] to be appointed by lot' was largely redundant in the eighteenth century, since it was unusual for gentlemen to ride their own mounts.[157] The primary exception to this was 'the gentlemen's purse', which only featured occasionally. When it was run at Carrigaline in July 1754 the young Edward Newenham rode his own horse unsuccessfully (into a distant second place), which may explain why owners generally preferred, when even this option was available, to delegate the task to a deputy, which is what happened when this choice was offered at Castlebar in August of the same year.[158]

Though the absence of regular reference to jockeys amidst the expansive volume of newspaper ink devoted to horse racing is emblematic of their lowly place in the social pecking order, the honourable mention accorded Paddy Murphy on the occasion of his death at Narraghmore, county Kildare, in 1760 indicates that the racing fraternity was well aware of the value of a good jockey.[159] It mirrored the appreciating realisation that racing in Ireland had nearly come of

PO, 6 Sept. 1748 (Mullingar), 19 Jan. 1759 (Curragh); *FDJ*, 3 Sept. 1748 (Cashel); Heber, *An historical list ... 1751*, pp 45–6, 126–7 (Clogheen, Castlebar); for examples of horses racing four heats see Heber, *An historical list ... 1751*, pp 65–5 (Assollas); *UA*, 9 Oct. 1753 (Lurgan); for the Jockey Club Purse of 1764 which required five heats see *Pubic Gazetteer*, 1 May, 16 June 1764. **154** James Medlicott's horse Buckinger was disqualified at Lacka, county Kildare, in 1753 because it 'ran the wrong side of a post': *UA*, 30 June 1753. **155** Resolution of Jockey Club, *UA*, 12 Apr. 1760. **156** John Murray's memorandum book, 1775 (NLS, Murray archive, MS 43018C f. 3). **157** *Dublin Evening Post*, 28 Aug. 1733. **158** *UA*, 6 July, 6 Aug. 1754. **159** *UA*, 25 Oct. 1760.

age. The establishment in 1747 of the Sportsmen's Club, its transmogrification in the 1750s into the Jockey Club, and the influence it brought to bear on the way that racing was conducted at the Curragh was one index of the sport's confidence, and of the emerging recognition in certain quarters that a still stronger regulatory body would be of benefit to the sport. It took a long time, and several organisational initiatives for this finally to come to pass, but Ireland was no different to England in this respect.[160] However, the near synchronous foundation on the two islands of clubs bearing the same name, with a disposition to perform an organisational and regulatory function, was a fair measure not only of the compatibility, but also of the comparable state of the sport in the two jurisdictions. This was underlined when, arising out of his assumption of responsibility for compiling the *Racing Calendar*, Reginald Heber decided to embrace Ireland within the expanded publication. Though he may have been guided by commercial considerations first and foremost, the presence of 30 Irish personages on the extensive subscription list to the 1751 volume, and Heber's complimentary reference to them suggests he too recognised the strides the sport had taken in Ireland in the course of the preceding decades, and that it would be to the benefit of racing in both islands if there was greater exchange and inter-action.[161]

Using the courses and meetings listed by Heber as a measure of their relative capacities, it is apparent that the sport of horse racing was conducted on a significantly smaller scale in Ireland (10 courses, 13 race meetings) at the midpoint of the eighteenth century than in England (73 courses, 109 race meetings), but that it was substantially in excess of Scotland (1 course, 1 meeting).[162] There were, it should be noted, more functioning racecourses in Ireland than the *Racing Calendar* knew about. Omissions have been detected in Heber's listing for 1751, and a closer perusal of the fuller newspaper record for 1755 has identified 18 race locations in Ireland in that year.[163] Since the number of multi-day events varied from year to year, the precise number is less crucial than the state of the sport, which was sufficiently robust in the early 1750s to sustain a long season extending from the spring meeting, which took place at the Curragh in April, through the summer and autumn to the end of season meetings at Ballinasloe, Corofin or Bagenalstown in the early winter. It was also better organised than at any point to date, and it is a measure of the sport's enhanced profile that racing was afforded unprecedented publicity in the most popular newspapers of the day – *Pue's Occurrences*, the *Universal Advertiser*, and the *Public Gazetteer*.

160 D'Arcy, *Horses, lords and racing men*, pp 2–8; Kelly, 'The pastime of the elite', pp 416–17. The assumption by the Jockey Club of responsibility for regulating horse racing in England was not achieved until the nineteenth century: see Mike Huggins, *Flat-racing and British society, 1790–1914: a social and economic history* (London, 1999), pp 174–203; Wray Vamplew, *The turf: a social and economic history of horse racing* (London, 1976), pp 77–109. **161** Heber, *An historical list of horse matches ... 1751*, preface, pp v–vii. **162** Ibid., pp 211–13. **163** Clogheen; Curragh (spring); Mullingar, Trim, Antrim, Carrigaline, Rathkeale, Limerick, Bellewstown, the Maze, Castlebar, Baltinglass, Killarney, Loughrea, Curragh, Boyle, Bagenalstown and Ringsend.

The 1750s was thus a boom time for the sport of horse racing in Ireland, and the Curragh set the pace. With financial assistance from the Jockey Club, the country's premier track offered larger and more appealing prizes from an impressive (by Irish standards) purse of between three and four hundred pounds a meeting, which ensured it attracted 'the prime' bloodstock in the country.[164] It also embraced the press, which was happy to act as the conduit of information. As a result, the Curragh races regained whatever social *éclat* they might have previously lost, and a day at the course was given the highest official imprimatur by the presence of the lord lieutenant, the marquess of Hartington, in 1755 and 1756.[165] As a consequence, not only did public interest in racing appreciate, but also competition improved as the number of owners eager to test the capacities of their star horses rose in parallel. Such was the sense of excitement that record numbers of horses were reported to be 'in train and preparing for the sod' in the spring of 1754.[166] The leading owners in the country in the 1750s were the earl of Antrim, Sir Edward O'Brien, Sir Ralph Gore, Sir Marmaduke Wyvill, Charles O'Neill, Thomas Walpole, and Maurice Keating, but they faced increasingly sharp competition from a host of established and new owners that included Charles Daly, John Hill Foster, Arthur Mervyn, William Henry Fortescue, John Browne, John Knox, Robert Burrowes, Sir Warren Crosby, the earl of Massereene, Thomas Newenham, Robert O'Callaghan, and others.[167] One positive consequence of this for the development of the sport was the greater emphasis that was placed on the rules. John Browne (from 1760 first Lord Monteagle), who ran a fine stable, exemplified this trend. He maintained that he lost out in 1761 when two of his horses were 'judged by some new rules in horse racing that I never before heard of', but he was so convinced that uniform rules were for the better he declined to sustain a protest. The organisers of the Rathkeale and the Carrigaline meetings in the summer of 1754 evidently thought likewise; they indicated in the published articles announcing their meeting that they would be guided in their actions 'by the established rules of the Curragh'.[168] And, in another indication of the desire for consistency, the organisers of the meeting at Broughshane signalled in 1757 that they would be guided in the weights that horses should bear by 'Mr Heber's book of horse races'.[169]

Encouraged by the example of the Curragh, and lured by the prospect of increased prize money, a variety of regional courses attracted unprecedented numbers of entrants during the 1750s. With a prestigious (and valuable) king's plate among its prizes, the Corporation of county Down horse breeders drew horses from as far south as the Curragh to the high-profile meeting it now alternated between the Maze and Downpatrick.[170] Others relied on the more familiar strat-

---

164 Kelly, 'The past time of the elite', pp 418–20; *UA*, 10 Sept. 1754; 12 Apr. 1755, *PO*, 20 Apr. 1756; *Public Gazetteer*, 22 Apr. 1760. 165 *UA*, 13 Sept. 1755; *PO*, 20 Apr. 1756; see also Barnard, *Making the grand figure*, p. 246. 166 *UA*, 26 Mar. 1754. 167 See Heber, *An historical list of horse matches … 1751–60*; *UA*, 1753–60. 168 *UA*, 11 Apr., 2 July 1754; Sir John Ainsworth (ed.), *Inchiquin manuscripts* (Dublin, 1961), p. 185. 169 *UA*, 6 Aug. 1757. 170 *UA*, 18 Sept. 1753.

egy of providing tempting headline prizes. Indicatively, the prize fund at Boyle, Loughrea and Castlebar was increased to between three hundred and four hundred pounds. The single richest race – a subscription purse for £120 (1754) rising to 150 guineas in 1755 – was run at Castlebar, but there was also a £100 race at Boyle, and daily purses of £50 at meetings such as Loughrea.[171] Another significant consequence of the increase in prize money, and the augmented number of owners and horses, was the emergence of Mullingar, Bellewstown and Trim in Leinster; Ballinsaloe, Boyle, Castlebar and Loughrea in Connaught, Clogheen and Carrigaline in Munster, and Broughshane in Ulster as significant regional centres of racing, albeit in some instances for a comparatively short period. Paradoxically, this diluted the sport's regional character, as owners responded by sending their horses further distances to compete.[172] This did not mean that one was not more likely to encounter the horses of Edward O'Brien in Munster and Connaught, and those of Lord Massereene in east Ulster, but they were also frequently entered for meetings in more far flung venues. Take O'Brien as an example; his horses are recorded competing (and usually winning) during the early and mid-1750s at Clogheen, Assollas, Limerick, Cashel, Rathkeale and Carrigaline in Munster; Ballinasloe, Castlebar, Eyrecourt, Gort, Loughrea, Tuam and Turloghmore in Connaught; Richhill, county Armagh, and at the Curragh. During the same time period, horses owned by Lord Massereene competed at the Maze, Downpatrick, Broughshane, Richhill and Antrim (all Ulster), Boyle, county Roscommon, and the Curragh. The earl of Antrim was still more venturesome; he sent horses to Clogheen (Munster), Boyle (Connaught), Trim, Drogheda and Mullingar (Leinster), and the Maze, Downpatrick, Richhill, Antrim and Broughshane (Ulster). Comparable patterns can be established with respect to other owners depending on their geographical place of origin.[173] The point is that the augmented number of courses, meetings, and prize money permitted individuals to achieve a measure of ascendancy within a region, from which they could mount an attempt at national dominance, which meant succeeding at the Curragh. As a result, success at the Curragh conferred a generous measure of social capital that had currency beyond the world of horse racing. When Sir Ralph Gore (Fig. 4) triumphed over Sir Edward O'Brien to win the king's plate for mares in September 1751, it was the cause of such 'great rejoicing' among his friends in Navan that a barrel of punch and a large tub of ale were made available to the populace to generate an appropriately celebratory mood.[174]

The press contrived to create the impression in the 1750s that horse racing was a joyous and engaging activity that promised those who attended 'extraordinary diversion'.[175] This was not an untruth, merely an exaggeration. Reports of violent altercations and assaults at horse races are unusual to be sure, but the

---

171 *UA*, 6 Aug. 1754, 22 July, 16 Aug. 1755, 8 Sept. 1759.   172 For example, it was reported in July 1754 which horses were being 'moved to Downpatrick' in advance of the races there: *UA*, 9 July 1754.   173 Based on an analysis of reported runners and owners in *UA*, 1753–9.   174 *Dublin Courant*, 10 Sept. 1751.   175 *UA*, 5 June, 14 Aug., 19 Sept. 1753.

Fig. 4 Equestrian portrait of Sir Ralph Gore (1725–1802), 6th baronet, later first earl of Ross, on his Bay Hunter. Gore was a key figure in the promotion and advancement of horse racing in Ireland in the 1750s (oil on canvas attributed to Thomas Spencer (1702–53), currently on show in Florence Court, county Fermanagh (The National Trust)).

'engagement between townsmen and mountaineers' reported at Wicklow races in the summer of 1753 in the course of which 'several persons were dangerously wounded' was an illustration of what could happen when ongoing rivalries were brought to the racecourse.[176] The more usual incidents were caused when a horse lost control, when a jockey was thrown or unseated and trampled underfoot, or when over-enthusiastic spectators encroached on the track in pursuit of the racing horses.[177]

---

176 *UA*, 16 June 1753.   **177** Mrs Delany to Anne Dewes, 10 July 1752 in Lady Llanover (ed.), *Autobiography and correspondence of Mrs Delany* (6 vols, London, 1861–2), iii, 136–8; *UA*, 8 Sept. 1753, 4 Nov. 1755. *FJ*, 22 Sept. 1764. In November 1755, it was deemed necessary by the organisers of racing at Ringsend 'to caution the public not to ride after the horses, in order to prevent

Horse racing was an inherently risky sport, as the injuries to which horses, riders, and, occasionally, spectators, were subject attest, but racing also inflicted severe financial injuries when enthusiasm prevailed over commonsense. This became more manifest in the 1750s also, as the sport assumed a higher profile, partly because of the increased prize money, but largely because the gambling that was integral to the sport became more daring. The closeness of the link between horse racing and gambling was underlined in 1754 when 'a gaming table, worth upwards of £40, known by the name of Rowly-Powly' was brought to Downpatrick for the duration of the race meeting. The intention of the owners of this apparatus was frustrated on this occasion by the intervention of 'the gentlemen of the sod' who seized, and burned, the offending table, but they were powerless to prevent race gambling, or to discourage the card-playing that was a feature of most such assemblies.[178] Because so much of this gambling was conducted privately, there is insufficient information with which to calculate the sums of money that changed hands at a typical meeting, but one can get some perspective from individual experiences, as Robert Clements' account of the fortunes of those in his circle at the Curragh in 1764 reveals:

> I returned last Sunday from the Curragh meeting, where I was as usual unsuccessful. I won every day upon the turf backing the field against the crack horse, but was every night broke by the round table. ... [Thomas] Conolly's horses were all beat as usual; he gave Lambert two hundred and twenty five g[uinea]s for his guelding the morning he was to run, and he was easily beat, tho' backed for much money against the field. However, he made it up at the hazard table having won about three hundred there. St Leger was cut up to the tune of thirteen hundred, which was won mostly by Kitty Burke. Harry Gore came off very well having won about two hundred and fifty.[179]

An equally helpful perspective on the financial expenditure the sport fostered is provided by the proliferation of matches during the 1750s.

The idea of two horses engaging in a test of speed and strength stretched back into antiquity. However, as horse racing became formalised in the eighteenth century, and competition came increasingly to focus on the racecourse, the three horse minimum rule discouraged match competition. Yet the idea did not disappear, and it was given something of a new lease on life by the surge in interest in the sport in the 1750s, as race organisers recognised that such events appealed to spectators, and rival owners yearned to test the quality of their bloodstock against each other rather than in open races. The organisers of the annual race meeting at Tralee in 1750 are a case in point; they opened the meeting with 'a match for

accidents'.　178 *UA*, 23 July 1754; more generally see Powell, *The politics of consumption*, pp 119–20.　179 Clements to Burton, 21 June 1764 (NLI, Killadoon papers, MS 36030/4), printed in A.P.W. Malcomson, *The Clements archive* (Dublin, 2010), p. 296.

Fig. 5 Silver punchbowl by William Williamson II, engraved by Daniel Pomarede, 1751, presented to mark the victory of Sir Ralph Gore's Black and all Black (otherwise Othello) over the ninth earl of March's Bajazet at the Curragh in September 1751 (Museum of Fine Arts, Boston).

one hundred guineas', which was small beer by comparison with the sum at stake when Sir Ralph Gore, by then one of the most influential figures of the Irish turf, matched his prize horse, Black and all Black (otherwise Othello), against the ninth earl of March's fabled Bajazet over four miles at the Curragh in September 1751.[180] Gore won 1,000 guineas, which was an unprecedented sum for an Irish match, and Black and all Black was for a time an equine celebrity memorialised on paper as well as in silver,[181] though the encounter's primary significance was that it restored the match to the heart of Irish racing (Fig. 5). As a consequence, many matches ensued over the following decade for sums ranging from £20 to 1000 guineas, and particular pairings that caught the public's imagination – one may instance the 1761 'match' between Beauchamp Bagenal's Prince Ferdinand

180 *Munster Journal*, 21 May 1750; Heber, *An historical list ...* 1751, p. 100; Sweeney, *Guide to the Irish turf*, p. 344. 181 The Black and all Black punchbowl, 1751, by William Williamson II and engraved by Daniel Pomarede (Fig. 5), is now in the Museum of Fine Arts, Boston; coloured engraving entitled 'A draught of the great match, which was run on the Curragh of Kildare near Dublin ... on 5 September 1751' by James Seymour and published in London by Henry Robert of Holborn: sold at Adam's, 30 April 2013; engraving of Ralph Gore's Othello (Black and all Black), by Henry Robert of original by Thomas Spencer: see Sweeney, *The Sweeney guide*, p. 103.

and Charles O'Neill's Hero – resulted in the laying of 'great bets' and were the subject of comment in the press.[182] Though their size might suggest otherwise, a substantial proportion of the wagers for £20 and £50 were laid by the likes of Charles O'Neill, Lord Antrim, Martin Dillon and Sir Patrick Bellew, who were sufficiently schooled in the perils of the sport to know that it was foolhardy to bet extravagantly on a match.[183] Others were less prudent. Edward Newenham is a case in point. A member of a middle-ranking aristocratic family, and the heir to a moderate inheritance, Newenham was seduced by the excitement of the turf not only to emulate his cousin Thomas by racing horses, but also to delude himself into believing that he could compete with those who were more experienced, knowledgeable and better circumstanced. By contemporary standards, Newenham did not bet extravagantly. He wagered 250 guineas in two matches in 1753 and 1756.[184] It was half what Arthur Mervyn and William Warren each staked in the legendary match between Warren's great horse Babraham, and Mervyn's Jupiter in 1759. It was also significantly less than the 400 guineas staked by John Hill Foster and the 350 plus by Sir Edward O'Brien, each in three matches, and in the same league as that wagered by Lord Massereene (200 guineas) and John Knox (200 guineas). Yet it was significantly in excess of the sums wagered in comparable circumstances during the 1750s by such *aficionados* of the turf as Sir Ralph Gore (175 guineas), John Browne (150 guineas), Lord Antrim (100 guineas), and William Henry Fortescue (100 guineas).[185] The problem for Newenham was that he did not have the resources to absorb such losses, with the result that his preparedness to venture such sums compounded the financial problems that obliged him, in 1756, to forsake horse racing completely, and to raise £4,000 against his properties.[186] It was a familiar strategy, and it could have devastating consequences. Significantly, this was the experience also of Sir Edward O'Brien, for several decades the most passionate and, ostensibly, most successful of Irish race owners.[187] From his base at Assollas, county Clare, O'Brien established an enviable stable of pedigree horses. These brought him many prizes over a period of three decades, and contributed to the improvement in the quality of Irish bloodstock, but the money he garnered was not commensurate with his outlay. O'Brien contrived either to minimise, or to ignore, the financial implications of his self-indulgence, choosing, in the manner of the addicted gambler, to defend his 'sole amusement' as essentially a benign recreation. He was able as a result to sustain

182 *Public Gazetteer*, 12 Sept. 1761. 183 *Munster Journal*, 17 July 1749; *UA*, 23 June, 4, 8 Sept., 9 Oct., 17 Nov. 1753, 4 May, 7, 21, 28 Sept. 1754, 14 Oct. 1755, 28 May, 7 Nov. 1758, 16 Oct., 11 Dec. 1759. 184 *UA*, 22 Sept. 1753, 10 Mar, 3 Apr. 1756. 185 *UA*, 3 Apr., 26 June, 22 Sept. 1753, 2 Apr. 1754, 10 Mar. 3, 6 Apr. 1756, 17 Sept. 1757, 28 July, 11 Sept. 1759, 3 May 1760; *Public Gazetteer*, 8, 15, 18 Sept. 1759, 19 Oct. 1760; Sweeney, *Guide to the Irish turf*, p. 346; *PO*, 16 Oct. 1759. 186 James Kelly, *Sir Edward Newenham, MP, 1734–1814: defender of the Protestant constitution* (Dublin, 2002), p. 33. 187 *DIB*, *sub nom*; Sweeney, *The Sweeney guide*, pp 49, 178. Among his many triumphs, Sir Edward won the £100 plate at the Curragh in 1732 and 1742: *PO*, 16 Sept. 1732, *Dublin Gazette*, 10 Apr. 1742, and purchased expensive English horses over several decades: *Dublin Evening Post*, 28 Jan. 1735; *UA*, 3 Nov. 1753.

the role of both patron and practitioner, equally at home at the local races at Assollas or Corofin as at the Curragh. This was tolerable as long as he could access the requisite resources, but it was apparent by the mid-1750s that he was in severe financial difficulties. Sir Edward limped on for a number of years until 1759, when he was obliged by his son, Lucius, 'to turn child', and accede to the appointment in January of trustees and, in August, to the humiliation of the sale by 'public cant' of his 'entire stud' at Assollas races. The man who had witnessed and contributed much to the development of horse racing in Ireland during his lifetime, concluded his life one of its more high-profile casualties.[188] Yet, O'Brien's cautionary life story did not cause other ambitious owners to proceed with greater circumspection. The coverage matches were accorded in the press indicates that this style of racing remained popular with owners and punters alike through the 1760s and beyond. Moreover, the sums staked – even at regional meetings such as Bellewstown, where bets in the order of 400 guineas were reported – indicated that the enthusiasm for the sport showed no signs of easing though clearly the trajectory of growth registered between 1730 and 1760 could hardly be sustained much longer.[189]

CONSOLIDATION, 1761–90

Consistent with its status as the most 'fashionable' recreational activity of 'the nobility and gentry', various suggestions were offered in the 1750s and 1760s as to how the sport might be developed to greater national advantage. It was, for example, suggested at one point that a network of 'training stables' might be established to facilitate the production of 'good riders', which would permit the sport to be 'carried on with more satisfaction and elegance'.[190] Utilitarian schemes of this nature were entirely in keeping with the commitment to improvement that informed public discourse, though they afforded insufficient recognition to the fact that the search for success on the racecourse not only secured the sport of horse racing a prominent place in the public sphere (a point underlined by the detailed coverage accorded the 'epidemical distemper' that afflicted horses in the winter of 1750–1, and by the ongoing interest in equine disease),[191] but also brought about an improvement in the quality of the country's equine bloodstock. The latter can be ascribed in considerable part to the readiness of owners like Edward O'Brien and Marmaduke Wyvill to spend heavily on the purchase of

188 *UA*, 3 Nov. 1753, 31 Aug. 1754, 4 Aug. 1759, 7 Oct. 1760; L.F. McNamara, 'Some matters touching Dromoland: letters of father and son, 1758–59', *North Munster Antiquarian Journal*, 28 (1986), pp 67, 70; D'Arcy, *Horses, lords and racing men*, p. 3. 189 See below pp 82, 84n, 87, 88, 101; *FJ*, 7 Sept. 1771. 190 *PO*, 25 Aug. 1759. 191 *Munster Journal*, 17, 24, 27, 31 Dec. 1750, 3, 7, 14, 31 Jan. 1751. In 1755, an Irish edition of William Gibson, *A new treatise on the diseases of horses* ... (3rd edn, Dublin, 1755) was published. An abridged version of the same was published in Dublin in 1756.

racers,[192] but quality breeding stock (Arabian horses were especially esteemed) was also imported in significant numbers over several decades.[193] Moreover, as the preoccupation with pedigree, bloodlines and the maintenance of stud books (which this encouraged) intensified, well bred stock made premium prices of 2,000 guineas, or more,[194] with the result that the willingness of gentlemen to pay more than they could reasonably afford for a prize-winning horse was balanced by the calculation that they would later recoup the cost in stud fees, and it is thus not coincidental that a preoccupation with breeding occurred in tandem with the rise in interest in racing.

There is no gainsaying the fact that the breeding and racing of horses was inextricably intertwined. The reservation of certain races to 'Irish bred' horses was a manifestation of this, but the connection was made still more explicit by the presence of stallions to 'be let out to mares' on race day at certain courses.[195] This was not common by comparison with the advertisement of the availability of quality breeding stock, which surged in the 1740s. Prompted by the realisation that there were sufficient horse owners willing to pay for the privilege of setting their mare to a good sire, increasingly larger sums were offered for good stallions. For example, Pierce Creagh paid Edward O'Brien 400 guineas in 1752 for the 'famous stallion Old England', but since he anticipated a fee of 5 guineas each time the stallion covered a mare he clearly calculated on recouping his investment.[196] Five guineas was towards the top end of the stud fees that were charged. Horses advertised at that fee invariably possessed a good pedigree and a winning record as a racer, which was something owners highlighted.[197] The most popular horse in this category was Bajazet, which was owned by Sims and Heney, a partnership that maintained a string of 'high-bred, high-priced horses', assembled 'at great expence', whose stud fees ranged during the 1750s between one and five guineas.[198] They were not the only operation of this kind. John Browne maintained an equally impressive stud at Breasy, near Castlebar, whose most valuable asset was an Arabian horse whose stud fee was ten guineas. Interestingly, this horse possessed neither a name nor a winning race record, but the fee was justified because of the high esteem in which Arabian horses were held. Otherwise, because a horse's record as a racer was deemed a reliable guide to its progeny's performance, the earning potential of a horse that was a proven winner could be considerable.[199]

192 *FDJ*, 27 Feb. 1747; *Munster Journal*, 3 May 1754. **193** *FDJ*, 24 May 1748; *Munster Journal*, 12 Mar., 15 May, 23 July 1750; *PO*, 26 May 1752; *UA*, 3 Feb., 9 Mar., 14 Aug. 1754, 13 May 1754; *Public Gazetteer*, 15 Apr. 1760, 21 Apr. 1761, 19 Apr. 1763; *FJ*, 6 Apr. 1765; *FLJ*, 22 July 1772. **194** *UA*, 21 Mar., 6 Apr. 1754, 25 Feb. 1758, 12 June 1759; *Munster Journal*, 16 July 1750; *Public Gazetteer*, 29 Mar. 1760, 19 July 1763; *FJ*, 22 Mar. 1766, 7 Apr. 1770; *BNL*, 5 Aug. 1768. **195** As at Clogheen, for example: see *Munster Journal*, 3 May 1754. **196** *PO*, 18 Nov. 1752; see also *Munster Journal*, 3 May 1750. **197** *UA*, 3 Apr. 1753, 14 Mar. 1754, 3 Apr. 1756, 24 Feb. 1759; *PO*, 3 Apr. 1753; *Public Gazetteer*, 29 Mar. 1760, 18 Apr. 1761, 19 Apr. 1763. **198** *UA*, 2 Apr., 7, 25 May 1754, 27 Jan. 1756, 23 Apr. 1757, 3 May 1760. **199** *UA*, 16 Mar. 1754, 3 Apr. 1756; *Public Gazetteer*, 29 Mar. 1760, 5 June 1764. For other notices advertising Arab horses see ibid., 2

Fig. 6 'Miss Doe a mare of Sir Edward O'Brien bart. she beat the duke of Bolton's famous horse Sterling', 1750s. Mezzotint by Richard Houston, from the copy sold at Whyte's auctioneers, January 2013 (by permission of Whyte's).

A majority of the horses at stud did not fit any of these categories of course. This notwithstanding, many owners were able to charge the still significant sum of two guineas, groom fee not included, but because there was an extensive menu of stallions to choose from, a majority could be had for the standard price of 'one guinea each mare, leaps and trial, and two shillings (English) to the groom', or for the still more reasonable 'half a guinea a mare, and one shilling to the groom'.[200] Since the fee was determined by reputation, the cost was commensurate with the perceived quality of the sire. The largest fees were paid for those stallions that were perceived most likely to produce top racers; the lower end of the market was occupied by mediocre, unproven or unfashionable sires. Yet, as the enterprise of Charles Varley, at Stockhole, Swords, county Dublin, attested, even average stallions possessed considerable earning power. He advertised Young Ramper, whose father Old Ramper was 'a famous running horse', in 1759 as 'every way qualified to breed fox hunters, as well as race and chapmen's horses' at the 'low price' of 'three crowns a mare' (plus 1*s.* 6*d.* to the groom).

Apr., 2 July 1754; *Munster Journal*, 3 May 1754, 15 May 1759.   **200** *FDJ*, 27 Feb. 1747; *UA*, 15 May 1749, 7 May 1754, 15 Sept. 1759; *Munster Journal*, 15 Mar. 1750, 15 May 1759; *PO*, 3 Apr. 1753; BNL, 26 Apr. 1768, 5 May 1769; *Ennis Chronicle*, 5 Apr., 13 May 1790, 28 Feb., 24 Mar., 4 Apr. 1791.

Other sires, targeted at producing good working horses, were available for less; Bomelbee, 'a famous draught horse', could be had for 'three half crowns English, per mare, and a shilling to the groom'.[201]

While the proliferation of notices bearing equine images and lyrically worded texts advertising the qualities of the sires at stud mirrored the high esteem in which horse racing was held at mid-century, the decision of Robert Fish of Kilcullen to highlight the proximity of his house and demesne to the Curragh in the notice published in 1760 announcing their availability to rent was a further illustration of the appreciating appeal of 'the turf'.[202] Its allure was echoed in the production, over and above the usual trophies, of visual images related to horses and horse racing. A striking example is Richard Houston's mezzotint 'Miss Doe, a mare of Sir Edward O'Brien bart.' (Fig. 6), which dates from the early 1750s when O'Brien was one of the dominant forces in Irish racing.[203] The fact that Houston, who was born in Dublin, plied his craft in London, where he achieved a measure of renown as a superior engraver of racing horses, is evidence that the racing fraternity in Ireland was not large enough to sustain a specialist in this area but the demand for equestrian images in the middle decades of the century did provide some with profitable opportunities.[204] The most remarkable was Robert Healy (1743–71), a young artist, and recent graduate of the Dublin Society school, who was given an opportunity to demonstrate his capacities as a sporting artist when Thomas Conolly,[205] who succeeded Edward O'Brien as the dominant owner of his generation, invited him in 1768–9 to prepare a series of pastels for Castletown House (Fig. 18). Though the nine monochrome drawings that resulted depict members of the Conolly household and staff engaged in various pursuits, six include horses and they are of such vivacity that Healy has been described (by Desmond Guinness) as 'the nearest there was to being an Irish Stubbs'.[206] This may flatter Healy somewhat, but the fact that he was commissioned to create such rich images for the most important Palladian house in

201 *UA*, 3 Feb. 1754. For Varley and his activities in the horse trade see Desmond Clarke (ed.), *The unfortunate husbandman: an account of the life and travels of a real farmer in Ireland, Scotland, England and America by Charles Varley* ... (London, 1964), p. 75. 202 *UA*, 5 Aug. 1760. 203 Richard Houston (1721/2–1775), 'Miss Doe a mare of Sir Edward O'Brien bart. she beat the Duke of Bolton's famous horse Sterling', mezzotint, *c*.1755. This print was sold at Whyte's auction of History, literature and collectibles in January 2013; see catalogue item 455. A print, also engraved in London, of the race between Bajazet and Othello (Black and all Black) in 1751 is titled 'A draught of the great match, which was run on the Curragh of Kildare near Dublin ... on 5 September 1751' by James Seymour and published by Henry Robert: a copy was sold at Adam's on 30 April 2013. 204 Houston (1721/2–75) plied his craft in London, where he achieved a measure of renown as a superior engraver of portraits as well as racing horses: see W.G. Strickland, *Dictionary of Irish artists* (2 vols, Shannon, 1969), i, 526–7; *ODNB sub nomine*. This point is reinforced by the fact that the pleasing series of equine portraits, which include Ralph Gore's Othello (Black and all Black), engraved in the 1750s were also prepared in England: see Sweeney, *The Sweeney guide*, plate 9, p. 103. 205 See below, pp 83–4. 206 Desmond Guinness, 'Robert Healy: an eighteenth-century Irish sporting artist', *Apollo*, 115:240 (Feb. 1982), pp 80–5; John Mulcahy, 'Lost to Castletown', *Irish Arts Review*, Summer 2012, pp 98–103; *DIB sub nomine*.

Map 3: Horse racing in Ireland, 1761–90: courses

the kingdom by the country's leading racehorse owner, was an eloquent statement of the status of the racehorse in Irish life.

Significant as this artistic endeavour was as a statement of the cultural capital that horse racing possessed, it was less economically and socially consequential than the number of functional racecourses and their distribution. A geospatial
illustration of known courses between 1761 and 1790 (Map 3) indicates that
racing was more evenly distributed across the island's landscape during these
three decades than was the case during the preceding thirty years (Map 2).
Leinster was still the heartland of horse racing, with 44 per cent of identified
courses, though in numerical terms it had 20 per cent fewer functioning courses.
The most striking spatial manifestation of this numerical decrease is the virtual
absence of a course in counties Louth and Wexford. However, since neither
county had previously sustained an active involvement in the sport, and since
there was an array of courses within accessible range, its impact was of the same
order, and significance, as the failure of courses at Finea (county Westmeath),
Myshall (county Carlow), and Rednah (county Wicklow), which contributed to
the net decline in the number of courses in counties Meath, Westmeath, Kildare,
Wicklow and Carlow by one or two.[207] It was, in other words, essentially a manifestation of consolidation rather than contraction.

The situation in Leinster was certainly more encouraging than the situation in
Connaught where the number of courses fell by a striking 40 per cent, from 15 to
9, during the same time period (see Table 2). The effects of this decline were most
manifest in county Galway, but the cessation of racing at Castleblakeney, Boyle
and Castlebar not only deprived Connaught of three significant courses, but also
of three major patrons – the Blakeneys, Lord Kingsborough and Lord Monteagle
– whose withdrawal from racing impacted the sport nationally as well as regionally. Munster did not experience an equivalent loss of patrons post 1760, though
there was a significant decline, in the order of 30 per cent, in the number of identifiable racecourses. In this case, the financial difficulties that obliged Sir Edward
O'Brien to embark on a severe programme of retrenchment contributed to the
decision to suspend racing at Assolas and Corofin in county Clare. The new course
at Ennis offered an alternative to people in the region, but the observation of one
of the O'Briens in 1763 that 'the races were … useless to the town …, hurtfull to
the country in general, and not very pleasureable to the idle people who attended
them' suggested that it did not get off to the best of starts, and that it would have
to proceed without the support of the O'Briens of Dromoland.[208] Elsewhere, the
decline in the number of courses in Munster was more obviously a consequence of
the fact, exemplified by the example of county Limerick, that the environment was
less favourable to smaller meetings. This had an impact also on south county Cork,
where the ongoing effort to identify a location that would sustain a major meeting

207 *Hibernian Journal*, 7 Oct. 1776 (Finae); *FLJ*, 26 June 1773 (Rednah); *Hibernian Journal*, 28
Sept. 1789 (Myshall). 208 Ainsworth (ed.), *The Inchiquin manuscripts*, p. 189; *Public Gazetteer*, 25
Oct. 1763, 26 May, 5 June 1764,

Table 2: Race meetings by province and county, 1761–90							
LEINSTER		**MUNSTER**		**CONNAUGHT**		**ULSTER**	
County	*Number*	*County*	*Number*	*County*	*Number*	*County*	*Number*
Louth	–	Kerry	2	Galway	5	Antrim	5
Meath	5	Cork	5	Roscommon	1	Down	7
Longford	3	Waterford	1	Mayo	1	Armagh	3
Westmeath	4	Limerick	2	Sligo	2	L'derry	1
Dublin	10	Tipperary	4	Leitrim	–	Fermanagh	2
Kildare	2	Clare	3			Cavan	1
Wicklow	2					Monaghan	2
King's County	2					Tyrone	1
Queen's County	1					Donegal	1
Kilkenny	4						
Carlow	4						
Wexford							
Total (%)	38 (44)		17 (20)		9 (10)		23 (26)

Source: *Freeman's Journal*, 1763–90; *Public Gazetteer*, 1761–68; *Hoey's Public Journal*, 1771–3; *Finn's Leinster Journal*, 1767–90; *Hibernian Journal*, 1773–90; *Dublin Gazette*, 1765, 1775; *Belfast News Letter*, 1763–90; *Faulkner's Dublin Journal*, 1778; *Volunteer Journal (Cork)*, 1783, 1786; *Dublin Morning Post*, 1785; *Dublin Evening Post*, 1786; *Saunder's Newsletter*, 1786; *Volunteer Evening Post*, 1787; *Clonmel Gazette*, 1788–90; *Ennis Chronicle*, 1789; *Dublin Chronicle*, 1787–90; *Dublin Weekly Journal*, 1790; Tony Sweeney et al., *The Sweeney guide to the Irish turf from 1501 to 2001* (Dublin, 2002).

in the environs of the country's second city continued to frustrate. However, as in Connaught, it was not only smaller meetings that failed to flourish that disappeared from view. Racing also ceased at Fethard and Clogheen, which were popular venues for a time with the population of south county Tipperary and environs.

Ulster was the only province in which the number of identified courses rose between 1761 and 1790. As a comparison of maps 2 and 3 reveals, this can be ascribed to two trends – the striking rise in interest in racing in counties Antrim and Down, and the penetration of the sport into the central and western parts of the province. Taking the situation first in east Ulster, it would appear that much of the energy and efforts allocated to the task of preparing new courses was not always well-conceived, as many enjoyed the briefest of existences. This is the case, for example, of courses at Ballyclare, county Antrim, and Kircubbin and Guilford in county Down, which may have hosted only one meeting.[209] Other

209 *BNL*, 27 Dec. 1787 (Ballyclare); 25 Sept. 1767 (Kircubbin); *Hibernian Journal*, 10 June 1776

venues proved more enduring; the courses at Broughshane and Antrim town sustained important regional meetings in mid-county Antrim through the 1760s and 1770s, while Ballymoney hosted a lively meeting, with cockfighting, for a decade between 1761 and 1771.[210] The situation was not altogether different in county Down. A successful race meeting was held at intervals at Comber between the mid-1750s and 1770s, at Castlewellan in the 1770s, and at Killileagh between 1781 and 1788.[211] However, these courses took a lowly second place to the meeting organised by the Corporation of Horse breeders in county Down, which continued to draw some of the finest horses in the country alternately to Downpatrick and the Maze (or Hillsborough as it was now known).[212]

Hillsborough and Downpatrick were unrivalled as Ulster's leading racecourses, but the increased popularity of the sport spawned nearly a dozen attempts between 1760 and 1790 to establish courses in the south, centre and western parts of the province (Table 2). Most were short-lived. None of the three attempts made in county Armagh (at Richhill, Middletown and Fathan, near Newry) lasted for more than a few years.[213] The situation was comparable at Clones (county Monaghan), Belturbet (county Cavan), and Lowtherstown (county Fermanagh), which together account for more than half of the identifiable courses established outside east Ulster. Others were more successful, though none of them put down lasting roots. It was unclear also which would emerge as the leading course in south Ulster, as Monaghan (1761–7), Clones (1777, 1779) and Aughnacloy (1775–82) each asserted its claim, but Enniskillen, which sustained a fitful pattern of racing through the 1760s and 1770s, emerged in the 1780s as the strongest location, and it seemed an established fixture on the national racing calendar by the early 1790s.[214] By contrast, though Londonderry races enjoyed considerable success during the lull that gripped several parts of the country when the America War of Independence dominated the political

(Guilford).   210 *BNL*, 23 Sept. 1763, 23 Sept. 1768, 12 Nov. 1776; *FLJ*, 16 Nov. 1776 (Broughshane); *BNL*, 6 Sept. 1763, 21 Sept. 1764, 27 Sept., 8 Oct. 1771, 13 July 1773, 30 Aug. 1774, 14 Oct. 1777, 24 Sept. 1779, 12 Sept. 1780, 28 Sept. 1781, 3 Oct. 1788, 2 Oct. 1789, 7 Oct. 1791 (Antrim); *BNL*, 11 Aug. 1761, 31 Aug. 1762, 20 June 1763, 17 Aug. 1764, 18 July 1766, 28 Aug. 1767, 5 Aug. 1768, 18 Aug. 1769, 3 Aug. 1770, 3 Sept. 1771; *Public Gazetteer*, 21 Aug. 1764 (Ballymoney).   211 *BNL*, 27 July 1756, 20 June 1775 (Comber); 3 Aug. 1773, 12 Aug. 1774, 8 Aug. 1775, 15 Aug. 1777, 7 Sept. 1779; *FLJ*, 13 Aug. 1774; *FJ*, 2 Sept. 1780 (Castlewellan); *BNL*, 31 July 1781, 30 July 1782, 22 July 1783, 6 Aug. 1784, 22 July 1785, 6 July 1786, 7 Aug. 1787, 18 July 1788; *FJ*, 10 Aug. 1784 (Killileagh).   212 *BNL*, June–Aug. 1760–90; *Public Gazetteer*, 8 Aug. 1761, 19 July 1763, 5 Aug. 1766, 4 Aug. 1767; *Hoey's Publick Journal*, 22 July 1771; *Dublin Morning Post*, 26 Mar. 1785; *FLJ*, 29 July 1772, 30 July 1774, 3 Aug. 1776, 6 Aug. 1788, 5 Aug. 1789; *FJ*, 31 July 1784; *Dublin Weekly Journal*, 31 July 1790.   213 *BNL*, 9 June 1761, 28 July 1769 (Richhill); 14 Sept. 1764 (Middleton); 27 June 1769, 16 Oct. 1770 (Fathan).   214 *BNL*, 23 June 1761, 4 Aug. 1767 (Monaghan); 5 Sept. 1777, 10 Aug. 1779 (Clones); 20 July 1784 (Lowtherstown); *Public Gazetteer*, 12 July 1763; *FLJ*, 28 July 1773, 29 June 1776, 11 July 1789; *Hibernian Journal*, 1 Sept. 1780; *FJ*, 11 July 1789, 2 July 1790; *BNL*, 27 Aug. 1784, 5 June 1787, 7 Aug. 1792 (Enniskillen); *Clonmel Gazette*, 24 July 1788; *Hibernian Journal*, 9 Sept. 1789 (Belturbet); *BNL*, 10 Oct. 1775, 30 July 1776, 22 July 1777, 31 July 1781, 24 Sept. 1784.

Fig. 7 Hugh Percy (formerly Smithson), eighteenth earl of Northumberland (1714–86) and lord lieutenant of Ireland, 1763–5, was a warm supporter of horse racing, and the donor of the gold cup, commonly known as the 'Northumberland Cup', that was one of the premier prizes in Irish racing (engraving after a portrait by Joshua Reynolds, in National Portrait Gallery, London).

horizon, its decline was as precipitous as its rise, and it had been replaced as the course of the north-west by Ballybofey by the late 1780s.[215]

Though this variegated pattern of regional rise and decline might suggest that the fortunes of racecourses, and by extension of horse racing, oscillated sharply between 1761 and 1790, the reality was that the sport consolidated its position as the island's most popular and best-organised recreation. It was not a picture of uninterrupted development to be sure, as following a period of fifteen or more years of robust growth spanning the 1750s and early 1760s, the level of public engagement declined beginning in the late 1760s. The sport experienced still greater difficulty during the second half of the 1770s, and while it embarked on a recovery in the early 1780s, the result was fitful and uneven. One reliable barometer of the state of the sport on the island is provided by the Curragh.

215 *BNL*, 27 June 1775, 30 July 1776, 15 Aug. 1777, 31 July 1778, 1 June 1779, 5 June 1781, 1 June 1784; *Hibernian Journal*, 9 July 1781 (Londonderry); *FLJ*, 9 Nov. 1776, 30 Oct. 1779, 23 Nov. 1782, 30 May 1787, 19 Nov. 1788; *Hibernian Journal*, 7 Nov. 1777; *BNL*, 4 Oct. 1776, 14 Nov. 1777, 5 Sept. 1788, 22 May 1789 (Ballybofey).

Building on what had been achieved in the 1750s, the course signalled its ambition to maintain its trajectory of growth by organising a stakes' race 'for 800 guineas' in September 1761, and it was enabled during the early 1760s, by combining high stake matches and the sponsorship of the Jockey Club, to offer the biggest and most attractive prizes. This ensured that success at the Curragh remained the primary object of the leading horse owners, which guaranteed it large and competitive fields for most of its races.[216] It also ensured that it remained unchallenged as the country's premier course, and its status, and, by extension, the status of the sport, was acknowledged when, following his appointment to the lord lieutenancy of Ireland in 1763, Hugh, the eighteenth earl of Northumberland (Fig. 7), visited the course, and donated 100 guineas from his salary towards the provision of a race prize (known for a time as 'the Northumberland purse').[217] He subsequently donated a 'gold cup', which augmented the number of prizes for which the Curragh was already envied.[218]

The Jockey Club was crucial to the improved profile of the Curragh during the 1750s because it not only proved a generous sponsor of races, but also embraced most of the key figures in Irish racing within its ranks. Having in 1759 opened a clubhouse in Kildare town, it seemed well placed to realise the ambition of some of its leading lights that it should become the regulating body of the sport in Ireland. However, its inability in 1764 to renew the seven-year sponsorship of the Jockey Club plates it had entered into in 1757, and affirmed in 1760, indicated that it could no longer access the resources required to sponsor racing to the tune of £200 per annum, and its status and influence began to diminish.[219] In other times, this might have spelled immediate problems for the Curragh course, but the Jockey Club contrived to sustain its financial support, albeit on a less regular and more obviously *ad hoc* basis, into the 1770s, and there were enough subscriber purses, sweepstakes and matches to ensure, with the king's and lord lieutenant's plates, that the Curragh did not have visible difficulty in scheduling races that attracted the best bloodstock on the island.[220] Moreover, it benefited in the early 1760s from the reinforcement of the cadre of owners who dominated the sport in the late 1750s – Arthur Mervyn, Sir Ralph Gore, Charles O'Neill, Thomas Burrowes, William Henry Fortescue, Thomas Knox, Lord Massereene, John St Leger, Lord Monteagle, John Hill Foster, Charles Daly and Lord Antrim – with a new generation of racing enthusiasts.[221] The most signifi-

216 *Public Gazetteer*, 18 Apr., 12 Sept. 1761, 25 Sept. 1762, 9, 26 Apr., 21 June, 17 Sept. 1763, 28 Apr. 1764. 217 *Public Gazetteer*, 18 June 1763, 14 Sept. 1765, 16 Sept. 1766. The fact that the allowance for the plate came from the lord lieutenant's allowance encouraged successive lords lieutenant to take an interest in horse racing, yet it was not uncontentious. The third Earl Hardwicke (lord lieutenant, 1801–6) objected strongly to the fact that the charge fell 'upon the lord lieutenant's income': A.P.W. Malcomson, *Nathaniel Clements: government and the governing elite in Ireland, 1725–75* (Dublin, 2005), p. 179. 218 *Clonmel Gazette*, 17 Nov. 1790. 219 *UA*, 12 Apr. 1760; *Public Gazetteer*, 16, 19 June 1764; Kelly, 'The pastime of the elite', pp 419–21; D'Arcy, *Horses, lords and racing men*, pp 6, 8. 220 *Public Gazetteer*, 21 Apr., 16, 19 June 1764, 22, 19 Apr. 1766; *FJ*, 21 May, 18 Apr., 23 Dec. 1769; *Hoey's Publick Journal*, 24 Apr. 1772; *FLJ*, 2 May 1772. 221 Extracted from

Fig. 8 Thomas Conolly (1738–1803) was the dominant racehorse owner from the 1760s and one of the chief patrons of racing (oil on canvas, by Anton Raphael Mengs, 1758, National Gallery of Ireland Collection).

cant was Thomas Conolly (Fig. 8), the heir to the vast Conolly of Castletown fortune, whose devotion to the turf matched that of Edward O'Brien, whose place he may be said to have taken.[222] It is a measure of Conolly's impact on

the cards of various meetings: see *Public Gazetteer*, 18 Apr., 12 Sept. 1761, 25 Sept. 1762, 9, 26 Apr., 21 June, 17 Sept. 1763, 28 Apr. 1764. The name of Charles Doherty/Dogherty can also be added to this list; he assumed control of the Doherty stud on the death of James Doherty in 1756: see above, pp 60, and *FJ*, 15 Apr. 1766, 15 Sept. 1767.   **222** A.P.W. Malcomson, 'The fall of the house of Conolly, 1758–1803' in Eoin Magennis and Allan Blackstock (eds), *Politics and political culture in Britain and Ireland, 1750–1850* (Belfast, 2007), pp 118–19; *Public Gazetteer*, 12 Sept. 1761, 9 Apr., 21 June 1763. Conolly was willing to stake heavily; in 1763, he wagered (and won) 500

racing in county Kildare that a new meeting was initiated at Celbridge, close to where he lived, within a few years of his return to Ireland from the grand tour.[223]

Conolly established himself as Ireland's leading racehorse owner in the 1760s with entrants in virtually every race meeting held on the Curragh. He did not always win the main prize, but his horses – Surly, Strongbow, Jolly Bacchus, Banker, Apollo, Richmond, Shoemaker, Lenox, Thumper, Ariadne, etc., etc. – were invariably competitive, and they won with enviable regularity.[224] The active involvement of Conolly, notwithstanding, horse racing experienced financial difficulties, comparable to those that gripped the exchequer, and the nation, during the 1760s and early 1770s, which was most obviously manifest in the contraction in the size of the purses, especially in the early 1770s, and the increased number of sweepstakes. Owners still ventured large sums in match races. These were sufficiently newsworthy to make the news columns on occasion, but their popularity did not make up for the loss to the sport caused by the exit of most of the generation of owners whose involvement helped make the 1750s and early 1760s a golden era in Irish racing, the contraction in the number of horses that were available to race, and the problems encountered by the Jockey Club.[225] These problems inevitably affected the quality of racing, but not its competitive character, as Thomas Conolly did not have it all his own way. He encountered stern competition in the 1770s from a number of Connaught owners – Lord Altamont, Denis Daly, James Daly, Denis Bowes Daly, Anthony Daly, William Power Keating Trench, Charles O'Hara, Xaverius Blake, John Kirwan, and others.[226] Yet these rivalries did not draw crowds in anything like their previous numbers, as John Murray observed when he visited the Curragh in June 1775:

> Though this day's races promised to be important ..., there was nothing like a crowd upon the road ... There appeared not to day so many ladies or fine carriages as might be expected upon the first course in the kingdom, and in this respect it falls short (not to speak of Newmarket) but of the inferior races of York, Edinb[urgh] and other places.[227]

---

guineas, and in 1764 200 guineas (which he lost) on his horses in two single matches. In 1775, on consecutive days he bet 1,000 guineas on Jolly Bacchus beating Paymaster, and 2,000 guineas on his horse Shoemaker beating Lord Drogheda's Chestnut Pope: Sweeney, *Sweeney's guide to the Irish turf*, p. 346; *Public Gazetteer*, 21 Apr. 1764; *Dublin Gazette*, 20 June 1775. See also, Patrick Walsh and A.P.W. Malcomson (eds), *The Conolly archive* (Dublin, 2010), pp 130–1, 224, 397; *FJ*, 26 Apr. 1770, 8 June 1771. **223** *Public Gazetteer*, 25 Sept. 1762. **224** *Public Gazetteer*, 14 Sept. 1765, 29 Apr., 14, 17 June, 13, 16 Sept. 1766, 30 Apr. 1768; *Hoey's Publick Journal*, 26 Apr., 13 Sept. 1771; *FLJ*, 10 June 1772; Sweeney, *Sweeney's guide to the Irish turf*, p. 347. **225** *Public Gazetteer*, 28 Apr. 1764, 15, 29 Apr. 1766; *Hoey's Publick Journal*, 19 Apr., 9 Sept. 1771; 22, 24 Apr., 11 Sept. 1772; *FJ*, 25 Apr. 1772; *FLJ*, 2 May, 10 June, 16 Sept. 1772; D'Arcy, *Horses, lords and racing men*, pp 8–9. **226** *FJ*, 18 Apr. 1769, 26 Apr. 1770; *Hoey's Publick Journal*, 19 Apr., 9 Sept. 1771, 7 June, 22 Oct. 1773, 15 June 1776; *FLJ*, 2 May, 10 June, 16 Sept. 1772, 1 May 1773, 4 May 1774. **227** John Murray's memorandum book, 1775 (NLS, Murray archive, MS 43018C ff 2–3); *Dublin Gazette*, 20 June 1775.

Though it is doubtful if many in Ireland would have accepted the implication that the Curragh was an 'inferior' course, Murray's description of the Curragh *before* it experienced the full impact of the fall off in interest in horse racing that was one manifestation of the political, economic and social crisis that gripped Ireland for the duration of the American War of Independence, indicates that the decline of the late 1770s was accentuated and not initiated by this crisis in the Atlantic world. The relative normalcy of the racing calendar in 1776 bears this out, and while the popularity of Londonderry races during the late 1770s suggests that the diminution in interest indicated by the reduced attention accorded racing in the press was not general, it was palpable for all that.[228]

By comparison with the competitive generation of racehorse owners who dominated the sport during the middle decades of the eighteenth century, Thomas Conolly was a selective patron of local courses. He did run horses in races at Celbridge (1762 and 1763), Eyrecourt (1762), Carlow (1772), Bellewstown (1773), Cloghan in King's county (1773), Rathkeale (1774) and the Maze (1775), but he was less involved in that sphere than Edward O'Brien, John Browne, James Dogherty and other leading owners had been in the 1750s and Charles Lambert, James Hewson, Charles Donnell and, James Daly and Lord Mounteagle were in the 1760s.[229] The prizes on offer at locations such as Celbridge (1761) and Mallow (1772, 1773) made visits to such courses potentially worthwhile, though £50 remained the standard purse for any meeting that aspired to attract other than local gentry.[230]

Race meetings that harboured such ambitions were also more likely to proffer inducements to incentivise gentlemen to bring their wives, and to the population at large to spend money on food and refreshments. As well as providing opportunities to imbibe (wine, beer and spirits) in the tents and booths on course, certain meetings continued the practice of organizing hunts (fox and buck), balls, and other diversions that were targeted at particular audiences.[231] The addition of horse racing to the attractions Mallow spa held out to prospective visitors was, for example, aimed at a different clientele than that which was drawn to cockfighting, which featured prominently among the diversions proffered at rural Ulster meetings.[232] Following the example of Mallow, Kilkenny made the fullest attempt to capitalise on the fact that it was a horse racing town

---

228 Above; *FLJ*, 27 Apr., 1 May, 15 June 1776; *Hibernian Journal*, 17 June, 18 Sept. 1776; D'Arcy, *Horses, lords and racing men*, pp 13–14. 229 Above, pp 60, 63–4; *Public Gazetteer*, 22 Sept. 1762, 6 Sept., 1 Oct. 1773; *FLJ*, 27 May 1772, 3 July, 2 Oct. 1773, 13 Aug. 1774; D'Arcy, *Horses, lords and racing men*, p. 15. 230 *Public Gazetteer*, 25 Sept. 1762; *FLJ*, 6 June 1772, 9 June 1773. For examples of typical £50 purses see *Public Gazetteer*, 26 May 1764; *Dublin Gazette*, 17 Aug. 1765; *FLJ*, 27 May 1772. 231 *BNL*, 11 Aug. 1761, 30 June 1763, 21 Sept. 1764, 4 Aug. 1767, 5 Aug. 1768, 29 May 1770, 30 July 1773, 8 July 1774, 10 Aug. 1775; *FLJ*, 10 June 1772, 25 Sept. 1773, 29 Oct. 1774; Middleton and Vamplew, 'Horse racing and the Yorkshire leisure calendar in the early eighteenth century', pp 275–6. 232 Below, pp 174–82, 188–92; *BNL*, 25 Feb., 4 Mar. 1766, 5 Aug. 1768, 6 May 1769, 1 June 1779, 5 June 1781, 22 July 1783, 22 July 1785, 22 May 1789. Cockfighting was also staged at Dunkerrin, county Tipperary: *FLJ*, 1 Apr. 1778.

by drawing attention from 1767 to the other distractions and diversions the town could offer racegoers who took accommodation for the duration of the week of racing. (These included a freak show, a display of 'curious wild beasts', concerts and comedy.)[233] Prospective attendees were also advised that 'beds' might be secured at 'no more than one guinea per person the week', which was the standard charge.[234] Prompted by the success of this initiative, and by the opportunities generated by the popularity of the nearby spa, which attracted 'respectable families from different parts of the kingdom', the village of Ballyspellan inaugurated a race meeting targeted at the ordinary rider, with a sweepstake match in 1772, and an even more democratic race for 'common hacks', which 'afforded great diversion to a very polite concourse of spectators'. This was horse racing for the edification of those who were drawn by ill health to the 'salutary waters and air' of Ballyspellan. Consequently, more effort was devoted to ensuring the availability of a 'good ordinary' and to providing an 'elegant dinner' than to the quality of the racing. The carnival mood the spa aspired to create was epitomised by the fact that in 1774 one of the diversions was the typical fairground activity of chasing a 'soaped pig'.[235]

If Ballyspellan exemplified horse racing as entertainment, there were many others who continued to be excited by the prospect of honest-to-goodness racing. Moreover, they were sufficient in number to sustain the local, low purse race meetings hosted during the 1770s at Moneese (county Cork), Turloghmore (county Galway), Rednah and Morragh (county Wicklow), Tullow (county Carlow), Thomastown (county Kilkenny), Maryborough (Queen's county), and, until they became more ambitious, at Callan and Longford.[236] Such meetings were exceeded by the number of locations, many of them with an established racing tradition, that continued to host meetings, or that resumed the practice after an interval. This category embraced some of the more iconic regional courses, among which Rathkeale, Gort, Tuam, Loughrea, Ballinrobe, Trim, Bellewstown, Cloghan, Callan, Athlone, Mullingar, Cashel and Nenagh stand out.[237] As illustrated by the thirteen individuals from Galway who in May 1773 promised to subscribe a prize of 130 guineas for 7 years, the organisers and subscribers who raised the money to enable most of these meetings to take place were genuine enthusiasts.[238] They did on occasion have the backing of local bodies – 'the town of Tralee' sponsored the opening race of the Tralee meeting in 1766; local landowners – the countess of Granard sponsored two of the prizes run for at Longford in 1779; and local interests, such as the freeholders who

233 *FLJ*, 17, 27 June 1767.   234 *FLJ*, 10 June 1772; *FDJ*, 14 May 1778.   235 *FLJ*, 25 July, 5 Aug. 1772, 8 May, 4 Aug. 1773, 10 Sept. 1774.   236 *FLJ*, 7 Oct. 1772, 26 June, 3 July, 25 Sept., 2 Oct. 1773, 29 Oct. 1774, 30 Oct. 1779; *Hibernian Journal*, 8 May 1776.   237 *FLJ*, 29 July, 5 Aug., 30 Sept., 3, 21 Oct. 1772, 3, 14 July, 4 Aug., 2 Oct. 1773, 18 June, 6, 10, 13 Aug., 15 Oct. 1774, 9 Aug., 13 Sept. 1775, 9 Sept. 1778; *Dublin Gazette*, 17 Aug. 1775; *Hibernian Journal*, 18 Aug. 1775, 17 July, 6 Sept., 7 Oct. 1776; *FDJ*, 14 May 1778.   238 *Hibernian Journal*, 26 May 1773.

were responsible for 'the freeholders purse' at Carlow in 1772, but there were fewer such races than there were sweepstakes.[239] This obliged organisers to be increasingly realistic in their attitudes and assessments. The enterprising organisers of Kilkenny races, for example, did not hesitate to attach reminders to their public notices alerting subscribers to pay their dues.[240] Others simply decommissioned courses. Recognising that its day was past, Maurice Keating partitioned 'the racecourse at Durrow' and let it be known in 1771 that it was available for rent 'for three lives, or years as may be agreed on'.[241] Four years later, having contrived with some success to revitalise the course, James Agar of Ringwood decided 'to drop Callan races' because he could not hope to compete with the better established meeting at nearby Kilkenny.[242] Agar's decision acknowledged the emergence of Kilkenny as the country's leading regional course. Its 1775 and 1776 races were particularly high-profile, and its course managers were quick to appreciate the importance of anchoring the meeting in the community by assigning the profits accruing from the race ball to the local Charitable Loan Society and by making the course available for use by the army, and by the Volunteers when they required an open space to host reviews.[243] These actions did not insulate the course from the difficulties racing encountered during the late 1770s and early 1780s, but they did help.

Using the Jockey Club, and race advertising as a barometer, it is apparent that horse racing emerged slowly in the 1780s out of the trough into which it had fallen in the late 1770s. The maintenance by the Curragh and the Corporation of Horse Breeders in county Down of the prestigious king's and lord lieutenant's plates ensured that both courses continued to attract the leading domestic owners, but sponsors and subscribers were elusive, and the prizes uninspiring. It is notable, for example, that in September 1780 the remnants of the Jockey Club – 'the members of the Coffee-house at Kildare' – supported a 'potatoe stakes' in which, 'for five guineas each', gentlemen competed in a race run over the best of three two-mile heats. A purse of 'forty-eight guineas (Coffee-house money)' was provided from the same source in 1781, but the absence of any mention of the Club or Coffee House in 1782 and 1783 indicates that the problems then gripping the sport continued to take a heavy toll.[244] This did not dissuade enthusiasts there and elsewhere from organising matches and meetings, but they were largely low-key, and few lived up to expectations.[245] This was the implication certainly of the report of the meeting at Ballincollig, county Cork, in the summer of 1783, which pointedly referred to the fact that

239 *Public Gazetteer*, 23 Sept. 1766; *FLJ*, 27 May 1772, 30 Oct. 1779.   **240** *FLJ*, 10 June 1772, 27 May 1775.   **241** *FLJ*, 2 Jan. 1771.   **242** *FLJ*, 10, 24 May 1775.   **243** *FLJ*, 28 May 1774, 27 May, 28 June, 1, 8 July 1775, 27 Jan., 6, 31 July, 3, 10 Aug. 1776, 30 June 1781.   **244** Kelly, 'The pastime of the elite', pp 421–2; *FJ*, 21 Sept. 1780, 21 June 1781, 6 Sept. 1783; *Hibernian Journal*, 22 June, 7 Nov. 1781, 20 Sept. 1782; *Volunteer Journal (Cork)*, 17 Apr. 1783.   **245** See *Hibernian Journal*, 12 May 1780 (match, county Tipperary), 18 Sept. 1780 (race meeting at Sligo), 20 Aug. 1781 (Longford), 7 Aug. 1782 (Trim); *FLJ*, 11 July 1781 (Callan), 29 Oct. 1783 (Loughrea); *FJ*, 27 July 1784 (Kilcock).

the event would have been more successful, and 'the plates would have been much more considerable' if support had been forthcoming from 'country gentlemen'. It was the implication also of the notice issued to gentlemen subscribers in advance of a meeting at Dungarvan requesting them to pay 'their subscriptions before the commencement of the races'.[246]

Though the ambitious attempt he spearheaded in 1777 both to re-structure and to re-focus the Jockey Club was mistimed,[247] Thomas Conolly remained a powerful figure in horse racing. The presence of so many of his horses at the Curragh in the 1780s indicates that he had no intention of ceding the limelight to others. His main competition emanated from Connaught, specifically from Denis Bowes Daly, who was the leading money winner for five years from 1784, and who took on 'the famous Count [Denis] O'Kelly of Epsom' at the Curragh in a match in that year. Conolly still possessed an impressive stable, and the fact that he won eight or nine successive Northumberland (Gold) Cups in the 1780s indicates that he could more than hold his own with Daly, John Kirwan, Giles Eyre, Robert Hamilton, Lord Powerscourt, Lord Clanwilliam, Lord Altamont and the other leading horse owners.[248] The problem for the sport was that public interest remained lacklustre. The establishment at some point in 1783 or 1784 of the Turf Club, in succession to the now defunct Jockey Club, indicated that the devotees of the sport were conscious of this fact, for while the new club was not in a position to resume where the Jockey Club had left off, with the ambitious structural and regulatory agenda delineated in 1777, its decision in 1784 to sponsor a gold cup race for its own members was a symbolically significant vote of confidence in the future.[249] It was not enough on its own to draw spectators back to the sport in substantial numbers, but the timing was good since it dovetailed with the lord lieutenancy of Charles Manners, fourth duke of Rutland (Fig. 9), whose enthusiasm for the sport provided an example that many status-conscious members of the Irish elite were happy to follow, as the report of his presence at the Curragh in April 1786 illustrates:

> The meeting at the Curragh last week was the best attended of any meeting that has been for some years; his grace, the duke of Rutland honouring it with his presence, contributed not a little to bring a great concourse of people; a great deal of money was sported in betting on the different matches, and there was deep hazard at the coffee room.[250]

246 *Volunteer Journal (Cork)*, 23 June 1783; *FLJ*, 10 Sept. 1783.   **247** D'Arcy, *Horses, lords and racing men*, pp 9–11.   **248** Kelly, 'The pastime of the elite', pp 421–2; Sweeney, *Sweeney guide to the Irish turf*, p. 189; *FJ*, 3 Aug. 1784; Curragh racing results for 1782, 1783 and 1784: *Hibernian Journal*, 20 Sept. 1782, 8 Sept. 1784; *FJ*, 21 Sept. 1782, 6 Sept. 1783, 10 June 1784; *Volunteer Journal (Cork)*, 17 Apr. 1783. Denis O'Kelly (*c.*1728–87) was originally from county Carlow. His most famous horse was Eclipse, which won eleven king's plates, and whose bloodline dominates racing to the present.   **249** D'Arcy, *Horses, lords and racing men*, pp 9–12; Kelly, 'The pastime of the elite', p. 422.   **250** *Saunders Newsletter*, 2 May 1786; *FJ*, 2 May 1786.

Fig. 9 Charles Manners, duke of Rutland (1754–87), lord lieutenant of Ireland, 1784–7, maintained the tradition of vice-regal interest in the turf, not only by attending the plate races at the Curragh, but also by running his own mare (engraving by W. Lane after a portrait by Richard Cosway, private collection).

Prompted by the lord lieutenant, and by his horse – the talented and tactfully named Anna Liffey – which won a sweepstake for three-year old fillies in 1786 and for four-year olds in 1787 – the Curragh became a fashionable place to be seen once again.[251] Moreover, racing also improved, as more owners ventured forth, and more horses were entered.[252]

Rutland's impact illustrated that vice-regal example still registered deeply with the elite, which is why his premature death in October 1787 deprived the sport of a valuable patron. Be that as it may, there were obvious limits to vice-regal influence, as the lord lieutenant could not be present on every occasion, and the public was disposed to be selective as to which meetings it attended. Indicatively, even the presence in September 1787 of the mare Jane Harrold, 'the most surprising three year old that has appeared on the Irish turf for many years', did not muster a good attendance.[253] It was observed ominously in certain

251 *Dublin Evening Post*, 27 Apr., 2 May 1786; *FLJ*, 10 May 1786; *Volunteer Evening Post*, 21 Apr. 1787. Rutland's horse was second in June 1787: *FLJ*, 23 June 1787. 252 *Hibernian Journal*, 13 Sept. 1786; *FJ*, 23 Sept. 1786, 21 June 1787; *Volunteer Evening Post*, 21 Apr. 1787. 253 For Rutland, see James Kelly, 'Residential and non-residential lords lieutenant – the viceroyalty, 1703–90' in Peter Gray and Olwen Purdue (eds), *The Irish lord lieutenancy, c.1541–1922* (Dublin, 2012),

circles that racing was in 'decline' because 'private gaming is so extensive', but this was overly reductive.[254] The availability of alternatives may well have satisfied those who perceived racing as no more than an opportunity to gamble, but in broader societal terms it was an early manifestation of the beginnings of the attitudinal sea-change that promoted a more moral lifestyle, which possessed more ominous implications for those sports that were less securely anchored socially than horse racing.[255]

Its recent vicissitudes notwithstanding, horse racing was secure as the leading sport in the kingdom as the 1780s drew to a close, for though some were disposed reflexively to dilate on 'the precarious state of the turf' on no stronger grounds than a below average attendance or the defeat of a favourite, their pessimism was unwarranted. The Curragh invariably put on the best day's racing of any course in the kingdom, and though the number present on a given day in the late 1780s fluctuated according to the time of the year, weather conditions, and the publicity it was afforded, it was still capable of attracting (as it demonstrated in the spring and summer of 1788) 'a larger concourse of people' than was 'usual for some times past'.[256] This bred confidence for the future,[257] which was encouraged by the visible improvement in regional and local racing.

Regional courses that negotiated the difficult early 1780s were generally well placed to take off when the environment improved. They included Kilkenny, which affirmed its position as the leading course in south Leinster in the late 1780s by organising a six-day meeting. Moreover, in a statement of intent, it offered a top prize of 100 guineas, and while it was not able to sustain this large purse for more than a few years, the organiser's commitment to high standards was made clear by its routine iteration that meetings would be conducted 'according to the king's plate articles'.[258] No other course made a comparable declaration, though the presence of active racing at Limerick and Rathkeale in county Limerick, and Ennis and Miltown Malbay in county Clare captured the ongoing strong commitment to the sport in the mid-west.[259] As was to be expected, given their geographical proximity, Denis Bowes Daly (Fig. 10), John Kirwan, Giles Eyre (Fig. 11) and others from among the strong Connaught

pp 85–8; James Kelly, *Prelude to Union: Anglo-Irish politics in the 1780* (Cork, 1992), pp 76–8; D'Arcy, *Horses, lords and racing men*, pp 56–7; *FLJ*, 22 Sept. 1787; *FJ*, 18 Sept. 1787. **254** *FJ*, 18 Sept. 1787. For more on the strength of gambling at this time see *Ennis Chronicle*, 30 July, 9 Aug. 1789. **255** See below, pp 192–200, for a fuller engagement with this point. **256** *FJ*, 1 May, 14 June 1788, 30 May 1789; *Clonmel Gazette*, 10, 28 Apr., 8 May, 16 June 1788; *FLJ*, 3 May, 21 June 1788. **257** *FLJ*, 3 Sept. 1788. **258** *FLJ*, 17 June 1786, 26 May, 7 July 1787, 4 June, 30 July 1788, 6, 27 June 1789, 23 June, 14 July 1790; *Clonmel Gazette*, 4 Aug. 1788; *Ennis Chronicle*, 6, 10 July 1789; *Dublin Weekly Journal*, 24 July 1790. **259** *FLJ*, 16 Aug. 1786, 16, 23 July 1788, 5 Aug. 1789; *Clonmel Gazette*, 3, 17, 21, 24 July 1788, 29 July 1789; *Ennis Chronicle*, 27, 30 July 1789 (Limerick); *Hibernian Journal*, 4 Oct. 1784, 30 Aug. 1790; *FLJ*, 8 Aug. 1787; *Ennis Chronicle*, 1, 4 June 1789; *Clonmel Gazette*, 4 June 1789 (Rathkeale); *Ennis Chronicle*, 30 July, 20, 31 Aug. 1789; *Munster Journal*, 23 Aug. 1789; *Hibernian Journal*, 29 Sept. 1790 (Ennis); *Ennis Chronicle*, 25 May, 16 Aug. 1789; *Clonmel Gazette*, 2 Oct. 1788 (Miltown Malbay).

Fig. 10 (*left*) Denis Bowes Daly (1745–1823) who was a member of both the Irish parliament and the United parliament between 1776 and 1818, and Ranger of the Curragh from 1788, was one of the leading racehorse owners in late eighteenth- and early nineteenth-century Ireland, and a key figure in the Turf Club (oil on canvas, attributed to Sir Joshua Reynolds, sold at Christie's London, 23 May 2012).

Fig. 11 Giles Eyre (1766–1830) of Eyrecourt was a significant regional horse owner in the late eighteenth, early nineteenth century. (The image is from I.M. Gantz, *Signpost to Eyrecourt*, portrait of the Eyre family (Bath, 1975)).

nexus of racehorse owners registered a prominent presence at the county Limerick and Clare meetings, but their most significant contribution was to the maintenance of courses at Loughrea and Eyrecourt, which carried the flag for racing in county Galway.[260] Mullingar, meanwhile, did likewise for the midlands, Ballybofey for the north-west, and Enniskillen for south Ulster.[261] As a consequence, most regions of the country could claim to possess a dominant course, and, where this did not suffice, or the area was wealthy enough to sustain additional racing, smaller, often short-lived, and still more regionally focused courses

260 *FLJ*, 29 Oct. 1783, 4 Nov. 1786, 3 Sept. 1788, 22 Aug. 1789, 4 Sept. 1790; *FJ*, 2 Nov. 1786; *Clonmel Gazette*, 4 Sept. 1788; *Ennis Chronicle*, 20 Aug., 26 Nov. 1789 (Loughrea); *FLJ*, 22 Sept. 1787; *FJ*, 11 Sept. 1787; *Clonmel Gazette*, 8 Sept. 1788; *Hibernian Journal*, 23 Oct. 1789; *Ennis Chronicle*, 26 Oct. 1789. 261 *Dublin Chronicle*, 26 June 1787; *FLJ*, 1, 4 July, 22 Sept. 1787, 26 June 1790; *FJ*, 24 June 1790; *Ennis Chronicle*, 6 July 1789; *Dublin Weekly Journal*, 26 June 1790.

continued to function. These have left less of an evidential footprint, but courses at Carlow, Myshall (county Carlow), Cork, Tipperary, Maryborough, Cashel, Tralee, Roscommon, Mallow, Longwood, Bellewstown, Birr, Leighlinbridge, Athlone, Turloghnore (north county Clare) and Sligo contrived not only to satisfy local needs but also to swell the racing calendar through the late 1780s.[262]

Their existence also corroborates the observation, offered in the *Clonmel Gazette* in the summer of 1788, that the country had finally shaken off the disinterest that had taken hold in the late 1770s:

> The many meetings advertised, and to be advertised for this season, promise that horse racing will henceforward be the favourite amusement of this nation; for some years Volunteering kept it at a stand; it is now rising like Phoenix from its ashes, countenanced and encouraged by the most respectable men of the kingdom. Kilkenny races ... succeed ours, after them Cork, Mallow, Tralee, Cashell, Rathkeal[e], Loughrea, Eyrecourt, and Ennis threaten the lover of the turf with a succession of sport for the season.[263]

Comments such as this both mirrored and complemented the extensive coverage the sport was accorded in the main newspapers, which prompted observations in 1789 to the effect that 'a spirit of horse racing seems to be the pervading rage of the present day, and the fashionable amusement of the season'.[264] This was sheer hyperbole, but such comments were indicative of the new-found confidence that characterised the sport at that moment. It also guided the decision of the organisers of the Curragh races to erect 'new railings', which gave the course a more agreeable, comfortable aspect, and in 1789 to introduce a second spring meeting.[265]

Since the Curragh was far from crowded during the two spring meetings that the course hosted in 1789, some pondered the wisdom of the decision to add an additional meeting to the racing calendar.[266] If so, they may have reconsidered in September of the same year when the lively pre-meeting speculation as to the likely winner of the Gold Cup, as the Northumberland Cup was now known, and the 1,000 guineas prize, brought a 'numerous and splendid' crowd to the course. The victory of John Dennis' horse Morgan Rattler brought Thomas

262 *FLJ*, 5, 29 Sept. 1787 (Carlow); *Hibernian Journal*, 28 Sept. 1789 (Myshall); *FLJ*, 29 Sept. 1787, 23 July 1788, 17 July 1790 (Cork); *FLJ*, 4 Aug. 1787 (Tipperary); *FLJ*, 18 June 1788, 20 June 1789, 24 July 1790 (Maryborough); *Clonmel Gazette*, 8 Sept. 1788; *FLJ*, 25 Oct. 1788, 16 Sept. 1789; *Hibernian Journal*, 28 Sept. 1789 (Cashel); *Clonmel Gazette*, 29 Sept. 1788 (Kerry/Tralee); *FJ*, 9 Oct. 1788, *FLJ*, 9 Sept. 1789 (Roscommon); *FLJ*, 25 Oct. 1788 (Mallow); *FJ*, 21 Oct. 1788, 1 Oct. 1789 (Longwood); *Ennis Chronicle*, 13 July 1789 (Bellewstown); *FLJ*, 14 Oct. 1789, 6 Oct. 1790 (Birr); *FLJ*, 10 Oct. 1789 (Leighlinbridge); *Hibernian Journal*, 16, 18 Aug. 1790 (Athlone); *Ennis Chronicle*, 11 June 1789 (Turloghmore); *Hibernian Journal*, 20 Oct. 1790 (Sligo). 263 *Clonmel Gazette*, 24 July 1788. 264 *Ennis Chronicle*, 21 Sept. 1789. 265 *FLJ*, 11, 25 Apr. 1789; *Hibernian Journal*, 22 Apr. 1789. 266 *FJ*, 8 Apr. 1790. There were two spring, one summer, and two autumn meetings in 1790.

Fig. 12 John Fane, tenth earl of Westmorland (1759–1841) was a
frequent presence at sports events in his capacity as lord lieutenant, 1789–94
(mezzotint by S.W. Reynolds and Samuel Cousins after a portrait by
Sir Thomas Lawrence, London, 1825 (National Portrait Gallery, London).

Conolly's streak of wins extending through the 1780s to an end, and Morgan
confirmed it was 'the first horse in Ireland' when he won the lord lieutenant's
plate ('the Northumberland purse') five days later.[267]

The loss of the Gold Cup did not signal the end of Thomas Conolly's long
engagement with the turf, but his era of dominance was over, and he was placed
no higher than fifth, behind John Dennis, Colonel Charles Lumm, Richard
Hamilton of the Curragh and Denis Bowes Daly, by one assessment of the leading owners in 1789. It was a questionable order as Lumm's Lady Emily (which
he had been given as a foal by Conolly) beat Morgan Rattler at the second
autumn meeting at the Curragh in 1789, but Morgan proved his superiority by
retaining the Gold Cup in 1790.[268] These rivalries generated excitement and
public interest, which the press encouraged, content in the realisation that when

267 *Ennis Chronicle*, 7, 10, 17, 21 Sept. 1789; *Hibernian Journal*, 2, 7, 9 Sept. 1789, 12 Nov. 1790;
Dublin Chronicle, 3 Sept. 1789; *FJ*, 10, 12, 17 Sept. 1789. 268 *Hibernian Journal*, 30 Oct. 1789, 30
Mar., 2, 23 Apr. 1790; *Dublin Weekly Journal*, 3, 24 Apr. 1790; *FJ*, 30 Mar., 1, 6, 8, 24 Apr. 1790;
Dublin Chronicle, 3,6,8 Apr. 1790.

the new lord lieutenant, John, earl of Westmorland (1789–94), let it be known that he enjoyed racing, the sport's place as the country's most respectable entertainment was secure (Fig. 12).[269]

Though the impression actively conveyed by the accounts of horse racing published in the press in 1790 was that it was a well-run, well-regulated sport, the reality could be different. Sometimes the problems related to the courses horses were required to negotiate. In 1790, a spectator was killed, three jockeys were 'dangerously injured', and three horses were 'incapacitated from ever appearing on the turf in future' because of deficiencies ('the shortness of the turns') in the Athlone course.[270] Seven years earlier, a man and a woman were killed, and a jockey and horse 'much hurt' because of the encroachment of spectators on the course at Mallow.[271] Accidents, fatal and otherwise, were an ongoing issue, and they served oftentimes to expose significant organisational deficiencies. No fatalities ensued when 'stages erected for the accommodation of gentlemen' collapsed within months of each other at Mullingar and Dunboyne in 1787, but the proximity of the two incidents was troubling, and indicative of a larger problem that the slowly appreciating concern with animal welfare did nothing to address.[272]

It is evident, based on the trend towards fewer heats and shorter races, that there was a slowly gathering appreciation in the second half of the eighteenth century of the physical demands racing placed upon horses, but the implications of this for the sport were far from universally acknowledged. It is notable, for example, that the failure to produce a clear winner after three heats at the Eyrecourt meeting in 1787 prompted a fourth, and when this proved inconclusive, plans to send the horses off for a fifth time were only abandoned because of the lateness of the hour and the realisation that the horses were 'greatly fatigued'.[273] Significantly, the judges and the gentlemen present were in agreement that this was the proper course of action. The failure of the judges chosen on the course in county Kerry in 1788 to rule decisively as to whether a horse that completed a race unopposed, having thrown its rider, could be adjudged to have won prompted an appeal to the Jockey Club.[274] Problems with officials were manifest at only a minority of races, but these and allied issues fuelled the perception in some quarters that the sport was rife with 'jobbing'. There is little evidence to suggest that racing was any more prone to the endemic jobbing impulse than other walks of life, but the criticism may have been a factor in prompting the Turf Club, which had evolved in the 1780s into a worthy successor to the Jockey Club, to seek to give effect to the ambitious regulatory agenda delineated

269 *FJ*, 1, 4 May, 10, 15 June, 4 Nov. 1790; *Hibernian Journal*, 3 May, 3, 11, 14, 18 June, 6 July, 6, 8, 13 Sept., 1, 3, 12 Nov. 1790; *Dublin Weekly Journal*, 5, 12, 19 June, 18 Sept., 6, 13 Nov. 1790. 270 *FJ*, 19 Aug. 1790. 271 *Volunteer Journal (Cork)*, 26 May 1783. 272 *Dublin Chronicle*, 26 June 1787; *FLJ*, 22 Sept. 1787. 273 *FJ*, 11 Sept. 1787. 274 *Clonmel Gazette*, 29 Sept. 1788. The extent of Irish appeals to the (English) Jockey Club is not clear, but it was not unusual: see Brailsford, *A taste for diversions*, p. 173.

in 1777. The most important outcome was the publication of 'The rules and orders of the Turf Club, 1790'. Though it may reasonably be surmised that this document built upon a pre-existing set of rules or articles (that eludes location), its preparation, and publication, was an earnest of the Club's commitment to ensure that the sport was pursued according to rule. To this end the 'rules' provided for the election of three stewards with 'full power to make such regulations as they think proper' to facilitate the operation of the Turf Club and Coffee house, and, still more importantly for the development of the sport, racing on the Curragh. Specifically, the stewards were empowered 'to determine [such] disputes' as might arise on the course. This was obviously important in so far as racing at the country's premier course was concerned, but the Turf Club did not conceive of this as the extent of their role. Confident in their knowledge of racing, and of its value if it was made available to the sport at large, the stewards let it be known that they 'were prepared to help adjudicate in disputes elsewhere, if invited to do so', while the Club, still more tentatively, asserted its claim to become the governing authority for the sport by proposing that it should be empowered 'not to permit any races to be run in this kingdom, unless a sworn judge from the Curragh attends at them'.[275] This was an authority the Club was not to exercise for some time, but its articulation was an unambiguous statement of intent, and it pointed the way towards the enhanced self-regulation that the prescient perceived was the logical next step for the sport. The fact that 'the rules and orders' were published in the first number of Patrick Sharkey's *Irish Racing Calendar*, which appeared annually from 1790, and that the *Calendar* both 'secured official Turf Club endorsement from the outset', and became 'a vital instrument in promoting awareness of the Turf Club, and its informal but growing authority, in developing acceptance of a unified code of conduct' was also significant. It was at once a statement of confidence in the future, and a pointer to the fact that the Turf Club was ready to assume leadership of the sport.[276]

Parallel with this, the peers and gentlemen who sought to improve the image of horse racing were anxious to identify some solution to the on-going problem of popular racing. Though primarily a matter for the civil authorities, popular racing had long been regarded nervously by respectable opinion, and it was the subject of parliamentary attention in 1739. Having concluded then that the increase in horse racing that had taken place in the 1730s had served 'to promote and encourage idleness and debauchery among ... farmers, artificers and day-labourers', MPs and peers proscribed races for wagers and prizes of less than £20.[277] Drafted with the specific intention of eliminating low-purse racing, the legislation was primarily tar-

---

275 D'Arcy, *Horses, lords and racing men*, pp 29–30, see also pp 25–7 and 345 for an account of the stewards; *Hibernian Journal*, 18 June 1790; Kelly, 'The pastime of the elite', pp 422–3. 276 *Irish racing calendar; containing an account of the plates, matches, and sweepstakes, run for in Ireland, in the year* by Pat. Sharkey, proprietor of the *Racing Calendar* (Dublin, 1790); Costello, *Kildare: saints, soldiers and horses*, p. 118; D'Arcy, *Horses, lords and racing men*, pp 12, 40. 277 13 George II, chap. 8; Barnard, *Making the grand figure*, pp 229–30. Interestingly, in legislation approved at

geted at venues like Glasnevin, which was then the most active course in the environs of the metropolis, Palmerstown, and Ringsend. The absence of any reference to racing at Glasnevin thereafter might be interpreted as evidence that the legislation had achieved its purpose, but the reality was that the law was soon ignored, and advertisements can be located from the mid-1740s alerting the public to forthcoming meetings at Crumlin and Finglas, and advising prospective entrants of the fees and other terms. As this suggests, the organisers of these race meetings sought to give the impression that they followed best practice through the entrance fees they charged, the prizes – bridle and saddle, silver spurs, £5 etc. – they offered, but the fact that they confined entry to horses that had 'never won above the value of ten pounds' testified to the popular character of the meeting to which they invited the public.[278] They certainly could attract substantial audiences, as the report of the Finglas meeting in 1749 attests:

> Last Saturday ended the races of Finglas, which held for a week, and afforded a great deal of diversion to a numerous concourse of people. The Tuesday's and Friday's plates were won by James Edwards, esq., bay gelding, Diamond, and the Wednesday's and Thursday's plates were won by Thomas Kean's grey gallway, Finglas Lad; and on Friday night a ball was given to the ladies by the gentlemen of the town, and genteel entertainment, where everything was conducted in a most elegant manner.[279]

The problem, from the perspective of the authorities, was that few popular meetings achieved the 'genteel' standard to which their organisers aspired. In 1747, at Kilmainham, 'three men were ... shot' when the intervention of the sub-sheriff and 'a party of soldiers' and the owner of lands adjoining Kilmainham Common prompted a confrontation with the 'great number of people assembled there to see a horse race'.[280] Though the landowner was the aggressor in this instance, the reflexive suspicion with which the authorities viewed low-purse meetings prompted the lord chief justice, Thomas Marlay, and the other justices of the Court of Kings Bench, to pronounce in 1750 'that for the future no horse races or games should be advertised in any of the Dublin newspapers, and that the judges on the next circuits are to give charges to the several grand juries to suppress all horse races and gaming that comes within the act of parliament'.[281] It is not apparent that the judges did as instructed, but even if they did it did not have the impact that those in authority anticipated.

Westminster in 1740, the minimum prize was set at £50 in order to prevent 'the excessive increase of horse races' and 'excessive and deceitful gaming'. Significantly, this act also addressed issues such as ownership, the weight to be carried by horses, and provided that owners could enter only one horse per race – issues not addressed in Irish law: 13 George II, chap. 19 (GB); 18 George II, chap. (GB); Tony Collins, John Martin and Wray Vamplew (eds), *Encyclopedia of traditional British rural sports* (Abingdon, 2005), p. 154; MacGregor, *Animal encounters*, pp 85–6.   **278** *FDJ*, 13 Aug. 1745, 17 Sept. 1748.   **279** *Munster Journal*, 5 Oct. 1749.   **280** *PO*, 3 Nov. 1747.   **281** *Munster Journal*, 12 Feb. 1750.

As the most popular venues in county Dublin, the organisers of the Finglas and Crumlin meetings concluded perceptively that it was not in their interest to set the law at defiance. Consistent with its stronger (and one presumes wealthier) support base, Finglas races raised their purses to 20 guineas in 1753. They succeeded for a time in attracting better horses, but they found it difficult to sustain this level of interest and prize money.[282] Crumlin likewise augmented its primary prize by introducing a £20 plate (in addition to the usual prizes of silver spurs, and the like), and in contrast to Finglas, which concentrated on racing, the organisers sought to enhance the appeal of the occasion by adding a trotting match and hurling to the menu of entertainments, and to meet the increased costs by levying a fee on stallholders selling wine and other goods.[283] This formula did not appeal to all, and a number of locations were emboldened to organise meetings where the prize money did not reach the threshold ordained by law. Meetings at Baldoyle in 1753 and 1754 and Rush, in north county Dublin, in 1754 provided great diversion in both localities. Neither they nor better organised meetings at Ringsend and Swords could raise the funding required to comply with the 1739 act, but the fact that the authorities chose to ignore this fact suggests that the periodic surge in anxiety that prompted public expressions of concern at such activity was then in remission.[284] This mood was not to endure, however, for though the races at Swords had achieved sufficient respectability by July 1771 to cause two baronets to enter horses for the £25 purse, and the authorities to turn a blind eye on racing at Howth in 1770, neither they nor the rising ranks of the respectable 'middling sort' were reconciled to the activity. Indeed, their unease at the loss of working time, particularly during the harvest season, the scenes of general dissipation, and 'the mischiefs which usually attend ... those kind of exhibitions so near the metropolis' was so unreserved that the decision of the lord mayor and sheriffs in 1771 to take 'down several tents' in order to 'put a stop to the horse racing intended to be exhibited' on Ringsend strand the first week of September was roundly applauded.[285] It was of a piece with the appreciating willingness of the authorities to intervene to discourage recreational activities that respectable opinion deemed disagreeable, and the mounting conviction, articulated in 1773, that legislation to prevent horse racing within twenty-five miles of the capital could only be beneficial:

> [It] will be a means of preventing murders, riots and robberies, which too frequently happen at those places, besides the loss of time and money of tradesmen and labourers to the very great injury of the public.[286]

Though no legislation was presented at that point, suggestions to the effect that Ireland should follow England, and forbid 'any race by horses, etc. for a smaller

282 *UA*, 30 Oct., 3 Nov. 1753.   **283** *UA*, 17 July, 18, 21 Aug. 1753; above, p. 64.   **284** *UA*, 28 Apr. 1753, 20 Apr., 26 Oct. 1754, 1 Feb., 4 Nov. 1755, 12 Sept. 1758; *The Public Gazetteer*, 24 May 1760; *FJ*, 31 July 1764.   **285** *FJ*, 28 July 1764, 23 Aug. 1768, 5 Sept. 1771; *Hoey's Publick Journal*, 9 Apr. 1770, 15 July 1771, 4 Sept. 1771.   **286** *Hibernian Journal*, 23 June 1773.

sum than fifty pounds' attested to the support for a prohibition in certain quarters.[287] It was assisted by the identification of Crumlin with 'the profanation of the sabbath', and racing generally with disorder, since it reinforced the respectable in the conviction that intervention was the only logical option.[288] The level of disorder encountered at the Maze, county Down, in the mid-1770s certainly gave cause for concern, and with reason, as the account later penned by Patrick Cunningham, a convert to Methodism, attested:

> The first day of the races presented a most shocking scene; perhaps not less than one hundred thousand people all confusion and uproar. This was occasioned by a quarrel between the men of Broomhedge and those of Hillsborough. They armed themselves with whatever weapons they could get, and rushed upon each other with the ferocity of wilds beasts, and fought with the greatest desperation. Such rage and clamour I never witnessed before. In a little time many of them were weltering in their blood. I remember one only killed dead on the spot, but several died afterwards of their wounds. ... How great must be the depravity of the human heart, when men can take delight in tearing each other to pieces, and for the sake of such sport, will venture on eternal damnation.[289]

Cunningham was witness here to a faction fight of the kind previously manifest at Wicklow races in 1753.[290] Such incidents were uncommon, but they reinforced the disposition, already entrenched in evangelical and respectable circles, that because horse racing and gaming were inseparable the former was 'destructive of honour, fame and fortune'. 'A single good act', it was observed in a panegyric on George, first Lord Lyttleton, was 'preferable to an Olympick triumph at Newmarket; the company of sober and rational creatures to that of pimps, grooms and jockeys, and a knowledge of ourselves to the most consummate judgement in dice, cards, hounds or horses'.[291]

For those who perceived gambling as fundamentally immoral, the intimacy of the link that bound it and horse racing was sufficient proof of the latter's sinfulness. This was too sweeping for a majority of the respectable, who were disposed to favour horse racing, but since they set their standard by the Curragh, they could find little in local meetings about which to enthuse. The successful interruption of racing at Booterstown in 1781, Clondalkin in 1787, and Lucan also in 1787, indicated that landowners and legal officials were at one on this, and that by the late 1780s the only races they were willing to tolerate in the neighbourhood of the capital were those organised by Lord Carhampton on Luttrellstown demesne.[292]

287 *Hoey's Publick Journal*, 11 Sept. 1772. **288** *FJ*, 30 Aug. 1770, 10 Sept. 1771. **289** *The life of Patrick Cunningham* (Belfast, 1806), p. 16. **290** Above, 68–9. **291** *Hoey's Publick Journal*, 17 Sept. 1773. For other criticism directed at horse racing see *FLJ*, 31 May 1775; *BNL*, 15 July 1791. **292** *FJ*, 7 July 1781, 18 Sept., 8 Oct. 1788, 25 Mar. 1790; *Dublin Chronicle*, 8 Sept., 6 Oct. 1787; *Dublin*

The esteem with which Luttrellstown was held in respectable circles was equalled only by the hostility with which they regarded Crumlin races. Having contrived with some success in the 1750s to reconcile popular and respectable sport, Crumlin Common had become firmly identified by the late 1780s with the violence, disorder, and lack of decorum that the elite associated with popular sport.[293] This was not entirely fair, but the convergence of religion and respectability was sufficiently close by then to permit those opposed to such popular recreations to seize the initiative in the public sphere. Indicatively, there was no single precipitating event. Indeed, though a number of spectators were injured in an incident on Crumlin Common in August 1788 when a horse ran into spectators, the annual race meeting was uneventful; 'the greatest order prevailed, notwithstanding the multitudes who appeared', it was observed.[294] However, the parish vestry of Crumlin was not content that racing should continue unchanged. Their disquiet had been mounting for years, and believing the races to be 'highly destructive of the property of the parishioners, and very injurious to the morals of the lower orders of the people', they vowed on 29 September 1788 to do what was necessary to 'suppress such illegal meetings'.[295] There was some public support for the vestry's resolutions when they were printed in the *Freeman's Journal*, because of the presumption that three local officials, who ought to have been enforcing the law, were taking backhanders, but this was of less consequence than the flood of hostile commentary published in the run-up to the 1789 meeting, which pointed out that it contravened the 1739 act, and that it encouraged 'idleness and dissipation, with the consequent drunkenness, riots, assaults, bloodshed and murders, which too frequently happen among the vulgar on such occasions'. Besieged by alarming assertions to the effect that the city was about to acquire 'a second edition of the fair of Donnybrook', the organisers of the race meeting did their utmost to ensure that all passed off smoothly, but when reports of the opening day indicated that this was far from being the case, a magistrate, 'accompanied by a strong party of the army' was dispatched 'to suppress the races', and when, his best efforts notwithstanding, racing was resumed, a further intervention was ordered, and the exercise repeated on the final day of the meeting.[296] Though the authorities had made their intentions clear, and they received the backing of 'all the gentlemen in that neighbourhood', the publication late in September 1790 of a notice to the effect that Crumlin races would recommence the week beginning 4 October put it up to the authorities, and they were not found wanting. The detention of the secretary and the clerk of the course deprived the meeting of organisers, and while this did not deter 'a number of people' from assembling with saddled horses with the intention of racing 'they were not permitted to start'.[297] Moreover, the authorities had another, decisive,

Weekly Journal, 27 Mar. 1790. **293** *FJ*, 30 Aug. 1770; D'Arcy, *Horses, lords and racing men*, p. 19. **294** *FJ*, 19 Aug., 20 Sept. 1788. **295** *FJ*, 4 Oct. 1788. **296** *FJ*, 9 Oct. 1788, 15, 17, 19, 22, 24, 26 Sept. 1789; *Hibernian Journal*, 16, 25, 28 Sept. 1789, 17 Sept. 1790; *FLJ*, 26 Sept. 1789; *Dublin Chronicle*, 24 Sept. 1789; F.E. Ball, *A history of the county of Dublin, part 4* (Dublin, 1906), p. 145. **297** *Hibernian Journal*, 22 Sept., 1, 13 Oct., 10 Nov. 1790; *FJ*, 5 Oct. 1790; *Dublin Weekly Journal*,

Map 4: Horse racing in Ireland, 1790s: courses

weapon in their disposal. A 'bill for preventing horse racing in the vicinity of Dublin' was presented by John Wolfe of Newlands to the House of Commons on 7 March 1791, and it is a measure of the support for the proposition at parliamentary level that it eased its way without difficulty into law in less than two months. With its enactment, parliament effectively 'put a stop to racing' 'for any public prize whatever within nine miles of [the] ... Castle of Dublin' by deeming 'any assembly of persons more than twelve in number at any horse race ... an unlawful assembly'.[298] It did not illegalise private matches, or trotting matches which continued, but the 'suppression of Crumlin, ... and other races' brought the most emblematic popular meeting on the racing calendar in the metropolitan area to an end.[299] It was a further milestone in the evolution of horse racing in Ireland.

MATURATION, 1791–*c*.1840

As Ireland embarked on the last decade of the eighteenth century, horse racing was, by some margin, the island's best-organised sport. Yet, as a comparison of a map of active racecourses in the 1790s (Map 4) with a similar map for the preceding three decades (Map 3) reveals, the consolidation that was a feature of the second half of the eighteenth century not only continued, it was intensified in the final decade of the century. This was not the only, and probably not the most important trend at work, which may be said to have hastened the maturation of the sport as it entered the nineteenth century. The confrontational character of the 1790s, which put an end to what Thomas Bartlett has identified as the 'moral economy' of the eighteenth century, also left a profound mark.[300] The effect of these developments on the sport was first manifest in the severe disruption to the existing pattern of race meetings that one can identify in the mid-1790s, which prompted a reduction in the number of listed race meetings from 25 in 1791 to 15 in 1795.[301] Moreover, this was but a foretaste of what was to happen in the dramatic final years of the decade, in 1798 and 1799, when racing all but ceased to take place as the country descended into rebellion, and the movement of horses was severely impeded. Horse racing resumed slowly thereafter, but it took a number of years for a pattern to be re-established, and when it did the sport

18 Sept. 1790.   **298** *The parliamentary register or history of the proceedings and debates of the Irish parliament* (17 vols, Dublin, 1782–1801), xi, 283; *FJ*, 8 Mar. 1791; *FLJ*, 23 Mar. 1791; James Kelly (ed.), *Proceedings of the Irish House of Lords* (3 vols, Dublin, 2008), ii, 232; 31 George III, chap 43. **299** *Hibernian Journal*, 1 June, 19 Aug. 1791; *Ennis Chronicle*, 26 May 1791, 26 Apr., 24 May 1792. **300** Thomas Bartlett, 'The end of moral economy: the Irish militia disturbances of 1793', *Past and Present*, 93 (1983), pp 43–64. See also M.J. Powell, 'Moral economy and popular protest in the late eighteenth century' in Michael Brown and Sean Patrick Donlan (eds), *Law and other legalities of Ireland, 1689–1850* (Aldershot, 2010), pp 231–53; S.J. Connolly, 'Violence and order in the eighteenth century' in Paul Ferguson, Patrick O'Flanagan and Kevin Whelan (eds), *Rural Ireland, 1600–1900: modernisation and change* (Cork, 1987), pp 42–61.   **301** D'Arcy, *Horses, lords and racing men*, pp 42, 344, table 3. These figures appertain to the meetings reported in the *Racing Calendar*, which

Table 3: Race meetings by province and county, 1791–1820							
LEINSTER		**MUNSTER**		**CONNAUGHT**		**ULSTER**	
County	*Number*	*County*	*Number*	*County*	*Number*	*County*	*Number*
Louth	1	Kerry	1	Galway	4	Antrim	1
Meath	4	Cork	5	Roscommon	3	Down	3
Longford	1	Waterford	5	Mayo	2	Armagh	1
Westmeath	4	Limerick	4	Sligo	–	L'derry	1
Dublin	–	Tipperary	5	Leitrim	–	Fermanagh	1
Kildare	3	Clare	3			Cavan	1
Wicklow	3					Monaghan	2
King's County	2					Tyrone	1
Queen's County	2					Donegal	1
Kilkenny	4						
Carlow	1						
Wexford	2						
Total (%) 27 (38)		23 (32)		9 (13)		12 (17)	

Source: *Hibernian Journal*, 1791–5; *Freeman's Journal*, 1791–1820; *Finn's Leinster Journal*, 1791–1820; *Dublin Chronicle*, 1791; *Dublin Weekly Journal*, 1791; *Clonmel Gazette*, 1791, 1793; *Cork Gazette*, 1791, 1794, 1796; *Dublin Evening Post*, 1799; *Ennis Chronicle*, 1791–2, 1818–20; Tony Sweeney et al., *The Sweeney guide to the Irish turf from 1501 to 2001* (Dublin 2002).

was visibly different. First, the distribution of courses had changed. Second, and more importantly, the primary social legacy of the end of the moral economy and the insurgency of the 1790s was a more suspicious and divided society, which was manifest on the racecourse in an expanding social and sectarian chasm between the elite and the masses that was a feature of the sport in the nineteenth century.

Viewed from a regional perspective, the consolidation of the sport of racing in the early 1790s is most evident in the province of Ulster where the cessation of racing at Ballybofey, following the earlier closure of the course at Londonderry, left Enniskillen as the leading Ulster course outside county Down.[302] Race meetings were conducted for a time at Ballyshannon, in south county Donegal. Belturbet, county Cavan, also continued its intermittent engagement with the sport in 1791, but other than a single meeting later in the decade at Ballyhackamore, on the outskirts of Belfast, the most striking feature of racing in the province was the disruption of the irregular network of local and regional meetings across the

are not complete.   **302** *FJ*, 14 July 1791, 10 Sept. 1793.

province (particularly in counties Antrim, Armagh, Monaghan and Down), which had carried the standard for racing in so many parts during the first three decades of the reign of George III. As a result, the venerable Corporation of Horse Breeders in county Down, which organised the iconic meetings at the Maze and Downpatrick, continued to act, as it had done for a century, as the torch-carrier for racing in the province. Its races continued to draw many of the kingdom's leading owners northwards (in 1791 they included Denis Bowes Daly, Charles Lumm, Robert Hamilton, John Knox and John Dennis), though apart from the king's plates, the standard prize (£60) was hardly tempting. Moreover, a review of results from the early 1790s suggests that, other than Francis Savage (a five-time steward of the Turf Club), whose horse Duchess of Leinster won the king's plate for six-year olds in 1791, local owners were hard-pressed to compete. The earl of Hillsborough and the Hon. Edward Ward did fly the flag on behalf of local landowners, but with modest success. However, even this did not blunt the strong competitive edge that was a feature of the sport in the province, based on the evidence of matches run at the Maze, and racing at Enniskillen in 1793.[303]

Next to the closure of so many courses in Ulster, the most notable change to the pattern of horse racing in the late eighteenth century was the cessation of the sport in county Dublin as a consequence of the legal prohibition introduced in 1790. Private matches continued to take place,[304] but the interdiction of organized racing within the environs of the city meant (as those who favoured the change hoped it would) that swathes of artisans and labourers who were not in a position to travel long distances were deprived of the opportunity to enjoy racing. This was the reality also for many in Connaught, where only Loughrea (1791–7) sustained a regular sequence of annual meetings. Racing took place in the early 1790s at Tuam (1792), Elphin (1791–3), Roscommon (1791–2), Loughlin (1792) – 'the stately seat' of Charles 12th Viscount Dillon – Castlebar (1792–3) and at Sligo (1790, 1792–4), where the incapacity of the Ormsby family to sustain their engagement with the sport replicated the pattern of many landed families.[305] Interestingly, in a pointer to a trend that was to become more manifest in the nineteenth century, the meetings at Elphin were targeted primarily at hunters, and the inclusion on the racecard of a sweepstake, 'gentlemen riding' (worth 200 guineas), and 'a most excellent hunt' was aimed at encouraging local participation.[306] The race meetings at Roscommon, Castlebar, Loughlin and Loughrea assumed a more conventional form, though Connaught owners were disproportionately represented.[307] The decline, from its mid-eighteenth-century peak, in the number of meetings in county Galway is particularly striking given the strength of the stables maintained

303 *Cork Gazette*, 3 Aug. 1791; *FLJ*, 30 July, 13 Aug. 1791, 2 May 1792, 11 Jan. 1794; *Clonmel Gazette*, 30 July 1791; *Hibernian Journal*, 3 Aug. 1792, 1 Aug. 1794, 20 July 1795; *FJ*, 10 Sept. 1793; D'Arcy, *Horses, lords and racing men*, p. 345. 304 *Hibernian Journal*, 1 June 1791, 4 May, 8 June 1792; *FJ*, 7, 13 Oct. 1790, 21 May 1793; *Ennis Chronicle*, 12 July 1790, 17 Mar., 29 Sept. 1791. 305 *Ennis Chronicle*, 12, 16, 30 Aug. 1792; *FJ*, 24, 28 Sept. 1793. 306 *FLJ*, 13 Apr. 1791, 30 Mar. 1792; *Hibernian Journal*, 30 Mar. 1792. 307 *Dublin Weekly Journal*, 17 Sept. 1791; *FLJ*, 19 Nov. 1791; *Ennis Chronicle*, 13 Aug. 1792; *Hibernian Journal*, 2 Nov. 1792, 25 Oct. 1793.

by Denis Bowes Daly, Anthony Daly, John Kirwan and other landowners from the county, but it was in keeping with the fact that their horizon was fixed on the national stage, even when, as was the case with Bowes Daly, he sent his horses to compete at Newmarket and other leading English courses.[308]

The pattern was not altogether different in Munster, though the focus on local horse owners was still more explicit. At Bandon, the decision of James Bernard of Castle Bernard to sponsor a plate for hunters owned by gentlemen resident in county Cork was emblematic of this trend, but more was required in order to establish a successful meeting. Bandon was dependent on the backing of the Bernards, who offered all the right signals when in 1792 they 'hosted the nobility and gentry who visited the races', and undertook to sponsor 'a racing plate to be run for at Bandon, for several years to come'. Such support could not be assumed, however, and its absence, or withdrawal, accounts for the brief existence of many meetings. Indeed, despite the optimism generated in 1792, the Bandon meeting did not survive for more than two years.[309] Ennis (1790–5), Cashel (1794–7), Rathkeale (1793) and Limerick (1791, 1793, 1796) were more enduring. They targeted the familiar combination of local, regional, and national owners, but the reservation at Limerick of a race for 'Limerick bred horses' was indicative of the fact that though the timing of regional meetings such as these, and Rathcormac, county Cork, required choreographing to enable horses, owners and riders from across the province and beyond to attend, organisers were largely reliant on local owners and riders, and the further down the racing pecking order one descends the greater the reliance. Local owners were the primary targets of low purse local meetings, such as Tralee, county Kerry, Assolas and Cood, county Clare, and Loughmore, county Limerick.[310] Accessibility was certainly a factor. Locations such as Tralee and Bandon required an additional effort that deterred many owners, but the geography of racing in Munster was such that Ennis, Cashel, Limerick and Rathkeale constituted an accessible circuit for lovers of the sport in the northern part of the province, while Rathcormac, Bandon, Tralee, Cork, Tramore and Dungarvan catered for the south and west.

As the province with the largest number of courses, Leinster remained the heartland of the sport of horse racing in Ireland. With five meetings, several king's plates, a long list of high-wager 'private matches', and the Gold Cup – 'the great glory of the turf' – the Curragh was unchallenged as the headquarters of Irish racing in the early 1790s.[311] Indicatively, it was the only course at which

308 For Kirwan see Ronan Lynch, *The Kirwans of Castlehacket, co. Galway: history, folklore and mythology in an Irish horse racing family* (Dublin, 2006), chapter 2.   309 *Cork Gazette*, 9 Feb. 1791; *Ennis Chronicle*, 30 May 1791, 30 July 1792; *FLJ*, 28 July 1792.   310 *FJ*, 17, 22 Oct. 1791, 30 July 1793 (Limerick); *Cork Gazette*, 29 Oct. 1791; *Hibernian Journal*, 4 Nov. 1791, 7 Sept. 1792 (Ennis); *FLJ*, 9 July 1791, *FJ*, 28 June 1791; *Clonmel Gazette*, 6 Aug. 1791 (Rathcormac); *Hibernian Journal*, 5 Sept. 1794 (Tralee); *Hibernian Journal*, 12 Aug. 1794, *FLJ*, 11 Oct. 1797 (Cashel); *Ennis Chronicle*, 13, 20 Oct. 1791 (Loughmore), 14, 21 July 1791 (Cood), 3 May, 5 July 1792 (Assolas).   311 This paragraph is constructed around the reports of the Curragh meetings 1791–6, and related commentary: *FJ*, 16, 20, 23 Apr., 7 May, 18, 21 June, 14 July, 15, 17, 20 Sept., 20 Oct., 1 Dec. 1791, 14, 16, 26 June 1792, 25, 27, 30 Apr., 2 May 1793; *Hibernian Journal*, 29 Apr., 2, 5, 13 May, 13 June, 19

the presence of the lord lieutenant was expected; indeed, the earl of Westmorland let it be known in advance that he would be present at the summer meeting in 1791. Vice-regal patronage notwithstanding, the unexpected death, also in 1791, of John Dennis' celebrated Morgan Rattler was a blow to the sport, but the effect was short lived and interest in the Gold Cup was soon as lively as ever. Most attention focussed on Master Bagot, Robert Hamilton's horse, which won the king's plate for four-year-olds in 1791, before taking the Gold Cup from Dennis in 1793. This not to suggest that the Curragh's fortunes were dependent on one race, but the focus on the Gold Cup in the press was indicative of the interest the race now generated among the general public, and of the prestige victory brought to the winning owner. Racing at the Curragh remained competitive as a result.[312] Indeed, in contrast to the 1760s and 1770s, when Thomas Conolly's stable was stronger than that of his rivals, and the 1780s when Denis Bowes Daly was in the ascendant, there was no equivalently dominant presence for the 1790s. Based on the number of horses bearing his colours entered to run, Conolly sharply reduced his stable in the early 1790s. Daly remained a powerful presence (he was the leading money-winner in 1793), but he faced stern competition from John Dennis (1789), Francis Savage (1790), Robert Hamilton (1791), John Kirwan (1792, 1796, 1797), and Charles Lumm (1794, 1795), who were the leading money winners during the rest of the decade. However, Daly's determination to outdo his rivals, and his resolve was rewarded when he was the leading money winner once more in 1798, 1799 and 1800. Further success in the early nineteenth century (1808, 1809, 1814 and 1818) confirmed his place at the forefront of Irish racing, but it is no less notable that his commitment to equine excellence in the field was matched by his support for best regulatory practice and by his active involvement in the Turf Club.[313]

Denis Bowes Daly's willingness to serve as a steward was indicative of the slowly appreciating acceptance within racing that the aspiration of the Turf Club to assume a regulatory role was beneficial. This is not to suggest that the Club did not encounter resistance. It was justifiably resented by some as unreasonably exclusivist because it refused to allow 'gentlemen, not members' access to the 'Coffee House at Kildare'. Others plainly disliked the fact that it bore so close a resemblance to a gentleman's club. Its reputation was not helped by the fact that relations with the Ranger of the Curragh were fractious in the 1790s, and degenerated, on occasion, into unedifying public bickering.[314] Yet, the realisation that it was in

Sept., 21 Oct. 1791, 25 Apr., 2, 8, 11 May 1792, 26, 29 Apr., 1 May, 14, 17, 19, 21 June, 9, 11, 13, 16, 20 Sept., 1 Nov. 1793, 24 Apr., 7 May, 18 June, 15 Sept., 31 Oct. 1794, 24, 28 Apr., 5 May, 11, 17, 25 June, 7 Aug., 2, 4 Nov. 1795; *Dublin Weekly Journal*, 7 May, 18, 25 June 1791; *Dublin Chronicle*, 5 May 1791; *FLJ*, 24 Sept., 2 Nov. 1791, 27 Apr. 1793, 17 Sept. 1794, 7 May 1796, 4 Nov. 1797. **312** *Ennis Chronicle*, 22 Nov. 1790, 14 Feb., 12 May, 29 Sept. 1791, 15 Nov. 1792. There were thirteen runners in the king's plate for three-year-olds in the second spring meeting in 1791: *FJ*, 5 May 1791. **313** *Ennis Chronicle*, 17 May 1792. For the leading money winners, and leaders in terms of races won see Sweeney, *Sweeney guide to the Irish turf*, pp 189–90, 203; see also pp 179–80; for the stewards of the Turf Club see D'Arcy, *Horses, lords and racing men*, pp 345–6. **314** D'Arcy,

the interest of the sport to have a body to which owners and organizers could appeal for the adjudication of differences, the resolution of disputes, the interpretation of the finer points of racing and the elaboration of appropriate regulations had increasing purchase in the 1790s. Its appeal was not yet general, but it can be identified in the decision of the race organisers at Bandon in 1792 to employ the weights 'fixed by the gentlemen stewards of the Turf Club', and the stewards at Cashel and Enniskillen in 1795 to employ 'a sworn judge from the Curragh'. It was still more manifestly in evidence in the transmission for adjudication of disputes from Loughrea in 1793 and Ballyshannon in 1792 and 1794, and, most significantly, in the adoption by the Corporation of Horse Breeders in county Down in 1797 of the rules and orders of the Turf Club.[315] This trend was encouraged by the realisation, as the Club assumed a more public identity in the 1790s, that it was not only advantageous administratively to have an Irish equivalent to the better known Jockey Club of England, but also that it was advantageous to the sport to be in a position to secure direction on a query from a domestic body when the alternative, previously pursued, was to approach the Jockey Club of England.[316]

The absence of reference in the contemporary record to tension between the Turf Club and regional and local courses suggests that such suspicion as may have been generated was kept within bounds. Owners certainly needed regional courses, and there were few parts of Leinster that were not within ready access of a course in the 1790s. Indeed, other than counties Longford, Louth and Dublin, every county in Leinster had an active course, though only Kilkenny, Birr, Trim, Leighlinbridge, Athlone and Mullingar possessed the capacity to put on a major meeting. The most dynamic regional course remained Kilkenny, which contrived, under the direction of a succession of well-connected treasurers, to maintain the reputation it had built up since the mid-1760s of combining good racing with attractive evening entertainment. To that dual end it provided a £100 purse 'for country-bred horses' which drew entries from the local gentry, and enough standard £50 and £60 purses to attract prominent owners such as Charles Lumm, Bowes Daly and John Kirwan. The ball in aid of The Charitable Society was a race week highlight, but visitors to the town in 1793 could also attend a double bill of 'the admired comedy *Wild Oats*' and *The Virgin unmask'd* performed by named actors brought 'at a very considerable expence' from Dublin and elsewhere.[317] This was richer fare than was available at other regional venues, though Birr also hosted elegant 'assemblies', and the revived Athlone meeting in the early 1790s sought, with some success, to attract a large attendance by providing good prizes. However, the success of the latter came at the expence of nearby Roscommon, which underlined the importance for a regional course of being able to draw on a

Horses, lords and racing men, p. 128; Kelly, 'The pastime of the elite', pp 421–2; *FJ*, 11 June, 24 Sept. 1791, 4 Oct. 1793; *Hibernian Journal*, 6 May 1791; *FLJ*, 28 Sept. 1791; *Ennis Chronicle*, 29 Nov. 1792. 315 D'Arcy, *Horses, lords and racing men*, pp 16, 34; *FJ*, 11 June, 24 Sept. 1791, 4 Oct., 24 Nov. 1792, 13 June 1793. 316 For the Jockey Club (of England) and its activities, including passing reference to determining on Irish appeals: see Vamplew, *The turf*, pp 77–109. 317 *FLJ*, 22 June, 9, 27 July 1791, 12 May, 20, 23, 30 June, 4 July 1792, 1, 19, 26 June 1793, 10 May, 7, 28 June 1794;

distinct geographical catchment and of identifying a defined calendar space.[318] This was not an issue for Birr, or Trim, or Mullingar, which also organised successful race meetings that attracted local as well as major owners in the early 1790s with the standard £50 purse, or Leighlinbridge, which offered £60 in 1792.[319]

Timing and geography were also important matters for local meetings though the fact that they offered purses in the region of £10 and £20 meant they were not competing with major regional or national meets for entrants. In keeping with the pattern of horse ownership among the gentry, middlemen and larger tenant farmers, the province of Leinster sustained more local meetings than other parts of the country. They were more reliant than their more high-profile regional peers on local support, and where this was forthcoming, as for example, from William, second Viscount Ashbrook (1744–1808), who was instrumental in the revival of racing for a time at Castle Durrow, Queen's county, it was generally sufficient to ensure a successful race meeting. With a prize for 'country horses' and a 'ten guinea cup' for the winner of a three-heat two-mile race reserved for 'his lordship's tenants', Durrow races were even more localised than Maryborough races, which in the mid-1790s confined entry to horses owned by the 'inhabitants of the Queen's county'.[320] Most local courses were not so exclusive, but the reservation of entry at Naas to 'half-bred horses', to horses that had not previous competed for prizes above £20, and to 'real hunters', which was a common specification (Baltinglass, county Wicklow, and Coolgreaney, county Wexford, Callan, county Kilkenny, were other examples), was calculated to appeal to ordinary horse owners within a particular catchment.[321] It was also illustrative of the fact that though the enhancement of bloodlines was crucial to the maturation of racing as a sport, thoroughbred racing was only one dimension, and for those who could not afford such expensive 'cattle' satisfaction was also to be gleaned from watching comparative plodders. The emergence of the cross-country steeplechase was further evidence of interest in the relatively ordinary,[322] which must be factored into any assessment of the appeal of racing. In what may reasonably be perceived as the final kick of popular racing in the Dublin area, the presence of 'crowds of equestrians ... from Dublin' at Kilcock in 1791, and 'of rude mechanics and apprentices' at Morragh, county Wicklow in 1792, indicates that the ban on racing in the environs of Dublin was to the advantage of popular meets within travelling distance of the capital in the early 1790s.[323]

Consistent with their location and focus (Map 4), most race meetings drew reasonable attendances in the early 1790s. There were exceptions, of course. The

FJ, 16, 21 July 1791, 7 July 1792, 4 July 1793; *Clonmel Gazette*, 29 June 1793. **318** *Hibernian Journal*, 8, 14 Sept. 1791; *FLJ*, 20 Aug. 1791; *Ennis Chronicle*, 13 Oct. 1791. **319** *FLJ*, 8 Oct. 1791; *Hibernian Journal*, 26 Sept., 7 Oct. 1791; *Clonmel Gazette*, 8 Oct. 1794 (Birr); *Hibernian Journal*, 12 Oct. 1792 (Trim); *Hibernian Journal*, 15 Aug. 1792 (Leighlinbridge); *FLJ*, 9 July 1791 (Mullingar). **320** *FLJ*, 22, 27 Oct. 1791, 4 Oct. 1794 (Durrow); *FLJ*, 8 July 1795 (Maryborough). **321** *Hibernian Journal*, 8 Oct. 1794 (Naas); *Dublin Weekly Journal*, 3 Dec. 1791 (Baltinglass); *Hibernian Journal*, 8 July 1793 (Coolgreaney); *FLJ*, 10 Oct. 1795, 25 June, 23 July 1796, 28 Oct. 1797. **322** *Hibernian Journal*, 25 Mar. 1793. **323** *FJ*, 25 June 1791, 29 May 1792, 23 May 1793;

disappointing crowd at Roscommon in 1791, which has been referred to, anticipated 'thin' attendances at several courses, including the Curragh and Kilkenny,
in 1792. This was gratifying for those who conceived of the sport as an incentive
to 'idleness, a neglect of all business, low gambling and dissipation', who revelled
in the prospect that 'the turf is rapidly on the decline'. Those for whom race
meetings were 'pregnant of every vice and productive of no one real good or
advantage' simply called upon the authorities to proscribe 'such exhibitions'.[324]
The authorities knew better than to take such moralistic interventions seriously,
or to rush to the conclusion that the sport was in decline, and they were proved
right as attendances recovered in 1793 and 1794.[325] It was a temporary respite,
however, as the polarisation of the country between radical and reactionary that
was a consequence of the politicisation of Irish society in the 1790s produced an
environment inimical to the sport. The most striking manifestation of this was
the interruption, or cessation, of racing at a number of well-established locations
– at Athlone in 1792; Castlebar in 1793; Trim in 1793; Mullingar in 1793;
Ballyshannon in 1793; Kilkenny in 1794; and Ennis in 1795. As a consequence,
the number of functioning courses fell to its lowest level in decades (the Curragh,
the Maze, Downpatrick, Cork, Cashel, Callan, Munney, Coolgreney, Loughrea,
Tramore and Enniskillen) in 1796–7, and it fell still further, to a minimal three
meetings, in 1798.[326]

In sporting terms, 1798 was a disaster, but it is hard to imagine how it could
be otherwise since much of Leinster and east Ulster was war-torn at crucial
points in the year. The clearest evidence of the scale of disruption is provided by
the fact that the *Irish Racing Calendar* was not published in 1798, and that the
king's plates, which were the highlight of the Curragh summer meeting, were
run in October. The usual schedule of racing was also not completed in 1799,
but the resolve of the devotees of the sport that normalcy should be restored was
in evidence at the Curragh. The season was inaugurated there in April 1799 with
the traditional spring Curragh meeting; there was also an autumn programme.[327]
Elsewhere, meetings were held in 1799 at Ballyhackamore, county Antrim, and
Dundalk, county Louth, and Down Royal. The situation in 1800 was still better;
12 meetings were held; yet the instability that gripped the country in the wake
of the rebellion was not easily cast off, and the racing calendar bore the scars for
a number of years, as meetings that might otherwise have happened did not take
place either because it was inopportune, or because (as was the case at Birr in
1800) 'there were no horses prepared to run'.[328]

Hibernian Journal, 13 June 1794.   **324** *FJ*, 3 July 1792; *Cork Gazette*, 22 July 1796.   **325** *FJ*, 27
Apr., 23 May 1793; *Hibernian Journal*, 13 June 1794.   **326** This observation is based on a reading of
the press and on the data extracted from the *Racing Calendar*, summarised in 'Irish racecourses, 1751–
2001' in Sweeney, *Sweeney guide to the Irish turf*, pp 54–70. As D'Arcy (*Horses, lords and racing men*,
p. 42) points out, Wetherby's *English Racing Calendar* reportedly wrongly that there was no racing in
Ireland in 1798; three meetings took place.   **327** D'Arcy, *Horses, lords and racing men*, pp 21–3; James
G. Patterson, *In the wake of the Great Rebellion: republicanism, agrarianism and banditry in Ireland after
1798* (Manchester, 2008), passim; *FLJ*, 18 May 1799; *FJ*, 26 Oct. 1799.   **328** Sweeney, *Sweeney*

Map 5: Horse racing in Ireland, early nineteenth century: courses

Table 4: Race meetings listed in the *Racing Calendar*, 1811			
LEINSTER	MUNSTER	CONNAUGHT	ULSTER
Curragh	Limerick	Roscommon	The Maze
Kilkenny	Limerick races	Westport	Monaghan
Birr	Rathkeale		L'derry
Longford	Mallow		Cootehill
Finae	Tramore		Clermont
	Mount Prospect		
Total 5	6	2	5

Source: *Freeman's Journal*, 3 Apr. 1811

These years of reduced racing were not a manifestation of the 'decline' the Cassandras had forecast in the mid-1790s, and those who embraced the moral message of evangelical religion and respectability aspired to bring about. The attachment to horse racing remained strong; its expression was merely interrupted, with the result that as the reverberations of rebellion and insurgency eased, the racing calendar gradually filled out. The most compelling measure of this transformation is the rise in the number of race meetings from 12 in 1800 to 20 in 1805, following which growth accelerated until it peaked at 31 in 1811. Other, perhaps more subjective, but still revealing indices are provided by the number of subscribers to the *Irish Racing Calendar*, which climbed during the same period from 346 to 680 to 1659, and by the rise in the membership of the Turf Club from 22 in 1800 to 35 in 1810.[329] While the subsequent fall-off in the number of race meetings (from 24 in 1815 to 13 in 1820) and in subscriptions to the *Irish Racing Calendar* (from 1166 to 646) suggests that the surge in racing that took place from 1805 can be attributed at least in part to the augmented military presence during the Napoleonic wars, the manner in which it was pursued indicates also that what took place was not simply the restoration and rebuilding of that which had been lost in the 1790s. In keeping with the evolution of the sport since the 1660s, it combined new and established patterns. Some venerable courses re-emerged to assume a place at the forefront of the sport; others remained closed because the patrons that had sustained them were either no more, or simply disinterested, while still others were displaced by new courses and new trends.

A useful starting point for an assessment of the state of the sport as the disruption of the late 1790s faded into memory is provided by the fact that the

guide to the Irish turf, pp 55, 60; Thomas C. Parsons to Parsons, 27 Sept. 1800 in A.P.W. Malcomson (ed.), *Calendar of the Rosse papers* (Dublin, 2008), p. 338.   **329** D'Arcy, *Horses, lords and racing men*, pp 28, 40–1, 42, 343; Charles Benson, 'The Dublin book trade' in J.H. Murphy (ed.), *History of the Irish book, volume 4: the nineteenth century* (Oxford, 2011), p. 30.

'races' listed in the *Sportsman's Calendar* of 1811 embraced eighteen locations –
five in Leinster, six in Munster, five in Ulster and two in Connaught. The calendar is not complete; it does not include information on minor courses and local
race meetings, but it does demonstrate that horse racing had not been deposed
from its position as the kingdom's primary national sport by its recent travails.[330]
Support for this conclusion is provided by comparing a map of the venues cited
in the *Racing Calendar* during the first two decades of the nineteenth century
(Map 5) with the pattern described above for the early 1790s (Map 4).
Significantly, the enforcement of the legal prohibition on racing within nine miles
of Dublin Castle introduced in 1790 meant there was still no racing in or near
the capital. There was some recovery in mid- and south-Ulster, which elevated
the number of courses in the northern province to double figures (Table 3),
though the official returns may understate the amount of actual racing that took
place, since the sport was also pursued at a number of other locations after a less
formal fashion. For example, the horse racing held on the common at
Carrickfergus during the annual fair attracted crowds estimated at between fifteen and twenty thousand until it 'ceased' *c.*1820, and yielded to a still-more
informal Christmas meeting on private lands that lasted for just over a decade
until it too ceased in the early 1830s.[331] Meanwhile at Greenlough, county
Londonderry, 'people ... assembled in thousands from various parts' on four to
six Saturdays during August and September to participate in various amusements, including horse racing, which was 'strenuously supported by the local
gentry' until 1814 when it too was discontinued.[332] Elsewhere, there was an
annual race at Rosapenna sands, county Donegal, at Broughshane, county
Antrim, Magheraboy, county Fermanagh,[333] and, after a still less structured fashion, in various parishes in counties Antrim and Londonderry.[334]

The absence of any formal record of these meetings, and still less of the participants and the results, indicates that these events were far removed from the
organised sport exemplified by the race for the king's plate at the Curragh. Be
that as it may, the fact that horse racing was pursued in an informal or *ad hoc*
manner at a number of locations is evidence of its popularity beyond the structured realm of the racecourse, and of the fact that though it became still more
manifestly the sport of the elite during this maturing phase, it sustained a large
popular audience. There is surprisingly little information with which one might
even attempt to reconstruct the racing experience of the ordinary public who
were drawn to the racecourse in great numbers in the early nineteenth century.
But it can reasonably be concluded that, as well as the drama of the sport, their

---

330 *FJ*, 3 Apr. 1811. It is noteworthy that racing was held at Charleville and Cork in 1812 (*Cork Advertiser*, 21, 25 July, 2, 3, Sept. 1812).   **331** Day and McWilliams (eds), *Ordnance survey memoirs: county Antrim*, xxxvii, 175–6.   **332** Day and McWilliams (eds), *Ordnance survey memoirs: county Londonderry*, xviii, 100, 122.   **333** Day and McWilliams (eds), *Ordnance survey memoirs: county Donegal*, xxxviii, 60; *county Antrim*, xiii, 95; *Ennis Chronicle*, 25 Mar. 1818.   **334** Day and McWilliams (eds), *Ordnance survey memoirs: county Londonderry*, vi, 17 (Artrea); xi, 54 (Drumboe);

The Maze/
Hillsborough
Downpatrick

Ballina
Castlebar
Castlebellingham
Longford
Bellewstown
Roscommon
Mullingar
Trim
Lusk
Ashbourne
Newcastle
Kilcock
Howth
Phoenix Park
Kingstown
Galway
Curragh
Naas
Bray
Loughrea
Frankford
Parsonstown
Maryborough
Punchestown
Mountfalcon
Athy
Wicklow
Ennis
Carlow
Limerick
Kilkenny
Kilmallock
Caher
Mallow
Fermoy
Tramore
Cork
Middleton
Kinsale

N

0   50 miles
0   80 km

Map 6: Horse racing in Ireland, 1830s: courses

presence was encouraged by the variety of recreational opportunities that such occasions offered, which was not only a palpable advance on what had occurred in the eighteenth century, but also comparable to that available at fairs and patterns. This is the implication of the description of Kilkenny races in 1828 provided by Humphrey O'Sullivan:

> There were plenty of tents and huts for eating and drinking there. The trick-o'-the-loop people were there and the thimble-riggers, sweep-stake bookies and wheel-o'-fortune men, jugglers and lottery-bag men, and a hundred other tricks not worth mentioning.[335]

The situation was comparable at the Broad Meadow at Enniskillen in the mid-1830s:

> The assemblage of personages was very considerable, together with numerous booths, gambling establishments and petty shows. The affair was kept up for a whole week each time and terminated by cot racing for prizes got up by subscription.[336]

Partly because of their enthusiasm for 'every kind of low game', the race-going populace was regarded by the elite with varying (but appreciating) levels of disdain. However, their participation was as crucial as that of the elite to the emergence of new (and generally short-lived) courses at Aughnacloy, Londonderry, Armagh, Cairnban (county Down), Emyvale (county Monaghan) and Kingscourt (county Cavan) in Ulster in the early nineteenth century, and it contributed in no small manner to the maintenance of racing, for 'half-bred racers and hunters', for longer periods at Enniskillen and Monaghan.[337] None of these locations rivalled the Maze or Downpatrick as the leading provincial venue in Ulster, though a riot at Downpatrick races in 1814 indicated that the racecourse could become a flashpoint for other social tensions. In this instance, disorder was precipitated when a private quarrel over money escalated, necessitating the intervention of a magistrate and a party of the army stationed nearby; this provoked a confrontation with the crowd, causing the army to open fire with live rounds as a result of which two died and seven were wounded.[338] This was the most serious incident on an Irish racecourse in the early nineteenth century, but

xiii, 50 (Layd); xxi, 60 (Desertmartin); *county Antrim*, xxi, 22 (Aghagallon); xxix, 151 (Kilbride). 335 *Cinnlae Amhlaoibh Uí Súilleabháin: the diary of Humphrey O'Sullivan ... 1827–36* ed., Michael McGrath (Irish Texts Society: 4 vols, London, 1928–31), ii, 49. 336 Day and McWilliams (eds), *Ordnance survey memoirs: county Fermanagh*, iv, 63–4; Mary Rogers, *Prospect of Fermanagh* (Enniskillen, 1982), p. 77. A cot race was a rowing race. 337 McGrath (ed.), *The diary of Humphrey O'Sullivan*, iv, 77; Sweeney, *The Sweeney guide*, pp 54, 61, 66; Desmond Chaloner, 'County life in Meath, 1810–17: extracts from the Kingscourt journals', *Ríocht na Midhe*, 8 (1987), p. 21; *FJ*, 22 Oct. 1818; *FLJ*, 14 Nov. 1818; Day and McWilliams (eds), *Ordnance survey memoirs: county Down*, iii, 74; Day and McWilliams (eds), *Ordnance survey memoirs: county Fermanagh*, iv, 63–4; Rogers, *Prospect of Fermanagh*, p. 77. 338 *FJ*, 30 July 1814.

the fact that racing ceased at Greenlough 'in consequence of tumult and quarrelling occasioned by excess of a drink and party animosities' suggests that rowdiness may have been less uncommon than the absence of reference to such matters in most accounts of racing may suggest.[339] It also indicates that the inclusion in certain race reports of the statement 'no disturbance took place' was not an irrelevant convention. Rather, it was a reflection of the fact that the social tensions that gripped early nineteenth-century Irish society were not left outside the racecourse.

One consequence of this for racecourses was the increased separation of the elite and *hoi polloi*, and the creation of discrete areas where subscribers, members, and others acceptable to the social elite could congregate, which freed them from the obligation to interact with their social inferiors. This development was assisted by the large numbers that were drawn to race meetings in the early nineteenth century, and to the tendency of the 'whole county' to attend the local race meeting. Because there is no data with which to make a valid comparison, it cannot be stated for certain that the estimated attendances of 10,000 at Cairnban, county Down, and 50,000 at Armagh in 1818 were unprecedented, or unusual, for regional meetings, but they provide some indication of the sport's popularity in Ulster at this time, and of the circumstances that encouraged the increased social stratification of racing crowds.[340]

Its impressive drawing power notwithstanding, Ulster possessed fewer racecourses at this time than either Leinster or Munster. Though the numerical margin between the provinces had diminished by the early nineteenth century, Leinster's ascendancy in the sport was secure, not least because the direction provided by the Turf Club ensured the Curragh was secure as the country's premier racing venue. There were many reasons – geographical, historical and organisational – for this, but the enduring popularity of the Gold Cup assisted the course rapidly to negotiate the debilitating legacy of the late 1790s, as it drew large crowds to the course, and encouraged large-scale betting – estimated at £50,000 in 1801 and 1803 – on the outcome. Though rivalries between owners, and the public's fascination with the horse of the year, fuelled this enthusiasm, there were fewer owners with the quality bloodstock required to compete at the Curragh in the early nineteenth century than was the case a decade earlier. Yet, the Curragh was still the preferred location of the country's leading owners, many of who stabled their horses in the various lodges that surrounded the course. Denis Bowes Daly's establishment – Athgarvan Lodge – was widely regarded as one of the finest, but other prominent owners who were drawn to the location included Robert Hamilton, John Whaley, Charles Lumm and William Westenra, second Baron Rossmore.[341] It was from these locations that the most ambitious Irish owners planned how they could take more than their share of racing's glittering prizes, both in Ireland, and

339 Day and McWilliams (eds), *Ordnance survey memoirs: county Londonderry*, xviii, 122. 340 *FJ*, 22 Oct. 1818; *FLJ*, 14 Nov. 1818; Chaloner, 'County life in Meath, 1810–17', p. 21. 341 See D'Arcy, *Horses, lords and racing men*, pp 48–54.

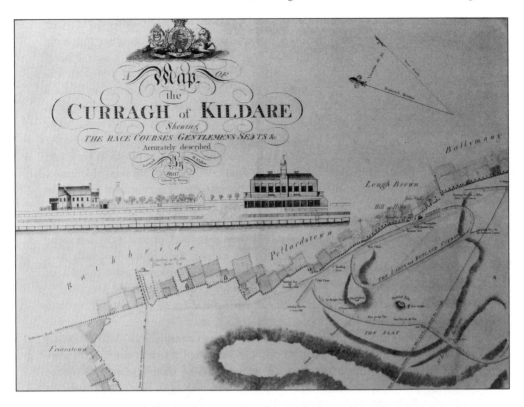

Fig. 13 Extract from *Map of the Curragh of Kildare showing the racecourses, gentlemen's seats, etc., accurately described by H[enry] Walker*, 1807. This illustrated extract from Walker's map shows not only the course options then available (the four-mile course, the Rutland course, the Conolly mile) but also the old stand and other buildings (photo by Paul Murphy from Walker's map).

in the case of ambitious individuals such as Bowes Daly and John Whaley, at Epsom and Newmarket in England.[342]

Next to the Gold Cup, the king's plates were the most high-profile races, but a significant early nineteenth-century addition, possibly prompted by a dilution in the ranks of subscribers, was the emergence of named stakes races. Bearing titles such as the Kildare Stakes, Lumm Stakes, Conolly Stakes, Kirwan Stakes, etc., these races combined with the now occasional race sponsored by the Turf Club, sweepstakes, handicap plates, the iconic king's plates and Gold Cup to continue to draw spectators in impressive numbers to the Curragh. The 'numerous' crowd present in 1801 indicates that this was an attractive menu at that

342 *FLJ*, 18, 25, 29 Apr., 16 Sept. 1801, 21 Sept. 1803; *FJ*, 5 May 1803; *Ennis Chronicle*, 25 Apr. 1818; Sweeney, *The Sweeney guide to the Irish turf*, pp 179–81.

moment, but the reduced prize money available and the smaller fields that became routine thereafter presented a problem.[343] This became acute following the conclusion of the Napoleonic wars when the combination of a severe post-war recession, the diminished tendency of the landed elite to travel to the Curragh from their estates or from England, and different recreational habits prompted a significant decline in the number of race meetings, and subscriptions to the *Irish Racing Calendar*. In an attempt to retain the public's interest, and to attract crowds, course organisers instituted new races. This was most manifest at the Curragh where, as well as sponsored cups (the Peel Cup, Royal Whip), and stakes (the Madrid Stakes, Wellington Stakes, Anglesey Stakes, Mulgrave Stakes), the Turf Club contrived to follow the example of Newmarket and establish Irish versions of English Classics.[344] It also contrived to follow the English precedent by adding pugilism to the menu of entertainments in the mid-1810s. It was, in so far as one can glean, the first time that the Curragh went down the latter route, and since it dovetailed with the emergence of Dan Donnelly as a national hero it may have had the desired impact as an exceptional 'assembly of noblemen and gentlemen' were present at the spring meeting in 1818.[345] However, it was a short-lived infatuation, and it proved no more enduring than the unsuccessful experiment in creating classic races.

The twenty years 1815–35 were difficult for the Curragh, and for Irish racing in general as the number of meetings was in deficit of its early nineteenth century peak, with the inevitable result that prize money, memberships, subscriptions and, not least, the condition of courses deteriorated. Though its position insulated it from the worst effects of the economic downturn then underway, the Curragh was not immune from its impact. The reputation of the course, and of racing in general, was certainly not assisted by ongoing internecine squabbles that depleted the energy and time of those charged with running the sport.[346] Yet, it is simplistic to characterise these years as 'a time of troubles'. The decision of George IV, a keen sportsman, to include the Curragh on his itinerary during his royal tour in 1821 was an explicit recognition of the course's place at the peak of the Irish racing pyramid. The preparation for the King's visit involved considerable expenditure to bring the decaying accommodation for visitors and spectators close to acceptable standard, but it provided the course, and the sport, with a welcome, if slow burning, boost. The King was greeted by Augustus, fourth duke of Leinster, in his capacity as head of the Turf Club, and his presentation of a Royal Whip, which was to be competed for over subsequent decades, served to affirm the value of the sport to an aristocratic elite whose involvement seemed on the wane.[347]

343 *FLJ*, 29 Apr., 2, 6 May 1801, 29 June, 28 Sept. 1803; *Ennis Chronicle*, 25 Mar., 25 Apr., 2 May, 17 Oct. 1818, 1 May, 12 June 1819.　　344 D'Arcy, *Horses, lords and racing men*, pp 58–63. 345 *FJ*, 10 Sept. 1814; below, pp 302–3; Dennis Brailsford, *Bareknuckles: a social history of prize fighting* (Cambridge, 1988), pp 18–9, 26–7, 31; *Ennis Chronicle*, 25 Mar. 1818.　　346 There were a number of particularly difficult episodes such as the Rossmore controversy and the Ruthven affair; see D'Arcy, *Horses, lords and racing men*, pp 64–92, 97–106, 112–24.　　347 The royal visit was

Despite the debilitating impact of the rows, differences, and disagreements that beset the Turf Club in the decades following the conclusion of the Napoleonic wars in Europe, racing continued to mature as a sport. This can be attributed in the first instance to the manner in which the stewards availed of the powers provided them under the Rules and Orders of the Turf Club. Though the regulations and practices that they followed appertained in the first instance to the manner in which racing was conducted at the Curragh, they were not without broader impact because of the tendency, already manifest in the 1790s, for courses to look to the Curragh as a guide to best practice increased in the early nineteenth century. Some of the instructions that were issued by the Curragh stewards on starting races on time, on the behaviour appropriate to the gallops, on the timely posting of racecards, course improvement, and on the prompt payment of wagers might have been implemented autochthonously at any course. Others were possessed of more obvious implications for the sport as a whole. The strong recommendation made in 1812, in response to a clash of fixtures, that the main race meetings should follow the schedule laid down by the Club was crucial in the emergence of a centralised racing calendar, and since it reduced the prospect of clashes injurious to the sport, it was an obvious improvement. The move towards embracing the Newmarket standard with respect to the length of races was also significant. However, it was signally less so than the implications of the increased recourse to the Turf Club as the arbiter of disputes, and the exercise by the stewards of the Club of that role, since it was a further tangible step on the journey towards the assumption by the Club of the regulatory function that defines the modern sport of horse racing.[348]

While the resilience of the Curragh, and the patience of the Turf Club stewards were crucial features of the maturation of the sport of horse racing in Ireland in the early nineteenth century, the sport was also shaped by the ongoing phenomenon of course rationalisation, which was another feature of the early nineteenth century that left no province untouched. As perhaps the most consistently well-organised regional racecourse in the country during the 1770s and 1780s, it was a matter of little surprise that racing resumed at Kilkenny in 1802, albeit after an interval of eight years, or that it offered an ambitious six-day programme that included a sweepstake for 'real hunters' to be ridden by 'members' of the three best-appointed gentlemen's clubs in the country, the Turf Club, and the Kilkenny Hunt. It was a novel formula that seemed well calculated to pay rich dividends, but the resuscitated meeting only functioned for two years before it ceased, and when it resumed again in 1808 it continued for four years before

described at great length: see *FLJ*, 5 Sept. 1821. Indicatively, when the lord lieutenant, the marquis of Anglesey, visited the Curragh in June 1828, he availed of the occasion to review the Eighth Hussars army regiment, 'putting them through a great number of evolutions', on his arrival, and to inspect 'the constabulary force of the three adjoining counties' after 'the termination of the sports of the day': *FLJ*, 21 June 1828; D'Arcy, *Horses, lords and racing men*, pp 93–7. 348 D'Arcy, *Horses, lords and racing men*, pp 29–40, 58 and passim.

it ceased once more. Closer inquiry is required before a definitive explanation can be advanced as to why this was so, but the unwillingness of sufficient numbers of the country elite to participate and to contribute in the selfless manner of their predecessors was a factor.[349] The emerging disinclination of the owners of quality bloodstock to enter their horses in regional meetings may also have been an issue, though the prize money on offer at Kilkenny was not derisory. Be that as it may, most of the horses that now competed at Kilkenny were locally owned, with the result that the seventeen-year interval between the cessation of racing at Kilkenny in 1811 and its resumption in 1828, as a four-day event, provided an opportunity that others contrived to avail of. It certainly worked to the advantage of the village of Johnstown (formerly Ballyspellan), which hosted racing in 1814 and in the late 1820s, Callan (revived in 1819), and Castletown (1833), all in county Kilkenny.[350] It may also have had a positive impact on the sport in the neighbouring counties of Carlow and Tipperary, and in Queen's county, which sustained a healthy number of local race meetings in the early nineteenth century, though here too the attrition rate was high, and courses such as Ballybrophy (Queen's county, 1807), Coolmoyne (county Tipperary, 1809–10), Lismore (county Waterford, 1810–11), and Carrick-on-Suir (county Tipperary, 1818–21) all flickered briefly before fading from view.[351]

The situation was comparable elsewhere. Across Leinster, courses at Wicklow, Maryborough, Longford, Trim, Moynalty, Athlone, Castlepollard, Kinnegad, Sallins, Athy, Dunlavin, Rathdrum, Frankford, Birr, Ballyhogue and Enniscorthy functioned for short periods with support from members of the landed elite, but failed for various reasons to carve out an enduring space on the landscape in the manner of Kilcock or Bellewstown; the latter capitalised on the acquisition of a king's plate in 1808 to become 'an established annual festival'.[352] The number of locations that hosted race meetings may suggest that the sport was more vibrant and dynamic in Leinster than was the case in reality. Yet despite the contraction that took place once the economic fortunes of the country took a nose dive, and the local elite withdrew from certain tracks, there were still more racecourses in Leinster in the 1830s than in any other province, and, the concentration in counties Kildare and Meath apart, they were more evenly distributed spatially than was the case elsewhere (Map 6).

In Munster, meanwhile, racing underwent a comparable process that contributed to the maturation of the sport. The two main courses in the province – Ennis and

349 *FLJ*, 6 Nov. 1802, 16 Apr. 1803, 28 May, 3, 6, 24 Aug. 1808.   350 McGrath (ed.), *Diary of Humphrey O'Sullivan*, ii, 49, 293, iii, 77; *FLJ*, 13, 31 Aug. 1808, 11 Sept. 1819, 29 Aug., 26, 29 Sept. 1827, 24 Sept., 21 June, 6, 17, 20 Sept., 1, 15 Oct., 1, 5, 12 Nov. 1828, 10 May 1833; Sweeney, *The Sweeney guide to the Irish turf*, pp 57, 63.   351 *FLJ*, 13 Aug. 1808, 3, 7 July 1819 (Carlow); *FLJ*, 19 May 1819, 20 Sept. 1820, 13 Oct. 1821 (Carrick-on-Suir); Sweeney, *The Sweeney guide to the Irish turf*, pp 55, 59, 65.   352 Chaloner, 'County life in Meath, 1810–17', p. 21; *FJ*, 28 May 1819, *FLJ*, 19 Apr. 1820 (Wicklow); *FLJ*, 28 Aug. 1819 (Maryborough); *FJ*, 30 June 1824 (Bellewstown); *FJ*, 21 Oct. 1829 (Longford); Sweeney, *The Sweeney guide to the Irish turf*, pp 54, 55, 56, 60, 61, 62, 66, 68, 70; D'Arcy, *Horses, lords and racing men*, pp 108–9.

Mallow – were venerable racing venues by the early nineteenth century. They maintained an impressive, albeit not continuous, sequence of meetings across the first four decades of the century, and were held in such esteem that local notables (MPs, office-holders and landowners) acknowledged the need to be seen to support the meeting by their presence by the 1820s.[353] Limerick sustained a comparable sequence of race meetings across three decades; as did Rathkeale during the first fifteen years. Tralee, by contrast, had faded from view by 1810, and racing did not resume in county Kerry until the inauguration of a course at Killarney in the mid-1820s. With an estimated '50,000 spectators' at Limerick's Newcastle course in 1819, it is clear that these locations possessed considerable drawing power, though, as in Ulster and Leinster, the quality of the racing sometimes left much to be desired. This was in keeping with the fact that most of the horses entered to run at Limerick, and elsewhere in the province (Ennis possibly excepted), were locally owned, and were seldom of the first rank.[354] Be that as it may, local notables were supportive of local racing, and they manifested this by providing purses for stakes races, by their presence on race days, and, as evidenced by the initiation of a four-day meeting at Carrick-on-Suir in 1819, by the willingness of some at least of 'the principal inhabitants' to assume organisational responsibility.[355] The interest in racing to which this attested was most in evidence at new courses. Cahir, county Tipperary, was one of the most significant, but it was less successful than Tramore, which was the major success story of racing in Munster, and the most successful manifestation of the phenomenon of strand racing whose emergence in the early nineteenth century dovetailed with the commencement of sea-bathing and recreational trips to the seaside.[356] Among the other beneficiaries of this trend were Dungarvan, Waterford and Youghal, though none of these locations sustained a continuous sequence of race meetings. In this respect, Munster was no different from Leinster and Ulster; a large proportion of its meetings – Kilmallock (1800, 1831–2), Nenagh (1814), Coolmoyne (1809–10), Carrick-on-Suir (1819–22), Charleville (1802–07, 1810, 1812), Liscarrol (1809), Lismore (1810–11) – were once-off or short-lived events that were not sustained for want of funds rather than spectators.[357] Moreover, in keeping with the pattern identified elsewhere, race organisers were disposed to innovate in anticipation that this might enable them better to negotiate this difficulty. In county Waterford, the inauguration in 1817 of a stee-

---

353 *FJ*, 21 July 1827; Sweeney, *The Sweeney guide to the Irish turf*, pp 61, 65. **354** See the racing cards at Rathkeale (*Ennis Chronicle*, 7 Jan. 1818); Limerick (*Ennis Chronicle*, 19, 23 Sept. 1818); Tramore (*FLJ*, 29 Aug. 1807), Cahir (*Ennis Chronicle*, 7 Oct. 1818), and Carrick-on-Suir (*FLJ*, 20 Sept. 1820). **355** *Ennis Chronicle*, 7 Jan., 6 June, 19, 23, 26 Sept. 1818; *FLJ*, 19 May, 28 Aug. 1819, 13 Oct. 1821; Sweeney, *The Sweeney guide to the Irish turf*, pp 64–5, 68. **356** Sweeney, *The Sweeney guide to the Irish turf*, pp 57, 70; *FLJ*, 17 June 1801, 8 Oct. 1806, 20 Aug. 1808, 29 Aug. 1809, 22 Aug. 1818 (Tramore); *Ennis Chronicle*, 7, 10 Oct. 1818; *FJ*, 16 June 1829 (Cahir); Kelly, 'Balneotherapeutic medicine', pp 138–9; Mary Davies, *That favourite resort: the story of Bray, county Wicklow* (Bray, 2007), p. 84. **357** *FLJ*, 30 Mar. 1803 (Youghal); *FLJ*, 19 May 1819, 20 Sept. 1820, 13 Oct. 1821 (Carrick-on-Suir); *FLJ*, 8 June 1803 (Charleville); Sweeney, *The Sweeney guide to the Irish turf*, pp 64–5, 68

Fig. 14 The Westmeath Challenge Urn, London 1834, mark of Charles Reily and George Storer. This large urn (115oz, 54cm high) depicts a hunt in full flight, galloping across the countryside above chased scrollwork in high relief, raised on a naturalistically cast cased leaf work scrolling circular base, with upturned lips. Sold at auction in October 2012 (image courtesy of Adam's).

plechase for hunters 'from different counties' to be run between Newtown and Bunmahon prompted a six-day meeting in 1819 at Bunmahon. It was organised by a consortium of local gentry, who put up most of the prizes, and it reflected the reality that the steeplechase was more in keeping with the profile of fox-hunting gentry than fine flat-racing.[358] The inauguration at Dungarvan in 1817 of a steeple-chase meeting in 1818 was a further demonstration of the expanding appeal of this form of racing.[359] Elsewhere, increasingly splendid silver trophies (sometimes weighting more than 100 ounces), such as the Westmeath Challenge Urn (Fig. 14) or the Meath Challenge Cup (Fig. 15), with the moulding of a horse on the lid, and scenes of horses in full flight on the body, attested to the attraction horse racing continued to exercise. Signally, both trophies were commissioned in the 1830s when the sport was on the eve of recovery from the trough into which it had descended

358 *FJ*, 22 Oct. 1818; *FLJ*, 2 Oct. 1819, 18 Oct., 8, 11 Nov. 1820.   **359** *Cork Advertiser*, 19 Nov. 1818.

Fig. 15 The Meath Challenge Cup, 1837, London 1833, mark of Jonathan Hayne. Large cup (102.5oz, 40cm high) with a fitted cover with figure of a horse finial on a chased ground, the lobed body finely decorated with intertwining acanthus leaves, and a racing scene to one side and engraved inscription to the other. The twin handles in the form of two horses rearing from the sides, raised on an upturned lip of vines and foliate, above fluted, leaf wrapped shaped circular spreading foot. Sold at auction in October 2012 (image courtesy of Adam's).

after 1815. Such prizes did not, to be sure, repay horse owners for the investment they put into the sport, but they reflected their confidence in the future. Moreover, the possession of such a prize, even for a season, was a source of sufficient wellbeing to convince many that not only was the expenditure justified but also that horse racing was intrinsic to their identity as a landed elite.

CONCLUSION

In April 1828, the 'races for the Kilmain Cup took place at Maiden Hill, county Mayo, in the presence of 'an immense concourse of people'. The fact that Maiden

Hill hosted such an impressive event illustrated that though Connaught had the fewest functioning courses of any province in the early nineteenth century, horse racing was no less firmly rooted there than it was elsewhere in the country. Indeed, the fact that four of Connaught's race-venues – Castlebar, Roscommon, Tuam, and Loughrea – were among the most important regional courses in the country in the 1830s was indicative of the fact that the now mature sport was deeply, if unevenly, anchored in the landscape. It was, to be sure, thinly represented in the south-west, the south-east, and across much of west and central Ulster (Map 6), but it had regained a foothold in Dublin (in the Phoenix Park, among other locations).[360] However, because there were fewer courses at the end of the Hanoverian era than at virtually any point since it commenced in 1714, the number of courses is only one of a variety of guides to the state of the sport at any point in time. Be that as it may, the rise in the number of courses during the first half of the eighteenth century constitutes a reliable benchmark against which one can track the spatial and infrastructural growth of the sport, bearing in mind that a variable proportion of the venues functioning at any given time were not only short lived but also un-viable. What this suggests is that, having experienced a period of extremely rapid expansion in the mid-eighteenth century, a subsequent phase of consolidation, and a phase of maturation, during which the number of race courses had fallen considerably from its eighteenth-century peak, the sport had arrived by the late 1830s at a point where in order to develop further it was necessary to embrace tighter regulation, to develop infrastructure, and to produce finer quality bloodstock.[361] It was not obvious where the sport was destined, but since it was patent that the standard of racing in Ireland in the 1830s was palpably in advance of where it had been a century earlier, there were considerable grounds for optimism. Furthermore, though there was still some resistance to accepting the Turf Club as the regulatory authority for the sport, horse racing was better organised and better administered than it had ever been, better indeed than other sports, and it was possessed of a proven agreed set of rules and customs.

In addition, horse racing also offered the spectator an engaging experience whether it was at Castlebar or at the Curragh. The meeting at Maiden Hill in 1828 may not have been entirely typical, but it is illustrative of a sport that was firmly socially anchored. Consistent with this, it is apparent from the extensive report of the proceedings at the county Mayo course that horse racing was not only popular because it was the country's most sophisticated sporting diversion but also because it was a red-letter day on the social calendar of rich and poor as the Hanoverian era neared its conclusion:

> ... The races for the Kilmain Cup took place on the race ground at Maiden Hill, and attracted an immense concourse of people. From the

360 *FLJ*, 18 June 1828. 361 Barnard, *Making the grand figure*, p. 247; Welcome, *Irish horse racing*, p. 12, citing Cheney's *Racing calendar* for 1750; Alexander Knox, *A history of the county of Down* ... (Dublin, 1875), p. 61.

stand house on which the band of the 3d Dragoons was stationed, the scene was animated and delightful beyond description; on each side a long line of carriages, jigs, jaunting cars, etc. was drawn up, filled with fashionable and elegantly dressed females; and the splendid uniforms of the Dragoon officers, intermixed with the moving mass of equestrians and pedestrians of every grade and hue, added considerably to the brilliancy of the *coup d'oeil*. Detachments of the Castlebar and Ballinrobe police ... cooperated with the stewards in preserving order; and we feel much gratification in stating, that notwithstanding the vast assemblage on the ground, not the slightest accident occurred. At four o'clock the first race commenced, and three horses, rode by Messrs Isidore Blake, Bowen Elwood and Lynch, started. Mr Blake's Rosette appeared to be the favourite, and the race was gallantly contested ... Mr Richard Blake of Garracloon rode the second heat with Mr Elwood, and after some excellent running, came in foremost, amid loud cheering from the populace. The leap racing then commenced, and afforded much amusement from the gallant manner in which the horses cleared the several leaps. It was won by Mr Blake's horse Tinker. But in consequence of not having entered in time, the cup was given to Mr Cuffe. The last race finished at eight o'clock, at which hour the gentry, whom the fineness of the day had tempted to remain, began to move off, and the merry sounds of the pipe and violin from many a booth invited the humble peasant to enter, where mirth and gaiety held many captive after night had closed upon the scene. ... Owing to the lateness of the hour at which the field sports terminated, the company did not begin to arrive till about eleven o'clock, and about twelve the rooms were completely filled. The Grand Jury room, which was fitted up very tastefully for the occasion, and hung round with festoons of laurel and evergreen, presented a scene of uncommon splendour and brilliancy. The rich dresses of the ladies, ...the gorgeous uniforms of the military, and the enlivening strains of the music, all contributed to fascinate and delight ... . Quadrille dancing and waltzing were kept up with great spirit till supper was announced, when the company retired to the Crown Court ... After supper, dancing was again resumed, and the company continued to enjoy the festive scene till an advanced hour ....[362]

362 *FJ*, 12 Apr. 1828.

2

Hunting

Individuals of every social class and rank hunted and killed animals, but hunting in its most developed and sophisticated sporting form was a privilege reserved for the elite.[1] In this respect hunting mirrored society, for though its elite practitioners were dependent on a veritable phalanx of helpers from the lower social orders – gamekeepers, beaters, grooms, dog-handlers, earthstoppers, etc. – to pursue the sport in the manner they deemed appropriate, they were also empowered to do so by the law, which upheld their exclusive entitlement to pursue the quarry they esteemed, to defend their lands against encroachment, and to penalise those whom they denominated poachers. The legal sanctions available were stern (though not as stern as the notorious 'black acts' that applied in England), but no attempt was made to confine the right to hunt *per se* to the elite, because there was an array of other animals in which those at or close to the apex of the social pyramid had less interest. They provided the quarry for those outside of the elite who not only hunted in a less structured fashion but in a manner that barely satisfied the contemporary definition of sport.

The most prized and, by extension, the most exclusive target of the huntsman was the stag – the male red deer – the pursuit of which was denominated 'the most gay, the most daring, and the most generous of all chases'.[2] The stag took precedence over the buck – the male fallow deer – which was the most popular ruminant quarry and the doe – the female of the same species.[3] The fox and the hare were also denominated 'noble chace', and in addition it was permitted by law to pursue otters, rabbits, badgers, wolves (until they became extinct), weasels and martins, and, because they fed on fish which were singled out for protection because of their economic significance,[4] herons, kites, cormorants, scaldcrows,[5] magpies and water

---

1 For the already classic analysis, locating Ireland with an *ancien regime* setting see S.J. Connolly, *Religion, law and power: the making of Protestant Ireland, 1660–1760* (Oxford, 1992). More broadly see, inter alia, J.C.D. Clark, *English society, 1688–1832: ideology, social structure, and political practice during the ancien regime* (Cambridge, 1985). 2 Arthur Stringer, *The experienc'd huntsman, or, a collection of observations upon the nature and chace of the stagg, buck, hare, fox, martern [sic] and otter...* (Belfast, 1714; 2nd ed., Dublin, 1780). A modern edition, from which most of the quotations cited in this chapter are drawn was published in 1977: *The experienced huntsman, by Arthur Stringer*, ed. James Fairley (Belfast, 1977), p. 40. 3 Ibid., pp 58–71; MacGregor, *Animal encounters*, p. 132. 4 See Andrew Sneddon, 'Legislating for economic development: Irish fisheries as a case study in the limitations of "improvement"' in D.W. Hayton, James Kelly and John Bergin (eds), *The eighteenth-century composite state: representative institutions in Ireland and Europe, 1689–1800* (Basingstoke, 2010), pp 136–59 for a recent consideration. 5 Scaldcrow/scalcrow was the name given in Ireland to the hooded crow (*corvus cornix*).

rats. Indeed, pretty much any feral animal that moved was a potential target, though it is striking that hunting was impelled less by the love of the chase than by the object of vermin control the further away one moved from the larger ruminant quadrupeds – game birds (the pheasant, partridge and grouse, particularly) excepted. The most noteworthy exception to this generalisation was the fox, which became the most popular quarry during the eighteenth century partly because it was more practical, and more economical than the deer, and partly because it provided 'a brave noble chace' between Michaelmas (29 September) and Lady day (24 March) 'for such who keep good horses and hounds'.[6]

As the reference to 'good horses and hounds' implies, hunting, like horse racing and cockfighting, was an expensive diversion when it was pursued at the highest level. It may not ordinarily have necessitated a financial commitment equivalent to that made by enthusiasts of the turf, but, good hunters, like good thoroughbreds, did not come cheap, and creating and stocking a deer park, maintaining a pack of quality hounds, and organising and hosting a hunt required a financial outlay in excess of the capacity of the stereotypical 'fox-hunting country squire' to maintain.[7] This had significant implications for the evolution of the sport in the eighteenth century.[8]

Because hunting was intrinsically a simple activity which pivoted on the chase, capture and (usually) the killing of an animal, it is tempting to assume that it possessed less capacity for change than other, more complex sports. It certainly did not experience anything during the seventeenth century comparable to the transformation to which it was subject in England as a consequence of the sharp diminution in the space available to keep, and, therefore, to pursue deer.[9] Yet hunting in Ireland was not unchanging. In keeping with the fact that it was the traditional recreation of the aristocracy and gentry, who maintained their own dog packs and deer herds, hunting was organised in an essentially individualist manner in the seventeenth and early eighteenth centuries. Subsequently, the sport was prompted by the accelerating associational impulse and by the growth in the allied sport of horse racing to assume a more organised form. The precise effects of these trends are not always easily disentangled, but the interaction with and, by extension, the impact of horse racing can be detected in the frequency with which race organisers in the second and third quarters of the eighteenth century included a hunt on the menu of alternative diversions they presented racegoers. It may be that the primary legacy of such sporting interaction was the taming of hunting – as evi-

6 Stringer, *The experienced huntsman*, pp 83, 86; Falkiner to [Trumbull], [1787] (NYPL, Trumbull papers, box 1). 7 For a wonderful dissection of the costs attendant on 'making the grand figure' in the hunting and racing realms see Barnard, *Making the grand figure*, chapter 7. Other than noting the financial commitment required, this chapter will largely eschew engaging with this dimension. 8 For an admittedly atypical illustration of the difficulty Lord Altham encountered sustaining the financial commitment required, see A. Roger Ekirch, *Birthright: the true story that inspired Kidnapped* (London, 2012), pp 32, 57. 9 Emma Griffin argues that 'the world of hunting never fully recovered from the events of the 1640s and 1650s', and that this was particularly manifest with respect to deer hunting: see Griffin, *Bloodsport: hunting in Britain since 1066*, pp 100–4; see also

denced by the appreciating reliance on 'bagged' foxes and 'carted' deer that purists lamented. But it is hardly coincidental, by the same token, that the inclusion of hunts on the menu of entertainments provided racegoers decreased as the hunt club emerged in the second half of the eighteenth century as the sport's most emblematical organisational manifestation. This did not result in the abandonment of the private pack of hounds though their size may have decreased. Hunt clubs continued to draw on private packs, but the club was the most significant structural innovation that hunting made in the eighteenth century, and the subscription pack, which it fostered, was indicative of the increasingly ordered way in which hunting was conducted.[10]

Like cockfighting and horse racing, which paved the way, the development of hunting both paralleled and profited from the emergence of a national and regional press. The newspaper facilitated hunts to promote and to publicise their activities and, by providing a modern medium with which to communicate with members and other interested parties, assisted clubs to recruit, to function as administrative and sporting organisations, and to serve as nodes of sociability. Indeed, by facilitating the assembly of groups of like-minded individuals, the press played a crucial role in the popularisation of the sport. This process was assisted by the increased focus on the fox, which was integral to the emergence of hunting in a recognisably modern form. Since what happened in Ireland in this respect echoed what happened in England during the same period, it cannot be suggested that the history of hunting was unique to Ireland. Yet, the country did not simply duplicate the pattern followed in Great Britain. There were differences that reflected the society in which it was pursued, and the colonial context in which hunting (and other sports) were conducted. There is, however, no reason to suggest that the treatment of animals in Ireland was any less exploitative than it was in England. Indeed, it can plausibly be suggested, based on the example of hunting alone, that the Irish replicated the abusive attitude of the English.[11] This is a subject requiring a more specific investigation than it is possible to provide here, but one of the advantages of exploring the history of the chase in the late early modern era is that it permits such broader conclusions, however tantalising they might be.

HUNTING IN THE LATE SEVENTEENTH AND EARLY EIGHTEENTH CENTURIES

Like Charles II, to whom he was devoted, the enthusiasm of James, first duke of Ormond (1610–88), Ireland's premier peer and long serving viceroy, for field

MacGregor, *Animal encounters*, pp 111–13.   10 See M.J. Powell, 'Hunting clubs and societies' in James Kelly and M.J. Powell (eds), *Clubs and societies in eighteenth-century Ireland* (Dublin, 2010), pp 392–408; Barnard, *Making the grand figure*, pp 244, 246; Lowe to [Baker], 13 Apr. 1754 (NLI, Baker papers: reports on private collections no. 351, p. 2566); Falkiner to Trumbull [1787] (NYLP, Trumbull papers, box 1).   11 For a larger engagement with this subject in its English context, see Diana Donald, *Picturing animals in Britain, 1750–1850* (London, 2008); MacGregor, *Animal*

Fig. 16 James, first duke of Ormonde (1610–88), lord lieutenant of Ireland, 1662–9, 1677–84, engraved by Robert Dunkarton from a pencil drawing by David Loggan (1815) (National Portrait Gallery).

sports not only ensured such recreational activity respectability but also encouraged others to engage in the pursuit. The observation by a member of Ormond's entourage that the lord deputy had pleasurably occupied himself 'hawking, hunting, coursing and horse racing' on the kingdom's primary racing venue, the Curragh, in the winter of 1662–3 attests to the centrality of the horse to such diversion, but it is also evident from this account that hunting offered more options than horse racing.[12] As a signature recreation of Europe's feudal nobility, hawking continued to appeal during the seventeenth century. It was evidently a favourite diversion of Sir George Rawdon (1604–84), one of the leading figures in Ulster politics during the Restoration era, for example, but it was visibly in decline.[13] The pursuit of the wolf, by contrast, was actively encouraged by the provision of a reward for each animal that was killed. With eradication in mind, the Cromwellian authorities inaugurated a programme of faunal cleansing in the

encounters, passim.   12 Barnard, *Making the grand figure*, p. 228. The member of Ormond's entourage who wrote of his experiences was E. Cooke. See also Hennessey, 'On the Curragh of Kildare', p. 353.   13 Edward McLysaght, *Irish life in the seventeenth century* (2nd edn, Shannon, 1969), pp 137–8, 140; Barnard, *Making the grand figure*, p. 237.

1650s, and though the campaign they initiated did not achieve its logical *denoue-ment* until the eighteenth century, the sharp decline in the number of wolves caught in the final decades of the seventeenth century, and in the number of wolfhounds in the country in the eighteenth is illustrative of its impact.[14] Hunting cannot, as the case of the wolf illustrates, always be separated from the aspiration to re-model the environment, the countryside particularly, in the improved mould that found increasing favour from the mid-seventeenth century.[15] But it was pur-sued by the elite primarily for recreational purposes, which may explain why the pursuit of the wolf, and, other than the otter and the fox, any birds or animal whose behaviour was incompatible with the economic, recreational or personal interests of mankind, was perceived inferior to the joy of the chase.

This is not to imply that every animal that was hunted was valueless as food. A haunch of venison was widely prized; game birds (partridges, pheasants) and hares were given as gifts, and perceived of as appropriate for the table of even the wealthiest.[16] Moreover, when the Irish Privy Council in 1662 sought to ensure there was sufficient game for the lord lieutenant 'within seven miles from the city of Dublin, as also within the bounds of the Curragh of Kildare, or within three miles distance from the same', it specifically proscribed the pursuit of 'pheasants, partridges, grows [grouse] and hares ... either by hawks, netts, set-ting dogs, grey-hounds or any other engine whatsoever'.[17] The absence of any reference to deer in this proclamation should not be misinterpreted; echoing Charles II, who sought with only partial success to undo the damage done to deer hunting in England during the Civil War and Protectorate, the duke of Ormond embarked in 1662 on the creation of a major deer park of some 2,000 acres – the Phoenix Park – when he commenced walling the acreage then in pos-session of the crown on the edge of the expanding city of Dublin, and stocking it with deer imported from England.[18] Elsewhere in the vicinity of the capital, Edward, second Viscount Loftus, maintained 'a very pleasant and commodious park, shutt up within a strong wall of lime and stone' at Rathfarnham, and there were at least three others 'within the space [of] 20, 12 and 9 miles of the cittie' by the late 1670s.[19] As this suggests, the possession of a well-stocked deer park

14 There is no agreement as to when the last wolf was killed in Ireland. It may have been as late as 1786, but the species was already very depleted well before then. For information on this, and the Cromwellian pursuit of wolves see Kieran Hickey, *Wolves in Ireland: a natural and cultural his-tory* (Dublin, 2011), pp 69–77, 103; see also MacGregor, *Animal encounters*, pp 137–8. 15 Barnard, *Making the grand figure*, pp 244, 246; idem, *Improving Ireland?: projectors, prophets and profiteers, 1641–1786* (Dublin, 2008), passim; Tyrawley to Townshend, 27 Oct. 1769 (Boston Public Library, Townshend papers, MS Eng.180(34)). 16 Barnard, *Making the grand figure*, p. 236; Dan Beaver, 'The great deer massacre: animals, honor, and communication in early modern England', *Journal of British Studies*, 38 (1999), pp 194–6. Indicatively, Stringer (*The experienced huntsman*, pp 116–18) devotes two sections of his book to 'breaking up a deer', and 'preserving and delivering venison'. 17 Kelly and Lyons (eds), *The proclamations of Ireland*, i, no. 80. 18 Griffin, *Bloodsport: hunting in Britain since 1066*, pp 104–5; MacGregor, *Animal encounters*, p. 113; Caesar Litton Falkiner, *Illustrations of Irish history and topography: mainly of the seventeenth century* (London, 1904), pp 52–60; Elizabeth Mayes (ed.), *Áras an Uachtaráin* (2nd edn, Dublin, 2013), p. 4. 19 Robert Ware,

was deemed the finest expression of the huntsman's commitment to his sport during the restoration era and beyond, in keeping with royal enthusiasm for the chase that lasted the duration of the Stuart dynasty.[20] As a result, a deer park featured prominently among the earl of Orrery's (1621–79) priorities when he lavished resources on creating a residence appropriate to the lord president of Munster, and others such as Edward, first Earl Conway of Killultagh (*c.*1623–83), who maintained 'a thousand brace of red, and fallow-deer' on three thousand acres of deer park at Partmore in south county Antrim, did likewise. It so happened that the favour of being allowed to hunt Orrery's deer did not prove as personally or politically advantageous either to him, or to his successors, as the lord president calculated, but the fact that Alan Brodrick (1656–1728), first Viscount Midleton, continued to offer the favour to friends and prospective allies into the second decade of the eighteenth century, and that a deer park was deemed integral to a well-appointed demesne, attests to its enduring register.[21]

Since chasing deer remained the acme of the hunting experience, it was inevitable that this quarry should feature prominently in the calculations of peers and MPs when they addressed the subject of preserving game in 1698. The Irish parliament was following in the footsteps of Westminster in so doing, since English legislators had sought repeatedly, most recently in 1691, to provide legal protection for deer.[22] Indicatively, Irish legislators in 1698 were guided in their actions by the landmark 1671 English act, which imposed a strict property threshold on those entitled to hunt by ordaining that no person could legally shoot deer except on his own ground or, 'being a Protestant, the ground of his master'. While this religious prohibition was consistent with the parallel effort, pursued under the umbrella of the 'penal laws', to preclude Catholics access to firearms, the Irish elite also aspired, following the pattern of their English and European equivalents, to establish a high social barrier by restricting the entitlement to hunt hare, grouse, quail, partridge, duck and other wild fowl they did not own to those possessed of freeholds worth more than £40 in value or real estate of £1000.[23] This proscription accurately mirrored the prevailing perception

'The history and antiquities of Dublin, collected from authentic records and the manuscript collections of Sir James Ware', 1678 (Armagh Public Library, Lodge MSS), pp 18–19; Finola O'Kane, *William Ashford's Mount Merrion: the absent point of view* (Tralee, 2012), p. 7. **20** MacGregor, *Animal encounters*, p. 113. **21** Barnard, *Making the grand figure*, p. 235; Stringer, *The experienced huntsman*, pp 4, 59. For Orrery, see P.M. Little, *Lord Broghill and the Cromwellian union with Ireland and Scotland* (Woodbridge, 2004), part 3; K.M. Lynch, *Roger Boyle, first earl of Orrery* (Knoxville, 1965), p. 106 ff. The implication, that landowners perceived that a demesne was not complete without a deer park, is reinforced by the presence of a deer park in the demesnes created by Thomas Fitzmaurice, twentieth Baron Kerry, and Sir Thomas Crosbie of Ardfert: Finola O'Kane, *Ireland and the picturesque: design, landscape painting and tourism in Ireland, 1700–1830* (London, 2013), pp 39–41, 50. **22** See *An act against unlawful hunting and stealing of deer and conies* (3 James I, chap 13); *An act for the explanation of … An act against unlawful hunting and stealing of deer and conies* (3 James I, chap 13); *An act to prevent the unlawful coursing, hunting and killing of deere* (13 Charles II, chap 10); *An act for the more effectual discovery and punishment of deer stealers* (3 and 4 William and Mary, chap 10). **23** Griffin, *Bloodsport: hunting in Britain since 1066*, pp

that hunting was the preserve of the elite, and that the law should echo this fact. Thus, as well as directing that a landowner's retainers must return all shot game to their masters, and empowering constables to seek out and to fine those who could not provide a satisfactory explanation if 'venison, hare, partridge, pheasant, pidgeon, fish, fowl or other game' were found on their premises, the final clause of the 1698 act specifically ordained that because 'great mischiefs do ensue by inferior tradesmen, apprentices, and other dissolute persons, neglecting their trades and employments' by engaging in hunting and fishing, such individuals were precluded from going 'to hunt, hawk, fish or fowl' other than when they were accompanied by their master.[24]

The fact that parliament frequently revisited this legislation in the half century that followed, and, in 1711 and 1737, sanctioned further enactments 'for the better preservation of game' points to the conclusion that the 1698 act was not as effective as its proponents anticipated. It also bears witness to the fact that the consensus within the English elite that hunting was their exclusive entitlement was shared in Ireland. Thus, though there were amendments to the law to provide rewards to encourage the killing of various species – otters, weasels, martins, herons, kites, cormorants, scal-crows, magpies and water-rats – that depleted game stocks, legislators did not seek, ever, to modify the law restricting hunting to the elite. Indicatively, in a further effort to protect red deer, 'which is like to be entirely destroyed for want of sufficient law to detect such persons as make it a great part of their business to kill and destroy the same', fines of 20s. for a first offence, and £5 for a second, were authorised in 1711.[25]

With a legislative framework in place, which mirrored the attitude of the elite that, 'birds and beasts of prey' apart, hunting was properly reserved for their enjoyment, members of the social elite were at liberty legally to pursue and kill those animals that represented the best sport. However, hunting was not immune to larger social and economic currents. The decline of the great deer parks, once sustained by Ormond, Orrery, Lord Conway, Baron Kerry and others, elicited genuine expressions of concern for the future of deer hunting in the early decades of the eighteenth century. Arthur Stringer, the author of a pioneering book on hunting published in Belfast in 1714, which served both as a guide and commentary, was one notable pessimist, but the establishment of smaller parks at Castlecoote and elsewhere indicated that if deer numbers declined as a consequence of the loss of a proportion of seventeenth-century deer parks, which was

112–13; MacGregor, *Animal encounters*, p. 107; 3 and 4 William and Mary, chap 10; Barnard, *Making the grand figure*, p. 235; C.I. McGrath, 'Securing the Protestant interest: the origins and purpose of the penal laws of 1695', *IHS*, 30 (1996), pp 25–46. **24** 10 William III, chap 8, sec. 19; Bullingbrook and Belcher, *An abridgement*, p. 395. **25** *An act for the better preservation of game*, 1711 (11 Anne chap 7); *An act for the better preservation of game*, 1737 (11 George II, chap 12); Bullingbrook and Belcher, *An abridgement*, pp 395–6. In addition, legislative initiatives, which failed to make it to the statute book, were pursued in 1707, 1710, 1711, 1715, 1717, 1721, 1723, 1725, 1727, 1733 and 1735: see Irish Legislation Database, 1692–1800, which can be accessed on the Queen's University website at http://www.qub.ac.uk/ild/.

the case in England, the pursuit of deer remained the premier manifestation of the sport of hunting.[26] This is the implication certainly of Stringer's identification of the stag and the buck as the favourite quarry of the serious huntsman, and of the generous space he gave them in his capacious guide to the sport in all its manifestations.[27] Whatever about the number, and condition, of the kingdom's deer parks, deer hunting certainly retained its appeal among the elite. Indicatively, the sports-loving lord justice, Charles, sixth marquess of Winchester, took advantage of the adjournment of parliament in October 1697 to head into the country 'for the diversion of hunting'; while Major-General Thomas Erle, who was commander in chief of the army at the accession of Queen Anne, and briefly a lord justice, enjoyed 'buck' hunting in county Kilkenny in 1702.[28]

It is not possible to estimate what proportion of the Irish public engaged in hunting, though the impression is that it exceeded the 'less than one per cent' estimate that has been proffered for England, or the quarry they targeted, though it difficult to believe that Ireland differed greatly from England, or that the fox was not increasingly favoured.[29] The presence of a pack of hounds at Killucan, county Westmeath, in 1697 had been interpreted as evidence that the fox was already a favourite target, but since the generality of hounds and hunter horses bred at this time were not fast enough to run down foxes it is likely that such packs pursued whatever quarry was at hand, including, but certainly not exclusively, the fox.[30] Based on its presence in Stringer's landmark work, his observation that 'the fox is a more noble chace than the hare', and his characterisation of it as 'a brave noble chace', it can be concluded that the fox had achieved sufficient prominence by 1714 to feature behind the stag and buck, and before the hare, martin, otter and badger in his listing of animals that the 'experience'd huntsman' enjoyed pursuing. Moreover, though Stringer's observation that it would best suit those 'who keep good horses and hounds' suggests that both the available horses and dogs were not always of the highest quality, fox-hunting was evidently on the increase. Indicatively, Arthur Weldon of Ralin, county Kildare enjoyed an eight-mile chase of a fox at Bishopscourt in 1726, and within a few years the vulpine pursuit was so well established that it was possible to speak of a fox-hunting 'season'.[31] Be that as it may, hunting was, as Martyn Powell has

26 Barnard, *Making the grand figure*, pp 236, 244, Lowry-Corry, *The history of two Ulster manors*, p. 149; O'Kane, *Ireland and the picturesque*, p. 150.   27 Stringer, *The experienced huntsman*, pp 41–72, and passim.   28 May to Blathwayt, 16 Oct. 1697 (NAI, May-Blathwayt correspondence, 1697–8, MS 3070); Erle to Lords justices, 13 July 1702 (NAI, Calendar of miscellaneous letters and papers prior to 1760, f. 23).   29 Griffin, *Bloodsport: hunting in Britain since 1066*, p. 124; Collins et al. (eds), *Encyclopedia of traditional British rural sports*, p. 113; MacGregor, *Animal encounters*, p. 134.   30 Tom Hunt, *Sport and society in Victorian Ireland: the case of Westmeath* (Cork, 2007), p. 11; Griffin, *Bloodsport: hunting in Britain since 1066*, pp 126–8; Stringer, *The experienced huntsman*, pp 86–7.   31 Stringer, *The experienced huntsman*, pp 73, 83, 86. 159; Earl of Mayo and W.B. Boulton, *A history of the Kildare Hunt* (London, 1913), pp 37–8; Griffin, *Bloodsport: hunting in Britain since 1066*, p. 125; *PO*, 5 Sept. 1741; *Munster Journal*, 22 May 1749.

Fig. 17 Kilruddery Hunt, *c.*1740. Oil painting in the possession of the earl of
Meath, at Kilruddery, county Wicklow. Reproduced from Constantia Maxwell,
County and town under the Georges (London, 1940), facing p. 33.

observed, typically 'conducted on a small scale' in the early eighteenth century,
in keeping with the fact that gentlemen 'kept their own packs of hounds, and
invited friends to take part [in a hunt] when they saw fit'.[32] This arrangement
had the merit of allowing individual hosts to set the tone, and to choose the
quarry, with the result that every hunt was not only different, but also that the
after-hunt entertainment, which was integral to the day's (or more precisely the
days') enjoyment (as most such meetings were conducted over a period of three
or more days), ranged from the raffish to the polite. Hunts from which women
were excluded were more likely to conform to the former pattern, but consistent
with the increased participation of ladies during the eighteenth century, hunts in
which members of both genders participated were conducted with less evidence
of the bibulousness for which such occasions were infamous. Greater decorum
did not ensure that women found hunting either tolerable or engaging. Mary
Ponsonby did not conceal her 'aversion' for the 'fox-hunting country squires' she
encountered at Kilcooley, county Tipperary, in the 1770s, but others, who were
not disposed to be so critical, took less exception.[33]

32 Powell, 'Hunting clubs and societies', p. 394.   33 Barnard, *Making the grand figure*, p. 245;
Mary Ponsonby to C.B. Ponsonby, 10 July [1780] (TCD, Barker–Ponsonby papers, P3/1/13); see
W.G. Neely, *Kilcooley: land and people in Tipperary* (Dublin, 1983), p. 64.

The sport of hunting was sustained by the enduring perception that it was not only a manly recreation but also that it was healthy, physically invigorating, and socially beneficial. This was the opinion, certainly, of Arthur Stringer, and, later, of the owner of *Finns's Leinster Journal*. In a world that accepted the stereotypical characterisation of urban living as effete, it was much to hunting's advantage that it was regarded as one of the 'noble, manly' recreations that appealed to men who recognised the benefits of vigorous exercise, and the social and societal merits of conviviality.[34] This image contrasted with the reality of many hunts, which combined a pedestrian daytime chase in the company of barking hounds, sweating horses, and a frightened fox fleeing for his very life with an evening devoted to over-eating and to bibulous excess. This link was already so firmly established by the beginnings of the eighteenth century that Stringer counselled huntsmen to embrace moderation, and though it may reasonably be assumed that those who shared his outlook, and his concerns for the future of the sport, were sufficiently self-possessed either not to indulge excessively in the first place or to embark on a more disciplined lifestyle when the moment of realisation dawned, the connection remained strong.[35] The tone, content and rhythm of the best-known hunting songs echoed to this reality,[36] and while raucous renditions of indifferent verse may have grated with those who subscribed to the code of improvement that achieved moral ascendancy as the experience of war and revolution migrated into memory following the successful negotiation of the Hanoverian succession in 1714, and to the politeness that it encouraged, the improvement in manner that was required did not appeal equally to all. Indeed, raucousness and the lifestyle of the Irish squirearchy were perceived as synonymous in some quarters, and hunting was integral to this lifestyle. 'A kennel of dogs is the *summum bonum* of many a rural squire', it was observed tellingly in the *Dublin Weekly Journal* in 1725.[37] Others offered comparable commentaries. Patrick Delany, who was an *intime* of Swift and the prime mover of *The Tribune*, a series of essays on moral questions, patriotism and government, observed censoriously that the lifestyle of those who hunted was characterised by excess. 'The whole business of the day', he pronounced in 1729, 'is to course down a hare, or some other worthy purchase; to get over a most enormous and immoderate dinner; and guzzle down a propor-

34 Barnard, *Making the grand figure*, p. 244; Stringer, *The experienc'd huntsman*, pp 138–40; *FLJ*, 4 Sept. 1774; Powell, 'Hunting clubs and societies', p. 405.   35 Barnard, *Making the grand figure*, pp 244, 246; Stringer, *The experienced huntsman*, pp 33, 37.   36 The most famous was The Kilruddery Hunt, which, its opening lines suggest, was penned in 1744: 'In seventeen hundred and forty-four,/The fifth of December, I think 'twas no more,/ At five in the morning, by most of the clocks,/We rode from Kilruddery in search of a fox. ...'. The song celebrates a foxhunt in county Wicklow in 1744, involving the hounds of Chaworth Brabazon, sixth earl of Meath, and describes the exploits of the leading sportsmen of the district. The words were by the actor Thomas Mozeen (d. 1768), an Englishman of French extraction who was on the Dublin stage, and it was sung to an old Irish tune (Celia O'Gara). The song was published in Thomas Mozeen, *A collection of miscellaneous essays* (London, 1762) with the title 'A description of a fox chase that happened in the county of Dublin with the earl of Meath's hounds'.   37 Quoted in Ekirch, *Birthright*, p. 20.

tionable quantity of wine'.[38] Delany exaggerated for rhetorical effect, of course, but there were enough instances of extravagance, and enough examples of rambunctious living to convince those who were repelled by the lifestyle that it was a symptom of a larger national malaise. The life of the unprincipled Arthur Annesley, fourth Baron Altham, whose kennel of hounds was one of his dearest possessions, and of the ineffectual James Barry, Lord Buttevant (later fifth earl of Barrymore), whose 'abilities reached little further than a pack of hounds or horses', and who habitually stayed up late 'drinking pretty hard' certainly gave verisimilitude to the caricature, and weight to the claims of those who concluded that it was symptomatic of a larger national malaise.[39] It is not apparent if Henry, fourth Baron Santry (whose trial for murder in 1739 was an extreme manifestation of the lack of personal discipline that an element of the Irish elite then indulged), hunted with equivalent passion, or that these Irish roués lived any more extravagantly than their English equivalents. George Edward Pakenham, who had experience of the lifestyle in both kingdoms, confided to his journal that Irish 'fox hunters live much after the same manner as in England and drink as hard'. Yet the negative image generated by Santry and the *habitués* of stereotypically raffish bodies such as the Dublin Hellfire Club made a deeper impression, and encouraged calls, akin to that famously made by Samuel Madden (1686–1765) in 1738, for a revolution in manners.[40]

Be that as it may, hunting, and the egregious behaviour it encouraged, was so firmly rooted on the Irish landscape by 1740 that it was impervious to admonitions to change. Moreover, members of parliament had no legislative remedy, for though most attempts that were made to revise the law in respect of the sport failed to make it onto the statute book, they were almost exclusively directed towards ensuring the availability of game for those of the elite who chose to hunt. They prioritised, as a result, those problems that were perceived to inhibit its successful practice, and did nothing either to discourage, or to proscribe, uncouth and disagreeable behaviour during the day, and still less to encourage decorum and moderation in the evening. Thus when parliament in 1737 finally responded positively to the attempt by Richard Lambart, the fourth earl of Cavan, to engage with problems in the sport, their priority was predictable – it was the discouragement of poaching and the illicit destruction of all type of game. To this end, they once more followed the example of Westminster, which had addressed the matter in 1707, and broadened their target to embrace 'higlers, cleavers and other

---

38 Patrick Delany, *The Tribune* (Dublin 1729), quoted in Ekirch, *Birthright*, p. 20.   39 Ekirch, *Birthright*, pp 20–38; Journal of George Edward Pakenham, 1737 in Edward McLysaght, 'Survey of documents in private keeping: Longford papers', *Analecta Hibernica*, 15 (1944), p. 120.   40 Journal of George Edward Pakenham, 1737, p. 120; David Ryan, *Blasphemers and blackguards: Ireland's hellfire clubs* (Dublin, 2012), pp 19–63; Neal Garnham, 'The trials of James Cotter and Henry, Baron Barry of Santry: two case studies in the administration of criminal justice in early eighteenth-century Ireland', *IHS*, 31 (1999), 328–52; Samuel Madden, *Reflections and resolutions proper for the gentlemen of Ireland, as to their conduct for the service of their country, as landlords, as masters of families, ...* (Dublin, 1738).

chapmen', who provided a commercial outlet for poached hares, pheasant, partridge and the like, and the bounties previously provided to encourage the apprehension of the augmented menu of natural predators (otters, weasels, herons etc., but not foxes) whose destruction they promoted.[41] This law did not go as far as some may have hoped for, but the fact that the issue was not revisited for some time thereafter suggests that there was a general consensus that the statute book did not require further reinforcement. The grand juries of counties Meath, Cork and Clare offer some – albeit limited – support for this conclusion, for though they intervened in the public sphere in 1749–50 to express unease at the level of poaching within their jurisdictions, and, in the case of counties Cork and Clare, to offer 'an additional reward' (of £2 and 2 guineas respectively) for information leading to the conviction of those responsible, their priority was to 'cause strictly to be put in execution all the statutes now in force for the preservation of the game', and not the ratification of new legislation.[42]

The effectiveness of such pronouncements, and the premises upon which they were based, may reasonably be questioned, as hunting assumed an increasingly, and recognizably, modern form. One significant change, which left its mark on the statute book, was the displacement of the net, hunting birds and game dogs as the primary means of game bird hunting by the gun. This was evidently sufficiently advanced by 1751 to cause parliament to provide for a specific shooting season for pheasants, partridge, quail and grouse.[43] The paucity of pertinent reference in the public sphere suggests that shooting game birds for sport was then in its infancy,[44] but the fact that parliament chose to intervene was evidence that the sport continued to evolve from the utilitarian skill out of which it emerged in the Middle Ages *en route* towards the emphatically recreational pursuit it had become by the mid-nineteenth century.[45] Viewed from this perspective, the identification in law of specific seasons for particular types of hunting was a manifestation of the modernisation of the sport that was a feature of the eighteenth century. It was also, clearly, another manifestation of the determination of the elite to preserve the exclusivity of the sport of hunting, which may have been pursued less successfully in Ireland than in England. The promise by grand juries of enhanced rewards did little, certainly, to deter poaching, though the absence of crime statistics means it is not possible to establish its pattern. This

---

41 Griffin, *Bloodsport: hunting in Britain since 1066*, p. 113; *An act for the better preservation of game*, 1737 (11 George II, chap 12). This was Cavan's fourth attempt to promote this legislation. He had previously proposed initiatives bearing the same title in 1727, 1733 and 1735. 42 *Dublin Courant*, 18 Mar. 1749; *Munster Journal*, 27 Aug., 29 Oct. 1750. 43 *An act for the better preservation of game*, 1751 (25 George II, chap 5) ordered a ban on shooting pheasants between 1 February and 1 September, and partridge, quail and grouse between 1 February and 1 August. 44 For example, *UA*, 18 Nov. 1755; *Hibernian Journal*, 24 Oct. 1791. 45 Griffin, *Bloodsport: hunting in Britain since 1066*, passim provides an excellent perspective on the modernisation of hunting, and pp 152–62 on the evolution of shooting, primarily focussed on the nineteenth century. For a glimpse at the sport in Ireland see *Ennis Chronicle*, 28 Nov. 1791; *Cork Advertiser*, 15 Sept. 1801; Falkiner to Turnbull, 28 Dec. 1792 (NYPL, Turnbull papers, box 1), and Knox, *A history of the county of Down*, p. 61.

notwithstanding, it is apparent that gentlemen sought more actively to combat poaching in the 1750s by offering rewards for the apprehension of those responsible, and by employing the press to publicise the availability of such rewards. One can instance Charles Massey, who responded to an incursion on 1 February 1751 onto his deer park at Doonass, county Clare, in the course of which 'a fine bald faced pet stag, and a brace of buck' were killed and skinned, by offering 'a reward of twenty pounds sterling over and above that allowed by act of parliament ... to any person or persons who shall discover the said offenders'.[46] John Hodges of Broadford, in the same county, was comparably animated; he called in 1750 upon 'all true sportsmen' to join with him in prosecuting those who pursued hares with greyhounds.[47] However, it is doubtful if this or other public attempts to rally sportsmen to do the necessary to secure game against interlopers had the desired effect. Certainly, the grand jury of county Meath returned in 1759 to a matter it had previously addressed a decade earlier, when it pronounced its intention 'to prosecute, with the utmost rigour, all disqualified persons who shall hereafter be found taking or destroying any partridge, grouse, hares, or other species of game', and offered a reward of 20s. additional to that provided by statute.[48] The fact that various sportsmen chose to echo this pronouncement is notable;[49] it contributed to the creation of the circumstances that facilitated the ratification by parliament in 1763 of a measure, which provided for substantially increased fines in a further effort to deter such infractions.[50]

Like the various grand jury resolutions referred to above, the 1763 enactment might be interpreted (in the manner of the notorious 'black act' approved at Westminster in 1723) as an oppressive act by a privileged interest, which accorded its recreational needs priority over the more fundamental needs of those of the population for whom hunting possessed a more obvious economic function.[51] Yet the example of the poachers who skinned the deer they killed in the deer park of Charles Massey in 1751, but left the carcass otherwise untouched, cautions against simplistic conclusions that poachers were exclusively, or even predominantly, motivated by the desire to secure food for the pot.[52] Moreover, it is no less simplistic to conclude that the elite sought only to safeguard its recreational privileges. This was a consideration of course, but many within its rank also recognised that hunting performed a broader social function, as the Grand Jury of Cork made clear. Addressing this matter in 1750, the jurors candidly avowed that they sought to protect game in order 'to encourage exercise and to encrease innocent rural diversions for the wealthy, by which means their health might be confirmed', but they also expressed the conviction, which was broadly acknowledged, that hunting was a social good because it

46 *Munster Journal*, 7, 11 Feb. 1751.   47 *Munster Journal*, 25 Jan. 1750.   48 *UA*, 10 Apr. 1759. 49 *BNL*, 14 July 1758; *UA*, 27 Feb. 1759.   50 *An act for the better preservation of game*, 1763 (3 George III, chap. 23).   51 See E.P. Thompson, *Whigs and hunters: the origin of the Black Act* (London, 1975); Pat Rogers, 'The Waltham blacks and the Black Act', *The Historical Journal*, 17 (1974), pp 465–86.   52 *Munster Journal*, 7 Feb. 1751.

encouraged landowners to reside 'upon their estates ... to the great emolument of the publick'.[53]

The broader social and economic dividends returned by hunting did not escape the organisers of horse racing, which, as we have seen (Chapter One), grew rapidly from the late 1720s. Conscious of the need to entertain, and eager to attract the squires and gentry for whom hunting was their primary recreation, a number of race organisers introduced hunting onto their programme. A meeting at Limerick in July 1731 was one of the first to make the attempt; they scheduled a buck-hunt on the morning of the third day of racing, when those attending a race meeting were traditionally at a loose end. The organisers of the ambitious race meeting at Athlone the same summer brought this a step further; they not only promised 'a buck hunt each morning' but also formally integrated the hunt into the racing calendar on Wednesday and Friday of their week-long gathering.[54] This raised the level of expectation, which may have been the reason why the meeting at Roscommon later that summer went one step further and promised 'buck and hare hunting each morning'.[55]

Buck-hunts were evidently the preferred choice of most gentlemen in Ireland at this time, but in keeping with the fact that from 1707 the law encouraged the pursuit of a variety of 'beasts of prey', the organisers of the race meeting at Castleblakeney in 1732 broke new ground when they scheduled 'a buck hunt [and] otter hunting' on the middle day of a three-day meeting in 1732, and an otter-hunt only in 1733. This attempt to combine the hunting of traditional and novel quarry must not have been a success, as it was not repeated, but the inclination to experiment was not exhausted.[56] The promise of 'a fox hunt every second day' at Maryborough, Queen's county, in 1733 is notable because until that point the absence of reference to fox-hunting suggests it still had a long way to go before it was viewed with general favour. It was evidently an expanding sport, as the references to a fox-hunting 'season' dating from this decade bear witness, but it was not until it was perceived by the organisers of racing as advantageous to their sport that it began to achieve a profile in the public sphere, inferior to that possessed by buck-hunting, but certainly in advance of the pursuit of otters and hares. Moreover, it rapidly grew in popularity. A fox-hunt was scheduled at the races held at Castlepollard, county Westmeath, in 1733, 'every morning' at Galway in 1735, 'each day' at Bonnet'srath, county Kilkenny, in 1737, on two of the five days on which racing was scheduled at Longwood, county Meath, in 1743, and at Mullingar in 1741, Kilmallock in 1749, and Richhill in 1754.[57] The augmented profile of fox-hunting was not entirely at the expense of the deer, moreover. First of all, the traditional hounds were, as the term 'buck-hound' attests, bred to chase deer, though they were not reserved exclusively for that quarry.[58] Second, the

---

53 *Munster Journal*, 27 Aug. 1750. 54 *PO*, 8, 29 June 1731. 55 *PO*, 21 Aug. 1731. 56 *PO*, 6 June 1732, 17 July 1733. 57 *FDJ*, 4 Sept. (Maryborough), 11 Sept. 1733 (Castlepollard), 9 Aug. 1737 (Bonnet'srath); *PO*, 12 Aug. 1735 (Galway), 5 Sept. 1741 (Mullingar); *Munster Journal*, 24 Aug. 1749 (Kilmallock). 58 See Mayo and Boulton, *A history of the Kildare Hunt*, pp 8–12 passim.

Fig. 18 *Thomas Conolly of Castletown hunting with friends*, 1769, by Robert Healy: chalk and gouache on paper (courtesy of the Yale Center for British Art, Paul Mellon Collection).

attachment to buck-hunting remained strong, and the fact that bucks and not foxes were chased at Eyrescourt in 1735, Tralee in 1739, 1740, 1748, 1749 and 1750, Assollas in 1740, Carlow in 1741 and 1747, Corofin and Castleblakeney in 1743, and Kilmallock in 1749 is indicative of the enduring appeal of bigger game.[59] The combination of 'fox-hunting and doe-hunting', which was offered twice during Bellewstown races in 1754, was possessed of novelty value to be sure, and like the decision of the meeting at Galway in 1735 to offer 'either buck hunting or fox-hunting', and of Kilfinane, county Limerick, to offer buck-hunting and cockfighting in July 1740, it set a precedent that others were disposed to imitate. Carlow and Longwood offered both, but it never really caught on and the trend increasingly was to focus on one or other.[60] More generally, whether there was a choice or not, the inclusion of hunting on the menu of diversions available to those who

59 *FDJ*, 7 July 1739, 13, 31 May 1740, 24 Mar. 1743, 3 Sept. 1748; *PO*, 25 June 1743, 4 July 1747; *Dublin Newsletter*, 15 Oct. 1743; *Munster Journal*, 21 May 1750; *UA*, 2 Nov. 1754. 60 *FDJ*, 15 July 1740; *PO*, 12 Aug. 1735, 5 Sept. 1741; *Dublin Newsletter*, 15 Oct. 1743; *UA*, 5 Oct. 1754; above, pp 54–5.

frequented race -meetings acknowledged the social reality that hunting and racing drew from the same social catchments, and that their common features meant they complemented each other.

Though the availability of an opportunity to hunt in the course of a race meeting was a clear illustration of the eagerness of the racing fraternity to reach out to those whose preference was the chase, hunting also brought something tangible to racing, in the form of the hunter horse, and endurance racing. Hunters did not appeal to horse owners whose goal was speed, and the courses that catered for thoroughbreds which best met that requirement, but there were many organisers, who could not aspire to attract horses of this quality who recognised this as an opportunity. The organisers of Enniskillen races were one of the first; they advertised in 1733 – for the modest prize of 'a pair of silver spurs' – a race exclusive to hunters 'that have ... been at the death of three brace of hares or [a leash of] foxes, last season'.[61] Enniskillen failed to catch on as a venue at this time, but the idea of reserving a race to hunters was recognised as a good one, since the same strategy was pursued at Gort the same year, and, though it did not feature annually thereafter, the idea of reserving a race to blooded hunters was perceived to possess sufficient merit to be resorted to at Ovens,

61 *PO*, 17 July 1733.

county Cork in 1749, Rathkeale, county Limerick in 1758, and Cashel, county Tipperary in 1778. However, it was also recognised that the requirement that a horse must 'have been fairly at the finding and killing of a lease [*sic*] of foxes or three brace of hares', which was the criterion set at Ovens, was too restrictive to be practical, and that it worked to the advantage neither of hunters nor of racing.[62] As a consequence, instead of reserving races for horses possessed of proven field experiences, race organisers targeted hunters in general, and advertised races specifically for 'real hunters' or 'hunters carrying' eleven stone, eleven stone seven pounds, or twelve stone. Since these weights were substantially in excess of those stipulated in other races, it simplified matters for owners while making it clear that hunters were deserving of a place on the racecourse. The import of the positive signal it gave was reinforced meanwhile by the number of racecourses that included races for hunters on their card.[63]

The commitment to improve the quality of Irish hunters evident on the racecourse was complemented by a parallel effort to improve breeding stock. The Corporation of the Horse Breeders in the county of Down was particularly active in this respect; it offered a prize of £10 in 1735 for 'the best stallion of the English foxhunter kind', and in 1748 it gave the idea of a race exclusively for hunters its influential *imprimatur* when it provided a £20 plate 'to be run for ... by hunters'.[64] By comparison with the prize money available to thoroughbreds at some of the more prestigious races in the country, these were not major sums, but they were not derisory either, and the fact that races reserved for hunters continued to be included on racecards throughout the second half of the eighteenth century was evidence of the esteem in which good hunter horses continued to be held.[65] Indeed, hunter-only races proved more enduring than the hunts that were once offered by race meetings to attract, and distract, spectators. The opportunity to hunt did not disappear entirely from race-meetings; men were still tempted by the prospect of buck-hunting, and could engage in this pursuit at Thurles in 1760, Tullow in 1773, and Miltown, county Clare in 1789.[66] However, the identification of the bagged fox as a suitable quarry, at Tullow in 1774 and Dungarvan in 1783, following its earlier adoption by individual organisers, was a pointer to the fact that race-day hunts were operating on borrowed time, and that the surge in enthusiasm for the pursuit of the fox, manifest in England, had not left Ireland untouched.[67]

62 *Dublin Evening Post*, 28 Aug. 1733; *PO*, 4 Sept. 1733; *Munster Journal*, 22 May 1749; *UA*, 29 Aug. 1758; *FDJ*, 14 May 1778. Lease is an error for 'leash'.   63 *FDJ*, 12 July 1737 (Painstown); *PO*, 6 Sept. 1748 (Mullingar), 6 Aug. 1751 (Gort); *Munster Journal*, 15 Mar. 1750 (Clogheen); *UA*, 26 July 1755 (Castlebar), 12 June 1757 (Baltinglass); 27 June 1758 (Trim).   64 *PO*, 22 Apr. 1735; *FDJ*, 3 Sept. 1748.   65 *Public Gazetteer*, 21 Oct. 1760 (Thurles); *FLJ*, 25 Sept. 1773 (Tullow); *Ennis Chronicle*, 25 May 1789 (Miltown); Falkiner to Turnbull, 15 Mar., 28 Dec. 1792 (NYPL, Turnbull papers, box 1).   66 *Public Gazetteer*, 26 May 1764 (Ennis); 23 Sept. 1766 (Tralee); *FLJ*, 6 June 1772 (Mallow); 10 June 1772 (Kilkenny); 29 Sept. 1787 (Carlow); *Clonmel Gazette*, 2 Oct. 1788 (Miltown); *Ennis Chronicle*, 1 Oct. 1789 (Cashel).   67 Lowe to Baker 13 Apr. 1754 (NLI, Baker papers, reports on private collections, no. 351, p. 2566); *FLJ*, 29 Oct. 1774, 10 Sept. 1783;

HUNT CLUBS AND THE EVOLUTION OF THE SPORT

It is tricky to identify the precise impact upon hunting of its association with horse racing. It is reasonable to conclude that both sports benefited from the close relationship that was the most obvious consequence of the invitation to hunt offered to racegoers. Yet the stimulus it provided those whose diversion of choice was hunting to re-imagine the way in which the sport was conducted was still more noteworthy. It necessitated a significant shift in thinking, which was informed by the burgeoning associational impulse that was the most tangible organisational product of the emergence of civil society then underway.[68] The most striking consequence of this for the sport of hunting was the inauguration of the hunt club, which expanded rapidly over a period of six decades to become the distinguishing, if not the defining, feature of the sport.

The appeal of the hunt club was increased by the fact that it possessed an underlying financial rationale. Hunting was costly when it was pursued by an individual because of its scale, recurring character and increasing size; it was reckoned in 1714 that the maintenance of a (small) pack of hounds, which necessitated the employment of a huntsman, and a dogs' boy, was in the region of £40. This had risen to £80 by the 1780s. Large packs, suitable for the hard riding that fox-hunting encouraged, cost a lot more.[69] Such outlays did not dissuade the passionate, but they were not always sustainable, and there were occasions when down-at-heel gentlemen and impoverished peers, such as Lord Altham (though he may properly be regarded as a special case), found them difficult to meet.[70] Moreover, the cost of maintaining a pack of hounds was only one, and, if the most regular, possibly not the largest expense likely to be incurred. A good horse, or, more precisely, a string of good horses was also a *desideratum*, necessitating an appreciating outlay as the quality of hunters improved, while the financial toll of the *ad hoc* rota that required individuals to host often substantial numbers of like-minded gentry and squires in their home for up to a week at a time while they engaged in the chase might also be considerable.[71] The order of the outlay inevitably varied; it was a matter ultimately for every individual, but it was of sufficient magnitude to heighten the attraction of the subscription pack, which provided clubs with their *raison d'être*. It also explains why cost must be factored into any explanation of the rapid emergence of the hunt club on the sporting landscape from the mid-eighteenth century.[72]

The hunt club was central to the growth of hunting, specifically fox-hunting, though it bears reiterating that the first clubs founded in Ireland were not estab-

Griffin, *Blood sport: hunting in Britain since 1066*, pp 125–7. **68** Kelly and Powell, 'Introduction' in Kelly and Powell (eds), *Clubs and societies in eighteenth-century Ireland*, pp 27–9. **69** Barnard, *Making the grand figure*, pp 246–7; Griffin, *Blood sport: hunting in Britain since 1066*, p. 128. Griffin suggests that some may have spent as much as £2,000 in early nineteenth-century England, which was above the capacity of all but a handful of Irish landowners. **70** Ekirch, *Birthright*, p. 57. **71** R.A. Richey, 'Landed society in mid-eighteenth century county Down' (QUB, PhD, 2000), p. 30. **72** See Powell, 'Hunting clubs and societies', p. 396.

lished with the sole object of chasing the fox. This notwithstanding, what has been said of England may also be said of Ireland: 'fox-hunting's status went from strength to strength during the second half of the Georgian era', and the hunt club was integral to this.[73] Based on the identification of a club in county Limerick in 1734, and another in county Cork in 1745 it would appear that the origins of the hunt club phenomenon in Ireland can be located in the surge in associational aggregation that has been located in the 1730s and 1740s.[74] Little survives of these early clubs, but the evident merits of the club structure encouraged others to follow the same route. The most high profile was the Kildare Hunt, whose precise year of foundation continues to elude, but one may safely concur with the conclusion of its historian that it involved some of the most notable families in the county,[75] and that it was bound up with the surge in interest in horse racing then underway, since the first demonstrable fact that can be established is that the club donated two silver cups, value 50 guineas, in August 1757 to be competed for at the Curragh in September of that year.[76] Significantly, the notice announcing the donation was signed on behalf of the club by Thomas Roan, in his capacity as 'clerk to the Kildare Hunt', which suggests that the young society possessed formal structures. This was to be expected of a body, which the following year offered a prize at the summer Curragh meeting for the horse carrying 9 stone that came home first in a race of three four mile heats.[77] Seven years later, the club was the grateful recipient of a 'silver cup' from the then lord lieutenant, Hugh Percy, duke of Northumberland, who was one of its (honorary) members.[78] It is not apparent if Northumberland's gift was presented to be competed for, but based on the existence of a number of receipts in the papers of Thomas Conolly, which indicate that the annual subscription was £5 13s. 9d. in the early 1760s, it can be assumed that by that date the club not only possessed an eminent membership drawn from among the best connected racehorse owners in the land, but also that its finances were sufficiently robust to permit it to present its own prizes.[79]

In the normal course of events the bulk of the income received in subscriptions was assigned by a hunt club to the maintenance of a pack of quality hounds, but since Conolly then, and William Brabazon Ponsonby (1744–1806) of Bishopscourt later, maintained large packs, and were willing (like others who

73 Brailsford, *A taste for diversions*, p. 61.   74 Kelly and Powell, 'Introduction', Powell, 'Hunting clubs and societies', D.F. Fleming, 'Clubs and societies in eighteenth-century Munster' in Kelly and Powell (eds), *Clubs and societies in eighteenth-century Ireland*, pp 27–9, 397, 441.   75 The historians of the County Kildare Hunt, the Earl of Mayo and W.B. Boulton, not only failed to identify the year of origin of the Kildare Hunt, they were inclined to the view (echoed by Con Costello (*Kildare: saints, soldiers and horses*, p. 146) that the Hunt did not come into being until 1804. The impression provided by Mayo and Boulton is that hunting was largely structured around the packs of Thomas Conolly at Castletown, the Ponsonbys at Bishopscourt and the Kennedys at Johnstown: see Mayo and Boulton, *A history of the Kildare Hunt*, pp 18 ff.   76 *UA*, 27 Aug. 1757. One of these cups is illustrated in Costello, *Kildare: saints, soldiers and horses*, p. 117.   77 *UA*, 21 July 1758.   78 *FJ*, 20 Apr. 1765.   79 TCD, Conolly papers, MS 3974–84/ 128–9.

enjoyed the same close relationship with their local club) to make them available it may be that the Kildare Hunt was in a position to adopt a more relaxed approach on this point than most subscription clubs. It may also have encouraged the establishment of a number of other clubs in the county – the Ballylinan Hunt, the Straffan Hounds, and the Union Hunt (which straddled counties Dublin, Kildare and Wicklow), the Kildare Merry Harriers, the Donadea Hunt and the Johnstown Hunt – each of which possessed a suitably eminent membership.[80] Be that as it may, the survival of even the most distinguished hunts could not be assumed. The disbanding in the late 1790s of the Bishopscourt Hunt, which was one of the main packs of an impressively aristocratic hunting nexus of Irish Whigs, was a significant moment, albeit one that mirrored the changing fortunes of Irish Whigs during that troubled decade.[81] On the positive side, it was almost certainly also a factor in the decision to re-organise or to reanimate the Kildare Hunt, which began in 1804, and which went on to become one of the leading hunts in the country in the nineteenth century.[82]

The involvement of the Union Hunt in a particularly lively pursuit of a doe across north county Kildare in 1789 indicates that though Thomas Conolly and the Kildare Hunt contributed in an important way to the promotion of fox-hunting (and to the improvement in the quality of foxhounds) in the county by introducing a prized foxhound from the pack of John, third duke of Rutland (1696–1779), the fox was not the only, and possibly not the primary quarry of hunts in that county until at least the 1790s.[83] The situation was not altogether different elsewhere. The Social Hunt of King's county which met for the duration of the week beginning 24 February 1800 at Birr captured the variety that gentlemen still craved when it promised a fox for those with foxhounds on Monday, Wednesday and Thursday, a hare hunt for harriers on Tuesday, Thursday and Saturday, and a main of cocks 'during the week'.[84] Others still preferred to chase deer. The popular Union Hunt, which assembled at Sallins, county Kildare at 9 a.m. on 21 March 1791, anticipated chasing a doe; this was the quarry also of Cahir Hunt in April 1792, of the Friendly Club of county Clare 1794, and of the Duhallow Hunt of county Cork in 1801, while the County Tipperary Hunt pursued a 'brace of deer', which were 'enlarged at Market-Hill near Fethard at midday' on 4 January 1789.[85]

80 Mayo and Boulton, *A history of the Kildare Hunt*, pp 48 56; *Hibernian Journal*, 1 Oct. 1790, 18 Mar. 1791, 15 Oct. 1792; Gerald Ponsonby, 'Bishopscourt and its owners', *Journal of the County Kildare Archaeological Society*, 8 (1915–17), pp 16–17. 81 Mayo and Boulton, *A history of the Kildare Hunt*, pp 39–47, 57–8; James Kelly, 'Elite political clubs, 1770–1800' in idem and M.P. Powell (eds), *Clubs and societies in eighteenth-century Ireland* (Dublin, 2010), pp 278–88. 82 Mayo and Boulton, *A history of the Kildare Hunt*, pp 59 ff; Costello, *Kildare: saints, soldiers and horses*, pp 146–50. 83 Mayo and Boulton, *A history of the Kildare Hunt*, pp 22–9; *FJ*, 4 Nov. 1790; Barnard, *Making the grand figure*, p. 244; 'Miscellanea', *Journal of the Kildare Archaeological and Historical Society*, 10 (1922–8), pp 154–5; *The Constitution*, 21 Dec. 1799, 25 Jan. 1800. For a useful introduction to the evolution and development of hunting dogs see MacGregor, *Animal encounters*, pp 116–21. 84 *The Constitution*, 15 Feb. 1800. 85 *Hibernian Journal*, 18 Mar. 1791; *Clonmel Gazette*,

The prominent part played by Thomas Conolly of Castletown, William Brabazon Ponsonby of Bishopscourt, Steuart Weldon of Kilmarony and Joseph Henry of Straffan at different points and in different hunt clubs in county Kildare is consistent with Martyn Powell's conclusion that few hunt clubs 'functioned or existed separate from the hunts patronized by landlords, as the club ... might not only emerge out of a hunt dominated by a particular landowner, but also maintain a close connection'.[86] The closeness of this link varied depending on the interest of individual landowners, and, still more significantly, the history of each hunt club, since, like racecourses, many flourished but briefly. It seems, for example, that Joseph Henry was a significant presence in the Union Hunt, which was at its most active in the years spanning the later 1780s and early 1790s, though two lesser lights, Cuthbert Hornidge and James Carlisle, were probably more instrumental in ensuring its smooth operation. Be that as it may, Henry was sufficiently committed to the sport to develop a club around his own pack some years later, and the Straffan Hounds, which resulted, were active in the same part of counties Wicklow and Kildare at the end of the decade.[87]

Other hunts, which were more fixed presences on the landscape, acted as an enduring focal point for the elite in a discrete area, or region. The County Down Hunt is a case in point. Founded in 1757, an analysis of the 134 men who were members between then and 1780 has established that 12 were MPs at some point, 17 were high sheriffs, and 36 were either peers or closely related to men of title. A majority (55 per cent of that total) were from county Down, but the club also attracted members from counties Antrim, Armagh, Louth and Tyrone.[88] The County Down Club possessed a strikingly high-profile membership, comparable (it may be surmised) to that of the Kildare Hunt, and, on a smaller scale, to the Ballylinan Hunt.[89] It attests also to the fact that though the emergence of the hunt club provided financial and organisational advantages to those who engaged in hunting, and drew larger numbers together to that end, thereby permitting hunts to grow in size, it did little in practice to dilute the determination of the social elite to pursue the sport in the company of their own kith and kin, because of the tight control most clubs maintained over membership. This was, to be sure, little more than a continuation in another form of the practice pursued when individual pack owners determined who to invite to their estates for a particular hunt.[90] On occasion, individuals like Joseph Henry might extend a general invitation to 'gentlemen who may wish to hunt with his hounds ... [to]

29 Dec. 1789, 18 Apr. 1792; *Ennis Chronicle*, 27 Feb. 1794; *Cork Advertiser*, 15 Aug. 1801. The Friendly Club normally pursued either a 'sporting buck' or a 'sporting deer': see *Ennis Chronicle*, 28 Apr., 29 Sept. 1791, 3 May, 22 Aug., 22 Nov. 1792, 27 Jan. 1794.   86 Powell, 'Hunting clubs and societies', p. 395.   87 'Miscellanea', *Journal of the Kildare Archaeological and Historical Society*, 10 (1922–8), p. 154; *Hibernian Journal*, 16 Mar. 1791, 15 Oct. 1792; *The Constitution*, 21 Dec. 1799, 25 Jan. 1800.   88 Richey, 'Landed society in county Down', p. 32. A list of members, 1757–72, is available in Knox, *A history of the county of Down*, pp 59–60.   89 Mayo and Boulton, *A history of the Kildare Hunt*, p. 51.   90 This point is reinforced by the third rule of the Ballylinan Hunt, which explicitly provided that 'each subscriber have the absolute command of the hounds and

do him the favour of coming to Straffan', but even these ostensibly public invitations were less open than they appeared, and most notices issued by hunts were published on the implicit understanding that they extended to a defined membership, which hunt clubs monitored closely.[91]

The means by which hunt clubs determined membership varied. The setting by the Ballylinan Hunt in 1780 of the subscription fee at 10 guineas, with an additional entrance fee of 5 guineas, constituted a formidable financial hurdle, which was augmented by the fact that one could reasonably anticipate paying 20 guineas in 1783 for 'a good huntsman's horse' and as much as 'sixty or perhaps an hundred guineas' a decade later for a fine one.[92] Other clubs employed the more direct method of vesting the right of admission in existing members, and while it is not clear what percentage of clubs followed the pattern of the North Rangers of County Louth in which case a single 'black bean' pre-empted admission, the inclusion in the regulations of the Duhallow Hunt of the provision 'one black bean in seven to exclude' suggests that it, or a recognisable variation, was commonly employed. In any event, the import of this system was that it tended to ensure that only those who were known, and deemed acceptable were admitted.[93] The process was not entirely unforgiving, however. Rules 13 and 17 of the North Rangers provided that if 'a candidate should be rejected, the person who proposes him may be at liberty to put him up a second time for balloting the same meeting, two clear days intervening between the days of setting up and balloting', while the Duhallow Hunt allowed a candidate to be re-nominated once twelve months had elapsed.[94] Since the North Rangers admitted 14 new members on one occasion (5 December 1774), albeit shortly after it was founded, 7 or 8 new members at the beginning of the new hunting season on several occasions (2 October 1775, 17 October 1782, 18 October 1792), and smaller numbers most other years between 1774 and 1797, it might be assumed that admission was a matter of routine, and essential to the maintenance of a healthy membership. However, because the profile of the general membership, and still more of the 'original members of the hunt', was identifiably exclusive socially and denominationally, and reserved to the nobility, gentry, and Church of Ireland clergy of the hunt's natural geographical hinterland, it is apparent that the means employed served the purpose that the members intended.[95] This was the case also of the Duhallow Hunt (founded in 1800), which comprised the equivalent social strata, and with the addition of army and naval officers, of

huntsman for a fortnight, turnabout, and that during his fortnight he be as much the master of them as if they were kept at his private expense': Mayo and Boulton, *A history of the Kildare Hunt*, p. 50. **91** *The Constitution*, 21 Dec. 1799; *Ennis Chronicle*, 8 Apr., 9 Aug., 29 Nov. 1790, 3 May, 22 Aug. 1792, 27 Feb. 1794. **92** Mayo and Boulton, *A history of the Kildare Hunt*, p. 54; Falkiner to Turnbull, 22 Dec. 1792 (NYPL, Turnbull papers, box 1). **93** J.R. Garstin, 'Records of the Northern Rangers Hunt Club, Dundalk, 1774', *Journal of the County Louth Archaeological Society*, 5 (1924), p. 234; James Grove-White, 'Extracts from old minute book of Duhallow Hunt, 1800 to 1808', *Journal of the Cork Historical and Archaeological Society*, 2nd series, 2 (1896), p. 50. **94** Garstin, 'Records of the Northern Rangers Hunt Club, Dundalk, 1774', p. 234; Grove-White, 'Extracts from old minute book of Duhallow Hunt, 1800 to 1808', p. 50. **95** Garstin, 'Records of

north-west county Cork.[96] The information is not available with which to venture a confident judgement with respect to other hunts, but the routine inclusion on notices announcing meetings of the Kilrush Hunt, the Miltown Chace, and the County Clare Hunt that 'gentlemen will be balloted for' suggests that there was a veritable lattice of clubs across the country, whose members were drawn from the elite, which was thereby permitted to ensure that, in its most organised form, hunting was, and remained, an elite recreation.[97] Control of membership certainly proved more direct (and presumably more effective) than the fiscal barrier posed by the requirement to pay an annual subscription, to possess an appropriate hunter, to purchase a club uniform, and to meet other expenses, in sustaining hunting's elite character.

The exclusivity to which hunt clubs aspired was underlined by their adoption of a set of 'rules and resolutions', equivalent to those adopted by dining, intellectual, improving and political clubs. This anchors them firmly in the associational world that took root in the eighteenth century, and connects them to the surge in the number of clubs of various forms that took place from the 1770s when hunt clubs achieved a national distribution.[98] It also emphasises the intimacy of the link that existed between hunting and sociability, and provides a useful perspective on what initially might appear puzzling about hunt clubs – the fact that their rules manifested a greater concern with the deportment of members in the club room than with the conduct of the chase. This can be illustrated by reference to the records of the Northern Rangers Hunt Club. Thus though rule 12, which pronounced that 'every member do appear in his uniform at the meetings and in the field under the penalty of five guineas', applied equally to the club room and the field, rule 4, which ordained that 'no more wine than 3 pints be allowed to each member after dinner', and rule 6, which stipulated that 'no game of chance be play'd in the eating room during meetings', appertained exclusively to the former.[99] These rules, and others appertaining to the still more crucial matter of the collection of subscriptions, the balloting of new members and the selection of officers,[100] the frequency of meetings, and the uniform members were required to wear were obviously crucial to the smooth functioning of the club room and to the proper deportment of members when they assembled, but they also suggest that the pleasures of sociability trumped the excitement of

the Northern Rangers Hunt Club', pp 235–7.   **96** Grove-White, 'Extracts from old minute book of Duhallow Hunt, 1800 to 1808', pp 51–3; *Cork Advertiser*, 15 Oct. 1801, 3 Mar. 1812.   **97** *Ennis Chronicle*, 11, 18 June, 6, 31 Aug., 7 Sept., 12, 22 Oct. 1789.   **98** Powell, 'Hunting clubs and societies', pp 394–5; Fleming, 'Clubs and societies in eighteenth-century Munster', p. 441.   **99** Garstin, 'Records of the Northern Rangers Hunt Club', pp 233–4. The fine levied by the Ballylinan Hunt on 'each gentleman appearing without the hunt uniform' was 'five English shillings': Mayo and Boulton, *A history of the Kildare Hunt*, p. 54.   **100** In most hunt clubs, a president and vice-president were appointed at every meeting ('the vice-president one day to be president the next'). The office of treasurer and secretary, which was filled annually or bi-annually, was the key office to the successful operation of the club: see Grove-White, 'Extracts from old minute book of Duhallow Hunt, 1800 to 1808', pp 50–1; Mayo and Boulton, *A history of the Kildare Hunt*, p. 54.

the chase for a significant proportion of members.[101] This certainly is the impression provided by the frequency with which clubs that did not possess a 'club-room' or 'club house', and they were to be found in places as far apart as Clane in county Kildare and Miltown Malbay in county Clare,[102] met in taverns, inns and other establishments associated with the purveying of food and alcohol.[103] Dining was, as this suggests, an integral feature of a day's hunting, and since the chase might commence at 9 or 10 a.m., most huntsmen were more than ready to sit down to dine at 4 p.m. This was the designated time for dinner for most clubs, and it had the merit of providing plenty of time for 'serious gourmandizing' as well as social bonding. The fact that from the late eighteenth century many clubs sustained a schedule of meetings and club dinners (and, eventually, balls) outside of the hunting season underlines the centrality of conviviality to the members of the club, and, by extension, of the appreciating importance of the club in the social and cultural life of the landed elite across Ireland.[104]

Be that as it may, the *raison d'être* of the hunt club was the promotion of hunting, no matter how appealing the prospect of convivial dining, and it is clear from surviving minute books that this dimension of the club's role was not overlooked. It is also evident from these records that the operation of hunt clubs was analogous to that of the Jockey Club, which contrived, albeit after a limited fashion, between the mid-1750s and the mid-1770s to perform the dual role of social club and administrative body for horse racing.[105] It was obviously more challenging to coordinate an equivalent in a sport such as hunting, given the autonomy enjoyed by individual hunt clubs and the inherently more contingent and less structured character of the sport, but it is notable that this did not deter an attempt in England to establish such an organization, and that the Game Association, which was founded to perform this role functioned as 'a quasi-national sporting body' for a time in the 1750s and 1760s. Moreover, when the Association collapsed, the fact that it was replaced in a number of shires by county associations indicated that there was a clearly perceived need for some organisation at provincial if not at national level.[106] The situation was not altogether different in Ireland, and it was a factor in the establishment in the mid-1770s of the Association of the Sportsmen's Club. Presided over by James, second duke of Leinster, who was its first president, William, second Baron Mountflorence, who was vice-president, and William Beckford, esquire, treasurer, the association supported the enforcement of the game

---

101 See Powell, 'Hunting clubs and societies', pp 394–402 for a more detailed engagement with the associational and sociable dimensions of the hunt club phenomenon. 102 *Ennis Chronicle*, 11 June 1789, 8 Apr. 1790; 'Miscellanea', *Journal of the Kildare Archaeological and Historical Society*, 10 (1922–8), pp 154–5; Powell, 'Hunting clubs and societies', pp 400–1. 103 The Kilkenny Hunt met at the Garter Inn, Kilkenny (*FLJ*, 27 Apr. 1776); the Merry Harriers at the Wheat Sheaf, Kilkenny (*FLJ*, 1 Nov. 1783); the County Tipperary Hunt at Smith's in Fethard (*Clonmel Gazette*, 29 Dec. 1789); the Kilrush Hunt met at Blackhall's (*Ennis Chronicle*, 6 Aug. 1789). 104 Powell, 'Hunting clubs and societies', pp 399, 401; *Ennis Chronicle*, 25 June, 6, 31 Aug. 1789, 8 Apr., 9 Aug. 1790, 14 Mar., 5 Apr. 1791, 17 Mar. 1794. 105 Kelly, 'The pastime of the elite', pp 417–22. 106 Brailsford, *A taste for diversions*, p. 23.

laws by promising 'to pay the sum of 20 guineas' to those who 'shall prosecute to conviction any person offending against' the said acts.[107] The support forthcoming from the Louth Harriers for the initiative suggested it was regarded in certain hunting circles as a good idea, but the absence of further reference suggests that it failed to prosper. Neither the sport of hunting nor society at large in Ireland was yet at a state of development to sustain a national organisation, though the absence of a body of this kind may have encouraged over-hunting, and contributed to a reported shortage of game in the early 1790s.[108]

There can be little question either but that the concerns of the sport might have been represented to advantage in the public and political sphere by a representative body of this kind as officials pondered the introduction in 1763 of an annual tax of £5 on a pack of hounds, and in 1799 succeeded in establishing a registration requirement, for the purpose of raising revenue, on those who kept a 'dog, gun or net' for the purpose of hunting.[109] In addition, as the sport's profile increased, religious and social improvers singled it out for criticism on various grounds including the infringement of the Sabbath.[110] In point of fact, hunting clubs, like the organisers of horse racing, were seldom vulnerable to the accusation that they failed to respect the Sabbath, as neither recreation was traditionally pursued of a Sunday.

A much more troublesome (and enduring) issue, which generated a lot of bad publicity for the sport, was the tendency of hunts to ignore farm boundaries, and to ride through fields, damaging stiles, gates, hedges and crops, in pursuit of their quarry. Since it was not only not illegal, but also regarded indulgently by generations of judges, most tenant-farmers seem to have been resigned to the losses they might incur, but voices were occasionally raised in protest when, as happened in 1782, the prospect for the harvest was poor. Having concluded that the 'damage done by sportsmen to the growing corn' in 'favourable seasons' was 'shameful', the *Hibernian Journal* pronounced decisively that in 'bad seasons' it ought not to be countenanced: 'No person should be allowed to pursue game in any field where the wheat or barley still remains annexed to its mother earth', it thundered. It is not clear what notice, if any, was taken of this pronouncement. The report, a decade later, when the ground was hard as a result of 'drought', that the Dublin Hunt directed that 'no riding over corn is allowed, under the penalty of a guinea for every field', suggests that there was greater sensitivity then to the plight of farmers, but, if so, it was far from general practice.[111] Moreover, there was no identifiably enduring change in behaviour. A satirical

---

107 The enduring nature of the elite's preoccupation with the law on hunting can be attested by the publication in 1780s and 1790s of two 'collections' of acts on this subject: *A collection of acts for the preservation of the game* (Dublin, 1785); *A collection of acts for the preservation of the game* (Dublin, 1794). 108 *Hibernian Journal*, 8 July 1776; *FJ*, 25 Jan. 1777, 8 Sept. 1791; Falkiner to Trumbull, 15 Mar. 1792 (NYPL, Trumbull papers, box 1). 109 *FJ*, 6 Dec. 1763, 8 June 1799; 39 George III, chap 62. The 1799 provision, in effect a licence to hunt, proved controversial as it was widely flouted: see *Ennis Chronicle*, 18 Aug., 2 Sept. 1818. For a list of licence holders in county Cork see *Cork Advertiser*, 2 Oct. 1812. 110 *FJ*, 24 Feb. 1767. 111 *Hibernian Journal*, 26 Aug. 1782, 7 Apr. 1790.

commentary published in September 1790 in response to a report that 'a certain country gentlemen' in county Kildare had organised the importation of 'a large number of ... true Welch, north English, Scotch and Mankish [*sic*] foxes in pairs of male and female' attested to the depth of the attitudinal chasm that divided farmers and hunters, and the cost to the former of the latter's self-indulgence.[112] Moreover, there was no evading the fact that those who worked the land could entertain no realistic prospect of recompense when the offending hunt included the owner of the soil among its members. The legality of the hunt's actions was never tested in the Irish courts, but the influential pronouncement in 1788 of Francis Buller, a judge of the English Court of King's Bench, that a hunter who pursued a fox across another man's land must not cause damage 'more than is absolutely necessary' did not encourage confidence in the prospect of a sympathetic hearing.[113] The perception of the general public that hunting was an 'excellent diversion', and that the longer and more imposing the hunt the better, was also of little assistance. In general terms, there was little farmers could do either to prepare for, or to mitigate the damage that would be caused to fields over thirty or more miles of countryside that were typically traversed in the course of a chase, lasting five or six hours, by a 'numerous company of gentlemen'.[114]

Farmers were possessed of more options when the quarry at issue was game birds. The corollary of the determination of the landed elite to reserve the most prized, and edible, game birds exclusively and entirely to themselves meant not only that tenants were precluded from hunting such game on the land that they farmed, but also that they were expected to preserve their lands, and to deter poachers, for the leisure of others. Some found this responsibility so disagreeable they responded, or so it was alleged, 'by destroying every nest they can conveniently put their foot in'. It also elicited prescient calls in certain quarters for a change in the law to allow 'farmers to kill on their own grounds, [and thereby to] turn the greatest enemies to the sports of the field into its friends and preservers'.[115] However, this ostensibly reasonable suggestion fell on deaf ears. Though the example of the Revolution in France ought to have encouraged caution, the kingdom's lawmakers in the 1790s were intent not only in perpetuating, but also in strengthening the game laws and the privileges they enshrined, with the result that some United Irishmen were prompted to condemn these laws as a 'badge of vassalage'. They were certainly encouraged in this stand by the decision of the County Down Hunt in 1792 to support the prosecution of a man for poaching a hare, which episode caused Wolfe Tone to resort, in the manner previously favoured by improvers and the polite, to his pen to criticise the bibulous country squires that were the mainstay of the hunt.[116]

112 *Hibernian Journal*, 17 Sept. 1790. 113 Griffin, *Blood sport: hunting in Britain since 1066*, p. 139. 114 *Dublin Morning Post*, 5 Feb. 1785; *FJ*, 27 Oct. 1791; *Cork Advertiser*, 3 Mar. 1812. 115 *FJ*, 3 May 1792; *Hibernian Journal*, 2 Sept. 1789. 116 Powell, *The politics of consumption*, pp 121–2; see T.W. Moody, R.B. McDowell and C.J. Woods (eds), *The writings of Wolfe Tone, 1763–98* (3 vols, Oxford, 1998–2007), i, 184.

The criticisms directed the way of hunting in the 1790s demonstrated that the corpus of law that sought to guarantee the privileged access of the elite to the game of the countryside, and facilitated them in the recreational pursuit of other animals, the fox most notably, which were regarded as vermin, was no longer accepted without demur by the public at large by the end of the eighteenth century. Nonetheless, the doyens of hunting were entirely at liberty to continue to enjoy the privilege because the broader consensus among the elite as to its value ensured that there was no prospect of the entitlement being challenged in law. It was not, for example, even raised as an issue during the animated discussion that resulted in the abolition of the Irish parliament and the inauguration of the United Kingdom of Great Britain and Ireland in January 1801.[117] Indeed, hunting not only remained firmly rooted attitudinally, it is a fair measure of its appeal that the number of hunt clubs, and, by implication, the number of devotees of the sport continued to grow through the second half of the 1780s and early 1790s. Moreover, other than the handful of political radicals already referred to, there were no strong voices, either individual or organisational, raised in opposition, and no identifiable strand of thought, or behaviour, prepared to oppose hunting in the manner that hastened the rapid marginalisation of cockfighting and bull-baiting at this very time.[118] Quite the opposite; as people grew more used to the idea of pursuing the fox to the extent of adopting some of the rituals of deer hunting (such as surrounding the kill, 'blooding' novice hunters, and taking various body parts – the tongue and brush notably – as trophies), interest in, and support for the claim that fox-hunting provided good sport, and that the pursuit of the fox was a beneficial activity, appreciated.[119] The following report, published in the *Freeman's Journal* in January 1792, certainly painted a positive picture:

> On Monday last, a very spirited fox-chase took place near Maynooth, which afforded high sport to a numerous field of well-appointed hunters. After a long and vigorous pursuit, in which the welkin[120] resounded with the continued cry of the hounds, and [the] powers of the horses were tried to the full, Reynard was taken alive, and saved from the fury of the dogs for a future day's sport.[121]

The fact that other commentators spoke in still more positive tones attested to the respectability with which hunting was regarded, and to the weakness of the alternative point of view.[122]

One consequence of the near total social acceptance of hunting was the generation of a parallel world of goods. The hunt club was crucial in this because, like a variety of other clubs and societies, most aspired to forge a distinct iden-

---

117 See P.M. Geoghegan, *The Irish Act of Union: a study in high politics, 1798–1801* (Dublin, 1999); G.C. Bolton, *The passing of the Irish Act of Union* (Oxford, 1966). 118 See below, pp 195–200, 230–32. 119 MacGregor, *Animal encounters*, p. 156. 120 An Old English term for clouds, sky, firmament (*OED*). 121 *FJ*, 7 Jan. 1792. 122 See the lyrical description leavened with poetic extracts in *FLJ*, 27 Feb. 1805; for another example, see *Cork Advertiser*, 3 Mar. 1812.

Fig. 19 Hunt Button, Dublin, *c*.1780. One of a set of twelve Irish silver buttons, 2.5cm diameter, each with a figure of a stag and inscribed 'The Northern Rangers'. The Northern Rangers Hunt Club, which continues, was founded in Dundalk in 1784. The buttons were part of a uniform. Sold at auction in October 2012 (image courtesy of Adam's).

tity. As a result, as well as the whips, saddles, boots, riding-breeches (jodhpurs) and other equine accoutrements, members of hunts chose to bedeck themselves in colourful bespoke jackets, studded with monogrammed buttons (see Fig. 19), caps and other recognisable gear. Most hunts took great pride in their uniform, and members honoured this by ensuring that they were well maintained. They also contrived, and with increasing frequency, as the proliferation of hunt clubs brought greater regularity to the sport, to acquire a distinctive horn, drinking glasses, hunt tables (see Fig. 20) and other furniture that was emblematical of the order, regularity and convenience that increasingly defined the chase. These artefacts were a demonstration both of the resources hunt clubs had at their disposal, and of the desire of those for whom hunting was a manifestation of exclusivity to bring a measure of elegance and sophistication to the field even if it was only really in evidence on the day at the places of assembly. They were facilitated in this endeavour by the fact that in its more exclusive organisational incarnations, hunting was identified as a quintessential elite activity, and those of that class who revered hunting, and who could afford it, emphasised the link by commissioning hunt scenes in oils to decorate their drawing rooms.[123] Much of this painting, exemplified by William Sadler's (*c*.1782–1839) depiction of a stag-hunt at Killarney, does not approach the standard of great art, but it was generally sufficiently well crafted to fit comfortably in one of the main public rooms of the 'big houses' that provided the focal point for many local and regional hunts.[124] Moreover, it dovetailed with, and reinforced the romance that the sport generated, which popular nineteenth-century authors and social observers of the likes of Thomas Crofton Croker were more than content to convey.[125]

If the proliferation of hunting scenes was one manifestation, an equally notable illustration of the permeation of the culture of hunting through society is provided by the emergence of greyhound racing, as an alternative activity for dogs that were once used all but exclusively for hunting hares. Another is provided by the enduring appeal of drag chacing. Neither greyhound racing nor drag chasing were particularly popular or (perhaps it is more accurate to state) well-publicised sports, despite their obvious links to hunting. Indeed, one is hard

123 See Donald, *Picturing animals*, part 4.   124 William Sadler's (*c*.1782–1839) depiction of a stag-hunt at Killarney was sold at Adam's in 2012, and bought by Muckross House, Killarney.   125 *Killarney legends*, ed. T. Crofton Croker (London, 1831), chapter 13.

Fig. 20 Irish mahogany
hunt table, *c.*1800.
Hunt table, 138cms by
255cms, with double
drop leaves, on square
chamfered leg supports.
Sold at auction in
October 2012 (image
courtesy of Adam's).

pressed to assemble an impressive evidential inventory of both. Of the two, greyhound racing was the more select, though the evolution of the greyhound from
a hunting specialist to a racing dog was well advanced when, in 1802, in county
Tipperary, Mr Langley's greyhound, Smart, aged 16 months, 'made a most
superior race, against Mr Riall's noted bitch, Nell'. Langley was acknowledged
as a trainer of note by this time as another of his dogs had earlier prevailed in a
race, the outcome of which was notable because it was determined by judges,
which suggests that this was already an organised sport with rules and procedures
to assist with the adjudication of difficult and disputed cases.[126]

The primary appeal of drag chasing rested in the fact that it combined elements of hunting (specifically fox-hunting) and horse racing (specifically the
match) in a hybrid activity pursued across country by horses and hounds. It also
appealed to those who liked to combine hunting and gambling. The order of the
bets laid down with respect to drag races varied, but reports to the effect that
'there were large bets depending' in a match pursued over 12 miles in counties
Tipperary and Kilkenny in 1765, that 600 guineas depended on the outcome of
a match run over six miles in north county Down twenty years later, and that a
chase between Castleknock and Cloghan Church in county Dublin was run for
100 guineas in 1789 provide a pointer to the sums that were at stake, as well as
the spatial extent of the sport, and the eagerness of participants to test the capacities of their packs, their horses and themselves.[127] Events of this nature were rare
by comparison with orthodox chases, whatever the animal quarry, but most
huntsmen accepted that they were part of a sporting continuum whose primary
manifestations were horse racing and, increasingly, fox-hunting.

It also embraced coursing; hare coursing may not have been 'very general', to
echo the pertinent judgment of a subsequent commentator, during the time period
with which this book engages, despite the apparent involvement of the duke of
Ormond's retainers in the pursuit in the 1660s. Indicatively, there is no contem-

126 *FLJ*, 16 May 1802.   127 *FJ*, 12 Oct. 1765; *Volunteer Journal (Cork)*, 7 Nov. 1785; *Ennis
Chronicle*, 12 Oct. 1789.

porary Irish equivalent to the public coursing club established at Swaffham, Norfolk, in 1776, but the sport developed in tandem with the targeted breeding of greyhounds.[128] It also provided a diversionary role, akin to hunting, for a breed of dog that was to flourish in the late nineteenth century, and was epitomised by Master McGrath, the famous dog owned by Charles Brownlow, the second Baron Lurgan (1831–82), whose achievements became the stuff of legend in the 1860s.[129]

The close relationship of hunting and racing remained a feature of both sports in the nineteenth century, but it assumed a different form to that which had obtained in the mid-eighteenth century when in order to encourage the gentry to attend, and divert them when they turned up, hunts were routinely timetabled for the mornings or mid-week during a race meeting. Few race meetings included an organised hunt in their schedule by the early nineteenth century, but most targeted the *aficionados* of the hunt by continuing to stage races exclusively for hunters, and, on occasion, for huntsmen. For their part, following on the earlier example of the Kildare Hunt, and the Dunlavin Hunt, which in 1755 provided a £30 cup for 'proved hunters, carrying 12 stone' at Baltinglass races, hunts such as the Miltown Chase, and County Clare Hunt (both county Clare) came to perceive the merit of sponsoring racing.[130] The minute of the Duhallow Hunt, which met at Mallow, on 7 September 1801, provides an illustration of this in practice:

> At a general meeting of the club, pursuant to public notice, William Wrixon, esq.,[131] reported to the club that the committee have taken into consideration the propriety of the Duhallow Hunt contributing for a purse to be run for at the ensuing Mallow races by county of Cork-bred hunters, and that the committee recommended it to the club to resolve the same. On proposing the said resolution to the club it was unanimously resolved that each member shall subscribe one guinea for the said purse, to be paid to William Wrixon Beecher, esq., steward.[132]

The sponsorship of trophies such as the Duhallow Hunt maiden plate for 'real hunters in the county of Cork', or later the Duhallow Hunt Cup, was manifestly of advantage to both hunting and racing, with the result that other hunts did likewise.[133] It was a synergistic relationship, in keeping with their shared interest in the promotion and advancement of equine sport. The precise configuration of the connexion was different then to what it had been in the eighteenth century but because both sports were better structured, more coherent, and more visible recreational activities than they had been at any point to date, they could justifiably look towards the future with optimism.

128 Above, pp 126–7; Collins et al. (eds), *Encyclopedia of traditional British rural sports*, p. 78. 129 Knox, *A history of the county of Down*, pp 58–9; Eamon Breathnach, *History lore and legend* (Waterford, [1987]). 130 Above, pp 41, 54–5; *UA*, 16 Aug. 1755; *Ennis Chronicle*, 28 June, 12 July, 13, 20, 23 Sept 1790. 131 Wrixon of Ballygiblin was a member of the committee that ran the club at this point: Grove-White, 'Extracts from old minute book of Duhallow Hunt, 1800 to 1808', p. 51. 132 Grove-White, 'Extracts from old minute book of Duhallow Hunt, 1800 to 1808', p. 53. 133 *Cork Advertiser*, 3 Sept., 22 Oct. 1801; *FLJ*, 16 Mar. 1808.

CONCLUSION

As the premier sports of the social, religious and ruling elite, horse racing and hunting were the two diversions most securely anchored in the Irish recreational landscape by the end of the Hanoverian era. This was so because both underwent significant change in the course of the eighteenth century, though neither did so to the extent that it can be said that they changed fundamentally during that time. They were, to be sure, more structured, and more organised in the early nineteenth century by comparison with a hundred-and-fifty years earlier. By implication, though it has long been maintained that 'fox-hunting as practised now began in the late eighteenth century' and that 'Hugo Meynell and the Quorn Hunt in Leicestershire' were responsible, there is little support for this theory in the Irish countryside. Evidence for fox-hunting in Ireland in the late seventeenth and early eighteenth centuries is not abundant, and the fact that 'a sporting buck' was released at Ballinahinch on St Patrick's Day in 1728 is consistent with the conclusion that though evidence can be located pointing to the existence of a designated fox-hunting season in the early 1730s, and perhaps earlier, the fox was not the pre-eminent quarry of hunters during the eighteenth century. It possessed a formidable, and, for many, more prized rival in the 'carted' deer. Be that as it may, the situation was ever changing and the activities of newly established clubs such as the Kilkenny Hunt tipped the balance in favour of the fox in the early nineteenth century. Under the guidance and direction of John Power, the Kilkenny Hunt set about from 1797 to build a strong pack of foxhounds, to which end they drew heavily on English imports.[134] They were following in the tracks of the Kildare Hunt in this respect, but as important as the introduction of new strains of hunting dog was to the development of the sport it must also be acknowledged that they were building on a domestic tradition of fox-hunting that can be traced back to the mid-seventeenth century, as evidence by Lord Castlehaven's observation in 1648 that he went 'early one morning a foxhunting as I was accustomed all the winter'.[135] Clearly, as Iris Middleton and Emma Griffin have pointed out, fox-hunting was not invented in the second half of the eighteenth century. Yet, Hugo Meynell's breeding practices were not without impact; they enhanced the speed and stamina of the dogs that were used, which benefited the sport, but this should be seen as part of an ongoing process (which included the improvement in the quality of horses) that was to continue into the nineteenth century.[136] Moreover, important as it was, it was hardly as transformative as the emergence of the hunt club.

Be that as it may, it is incomplete as well as anachronistic to think of hunting in Ireland in the early nineteenth century exclusively in terms of fox-hunt-

134 Sir John Power, *Memoir of the Kilkenny hunt* (2nd edn, Dublin. 1911), p. 6.   135 Power, *Memoir of the Kilkenny hunt*, appendix 4.   136 I.M. Middleton, 'The origins of English fox-hunting and the myth of Hugo Meynell and the Quorn', *Sport in History*, 25 (2005), pp 1–16; Griffin, *Blood sport: hunting in Britain since 1066*, pp 125–8; MacGregor, *Animal encounters*, p. 155; *FLJ*, 26 Mar. 1828.

ing and the hunt club, and of the sport as an exclusively elite recreation. The picture of hunting presented by Robert Devereux of Carigmenan, county Wexford, in 1779 and the memoirists who collected information on recreational practice in Ulster on behalf of the Ordnance Survey in the 1830s indicates that hunting was pursued by and across all levels of society. Devereux certainly sought to convey the impression that there was plenty of quarry in the south east for those who were interested:

> The healthy youth who rural sport admires,
> Can here content his heart's most fond desires;
> Whether he would the wily *fox* pursue,
> With well-tongued hounds, quite steady, fleet, and true;
> Or would he rather chase the timid *hare*,
> Following the various mazes of its fear;
> Or, do the pleasures of the gun engage,
> Against the feather'd race fierce war to wage,
> If in a boat he goes, he cannot fail
> Charg'd to return with *widgeon*, *duck*, and *teal*;
> Or, if he likes, the *long bill'd cock* to flush
> Numbers he'll find in every hedge and bush;
> And to plump *partridges*, a plenteous store,
> Equal in taste to those of Perigord,
> Does he the silent angler's care prefer?
> The stream his pleasure's ready to confer,
> Where patiently he marks the well-made fly.
> And fills his basket with the shining *fry*.[137]

This idealised perspective does not accord with the reality of a sport that was by no means open to all. The reality was more apparent from the commentaries offered by the memoirists working for the Ordnance Survey in Ulster. However, it is also clear from both these and other sources that interest and engagement in the sport percolated deeply through society. The Antrim Hunt sat proudly at the top of the sporting social pyramid in Ulster in the early nineteenth-century. Presided over by George, second marquess of Donegall, it enjoyed the luxury of 'a splendid hunting establishment at his seat at Fisherwick' between its foundation in 1815 and 1835, when the financial problems of the Donegall family hastened the break up of 'the hunting establishment' and the loss of the income that went with it. This was 'a serious loss to [the grange] of Doagh', in county Antrim, but elsewhere in the province the continuing commitment of the elite to their 'hounds and hunters', and to a network of clubs sustained a pattern of elaborate chases, such as took place at Broughshane where the Carrick Hunt ven-

137 Coleman, 'Hurling in the Co. Wexford in 1779', p. 118. The italicisation is this author's.

tured every February into the 1830s, and in county Down where the Down Hunt was a veritable institution.[138]

Hunting was also pursued, albeit in a less-structured manner, by the large numbers of the population – in south Ulster especially – for whom this was 'their favourite sport'. The generality of the populace did not have the resources to procure well-bred hunters, or bespoke uniforms with silver monogrammed buttons, but they availed of the opportunities available to them to fish, to fowl, and to hunt foxes and hares in their own way.[139] Moreover, there were occasions, such as those provided by the County Down Hunt, by subscription packs that 'were billeted throughout the country', and by individual owners like Watson of Brookhill, county Antrim, and John Gordon of Sheepbridge, county Down, when 'the country people' could engage vicariously in the thrill of the chase.[140] These occasions may not have contravened the hierarchical exclusivity that was integral to the organised structured sport of hunting, but the enthusiastic involvement of country people in various ways was an illustration of the fact that hunting sustained not only deep roots in the countryside, but also a fond place in the hearts of a majority of countrymen as the Hanoverian era drew to a close.

138 Day and McWilliams (eds), *Ordnance survey memoirs, county Antrim*, xxix, 68 (Grange of Doagh), xiii, 95 (Racavan); Day and McWilliams (eds), *Ordnance survey memoirs, county Down*, xvii, 17–8 (Ballee).   139 Day and McWilliams (eds), *Ordnance survey memoirs, county Antrim*, x, 40 (Islandmagee), xxxii, 68 (Glenwhirry); Day and McWilliams (eds), *Ordnance survey memoirs, county Fermanagh*, xiv, 24 (Cleenish); xiv, 43 (Derryvullan); xiv, 66 (Drumkeeran); xiv, 99 (Magheracross); xiv, 129 (Trory); Day and McWilliams (eds), *Ordnance survey memoirs, county Monaghan*, xl, 109 (Donaghmoyne).   140 Day and McWilliams (eds), *Ordnance survey memoirs, county Down*, iii, 74 (Newry); xvii, 17–18 (Ballee); Day and McWilliams (eds), *Ordnance survey memoirs, county Antrim*, xxi, 109 (Magheragall); Day and McWilliams (eds), *Ordnance survey memoirs, county Londonderry*, vi, 10 (Magherafelt).

3

Cockfighting

Horse racing was the most organised, most respectable and, by a large margin, the most publicised sporting activity in eighteenth-century Ireland. Its closest rival was cockfighting, which was pursued with comparable enthusiasm over large parts of the provinces of Ulster, Leinster and in smaller pockets in the provinces of Munster and Connaught during the second half of the century. However, whereas there is a modest (but helpful) literature upon which one can draw to assist with tracing the emergence and development of Irish horse racing,[1] the historiographical landscape is featureless when it comes to cockfighting. There is an obvious reason for this. Though cockfighting continued to be pursued in parts of the country until at least the mid-twentieth century,[2] it was done covertly, away from the prying eyes of the authorities because, in direct contrast to horse racing, which remained the favoured sport of the elite, it became an illegal activity. The proscription of cockfighting in 1835 accelerated a trend that can be traced to the final decades of the eighteenth century when the respectable, who previously tolerated when they did not encourage the activity, not only distanced themselves but also actively urged its discontinuance. This was a critical moment in the history of the sport. Prior to this moment, cockfighting seemed as firmly anchored in Irish society as horse racing, and its Irish advocates as persuaded as its practitioners elsewhere that it possessed a venerable genealogy reaching back into classical antiquity,[3] when the reality was that it flourished for little more than half a century, and that its experience was emblematical of one of the truisms of the history of so many recreational sports – their temporal transience.

BACKGROUND AND DEVELOPMENT TO 1760

By comparison with England, where there is clear evidence that cockfighting was firmly established as a recreational pursuit by the second half of the sixteenth

1 See above, p. 21. 2 Neal Garnham, 'The survival of popular blood sports in Victorian Ulster', *PRIA*, 107C (2007), pp 107–26 passim; George Ryley Scott, *The history of cock-fighting* (London, [1957]), pp 173–4; P. Ó Crannlaighe, 'Cock-fighting', *The Bell*, 9:6 (Mar. 1945), pp 510–13; P. Beacey, 'Prelude to a cockfight', *The Bell*, 11:1 (Oct. 1945), pp 574–6. Scott, Ó Crannlaighe and Beacey mention illegal cockfighting in Donegal, Tyrone, and unspecified parts of Munster. 3 See R[obert] H[owlett], *The royal pastime of cock-fighting ... to which is prefixed a short treatise, wherein cocking is proved not only ancient and honourable, but also useful, and profitable* (London, 1709; reprint edn, Liss, Hampshire, 1973), preface.

century, there is a striking absence of reference to cockfighting in early modern Ireland.[4] Yet because cockfighting was the recipient of sufficient royal favour[5] to accommodate the construction of 'cockpits' in the Westminster and Whitehall areas of London during the reigns of the Tudor and early Stuart monarchs, it is improbable that the New English officials in Ireland opposed its pursuit. Be that as it may, it was not commonplace, if it occurred at all.[6] It certainly did not possess sufficient profile to warrant the construction of a purpose-built cockpit in the style of those built in Whitehall (London) in 1533–4, or the publication of an Irish edition of George Wilson's defence of the antiquity of cockfighting, *The commendation of cockes* (1607), or any of the many editions of Gervase Markham's *Country contentments, or, the husbandman's recreations*, which commended 'the use of the fighting cock' among a number of diversions that included hunting, hawking, coursing with greyhounds, shooting and angling.[7] It may also be significant that the infamous Cromwellian ordinance of 1654 'prohibiting cock-matches' on the grounds that they 'tend ... to the disturbance of the public peace, and are commonly accompanied with gaming, drinking, swearing, quarrelling and other dissolute practices' applied only to England and Wales.[8] In any event, the palpable relaxation in attitude towards recreational activity in general, and sports like horse racing and cockfighting, that followed the restoration of the monarchy in 1660 did not precipitate an identifiable surge in interest in cockfighting in Ireland.[9] This contrasts strikingly with horse racing,[10] and with the situation in England where royal example encouraged a great 'variety of people, from parliament man ... to the poorest [ap]prentices' to frequent the various cockpits that were opened. It also gave cockfighting respectability, for while Samuel Pepys was plainly uncomfortable with 'the mixed rabble of people' that he encountered in London's cockpits, and the inherent violence of the sport, others found the environment and the activity exhilarating. Like Charles II, whose presence at the royal cockpit at Newmarket during the annual spring race meeting gave cock-

4 Walter Gilbey, *Sport in the olden time* (reprint, Liss, Hampshire, 1975), pp 1–4, 5; Brailsford, *Sport and society: Elizabeth to Anne*, p. 204; Griffin, *England's revelry*, pp 33–4. 5 Various claims have been made in respect of Henry VIII, and James I (Gilbey, *Sport in the olden time*, pp 8–9, 16–7). 6 Gilbey, *Sport in the olden time*, pp 6–16; MacGregor, *Animal encounters*, pp 248–50. 7 MacGregor, *Animal encounters*, pp 230–1; George Wilson, *The commendation of cockes, and cock-fighting, wherein is shewed, that cocke-fighting was before the comming of Christ* (London, 1607); Gervase Markham (1568?–1637), *Country contentments, or, the husbandman's recreations: containing the wholesome experience, in which any ought to recreate himself, after the toyl of more serious business ...* (4th edn, London, 1631). 8 *An ordinance prohibiting cock-matches* (London, 1654); Gilbey, *Sport in the olden time*, pp 27–9; Joseph Batty, *Cock-fighting ban of Oliver Cromwell* (second ed., Midhurst, West Sussex, 2005), pp 18–20. The prohibition on cockfighting was affirmed in further ordinances issued in 1656 (Gilbey, op. cit., p. 28), but it must be noted, as Dennis Brailsford has observed, that by comparison with bear-baiting, the prohibition was not firmly enforced (Brailsford, *Sport and society: Elizabeth to Anne*, pp 138, 204). 9 Significantly, Edward MacLysaght produces no evidence of cockfighting in the period in *Irish life in the seventeenth century* (2nd edn, Cork, 1950). The references he cites relate to the eighteenth century (MacLysaght, op. cit., p 149). 10 See above, pp 31–3.

fighting the all-important royal endorsement, they were drawn by the drama of the pit, by the excitement of gambling, and, one may reasonably assume, by the intrinsically gladiatorial character of a battle of cocks.[11]

As a consequence of the appreciating public interest, cockfighting became more organised and more structured. The inauguration of an annual main at the royal cockpit at Westminster is one salient indicator of this tendency, for while the suggestion that 'the earliest code of laws governing the sport' dates from this period has reasonably been queried, there is no evading the fact that the 'battles of cocks' described by Pepys were not unregulated free-for-alls.[12] This was crucial because gambling was integral to the appeal of the sport, and individuals would not continue to hazard money if they were not persuaded that the contests on which they ventured their resources were not conducted in a manner that offered them at least a reasonable chance of advantage.

Cockfighting also derived credibility from the interventions of respected authorities and authors, like Charles Cotton (1630–87), whose guide to gaming published in 1674 depicted cockfighting as 'a sport or pastime ... full of delight and pleasure, that I know not any game in that respect to be preferred before it'.[13] Cotton revealed the rising esteem in which cockfighting was held by referring to it in the same manner as he did horse racing, and the fact that Richard Blome did likewise in his 1686 publication, *The gentleman's recreation*, attested to its improving fortunes. In practice, the popularity of cockfighting derived in no small part from the fact that it appealed across social boundaries, though this did not mean that the elite and the populace mixed together in the cockpit. The publication by Robert Howlett in 1709 of a discourse on the 'royal pastime of cockfighting', which served at once as a guide to the care of cocks, a source of information on how to ready them for battle, a *vade mecum* to the rules and procedures to be followed at a main, and a paean of 'praise to the fighting cock', was unambiguously targeted at 'person[s] of honour'.[14] It had little to offer the 'bakers, brewers, butchers, draymen, and what not' whose presence Pepys had found discomforting, though they were an important constituency of the audience that sustained the expanding number of cockpits in late seventeenth-century London, and elsewhere.[15] Indeed, they were a visible manifestation of the fact that in late seventeenth and in eighteenth-century England, cockfighting, 'like horse racing, pugilism, and cricket ... drew support from a very wide spectrum

11 Brailsford, *Sport and society: Elizabeth to Anne*, pp 203, 206, 214; Gilbey, *Sport in the olden time*, pp 31–2; Robert Latham and William Matthews (eds), *The diary of Samuel Pepys* (10 vols, London, 1970–83), iv, 427–8, ix, 154. 12 Gilbey, *Sport in the olden time*, p. 29; *The diary of Samuel Pepys*, iv, 428. 13 Charles Cotton, *The compleat gamester: or, instructions how to play at billiards, trucks, bowls, and chess, together with all manner of usual and most gentile games either on cards or dice, to which is added, the arts and mysteries of riding, racing, archery, and cock-fighting* (London, 1674). It was a work of enduring appeal, as further editions were published in 1676, 1680, 1687, 1709, 1710, 1721, 1725, all in London; Brailsford, *Sport and society: Elizabeth to Anne*, p. 214. 14 H[owlett], *The royal pastime of cockfighting ....* 15 *The diary of Samuel Pepys*, iv, 428; I.C. Peate, *The Denbigh cockpit and cockfighting in Wales* (Cardiff, 1970).

of society', which was key to its popularity, and, it might be added, to the absence of a vigorous public critique.[16] Thus at a 'plebeian level', as Dennis Brailsford has noted, 'cockfighting was virtually universal at Shrovetide'. It was then that one was most likely to encounter 'shake bag' contests when unmatched cocks were set to fight with little of the ceremony that characterised a cockpit encounter.[17] However, as one ascended the social pyramid, the emphasis shifted, and formality and order became increasingly normative. At this level, cockfighting was an organised, competitive sport, pursued by peers of the realm and by gentlemen with the resources and know-how to assemble large numbers of selectively bred cocks, from which they culled only those who demonstrated an above average capacity to fight. They also employed cock masters and feeders who with great care and deliberation fed, coached and physically prepared the birds that were presented to fight because, as well as the bird's life, the money, honour and reputation of its owner was at issue each time it entered a cockpit.[18]

Given the close cultural links that bound the anglophone communities in both kingdoms, it was logical that Ireland should follow Britain in embracing cockfighting as a recreational activity. Because of the fragmentary character of the evidential record, it is not possible at present either to identify when cockfighting commenced, or where it first put down roots. It may be surmised, based purely on the fact that it must have taken a number of decades to arrive at a critical mass to permit the organisation of competitive cockfights, that this process spanned the final decades of the seventeenth and early decades of the eighteenth centuries. It may also reasonably be surmised that the earliest cockfights resembled the local and random 'shake bag' contests that were commonplace in provincial England, and that, as well as gentry and nobility, a significant proportion of the practitioners were individuals of modest means, who kept a few fighting cocks, which they presented to fight for relatively small sums. This, inevitably, was too informal for the peers and substantial landowners whose knowledge and understanding of cockfighting derived directly, or by report, from the 'great cocking' matches held in England. A direct connection remains to be established, but the presence of Henry (O'Brien), seventh Lord Thomond, George (Villiers), fourth Viscount Grandison, and others at one such event in 1687 when 'thousands' was bet on the outcome provides some evidence of the involvement of members of the Irish peerage in English cockfighting. Moreover, the emergence of 'battles royal' and team encounters involving the gentlemen of towns or counties must have impressed Irish gentlemen, and encouraged them to attempt to do likewise.[19] The successful inauguration of a steadily expanding schedule of horse races may also have served as an incentive, both because of the close links between horse racing and cockfighting epitomised by the presence of the royal cockpit at Newmarket, and because horse racing established an organisational

16 Griffin, *England's revelry*, p. 14; Brailsford, *A taste for diversions*, pp 21, 23.   17 MacGregor, *Animal encounters*, pp 246–7.   18 Brailsford, *A taste for diversions*, pp 21, 77–8; MacGregor, *Animal encounters*, pp 232–42.   19 Gilbey, *Sport in the olden time*, pp 41–2, 55.

precedent that other sports could follow. Furthermore, the growth of horse racing demonstrated the usefulness of the newspaper press as a means of conveying information and promoting involvement. It is certainly hardly a coincidence that the first identifiable report of a cockfight involving two Irish regional teams was published when reports of horse racing meetings were already a standard feature in the Irish press.[20] This encounter, between the gentlemen of the city of Londonderry and the town of Strabane on 10 April 1730, was printed in George Faulkner's *Dublin Journal* in a manner that made it clear it was carried because the result was deemed newsworthy, not because cockfighting was new or novel:

> Yesterday the gentlemen of the city of Londonderry came to this town [Strabane] according to an agreement some time ago made, and fought seven cocks for above one hundred pounds sterling. Strabane had the fortune to win every battle tho' Derry fought extraordinary good fowls; the case being so uncommon in seven battles not to lose one that the putting it in your paper will oblige many...[21]

In keeping with the tone of this story, neither George Faulkner nor any other newspaper proprietor deemed it worthwhile in the years immediately following to allocate space either to upcoming or completed matches. Cockfights, evidently, were not of sufficient public interest to merit inclusion in the short Irish news columns of the main news sheets unless the event being reported was unusual or newsworthy for some other reason. This was the case, certainly, of the publication by the *Belfast News Letter* in March 1739 of a detailed account of a match in the neighbourhood of Randalstown between Randal Mac Donnell, who maintained 'above sixty cocks', and 'three gentlemen from the parish of Dunean[e]',[22] in which victory went to Mac Donnell by 7 battles to 4. Since the stakes at issue in this instance were an unremarkable 'three guineas a battle and seven guineas' the main, it is improbable that the encounter would have excited any attention outside of its immediate hinterland but for the imprudent claim, offered on behalf of the winning Mac Donnell team (and assumed reasonably by their opponents to emanate directly from Randal Mac Donnell), that their higher quality cocks, which bore individual names, 'would undoubtedly have gained the whole had not the opposite party most ungenerously and surreptitiously fought his own blood against him, ... contrary to the rules of cocking'. This was a serious alle-

---

20 Above, pp 40–2. 21 *FDJ*, 14 Apr. 1730; see also D.F. Fleming, 'Diversions of the people: sociability among the orders of early eighteenth-century Ireland', *Eighteenth-Century Ireland*, 17 (2002), pp 109–10. It may be noted at this point that cockfights between representative teams were well established in England. For example, 'the gentlemen of Essex and the Gentlemen of London' met at the cockpit 'by the bowling-green behind Gray's Inn' in 1709: *Daily Courant*, 24 Jan. 1809, printed in W.B. Ewald (ed.), *The newsmen of Queen Anne* (Oxford, 1956), p. 166. 22 Duneane parish is in the barony of Upper Toome, six miles from Randalstown, county Antrim.

gation, but Mac Donnell was so convinced his opponents had transgressed that he pronounced portentously that the conduct of the team from Duneane 'tend[ed] to the manifest destruction of that noble diversion'. He clearly sincerely felt 'his profound skill in that science', and his judgment 'that his cocks are of the true ginger kind, and the best that ever flew' had been challenged. As a result, as well as seeking to mitigate the blow to his elevated self esteem caused by losing four battles to 'the gentlemen of Dunean[e]', he accused his opponent of cheating, and sought to restore his reputation as the owner of the best cocks in the region by challenging 'some cockers in the county of Derry to shew six staff of cocks on 2 April next for fifty pounds the main'.[23] It is not apparent if Mac Donnell's challenge was taken up, but the gentlemen of Duneane demonstrated that they were not prepared to be cowed into submission, or to have their reputation impugned, by presenting a detailed reply in which they dilated at length on the battles that had been fought and the qualities of the fowl at the heart of the dispute, and, with still more impact, accused Mac Donnell of disingenuousness, pomposity and of 'ostentation intirely unworthy a generous sportsman'. They also expressed confidence in their own cocks and, by extension, questioned Mac Donnell's judgment by declaring that they were prepared to renew the rivalry with him on any occasion for the augmented stakes of five guineas the battle and fifty guineas the main.[24]

Though the details of the Mac Donnell–Duneane spat just described are primarily of interest for what they reveal of competitive cockfighting in the 1740s, they also manifest how personal sensitivities could generate disagreement, and, among an elite quick to take offence and preoccupied with personal reputation, escalate easily into life-endangering affairs of honour.[25] Human competitiveness was certainly a crucial dynamic in the sport of cockfighting, for though the cocks that were set against each other in mortal combat were genetically and behaviourally predisposed to fight, the 'battles' they pursued were first and foremost a product of human agency. During the second quarter of the eighteenth century, when the local and regional rivalries that provided the primary dynamic for the sport during its Irish heyday were still protean, competition took different forms. It could, for example, follow the intrinsically local pattern manifested at Strabane in 1730. This was emulated by the nexus of gentlemen from the city of Cork and the popular spa town of Mallow who undertook to assemble an impressive 21 pair of cocks at the latter location at Whitsuntide in 1737 and to guarantee a stake of £5 a battle and 100 guineas the main.[26] However, it could also assume an inter-provincial form as when, in 1741, two teams, describing themselves as 'the gentlemen of the province of Munster, and the gentlemen of the city and

23 *BNL*, 13 Mar. 1739/40. The report is printed in Thomas McTear, 'Personal recollections of the beginning of the century', *UJA*, 2nd series, 5 (1899), p. 70.   24 *BNL*, 27 Mar. 1740.   25 See James Kelly, *'That damn'd thing called honour': duelling in Ireland, 1580–1860* (Cork, 1992).   26 *Dublin Daily Advertizer*, 19 Mar. 1737; James Kelly, 'Drinking the waters: balneotherapeutic medicine in Ireland, 1660–1850', *Studia Hibernica*, 35 (2008–9), pp 117–18.

	DUBLIN	LEINSTER	MUNSTER	ULSTER	CONNACHT	TOTAL
			Table 5: Cockfighting: reported mains, 1741–60			
1741	1	1				2
1743		1				1
1744	1		1			2
1747	2					2
1748	1				1	2
1751	1	1				2
1753	2	3		1		6
1754	5			1		6
1755	5	3				8
1756	3			1	1	5
1757	1	11				12
1758	3	1				4
1759	2	1				3
1760	2	3		4		9
Total	29	25	1	7	2	64

Source: *Faulkner's Dublin Journal*, 1741, 1744, 1748; *Dublin Newsletter*, 1743; *Dublin Courant*, 1747, 1751; *Munster Journal*, 1751; *Pue's Occurrences*, 1748, 1753; *Universal Advertiser*, 1753–60; *Belfast News Letter*, 1753–60; *Public Gazetteer*, 1760.

county of Dublin' embarked on a week-long match in Dublin for ten guineas a battle and two hundred guineas the main.[27]

Significantly, this event took place in Crofton's Cockpit Royal on Cork Hill, close to Dublin Castle, which was acknowledged before the middle of the century as the premier cockfighting location in the country. Though little is known of the location of the venue (other than that it was accessed for a time through the Hoop Tavern), the date upon which it was established, its capacity, configuration and its proprietor – the eponymous Crofton – it was probably a recent undertaking, since the first identified reference dates from January 1737. Another announcement made in 1738 does not name the participants in the scheduled multi-day match.[28] The absence of reference in the publicity announcing the event to 'the old cockpit royal in Cook Street' is less notable, though it conveniently ignored the fact that the city already possessed a cockpit, which, it may reasonably be assumed, was not as well appointed as the Cork Hill pit.[29] Be that as it may, the new 'Cockpit Royal' had to win over the cockfighting audience,

27 *FDJ*, 7 Feb. 1741.   28 'The Cock-pit Royal' is referred to in *Dublin Daily Advertiser*, 17 Jan. 1737; Colm Lennon, *Irish historic towns atlas no. 19: Dublin, part 2, 1610 to 1756* (Dublin, 2008), section no. 21.   29 *UA*, 2 July 1754.

and the absence of specific detail in the 1738 announcement suggests not only that it sought to encourage entrants, but also that it was not yet firmly established as a prime recreational venue in the public mind. However, it had the advantage of a city-centre location and, based on its commercial relationship with two of the capital's premier coffee houses, close links to other major centres of male sociability:

> At the Cockpit Royal on Cork Hill, on Tuesday, Wednesday, Thursday, Friday and Saturday next, will be a cock match, for ten guineas a battle, and two hundred guineas the odd battle. No person whatever to be admitted without a ticket, which may be had at Lucas's or the Globe Coffee houses, at a British half crown each. No odd money will be taken. Beginning at 12 each day.[30]

Whatever the outcome, the confidence with which Crofton announced his presence supports the conclusion that he believed that Dublin was ready for a modern cockpit, and that his conformed to the recognised form that such locations assumed; it was 'a circular place with rows of seats one above another and a platform in the middle lighted by a lustre'.[31] Indicatively, Crofton's confidence was a herald of what was to come as the Cockpit Royal quickly established itself as the most popular cockfighting venue in the country, and the only one whose matches were routinely advertised, and reported, in the press. It also sustains the impression that cockfighting was a fast-growing sport. Indicatively, the Cockpit Royal hosted a 'grand cock match' over five days in the mid-1740s between the gentlemen of Munster and Leinster for the largest sum – 'forty guineas a battle and 500 guineas the odd battle', or main – publicly fought for in Ireland to that point.[32]

Given the sums involved on this occasion, one might have assumed that it would have set the tone for future matches at this and other venues, and that team competition would have become the norm, whereas the dominant form of combat during the remainder of the 1740s and early 1750s was between individuals. Since this was common practice in the countryside – as instanced by the three-day match at Castle Lyons, county Cork in January 1744, between Lord Buttevant and the Manserghs of Macrony[33] – it was to be expected that the Royal Cockpit would also host matches between the owners of large numbers of fighting cocks, but the evident preference at this moment for matches of this type over county or regional matches is still striking. There is no obvious reason as to why this should be, but it was almost certainly bound up with the ambitions in the late 1740s of a number of wealthy fighting-cock owners of whom

30 *Dublin Newsletter*, 4 Mar. 1738; John Gilbert, *History of the city of Dublin* (3 vols, Dublin, 1859–61), ii, 16.   31 *The diary of Sylas Neville, 1767–88*, ed. Basil Cozens-Hardy (Oxford, 1950), p. 2.   32 *FDJ*, 20 Mar. 1744.   33 Pearde to Price, 31 Jan. 1744 (NLW, Puleston papers, MS 3579 f. 67); GEC, *The complete peerage*, ii, 44–5.

Chaworth Brabazon (1686–1763), sixth earl of Meath, stands pre-eminent. As the one-time MP for county Dublin (1713–14), a senior peer and privy councillor, and the beneficiary of a large rent roll from his Dublin properties, Meath does not conform to the traditional raffish image of the gentry 'cocker'.[34] Neither does Sir Laurence Parsons (1712–56), whose improvements to Birr Castle suggest he was a man of 'civilised taste' and financial prudence.[35] However, both were keen sportsmen. Parsons ran a mare in the blue ribband king's plate at the Curragh in 1738, and since he, like the wealthier earl of Meath, clearly found the hurly-burly of the cockpit more to his liking than the verbal jousting of the political arena, he showed no hesitation in pitting his best fowl against those of the earl of Meath (which he did in 1751 and 1753 (twice)) and other cockfighting enthusiasts, most of whom were less socially eminent.[36] Of course, wealth and status were no guarantee of success in the cockpit, though the willingness of both to wager '40 guineas a battle and 400 guineas the main' in the 'grand match' won by Parsons in April 1753 vividly demonstrated that money was an important consideration and that, no less than horse racing, cockfighting at the highest level was not a sport for those with shallow pockets.[37] Such outlays may also have prompted Meath and Parsons to show caution, since having dominated the Cockpit Royal for six years by that point, Meath, followed shortly afterwards by Parsons, ceded the honour to others, among whom Gorges Lowther (1713–92) of Kilbrew, county Meath, the MP for Ratoath, 1739–50, and county Meath, 1761–92, stands pre-eminent. Like Parsons and Meath, Lowther was not an active parliamentarian; indeed, it was said of him by one acute observer of what was required to succeed in the political arena that 'his voice is much better adapted to the sports of the field, or the riots of a cock-pit, than to oratorical exhibitions or displays of eloquence', but Lowther took little notice of what others thought. He fought, and prevailed in his first recorded cockfight in the Cork Hill cockpit in 1754, and though he did not grace the same arena frequently thereafter, he remained a visible and active presence in the sport through the 1760s and the 1770s when his main rival for the accolade of leading individual fighting-cock owner was William Henry Burton of Burton Hall, county Carlow.[38]

Meath, Parsons, Lowther and Burton were the most active of the high profile individuals who pursued the sport of cockfighting. Their involvement in the sport was on a scale sufficient to allow them to assemble a team of fighting cocks from their own flocks; those who did not possess flocks of sufficient magnitude had little alternative but to opt for the team-based competition that emerged in

34 GEC, *The complete peerage*, viii, 615–16; Edith Johnston-Liik, *History of the Irish parliament, 1692–1800* (6 vols, Dublin, 2001), iii, 256.   35 A.P.W. Malcomson (ed.), *Calendar of the Rosse papers* (Dublin, 2008), p. xii; Johnston-Liik, *History of the Irish parliament*, vi, 22.   36 The earl of Meath fought Captain Vernon in 1747, and Mr Worthington in 1748 (*Dublin Courant*, 28 Feb. 1747; *FDJ*, 29 Mar. 1748).   37 *Dublin Courant*, 28 Feb. 1747, 28 Mar. 1748; *FDJ*, 29 Mar. 1748; *Munster Journal*, 11 Mar. 1751; *UA*, 10 Mar., 17 Apr. 1753.   38 Johnston-Liik, *History of the Irish parliament*, v, 128–30; *UA*, 21, 23 Mar. 1754; Falkland [J.R. Scott], *A review of the principal characters of the Irish House of Commons* (Dublin, 1789), pp 137–40.

the late 1750s as an expression of the sport in its most structured and organised form. The emergence of team cockfighting may be ascribed in part to the costs associated with building and maintaining a flock of quality cocks large enough to sustain the extended multi-day events that were increasingly favoured from that point, but it is also likely that team competition supplanted individual competition because it was a more successful means of generating the public interest that defined a popular sport.

One cannot ascribe the increased participation in cockfighting that was a feature of the 1740s and 1750s to a single factor, organisational or otherwise, because there were a number of converging trends that shaped the sport. The most consequential was the generation of an infrastructure, of which the most visible, and important, manifestation was the increased number of dedicated cockpits. It is not possible at present to offer a *secure* statistical perspective on this, but it is notable that the success of the Royal Cockpit on Cork Hill, Dublin, did not force the closure of the 'old Cockpit Royal' on Cook Street. Indeed, the latter served for a time in the mid-1750s as a genuine rival to the Cork Hill location, by providing the venue for mains involving 'the gentlemen of county and city of Dublin and of county Wicklow'.[39] However, it surrendered that match-up to its more modern rival in 1755, and though it continued to host team events thereafter, it is significant that it appealed primarily to the tried and trusted, but now less popular, practice of hosting matches between individual gentlemen.[40]

It is unlikely, given the comparatively small number of meetings it staged by comparison with the Cockpit Royal, that the Cook Street venue was a highly profitable enterprise. Yet cockfighting was sufficiently popular and, by implication, sufficiently lucrative to encourage tavern and inn owners to host matches. Irish tavern owners did not promote cockfighting with the same energy as their English counterparts, though it may be that most were content to provide the location for 'shake bag' events that met the needs of the majority of owners who kept a few fighting cocks as a hobby, and who have made little impression in the evidential record.[41] There are a number of exceptions. The preparedness of John Dillon, who ran the Sign of Cork in Dolphin's Barn on the southern outskirts of Dublin city, to host a 'grand cock-match' in 1757, and his willingness in 1758 to share the regular main between the gentlemen of the county of Kildare and Dublin with the Cockpit Royal on Cork Hill indicates that taverns and inns were not off limits as venues for major matches. However, since few events of this kind have been identified, it may be that those tavern owners and innkeepers that promoted the sport normally restricted their involvement to local owners, which was critical to the survival of the sport at the level below that of the major owners, and the representative teams that featured disproportionately in the newspapers.[42]

---

39 Gilbert, *History of the city of Dublin*, i, 313; *UA*, 20 Apr. 1754, 4 Jan. 1755.   40 *UA*, 2 July 1754, 19 Apr. 1755, 6 Apr. 1756.   41 I.M. Middleton, 'Cockfighting in Yorkshire during the early eighteenth century', *Northern History*, 40 (2003), pp 136–8; Brailsford, *A taste of diversions*, pp 108, 110.   42 *UA*, 3 May 1757, 13 June 1758.

The best-known Dublin-based cockpits were privately owned, commercial undertakings. This was the case also of the 'new cock pits' built in 1755 with 'all conviencies [*sic*], the same as in the royal cock pit in Dublin,' in Naas and Athy.[43] A still most striking illustration of the emergence of the sport of cockfighting in the middle decades of the century is provided by the decision of the Corporation of Kilkenny, in 1747, to 'order ... that a cockpit be built, and that the sum of £20 be given by this city for building the same, provided a convenient place be got for building it upon the city ground'. The latter condition did not present a difficulty; a site was quickly located on St Mary's Lane, near St Mary's Church, thereby providing Kilkenny with what was, in effect, a 'municipal cockpit'.[44] As expected, the presence of the cockpit encouraged cockfighting, not only in the locality but also in the region (the most striking manifestation of this was 'the annual stag match' that took place at the venue 'between the gentlemen of the counties of Carlow and Kilkenny'). It also gave impetus to what others contrived eagerly to affirm, that cockfighting was not only popular, but also highly respectable.[45] This was the implication, certainly, of the establishment of a cockpit at Limerick (1747), and of the 'great appearance of gentlemen' at the 'decision' of the keenly contested match between Alexander Mac Donnell (1713–75), the fifth earl of Antrim, who was governor of the county that gave him his title, and the gentlemen of Derry, which took place in Derry in April 1754.[46]

This was not the unanimous view, however; there were some who continued to look upon cockfighting with disfavour. The invocation of 'cockfighting' in the title of a verse satire directed at Charles Lucas, the radical firebrand, whose determined challenge to the authority of the aldermen of Dublin Corporation in 1748–9 was a *cause célèbre*, was symptomatic of the enduring strand of orthodox opinion that conceived of the sport as bloody and disruptive.[47] The 'bloody quarrel ... wherein one man was killed on the spot, another so much wounded, and several others were terribly cut and battered' at a cockfight in a 'whiskey house' at Dunnamanagh, county Tyrone, late in January 1753 certainly served to affirm such negative impressions.[48] It may even have guided Nathaniel Nisbitt, a land agent based at nearby Lifford, county Donegal, who when addressing the issue of the fair held in the busy market town of St Johnston in April 1758 informed the earl of Abercorn that he would 'allow neither cockfight, nor horse race, though the people of the town were all for it, as all towns are indeed'.[49]

43 *UA*, 12 Apr., 10, 17 May 1755. 44 J.G.A. Prim, 'Olden popular pastimes in Kilkenny', *Transactions of the Kilkenny Archaeological Society*, 2 (1852–3), p. 325; P. Walsh, 'Eighteenth-century Kilkenny', *Old Kilkenny Review*, 17 (1965), pp 42–3; John Bradley, 'Kilkenny' in *Irish historic town atlas, volume II: Maynooth, Downpatrick, Bray, Kilkenny, Fethard, Trim* (Dublin, 2005), section no. 21. 45 *UA*, 19, 23, June 1753; *Public Gazetteer*, 10 June 1760, 9 June 1761. 46 Eamon O'Flaherty, 'Limerick' in *Irish historic town atlas, volume III: Derry-Londonderry, Dundalk, Armagh, Tuam, Limerick* (Dublin, 2012), section no. 21; *UA*, 27, 30 Apr. 1754; GEC, *The complete peerage*, i, 176. 47 *Cock-fighting display'd, or Lucas cut down* (Dublin, 1749); for Lucas and the Lucas affair see Sean Murphy, 'The Lucas affair: a study in municipal and electoral politics in Dublin, 1742–49' (MA, UCD, 1981). 48 *UA*, 6 Feb. 1753. 49 Quoted in W.H. Crawford, 'The political econ-

Fig. 21 John, Lord Eyre (1720–81), MP for Galway borough, 1748–68, was one of the most active patrons of cockfighting, and the host of many mains at his Eyrecourt residence (image from I.M. Gantz, *Signpost to Eyrecourt*, portrait of the Eyre family (Bath, 1975)).

Though cockfighting continued to sustain a negative image in some quarters, the increasing participation in the sport, the greater willingness of the owners of fighting cocks to pool their birds, and the publication of Irish editions of standard guides such as Thomas Fairfax's *Complete sportsman*, which purported to present 'the very best instructions' for the 'breeding and the management of game-cocks', accented the trend towards greater uniformity in the manner in which the sport was conducted that was another feature of the middle decades of the eighteenth century.[50] As already indicated, this did not require individuals, with the resources and the interest to sustain a flock of quality cocks, to forsake their own private ambitions. The capacity of the fifth earl of Antrim to muster 31 cocks to take on a team comprising the gentlemen of Derry in 1754 is illustrative of his commitment to the sport. He was not alone in so doing, but it was increasingly difficult to sustain this level of engagement in a world of intensify-

omy of linen' in idem, *The impact of the domestic linen industry in Ulster* (Belfast, 2005), pp 97–8.
50 Thomas Fairfax, *The complete sportsman: or country gentleman's recreation, containing the very best instructions under the following head, viz., of breeding and the management of game cocks* ... (Dublin, 1764). First published in London on 1758, this title was frequently reprinted between 1758 and 1766.

ing competition. It may be that it is not without significance also that Antrim lost this particular match, albeit by the smallest margin.[51]

John Eyre, who represented Galway borough in the Irish House of Commons for twenty years before he was ennobled in 1768, was another who contrived to sustain his 'great passion for cockfighting', in his case by hosting matches at Eyrecourt, county Galway. Eyre's enthusiasm for 'cocking' dovetailed with his lifestyle, which was memorably recorded for posterity by Richard Cumberland, the dramatist and Ulster secretary in the earl of Halifax administration (1761–3), who observed witheringly of Eyre that he 'lived in an enviable independence as to reading, and, of course, he had no books'. Eyre's disinterest in print made for a dining experience that (according to Cumberland) wanted for refinement and lively conversation, but his reputation as a host was widely admired among the rural gentry of which he was an archtype, and it was a significant consideration in attracting a team of Queen's county gentlemen and twenty-one cocks to Eyrecourt to participate in a four-day long main in April 1748, and a still-more representative gathering from Munster and Connaught who competed in a rare inter-provincial main in 1756.[52]

Eyre's bacchanalian propensities have almost certainly been inflated by the habitual predilection of memoirists to exaggerate, but private communications emanating from other locations to the effect that the assembled company generally 'drank hard' in the long evenings that followed a day's cockfighting suggest not only that such occasions lent themselves to bibulous excess, but also that it was integral to the homo-social appeal of such events.[53] Moreover, it may have become more prevalent because of the increased number of long mains that were a consequence of the emergence of baronial, county and, occasionally, of provincial and, even, reputedly, of national teams. Support for this suggestion is provided by the profile of the 'grand cock' or 'grand stag matches' of three to five days which took place in Leinster – then the main centre of cockfighting – during the 1750s.[54]

Long mains necessarily demanded greater numbers of quality fighting-cocks on each side (21 or 31 were the most common numbers, but mains of 15, 16, 18, 22, 23, 24, 30, 37 and 41 pair are also recorded) than it was within the capacity of other than a handful of Irish owners to assemble.[55] As a consequence, following the pattern established in England, interested parties in individual counties came together to constitute teams. While the denomination of these aggregations

51 *UA*, 27 Apr. 1754; GEC, *The complete peerage*, i, 176. **52** Johnston-Liik, *History of the Irish parliament*, iv, 126–7; GEC, *The complete peerage*, v, 227; Ida Gantz, *Signpost to Eyrecourt: portrait of the Eyre family* ... (Kingsmead, 1975); *PO*, 9 Apr. 1748; *UA*, 13 Mar. 1756. **53** *Memoirs of Richard Cumberland* (2 vols, London, 1807), pp 280–1; Pearde to Price, 31 Jan. 1744 (NLW, Puleston papers, MS 3579 f. 67). **54** See *UA*, 6 Apr. 1756, 3 May 1757, 21 Mar. 1758, 27 Mar. 1759. **55** *Dublin Courant*, 28 Feb., 28 Mar. 1747; *FDJ*, 29 Mar. 1748; *PO*, 9 Apr. 1748; *Munster Journal*, 11 Mar. 1751; *UA*, 10 Mar., 7, 28 Apr., 19 June 1753, 27 Apr. 1754, 12 Apr., 3, 10, 27 May 1755; *BNL*, 18 Mar., 8 July 1760, 10 Apr., 16 June 1761, 30 Apr., 11 May, 30 July 1762, 19 Apr., 10 May, 5, 15 July 1763, 17, 20, 27 Apr., 11 May, 8 June 1764, 1 Mar., 26 Apr., 21 May 1765.

of individuals as 'county' teams is problematical to say the least, the invocation of county identity was appropriate (and significant) since it drew on a core administrative unit with which the public was already familiar. Moreover, it both anticipated and fostered a geo-spatial allegiance and identity that remains one of the cornerstones of sporting competition to the present.[56] As a result, before the 1750s was over, county teams representing Dublin, Meath, Westmeath, Carlow, Kilkenny, Wicklow, Kildare, Queen's county, Derry, Donegal, Tyrone and Antrim, and in the case of one city, Dublin, were brought into being and cockfighting had emerged for the first time as a truly high-profile sport. It is not apparent who comprised these teams or how they were assembled (since there are no lists of participants with which one might even attempt a prosopographical analysis), but the fact that the Cockpit Royal on Cork Hill was, by some margin, the most popular venue attests both to its importance to the sport as well as to Dublin's dominant position in Leinster.[57] This was by no means total, and one of the revealing indices of the growing popularity of cockfighting, physically manifested by the construction of dedicated cockpits in Kilkenny, Naas and Athy, is provided by the decision to host representative matches in each of these locations.[58] In addition, a number of counties sustained strong intra-county rivalries. In county Wexford, for example, Enniscorthy prevailed over Wexford in 'the great cock match' involving 21 cocks on each side for 10 guineas per battle and 100 guineas the main fought in April 1753.[59] In county Meath, the gentlemen of the baronies of Navan and Kells met for a three-day match in 1755.[60] Outside of Leinster, the only other province where cockfighting was sufficiently organised to produce local and county teams was Ulster. In 1753, 28 of the 31 pair of cocks produced by the gentlemen of the counties of Antrim and Derry gathered at Coleraine in April 1753 'fell in' (or were deemed eligible to compete); while in May 1754 a grand stag[61] match between 'the gentlemen of the counties of Donegal and Tyrone', which was held at Clady, was won comfortably by the former.[62]

Though the extant evidence points to the conclusion that cockfighting emerged as an organised sport in the province of Leinster first, it was soon emulated by Ulster. An important moment was reached at Dromore, county Down in 1760, when representatives of Moira and Dunaghclony on the one side and

---

56 See Brailsford, '*A taste for diversions*', pp 186–7.   57 The known matches at the Cockpit Royal in Cork Hill involved Dublin v Wicklow (*UA*, 11, 20 Apr. 1754, 4 Jan., 19 Apr. 1755, 23 May 1758); Carlow v Wicklow (*UA*, 1 June 1754); Dublin v Kildare (*UA*, 1 Feb., 29 Mar. 1755, 30 Jan. 1756); Kildare v Queen's county and Kilkenny (*UA*, 10, 27 May 1755, 21 Mar. 1758); Wicklow v Kilkenny (*UA*, 27 Mar. 1759, 8 Mar. 1760); Kildare v Meath (*UA*, 22 May 1759); Wicklow v Kildare (*UA*, 29 Dec. 1759, 8 Mar. 1760).   58 County Carlow v Kilkenny city (*UA*, 19, 23 June 1753); Dublin v Naas (*UA*, 12 Apr., 3 May 1753); Kildare v Queen's county and county Kilkenny (*UA*, 10, 27 May 1755).   59 *UA*, 7 Apr. 1753.   60 *UA*, 17 May 1755.   61 Cocks sent to fight as yearlings were known as stags. Usually cocks were not presented to fight until they had reached 2 years, or above (MacGregor, *Animal encounters*, p. 242).   62 *UA*, 28 Apr. 1753, 1 June 1754. The report of the meeting between counties Donegal and Tyrone locates it at Clody, but as no location of that name has been identified in the designated area it is deemed an error for Clady.

Dromore on the other met twice, in April and July, at the local cockpit in mains of 31 battles, which were fought for the modest stakes of 4 guineas the battle and 30 and 40 guineas the main. In the same year at Tandragee, county Armagh, a gathering of local gentlemen and a team from nearby Aston pitted their best cocks against each other over three days in June for two guineas a battle and £40 the main.[63] These were palpably smaller stakes than those ventured by the major cockfighting patrons, which peaked in 1756 at 40 guineas a battle and 500 guineas the main when the earl of Antrim met William Burton.[64] However, they were not inconsistent with the stakes offered in team competition generally, which ranged during the 1750s between one and 10 guineas a battle (with 4 being the most usual amount) and 20 to 100 guineas the main.

Encouraged by the larger numbers of participants,[65] by the commercial imperative of attracting paying customers, by the sums of money at issue, whether staked by the owners or bet by spectators, and by the longer average duration of mains, cockfighting was conducted increasingly according to the received rules of the sport. This was not invariable. The 'shake bag ... match, consisting of seven battles' conducted on George's Quay in Dublin in 1755 between a body of Welsh and Irish gentlemen was evidence of the abiding appeal of the random, but such events were deviations from the increasing regularity that was then in evidence.[66] Five-day mains certainly assisted in this process, as it permitted the timetabling of a 'shew day', which became an integral part of the programme of a well-run main. It provided time for the appointed judges to weigh and pair birds according to size and weight, for gamblers and *cognoscenti* of the cockpit to assess the relative merits of the combatants both in the individual battles and overall main and to offer odds,[67] and, not least, for the owners of cocks to make final preparations for the battles ahead. The pattern in Leinster, as exemplified by the Carlow–Kilkenny match that was held in Kilkenny city in 1753, was to allocate the Monday to the showing of cocks, and to devote the remainder of the week to battles, which, in this instance, averaged a modest four or five a day.[68] In Ulster, by contrast, the preferred show day was the Saturday prior to the week in which fighting was to take place. This meant, inevitably, that those who travelled to be present at a long main incurred the extra expense of diverting themselves on the Sabbath, since cockfights never occurred on Sunday, or (as happened in 1756) on days appointed for a general fast.[69] Moreover, the tendency at some meetings to schedule bye battles (involving unmatched cocks) after the main was complete

63 *BNL*, 18 Mar., 15 Apr., 3 June, 8 July 1760. **64** *UA*, 17 Feb. 1756. **65** See the comment included with the reports of the match between the earl of Antrim and the gentlemen of Derry (*UA*, 27 April 1754). **66** *UA*, 25 June 1755. **67** Brailsford, *A taste for diversions*, pp 184–5. For example the advertised odds in the grand cock match involving the gentlemen of counties Antrim and Derry in April 1753 were three to two on Antrim for day one, and two to one for the main (*UA*, 28 April 1753). **68** *UA*, 19 June 1753. By contrast, nine battles were fought on day one of the grand cock match involving the gentlemen of counties Antrim and Derry in Apr. 1753 (ibid., 28 Apr. 1753), and 8 and 9 at the three-day Easter meeting held at Dromore in April 1760 (*BNL*, 15 Apr. 1760). **69** See Middleton, 'Cockfighting in Yorkshire', pp 144–5; *UA*, 30 Jan. 1756.

ensured that many meetings ran the full duration of the week. This was, to be sure, not the priority of the gentlemen who guided cockfighting, whose object was to attract men of their own station to the cockpit, and 'genteel company' to enjoy the 'diversion' that was increasingly prioritised from the mid-1750s.[70] However, it was potentially a boon to the keepers of local hostelries, who stood to gain most from such assemblies, and some locations were quick to capitalise. One may instance the main held in Kilkenny city in the summer of 1760, which advertised the availability of 'a good ordinary each day', and scheduled 'a grand entertainment' in a local hostelry in the evenings.[71] The provision of such diversions demanded that matches were conducted according to a set schedule, which was increasingly the case. Mains at the Cockpit Royal on Cork Hill, for example, commenced 'precisely at noon' for a time, though this was not sustained. Moreover, the starting time did not mutate according to the seasons and the availability of light, which was the case in parts of England. Like other Irish venues, matches at the Cockpit Royal might commence at twelve noon, twelve thirty, or at one o'clock.[72]

Given the growth of cockfighting, and the eagerness of those who followed the sport closely to take every factor into consideration as they determined on which bird to bet, it became the practice also to alert the public to the name of 'the feeder' employed to prepare cocks in advance of a main. As the title suggests, one of the purposes of the feeder was to ensure that cocks were properly nourished, but they were also tasked with training (usually for nine days) prior to a main. This was a critical responsibility, and some evidently were so skilled in the role that the feeder's name was included on the publicity announcing a match, presumably because it was information that punters deemed relevant. Though the possibility that feeders handled birds in the cockpit cannot be ruled-out, it was more usual for the feeder's role to end with the delivery of the cocks for showing and matching prior to the commencement of the main. It was certainly the practice in England in the early nineteenth century to entrust the management of the weighed and matched birds in the cock-pit to a 'setter-to', who performed the vital function, which might determine the outcome, of setting (or introducing) the cock to battle. Other than their names, little information is available on the backgrounds, attributes, earnings, and impact of feeders, but given the frequency with which some individuals were resorted to it is clear that a small number were in great demand, and were (presumably) remunerated accordingly.[73] The first iden-

70 See *UA*, 27 Apr. 1754, 12 Apr. 1755, for evidence for the prioritisation of the attendance of 'gentlemen' at venues across the country. 71 *UA*, 11 Apr. 1754, 3 May 1757. 72 *UA*, 11 Apr., 2 July 1754, 4 Jan., 1 Feb., 19 Apr., 29 May 1755, 30 Jan., 6 Apr. 1756, 3 May 1757, 21 Mar., 23 May 1758, 27 Mar., 22 May, 29 Dec. 1759, 8 Mar. 1760; George Jobey, 'Cockfighting in Northumberland and Durham during the eighteenth and nineteenth centuries', *Archaeologia Aeliana*, 5th series, 20 (1992), p. 6. 73 MacGregor, *Animal encounters*, pp 242–4; Jobey, 'Cockfighting in Northumberland and Durham', p. 8; H[owlett], *The royal pastime of cockfighting*, passim; Collins et al. (eds), *Encyclopedia of traditional British rural sports*, pp 70, 71; below, p. 194.

tified reference to the engagement of named feeders in Ireland appertains to the long main held at the Cook Street cockpit in 1754, the second to the local meeting between Navan and Kells, which was held at Kells in May 1755, and it is a measure of the esteem in which individual feeders were held by the cockfighting fraternity that before the decade was out their names were published in notices of upcoming mains and, when the feeder was deemed to have played a significant part in the outcome, in accounts of particular victories.[74]

Because so much rested on the outcome, and the large sums that stood to be won or lost as a consequence, it was appropriate that cockfighting (like horse racing) possessed an agreed set of rules. However, unlike horse racing, in which case the Jockey Club might be appealed to as the arbiter of what was appropriate, there was no equivalent body to assume that role in the case of cockfighting.[75] It was, in so far as one can establish, an inherently less structured sport, though it is self-evident that the increasing number of inter-county mains that took place demanded considerable organisation if they were to run smoothly. Of course, cockfighting did not function in isolation, and, no less than hunting, it was not unaffected by the emerging civil society that provided the spur for the burgeoning number of clubs and societies that were a feature of the middle and later eighteenth century.[76]

More specifically, the appreciating order detectible in the manner in which cockfighting was conducted was both accented and influenced by the close relationship it enjoyed with horse racing. This was not a new or unheralded juncture. It can be traced in England to the royal cockpit frequented by Charles II at Newmarket; it was commonplace at Newmarket also to hold cockfights 'in conjunction with horse racing' by the mid-eighteenth century, and the practice was encouraged, Dennis Brailsford has pointed out, by 'the development of inter-county competition'.[77] These were not the only influences at play in Ireland. The decision of the organizers of racing at Kilfinane (county Limerick) in 1740 and Carlow in 1741 to include 'a match of cock fighting' as part of the programme of racing held in the third week of September was prompted in the first instance by the wish to provide some entertainment during the mid-week break that was a feature of many race meetings. This additional entertainment was targeted at men. The women present were promised 'balls and plays every night'.[78] Cockfighting was, of course, but one of a number of 'diversions' offered at race meetings to distract and to divert spectators. Buck-hunting and fox-hunting also featured prominently.[79] For example, attendees at Longwood races, county Meath, in 1743 were promised 'fox hunting and several matches of cockfighting'.

---

74 *UA*, 11 Apr. 1754, 17 May 1755; more generally see Jobey, 'Cockfighting in Northumberland and Durham', p. 8.   75 James Kelly, 'The pastime of the elite: clubs and societies and the promotion of horse racing', pp 417–20.   76 See James Kelly and Martyn J. Powell, 'Introduction' in idem (eds), *Clubs and societies in eighteenth-century Ireland*, pp 28–30.   77 Middleton, 'Cockfighting in Yorkshire', pp 142–3; Ewald, *The newsmen of Queen Anne*, p. 165; Brailsford, *A taste for diversions*, p. 22.   78 *FDJ*, 15 July 1740; *PO*, 5 Sept. 1741.   79 See above, pp 137–9.

At Baltinglass in 1757 'hunting and cockfighting in the morning and balls at night' were promised over six days to those who attending the race meeting at that location. Variety doubtlessly had its attractions, but cockfighting was especially appealing to those drawn to the turf, and it was the only diversion offered at Ratoath, county Meath, Ballymacash, county Antrim, and at Antrim races in 1755 when it was credited with drawing a 'greater' number of gentlemen to the venue than was previously the case.[80] Horse racing was also quick to capitalise on the emergence of inter-county cockfighting, which was not long established on the sporting landscape when Mullingar offered those who were drawn by the prospect of competitive racing the diversion of a cockfight involving the gentlemen of King's county and the gentlemen of Westmeath. The better-established meeting at Trim went one better; it provided spectators with an opportunity from the late 1750s to watch the gentlemen of county Meath take on a team from a different county every year in a match extending over four of the meeting's five days.[81] By then cockfighting had become a standard feature of certain race meetings, as the organisers of Navan races made known when they pronounced in April 1760 that the annual race meeting would include 'cockfighting as usual'.[82]

The increasing closeness of cockfighting and horse racing evident on Ireland's racecourses in the 1750s was acknowledged by Reginald Heber, on his assumption of the editorship of the *Racing Calendar* following the death in 1750 of John Cheney. Heber's decision to include Irish race meetings in the *Calendar* was well judged given the increasing popularity of horse racing in Ireland,[83] but he also did cockfighting a considerable service by making the 'Rules and orders for cocking', which Cheney had previously published in 1743 for his English target-audience, available in Ireland.[84] The rules contained in the landmark 1751 edition of the publication, which served as the standard guide for several generations, had evolved over time and did not (in so far as it is possible to tell) prompt any significant alteration in the manner in which cockfights were conducted at the elite level of the sport in Ireland. However, their availability was of further assistance in regularising the sport and in promoting a diversion that had, in the space of a few decades, taken firm root on the sporting landscape.

THE GROWTH OF THE SPORT IN ULSTER IN THE 1760s AND 1770s

With a recognised code of rules governing showing, fighting, betting and deportment in the cockpit, a growing network of venues, an expanding lattice of com-

80 *Dublin Newsletter*, 15 Oct. 1743; *UA*, 17 June 1755, 12 June 1757; *Dublin Courant*, 10 Sept. 1751; *BNL*, 28 May 1756; George Benn, *History of Belfast* (Belfast, 1877), p. 491. 81 *UA*, 27 June 1758, 2 June 1759, 12 Apr., 19 July 1760; *PO*, 14 May 1753. 82 *Public Gazetteer*, 15 Apr. 1760. 83 See above, p. 66. 84 Heber, *An historical list of horse-matches, and of plates and prizes run for in Great Britain and Ireland, 1751*, pp 149–53; Middleton, 'Cockfighting in Yorkshire', p. 133; Brailsford, *A taste for diversions*, pp 21–2. The rules are also printed in Gilbey, *Sport in the olden time*, pp 104–7.

	DUBLIN	LEINSTER	MUNSTER	ULSTER	CONNACHT	TOTAL
			Table 6: Cockfighting: reported mains, 1761–80			
1761		1		2		3
1762				6		6
1763	1			9		10
1764		1		9		10
1765				11		11
1766				6	1	7
1767	2	1	1	13		17
1768	2			5		7
1769				5		5
1770	1			4		5
1771	2	3		3		8
1772		2		3		5
1773	3	4	3	2		12
1774	2	3		2		7
1775	4	2		2		8
1776	1	3		1		5
1777		1		6		7
1778	1	2		4		7
1779		1	1	7		9
1780	1			3		4
Total	20	24	5	103	1	153

Source: *Belfast News Letter*, 1762–80; *Public Gazetteer*, 1761–8; *Dublin Gazette*, 1763; *Dublin Chronicle*, 1770; *Hoey's Publick Journal*, 1771–3; *Finn's Leinster Journal*, 1767–80; *Freeman's Journal*, 1767–80; *Hibernian Journal*, 1772–80; *Faulkner's Dublin Journal*, 1778

mitted and enthusiastic owners, an increasing number of eager followers and the financial incentive provided by gambling, cockfighting was well positioned to continue to grow when George III ascended the throne in 1760. Because the press is the primary source of information on the sport, and the information that can be extracted from that quarter is unforthcoming on the personalities that organised and promoted cockfighting regionally and nationally, the picture that can be constructed is incomplete, but certain trends seem clear. The most striking is the rapid growth that took place in the sport in Ulster.

Though the scheduling in the 1750s of representative matches involving Ulster counties indicates that cockfighting was already an established feature of the social landscape of the province by that point, the sport grew at an unprecedented pace in the 1760s (Table 6). The most obvious index of this growth is the

number of venues that advertised meetings. Following the example set by
Dromore, which hosted matches between local teams (Banbridge, Donaghcloney
and Dromore) in the county, the venue took a major step forward when in April
1762 it hosted the first recorded representative match between the gentlemen of
counties Antrim and Down.[85] While there is no evidence confirming that the
'great fighting' that was promised ensued, the example of Dromore encouraged
other towns to do likewise, and over the following three years mains were held
at Banbridge, Hillsborough (2), Strangford and Waringstown in county Down;
Acton, Lurgan, Newry (3) and Portadown (2) in county Armagh; Antrim,
Ballinderry, Belfast (2), Ballyclare, Carrickfergus (4) and Randalstown (2) in
county Antrim; and Benburb, Coagh and Stewartstown (2) in county Tyrone
(3).[86] Some 55 per cent of these meetings were of an inter-county character; the
rest involved local teams or were open invitations, but when set alongside the
cockfighting provided annually at Ballymoney and Broughshane races,[87] it is clear
that the enthusiasm for the sport manifest in east and mid-Ulster in the early
1760s exceeded that previously only identifiable in Dublin and parts of Leinster.
Moreover, it appreciated further in the decade-and-a-half that followed, as in
addition to those places that hosted matches between 1762 and 1765, which continued active in the sport (Dromore, Banbridge, Portadown (3), Belfast,
Stewartstown (2), Lurgan, Hillsborough (2), Carrickfergus (2), Newry (5) and
Antrim), mains were conducted between 1766 and 1780 at Bellaghy (2),
Dungiven and Moneymore (2) in county Londonderry; Connor, Crebilly, Larne
and Toome (2) in county Antrim; Ardmillen, Guilford (3), Downpatrick (5),
Killinchy, Moira and Killileagh (3) and Saintfield in county Down; Monaghan
(2), county Monaghan; Charlemont and Jonesborough Fair in county Armagh;
Moy and Strabane (2) in county Tyrone; Glasslough, county Monaghan; and
Lifford, county Donegal.[88]

In addition, cockfighting and horse racing consolidated their already close
bond. Ballymoney races continued to feature cockfighting 'on the morning of
each day's' meeting through the 1760s,[89] and when this meeting was discontinued in the early 1770s, the decision of the organisers of Londonderry races,
which filled the vacant space in the racing calendar, to feature 'a main of cocks'
during its racing week, attested to the continuing appeal of cockfighting to racegoers and to gamblers in the region.[90] The closeness of the link was highlighted
by the decision to host a joint 'horse racing and cockfighting' meet at Killileagh
in April 1779,[91] which featured 'a main of 21 cocks ... to be fought between the

85 *BNL*, 10 Apr., 16 June 1761, 6 Apr. 1762.   86 *BNL*, 1762–5 passim.   87 For evidence of cockfighting at Ballymoney races during the early 1760s, see *BNL*, 16 July 1762, 30 June 1763, 29 June
1764, 21 June 1765, and for Broughshane, op. cit. 23 Sept. 1763.   88 *BNL*, 1766–80 passim.   89
BNL, 28 Feb., 1 July 1766, 10 July 1767, 28 June 1768, 16 May 1769.   90 *BNL*, 30 May, 2 June
1775, 13 Apr., 1 June 1779, 5, 9 June 1780; T.H. Mullin, *Ulster's historic city: Derry/ Londonderry*
(Coleraine, 1986), p. 67.   91 *BNL*, 2, 13 Apr. 1779; 'Local historic scraps', *Ulster Journal of
Archaeology*, 2nd series, 14 (1908), p. 135.

county of Down and county Antrim for four guineas each and sixty the main'. But the clearest indication of the reputation of the sport at that point was provided by the fact that the Maze races, organised by the oldest horse club in the kingdom, the Corporation of Horse Breeders in the County of Down, facilitated a long main of 31 cocks between the gentlemen of counties Armagh and Antrim in 1779 on the morning of each race day, and that this was continued, albeit in a somewhat pared back fashion there, and at Killileagh, into the early 1780s.[92]

Though the intermittent nature of the data with which one has to work, vitiates any attempt to construct a secure geo-temporal interpretation of cockfighting in Ulster in the second half of the eighteenth century, the advertising engaged in by the organisers of inter-county meetings suggests not only that the number of cockfights in the province increased during the 1760s and 1770s but also that the sport spread west and southwards from its original heartland in counties Antrim and Down. This process was assisted in no small way by the improvement in facilities, by the insistence on a code of personal behaviour in the cockpit, and by the adoption, and implementation, of 'rules for cocking' that ensured the sport was conducted in an increasingly orderly fashion.

The provision of dedicated cockpits was obviously crucial to the growth of the sport. Based on the number of references to the existence of a pit in the notices alerting the public to an upcoming main, it seems that a network of some twenty pits was put in place in Ulster in little over a decade spanning the 1760s.[93] It may be that the pits resorted to outside the larger urban centres were makeshift, temporary venues. The facilities available at Dromore, Newry, Portadown, Hillsborough, Downpatrick, Coagh and Toome were more enduring, and commodious. Moreover, this was increasingly the expectation, and it was an expectation organisers with access to good facilities did not hesitate to make known they could meet. As a result, notices and advertisements carrying the information that 'there will be a good pay pit', 'a very good pit', or simply 'a regular pit', 'a good regular pit with all good accommodation for gentlemen' featured commonly during the 1760s.[94] Some locations were still more forthcoming. The organizers of a main at Stewartstown, county Tyrone, between the gentlemen of county Armagh and county Antrim in April 1764, made it known that their pit possessed seating for the comfort of those who attended.[95] Determined to alert the public to the superior quality of their facilities, the organisers of the match between the gentlemen of counties Antrim and Down at Ballinderry,

---

92 *BNL*, 29 June 1779, 10 July, 3 Aug. 1781, 22 July 1783. **93** Dedicated pits existed at the following locations by the date indicated: Dromore (10 Apr. 1761); Randalstown (30 Apr. 1762); Portadown (11 May 1762); Ballyclare (18 Feb. 1763); Belfast (5 Apr. 1763); Stewartstown (19 Apr. 1763); Hillsborough (15 July 1763); Strangford (13 Apr. 1764); Newry (11 May 1764); Ballinderry (8 June 1764); Cookstown (12 Feb. 1765); Antrim (21 May 1765); Moneymore (7 May 1766); Toome (18 May 1766); Guilford (25 Mar. 1768); Downpatrick (1 July 1766); Connor (19 Feb. 1773); Dungiven (10 May 1774). All references are from the *BNL*, by the date given. **94** *BNL*, 30 Apr. 1762, 11 May 1762, 11, 18 Feb., 10 Apr., 17 July 1763, 13 Apr. 1764, 7 Mar., 3 June 1766, 14 Apr. 1769, 24 July 1770. **95** *BNL*, 27 Apr. 1764.

county Antrim, later the same year announced that 'there will be a very good stone and lime wall about the pit, and regularly seated', while the pit at Coagh (near Cookstown), county Tyrone, was described as 'inferior to none in the north'; that at Hillsborough as 'well enclosed [and] fit to accommodate gentlemen during the time of the battles', and that at Toome, county Antrim, as simply 'well enclosed'.[96]

As the standard of the facilities improved, and purpose-built cockpits became commonplace, the focus of organisers shifted from the cockpit to general amenities on the reasonable assumption that this would assist them to attract the respectable audience to which all venues aspired. In this context, it was no longer sufficient to promise 'a pay pit with every other good accommodation for gentlemen'; the more ambitious cockpit owners reached out to potential attendees, and their families, with the promises of entertainment and services.[97] The quality of what was offered varied greatly. The organisers at Portadown scheduled 'a ball for the ladies' on the evening of the second of three fighting days in May 1762.[98] At Acton, county Armagh, in July 1765, patrons were promised 'an assembly, conducted in the grandest manner at the Newmarket House in Newry every evening' for the consideration of one shilling per person during the extra long main of 41 cocks scheduled for that venue,[99] while it became commonplace from the mid-1760s, following the example previously set in Leinster, to provide each day 'a genteel ordinary', 'a grand ordinary' or 'grand ordinaries', sometimes, but not always, at an advertised location.[100] Portadown set the highest standards in this respect. In 1768, it promised 'a good ordinary each day, and an assembly for the ladies on Tuesday and Thursday, with different diversions every morning of foot racing, dancing for shifts, grinning for tobacco etc.'[101] Recognising that the onus was on them to entertain visitors, other locations followed suit. The long main held at Stewartstown in May 1770 included a ball at the market house for which tickets could be purchased. Bellaghy, county Derry, went one better in 1771; it promised 'a ball each night for the ladies', which became a standard feature at a number of locations.[102] Meanwhile, in an acknowledgement of a recurring problem, and one that could be particularly acute in rural locations, patrons attending the main held at Glasslough, county Monaghan, in 1771 could avail of lodgings 'for a guinea each bed', 'a good ordinary each day, and publick breakfast at the house of James Brenan, publican'. Those attending a main at Charlemont, county Armagh, in 1773, were assured that 'good accommodation' was available, though no indication was given of its cost or location.[103] A number of venues went still further. Gentlemen attending the main at Tullhog, county Tyrone, were promised 'good accommodation, ordinaries will be prepared, and grass for horses on very moderate terms'.[104]

96 *BNL*, 8 June 1764, 12 Feb., 4 July 1765, 18 Mar. 1766. 97 *BNL*, 30 Apr. 1762. 98 *BNL*, 11 May 1762. 99 *BNL*, 2, 5 July 1765. 100 *BNL*, 2, 5 July 1765, 18, 25 Mar., 3 June 1766, 12 June 1770, 18 Apr. 1775. 101 *BNL*, 21 June 1768. 102 *BNL*, 27 Apr. 1770, 10, 14 May 1771, 14 Feb., 10, 14 Apr. 1772. 103 *BNL*, 10 May 1771, 16 July 1773; *FJ*, 16 May 1771. 104 *BNL*, 28

Such announcements were targeted directly at gentlemen. Based on the statement attached to the advertisement in 1779 of a main at Moy, county Tyrone, involving the gentlemen of Tyrone and Armagh, which pronounced that 'there is no other parties to be concerned but the gentlemen of the above named counties', it may be suggested that the aspiration to exclusivity was achieved at certain locations.[105] However, it is also manifest that cockfighting was not a socially exclusive sport, and that the organizers of most mains had no difficulty with this reality. For those of the public for whom assemblies, balls and expensive ordinaries in local taverns held little appeal, or were above their income level, other provision was made. It is not apparent if an appropriate range of foodstuffs could be purchased at the 'tents, booths and stands' that were a familiar presence at certain venues, but alcohol certainly was, and organisers sought both to regulate this activity and to profit from it either by reserving the entitlement to local providers, or by insisting that those who operated a tent, booth or stand paid for the privilege. The fee ordained at Toome in 1766 was 6s. 6½d., rising to 8s. 3d. in 1767. The organisers at Ballymena demanded a similar sum (8s. 1½d.), also in 1767, but as the appeal of cockfighting grew the price rose, and the tariff of half a guinea set at Portadown in 1768 was the standard charge in the 1770s.[106]

This was a realistic fee, and it provides some indication not only of the potential benefit to a local economy of a well-attended cockfight, but also of the profit that could be made by the canny owner of a cockpit and of a nearby inn or tavern. Cockpit owners were the primary beneficiary of the entrance fee charged for admission to the pit, and the fact that a fee was levied was indicative of the secure financial grounds upon which the sport stood during the 1770s. The charge levied on those seeking admission to a cockpit averaged more than 2s. during the mid-1770s; subsequently, it fell back to the modest figure, by comparison, of 1s. 1d. in the later years of the decade.[107]

These were not minor sums even for gentlemen, but they served the useful function of excluding the more rambunctious social elements from the cockpit, which contributed in turn to mitigate the likelihood of disorder or disruption. Based upon the frequency with which warnings were issued on this very subject in the 1760s, this was then a matter of some concern. Indicatively, the organizers of a main at Belfast in April 1763 warned specifically that 'no drunken riotous person [would] be admitted into the pit', and that those who did 'misbehave in the time of fighting will be hoist in the creel' over the pit, which was the ultimate sanction generally reserved for those who were guilty of the most grievous offence one could commit in the cockpit – the failure to one pay one's debts on demand.[108] Stern though this sanction was, bad behaviour could not simply be sanctioned out of existence, but it is a measure of the skill with which the owners

May 1776. **105** *BNL*, 1 June 1779. **106** *BNL*, 18, 25 Mar. 1766, 15 May, 23 June 1767, 21 June 1768, 28 May 1776. **107** *BNL*, 18 Apr. 1775, 2, 20 May 1777, 15 May, 7 July 1777. **108** *BNL*, 5 Apr. 1763. For an artist's impression of what it meant to be hoist in the creel see William Hogarth's famous image of the Cockpit Royal, 1758, printed in Hogarth's works.

of pits judged their clientele that they contrived successfully to exclude most of those who might be 'disorderly', and to focus their energies on the regulation of the behaviour of those who were admitted, which could be problematical on occasion.[109] With the redress of this problem in mind, the owners of the Newry Cockpit ordained in 1764 that 'no body [would] be admitted to the pit with either a whip or staff'.[110] The organisers of the main at Ballinderry, county Antrim, in June the same year extended this prohibition to include 'gentlemen' in an attempt to make it explicitly clear to all that 'good order is expected in every particular'.[111] These directives appear to have had the requisite impact as equivalent instructions were seldom issued after 1765,[112] and main's organisers were content to pronounce that in the event 'all disputes are to be determined by judges', who, it was broadly accepted, were crucial to the success of the sport.[113]

The primary function of judges was to adjudicate 'all disputes about bets',[114] but the realisation that they were integral to a properly conducted main was crucial to the credibility of the sport and, by extension, to its survival because, as with horse racing, money generated by gambling and distributed in the form of prize money was essential if it was to continue to function. Significantly, though long mains of 31 cocks were normative in Ulster during the 1760s and 1770s,[115] the sums at issue were not only more moderate than the sums available at equivalent representative mains in Leinster, but also smaller than those wagered when individual cockers competed. Most battles were fought in Ulster for sums of the order of 2, 4, 5 and 6 guineas; 4 and 5 guineas per battle were the favoured amounts, and only a small number were fought for the larger sums of 6, 8 and 10 guineas. Mains, or odd battles, were generally fought for sums in proportion; 40 or 50 guineas was the standard sum, but this could range, depending on whether the contest involved local or inter-county teams, between 20 and 100 guineas, and, on occasion, might achieve levels considerably in excess of the latter sum. For example, the main advertised for Guilford, county Down, in March 1766 between the gentlemen of county Down and county Armagh was scheduled to be fought 'for 5 guineas a battle and 400 guineas' the main; that at Lifford, county Donegal, between teams representing county Fermanagh and county Donegal in 1774 promised 'ten guineas a battle and 500 guineas the main'. The most valuable of all, which was fought at Acton, in county Armagh in July 1765, was 'for 20 guineas each battle and one thousand guineas the main'.[116]

---

109 *BNL*, 19 Apr., 10 May 1763.   110 *BNL*, 11 May 1764.   111 *BNL*, 8 June 1764.   112 *BNL*, 12 Feb. 1765.   113 *BNL*, 5, 19 Apr. 1763, 27 Apr. 1770, 19 Feb. 1773, 13 Mar. 1778.   114 *BNL*, 5 Apr. 1763.   115 Mains of 21 cocks were not unusual; there were occasional short mains of 9, 11, 13 and 15 cocks (*BNL*, 18 Feb. 1763, 13, 20 Apr. 1764, 15 June 1764, 21 May 1765) and extra long mains of 41 cocks and stags (Tyrone v Londonderry, *BNL*, 28 May 1776), of 21 cocks and 21 stags (Monaghan v Dungiven at Dungiven in May 1774, and Killileagh v Lecale, Mar. 1780 (*BNL*, 10 May 1774, 17 Mar. 1780)), and even 31 stags and 21 cocks (Killinchy v Saintfield at Ardmillen (*BNL*, 7 July, 1778)). They constituted a small proportion of the advertised total, and they generally involved local rather than county teams.   116 *BNL*, 2, 5 July 1765, 25 Mar. 1766; *FLJ*, 19 Mar. 1774.

Though not unusual by English standards,[117] or even by the standards of the sums on offer in Ireland in the early nineteenth century,[118] this was the largest recorded prize offered at a main in Ulster in the eighteenth century. It is difficult, for that reason, to interpret its significance. It is notable that it was not an inter-county representative event. Yet, it does not diminish the impression provided by the proliferation of locations at which cockfighting was conducted, and the ordinariness of the sums generally on offer as prize-money, that cockfighting was less socially exclusive in Ulster than was the case elsewhere in the country. There are no hard data with which to demonstrate this, but it is consistent with Edward Wakefield's later observation that in Ulster's religiously cleaved society, cockfighting (along with horse racing, bull-baiting and long bullets) was one of the 'favourite amusements' of the 'class sprung from English progenitors ... and the descendants of the Scotch [*sic*]'.[119] It is also notable in this context that though eight of the province's nine counties (Cavan is the sole exception) fielded representative teams, the number of inter-county mains in which these counties participated in the years 1761–80 indicate that the sport was most deeply rooted in counties Down (24), Armagh (24), Tyrone (21) and Antrim (14). By comparison, counties Londonderry (8), Monaghan (6), Donegal (5) and Fermanagh (2) were less visible on the expanding inter-county circuit, presumably because they had a smaller number of fighting cocks and cockers to draw upon, although they achieved greater visibility over time. This was consistent with the movement of the heartland of cockfighting during the same time period westwards towards the centre of the province, for though the comparability of the figures for the years 1781–92 might suggest an enduring commitment to cockfighting in east Ulster, it is significant that the number of inter-county mains in which Down (16), and Antrim (20) featured was exceeded then by Armagh (24), Tyrone (26), and Londonderry (18). Even county Fermanagh (9) registered a firm presence, which left only counties Monaghan (3), Donegal (2) and Cavan (0) in their traditional place as outliers.[120]

The maintenance of a strong inter-country competitive dimension was crucial to the wellbeing of cockfighting as a sport in Ulster in the second half of the eighteenth century. The fact that 'the gentlemen of county Tyrone' were required to pay a 'forfeit' when they were unable to fulfil their undertaking to meet the gentlemen of Monaghan on 6 May 1767 is evidence that this sanction was not only acknowledged as a useful means of ensuring teams took their com-

---

117 The largest prize recorded in north-east England was 1,000 guineas a battle and 5,000 guineas the main in 1830. This was exceptional, but the normal monetary prizes on offer of 10 to 20 guineas the battle and 500 guineas the main or odd battle was still above the Irish level: Jobey, 'Cockfighting in Northumberland and Durham', pp 15–16. By contrast, the more modest sums proffered in Devonshire compare favourably with those available in Ulster: see J.H. Porter, 'Cockfighting in the eighteenth and nineteenth centuries: from popularity to suppression', *Reported Transactions of the Devonshire Association for the Advancement of Science*, 118 (1986), pp 66–7. 118 Below, p. 202. 119 Edward Wakefield, *An account of Ireland, statistical and political* (2 vols, London, 1812), p. 738. 120 *BNL*, 1760–92 passim; see Table 6.

mitments seriously but also that the rules had teeth.[121] Significantly, it existed side by side with an only slightly less visible tradition of local cockfighting based on barony, town and parish, much of which was also centred on the expanding network of cockpits among which Dromore, Newry and Downpatrick were particularly notable. Indeed, Dromore played host to successive mains involving local teams from north and mid county Down, including Moira, Magharalin, Donaghcloney, Dromore and Banbridge. Newry and Banbridge appealed to the gentlemen of Donaghcloney, Rathfriland, Loughbrickland, Banbridge and Newry.[122] Downpatrick was for a long time the preferred location of the gentlemen of Kinalarty and Lecale, who committed in 1766 to an annual main for seven years, and to groups from Downpatrick, Killinchy, Killileagh and Castlereagh.[123] Other venues to host local mains include Antrim, Belfast, Larne and Crebilly (county Antrim), Killinchy, Killileagh and Strangford (county Down) and Dungiven (county Londonderry).[124] But perhaps the outstanding example of a local meeting that mirrored the enthusiasm for cockfighting that was a feature of Ulster society between 1760 and 1790, and its percolation into the core of Ulster society, was Carrickfergus fair. Eager to present a welcoming attitude, and to foster a reputation for fairness, the organisers made it publicly known in 1763 and 1764 not only that they would not countenance the 'breaking of pits', 'disorder' in the cockpit, or the admission of any individual 'into the cockpit with either whip, spurs or stick', but also that 'any strangers that bring cocks may depend on having the height of justice doing them'. It was a successful formula, as the combination of cockfighting involving a local team or teams in the morning, horse racing in the evening, and an array of small prizes contributed to the fair's popularity, and epitomised the popular base upon which the appeal of cockfighting in Ulster was grounded.[125]

THE LIMITS OF COCKFIGHTING REVEALED: THE 1760s AND 1770s IN LEINSTER AND MUNSTER

Though the sport of cockfighting was international, a fact exemplified by the adoption in Ireland of a set of rules that took their origin in England, there are many reasons why the sport was pursued in a manner that reflected the regional, indeed local disposition, of its practitioners. The difficulty of transporting cocks significant distances was an obvious, and important, consideration,[126] but it was

---

121 *BNL*, 8 May 1767. **122** Above, pp 170–1; *BNL*, 10 Apr., 16 June 1761, 23 Mar. 1762, 1 Mar., 24 Apr. 1765, 27, 31 Mar. 1767. **123** *BNL*, 1 July 1766, 8 May 1767, 14 Apr. 1769, 10 Apr., 24 July 1770, 28 May 1779. **124** *BNL*, 5 Apr. 1763, 13, 30 Apr. 1764, 23 June 1767, 12 June 1770, 10 May 1774, 18 Apr. 1775, 13 Mar. 1778, 28 May 1779, 17 Mar. 1780. **125** *BNL*, 24 Apr., 12 June 1764, 26 Apr., 14 May 1765, 31 May 1768, 21 June 1771. **126** Cocks were transported from place to place in bags, which, while tolerable for a short period, was not conducive to their well-being when the journey was long: see Gilbey, *Sport in the olden time*, p. 33; Jobey, 'Cockfighting in Northumberland and Durham', p. 12.

less consequential in the Irish context than the inherent regionality of the sport. The clearest evidence for this is provided by the fact that while local (barony and town) teams generally confined their movements to the county in which they were located, inter-county competition was fundamentally province-based. It is striking, the rare inter-provincial mains apart, that there was only one inter-county main between an Ulster and Leinster county in the 1750s, and that (involving counties Armagh and Meath) took place in 1758 in the atypical environment (for an inter-county match) of Trim races.[127] The staging in Belfast five years later of a main between the gentlemen of county Down and county Louth involving 11 cocks and 11 stags on each side, and, in Monaghan town in 1768, of a long main of 31 pair of cocks between the gentlemen of Louth and Monaghan could be interpreted as evidence of the readiness of the champions of cockfighting in Ulster to embrace county Louth within the Ulster sphere, but that would be to accord these matches too much significance as they were rare and isolated events.[128] The introspective focus of the sport persisted, with the result that instead of evolving in a manner that might have fostered the generation of a national organisation whose jurisdiction was island-wide, cockfighting remained fundamentally regional, even local in outlook, and it failed to pupate into a definably national sport in the manner of horse racing. The most salient early indicator of this is provided by the reinvigoration in the 1770s of the phenomenon of the individual cocker, which was essentially regressive, and which contributed over time to the sport's marginalisation. These trends were first manifest in the weakening presence of the sport in the main urban centres of Dublin and Cork. Evidence on the conduct of the sport in Cork is elusive, but the fact that the cockpit in the city was used as a public lecture room in 1769 suggests that it was no longer a centre of sports activity.[129] There is more evidence with which to attempt to construct the history of the sport in Dublin, where its declining fortunes were a prelude to a slower, inexorable, contraction in the province of Leinster.

On the face of it, cockfighting in Leinster in the early 1760s was in a strong position, and well placed to build on the impressive growth it had registered in the course of the previous decade. Indeed, following the example set by the Jockey Club, it seemed that the gentlemen who congregated at the Cockpit Royal harboured ambitions to evolve into the governing body of the sport when, in 1766, they responded to the problem of cock theft with the offer of a reward for the conviction of those responsible:

> At a meeting of several gentlemen in the Cockpit Royal, Dublin, it was unanimously agreed, and a subscription entered into for that purpose, to prosecute any person or persons who shall be detected in stealing any game cock or hen, the property of any person, and that any such person

---

127 *UA*, 27 June 1758.   **128** *BNL*, 15 June 1764, 16 Feb. 1768.   **129** 'Dr Caulfield's notes on Cork events in 1769 and 1781', *Journal of the Cork Archaeological and Historical Society*, 11 (1905), p. 146.

convicted shall on its occurrence entitle the person prosecuting to a reward
of £5 over and above any expenses they might incur in pursuing and
prosecuting. The money to be paid by Richard Robbins esq., Anglesea St.
Dublin.[130]

However, this intervention was unique. Instead of embarking on an era of organisational, infrastructural and participatory expansion, with the Cockpit Royal as
its headquarters and Dublin as its centre, the sport embarked on an era of stag-
nation in the capital. The growth that followed was regional, with the result that
rather than evolving into a recreational activity with a truly national presence,
older, regional patterns of competition persisted. These left the sport vulnerable
to the accusation, then rarely heard but identifiably present, that cockfighting was
intrinsically barbarous and behaviourally uncouth, and that it should actively be
discouraged.

One of the significant setbacks that cockfighting experienced in the 1760s was
caused by the re-location in 1763 of the Cockpit Royal, which moved from Cork
Hill to Essex Street. It is not clear precisely what prompted this, but because it
coincided with the extensive acquisition by the Wide Streets Commissioners of
property in the area, street redevelopment may well have been the key factor.[131]
On the face of it, a move of approximately a hundred metres was not of major
consequence. The Cockpit Royal announced its reopening in the ultra-respectable
Dublin Gazette in May 1763 with 'a grand stag match' for ten guineas a battle
and 100 guineas the main, or odd battle' between Richard Robbins and Benjamin
Burton, two acknowledged champions of the sport.[132] Moreover, the cockpit continued to host mains through the 1770s and early 1780s (and thereafter), but it
did not occupy the dominant place in the sport possessed by its Cork Hill pred-
ecessor.[133] The evidence for this is tantalising but it is implicit in the increased
disinclination to mention the venue when the results of inter-county mains were
reported in the press.[134] Furthermore, the generally undistinguished character of
the mains that were publicised as taking place at the Cockpit Royal indicates not
only that the glory days of the 1750s were no more but also that interest in cockfighting in the capital was in decline. The Dublin that prioritised wide streets,
improvement and respectable associative culture was not hostile in principle to
blood sports, but it perceived cockfighting and the behaviour it promoted with
mounting unease. Most cockers may have concluded when the move was mooted
that relocation to Essex Street was merely a minor inconvenience, but in practice

130 *BNL*, 7, 18 Mar. 1766. The theft of cocks was not unique to Ireland. It was also a problem in
north-east England, where it prompted notices of reward: Jobey, 'Cockfighting in Northumberland
and Durham', p. 12.   131 Gilbert, *History of Dublin*, ii, 21–2; Edward McParland, 'The Wide
Streets Commissioners: their importance for Dublin architecture in the late eighteenth-early nineteenth century', *Bulletin of the Irish Georgian Society*, 15:1 (1972), pp 1–32.   132 *Dublin Gazette*, 3
May 1763.   133 *FDJ*, 14 May 1778; *Saunders Newsletter*, 3 Feb. 1786.   134 *FLJ*, 17 Feb., 14 May
1768, 6 Apr. 1776; *Public Gazetteer*, 16 Feb. 1768; *Dublin Chronicle*, 20 Feb. 1770; *Hibernian
Journal*, 15 June 1774, 21 June 1780; *FJ*, 22 Feb. 1770, 16 June 1774, 15 Apr. 1777.

it mirrored the attitudinal marginalisation of cockfighting (and other blood sports) already underway in the capital since it served to remove the primary cockpit in the kingdom from its prominent location close to Dublin Castle and the hustle and bustle of one of the city's main thoroughfares to a lesser, albeit still central, street where it was palpably less visible.

Outside of the capital, the continuing prominence of cockfighting is consistent with the conclusion that provincial opinion was less attitudinally ambivalent towards the sport. It is not possible fully to construct a comprehensive geospatial picture, but accounts of 'great cock matches', 'grand cock matches' and 'great mains' suggest that the commitment to cockfighting manifest in provincial Ulster was replicated, albeit with lesser intensity, across much of provincial Leinster, parts of provincial Munster, and in a handful of locations in Connaught during the 1760s and early 1770s. Based on identified inter-county encounters, it is demonstrable that there was sufficient interest in cockfighting in Meath (9), Carlow (5), Kildare (4), Wicklow (4), Queen's county (3), King's county (2), Dublin (2), Wexford (2), Kilkenny (2), Westmeath (1) and Louth (1) to permit the assembly of county teams, but, by comparison with Ulster, where inter-county mains were commonplace, the number of recorded matches, signalled above in brackets, involving Leinster counties was modest (Table 6). Indeed, counties Westmeath[135] and Louth featured in only one match. This notwithstanding, it cannot be assumed that interest in cockfighting in county Louth went into rapid decline following the last identifiable appearance of a county team in 1768,[136] as there was sufficient interest in the sport in Drogheda to justify the construction in Pillory Street of a 'new cockpit' in 1773, when a town team lost 10:8 to county Monaghan. The following April, Drogheda lost again, by 17 battles to 13, in a long main to a team from county Meath,[137] and though it lost once more in July 1776, the consensus on this occasion was that this was a particularly exciting encounter:

> There was lately fought in Drogheda, a most extraordinary main of cocks, between the gentlemen of the county of Meath and the town of Drogheda, there was forty-five cocks shown of each side for the main, thirty-nine of which fell in, twenty of which were won by Meath, and nineteen by Drogheda; three bye battles were also made, in order to make seven battles every day during the week, two of which were won by Meath. There was excellent fighting during the week, and very closely fought; the cocks were in good condition on both sides. John Johnson feeder for Meath; John Oldred for Drogheda.[138]

---

135 Significantly, Athlone had a cockpit in 1780: Harman Murtagh, *Athlone* in *Irish historic town atlas, volume I: Kildare, Carrickfergus, Bandon, Kells, Mullingar, Athlone* (Dublin, 1996), section no. 21. 136 Above, p. 183; *BNL*, 16 Feb. 1768. 137 *Hibernian Journal*, 11 June 1773, 13 Apr. 1774. 138 *FLJ*, 10 July 1776.

As the Leinster county with the strongest cockfighting profile, the readiness of the gentlemen of county Meath to field a team against Drogheda, and the closeness of the ensuing contests, offers a salutary caution against assuming that the failure of a county regularly to engage in inter-county mains is an entirely reliable guide to the strength of cockfighting in that geographical area, but it does allow some comparisons to be drawn. Moreover, it sustains the conclusion that by the 1770s the sport was weak in county Westmeath,[139] in decline in county Dublin,[140] and that it was heavily reliant elsewhere in the province on a far from dependable combination of enthusiasts and those with a passing interest. It is not possible even to estimate their number, but it was large enough, and it could count on sufficient local support, to sustain an active cockpit at a variety of locations.

One of the regionally important cockpits was located at Birr, which was the preferred venue for meetings between teams from Galway and from King's and Queen's counties.[141] Birr was only modestly active by comparison with the southeastern towns of Ross and Wexford. Indeed, the cockfighting community in county Wexford was perhaps the liveliest in the whole province by the 1770s, as it was responsible not only for the construction of a new cockpit in Wexford in 1778, but also for sustaining one of the most active competitive rivalries (between Wexford and New Ross) in the sport. This was one of the most significant developments in the sport of cockfighting in the 1770s, since as well as promoting the diversion within the county, it supported the forging of competitive links with the towns of Waterford and Clonmel, and sustained an inter-county contest between Wexford and Waterford that, based on the substantial sums ventured as prize money for battles and mains, was keenly contested.[142] Elsewhere, inter-county mains were conducted at Maynooth in 1771 and, particularly successfully, at Athy in 1773;[143] but they were exceeded in the number reported by short mains at Kildare town in 1773 involving teams from Kildare and Kilcullenbridge; at Ballynakill in 1774 between the gentlemen of Kilkenny and Ballynakill on the one side and the town of Ossory on the other; at Castletown, Queen's county in 1776 between the gentlemen of Castletown and Upperwoods; and at Dunkerrin races in 1778 between the gentlemen of Dunkerrin and Shrinrone, county Offaly.[144]

While the links forged across the Shannon by the managers of Birr cockpit, and into Munster by the enthusiasts of cockfighting in county Wexford were welcomed by the champions of the sport, the practical reality was that cock-

139 The only record for county Westmeath (a main for 200 guineas against county Meath) dates from 1784: *Hibernian Journal*, 19 June 1784.   140 It is a measure of the decline of cockfighting in county Dublin that one of the more intriguing and short-lived initiatives was the inclusion of cockfighting at Booterstown races in 1773: *Hibernian Journal*, 9 June 1773.   141 *Public Gazetteer*, 28 July 1764; *FLJ*, 26 June 1773, 16 Feb. 1774; *FJ*, 29 June 1773.   142 *FLJ*, 23 Feb., 6 Mar. 1771, 29 Apr., 2, 6, 9 May 1772, 10, 31 May, 3, 7 June 1775, 15 May, 8 June 1776, 15 May 1779; *Hibernian Journal*, 2 June 1775. The sums ventured in these rivalries frequently ranged between 200 and 500 guineas for the main.   143 *FJ*, 4 June 1771; *FLJ*, 3, 17, 21 July 1773.   144 *FLJ*, 21 Apr. 1773, 23 Apr. 1774, 27 Apr. 1776, 1 Apr. 1778.

fighting in Connaught hardly extended outside its Eyrecourt fastness, and that its horizon did not extend further than Birr.[145] It is noteworthy that a short main of thirteen cocks 'between the officers quartered there and the gentlemen' of the town took place in Sligo in 1766, and that Tuam racecourse staged a cockfight in 1767, but these were one-off events.[146] The situation in Munster was less fragile. Cockfighting was sufficiently developed in three counties – Waterford, Tipperary and Clare – to permit them to participate at least once in an inter-county main in the 1770s, but this hardly captures the liveliness of the sport in those counties, in parts of county Cork or in Limerick city. A small number of individuals successfully sustained activity at an impressive level in each of these counties through the 1770s, if the occurrence of both inter- and intra-county mains at Nenagh, Tallow, and Waterford is an accurate guide.[147]

Though the visibility of cockfighting in areas not previously identified as part of the sport's heartland mitigated the impact of the contraction identifiable in parts of the province of Leinster, it would have been still more acute but for the re-emergence of individual owners, and their reoccupation of the space left vacant by the decline in inter-county competition. As had been the case some decades earlier when individuals had previously dominated the sport,[148] the cost of maintaining a flock of well-bred and well-tended fighting cocks was sufficiently large to ensure that the number of individuals prepared to make the investment required was small. Moreover, the passing of the generation of owners that had dominated the sport in the 1740s and 1750s, the redoubtable Gorges Lowther excepted, meant that a new generation of competitors had emerged. Lowther's most formidable rival was William Henry Burton of Burton Hall, county Carlow, and MP for the county from 1768, whose father Benjamin (1709–67) competed actively in the 1750s.[149] In keeping with the fact that he was the more experienced cocker, Lowther prevailed in the three long mains that the two fought in 1767 and 1771, but Burton possessed a steely determination and he achieved a resounding (home) victory, 20 battles to 9, at Carlow in 1772.[150] Earlier, Burton had demonstrated his aggressive intent by taking on, and defeating, Richard Longfield of Castlemary, county Cork, in 1767, but a comprehensive loss in the same year to Richard Robbins at Dublin highlighted how difficult it was to build and, having done so, to maintain a winning flock.[151] Moreover, he had less stamina for battle than Lowther who soon regrouped, and, following Burton's apparent withdrawal from the sport, (Lowther) engaged between March 1773 and May 1775 in five long mains with another pretender, William Warren, in which he prevailed on each occasion.[152]

145 *Public Gazetteer*, 28 July 1764; *FLJ*, 26 June 1773. **146** *Public Gazetteer*, 17 May 1766; J.A. Claffey, 'Tuam', *Irish historic town atlas*, iii, section no. 21. **147** *FLJ*, 21 Apr., 8, 11 May 1773, 7 Apr. 1779; O'Flaherty, 'Limerick', *Irish historic town atlas*, iii, section no. 21. **148** Above, pp 164–6. **149** Johnston-Liik, *History of the Irish parliament, 1692–1800*, iii, 318–20, 330–1. **150** *FJ*, 3 Feb. 1767, 5 Mar., 6 May 1771; *FLJ*, 6 Mar. 1771, 6 Mar. 1772; *Hoey's Publick Journal*, 6 May 1771, 17 Feb. 1772; *Hibernian Journal*, 21 Feb. 1772. **151** *FLJ*, 6, 11, 14 Mar. 1767; *Public Gazetteer*, 10 Mar. 1767; C.B. Gibson, *The history of the county and city of Cork* (2 vols, Cork, 1861), ii, 206; *FJ*, 12 May 1767. **152** *FJ*, 2 Mar. 1773; *FLJ*, 3 Mar., 5 May 1773, 22 Feb., 13

Gorges Lowther was deserving of the reputation he acquired as that of a man for whom his fighting cocks were an obsession. Others did not possess either the same drive or knowledge of birds. Yet the passion that drove Lowther also animated William Henry Burton, soldiers such as Cornet Conyrs, Henry Thomas Butler, Lord Ikerrin (1746–1813) of Mount Juliet (who succeeded his father as second earl of Carrick in 1774) and Haydocke Evans Morres (1743–76), the MP for Kilkenny, and was crucial in ensuring that the Kilkenny cockpit continued to function as a lively venue during the 1760s and 1770s.[153] Elsewhere, others, less socially eminent, made an equally significant contribution to the maintenance of cockfighting in places as diverse as Dublin, Tallow, county Waterford, and Dunlavin, county Wicklow.[154] Otherwise, the distinct signs of contraction that one can identify in the sport's marginalisation in major urban centres, which prompted Oliver Goldsmith to observe of cockfighting in London that it 'is declining every day', might have percolated still more deeply.[155] As it was, the sport in Ireland entered the 1780s in ostensible good health. It remained a strong popular recreation in Ulster and a prominent activity across much of Leinster. It was also possessed of committed devotees in Munster and in county Galway. However, there were storm clouds on the horizon. The most significant was its decline in the capital, which had long served not only as the location of the kingdom's primary cockpit but also as a gathering place for the leaders of the sport. Indivisible from this were signs that the esteem with which the sport was regarded by respectable opinion was ebbing. There was no reason for particular concern at that moment. The publication by Richard Singleton, at the Fighting Cocks on Cork Hill, one of the leading cutlers and corkscrew makers in the country, of a billhead in which he advertised 'silver and steel cockspurs' for sale alongside a variety of 'plated and polished steel bitts, spurs stirrups, bridles [and] buckles' for horses was evidence of how firmly anchored cockfighting was in the commercial life of the city. The situation was comparable in Belfast, though it is significant that their main retail outlet for cockspurs was the town's ironmonger.[156] Be that as it may, however one seeks to interpret the evidential runes, the fact remains that the future of the sport was less secure when the 1780s commenced than it had been a decade earlier.

COCKFIGHTING IN ULSTER IN THE 1780s

The shift inland in the southern heartland of cockfighting in Leinster that is one of the more striking features of the trajectory of the sport in the 1770s mirrored

May 1775; *Hoey's Publick Journal*, 3 May 1773; *Hibernian Journal*, 3 May 1773, 21 Feb. 1774.　**153** *FLJ*, 7, 11 Mar. 1767; *FJ*, 2 July 1771; GEC, *The complete peerage*, iii, 60–1; Johnston-Liik, *History of the Irish parliament, 1692–1800*, v, 318.　**154** *FJ*, 24 Jan. 1775; *FLJ*, 21 Apr. 1773, 25 Jan. 1775, 20 May 1778; *Hibernian Journal*, 14 July 1775.　**155** Oliver Goldsmith, *History of the earth*, v, 163, cited in *OED*, sub cockfighting.　**156** Billhead of Richard Singleton, [1770s] printed in Barnard, *Making the grand figure*, p. 248. Singleton subsequently conducted his business from 7 Exchange Street (*Dublin Directory*, 1783, p. 72); Benn, *History of Belfast*, p. 591.

	DUBLIN	LEINSTER	MUNSTER	ULSTER	CONNACHT	TOTAL
1761		1		2		3
1781				3		3
1782				3		3
1783				8		8
1784		1		8		9
1785				9		9
1786	1			10		11
1787				9		9
1788		1		11		12
1789				6		6
1790				8		8
1791		1		2		3
1792		1		1		2
1793				1		1
Total	1	4	0	79	0	84

Table 7: Cockfighting: reported mains, 1781–93

Source: *Belfast News Letter*, 1781–93; *Finn's Leinster Journal*, 1781–93; *Freeman's Journal*, 1781–93; *Saunders Newsletter*, 1786

the trend already under way in Ulster, which intensified in the 1780s. As was the case in Leinster, this geospatial shift did not precipitate the total cessation of cockfighting in an urban centre where it was previously well established, but it is notable that the number of reported mains fell appreciably in previously core areas. Based on an analysis of the mains advertised and reported in the *Belfast News Letter* between 1781 and 1792, organised cockfighting continued to take place in county Down (Dromore (1), Hillsborough (1), and Killileagh (5)), county Antrim (Antrim (1), Ballyclare (1) Ballymoney (3), Ballinderry (3), Belfast (1)), county Londonderry (Coagh (8), Moneymore (3), Moy (3), and Stewartstown (2)), and county Armagh (Portadown (4), and Tandragee (1)), but the number of reports, indicated in brackets, was significantly in arrears at several venues, and in the case of Belfast, it is notable that the one reported main was held at Malone, close to but not in the city.[157] Moreover, the number of established locations was exceeded by the number of locations that advertised a main for the first time. These included Enniskillen (4) and Maguiresbridge (2) in county Fermanagh; Aughnacloy (5), Caledon (1) and Coalisland (2) in county Tyrone; Ahoghill (1), Castledawson (1) and Magherafelt in county Londonderry (1); Armagh (1), Richhill (1), Maghery

157 *BNL*, 26 Mar. 1784.

(1), Blackwatertown (3) and Tynan in county Armagh (1); Crumlin (2), Conner (1) and Glenavy (4) in county Antrim; Magheralin (2), Newtownards (1), Rathfryland (3) and Ballydugan (1) in county Down, and Ballybofey (3) in county Donegal. Interestingly, though the number of advertised mains held at these venues – both new and established – ranged between one and eight, the number of mains in new locations exceeded that at established locations though the average number hosted at the latter was greater.[158]

The identifiable increase in the number and in the geo-spatial spread of the locations in which cockfighting was conducted notwithstanding, the organisers of the sport in the 1780s continued to conduct the sport according to the established rules of cocking. These had achieved general acceptance by this point, but it was still deemed appropriate to announce that this was the case on occasion. Thus the organisers of inter-county mains between the gentlemen of counties Tyrone and Derry at Magherafelt in April 1784, and between Tyrone and Down at Moneymore in August 1786, included in the advertisements announcing the dates on which they would be held a statement to the effect that 'there will be a good pit, reputable judges and everything conducted with the greatest regularity'. The organisers of the main at Moy, county Tyrone, announced publicly through the late 1780s that 'judges [would be] appointed each day', and those of 'the great cock match …[to be] fought in Blackwaterstown, near Armagh' in 1790 that 'proper judges' would be appointed.[159] In so far as one can tell, these pronouncements had no impact on the manner in which mains were conducted, and the sport in Ulster was pursued free of discernible controversy or disorder. This was facilitated, doubtlessly, by the fact that the inter-county main was still the highest expression of the sport. Taking those matches advertised in the *Belfast News Letter* as a guide, an imposing 76 per cent of events were inter-county mains. The remaining 24 per cent was divided, not altogether equally, between local mains, open mains, which welcomed all-comers, and mains held at race meetings, of which Killileagh, Ballbofey and Enniskillen races were the most notable; there cockfighting served largely as a diversion from the primary activity which was horse racing.[160] Moreover, most mains followed a familiar pattern; from the various fighting cocks that were assembled, 21 or 31 pair were identified and presented the Saturday previous to the week in which fighting took place.

This regular mode of proceeding ensured that mains were concluded within the allotted 4–5 days, while providing scope for the addition of stag and bye battles. These added to the spectacle of the main, and they became an increasingly common feature in the second half of the 1780s.[161] Since there was no identifi-

---

158 *BNL*, 1781–92 passim. According to these figures 37 mains were held in 14 established venues and 41 at 21 new locations.   159 *BNL*, 23 Apr. 1784, 11 Aug. 1786, 24 July 1787, 6 June 1788, 17 Mar. 1789, 19 Mar. 1790.   160 Above, pp 54–5; *BNL*, 14 Aug. 1781, 2 May 1786, 20 Apr. 1787, 22 May 1789, 7 Aug. 1792; *The Sporting Magazine*, Aug. 1792, p. 308.   161 For examples, see *BNL*, 14 May, 11 June 1782, 16 Apr., 21, 25 May, 20 July 1784, 15 Mar., 15 July 1785, 21, 24 Feb., 11 Apr., 23 May, 2 June 1786, 27 Mar., 11, 22 May, 8, 26 June, 24 July 1787, 29 Apr., 6, 20 May,

able alteration in the manner in which mains were conducted, and the sums for which battles and mains were fought rarely deviated in the early and mid-1780s from the 4 guinea-£5 standard for the former, and the 50 to 100 guineas standard for the latter that was normative in Ulster, it may plausibly be concluded that the increase in the total number of battles was prompted by the desire to attract spectators by expanding the entertainment factor of the occasion. More battles certainly provided more diversion. This would also account for the decision of the organisers of the race meeting at Killileagh (which traditionally combined an orthodox main with horse racing) to experiment with the format, and, in 1788, to augment the traditional match involving the gentlemen of Lecale and Killileagh with a battle royale.[162] All-in cockfighting was a rarity in Ireland,[163] but it was necessary by the late 1780s to spice up the fare, and to sell the sport to an increasingly disinterested public. This approach assumed a familiar form at Antrim in 1786 when the organisers of a local main between the gentlemen of Killead and Ahogill announced below the notice heralding the event that 'there is a large and commodious pit now building', but this lacked novelty, and it does not appear to have had the hoped for impact.[164] Disposed to attempt some thing different, the owners of the well-established cockpit at Portadown organised a main in which a team from county Antrim fought a combined team from Down and Armagh for the large stakes (by Ulster standards) of '500 guineas the main or odd battle and 5 guineas a cock'.[165]

The implication, the augmented number of cockfights and venues notwithstanding, that the sport encountered increasing difficulty in the 1780s in attracting audiences equivalent to those present in the 1760s and 1770s is strengthened by other changes in the manner in which the sport was conducted. One of these was a change to the way in which cockfights were advertised. Following the inauguration in the 1750s of the practice of advertising cockfighting in the *Belfast News Letter*, it was commonplace for advertisements announcing an upcoming main to feature in only one issue of the paper. This changed in the mid-1780s, when advertisements announcing forthcoming mains included a statement to the effect that the advertisement would 'be continued' twice, three, four, six or more times, or from the date of initial insertion to the completion of the main.[166] Since the repetition of advertisements and comparable notices was commonplace in many walks of commercial endeavour, its adoption by the cockfighting fraternity may seem barely noteworthy in and of itself. However, since it was accompanied by the still-more indicative trend of eliminating prize money for each battle and reserving the total prize on offer for the main, it is reasonable to conclude that the change was commercially motivated. The consolidation of prize money did not represent a

6 June 1788, 17 Mar., 24 Apr. 1789, 9 Feb., 7 May 1790. **162** *BNL*, 31 May 1785, 2 May 1786, 16 May 1788. **163** Another instance described, by Jonah Barrington, suggests it may have been more common in the less regulated world of shake bag and informal cockfights: Jonah Barrington, *Personal sketches of his own time* (3 vols, London, 1827–32), i, 70. **164** *BNL*, 6 June 1786. **165** *BNL*, 4 Apr. 1786. **166** *BNL*, 21, 25 May, 20 July 1784, 8 Feb., 15 July 1785, 24 July 1787.

major break with precedent either, as divers mains had been fought for a single prize over the years. However, meetings organised along these lines became more common in Ulster in the early and mid-1780s, when the practice became standard, and before the decade was out only a small proportion of advertised fights indicated that the winners of individual battles would benefit financially.[167]

These trends do not necessarily imply that cockfighting in Ulster was already in irrevocable decline, but they do suggest that, as in Leinster, it was at a point where it was seeking to identify ways that would enable it to retain both the respectability and the visibility that it had enjoyed over several decades. This did not mean that the sport was haemorrhaging support, either at the elite level or on the ground. Cockfighting was, as John Tennent (1772–1813) observed in his journal of his time as an apprentice in Coleraine, one of the 'amusements which are so pleasing to young apprentices, tradesmen, etc', but it is notable, having once engaged enthusiastically in the diversion, that Tennent no longer found it entertaining: 'Now more sober sentiments has taken place of those giddy and foolish thou[gh]th that possessed me, which made me think happiness consisted in foolish and idle play', he confided to his journal in April 1790.[168] Tennent was not representative of all of society, but he did reflect the attitude of an emerging generation, and a world-view identifiable with the growing ranks of the middling sort and an emerging evangelical Christian morality that was disposed to look censoriously upon sports such as cockfighting.[169]

EXPLAINING THE SHIFT IN OPINION

The rapidly diminishing enthusiasm for cockfighting identifiable in Ireland in the 1780s is not easily explained. An explanation would not be necessary, of course, if one embraced the once dominant anthropocentric perspective, which presumed that history is a story of progress and betterment, since one could account for the change as an inevitable consequence of societal evolution. However, this variant on the Whig interpretation of history begs more questions than it answers. It is also unsatisfactory to ascribe the decline of cockfighting to 'human feeling', specifically to an emerging humanitarian sentiment that concluded it was morally wrong to abuse animals, since, as Emma Griffin and others have persuasively pointed out, it does not accord with the facts. Insouciance towards the suffering of animals, inherent in cockfighting, long survived the decline of that sport.[170]

---

167 *BNL*, 14 May 1782, 1 Apr., 27 June 1783, 16, 23 Apr., 21, 25 May, 15 June, 20 July 1784, 8 Feb., 27 May 1785, 21, 24 Feb., 2 June, 11 Aug. 1786, 27 Mar., 22 May, 25 Dec. 1787, 29 Apr., 6 June, 15 July 1788, 17 Mar., 24 Apr., 22, 26 May 1789, 9 Feb., 12, 19 Mar., 27 Apr., 7 May 1790.   168 Leanne Calvert (ed.), 'The journal of John Tennent, 1786–90', *Analecta Hibernica*, 43 (2012), pp 117–18.   169 For some broad contextual observations see Kelly, 'The emergence of the middle class and the decline of duelling', pp 89–93; and for the specific world of Ulster Presbyterianism, Holmes, *The shaping of Ulster Presbyterian belief and practice*, chapters 3 and 6.   170 Griffin, *England's revelry*, pp 114–18; *eadem*, 'Popular culture in industrializing England',

Moreover, one will search in vain in the eighteenth (or the early nineteenth) century in Ireland for 'a growth in humanitarian sentiment' (to invoke Ronald Hutton's phrase) robust enough to account for what happened, though, interestingly, the reduction in the space allocated to cockfighting in the public realm in Ireland precedes its occurrence in England.[171] This notwithstanding, the weight of evidence supports the conclusion that in Ireland, as in England, the disquiet articulated on the subject of animal suffering was selective, particular, and seldom, if ever, consolidated into a unified conception of animals as sentient creatures, with all that that implied.[172]

One does not seek either to overlook or to minimise the import of the condemnations proffered in response to reports of egregious animal abuse, or the genuine feelings of revulsion generated by the number of birds that died in the cause of cockfighting, but such sentiment had limited purchase, because, individuals excepted, eighteenth-century society was only inching towards a concept of cruel and unreasonable treatment with reference to animals. The press did not, to be sure, describe what went on in the cockpit in other than general terms, and rarely if ever detailed the manner in which individual fighting cocks died, but it unhesitatingly echoed the prevailing view that a main was an affirming and joyful sporting and social occasion. Witness, for example, the concluding sentence of the celebratory report of the 'grand cock match between the gentlemen of the counties of Kildare and Wicklow' that took place in Athy in July 1773:

> There never was seen finer cockfighting, nor a more numerous meeting of ladies and gentlemen in said town, who were all highly pleased with the regularity and elegance of the balls and assemblies, and parted with the utmost harmony and good humour.[173]

There is no suggestion here, or in any of the multiplicity of reports of cockfights carried in the main newspapers of Dublin, Belfast and Kilkenny published over half a century, and still less in the advertisements announcing forthcoming matches, that either the organisers, owners, spectators or gamblers, whose money fuelled the sport, were even faintly troubled by the fact that cockfighting involved the organised setting of aggressive birds against each other and that victory was achieved when one killed, or at the least, so incapacitated the other that it could no longer fight back. There was little uneasiness either with the fact that

Historical Journal, 45 (2002), 619–35; MacGregor, *Animal encounters*, chapter 5; Donald, *Picturing animals*, chapter 7. **171** Ronald Hutton, *The stations of the sun: a history of the ritual year in Britain* (Oxford, 1996), p. 357, cited in Griffin, op. cit., p. 114. See also Keith Thomas, *Man and the natural world: a history of the modern sensibility* (Oxford, 1983), p. 159. **172** In other words disquiet was occasionally expressed at 'the cruelty of those savages who drive animals through the city from Smithfield', and at individual acts of egregious cruelty, but other than the regulation approved in the 1780s prohibiting the use of 'any other instrument than whips' to drive livestock, on pain of a fine, there was no sanction: see *FJ*, 10 July 1790, and for examples of cruelty, *Public Gazetteer*, 12 Apr. 1766; *Hoey's Public Journal*, 2 Nov. 1772. **173** *Hibernian Journal*, 21 July 1773.

the preparation of birds to fight involved forced feeding, sweating (or stoving), the cutting of feathers, removal of combs and wattles (dubbing), and the paring of the bird's natural spurs to permit the fixing of a still more destructive metal equivalent (heeling), which were readily purchasable in silver, or in steel at the affordable price of 8*s*. for six pair,[174] in order to turn instinctively belligerent birds into efficient killers.[175] This is true also of the practice of setting a young fighting cock 'to tear' up another that had been injured beyond recovery in the cockpit 'to see if he is true game'. This practice disturbed those like Sylas Neville, the mid-eighteenth-century diarist, who visited the London cockpit in 1787.[176] Yet the treatment of fighting cocks must not be depicted in a mono-chromatically negative light. The most influential manuals on bird welfare make it clear that the owners of cocks and their feeders were not unfeeling. Many evi-dently cared deeply for their birds, and lavished care and attention on those groomed for the cockpit. They also contrived (albeit when it was in their inter-est to do so) to cure injured birds.[177] It may not have been true of all, but most owners and feeders were informed and knowledgeable men, who knew exactly what to do to get the most out of a fighting cock, but the facility with which they disposed of those who did not make the grade demonstrates that they were not sentimental. It was this quality that separated the superior feeders from the ordinary, and that explains why a handful, among whom John Ouldred and John Scott stand out, were in heavy demand.[178] It is a fair measure of the relationship some owners and feeders built up with their birds that some fighting cocks were given individual names, and those that proved especially combative, and survived a career in the cockpit, were selected, and protected, for breeding. This was pretty much as far as it went, however. Fighting cocks were judged on their capacity to kill and their willingness to fight to the death, and the anticipated outcome in each instance that two birds were set to fight was that at least one of the two participants would die; in battles royale and Welsh mains (in which the birds that were admitted to compete fought a series of rounds, and the final eight fought together until there was only one victor) the chances of survival were much smaller.[179] A cock that declined to fight or that failed to show appropriate belligerence in the cockpit was as likely as not to have its neck wrung, which was the usual fate also of injured victors whose owners were not prepared to vest the time or effort to nurse them back to health. To put it in perspective, no Irish fighting cock was held in sufficient esteem either by its owner or by society to

---

174 This was the price paid by Thomas Kingsbury, MD, in 1732: Kingsbury to [Price], 27 Apr. 1732 (NLW, Puleston papers, MS 3584 f. 18); more generally see MacGregor, *Animal encounters*, p. 242.   175 Howlett, *The royal pastime of cockfighting*, pp 42–64 passim; Gilbey, *Sport in the olden time*, pp 47–9; Collins et al. (eds), *Encyclopedia of traditional British rural sports*, pp 70, 71; MacGregor, *Animal encounters*, pp 233–7.   176 Cozens-Hardy, *The diary of Sylas Neville*, pp 2–3. 177 Howlett, *The royal pastime of cockfighting*, passim.   178 *Dublin Gazette*, 3 May 1763; *FLJ*, 17 Feb. 1768, 10 July 1776; *Hibernian Journal*, 13 Apr., 15 June 1774; *FDJ*, 14 May 1778. Other feed-ers mentioned include John Johnson, Henry Browne, Simon Prescot, and Patrick Grogan.   179 MacGregor, *Animal encounters*, pp 247–8.

have its image recorded in oils, watercolours or even printer's ink. In this respect, the cock compared negatively with the horse or even the stag.[180]

Though one will seek in vain for evidence of a general or developed concern for the welfare of key sporting animals,[181] one should not conclude from this that the strand of opinion that was prompted by genuine antipathy to offer a critique of cockfighting and the behaviours it promoted and encouraged made no impression. Unlike bull-baiting and throwing at cocks, which the authorities sought actively to interdict,[182] cockfighting operated free of official sanction during the eighteenth century, but because it was possessed of a host of disagreeable features – blood-letting, brutality, violence, cruelty, gambling, loss of personal control – it was not immune from criticism. It was secure from sanction so long as it retained the support of the respectable,[183] but this could not be assumed, not only because opinion was mutable on this and related subjects, but also because of the deeply-held aspiration of those who were motivated by the ideals of societal improvement – secular as well as religious – to rid society of practices and diversions they deemed incompatible with a disciplined, orderly and godly lifestyle. Moreover, there was increasing interest in order, conformity, rules, personal decorum and other values that the nascent middle class esteemed as the eighteenth century progressed.[184] This attitude can be detected in the negative response of Nathaniel Nisbett, the earl of Abercorn's agent, in 1758 to the suggestion that cockfighting and horse racing should be allowed at St Johnstown market.[185] It was articulated explicitly five years later in the response to an advertisement in the *Belfast News Letter* announcing 'a main of 31 cocks' involving 'the gentlemen of the town of Belfast and the gentlemen of Malone and Derriaghy'.[186] Persuaded that it was of public advantage 'to put a stop to this source of wickedness and cruelty', which he had 'ever considered as very pernicious to society', an anonymous commentator lucidly outlined the case against cockfighting on two grounds, which informed much of the criticism that was to follow. In the first place, he criticised it as dehumanising and cruel:

> This sanguinary pastime has a manifest tendency to extinguish *compassion*, one of the finest feelings of the human heart, and to beget savageness of disposition in its room. Tho' we are permitted the use and service of creatures of a subordinate rank, we are not therefore allowed to abuse them. It would, perhaps, be a very difficult matter for us to justify our taking away the life of any inoffensive animal, if we could not plead a particular permission; but surely the benevolent Author thereof never intended by it to countenance us in acts of cruelty and wanton barbarity to his creatures of an inferior order. We are commanded, if we find a bird's nest in the

180 See above, pp 41, 55, 69, 75, 151. 181 Griffin, *England's revelry*, pp 114–19. 182 Chapter 4 below. 183 See Brailsford, *A taste for diversions*, pp 60–1; Griffin, *England's revelry*, pp 123–4, 162. 184 See Brailsford, *Sport and society: Elizabeth to Anne*, p. 156; Kelly, 'The decline of duelling and the emergence of the middle class', pp 89–95. 185 Above, n. 49. 186 *BNL*, 5 Apr. 1763.

way, not to take the dam with the young; and the most valuable temporal reward is annexed to the observance of this precept, *health and the prolonging of our days*. Indeed, it may be affirmed, that in proportion as men are accustomed to cruelty to animals of a lower species, they lose humanity to their fellow creatures; and it is upon this principle that the *law* prohibits a particular set of men from being jurors on certain occasions: beside, a train of horrid vices which attends cockfighting, the shocking crime of murder is often committed there, and, it is not surprising, that such an effect should ensue therefrom.[187]

And second, he objected to the fact that it discouraged industry and promoted profligacy among those who could least afford it, and served 'to seduce the youthful and inexperienced, or any person whatever, into the paths of vice and idleness':

> By these cock matches, a door is opened for, at least a week of idleness, drunkenness, and immortality of every kind. It must be confessed that the lower sort of tradesmen have too strong a tendency to assemble at these places, wherefore every opportunity of such meetings ought to be cut off.[188]

These were, the writer avowed, compelling reasons why the proposed cockfight should not proceed, but the terse rejection by 'the gentlemen of Belfast' of his call to abandon the event indicated that his was very much the minority view at this point.[189] Moreover, it remained so for some time, though the occasional critic ventured forth with similar sentiments. A notable intervention in the *Freeman's Journal* in 1764 rejected the distinction 'gentlemen' sought to draw between bull-baiting, throwing at cocks and cockfighting. Addressing those of that rank who supported cockfighting, the writer called upon them 'to recollect', convinced that if they did so:

> They would find it full as barbarous to set two poor animals a fighting, to cut, mangle, and kill each other with weapons tied for that purpose to their feet, as to fasten one of the same species to a stake and knock him in the head with a club. I think the last is really the least cruel.[190]

This author had no scruple in labelling cockfighting 'an inhuman custom'; those who were less sure criticised it more meekly as 'an unprofitable and unmanly diversion'. These were legitimate criticisms, but the continuing ability of those who oversaw the sport at its most organised level to ensure that inter-county mains were properly conducted and that the rules were observed insulated cockfighting against its sharpest critics and the possibility of political intervention.[191]

187 *BNL*, 12 Apr. 1763; *The Public Gazetteer*, 16 Apr. 1763. 188 Ibid. 189 *BNL*, 15 Apr. 1763. 190 *FJ*, 14 Jan. 1764. 191 *BNL*, 12 May 1767; above, pp 171–2, 179–80.

Protected as a result from accusations that it was either barbarous or badly organised, cockfighting was permitted to expand *largely* criticism-free until the early 1770s when the declension of the sport in Dublin, epitomised by the travails of the Cockpit Royal, emboldened its critics. Significantly, few targeted the sport *per se*, or objected on the grounds that it was ethically wrong to train birds to kill; instead they adopted an anthropocentric perspective, and alleged that cockfighting was dele-terious because it encouraged humans to gamble and to engage in practices that were sinful and immoral. This argument would have been difficult to counter at any time; the task was exacerbated in the 1770s because of the level of public unease at the number of illegal gambling dens in the capital and, specifically, the struggling Royal Cockpit, which was targeted for specific criticism because it was used 'for the profligate purpose of gaming throughout the night'. The city sheriff, Blennerhassett Grove, did his utmost to prevent such practices. The dispersal 'of a very numerous company at 12 o'clock on[e] Saturday night' late in 1770 elicited calls for 'judicial' intervention and the 'exemplary suppression of that nursery of vice and public dis-order'.[192] This was a step too far. As a result, the problem may have worsened, obliging Grove's successor, James Shiel, to intervene, and commit 'a numerous ban-ditti of vagrants [detected] playing at hazard' in the same venue in 1773. This rein-forced the conviction, previously articulated, that 'if the law was put in force against the person' who oversaw what was now denominated 'that school of wickedness', it would be a public good. It also served as a rallying cry for those who contended that exemplary action 'would not only overthrow a nuisance of the most infamous kind, but [also] deter others from following the like practices'.[193]

The effective withdrawal of cockfighting from the capital during the 1770s to the more accepting environment of provincial Leinster eased the criticism to which the sport was subject by reason of its association with gambling, but the relief was short lived. Its cause was not assisted to be sure by reports of the involvement of cocks in encounters that seemed to exemplify the egregious cru-elty with which cockfighting was increasingly identified – reports like that pub-lished in the summer of 1779 involving a cock, owned by James Farrell, a sales master from West Arran Street Dublin, and a cat:

> Last Friday evening a most extraordinary battle was fought at Smithfield for a wager of 3 guineas between a buck cat and a game cock. The cock was steeled and his head rubbed with the blood of a mouse. They fought for six minutes, during which time the cock defended himself from the talons of the cat with dexterity, and was set for victory, as the cat's head was cut in several places by the gaff of the cock, but at length the cat got the cock's head entirely in his mouth, upon which the cock rose and stuck the gaffs in his antagonists throat cutting the same entirely across. The cock died instantly, and the cat one hour and a quarter later.[194]

192 *FJ*, 9, 27 Nov. 1770. For further linking of cockfighting and gambling see *BNL*, 1 Apr. 1767.
193 *Hoey's Publick Journal*, 7 Apr. 1773; *FJ*, 4 July 1771. 194 *FLJ*, 10 July 1779.

This was a singular event, but its occurrence reinforced the association, that was increasingly made, between cockfighting and cruelty, and it diminished the capacity of those who were disposed to do so to defend the integrity and value of the sport. Conscious of the changing public mood, a number of gentlemen began to distance themselves from cockfighting in favour of horse racing, but those who conceived of all such diversions as morally problematic, and who believed that cockfighting and race meetings were equally an 'outlet for gamblers, sharpers and pickpockets', were unconvinced. Nonetheless, the perception, cultivated by those advocating moral reformation, that horse racing was the sport of gentlemen, and cockfighting that of 'idle vagabonds' gained weight.[195] Such views had more obvious purchase among those who set the social tone in larger urban centres, but the percolation of such ideas could not be corralled and it was not long before they had penetrated the heartland of cocking. Saliently, when a group of individuals styling themselves 'gentlemen' announced a main of cocks at Ballymoney, county Antrim, on 8 April 1783, their notice was contradicted by 'the inhabitants ... as neither they [n]or any gentlemen are concerned in said main'.[196] Since the devotees of cocking had plenty of events from which to choose, they had no reason to dwell on the resistance to this attempt to hold a main in one of their sport's traditional bastions, but there was no escaping the fact that the environment was incrementally unsympathetic to their diversion. This was yet to reach critical proportion, but the publication during the 1780s of news and opinion columns, drawn from the London press, applauding the fact that cockfighting was in 'decline', and calling upon the authorities to ensure that there will 'no longer ... be any temptation to it held out, as from authority', by closing 'the royal cockpit in St James Park', was indicative of the growing assertiveness of the contrary voice.[197] There was mounting support, in particular, for the view that the young should forsake dissolute recreations such as 'fox-hunting and cockfighting' for more wholesome activities, and a greater willingness to caricature the 'jontlemen' who were preoccupied with the 'bravery' of their cocks as 'poor, proud, and dissipated' squireens who failed to live up to either their family or societal responsibilities.[198]

Since they represented the sport in its most sophisticated and well-regulated incarnation, most criticism of cockfighting was not targeted at inter-county mains, but at the less structured displays, which were encountered in the grounds of taverns and makeshift cockpits. Inns and taverns were an obvious target for moral reformers because they were the focal point of a variety of the societal ills they sought to eradicate, and, encouraged by the example of France, where (it was asserted) the licensing laws empowered the authorities to prohibit such activities, there were mounting calls in the late 1780s simply to prohibit gambling and allied activities in taverns and other public houses:

---

195 *BNL*, 15 Apr. 1775.   196 *BNL*, 11, 15 Apr. 1783.   197 *BNL*, 2 May 1786.   198 *BNL*, 16 May 1786; *FLJ*, 10 Jan. 1789. The latter column is reprinted from the *Dublin Evening Packet*; see also Holmes, *The shaping of Ulster Presbyterian belief and practice*, pp 177–8.

To allow any kind of gambling should be a forfeiture of licence, as cards, skittles, nine pins, cockfighting, races by men or women, for ale or other things, cudgelling, pugilism, bull baiting, and calling of drinking for wagers.[199]

Attracted by the prospect of being able, at a stroke, to curb a host of popular practices that those who pursued a vision of an orderly society aspired to bring about, and secure in the presumption that 'the primary object of every legislator should be the good morals of the people', calls for the regulation of taverns and public houses multiplied.[200] A significant moment was reached in May 1789 when five landowners from east and south county Antrim, which had been disturbed by robberies and petty larcenies, concluded simplistically that these criminal activities were linked to the predilection for cockfighting, horse racing, gaming and other diversions whereby 'the morals of the lower orders are very much hurt'.[201] Determined to attempt to impose order on their communities, and persuaded that the eradication of unwholesome recreations was critical, the landowners, guided by Richard Gervais Ker of Red Hall, Ballycarry, prevailed on the 'jurors impanelled at a court leet in Ballycarry on 21 May, and other principled inhabitants of the manor of Broad Island' to 'pledge ourselves in the most determined manner that we will exert out utmost activity and influence in our several families and departments' towards

the laudable purpose of suppressing cockfighting, pony horse racing, and other lawless meetings in their respective neighbourhoods, fully sensible of the many evils arising from such illegal assemblies as hostile to the tranquillity of the country as they are destructive to industry and good morals.[202]

There was support for this initiative in the community, but the press was ambivalent. Though conscious of the impact of the argument proffered by those who deemed cockfighting 'repugnant to humanity, and fraught with injury to society, by promoting a spirit of cruelty, gaming and idleness', the *Belfast News Letter* was still loath, it made clear in the spring of 1790, 'to enter fully into the subject', probably because the sport still possessed many supporters whom it wished not to alienate.[203] A further indication of societal ambivalence is provided by the fact that though two members of Freemasons Lodge 418 were censured in 1794 for attending cockfights, two members of the same lodge objected to the inclusion in the bye-laws of 'a clause against cockfighting' a year later.[204] Such rear-guard

199 *BNL*, 11 Sept. 1787. 200 *BNL*, 23 May 1788. 201 *BNL*, 5 May 1789. The parish concerned embraced Larne, Glynn, Islandmagee, Templecorran (Broad Island), Killroot and Kilead. The landowners were Conway Richard Dobbs, Richard Gervais (or Jervis) Ker, Marriott Dalway, George Anson McClaverty and Richard Kingsmill. It may be noted that Ker was high sheriff of county Antrim in 1791: see PRONI, Ker papers, D2651. 202 *BNL*, 2 June 1789. 203 *BNL*, 2 Apr. 1790. 204 Petri Mirala, *Freemasonry in Ulster, 1733–1813: a social and political history of the*

actions may not have been unusual, or unanticipated from the devotees of the cockpit, but there was no evading the fact that the tide of respectable opinion was in favour of the sport's opponents by the early 1790s. The assembled magistrates of Belfast indicated as much when on 17 April 1791 they 'unanimously resolved not to certify in future for any publican' who failed to meet four basic criteria, one of which involved having 'heretofore encouraged cockfighting etc'.[205]

Such actions, which anticipated a similar initiative by the magistrates of Staffordshire by a number of months, were welcomed by the critics of cock-fighting, who were emboldened by the tide of sentiment in their favour to high-light the positive attributes of the cockerel and to present increasingly uncompromising critiques of those who continued to pursue 'a mode of diver-sion, so cruel as that of cockfighting'. One of the most passionate interventions of this kind took the form of a letter to the editor of the *Belfast News Letter* in March 1792:

> It is disgraceful to humanity that so many of these noble animals should be murdered for the sport and pleasure, the noise and nonsense, the pro-phane cursing and swearing of those who have the effrontery to call them-selves with all their impiety, Christians, men of benevolence and morality.[206]

Cockfighting was not without defenders, but apart from the authors of various guides to country sports, who assumed cocking was a legitimate activity, few voices were raised loud in support, and still fewer were prepared to take the argument into the public sphere.[207] An interesting, if somewhat ironic, anony-mous intervention did proffer a defence of the sport (and other traditional and customary activities) as socially integrative on the grounds that they brought indi-viduals of different social stations together, but it is a measure of how far the pendulum of opinion had swung in the other direction that this voice was barely heard above the chorus of contrary views.[208]

DECLINE

Consistent with the ebbing current of opinion, there was a sharp decline in the number of cockfights reported in the Irish press from the early 1790s. Though this mirrors the situation in Devonshire,[209] it is not without interpretative diffi-culties. Assuming that the press accurately captured the pattern of cockfighting,

masonic brotherhood in the north of Ireland (Dublin, 2007), pp 89, 90. **205** *BNL*, 29 Apr. 1791. **206** *BNL*, 20 Mar. 1792. See also *Ennis Chronicle*, 16 May 1791. **207** *The sportsman's dictionary, or the gentleman's companion for town and country containing full and particular instructions for … cock-ing* …. etc (Dublin, 1792). This work, which was printed by Peter Hoey, retailed at a not incon-siderable 5s. 5d. **208** *BNL*, 25 May 1792. **209** Porter, 'Cockfighting in the eighteenth and nineteenth centuries', p. 67.

the number of high-profile inter-county mains fell dramatically in the early 1790s
in both its provincial heartlands. Since this trend had been under way in Leinster
for some time (Table 7), the fact that the three mains advertised in *Finn's
Leinster Journal* between 1788 and 1792 were not inter-county events is not surprising.[210] However, the scale of the collape in Ulster was so pronounced (Table
7) that one feels obliged to question the reliability of the data. It could be that
the absence of advertisements and reports in the *Belfast News Letter*, which was
for decades the paper of record for cockfighting in the province, indicates that
the ongoing disengagement of the gentry, who were the mainstay of the sport in
the province for half a century, had arrived at a point by 1792 when it was
simply no longer possible to sustain the traditional round of inter-county mains.
Alternatively, it may be that some inter-county mains continued to take place,
but were not reported either because those who were involved did not bring
them to the notice of the press, or because the press (meaning the *Belfast News
Letter*) had finally decided no longer to carry such advertising. It is noteworthy
in this context that the formation of county teams did not come to a complete
stop, though there may have been a hiatus of some years, spanning the mid and
late 1790s, since the next identifiable references to county teams in Ulster (for
counties Armagh, Antrim and Fermanagh) date from the early nineteenth century. What is clear is that cockfighting did not simply cease. However, it was no
longer conducted in the organised, high-profile manner that was indicative of a
sport when it was held in general favour by respectable opinion. It continued to
be pursued in the random way that it had long been pursued by those, mostly
though not exclusively below the rank of gentleman, who kept a handful of
cocks.[211] It is difficult to penetrate the sport at this social level, but, based upon
the description provided by Thomas McTear of cocking in Belfast 'about 1808',
it would appear that it appealed to a minority across a broad social catchment.
From his residence on Watling Street, McTear had a full view of an open-air pit
in 'a large yard' entered from Hill Street in the city:

> This yard contained a cockpit uncovered, and from the back windows of
> the house, we had a fine view of this cruel sport. The fights were very
> frequent, and were attended by gentlemen of the town, as well as by
> poorer people; and no one had any idea that ... cockfighting was anything
> else than a most proper and gentlemanly amusement.[212]

McTear's contention that cockfighting was a 'proper and gentlemanly amusement' is patently misleading, but the account he provides is revealing of the

---

210 *FLJ*, 7 June 1788, 20 Apr. 1791, 18 Apr. 1792. These mains involved local teams or were open
events. 211 As instanced, for example, by the incident recounted by John Tennent, on 8 Mar. 1789:
see Calvert (ed.), 'Diary of John Tennent', p. 88. Furthermore, William Sinclair (1760–1807), the
Belfast linen manufacturer and political activist, kept fighting cocks (*DIB sub. nom.*). 212 McTear,
'Personal recollections of the beginning of the century', p. 70. See also Benn, *History of Belfast*, ii,
95, which refers to schoolboys with 'game cocks' bearing evidence of having been fighting.

enduring attachment to the sport. This was no longer sufficient, or strong enough, to withstand the penetration of an ethical morality, which proffered a persuasive new definition of respectability, but it was strong enough to sustain the sport in Belfast and at other locations for as long as it was not illegal to possess fighting cocks.

This dramatic shift in attitude notwithstanding, there were still enough *aficionados* of the sport among the gentry in Leinster to permit a low-key main of stags at Durrow in 1794 between the gentlemen of Queen's county and Kilkenny for 2 guineas a battle and 40 guineas the main.[213] The sharp deterioration in the political environment in the mid and late 1790s disturbed even this pattern of local meetings. But once the country was restored to a measure of normality in the aftermath of the 1798 Rebellion, cockfighting experienced a short-lived resurgence in the midlands, symbolised by the new cockpit that was erected in Maynooth.[214] The way forward was pointed by the gentlemen of King's county who organised 'a main of cocks' during a 'hunt meet' at Birr in February 1800, and 'a main of stags' in the same town in June 1800 when Kings' county competed with the gentlemen of county Tipperary for the not inconsiderable sum of 5 guineas a battle and 200 guineas the main.[215] This set the pattern for what was to follow, and a 'grand stag' match featuring a team from King's county and an Ulster team (drawn from counties Armagh, Antrim or Fermanagh) was fought in Dublin annually between 1808 and 1819. At least three of these long mains were held in the Cockpit Royal in Essex Street (1808, 1815, 1817).[216]

By 1819, the Cockpit Royal had moved to Wellington Quay, mid-way between Essex Bridge and the New Metal Bridge. The fact that the pit successfully negotiated yet another change of location was testimony to the enduring appeal of cockfighting, but it was still more significant that the King's county match was a once-off event. Dublin was not the sole urban venue, of course; the municipal pit in Kilkenny also continued to function. Moreover, the fact that the sums at stake in the 'grand stag' matches were of the order of 20 guineas a battle and 1,000 guineas the main or odd battle is further proof of the attachment to the sport among elements of respectable opinion, though the discontinuation of the practice of holding mains at gentlemen's houses before race days was a further indication of their continuing disengagement.[217] Pre-race mains were emblematic of the traditional bonds that bound cockfighting and horse racing, but the link became increasingly difficult to sustain in the early nineteenth century, and as the preparedness of gentlemen to defy respectability diminished, so the connection weakened. The exclusion in 1819 of 'The rules for matching and fighting cocks in Ireland', which had been carried in the *Irish Racing Calendar* since its inception, brought to an end a link that could be traced (via the *Racing Calendar*) back to the

213 *FLJ*, 19 July 1794. 214 J.H. Andrews, *Kildare, Irish historic town atlas*, i, section no. 21. 215 *The Constitution*, 15 Feb., 3 May 1800. 216 The 1813 main was held at the Farming Repository, St Stephen's Green: *FJ*, 27 May 1813. 217 *FJ*, 13 July 1808, 27 May 1813, 22 May 1816, 20 June 1817, 21 May 1819; Walsh, 'Eighteenth-century Kilkenny', p. 47.

mid-eighteenth century, and though more symbolic than serious, it mirrored the decline of the sport as a recognised, respectable and popular recreation.²¹⁸

THE END?

Though the formal severance of the link between horse racing and cockfighting was an indicative consequence of the disengagement of respectable opinion from the sport, cockfighting was sufficiently firmly entrenched among the population at large to survive as a demotic recreation for a further generation. This can be demonstrated by Easter week in Dungiven, county Londonderry, the 'greater part' of which was 'still ... devoted to the royal sport of cockfighting' in 1821.²¹⁹ However, even here social forces were at work detaching the unenthusiastic, and discouraging the *aficionados* from maintaining their involvement at its previous level. The impact of these forces varied from parish to parish and county to county across the province, but it is notable that they proceeded at a faster pace in Ulster than they did in the sport's English heartland.²²⁰ There were locations, like Bovedy, in the parish of Maghera, county Londonderry, where cockfighting survived as a feature of the annual Christmas Day fair into the 1830s. In the parish of Drumkeeran, county Fermanagh, the Grange of Ballyscullion, and the parishes of Derrykeighan, Drumtillagh, Raloo, Loughguile, Kilwaughter, and Carncastle and Killyglen (all in county Antrim), cockfighting was still sufficiently popular then to warrant being described as either the 'chief amusement', a 'favourite amusement' or one of the 'principal amusements' of the people, but these were exceptional.²²¹ Moreover, they were exceeded by that date by the number of parishes in which cockfighting was either 'given up', 'nearly given up', 'much given up', 'giving way', 'declining' 'almost disappearing', 'very rare', 'falling greatly into disuse' or confined to 'a day or two at' Easter, to Easter Mondays, or even in certain instances (the south county Antrim parish of Camlin, for example) to 'the morning of Easter Monday'.²²² Cockfighting was also accommodated in the parish

218 Welcome, *Irish horse racing*, p. 18; Costello, *Kildare: saints, soldiers and horses*, pp 119, 120; John Feehan, *Cuirrech Lifé: the Curragh of Kildare* (Dublin, [2009]), p. 63. The lawn of Denis Bowes Daly's house Athgarvan Lodge, which was on the edge of the Curragh, was a favoured location. **219** Day and McWilliams (eds), *Ordnance survey memoirs: county Londonderry*, xxx, 11.   **220** Brailsford, *A taste for diversions*, pp 185–6.   **221** Day and McWilliams (eds), *Ordnance survey memoirs: county Londonderry*, xviii, 100 (Maghera); idem, *Ordnance survey memoirs: county Fermanagh*, xiv, 66 (Drumkeeran); idem, *Ordnance survey memoirs: county Antrim*, x, 5 (Carncastle and Killyglen); x, 115 (Kilwaughter); xiii, 65 (Loughguile); xvi, 86 (Derrykeighan); xvi, 99 (Drumtillagh); xix, 7 (Grange of Ballyscullion); xxxii, 84, 103, 127 (Raloo).   **222** Day and McWilliams (eds), *Ordnance survey memoirs: county Antrim*, xiii, 56 (Granges of Layd and Inispollen); xix, 135 (Grange of Shilvodan); xxvi, 106 (Templecoran); xiii, 95 (Racavan); viii, 113 (Derryaghy); xxi, 70 (Camlin); x, 40 (Islandmagee); xxvi, 28 (Glynn); viii, 15 (Blaris); xxix, 48 (Antrim); xxiii, 133 (Rasharkin); xxiv, 17 (Ballintoy); idem, *Ordnance survey memoirs: county Londonderry*, vi, 10 (Magherafelt); xi, 11 (Aghanloo); vi, 55–6 (Ballyscullion); idem, *Ordnance survey memoirs: county Tyrone*, xx, 12 (Ballinderry); xx, 18 (Ballyclog); idem, *Ordnance survey memoirs:*

of Trory, county Fermanagh, on Whit Monday,[223] but this was unusual, and it was of palpably less significance than the fact that the sport was becoming increasingly marginalised socially as well as geographically. It is notable, for instance, that cock-fighting had all but disappeared by the early 1830s as a popular recreation from the more peripheral provincial counties of Donegal, Fermanagh and Monaghan, and that there is no evidence that it sustained a distinct presence in counties Armagh, Tyrone and Down.[224] Socially, its decline can be measured by reports to the effect that the sport was 'confined to the Roman Catholics' in the south county Antrim parish of Tullruskin in 1833; that it was 'only resorted to by the more profligate' in the mid-Antrim parish of Kirkinriola in 1832; and that the denizens of the surviving cockpits of Belfast were described in 1835 as 'the very lowest and most abandoned descriptions of persons'.[225]

The changing social profile of those who participated in cockfighting was directly attributable, it was observed cryptically of the inhabitants of the parish of Aghanloo, county Londonderry, 'to the gradual increase of seriousness in the general character of the parishioners'.[226] This was, it can justifiably be observed, an inherently subjective assessment, but it echoes the broader secular trend, whose roots can be traced at least to the 1780s, that was accented during the 1820s by a combination of greater receptivity to the directions of the clergy, and, in an environment of more visible religiosity, to the greater readiness of Catholic priests and Protestant ministers to instruct their flocks as to how they should behave. These clerical instructions were was not directed solely at cockfighting, of course, or confined to the province of Ulster. Humphrey O'Sullivan noted the same tendency in county Kilkenny, where cockfighting was pursued on Sundays and holidays. From a clerical perspective, regardless of the denomination, such demotic recreations as dancing, hurling, card-playing and cockfighting not only were not consistent with the divine injunction to keep the Sabbath holy, but also did not meet their definition of edifying behaviour to which all should aspire. The clergy did not hesitate, as a result, to preach against them, and, when and where possible, to seek actively to prevent their occurrence.[227]

The religious did not act on their own in this pursuit, of course, and they might not have tried, still less have succeeded, if they did not have the warm

county Fermanagh, xiv, 43 (Derryvullan); xiv, 24 (Cleenish); idem, *Ordnance survey memoirs: county Monaghan*, xl, 82 (Ballybay); idem, *Ordnance survey memoirs: county Donegal*, xxxviii, 17 (Clonmany).   223 Day and McWilliams (eds), *Ordnance survey memoirs: county Fermanagh*, xiv, 129. 224 As note 219.   225 Day and McWilliams (eds), *Ordnance survey memoirs: county Antrim*, xxi, 138 (Tullrusk); xxiii, 107 (Kirkinriola); viii, 15 (Blaris).   226 Day and McWilliams (eds), *Ordnance survey memoirs: county Londonderry*, xi, 11 (Aghanloo).   227 Holmes, *The shaping of Ulster Presbyterian belief and practice*, part 4; S.J. Connolly, *Priests and people in pre-Famine Ireland* (Dublin, 1982), p. 168; *Carlow in 1798: an autobiography of William Farrell of Carlow* ed. R.J. McHugh (Dublin, 1949), p. 39; McGrath, *Diary of Humphrey O'Sullivan*, i, 245, iii, 53, iv, 91; Day and McWilliams (eds), *Ordnance survey memoirs: county Antrim*, xix, 104–5 (Durane); xxi, 22 (Aghagallon); xiii, 54 (Layd); xxiii, 16–17 (Ahoghill); idem, *Ordnance survey memoirs: county Londonderry*, xi, 109 (Magilligan); xxii, 70; (Macosquin); xxxi, 60 (Desertmartin).

support both of an expanding public constituency, and of the agents of the state. Based on the observations of the memoirists employed in Ulster by the Ordnance Survey, a good case can be made that the former was the more important. The clearest evidence for this is provided by the large number of parishes across the province whose residents had either forsaken cockfighting totally, or were in the process of doing so when the Ordnance Survey memoirist visited in the 1830s.[228] In several locations, cockfighting was openly described as 'disgraceful' or 'disreputable' with the result that it was either confined to 'the remote part of the parish' (as in Maghera, county Londonderry) or 'followed by none but the lower class', which was the case in Enniskillen, county Fermanagh, and in county Down.[229] This was not the profile of a thriving recreational activity, and the decision of parliament in 1835 to approve the Cruelty to Animals Act, and sanctions of £5 a day for operating a cockpit, dealt it a direct blow by signalling the end of cockfighting as a legal pastime.[230] The response to this legislation varied across the United Kingdom, but it is significant that magistrates in country Antrim were prompted to intervene actively to prevent what 'was at one time a favourite amusement', and that their intervention delivered a *coup de grâce* to the sport in the region.[231] Before the decade was out it was reported from parishes in counties Antrim and Londonderry where until recently cockfighting was 'a very favourite amusement at Easter', or 'formerly carried to an almost incredible extent' that the sport had 'almost disappeared'.[232] This was the assessment also of the near contemporary historian of county Down; addressing the situation of the sport in the 1870s, Alexander Knox observed what was once 'a favourite

---

228 Day and McWilliams (eds), *Ordnance survey memoirs: county Antrim*, xxix, 77 (Grange of Doagh); xxix, 151 (Kilbride); xix, 61 (Drummaul); idem, *Ordnance survey memoirs: county Londonderry*, xxii. 52 (Ballyrashrane); xxxiii, 164 (Killowen).   **229** Day and McWilliams (eds), *Ordnance survey memoirs: county Antrim*, xvi, 48 (Billy); xvi, 129 (Kilraghts); idem, *Ordnance survey memoirs: county Londonderry*, xviii, 73 (Maghera); idem, *Ordnance survey memoirs: county Fermanagh*, iv, 63–4 (Enniskillen); Alexander Knox maintained that when the sport was played it 'was principally confined to the lower classes of the people': Knox, *A history of the county of Down*, p. 58.   **230** 5 and 6 William IV, c. 59. sec. 3. The clause ran as follows: 'And whereas cruelties are greatly promoted and encouraged by persons keeping houses, rooms, pits, grounds, or other places for the fighting or baiting of dogs, bulls, bears, or other animals, and for fighting cocks, and by persons aiding or assisting therein, and the same are great nuisances and annoyances to the neighbourhood in which they are situate, and tend to demoralize those who frequent such places; "be it therefore enacted, that from and after the passing of this act, if any person shall keep or use any house, room, pit, ground, or other place for the purpose of running, baiting, or fighting any bull, bear, badger, dog, or other animal (whether of domestic or wild nature or kind), or for cockfighting, or in which any bull, bear, badger, dog, or other such animal shall be baited, run, or fought, every such person shall be liable to a penalty not exceeding five pounds nor less than ten shillings for every day in which he shall so keep and use such house, room, pit, ground, or place for any of the purposes aforesaid"'.   **231** Collins et al. (eds), *Encyclopedia of traditional British rural sports*, p. 73; Day and McWilliams (eds), *Ordnance survey memoirs: county Antrim*, xxix, 29 (Antrim); xxxv, 68 (Grange of Muckamore).   **232** Day and McWilliams (eds), *Ordnance survey memoirs: county Antrim*, ii, 9 (Ballymartin); ii, 62 (Carnmoney); xxxv, 122 (Templepatrick); idem, *Ordnance survey memoirs: county Londonderry*, vi, 17 (Artrea). This was also the case in county Down

amusement' was 'now very rarely practised' 'partly from a change of taste, and partly from the strictness with which the laws made for its suppression are enforced'.[233]

The attitudinal and behavioural change of which the demise of cockfighting was a manifestation achieved organisational expression in the foundation in 1824 of the Society for the Prevention of the Cruelty to Animals. It epitomised the commitment and respectability that defined the Victorian era in Britain, and the emerging belief that since it was no longer legitimate to set fighting cocks at each other that the law against blood sports should be strengthened.[234] The ensuing 1849 prevention of cruelty to animals act extended the sanctions against those engaged in cockfighting to include those attending or assisting a fight.[235] Problems with the enforcement of the law, and the devotion of individuals to the sport ensured that cockfighting persisted thereafter in a covert capacity, but it was pursued by a modest number of devotees. The assertion by *The Anglo-Celt* newspaper in 1851 that cockfighting was a 'savage game' and a manifestation of 'primitive barbarism' that could not be condoned or tolerated mirrored opinion at large, but it is noteworthy that the paper was prompted to offer this observation by reports of a planned cockfight at Tullyvin, county Cavan.[236] Moreover, the die-hard cockers were determined to continue regardless of contrary opinion, and regardless of the fact that the withdrawal of public approval, and the intervention of parliament, had deprived the recreation of the endorsement required to permit it even to be deemed a sport.[237] Cockfighting was not unique in this respect, of course, but whereas throwing at cocks and bull-baiting, to which we now turn, were also subject to the coercive sanction of law, cockfighting was unique in the tableau of eighteenth-century recreational activities in the manner and speed with which it was transformed from a respected sport to a reprobated activity.

233 Knox, *A history of the county of Down*, p. 58.   234 Garnham, 'The survival of popular blood sports in Victorian Ulster', pp 107–26 passim.   235 12 and 13 Victoria, c. 92, sec. 33.   236 *The Anglo-Celt*, 24 July 1851.   237 As note 2 above; Porter, 'Cockfighting in the eighteenth and nineteenth centuries', pp 69–70.

4

Throwing at cocks, bull-baiting, bear-baiting and other animal blood sports

Unlike cockfighting, which enjoyed six decades of respectability, during which it flourished as a recreational and gambling sport, throwing at cocks, bull-baiting and allied blood sports (bear-baiting and dogfighting) were pursued beyond the boundaries of social acceptability. Viewed with hostility by the nexus of opinion formers, municipal officials and civil administrators who were increasingly influential arbiters of what was acceptable, they contravened the expanding vision of an ordered public arena to which both the middling sort and the elite aspired. A number of reasons can be adduced to explain why this was so; one of the most important was social class; another was location. Throwing at cocks and bull-baiting were emphatically plebeian recreations, which were pursued primarily in larger towns. As a result, they collided directly, and with increasing intensity as the eighteenth century progressed, with the aspiration of municipal officials, and the middling sort from whom they were largely drawn, to take control of urban public spaces in order, first to eradicate practices they deemed unrefined, and, secondly, to transform them into the ordered, polite civic areas that conformed to their *beau idéal*. This was not an uncontested vision, of course. It met with resistance within the elite from, among others, boisterous elements among the student population of Trinity College, and the pinkindindies, macaroni and other manifestations of elite rowdiness that populated the streets of the capital, and to a lesser extent other centres, during the eighteenth century.[1] Nevertheless, it grew in influence and authority because it possessed more purchase than the alternative, and because it was more obviously in keeping with the commitment to improvement, manners, and self- and social discipline inherent in the vision of a civil society then emerging.[2] This is not to imply that its triumph was assured, still less fully realised before the eighteenth century's end. As well as those of the elite for whom it held little appeal, the vision of an ordered public space was fundamentally incompatible with the traditional social order that the practitioners of plebeian sports favoured, but

1 See David Ryan, *Blasphemers and blackguards: the Irish hellfire clubs* (Dublin, 2012), chapter 5 for a recent consideration. The classic, if not entirely reliable, account is John Edward Walsh, *Sketches of Ireland sixty years ago* (Dublin, 1847); for Trinity students, see Constantia Maxwell, *Dublin under the Georges, 1714–1830* (London, 1937), pp 151–2, 157–8, and Jonah Barrington, *Personal sketches of his own time* (3 vols, London, 1827–32). 2 Barnard, *Improving Ireland?: projectors, prophets and profiteers, 1641–1786*, passim; G.J. Barker-Benfield, *The culture of sensibility: sex and society in eighteenth-century Britain* (Chicago, 2002); James Kelly and M.J. Powell (eds), *Clubs and societies in eighteenth-century Ireland* (Dublin, 2010).

the forces of custom and practice that legitimised the conduct of such sports in public spaces were put on the defensive in the course of the eighteenth century. With the impetus secured from their dominance in the public sphere, and their ascendancy in municipal and local government, the proponents of respectability and order seized the initiative, and pressed forward, with complete moral conviction, first to confine and then to eliminate the practices that they deemed behaviourally retrograde or simply undesirable.

In Ireland as in England, the fundamental issue was not whether it was reasonable or not to brutalise animals in the name of entertainment, but social power. It was in its essence a cultural struggle to determine whose social vision and whose recreational practices were acceptable, and, since the arena in which these diversions were conducted was a public one, it was also a contest to determine who controlled the streets and public spaces on the Irish urban landscape. By accomplishing their object, first, of confining, and, finally, of eliminating throwing at cocks and bull-baiting, the middling sort took a significant step towards the achievement of their vision of an ordered and regulated communal space that echoed to their values. Throwing at cocks and bull-baiting might be characterised as emblematic of a robust demotic culture, but they were unable to sustain the case in favour of such customary plebeian practices in the public sphere, and because of this they functioned in retreat from at least the middle decades of the eighteenth century.

THROWING AT COCKS

By comparison with cockfighting, which confidently claimed a long historical lineage,[3] the origins of the practice of throwing at cocks were nebulous and contested. Whereas the presence in most substantial towns of bullrings, albeit in some instances in a derelict or neglected state, was tangible evidence of the venerability of bull-baiting, there was no equivalent physical evidence to support the conclusion that throwing at cocks possessed a comparable ancestry. As a consequence, there was considerable conjecture as to how it came in to being. Indeed, one commentator admitted to be baffled, conceding in 1764 'whence that custom first took its rise amongst us I know not'.[4] Be that as it may, the common assumption was that throwing at cocks possessed deep roots, and various theories were offered, though none provided an explanation for its presence in Ireland. The most pervasive general theory attributed the practice to a religiously motivated desire for revenge on the cockerel because of its role in the story of Peter's denial of Jesus, but the religious minded were not *ad idem* on this point as the cockerel's use as a symbol of Pontius Pilate was also invoked.[5] However, since religion was not appealed to in the public discussion of throwing at cocks that took place in eighteenth-century Ireland, it is improbable that its Irish prac-

3 For cockfighting see Chapter 3.   4 *FJ*, 14 Jan. 1764.   5 Brailsford, *A taste for diversions*, p. 15.

titioners rationalised their actions by reference either to the life of Christ or to scripture. Such explanations as were advanced were historical, but of a kind that echoed the perception that throwing at cocks was a 'barbarous' relic of a bygone era.[6] Thus in response to a question posed in the short lived *Dublin Chronicle* in 1770 as to 'how old, and from whence is the custom of throwing at cocks on Shrove-Tuesday?', the newspaper ascribed its origins to an incident that had happened in England late in the first millennium when the crowing of cockerels frustrated an attempt by the Anglo-Saxons to overturn the Danish yoke:

> When the Danes were masters of England, and lorded over the natives of the island, the inhabitants of a certain great city, grown weary of their slavery, had formed a conspiracy to murder their masters in one bloody night, and twelve men had undertaken to enter the town house by a stratagem, and seizing the arms, surprise the guards which kept it; at which time their fellows, upon a signal given, were to come out of their houses, and murder all opposers. But when they were putting it in execution, the unusual crowing and fluttering of the cocks about the place they attempted to enter at, discovered their design, upon which the Danes became so enraged, that they doubled their cruelty, and used them with more severity than ever. Soon after, they were forced from the Danish yoke, and to revenge themselves on the cocks for the misfortune they involved them in, instituted this custom of knocking them on the head on Shrove Tuesday, the day on which it happened. This sport, though at first only practised in one city, in process of time became the natural divertissement, and has continued ever since the Danes first lost England.[7]

'Be that as it may', another correspondent observed referring to this legend, it did not 'justify cruelty'.[8] It also contained sufficient generic elements, and insufficient detail to be entirely convincing, which caused the sceptical to conclude that it was apocryphal. This did not precipitate the abandonment of what one may call the Danish origin-myth of throwing at cocks, but it did provide space for alternatives that possessed more contemporary currency. In an article entitled 'An enquiry into the original meaning of cock-throwing', published in 1793 in *Anthologia Hibernica*, an anonymous author proffered the suggestion, ostensibly constructed on the fact that the Latin for 'cock/s' (*gallus, galli*) was the same as that for Gaul (*Gallus*) and the Gauls (*Galli*), that the sport originated in the reign of Edward III (1312–77) and that 'gallicide, or cock throwing, was first introduced by way of contempt to the French, and to exasperate the minds of the people against that nation':

> Our ingenious forefathers invented this emblematical way of expressing their derision and resentment towards that nation. Poor *Monsieur* at the

6 *FJ*, 17 Feb. 1776.   7 *Dublin Chronicle*, 27 Feb. 1770.   8 *FJ*, 17 Feb. 1776.

stake was pelted by men and boys in a very rough and hostile manner. The brawny arm that demolished the greatest number of the enemy gained the honour of being the hero and champion of its country. The engagement generally continued the whole day, and the courageous brave English always came off conquerors.[9]

As appealing as this explanation may have been to the editor, and readers, of *Anthologia Hibernica* in the context of the re-commencement in February 1793 of hostilities between Britain and revolutionary France, it was a rather transparent attempt to update an old and, intrinsically, redundant folk belief linking the origins of the sport to the Danish intrusion more than a millennium previously. Be that as it may, it possessed sufficient purchase in Ireland to merit inclusion in Amhlaoibh Ó Súileabháin's (Humphrey O'Sullivan) diary of his life in county Kilkenny a generation later. Yet the fact that Ó Súileabháin denominated throwing at cocks 'an English practice' is evidence not only of his own discomfort with this expression of 'the intense hatred [the English] had for Frenchmen' but also of the difficulty Irish middle-class literate opinion experienced when they sought to account for the practice.[10]

This was not something that troubled those who pursued the sport, and since there is no evidence to suggest that throwing at cocks commenced in Ireland in either the early medieval or late medieval period,[11] it can reasonably be concluded that its Irish practitioners were more committed to the pursuit of the recreation than to pondering its symbolic meaning or its antiquity. This does not provide a clue as to when the practice of throwing at cocks commenced in Ireland, but if the absence of reference to the diversion among the 'unlawfull games' ('bull baytinges, beare baytinges and other uncivill and unlawful games and exercises') and 'divers new vaine customes' that Dublin Corporation aspired to proscribe in the second decade of the seventeenth century is not misleading, it postdates 1620.[12] By a process of elimination, one can hypothesise that it was introduced as part of the substantial movement of English migrants to Dublin in the middle decades of the seventeenth century, which was crucial to the growth and anglicisation of the city.

Too little is known about the social make-up and cultural practices of the English migrants whose arrival transformed Dublin into a predominantly Protestant city by 1660 to suggest how and when throwing at cocks took root.[13]

9 'An enquiry into the original meaning of cock-throwing on Shrove-Tuesday', *Anthologia Hibernica*, 2 (July 1793), pp 19–21. This explanation was previously iterated in *The Gentleman's Magazine* (1737), from which it is apparent that it possessed a long intellectual genealogy. 10 McGrath (ed.), *Diary of Humphrey O'Sullivan*, iii, 19. 11 This is in contradistinction to England 'where it appears to have been widespread in the fifteenth and sixteenth centuries, and was played by all classes of society, including royalty': Collins et al. (eds), *Encyclopedia of traditional British rural sports*, p. 75. 12 Gilbert (ed.), *Calendar of ancient records of Dublin*, iii, pp xi–ii, 20, 39–40, 123–4. 13 Nuala T. Burke, 'Dublin 1600–1800: a study in urban morphogenesis' (PhD, TCD, 1972), chapters 4–6.

It may be that it was as much a consequence of cultural diffusion as of demographic transfer, but the incentives provided for by parliament in 1662 to encourage artisans, craftsmen and traders 'to inhabit and plant in the kingdom of Ireland' provides one possible point of entry of English recreational habits.[14] Indeed, it might be observed, following Dennis Brailsford, that if 'the free atmosphere of the post-Restoration era' in England 'gave ... traditional festivals an opportunity to develop their more barbarous potentials', the adoption in Ireland of the practice of throwing at cocks was an illustration of the same impulse in action in Ireland.[15] Throwing at cocks was certainly not of such complexity that it necessitated the transfer of an intricate set of ideas or habits, since, at its most basic, it involved little more than tethering a cockerel with a rope or hempen chords to a post or stone pillar in order to provide a target; then, for a penny or comparably modest sum, an individual purchased the right to throw a stick or staff at the bird in the anticipation that if he succeeded in striking a mortal blow, the bird was his; alternatively, if he managed to knock the bird off its feet he was entitled to claim possession if he was quick and agile enough to take it into his grasp before the bird righted itself.[16] There was room within this loose framework for some variation, but the rude simplicity of the sport appealed particularly to the apprentices, servants and young men with whom it was most closely identified. They treasured the entitlement to cast off the rules and restrictions by which they were habitually bound on Shrove Tuesday, and the days leading thereto, which was the season when throwing at cocks was commonly practised.

Shrove Tuesday had evolved by the early seventeenth century into a key date in the annual calendar of apprentices in London and English regional cities; it was a day characterised by 'licensed misrule' as the rules and conventions that bound apprentices, servants and other males in equivalently dependent positions were momentarily relaxed and they were indulged in their wish to recreate on the streets and greens of towns and cities.[17] There is insufficient evidence to suggest that the situation was similar in Ireland, but the concern expressed in Dublin in 1620 that apprentices and servants were being tempted into 'vice and idleness, to the decaie and impoverishing of their masters and other the cittizens' by engaging in bear- and bull-baiting suggests that there was a comparable impulse at work

---

14 14 and 15 Charles II, chap 12: *An act for encouragement of Protestant strangers, and others, to inhabit and plant in the kingdom of Ireland*; saliently, this act was renewed in 1692. Patrick Fagan, 'The demography of Dublin in the eighteenth century', *Eighteenth-century Ireland*, 6 (1991), pp 121–56; David Dickson, 'The demographic implications of the growth of Dublin 1650–1850' in Richard Lawton and R.W. Lee (eds), *Urban population development in western Europe* (Liverpool, 1989), pp 178–89.   **15** Brailsford, *Sports and society: Elizabeth to Anne*, pp 202–3.   **16** McGrath (ed.), *Diary of Humphrey O'Sullivan*, iii, 19; Griffin, *England's revelry*, p. 34; Brailsford, *Sports and society: Elizabeth to Anne*, pp 15–18; Samuel McSkimmin, *The history and antiquities of the county of the town of Carrickfergus, from the earliest records till 1839: also a statistical survey of said county* (Belfast, 1909), p. 351. For a pithy description of the variable ways in which the sport was played see Collins et al. (eds), *Encyclopedia of traditional British rural sports*, p. 75.   **17** Brailsford, *A taste for diversions*, pp 15, 16; Griffin, *England's revelry*, pp 35, 98.

even if it did not then follow the same pattern.[18] The most obvious difference was that of scale, but as Irish urban spaces expanded as a consequence of immigration, and specialised industrial quarters emerged, the likelihood of artisans, servants and apprentices emulating the cultural practices of their English equivalents increased.[19] The process remains elusive, and the particulars of the embrace of throwing at cocks particularly opaque, but the general imitation of English recreational practices across the island, commented upon by one observer in 1732, encouraged comparable pursuits, of which throwing at cocks was one.[20] It is not possible confidently to map the geospatial extent of throwing at cocks in Ireland, but definite evidence for its presence in Dublin, Belfast, Ballymena, Londonderry, Kilkenny and Cork suggests not only that it was an urban activity, but also that it required a critical plebeian mass with anglicised cultural roots to flourish.[21] This was certainly in place by the beginning of the eighteenth century, from when there is clear evidence that recreation was being practised. As a result when the authorities in Ireland sought to emulate the example of various provincial municipalities in England and effect its eradication, they quickly learned that this would not be a simple or straightforward matter because the practitioners of the sport were too devoted to its retention readily to comply.[22]

The first identified attempt to curb the urban plebeian enthusiasm for throwing at cocks in Ireland dates from 1726. It emanated with Londonderry corporation, and it provided for a fine of 5s. for those who threw at cocks within the city walls.[23] A quarter century later, the sovereign of Belfast signalled his intention to combat the practice when in February 1750 he 'issued warrants to the several constables there to apprehend all persons who shall fight, set up, or throw at cocks on Shrove Tuesday next in the town of Belfast or within two miles thereof'.[24] As if liberated by this example, the lord mayor of Dublin, Thomas Taylor, issued a proclamation on 16 February 1751 proscribing 'the inhuman custom of throwing at cocks in the street' in the capital, on the grounds that it was injurious not only to 'the lives of … poor creatures but [also to] the limbs of many … spectators', and 'commanding the several constables of the city to be vigilant in apprehending such persons' as might challenge his order.[25] Meanwhile,

18 Gilbert (ed.), *Calendar of ancient records of Dublin*, iii, 124. 19 For insights into this process in Dublin see Burke, 'Dublin 1600–1800: a study in urban morphogenesis', chapters 4 and 5; eadem, 'An early modern Dublin suburb: the estate of Francis Aungier, Earl of Longford', *Irish Geography*, 6:4 (1972), pp 365–85; Brendan Twomey, *Smithfield and the parish of St Paul, Dublin, 1698–1750* (Dublin, 2005); James Kelly, *The Liberty and Ormond boys* (Dublin, 2006), pp 11–21. 20 'Description of Dublin, 1732' in Gilbert (ed.), *Calendar of ancient records of Dublin*, x, 527. 21 *BNL*, 7 Feb. 1750; *Munster Journal*, 18 Feb., 7 Mar. 1751; Mullin, *Derry/Londonderry*, p. 67; *FLJ*, 4 Mar. 1767; *Tucker's Cork Remembrance*, p. 155. 22 Griffin, *England's revelry*, pp 99–101. Norwich commenced its campaign to defeat the throwing at cocks in 1719; it was followed by Portsmouth in 1720, and in the 1750s 'towns everywhere were beginning to take steps to end the custom'. 23 Mullin, *Derry/Londonderry*, p. 67. 24 *BNL*, 23 Feb. 1750. 25 *Dublin Courant*, 19 Feb. 1751; *Munster Journal*, 18 Feb. 1751; *PO*, 19 Feb. 1751. Interestingly, these interventions anticipated (albeit by a small margin) the decision to prohibit throwing at cocks in London in 1762:

in Ballymena, which possessed a less developed structure of local government, 'the gentlemen there' took a quite different tack. Instead of seeking simply to ban the practice, they 'promoted a battle royal of cocks to prevent the barbarous custom of throwing at them; which battle consisted of 21 cocks in one pit; the owner of each cock putting in an English shilling, which money and cocks were given to the poor, except the surviving one'.[26] Cockfighting was, it might be suggested, a rather obvious diversionary tactic, and it may be that it succeeded since no further mention is made of the sport of throwing at cocks in that jurisdiction. It became quickly apparent though that the task of eradicating the diversion in larger towns and cities would not easily be accomplished, though this did not dissuade either the sovereign of Belfast or successive lord mayors of Dublin from trying. Indicatively, the lord mayor, Charles Barton, signalled his resolve in 1753 by reiterating the commitment to take up 'all persons who shall be found guilty of the barbarous practice of throwing at cocks', and it is a measure of his determination to ensure that his instruction was not ignored that soldiers in the Royal Barracks were requested to be at the ready to assist with the policing of the city on Shrove Tuesday, 3 March, should they be called upon.[27]

It so happened that the military were not called upon to disperse the 'great number of idle vagrants [who] assembled' in Christ-Church Yard on Shrove Tuesday for the purpose' of throwing at cocks because the task was performed satisfactorily by 'the sub-sheriff of the county ... attended by a party of constables'.[28] However, the body of people – variously described as a 'great mob' and as 'several disorderly persons' – that gathered the same day at Oxmantown Green both to partake in and to view the same activity, presented a more deliberate act of defiance, which the authorities were not willing to ignore. Inevitably, a confrontation resulted. Angered by the actions of 'some soldiers, endeavouring to disperse them, a fray ensued, in which several persons were dangerously wounded'. This was not unusual; relations between the citizenry of the city and the military garrison were inherently volatile, and it took little to ignite this combustible tinder. The spark was provided, on this occasion, by the butchers of Ormond market. They were the primary constituency of one of the city's leading factions – the Ormond Boys – and they were provoked by the altercation at Oxmantown Green to animate their own ongoing confrontation with the army. The sequence of events is unclear, but later that same day 'a disturbance happened and much mischief was done, on Ormond Quay, in a quarrel on the like account between several soldiers and butchers, which was renewed the next day with great violence, and many wounded on both sides'.[29]

These were troubling events because they manifested how an ostensibly peripheral customary diversion such as throwing at cocks could plunge the main

Vic Gattrell, *City of laughter: sex and society in eighteenth-century London* (London, 2006), p. 105. **26** *Munster Journal*, 7 Mar. 1751. **27** *BNL*, 27 Feb., 6 Mar. 1753; *PO*, 6 Mar. 1753; *UA*, 6 Mar. 1763. **28** *Universal, Advertiser*, 10 Mar. 1763. **29** *UA*, 10 Mar. 1753; *PO*, 10 Mar. 1753; Kelly, *Liberty and Ormond boys*, pp 27–33 passim.

urban centre of the country into violent disorder. In other circumstances, this might have sparked off a sustained phase of violence between the citizenry and the military, but the Ormond Boys were not in one of their active phases, and besides, the brevity of the season for throwing at cocks ensured that the cause of the confrontation soon disappeared from view.[30] Be that as it may, the authorities had no intention either of backing down or even of reconsidering the appositeness of the policy upon which they were embarked. The reiteration (by Hans Bailie) in 1755, (by John Forbes) in 1757, and (by John Tew) in 1759 of previous lord mayoral proclamations 'prohibiting the inhuman practice of throwing at cocks on Shrove Tuesday' was an earnest of their commitment, though the fact that it was necessary to reiterate the prohibition attested to the enduring appeal of the sport to artisans, apprentices and servants.[31]

The social and attitudinal cleavage to which this bore witness was reinforced during the 1760s, and afterwards, by the intensification of the campaign waged against the mistreatment of animals in the public sphere. The embrace by the *Freeman's Journal* – which quickly carved out a niche as the country's most liberal political voice following the publication of its first issue in September 1763 – of the cause of animal welfare was notable in this respect. The *Journal*'s most material contribution to the embryonic debate on this subject was a series of articles on behalf of a number of 'inoffensive harmless animal[s]', which were published in the winter of 1763–4. Taking as his starting point the fast-emerging consensus among the 'middling sort' that the 'throwing at cocks at Shrove-tide' was a 'barbarous inhuman custom', the author, who sheltered behind the *nom de plume* of 'An Englishman', called on those in power to taken on board that 'almost every body in a higher sphere in life condemns it'. Specifically, he called upon magistrates to set an example:

> It is in a magistrate's power to suppress it, which might easily be done by going in person with his proper constables to those places of resort where these idle miscreants are entertaining themselves with such acts of cruelty, rescue these poor birds out of their merciless hands, and set the vagabonds in stocks who should dare to murmur at his proceedings. Was this once or twice put into practice, it might have a great influence on the common sort; they would perceive by it that what they were doing was not only disapproved of, but punished and fear might bring that to pass, which reason and persuasion could never accomplish, for all that could be said to such wretches would not have the least weight, and the magistrate's rod would do more in this case than a Cicero's tongue.[32]

Though the author's confidence that throwing at cocks could be 'easily' suppressed was misplaced, his advocacy of intervention to discourage the sport was

30 Kelly, *Liberty and Ormond boys*, p. 39.   31 *UA*, 11 Feb. 1755; *PO*, 22 Feb. 1757, 25 Dec. 1759. 32 *FJ*, 14 Jan. 1764.

not unreciprocated. It mirrored the shared insight of the warmest critics of blood sports that throwing at cocks and bull-baiting were equally egregious, and that cockfighting was the least exceptionable of the three. (Indeed, some opponents of throwing at cocks were prepared to denominate cockfighting a 'genteel entertainment' and not only by comparison.)[33] As a consequence, hostile commentaries often considered both together.[34]

In keeping with the slowly appreciating sensitivity on the subject of cruelty to animals,[35] one of the most effective weapons in the armoury of those who aspired to put an end to what was *now* routinely denominated the 'barbarous' and 'inhuman' practice of 'throwing at cocks' was to dwell on the sheer brutality of the sport.[36] Writing in 1767 in *Finn's Leinster Journal*, a correspondent observed of Shrove Tuesday that it was the 'day on which there is more wanton cruelty committed in this civilized nation than ... is to be found in all the other nations of Europe'. He painted a disturbing picture:

> Our streets crowded with creatures seemingly of the human kind, gratifying their barbarity with the sight of a poor defenceless animal, tied to a stake and there pelted at with clubs, till it expires in the greatest of agonizing pain, with all its bones crushed, and its poor tender flesh beat to a jelly.[37]

Nine years later another commentator penned a similarly arresting description:

> Ye who have seen the heavy blows given to one of these poor animals at the *stake* of *torture*, and heard his piercing screams; who have seen his violent but vain struggles to get loose, seen his toes battered, his wings flagged, perhaps broke; his beak dropping gore, and his body by slow degrees sinking through bitter anguish into the ground, need not be informed of so shocking a spectacle. How base such treatment of a weak, defenceless animal, yet brave by nature, and courageous even to death against his equal.[38]

Persuaded that those who were responsible for such abusive excess were deserving of being treated in a comparable manner (transportation to the Caribbean plantations to ease the lot of slaves there was one suggestion), critics of the sport appealed increasingly to their readers' humanitarian instincts, and invoked the many 'useful' qualities of cockerels in support of their contention that Ireland must urgently follow the example of 'all civilized nations in Europe' and forsake 'that wicked vandal custom of throwing at cocks on Shrove Tuesday'.[39] It is difficult to assess the impact of such interventions, which were largely confined to

33 *Anthologia Hibernia*, ii (1793), p. 21. 34 *BNL*, 23 Dec. 1766. 35 See also pp 227–8; Brailsford, *Sport and society: Elizabeth to Anne*, pp 214–19. 36 *BNL*, 2 Nov. 1770. 37 *FLJ*, 4 Feb. 1767. 38 *FJ*, 17 Feb. 1776. 39 *BNL*, 27 Feb. 1767; *FLJ*, 4 Feb. 1767.

the brief spring season when the issue was topical. Yet the fact that such sentiments were published in newspapers based in Dublin, Belfast and Kilkenny suggests that the press echoed a growing current of opinion.

The re-publication in 1769 by Peter and William Wilson of Dublin of 'the substance of two sermons' opposed to throwing at cocks originally delivered in London eight years earlier supports this conclusion,[40] but this was tangibly less consequential than the augmented willingness of local officials to take action 'to suppress the inhuman practice'. A significant moment was reached in March 1765 when 'the mayor of Cork, attended by a guard of soldiers, went round the different parts of the city' and committed 'several persons' whom 'he detected in that wicked practice' to the city bridewell.[41] Two years later, the mayor of Kilkenny, Thomas Butler, was prematurely credited with having 'abolished' the 'scandalous-cruel custom' in that town by reason of his having 'perambulated ... all the lanes and bye places' where the sport was commonly conducted, and, by his presence, with striking 'panick into the minds' of those gathered at those locations for this very purpose.[42] In practice, neither intervention registered the impact initially attributed to it. Instances of 'throwing at cocks' were reported in both cities in the early 1770s, prompting Anthony Blunt, the mayor of Kilkenny in 1770–1, to supplement the by-now familiar condemnation that officials routinely offered with an appeal to 'all heads of families to keep their children and servants at home' on Shrove Tuesday and the days preceding 'as I am determined to apprehend, and punish with the utmost severity, all persons who shall be found assembling for the above infamous practices'.[43] Various office holders in Dublin likewise sought to tighten the screw with still more mixed success, as the report that 'a boy had his leg broke in Oxmantown Green by the blow of a stick' during a session of throwing at cocks in February 1773 indicates, but they contrived to make it difficult for those who sought to assemble annually at familiar locations.[44] As a consequence, reports of the playing of the sport declined from the mid-1770s, which encouraged observers to conclude that throwing at cocks 'is gradually growing out of use'. This was, it was perceptively observed in one quarter in Belfast in 1788, part of a wider cultural shift that caused the respectable to deem the practice 'barbarous' and encouraged apprentices and others to manifest 'their contempt of old customs', which hastened its decline and the diminishing popularity also of cockfighting.[45] Indicatively, it was later recalled, 'the barbarous custom of throwing at a cock fastened to a stake with sticks' on Shrove Tuesday ceased at Carrickfergus 'about the year 1794'.[46]

40 *Clemency to brutes: the substance of two sermons preached on a Shrove-Tuesday, with a particular view to dissuade from that species of cruelty annually practised, the throwing of cocks* (London, 1761; Dublin, 1769). 41 *Dublin Gazette*, 2 Mar. 1765. 42 *FLJ*, 4 Mar. 1767. 43 *FLJ*, 9 Feb. 1771; Tucker's *Cork Remembrance*, p 155; Gibson, *History of the county of the city of Cork*, ii, 206. 44 *FLJ*, 3 Mar. 1773, 19 Feb. 1774; *Hibernian Journal*, 21 Feb. 1774. 45 *BNL*, 15 Feb. 1788; McGrath (ed.), *The diary of Humphrey O'Sullivan*, iii, 19; above, pp 198–9. 46 Day and McWilliams (eds), *Ordnance survey memoirs: county Antrim*, xxxvi, 76–7; McSkimmin, *The history and antiquities of the county of the town of Carrickfergus*, p. 351.

But if, as one commentator noted gleefully in 1793, the sport of throwing at cocks was 'dying', it was too deeply rooted simply to disappear, and condemnations of the practice as socially regressive continued to possess currency. Such sports served, one censorious essayist observed, to 'inspire the minds of children and young people with a savage disposition and se[ve]rity of temper highly pleased with acts of barbarity and cruelty'.[47] From those who were unwilling to allow the tide of cultural change take its inevitable course, there were calls upon legislators to intervene. One commentator pronounced in 1793 that assembly for the purpose of throwing at cocks should be deemed 'riotous' by law, and 'indictable at assizes or sessions' by an 'express statute'; a law to this effect would, so the argument ran, assist a magistrate tasked with the maintenance of law and order, since it must be beneficial if he was empowered 'to proceed with vigour and efficacy, and at the same time with caution, prudence, and clemency – not to leave his conduct to be arraigned or defended upon doubtful implication of what is law, and what is not'. It would be possible then, the author concluded, justly to penalise the 'savage' who 'can without feeling or remorse, tie this generous creature to a stake, throw at him with clubs, and not give over while there is appearance of life in him'.[48] In point of fact, legislative intervention was not necessary. Throwing at cocks was in irrevocable decline. In 1810, the *Freeman's Journal* observed that 'the barbarous custom of throwing at cocks' was virtually abandoned. Amhlaoibh Ó Súileabháin observed in 1831 that he had not seen the practice in 'the past thirty years'. Ireland in this respect mirrored England, where, according to the *Monthly Magazine* in the late 1790s, throwing at cocks was pronounced 'nearly extinct'. This was premature. As in England, the practice persisted among small local groups into the early nineteenth century, but it was seldom referred to publicly, and it had all but disappeared in Dublin and its environs and in Kilkenny.[49]

The elimination of throwing at cocks dealt a blow to the once-vigorous plebeian culture, which tolerated when it did not explicitly valorise practices that involved aggressive and vulgar demonstrations of violence towards animals in the public arena. By contrast, it represented a triumph for the emerging middle–class ethos that esteemed and promoted respectability, decorum and public discipline. Viewed from this perspective, much more so than in the case of cockfighting, the eradication of throwing at cocks was a victory for those who advanced a less abusive, more humanitarian attitude towards animals and promoted animal welfare. Throwing at cocks was, to be sure, a more inviting target than cockfighting, because of its 'perceived unfairness … . For many who could usually accept the pain or death of an animal in sport, the fact that here the bird had neither means of defending itself nor of escape was objectionable'.[50] This is not to suggest that

47 *Anthologia Hibernica*, 2 (July 1793), p. 21.   **48** 'On a barbarous popular sport', *Anthologia Hibernica*, 2 (Oct. 1793), pp 247–8.   **49** *Monthly Magazine*, 1797 cited in Collins et al. (eds), *Encyclopedia of traditional British rural sports*, pp 75; *FJ*, 8 Mar. 1810; McGrath (ed.), *The diary of Humphrey O'Sullivan*, iii, 19; Brailsford, *A taste for diversions*, pp 181–2.   **50** Brailsford, *A taste for*

animal welfare was a priority with those who called for the elimination of the sport; rather it was a beneficial side-effect. In Ireland, as in England, 'disorder rather than cruelty ... [w]as the authorities' central concern'; in other words, animal welfare took a distant second place to public order, as evidenced by the, by comparison, modest notice accorded the collateral injuries inflicted on spectators and passers-by.[51] Reduced to its essence, the campaign to effect the exclusion of throwing at cocks from the public arena was, in the first instance, a matter of social control, and the regulation of plebeian behaviour. The achievement of that object did not confer victory in the ongoing struggle for control of public space to the growing middling sort and their allies in the state and municipal bureaucracies, but it was a significant milestone on the way. There were others yet to be reached, and one of these involved the no less problematical practice of bull-baiting, which was another recreational activity upon which plebeian and middling sort values collided.

BULL-BAITING

If throwing at cocks was the first of the sports involving the abuse of animals to be excluded from the public arena, and effectively eliminated as a recreational activity, it was followed soon after by bull-baiting. Significantly, in Ireland as well as England, these two recreational activities were commonly twinned in the fierce denunciations of 'barbarous' plebeian practices that became normative as the eighteenth century advanced, and as the respectable middle-class morality that achieved ascendancy in the nineteenth century gained an increasingly firm foothold.[52] This is as might be expected since as well its inherently violent nature, bull-baiting could equally be perceived to represent an affront to the vision of ordered public spaces that respectable opinion craved. This was particularly true of Ireland because the form of bull-baiting that was practised, in Dublin and Cork particularly, was something of a cross between traditional bull-baiting in a bullring, and bull running, and was, as a result, more likely to inconvenience the general public, to result in serious injury to passers-by as well as participants, and to bring about damage to property. It also involved the brutalisation of animals, which was a further consideration that was a source of revulsion in certain quarters.

Despite the liberal amounts of scorn poured on those who engaged in the practice in the eighteenth century, bull-baiting could reasonably lay claim to a long and respectable ancestry in Ireland, as well as in England. It was thus dif-

diversions, p. 16. **51** Griffin, *England's revelry*, p. 102. **52** Griffin, *England's revelry*, p. 113; Kelly, 'The emergence of the middle class and the decline of duelling', pp 89–93; Leonore Davidoff and Catherine Hall, *Family fortunes: men and women of the English middle class, 1780–1850* (London, 2002); for a popular, critical and readable view of the transition see Ben Wilson, *Decency and disorder: the age of cant, 1789–1837* (London, 2007).

ferent to cockfighting and to throwing at cocks, neither of which could convincingly sustain any such claim. In its classic form, bull-baiting involved the tethering of a bull to a stake with a rope of variable length (five yards was usual). This
allowed the bull to move in a circle of some thirty feet, outside of which spectators gathered, and the dogs (bulldogs and mastiffs) which were set on the bull
lined up. Bulldogs, which, as their name indicates, were the dogs of choice for
this sport, were trained to attack and tear the bull, which sought in turn to defend
itself by goring, butting and kicking its assailants. Bull-baiting was, as this suggests, a violent, brutal activity, and the assumption was that dogs would be
injured and that the bull would die a bloody, turbulent death.[53] It derived its
legitimacy as a sport from the belief that baiting served to relax and tenderise
meat thereby making it more suited to human consumption, and it was the combination of entertainment and utility that prompted the construction of bullrings
in towns and cities across Britain and Ireland in the high Middle Ages.[54] Indeed,
it is a measure of the esteem in which bull-baiting was held, that the position of
'Mayor of the Bull-ring', which was an office to which individuals in Dublin were
elected by the citizens, was created. In so far as he had a particular function, the
duties of the Mayor of the Bull-ring were largely ceremonial; ostensibly charged
with providing direction to, and policing the behaviour 'of the batchelers and the
unwedded youth of the civitie', and accorded a place of prominence in the festiv-
ities held on May Day, and the eve of the festivals of St Peter and Corpus
Christi, he had jurisdiction over the bullring in the Cornmarket 'to which the
bulles that are yearlie bated be usuallie tied'. This arrangement was persisted with
in the capital until the late sixteenth century when the pageants that were a feature of festival days were discontinued, and the Corporation came increasingly to
look with disfavour on all sporting activity, but with particular hostility upon 'bull
baytinges', which was mentioned by name in 1620 (alongside 'beare baytinges') as
one of the 'uncivill and unlawful games and exercises' that it aspired to eliminate.
In this climate the office of Mayor of the Bull-ring was increasingly anomalous,
and it was allowed to 'fall ... into desuetude' about the same time as the city's
bullring, which was last referred to as a tenement in 1632.[55] By 1651, when the
master, wardens and corporation of butchers of the city petitioned for the restoration to them of 'the fleshambles belonging to this cittie', it was apparent that bull-
baiting was no longer a current practice as the butchers promised in return to
keep up 'the custome of bull-baiteings as it was aunciently used'.[56] They were
only partly successful, if at all. According to Robert Ware, the bullring was
'removed to St Thomas St', where bull-baiting may have survived as a Christmas

---

53 Brailsford, *A taste for diversions*, pp 17–18; R.W. Malcolmson, *Popular recreation in English society, 1700–1850* (Cambridge, 1973), pp 45–6, 63.   **54** Griffin, *England's revelry*, p. 60; Collins et al.
(eds), *Encyclopedia of traditional British rural sports*, pp 51–2.   **55** Gilbert (ed.), *Calendar of ancient
records of Dublin*, ii, p. v, iii, 123–4 Gilbert, *History of the city of Dublin*, i, 153, 250–1; H.B. Clarke,
Irish historic towns atlas no. 11: Dublin, part 1, to 1610 (Dublin, 2002), section no. 21; Lennon, *Irish
historic towns atlas no. 19: Dublin, part 2, 1610 to 1756*, section no. 21.   **56** Gilbert (ed.), *Calendar
of ancient records of Dublin*, iv, 13–4.

diversion, but the imprecision in his account, which dates from 1678, suggests that it was a pale shadow of the vigorous sport it once was.[57]

The decline of the ancient sport of bull-baiting in Dublin to which the history of the office of Mayor of the Bull-ring bears witness was seemingly replicated in Drogheda, since the earliest identified reference to the bullring in that town, dating from 1657/8, refers to it in a manner that suggests it no longer served the function for which it had been established.[58] A comparable situation may have obtained in Navan,[59] but there is evidence to suggest that, as in England, bull-baiting survived intact for far longer in other urban centres where it established firm roots in the high middle ages.[60] Wexford, Carrickfergus and Derry/Londonderry are cases in point. In Wexford, the charter establishing the guild of butchers in 1621 provided for the presentation by the guild in perpetuity of two bulls for 'bull bayting at the Common playne of Wexford, ye[a]rly for ever, ... at Barttemas day [24 August] and Hallantyde [21 November]'. This undertaking was not honoured in perpetuity as promised, but the presence of a bullring in the town suggests that bull-baiting was popular there well into the eighteenth century. The erection at some point after 1770 of a fountain in the bullring implies that the sport had fallen out of favour by that point, but it is not inconsistent with the conclusion that bull-baiting was long pursued in that town.[61] Meanwhile, in Carrickfergus, county Antrim, it was long customary after swearing the mayor elect into office to fasten a bull to a ring in the market place, and to bait him with dogs. This was persisted with into the late eighteenth century, and perhaps later, as bull-baiting was practised in the town, and in the nearby locality of Belfast, into the early nineteenth century.[62] Comparable indulgence was in evidence in Londonderry, though the city corporation determined in 1696, as part of a broader process of locating violent sports outside of the old city, to proscribe bull-baiting within the city walls, and to relocate the ring and staple in the cow market.[63] Support for the sport was also manifest in Athlone,[64] Tuam,[65] Naas[66] and in Kilkenny, where, in a replication of Dublin and of the encouragement accorded cockfighting, the corporation autho-

57 Robert Ware, 'The history and antiquities of Dublin, collected from authentic records and the manuscript collections of Sir James Ware', 1678 (Armagh Public Library, Lodge MSS), p. 59. 58 T. Gogarty (ed.), *Council book of the Corporation of Drogheda* (Drogheda, 1915), p. 54; Michael McEvoy, *Return to the bull ring* (Drogheda, 1997), p. 4. 59 'Answer to queries', *UJA*, 8 (1860), p. 236. 60 Malcolmson, *Popular recreation in English society*, pp 66–8, 122–3. 61 P.H. Hore, *History of the town and county of Wexford* (London, 1906), pp 236–8. 62 McSkimmin, *The history and antiquities of the county of the town of Carrickfergus*, pp 266–7; 'Answer to queries', *UJA*, 8 (1860), pp 236–7; 'Answer to queries', *UJA*, 9 (1861–2), p. 148. 63 Mullin, *Derry/Londonderry*, p. 67. 64 Evidence for the sport in Athlone is scant, but there was a bullring on Lower Road South in the early nineteenth century: Harman Murtagh, 'Athlone' in *Irish historic towns atlas, volume I: Kildare, Carrickfergus, Bandon, Kells, Mullingar, Athlone* (Dublin, 1996), section no. 21. 65 Evidence for the sport in Tuam is scant, but there was a bullring on Vicar St. West, and it is retrospectively noted in the Town Commissioners minutes for 29 July 1873: J.A. Claffey, 'Tuam' in *Irish historic towns atlas, volume III: Derry-Londonderry, Dundalk, Armagh, Tuam, Limerick* (Dublin, 2008), section no. 21. 66 In Naas the bull, which was presented by the town sovereign, was baited at the Market Cross in the centre of the town. In 1743, the bull cost £3, and forty years later a sum was

rised the establishment of a committee to look after the sport. It also authorised the high constable of the town to function as 'the Lord of the Bull-ring', which was located in the square near St Francis' Abbey known as the 'Ring', and persisted with the use of the appellation 'Mayor of the Bull-ring' until the late eighteenth century. Indeed, it may be that the title was coeval with the bullring, which continued in use into the nineteenth century. The last recorded instance of bull-baiting in Kilkenny dates from 1837.[67]

As these different urban experiences attest, the sport of bull-baiting negotiated the elimination of the practice in certain east-coast urban centres in the seventeenth century, and flourished during the eighteenth century in those locations where local officials either tolerated or encouraged the sport. It is less than entirely clear why they did so. The strength of tradition was obviously a factor, but this was hardly sufficient on its own to sustain the activity and it is improbable that it would have survived for so long but for the fact that it was perceived by those of the elite who paid for or subsidised the activity as a gesture to the disempowered urban poor. This conclusion is reinforced by the fact that it was not unusual for a bait to take place within days of the election of a sovereign, portrieve or mayor to head the municipality, or, once the setting of dogs on the tethered bull had concluded, for the animal to be slaughtered and portioned for distribution among the citizenry.[68] However, one must not overlook the recreational dimension of such occasions. Precise descriptions of the manner in which bulls were baited in individual Irish towns are not always readily locatable, but Archibald Hamilton Rowan's account, which dates from when the sport was in retreat, offers a good sense of the attraction of the activity to spectators as well as to participants:

> A bull is procured, the wilder the better for the sport, and fastened to a stake by a rope about ten yards long, in any commodious place. The spectators make a ring around him, the hardiest in the front, as their duty is when a dog is thrown into the air, to run within the ring and by catching him to prevent him receiving any injury from the fall. The bull's horns seldom pierce the skin of the dog, but it frequently happens that men are hurt. Each person possessed of a dog brings him on a chain; there are never more than two, but generally one dog let on the bull at the time. Should a dog attack a bull anywhere but in front, he is taken up and turned out of the ring. The dog acquires the greatest favour who most fre-

still being voted by the Corporation to pay for the rope by which the bull was tied: Costello, *Kildare: saints, soldiers and horses*, p. 46.   **67** NLI, Walsh news-cuttings, MS 14026; P. Walsh, 'Eighteenth-century Kilkenny', *Old Kilkenny Review*, 17 (1968), p. 43; *Irish historic town atlas, vol. II: Maynooth. Downpatrick, Bray, Kilkenny, Fethard, Trim* (Dublin, 2005), Kilkenny, no. 21; S.J. Connolly, 'Popular culture in pre-Famine Ireland' in C.J. Byrne and M.R. Harry (eds), *Talamh an Eisc: Canadian and Irish essays* (Halifax, Nova Scotia, 1986), p. 15.   **68** Costello, *Kildare: saints, soldiers and horses*, p. 46; McSkimmin, *The history and antiquities of the county of the town of Carrickfergus*, p. 267.

quently pins the bull, that is, seizes him by the upper lip, between the nostrils, and ... the man who had caught the most dogs has plainly been the most intrepid.[69]

Since bull-baiting was 'an amusement, I am not ashamed to say I have frequently assisted at in both England and France', Hamilton Rowan's testimony cannot be taken without some discount. It should also be noted that it was offered in the context of a controversial court case.[70] Still more significantly, Rowan provides a misleading perspective on the sport in the capital, since, in contradistinction to the urban centres referred to above and the impression his ebullient description provided, municipal officials in Dublin sought to discourage the practice. As a result, bull-baiting in the classic form described by Hamilton Rowan was seldom pursued in the capital. However, the plebeian interest in the pursuit survived and it was channelled in the direction of bull running.

Dublin was not unique in the direction it took. 'Bull running, a specialised form of baiting where the bull was chivvied through the barricaded streets of the town', was long practised in the English towns of Tutbury (Staffordshire) and Stamford (Lincolnshire).[71] Dublin had no identifiable links with either place, and it evolved its own style of bull-baiting, which forged elements of bull running and traditional bull-baiting in a unique combination. The differences were touched upon by an English visitor who was familiar with both:

> In most parts of England (where ... bull-baiting is ... in fashion) they tie the bull down to a ring or stake, and never permit more than one dog to attack him at a time; a hole is also made in the ground for the creature to put his nose into, which prevents the dog seizing him in that part. After they have thus exercis'd him for an hour or two, he is led away.
>
> The custom here is quite different. ... Here, and to be sure in many other places, they generally set three, four, and sometimes five dogs on the bull at once. A rope is indeed tied round his neck, but they let him run loose through the whole town, the dogs tearing and pursuing him all the way ... Not long ago, a bull thus baited for some hours, at last through weariness and pain fell down in the street; the savages who followed him beat him with sticks to make him rise, which not being able to do, they set several dogs on him at once. This not taking effect, they then placed

69 *The trial of James Vance, esquire, one of the high sheriffs of the city of Dublin, on Thursday, the 25th February 1790, at the commissioner of oyer and terminer* ... (Dublin, 1790); Costello, *Kildare: saints, soldiers and horses*, pp 45–6. **70** R.B. McDowell, 'Introduction' in *The autobiography of Archibald Hamilton Rowan*, ed., William H. Drummond (repr., Shannon, 1972), p. vii; below, pp 230–1. **71** Brailsford, *A taste for diversion*, p. 19; Malcolmson, *Popular recreations*, pp 66–7; M.W. Walsh, 'November bull running in Stamford, Lincolnshire', *Journal of Popular Culture*, 30 (2004), pp 233–47; Collins et al. (eds), *Encyclopedia of traditional British rural sports*, pp 52–3.

a heap of straw and furs[72] under his head, which they set fire to, the pain of which I believe effected their purpose ...[73]

In common with the adoption of the sport of throwing at cocks, there is insufficient information to allow one confidently to suggest how and when this distinctly Irish style of bull-baiting evolved. However, based upon the reference in the description of life in Dublin in 1732, previously cited, and a newspaper report the same year of the lord mayor's response to information about a riot on Oxmantown Green caused by a 'mob' which had taken 'a bull by force out of Smithfield Market, and set ... dogs at him', there are solid grounds for concluding that it was firmly anchored by that date.[74] Indicatively, the latter event was reported not because it was new or unusual, but because the detention in the new Bridewell of two soldiers from the nearby garrison who joined in the bull beat prompted a failed rescue by 'a party of the soldiers from the barracks'.[75] The report is revealing, nonetheless, because it demonstrates that the practitioners of bull-baiting in Dublin felt entirely justified during the bull-baiting season, which was in November and December,[76] in seizing a bull and baiting it openly on the streets of the city.

The authorities contrived as best they could to combat this practice, but if the incidents reported during the 1730s are an accurate guide, it is a measure of their general ineffectiveness, and of the resistance they encountered that the lord mayor or sheriff ran a serious risk of assault if they intervened. These were dangerous occasions also for spectators and passers-by, and collateral injuries were not unusual.[77] It was only a matter of time therefore before the matter attracted official notice, as in November 1738 when it featured on the agenda of the Common Council of Dublin Corporation. Animated by reports that

> the peace and quiet of this city hath of late been greatly disturbed by a great number of idle, wicked and disorderly persons resorting in and about Smithfield, there making tumults and riots, disturbing the market, and from thence frequently on Mondays and Thursdays by force take one or more bulls to beat, which occasions many disorders to the hazard of the lives of several of his majesty's subjects, and to the destruction of the peace and welfare of this city,

the Common Council appealed to the board of aldermen to approve an initiative to apprehend and prosecute those responsible 'in such exemplary manner as may

72 *Lege* furze.   73 *FJ*, 1 June 1764.   74 'Description of Dublin, 1732' in Gilbert (ed.), *Calendar of ancient records of Dublin*, x, 527; *PO*, 18 Nov. 1732. Significantly, in 1731 a violent 'quarrel', necessitating the intervention of the high sheriff and the guard, between the butchers and the weavers was 'occasion'd by some weavers taking away a bull from the butchers, as they were driving him from the market': *FDJ*, 2 Jan. 1731.   75 *PO*, 18, 28 Nov. 1732.   76 *FJ*, 20 Dec. 1775. 77 *Dublin Evening Post*, 2 Nov. 1734; *Dublin Gazette*, 6 Nov. 1739, 8 June 1742.

deter any others from daring to commit the like outrage'.[78] The aldermen did not respond with the anticipated urgency to this intervention, but it is a measure of the seriousness with which the problem was regarded that the constables of the city aspired for a time thereafter, by devoting close attention to Smithfield on market day, 'to prevent the rioters of the city from hunting bulls'.[79] They were not entirely unsuccessful, but the demotic desire for excitement was stronger, and before long bulls were being taken from Smithfield market virtually at will.

The mob did not have it all its own way, however. It was sometimes interrupted in the act by the lord mayor and a party of soldiers; a number of offenders were publicly whipped, others were committed to prison *pour encourager les autres* during the 1740s and 1750s, but the attachment to bull-baiting was not easily broken.[80] Indeed, based on the claim, made at the end of George II's reign, that 'every journeyman butcher, shoemaker, or other low artificer' had one or more bulldogs, it was expanding rather than contracting.[81] Moreover, those seeking bulls to beat brought a measure of resourcefulness, determination, and ruthlessness to bear that the authorities struggled to equal. The practitioners of bull-baiting did not, for example, confine themselves to Smithfield on market day; bulls were brought from farms on the outskirts of the city, taken from 'countrymen' *en route* to market, and even seized 'with dreadful imprecations' from sale-master's yards.[82] Each of these interventions, when they occurred, had obvious financial consequences for the owner of the animal that was taken, but this mattered little to those who orchestrated such interventions. Their devotion to their dogs and to the thrill of bull-baiting was so complete they were impervious to the impact upon wider society of the annual season of bull-baiting, and of the combination of apprehension and alarm generated in the mind of the public by the death, injury and material damage that were a regular feature of the reports of such events. The number of such incidents was not especially large, but they forged an indelible impression of lawlessness and delinquency. Moreover, they were assured of a ready conduit into the public sphere, as stories of the heroic efforts of individual lords mayor dispersing baying mobs and taking angry bulls off the street made only slightly less compelling copy than dramatic accounts of bulls, 'driven to madness by the populace,' inflicting life-threatening injuries on innocent urban dwellers. They were complemented by troubling stories of the wanton destruction of property, and shocking narratives of the brutal, painful deaths to which these animals were subject. The perception created, and embraced by the middling sort, was that bull-baiting served only to gratify the baser instincts of artificers for whom the drama of pursuing a bull to a brutal death was an antidote against an otherwise humdrum existence.[83]

78 Gilbert (ed.), *Calendar of ancient records of Dublin*, viii, 315–16.　79 Gilbert (ed.), *Calendar of ancient records of Dublin*, ix, 31.　80 *FDJ*, 4 Oct. 1748; *PO*, 6 Dec. 1748; *Munster Journal*, 27 Nov. 1749, 29 Jan. 1750; *UA*, 6 Oct. 1753; *Public Gazetteer*, 12 Dec. 1758, 21 Oct. 1760.　81 *UA*, 30 Jan. 1760.　82 *Dublin Gazette*, 18 Dec. 1742; *PO*, 23 Nov. 1756; *Public Gazetteer*, 19 Oct. 1762. 83 *FDJ*, 4 Oct. 1748; *PO*, 6 Dec. 1748, 23 Nov. 1756; *Munster Journal*, 27 Nov. 1749; *Public*

This complex of forces served to ensure that the initiative in public discourse on the subject of bull-baiting remained firmly with the opponents of the sport, and that the grand narrative in the public sphere echoed the preoccupations and concerns of the advocates of law and order rather than the recreational imperatives of the bull-baiters. Moreover, the dominance of the former in the public realm was more clearly drawn as a result of a number of significant interventions in the 1760s. Because these interventions were separate rather than concerted, they were not part of either a structured or focused initiative, but they served to accentuate trends already in train, and, combined, to amplify and to reinforce the already firmly rooted impression that bull-baiting was not only 'barbarous', 'inhuman', 'cruel' and 'dangerous' but also socially regressive.[84] It was, it was pointed out, 'productive of drunkenness, idleness and quarrelling, by which much mischief is done and much labour lost to the kingdom, whole weeks in some places being employed in this inhumane sport, and attended to by crouds, whose families must want that support which might be earned in the time'. It served also, the author of these critical remarks continued, to 'keep up a spirit of ferocity' that was not confined to the economic or social realm out of which bull beating emanated, but which permeated society at large. This was illustrated by reference to the injuries inflicted by the dogs that were trained to attack bulls, which were responsible for many 'melancholy instances ... of defenceless passengers being torn to pieces'.[85] These were subjects of genuine, and legitimate, social concern. The challenge was to identify solutions. Various ideas were floated, the common denominator of which was the demand for greater regulation and augmented sanction. Thus, it was confidently avowed, the 'intollerable nusance' caused by the proliferation of dangerous dogs would be eased if parliament required the owner of 'every bull-dog' to pay 15s. annually.[86] The imprecision of the law as it stood was also highlighted; one commentator acknowledged pertinently that if bull-baiting was legally 'permitted', this did not mean it was 'to be executed in the shocking manner I have so frequently seen it done'; those responsible could surely be pursued under the laws against 'riotous and unlawful assembly'.[87] This was more problematic in practice than on paper, as those who were more legally aware acknowledged, but mounting antipathy to the reality of animal sport in its various violent manifestations not only sustained general calls upon magistrates to adopt a more interventionist position, but also specific suggestions that they should be empowered to take those responsible for riotous assembly 'into custody', and to determine that the 'able young fellows' among their number were 'immediately selected and sent on board any ship of war' and into 'the marine service'.[88]

This was a draconian suggestion, which probably explains why it was not taken up and pursued. However, it seemed to some that the reluctance of the authorities to take decisive action contributed to the greater daring of those who

Gazetteer, 12 Dec. 1758, 21 Oct. 1760, 31 Jan. 1761, 25 June 1763; *UA*, 6 Oct. 1753; *Dublin Gazette*, 8 June 1742. **84** *UA*, 30 Jan. 1760; *FJ*, 4 Jan. 1764. **85** *UA*, 30 Jan. 1760. **86** Ibid. **87** *FJ*, 4 Jan. 1764. **88** *FJ*, 14 Jan. 1764; *The Public Gazetteer*, 27 May 1760.

engaged in bull-baiting. The evidence in support of this position was ambiguous at best, but the perception that this was so was reinforced by the experience of the residents of Dolphin's Barn, Marrowbone Lane, Brown Street, Weaver's Square 'and parts adjacent' in November 1766:

> On Sunday morning last, they had a mad bull in the streets, with a number of dogs at him, and continued driving him from street to street, until they killed him; then they turned out another, and so on, until they finished five or six fine large bulls, every one of which they forcibly took from the countrymen who were bringing them to market... When the beast is dead, they leave him lying in the street, so frightful a sight that neither horse nor carriage will pass him without the greatest danger of the rider getting his limbs, neck, or skull broke ...[89]

The tangible sense of outrage suffusing the reports of this event indicates that it shocked the residents of the south-western part of the city, who had little previous experience of the 'dangerous practice of bull-hunting'. This is not to suggest that they were shielded from the more violent features of urban living. Nearby Long Lane was a favourite rendezvous point of the Liberty and Ormond Boys, but the gravitation of bull-baiting to the city's outskirts, itself a consequence of the increased determination of the authorities to suppress the activity in the city core, came at a price.[90] Moreover, it had to be paid, and repaid, as the impact of the efforts of sheriff William Lightburne (1766–7), and mayor Sir Anthony King (1778–9) to prevent bulls being taken from Smithfield, and bull-baiting in such central locations as St Mary's Abbey, compelled the committed baiters to move further afield (to Glasnevin and Finglas) in search of bulls, and to resort to previously unmentioned locations such as Kevin's Port and the Little Green for space to pursue their favoured diversion.[91]

The flexibility evident in the manner in which the sport was pursued was not confined to its metropolitan practitioners. Evidence from Waterford and Cork suggest that the authorities in these jurisdictions were no less eager than those in the metropolis to combat the sport. It is also apparent, based on a still-thinner corpus of evidence than it has been possible to assemble with respect to the capital, that bull-baiting was 'much practiced' in both cities in the 1760s and 1770s. Certainly, this was the message conveyed from Waterford in December 1769 when the mayor (Bolton Lee) of the city, 'with a party of the army, lodged in gaol, several boys that were driving a bull through the streets'.[92] The challenge posed the authorities in Cork was more formidable, as the following account of an incident in that city in the summer of 1770 attests:

89 *FJ*, 29 Nov., 16 Dec. 1766. 90 *FJ*, 16 Dec. 1766; Kelly, *The Liberty and Ormond Boys*, pp 42–4. 91 *Dublin Mercury*, 14 Oct., 27 Dec. 1766; *FJ*, 17 Dec. 1768, 5 Dec. 1769, 20 Dec. 1775; *Hoey's Publick Journal*, 19 Oct. 1772. 92 *FJ*, 23 Dec. 1769.

Some inhuman savages forcibly took a bull in the north suburbs, and after having driven him through the city with dogs, had him baited in the south suburbs for some hours, when the tormented creature ran from their carnage back into the city, which obliged the inhabitants to shut up their shops, and put an end to all business; the bull being unable to proceed further than Broad Lane, was there, and near the Exchange, baited by dogs and their brother brutes, armed with sticks, for near five hours; and after having frightened four pregnant women into fits, tossed a horse nearly as high as assign-post, threw a decrepid beggar and a standing of stockings into the kennel, gave up the remains of his tortured life in a narrow lane, much to the disappointment of his savage persecutors, and to the loss of his owner.[93]

A further incident in which a man 'narrowly escaped being killed' elicited an emotional plea, published as the 'wish' of the 'lovers and humanity and justice', that steps were taken urgently 'to prevent the savage amusement of bull-baiting' in Cork, and while there is no evidence to suggest that it had the desired impact, it echoed the wish of respectable opinion that an end should be put to a recreation they identified as damaging to the local economy, dangerous to individuals, and anti-humanitarian.[94] Bull-baiting in Ireland, a self-styled advocate of urban improvement, Philo-urbanus, observed in the *Freeman's Journal* in September 1770, 'exceed[ed] even the brutality of the bull-feast in Portugal'.[95]

Because bullfighting and bull-baiting were fundamentally different recreational activities, this was not a comparison that could be sustained, but the willingness to make the analogy is testament to the readiness of those who deemed bull-baiting a 'nuisance', to caricature its practitioners in the 1770s as 'wanton, idle vagabonds' as bereft of 'compassion, as the dogs they nurture for these devilish purposes'.[96] It was perhaps inevitable in this changing context that the authorities were in receipt of information from the public that assisted them to combat the activity,[97] but, in the broader realm, the anti-bull-baiting cause derived greater impetus from the relentless publicising of the sheer brutality of the sport. Inevitably, accounts of the injuries inflicted on innocent passers-by were afforded generous coverage in the press, but as significant as these were they occurred with such regularity that they registered less impact in the mid- and late-1770s than reports highlighting the inherent abusiveness of the recreation.[98] The following account was conveyed to the editor of the *Freeman's Journal* from Lurgan Street, Dublin, in December 1775:

I happened to meet the other day one of them ['poor creatures'] after having been beat in such a manner that I was for some time at a loss to

---

93 Tuckey's *Cork Remembrancer*, pp 156–7; Gibson, *History of Cork*, pp 206–7. 94 Tuckey's *Cork Remembrancer*, p. 158. 95 *FJ*, 8 Sept. 1770. 96 *FJ*, 8 Sept., 13 Nov. 1770, 20 Oct. 1774, 20 Dec. 1775, 31 Oct. 1776; *Hibernian Journal*, 19 Oct. 1774. 97 *FJ*, 13 Nov. 1770. 98 For accounts of injuries in the 1770s, see *Hibernian Journal*, 19 Oct. 1774.

conceive what animal it was. The sight was shocking; the nose of the creature hanging by the skin, one of its eyes almost out, and the breast torn
in a dreadful manner.[99]

Such encounters may have been traumatising for the individual concerned, but
the plenitude of instances of animal abuse – the casual egregious brutality of
penny boys and drivers who broke bones without a thought; the profound insouciance of carmen who tied calves down in such a manner that their heads were
abraded by the wheels of the vehicles in which they were carried; the calculated
torture inflicted by bored men in slaughter houses; the extracting of fat from
sheep while still alive, and so on – reinforce the caution previously offered about
ascribing too much weight to hostile testimony that chimed with the views of the
newspaper proprietor who ushered it into the public realm.[100] It is important not
to do so, moreover, lest one is led to assume that the dawning concern about
animal welfare, to which the reports of instances of egregious abuse attest, meant
that by the mid-1770s bull-baiting was embarked, inexorably, on a journey whose
inevitable destination was elimination. This was to happen within a generation,
it is true, but it could not be assumed then that it was either inevitable or immi-
nent because bull-baiting still drew on a deep reservoir of popular support, and,
most importantly, because it was sufficiently responsive to attempt, in the face of
mounting criticism, to reinvent itself in a manner that, its advocates hoped,
would disarm its critics and give it a new lease on life.

The first clear indication that the recreational activity that was bull-baiting
was capable of adjusting in a manner that might disarm its increasingly voluble
critics was provided by a report in advance of a bull-beat that was scheduled for
the Phoenix Park in Dublin in August 1779:

> The *penny boys* of Smithfield, we are informed, are to have a bull beat
> next Sunday evening at the Fifteen Acres, and have laid a considerable
> bett with the hurlers of the Phoenix Park that they draw a greater number
> of spectators than their opponents. Which ever side has less than ten
> thousand loses the wager. The *penny boys* hope that on this occasion, their
> friends round the markets etc. will exert themselves for the honour of the
> steel, and they advise all those that intend to bring dogs, to enter them
> two days before with F—t—ns (who is appointed register) opposite
> Island-bridge gate, as none will be admitted to play at the bull but such
> as are so entered; and they too, according to their rotation in the book.
> There will be tents on the ground, with variety of entertainment; and as
> this diversion is purposed [sic] to be continued every Sunday throughout
> the year, they expect suitable encouragement by a numerous appearance
> of the *mob*.[101]

99 *FJ*, 20 Dec. 1775. 100 *Hibernian Journal*, 15 Aug. 1776; *FLJ*, 18 Mar. 1778; *Volunteer Evening
Post*, 4 Jan., 10 May 1787; above, pp 217–18. 101 *FJ*, 14 Aug. 1779.

While it may appear, on first glance, that the event planned for the Phoenix Park had more in common with the organised bull-baiting that functioned with municipal approval in certain locations in Ireland and, still more in England, than with the ostensibly random bull-beats pursued in Dublin and its environs for half a century it would be unwise to draw too bold a line, since this was evidently a plebeian event – albeit one that was run on more formal lines than normal street beats. Moreover, it was clearly more than just a once-off occasion organised for the simple purpose of winning a bet. A lot of thought went into preparing for this event, and while it is impossible in the absence of further information to conclude definitively what was the calculation, it is hardly a coincidence that this initiative took place in the context of the sustained, and successful, effort by the civil authorities in the late 1770s to pursue, prosecute, and penalise those who engaged in street bull-baiting, that, if it was sustained, augured badly for its future.[102]

Assuming that this is a correct reading of the record, it can plausibly be surmised that the bull-beat organised for the Phoenix Park in August 1779 was an inaugural event organised by those among the *penny boys*, who had concluded that the sport had to change. It was certainly necessary, if it was to survive, to disengage from a confrontation with the authorities the 'penny boys' could not win, and from encounters with the respectable that served only to reinforce the hostility with which bull-beating was regarded in the public sphere, since the attempt to identify new locations where the sport might be pursued had palpably failed to secure the sport against debilitating criticism.[103] If this interpretation is correct, and it is supported by the fact that bull-baiting virtually disappeared from the streets of the city during 1779 and 1780, it offered its loyal practitioners only a temporary respite. The authorities may have welcomed the fact that they did not have to engage in the annual seasonal confrontation with the *aficionados* of bull-baiting during either year, but there were others whose vision of a reformed society was more complete, who were not content with the removal of bull-baiting from the streets of the capital. They sought nothing less than its elimination, and having brought sufficient pressure to bear to force the sport out of the Phoenix Park in 1780, they did not hesitate to call upon the authorities to take the next step, and proscribe the sport. A commentary published in the *Freeman's Journal* in January 1781 laid bare their unhappiness that bull-baiting still continued in a location contiguous to the Phoenix Park:

> Every Sunday, for a long time past, a set of impious vagrants continue to assemble near Island-bridge for the inhuman diversion of bull-beating. This being a favourite pastime, it seems, of the lower class of people, thither every denomination of vagabond resort, much to the terror of the

102 *Hibernian Journal*, 23 Oct. 1776 (two 'ringleaders' were taken into custody and sent to Newgate); ibid., 22 Oct. 1777 (John Lawlor was committed to Kilmainham gaol for his involvement in a bull-beat at Grangegorman); ibid., 17 Dec. 1777 (two persons were taken up and lodged in Newgate and the bull released).   103 *FLJ*, 2 Nov. 1776, 25 Nov. 1778.

entire neighbourhood, and for the abominable and profane purpose of breaking the holy Sabbath day. It is not a little surprising how so infamous a nuisance has so long passed unobserved by our vigilant and active magistrates, without being totally suppressed.[104]

From what it is possible to establish, this call to the city's law officers to move against bull-baiting in the environs of the Phoenix Park did not precipitate the strong response the opponents of bull-baiting desired, but it did signal the end of the *modus vivendi* that had obtained for a number of years. The reporting of a bull-beat in February 1782 in which a woman was 'much hurt' on Lower Abbey Street, and another in November 1784 indicated that street bull-baiting still had its devotees, and that they were not disinclined, in the absence of an alternative location, to bring bull-baiting back to the main thoroughfares of the city, but the small number of reported beats dating from the mid-1780s suggests that the sport drew on a narrower constituency of supporters than was the case when it was at its height.[105]

Moreover, the public perception that the sport was gratuitously violent was firmly fixed. The death of two journeymen butchers from Dublin, who travelled to Finglas on St Stephen's Day – a day traditionally devoted to the sport in certain quarters – in 1787 in search of a bull merely affirmed what was generally assumed to be the case, and it was unsurprising that the persons who were brought to trial arising out of the incident were acquitted.[106] Significantly, the victims elicited little public sympathy, and it was no coincidence that the response was similar two years later, when a bull-beat organised for a field in the North Lotts also turned violent. On this occasion, the city sheriff, James Vance, and the divisional police justice, alderman John Carleton, with a sergeant and twelve men from the main guard, intervened following a complaint from 'several respectable citizens', who were alarmed by the behaviour of the 'riotous and disorderly mob … [that] paraded through Abbey Street, on their way to the Lotts'. Angered by the intervention, and by the apprehension of two of their number, the crowd commenced stoning the military, which responded by opening fire and killing three unarmed men. This prompted an enormous outcry among those whose sensitivities were already in a heightened state because of the perception, generated by the controversial inauguration three years earlier of a Dublin police force, that the authorities were disposed to countenance the use of excessive force when they encountered even minor breaches of public order.[107] The liberal press and Whig commentators rallied in support of the traditional liberties of the subject but they were out-argued by a phalanx of conservative voices which pointed

104 *FJ*, 16 Jan. 1781.   105 *Hibernian Journal*, 13 Feb. 1782; *Volunteer Evening Post*, 6 Nov. 1784. 106 Brian Henry, *Dublin hanged: crime, law enforcement and punishment in late eighteenth-century Dublin* (Dublin, 1994), p. 95; *FJ*, 3 Jan. 1788.   107 Stanley H. Palmer, *Police and protest in England and Ireland, 1780–1850* (Cambridge, 1988), pp 92–134; Drummond (ed.), *The autobiography of Archibald Hamilton Rowan*, pp 103–6.

out reasonably that it was 'the duty of every good and active magistrate, particularly in large and populous cities, to use his utmost exertions, especially when called on, as was the present case, to oppose and disperse such unlawful meetings'.[108] The case went to trial, but the outcome was never in doubt. Sheriff Vance was promptly acquitted of the charge of murder by a jury, which was simply not prepared any longer to indulge the violence and riotousness, or to negotiate the personal danger, that bull-baiting permitted.[109]

Though the events of winter of 1789 demonstrated with unheralded clarity that the authorities' efforts to suppress bull-baiting had the support of the respectable citizenry of Dublin, it made little impression on the socio-cultural groups for whom bull-baiting was intrinsic to their identity. Obliged to look to the city margins for a suitable venue, they identified a location in Irishtown where they assembled in the winter of 1792, but after a number of Sundays of uninterrupted revelry they were obliged, by the intervention of the high constable (acting on the instruction of the lord mayor, John Carleton) and the gentlemen of the Sandymount Association, to cease their activities.[110] Nothing if not resourceful, the die-hards shifted the focus of their play to Donnybrook Common, to the 'annoyance of the neighbourhood', and to a chorus of further calls to the authorities to intervene.[111] It is not apparent if the complainants secured the response they desired in this instance, but it was clear by that point that while the authorities throughout the county did not have the resources, or possess a system of intelligence gathering that would permit them to prevent bull-beats taking place,[112] their willingness to intervene to disrupt, interrupt or to prevent such events ensured that it was increasingly difficult for the practitioners of beating to pursue the activity. Moreover, the authorities' capacity to respond continued to improve. The hated Dublin police force established in 1786 was controversially abolished in 1795, but a new expanded and enhanced body – the first version of what was to become a constabulary in 1816 – was brought into being in 1808.[113] This empowered the authorities both to respond more promptly and effectively when bull-beats were brought to their notice. Moreover, in keeping with the now widely accepted view that bull-baiting was 'barbarous', that those who revelled in an activity whose object was to reduce a useful animal to a 'poor mangled' state, revolting to ordinary sensibility, were mere 'ruffians' and 'miscreants', and that the pursuit of such activity on the Sabbath was profanation of the worst order, they were now encouraged to take new and additional steps actively to eradicate 'that disgraceful Gothic barbarity'.[114] Thus the mayor of Waterford, Samuel King,

108 *FJ*, 29, 31 Dec. 1789; *Clonmel Gazette*, 29 Dec. 1789; Henry, *Dublin hanged*, p. 95. 109 *FJ*, 2 Mar. 1790; *The trial of James Vance, esquire, one of the high sheriffs of the city of Dublin, on Thursday, the 25th February 1790, at the commissioner of oyer and terminer* ..., passim; Henry, *Dublin hanged*, p. 95. 110 *Dublin Chronicle*, 27 Nov. 1792; *FJ*, 29 Nov. 1792; 'Answers to queries', *UJA*, 8 (1860), p. 236. 111 *FJ*, 6 Dec. 1792. 112 There was a further series of bull-beats in Irishtown in 1793, for example, which elicited further calls on the authorities to prevent such 'wicked sports': *FJ*, 23 Nov. 1793. 113 Palmer, *Police and protest in England and Ireland*, pp 135–40, 148–59; Galen Broeker, *Rural disorder and police reform in Ireland, 1812–36* (London, 1970), passim. 114 *FJ*, 23

was applauded when in October 1800 he announced in advance of the bull-baiting season his intention not only to 'punish all persons exemplarily' who engaged
in the activity, but also 'to kill the bull, destroy the hide, and take up the followers, as rioters and disturbers of the public peace'.[115] Even this stern pronouncement was not sufficient to bring about the end of bull-baiting in Waterford, but
it took place increasingly in the teeth of official resistance. Thus when, in 1808,
'a mob ... engaged at Upper Calreen in the savage *divarshion* of baiting a bull' it
was interrupted by a posse of constables. The constables were 'set upon, pelted
with stones, knocked down, and finally routed leaving savagedom in possession of
the field', but it was a pyrrhic victory.[116] Indicatively, in Carrickfergus the same
year, the baiting of bulls, which had long been indulged by the authorities in the
town, 'was discontinued', and the acquiescence of those who might otherwise have
objected was bought by the purchase and slaughter of a bull, and by the distribution of its meat 'amongst the poor'. As a result, when in 1812, a local eminence,
Arthur Chichester, sought to resuscitate the sport, the mayor intervened decisively
in order to pre-empt its revival.[117]

While the authorities at Carrickfergus deployed a prudent blend of incentive
and sanction effectively to eliminate bull-baiting within their jurisdiction, the ease
with which they got their way was due in no small part to the fact that the environment across the British Isles was increasingly disposed to favour prescription,
and to the fact that the sport had visibly contracted in virtually all regions. This
accounts for the fact that the annual bull-beats that were once a feature of the
recreational calendar in parts of rural Ulster were simply 'relinquished', while
other less heatedly contested but still controversial sports such as cockfighting
persisted for another generation.[118] The most notable regional deviation from this
pattern was the English west midlands, where bull-baiting withstood the campaign to effect its extirpation until the 1830s.[119] The situation was still more
select in Ireland, though traditional bull-beats were recorded in Cork as late as
1819, in Shruel, county Longford, in 1819, in Callan, county Kilkenny, in 1828,
and, finally, in Kilkenny city in 1837.[120]

By then the chorus of voices raised against bull-baiting monopolised the
engagement, such as it was, with the sport in the public sphere.[121] In keeping
with this, parliament bowed to the weight of public sentiment and manifested its
increasing readiness to engage with the matter. Legislation to proscribe bull-baiting was proposed in 1800, and while the failure of this initiative, and subsequent
initiatives in 1802 and 1809, attested to the enduring resistance to the idea of

Nov. 1793.   **115** *FJ*, 11 Oct. 1800.   **116** Patrick Power, 'A Carrickman's diary, 1787–1809', *Journal
of the Waterford and South-East of Ireland Archaeological Society*, 15 (1912), p. 128.   **117** Costello,
Kildare: saints, soldiers and horses, p. 46; McSkimmin, *The history of Carrickfergus*, p. 267 and note;
Day and McWilliams (eds), *Ordnance survey memoirs: county Antrim*, xxxvii, 175.   **118** Day and
McWilliams (eds), *Ordnance survey memoirs: county Antrim*, viii, 113.   **119** Brailsford, *A taste for
diversions*, p. 183; Griffin, *England's revelry*, pp 151, 154, 235–49.   **120** Connolly, 'Popular culture
in pre-Famine Ireland', p. 15.   **121** Griffin, *England's revelry*, pp 126–9; Brailsford, *A taste for
diversions*, pp 58–9.

protecting animals by law, opinion gradually came round. Bull-baiting was not explicitly referred to in Richard Martin's famous measure of 1822 'to prevent cruelty to horses and cattle', though some provincial magistrates evidently concluded that it was. In fact it was only with the ratification in 1835 of the landmark *Act to consolidate and amend the several laws relating to the cruel and improper treatment of animals, and the mischiefs arising from the driving of cattle* ... that the baiting, fighting, and running of bulls was formally proscribed. Since bull-baiting had effectively been eliminated by then this enactment was first and foremost, Emma Griffin has pertinently observed, 'an ideological statement rather than a political act'. However, the act conveyed an important cultural message, and drew more narrowly the parameters of the animal kingdom humans were at liberty to use for their own purposes, and what was tolerable in the pursuit of recreational diversion.[122]

If all of this suggests that the elimination of bull-baiting was a quintessential manifestation of the triumph of the cult of improvement that permeated discourse in the eighteenth century and that achieved a measure of cultural, religious and legal ascendancy with the emergence of a powerful middling sort, this is only the more tangible, recoverable part of the significant cultural shift that is at issue. What is less visible, less explicably, but as important, Griffin properly observes, was the transformation in disposition and attitude that took place among the plebeian practitioners of bull-baiting, since something important happened there also. In order properly to engage with this it will be necessary first to reconstruct the 'nebulous and unquantifiable domain of plebeian cultural tastes'. In its absence, any account of the demise of bull-baiting that may be presented will be incomplete, but even an incomplete account (such as this) attests to the importance of this seasonal recreational activity to those who practised it, and to the fact that the key to the survival of any recreational sport was less the devotion of its practitioners than societal acceptance. Bull-baiting failed to achieve that degree of acceptance partly because it failed to adjust to survive in an era that was attitudinally different to that which had spawned it. This was the price of survival. Its inability to pay that price ensured its elimination because, like throwing at cocks, it no longer reflected the mood of the public, and any sport that was reduced to this situation was destined, like any anachronistic practice, belief or custom, first, to decline and, then, to disappear.

BEAR-BAITING AND DOGFIGHTING

Bull-baiting and throwing at cocks were forced out of existence because they collided directly with the appreciating societal conviction that such sports were bar-

---

122 Griffin, *England's revelry*, pp 233–4; Shevawn Lynam, *Humanity Dick: a biography of Richard Martin, MP, 1754–1834* (London, 1975), pp 197–225; Collins et al. (eds), *Encyclopedia of traditional British rural sports*, p. 52.

barous. These, cockfighting and hunting excepted, there is little evidence to suggest that there was much enthusiasm for animal blood sports in Ireland, or that such traditional animal blood sports as bear-baiting, badger-digging and dog-fighting, for which there is an ample record in England, were conducted other than occasionally, if at all.[123] There is no evidence, for example, that bear-baiting, which was explicitly denominated an 'unlawful game' by Dublin Corporation in 1620, and retained a topographical presence in the 'bear-garden' located on Smock Alley, was actively pursued then or thereafter, and it is surely significant that no attempt was made to imitate the unsuccessful English attempt in 1724 formally to ban the pursuit.[124] This notwithstanding, the impulse survived, and while it was not indulged as frequently in Ireland as it was in England, one can suggest a possible Irish attempt to follow in the footsteps of mid-eighteenth century Liverpool, which 'provide[d] a bear for baiting at mayoral election times', in the decision of the lord mayor of Cork, Noblett Phillips, to authorise an exhibition of 'bear beating' in the county courthouse on 16 January 1769. Phillips did not offer a rationale for his decision, but it may be conjectured that it was a misconceived attempt to counter the rising tide of criticism with respect to blood sports. The lord mayor was certainly aware that he was courting controversy, because it was made clear in advance of the event that the baiting would be pursued in an orderly fashion 'by one dog at a time, ... [and] if any person attempts to set the second dog on the bear, the owners have liberty ... to kill the dog, and take the law of the owner [sic]'. It is not recorded if everything went as choreographed, but the savagely ironic response of Humanus, who articulated the sentiment of respectable society in a contribution to the *Freeman's Journal*, demonstrated that Phillips had seriously miscalculated if he assumed he could steer a safe route between the pro- and anti-blood sports lobby, and that he could do so in a manner that would bring about the revival of near moribund forms of blood sports such as bear-baiting.[125] Moreover, the fact that there was no repeat performance suggests that officials, even those as well placed as the lord mayor of Cork, who evidently harboured few reservations, recognised that the issue stoked irreconcilable emotions that it was not in their interest to disturb. Be that as it may, the fact that the chief magistrate of the kingdom's second-largest city gave his *imprimatur* to a public bear-beat, and that it was hosted in a public building does raise the spectre that bear-baiting was conducted covertly.

This was the case certainly with dogfighting, which was linked with bull-baiting in parts of rural Ulster. Evidence for the practice is also elusive but the statement in the Ordnance Survey memoir for the parish of Maghera, county Londonderry, that 'the villagers ... were formerly very fond of fighting their dogs

123 See MacGregor, *Animal encounters*, passim.   124 Gilbert (ed.), *Calendar of ancient records of Dublin*, iii, 123–4; Gilbert, *History of Dublin*, ii, 79; Linzi Simpson, *Smock Alley Theatre: evolution of a building* (Dublin, 1996), p. 12; Collins et al. (eds), *Encyclopedia of traditional British rural sports*, p. 43; MacGregor, *Animal encounters*, pp 198–227.   125 Collins et al. (eds), *Encyclopedia of traditional British rural sports*, p. 43; *FJ*, 24 Jan. 1769.

with one another', and that 'they kept many large bulldogs', which was the dog of choice for bull-beats, suggests that the communities, urban and rural, that sustained bull-baiting may also have sustained dogfighting. More evidence is required before one might attempt, even tentatively, to map the practice, but the tantalising observation that the sport was 'decreasing' in Maghera in 1830 conforms to the broader history of blood sports, and indicates that diversions like cockfighting, dogfighting, badger-baiting and bear-baiting could only have survived from then on as underground pursuits.[126] It is also in keeping with the conclusion, previously offered with respect to cockfighting, that such sports declined more rapidly in Ireland than in England. Indicatively, dogfighting and other blood sports may have grown in popularity in England in the late 1810s and 1820s.[127]

If, as this suggests, the early nineteenth century was a transitional moment in the history of sport in Ireland because many once firmly established activities were either in decline or being forced underground, there was a number of related emerging niche sports. One of those most frequently encountered by the Ordnance Survey memoirists as they made their way around the province of Ulster was shooting at domestic fowl. This may well have been indebted in the first instance to the aristocratic sport of bird shooting, but it took the more obviously sporting form in early nineteenth-century Ulster of 'shooting at a mark for a prize'. Based on the references that have been identified, it was mainly practised at festive occasions, primarily Christmas time, when the prize that was competed for was the appropriately seasonal fare of a goose or turkey. In some locations, various domestic birds (chickens, geese and turkeys) provided the target, but in these instances logic, and the resources available to the communities that hosted such events, required that those who participated paid 'a certain sum to the owner of the fowl for a shot at him'.[128]

CONCLUSION

When William Herbert came to publish his entertaining *pot pourri* of social and cultural reminiscences of life in Ireland in 1836, he specifically mentioned bull-baiting and throwing at cocks among a number of what he deemed 'vile sports', once 'practised with impunity to the odious actors and abettors' that were now no more. Like most nineteenth-century authors, Herbert did not feel the need to enter into a complex socio-cultural explanation as to why these, and other, 'brutal practices' had disappeared. He ascribed their elimination gratefully to 'our protectors of the peace, the police', without any apparent consciousness of the fact

---

126 Day and McWilliams, *Ordnance survey memoirs, county Londonderry*, xviii, 18.   127 Brailsford, *A taste for diversons*, pp 184–5.   128 Day and McWilliams, *Ordnance survey memoirs, county Fermanagh*, iv, 130; Day and McWilliams, *Ordnance survey memoirs, county Antrim*, x, 40, xxvi, 67–8; xxxiii, 14, xxxvii, 77; Day and McWilliams, *Ordnance survey memoirs, county Londonderry*, xxviii, 18, 27.

that in so doing he echoed the desire of the middling sort during the eighteenth century that wanted rid of such sports both because they offended their perception of what was polite and decorous, and because their occurrence in public spaces – streets, greens, commons, parks – intruded in a wholly disagreeable, and at times threatening, manner into spaces they believed should reflect their more ordered approach to, and orderly attitude towards life.[129] The struggle for cultural dominance, of which the manner in which people deported themselves in public was a crucial aspect, was essentially over when Herbert addressed the matter. But for most of the eighteenth century it was one of the most significant socio-cultural struggles fought out in Irish society. In achieving victory, the middling sort took an important step towards the creation of a public space that was more ordered, and by extension, more modern. In so doing they successfully imposed their view on the apprentices, labourers, cattle-drivers, servants and others for whom throwing at cocks and bull-baiting were adrenaline-boosting recreations; the price the society at large paid was the loss of two traditional blood sports.

129 William Herbert, *Irish varieties* (Dublin, 1836), pp 90–1.

5

Hurling, commons and football

Though team sport was a feature of the recreational landscape of late early modern Ireland, as the presence of county and baronial teams in cockfighting attests, sports conducted by teams were a less than dominant presence. This may be ascribed to the fact that the number and variety of team sports was small. Cockfighting has already been referred to, but a cockfighting team was essentially an aggregation of individuals who engaged in a common pursuit that they might well have pursued separately; it was not, in other words, an intrinsic team activity, which, for the purpose of this study, is identified as a number of players operating as a unit, and combining a variety of skills, attributes and functions within a shared set of rules or conventions, which defined the sport.

The main team sports played in late early modern Ireland were hurling (*iomáin*), commons and football. Though they bear comparison respectively with the modern sports of hurling, shinty and Gaelic football, and are commonly identified as their antecedents, each was fundamentally reshaped in order to comply with the requirements of modern team sports when they were codified during the 'sporting revolution' of the late nineteenth century. As demotic sports, they were not codified in any recognizable sense, with the result that they accommodated a variety of arrangements, patterns, and practices (as in the number that constituted a team, the duration of a game, and the dimensions and nature of the playing area). This complicates any attempt either to define or precisely to describe them. It also heightens the challenge presented by the fact that there are many aspects of all three that are resistant to recovery and reconstruction, and by the legacy of a tradition of writing on these sports which has combined a positivist attitude with an asynchronous engagement with the evidence that can be drawn upon to reconstruct their histories.[1]

Of the three team sports that are addressed in this chapter, hurling was the most popular. In keeping with its putative origins, which have been enthusiastically (if not always convincingly) linked to the foundation myths of Celtic Ireland,[2] it is the sport that is identified most closely with the indigenous population,

---

1 For a recent example, which conflates folklore, history and historiography, and advances unproven claims that 'both cross-country hurling and the game of camán (commons) were played in virtually every parish' in county Donegal in the nineteenth century, see Martin McGonigle, 'Hurling in Donegal before the GAA', *Donegal Annual*, 64 (2012), pp 39–51. 2 See S.J. King, *A history of hurling* (Dublin, 1996), pp 1–6; Philip Fogarty, *Tipperary's GAA story* (Thurles, 1960), p. 15; Marcus de Búrca, *The GAA: a history* (Dublin, 1980), pp 1–2; Art Ó Maolfabhail, *Camán: two thousand years of hurling in Ireland* (Dundalk, 1973), pp 10–11.

though such attempts as have been made to map it in the eighteenth century suggest that it was a regional rather than a national sport. It was played competitively in some thirteen or fourteen counties on the southern half of the island, and pursued vigorously within a compact geographic region that embraced south Leinster, north and east Munster, and parts of south Connaught (see Maps 7 and 8).[3] Commons bears comparison with hurling in that it was also played with a stick and a small ball. It too has been accorded a Celtic ancestry, but in so far as can be established the two sports may not have overlapped geographically by the eighteenth century, and seem not to have engaged in any form of sporting or competitive interaction, not least because they were played at different times of the year. Commons certainly enjoyed a distinctly northern spatial distribution,[4] which cut it off from hurling, and it may also have sustained a smaller, and narrower community of adherents (Map 9). Football, by comparison could, and did, draw on a broader social as well as geographical catchment, and while there is insufficient evidence with which confidently to present this cartographically, it may have expanded from a comparatively small geographical area in north Leinster in the late seventeenth century to embrace north and east Leinster, Dublin, east and south Ulster, and north Connaught by the early nineteenth century. Its identification with the Old English suggests it shared a common ancestry with the popular football played in England, which ultimately provided the foundations for Association Football. Its particular popularity in county Dublin suggests also that, next to horse racing, which had the advantages of superior organisation and greater respectability, it may have possessed the urban appeal that Peter Borsay has identified as one of the prerequisites for the successful emergence of football as one of the defining pursuits of the modern era of mass recreational sports.[5] This may be true of sport in England, the United States and other industrialised societies, but the successful codification of hurling and Gaelic football, which were primarily rural recreations, in late nineteenth-century Ireland would suggest that this was not invariably the case.

HURLING

In common with so much of popular culture in this era, the history of hurling has largely to be elicited from a corpus of source material that was constructed by social interests who, to invoke the oft-quoted words of Arthur Young, perceived the sport as 'the cricket of savages'.[6] The challenges posed by source material that has to be read against the grain notwithstanding, it is apparent from the failure of the attempts to effect its elimination across a number of centuries that hurling was a deeply-rooted popular recreational pastime. Galway

3 See also Kevin Whelan, 'The geography of hurling', *History Ireland*, 1 no. 1 (1993), pp 27–31, fig. 2.   4 Ibid., fig. 1.   5 Peter Borsay, *A history of leisure: the British experience since 1500* (London, 2006).   6 Arthur Young, *Tour of Ireland* (2 vols, London, 1890), ii, 147.

Corporation's relationship with the sport in the sixteenth century is a case in point. Prompted by a complex of essentially utilitarian motives (of which the desire to promote practical skills such as the accurate use of the long bow is most readily identifiable), the Corporation ordained in 1527 not only that men were forbidden to play 'at choyttes [quoits]', but also that they must devote 'no tyme to use ne occupye the horlinge of the litill balle with hockie stickes or staves, nor use no hande balle to playe without the walles, but onely the great foote balle'.[7] Neither the circumstances that prompted this intervention, nor the reaction it generated offer a reliable pointer to the popularity of hurling in the environs of Galway in the early sixteenth century, but it may reasonably be concluded from the preferential allusion to 'great foote balle', and a subsequent royal reference to 'unlawful games', that the considerations that guided the leaders of this munici-pality were cultural as well as practical. Be that as it may, the Tudor authorities, local and national, were obliged to learn that popular recreations could not simply be regulated out of existence, though their intervention was not without impact.

Like their Stuart and Hanoverian successors, the actions of the Tudor author-ities had a considerable bearing on which sports were played, and where. However, unlike bull-baiting and throwing at cocks, which were targeted for elimination in the eighteenth century because their practitioners' wish to pursue them within a built up urban environment collided with the desire of the respectable for social order, this was a less crucial consideration for hurling and football. Both games required open spaces if they were to be played properly, which meant they did not encounter quite the same animosity. This is not to imply that hurling was exclusively a country sport, or that the impulse to play hurling was monopolised by rural dwellers, but rather that because the space required to play a team sport such as hurling was not available in the walled towns that dominated Ireland's urban landscape at the beginning of the early modern era, the attempt by local authorities to expel it from the crowded and keenly contested urban, and suburban, spaces that other sports sought, contro-versially, to occupy proved advantageous in the longer term.[8] The fact that hurl-ing was suited to public commons and fair greens permitted it not only to acquire influential patrons that eased the issue of its problematical relationship with the ruling elite for much of the eighteenth century, but also to flourish proximate to urban environments that one might deem uncongenial *a priori*. However, this seemed an unlikely prospect in the sixteenth century as the burghers of Cork made clear when in 1631 they addressed the matter of sport within the city walls, and resolved that 'hurling upon the streets ... be given over':

Whereas there hath been in former times used in this city a very bar-barous and uncivil kind of sport upon Easter Tuesdays, May days,

7 O'Sullivan, *Old Galway: the history of a Norman colony in Ireland*, p. 441; Pat O'Leary (ed.), *Killeenadeema Aille: history and heritage* (Loughrea, 2009), p. 250. 8 See above, pp 238–40.

Whitson Tuesday, *viz.*, tossing of great balls, and hurling in the open streets with the small ball, great mischiefs have oftentimes happened, as the death of men, and many wounded and maimed in these sports, and many quarrels have followed, which were like to break out into a general tumult within the city, we therefore, the Mayor, etc., for abolishing these sports and preventing the mischiefs, and the rather that we have received directions from the right hon[ourable] the Lord President, for abolishing of all such unlawful plays, ordain for a bye-law that said tossing and hurling in the street shall not be used the days aforesaid, nor any other, upon pain of 40s. And likewise that any mayor, etc., that shall permit hereafter such sports shall forfeit £20 ster[ling], and every sheriff £10.[9]

These were sizeable sanctions (much stiffer certainly than the 8*d.* authorised by Galway Corporation, albeit over a century earlier). More significantly, the resolution echoed the anglicisation of Ireland's urban spaces then under way, and the broader political, economic and cultural anglicisation that was a feature of the seventeenth century.[10]

If its spatial and cultural peripheralization in the expanding urban sphere of early seventeenth-century Ireland was potentially ominous as far as hurling was concerned, its future was not assisted by the disposition of members of the anglophone elite, who consolidated their command of the countryside as a consequence of the Cromwellian plantation, to perceive the game, not as a spirited recreational activity, but as a convenient cloak for sedition. The powerful Lord President of Munster, the earl of Orrery, articulated this view with characteristic directness; his observation in 1667 that Catholics were gathering in 'great meetings' in county Tipperary 'under pretext of a hurling match' when their real intention was to pursue a conspiracy aimed at subverting the Protestant interest was an early articulation of a point of view that was to endure.[11] What is no less striking about this letter than the suspicion Orrery brought to bear is the easy manner in which he referred to hurling, because it suggests that it was a familiar presence on the landscape of north Munster. This conclusion is given added authority by the observation of the anonymous author of a pamphlet published less than a decade later that 'the common sort meet oftentimes in great numbers (in plain meadows or ground) to recreate themselves at a game called bandy, with balls and crooked sticks, much after the manner of our play at stoe-ball'.[12] This

9 Richard Caulfield, *Council book of the corporation of Cork from 1609 to 1643 and from 1690 to 1800* (Guilford, 1876), p. 157.   10 For perspectives on these larger forces see Raymond Gillespie, *Seventeenth-century Ireland; making Ireland modern* (Dublin, 2005); Nicholas Canny, *Making Ireland British, 1580–1650* (Oxford, 2001); Raymond Gillespie, *The transformation of the Irish economy, 1550–1700* (Dundalk, 1991); Toby Barnard, *A new anatomy of Ireland: the Irish Protestants, 1649–1770* (London, 2003); J.H. Ohlmeyer, *Making Ireland English: the Irish aristocracy of the seventeenth century* (London, 2012).   11 Orrery to [ ], 9 May 1667, cited in Liam P. Ó Caithnia, *Scéal na hIomána ó thosach ama go 1884* (Baile Átha Cliath, 1980), p. 4.   12 *The present state of Ireland* (London, 1676), p. 153. Bandy ball was a game in which teams aimed to drive a small wooden

Fig. 22 John Dunton (1659–1732) was a bookseller and author, whose memoirs (published and unpublished) of his experiences in Ireland in the 1690s offer an informative perspective on otherwise poorly chronicled areas including sport (engraving by M. Van der Gucht from a drawing by E. Knight, from the frontispiece to *The life and errors of John Dunton* (2 vols, London, 1705)).

was the impression also of Thomas Dineley; writing in 1681, he sustained his pejorative characterisation of the Irish as lazy by reference to their devotion to playing games, the chief field manifestations of which 'in the meadows [were] bandy and stoeball'.[13]

ball with sticks, curved in the manner of a hockey stick, through their opponents goal. It took different forms depending on geography and local custom. The sport was popular in Devon, Wiltshire, and in variant forms, in Suffolk and Norfolk. The game is a forerunner of field and ice hockey (Collins et al. (eds), *Encyclopaedia of traditional British rural sports*, p 39; *OED*). Stoeball, stowball, stoball, stob-ball, stobball was an English game played with a ball and bent stick, which has been described as 'both similar to and a forerunner of cricket'. It is variously, and largely imprecisely described, but one of the most informative descriptions is by John Aubrey, who observed as follows: 'Stobball-play is peculiar to North Wilts, North Gloucestershire, and a little part of Somerset near Bath. They smite a ball, stuffed very hard with quills and covered with soale leather, with a staffe, commonly made of withy, about 3 [feet] and a halfe long ... A stobball-ball is of about four inches diameter, and as hard as a stone.' The bat was light and shaped like a hockey stick, much like the bats used in bandy (Collins, op cit., pp 252–3).   13 E.P. Shirley, 'Extracts from the journal of Thomas Dineley', *Journal of the Kilkenny and South East of Ireland Archaeological Society*, new ser. 1 (1856–7), p. 182.

Dineley's disinclination to describe the sport he observed, and to characterise those who engaged in recreational activity as lazy, was a manifestation of the instinctive antipathy with which sport in general, and indigenous Irish sports in particular were then regarded by the dominant Protestant interest in Ireland. Be that as it may, hurling continued to be played, and it was observed more sympathetically by John Dunton (1659–1732), the English publisher, who included an extended description in his racy, but informative, account of his experiences in Ireland in 1698, which is the fullest available of the sport as it was pursued at the end of the seventeenth century:

One exercise they use much is theire hurleing, which has something in it not unlike the play called mall.[14] When their cows are casting their haire, they pull it of[f] their backs and with their hands work it into large balls which will grow verie hard.[15] This ball they use at the hurleings, which they strike with a stick, call'd commaan, about three foote and an halfe long in the handle. At the lower end it is crooked and about three inches broad, and on this broad part you may sometimes see one of the gamesters carry the ball tossing it for 40 or 50 yards in spight of all the adverse players; and when he is like to loose it, he generally gives it a great stroak to drive it towards the goale. Sometimes if he miss his blow at the ball, he knocks one of the opposers down, at which noe resentment is to be shewn. They seldome come off without broken heads or shins in which the[y] glory verie much. At this sport sometimes one parrish or barony challenges another; they pick out ten, twelve, or twenty players of a side, and the prize is generally a barrel or two of ale, which is brought into the field and drank off by the victors on the spot, tho the vanquisht are not without a share of it too. This commonly is upon some verie large plaine, the barer of grass the better, and the goals are 200 or 300 yards one from the

14 Mall involved shooting a ball with a stick through a hoop or 'high arch of iron, one of which was located at either end of a court or playing alley: see Joseph Strutt, *The sports and pastimes of the people of England* (2nd edn, London, 1810), p. 96. 15 Dunton's description of the ball used in hurling makes no reference to a covering. This may reflect the practice, but it is notable that the ball referred to by Coquebert de Montbret in 1791 was 'covered with leather', which suggests that the introduction of a leather covering may have been an eighteenth-century innovation. This is consistent with the considerably older dating ascribed by A.T. Lucas, and Ó Caithnia, to the 'hair hurling balls' discovered in Limerick and Kerry, which possessed a covering made of plaited horsehair cord. One may legitimately question how long these would retain their integrity if struck repeatedly: Síle Ní Chinnéide, 'Coquebert de Montbret's impressions of Galway city and county in the year 1791', *Journal of the Galway Archaeological and Historical Society*, 25 (1952), p. 11; A.T. Lucas, 'Hair hurling balls', *Journal of the Cork Archaeological and Historical Society*, series 2, 57 (1952), pp 99–104; idem, 'Two recent finds: hair hurling ball from county Limerick', *Journal of the Cork Archaeological and Historical Society*, series 2, 58 (1954), pp 78–9; idem, 'Hair hurling balls from county Limerick and county Tipperary', *Journal of the Cork Archaeological and Historical Society*, series 2, 76 (1971), pp 79–80; idem., 'Hair hurling ball from Aughrim, county Kerry', *Journal of the Cork Archaeological and Historical Society*, series 2, 82 (1977), pp 30–2.

other, and which ever partie drives the ball beyond the other's goale wins the day. Their champions are of the younger and most active among them, and their kindred and mistresses are frequently spectators of their address. Two or three bagg pipes attend the conquerors at the barrell's head, and then play them out of the field. Att some of these meetings two thousand have been present together.[16]

Dunton's acknowledgement that it took skill to hurl well, strength to bear the blows that were a feature of the game, and organisation to stage what was clearly already an important communal occasion in which teams of equal but variable size contested for superiority contrasted sharply with the prevailing tendency of the literate when it came to popular sports. He is less forthcoming on the rules of the game, and on the manner in which scores were achieved, but the comparison he draws with mall and the large and undefined size of the playing area indicates that victory was achieved by the team that succeeded in penetrating the defences of their rivals and placing the hair ball, or *sliotar*, in the small goal of their opponents, and that this was a test of strength as well as skill. It may also be concluded from Dunton's tantalising but useful account that because one score effectively determined the outcome that little quarter was asked or given, and that, in common with faction fighting, the sport demanded not only that those who engaged did not shirk physicality, but also that they were predisposed to aggression.[17] This is partially substantiated by a description in verse penned eighty years later of the sport as it was then played in county Wexford. Written by Robert Devereux of Carrigmenan in the county, and printed in 1779, it offers a fuller perspective on the manner in which teams were organised, as well as the physicality of the game:

> Just as the army has its van and rear,
> Besides those who the brunt of battle bear,
> So here the lads must in three bands divide,
> The discipline's the same on either side,
> One score, and one's the number most complete.
> Seven guard the goal while seven brave the heat
> Of the mid play; the other seven drive
> At th'adverse goal, and keep the game alive. ...
> ... this happy soul,
>   Drives it directly o'er the adverse goal,
> Now diff'rent shouts from all sides rends the sky.
> Glory to one, to t'other, danger nigh.
> With greatest speed the goal they crowd around.
> Where scarce three standing men are to be found,

16 John Dunton, *Teague land: or a merry ramble to the wild Irish: letters from Ireland, 1698*, ed. Edward McLysaght (Dublin, 1982), pp 91–2. 17 Ibid.

In dread confusion heap'd upon the plain,
They stretch each sinew, swell up every vein,
This wont retire, and t'other can't advance.[18]

While it is manifest from Dunton's limpid prose and Devereux's functional verse that hurling was a robust game, it is apparent also that this was a feature of the sport that knowledgeable spectators relished. Football was played in England at this time with equivalent ardour. John Dunton did not draw a direct comparison, but it is implicit in his comments.[19]

Dunton was also conscious of the fact that a majority of the Protestant interest in Ireland were disposed instinctively to look with unease upon all manifestations of collective indigenous expression. They certainly felt justified in their suspicions in the aftermath of the ordeal they were put through when the Catholic supporters of a Stuart succession (Jacobites) seized control of the kingdom following the deposition of James II late in 1688, and proceeded to set a process in train that sought to pave the way for the attainder of some three thousand Protestants who had withdrawn their loyalty.[20] The corpus of anti-Jacobite and anti-Catholic regulations retrospectively denominated the 'penal laws' that was one consequence of this experience has frequently been examined.[21] More recently, the vigour of the ideological hostility towards the Irish language has also elicited attention, but the efforts that were made to discourage team sport has largely been overlooked outside of specialised sports histories, which usually characterise the regulation as merely another obstacle that the sport triumphantly hurdled.[22] This oversight can be accounted for by the fact that the regulation enacted by the Irish parliament in 1695 proscribing 'tumultuous and disorderly meetings, which have been and frequently are used on the Lord's day under pretence of hurling, communing, [and] foot-ball playing' was approved as part of a sabbatarian initiative.[23] However, the distinction between sabbatarian and penal legislation can be fine, and it is significant that in 1719 when Irish Protestants were in the throes of one of their periodic invasion scares that, as well as the law

18 J. Coleman, 'Hurling in the Co. Wexford in 1779', *Journal of the Waterford and South-East of Ireland Archaeological Society*, 12 (1909), p. 117. 19 As evidenced by the observation of English vernacular football reported by a participant in 1807: 'many times have I had my shins broken in playing at football': Brailsford, *A taste for diversions*, p. 63. 20 See J.G. Simms, *Jacobite Ireland, 1685–90* (London, 1966). 21 See James Kelly, 'Sustaining a confessional state: the Irish parliament and Catholicism' in idem, David Hayton and John Bergin (eds), *The eighteenth-century composite state: representative institutions in Ireland and Europe, 1689–1800* (Basingstoke, 2010), pp 44–77; idem, 'The historiography of the Penal Laws' in John Bergin et al. (eds), *New perspectives on the penal laws*, Eighteenth-Century Ireland: special issue no. 1 (Dublin, 2011), pp 27–52; James Kelly, 'Protestants and the Irish language' in idem and Ciarán Mac Murchaidh (eds), *Irish and English: essays on the linguistic and cultural frontier, 1600–1900* (Dublin, 2012), pp 189–217. 22 See de Búrca, *The GAA: a history*, p. 3. 23 Act for the better observation of the Lord's day, commonly called Sunday: 7 William III, chap 17. For an informed discussion of this context see Toby Barnard, 'Reforming Irish manners: the religious societies in Dublin during the 1690s', *Historical Journal*, 35:4 (1992), pp 805–38.

against Catholics bearing arms and requiring Catholic clergy to be registered, the authorities instructed 'all sheriffs, justices of the peace, magistrates and other officers to suppress ... all tumultuous and numerous meetings, under pretence of foot-ball playing, hurling, communing or other sports'.[24]

The targeting of hurling in 1719 was a once off. Yet the fact that sports events were embraced within this general instruction to officials to be on the *qui vive* was emblematical of the panic to which Irish Protestants were susceptible, and their instinctive conviction that large gatherings of Catholics were implicitly subversive. This susceptibility was insufficient on its own either to cause the authorities to clamp down consistently on gatherings with a sporting purpose, or to discourage the communities that engaged in such activity from play, but it did ensure that the games of hurling that were adverted to in the public sphere were disproportionately those that resulted in a disturbance of the peace. The nature of the disturbance inevitably varied. Moreover, they were relatively few in number, but because a high proportion of the occasions in which hurling was mentioned involved riots, altercations or physical exchanges in the course of which an individual was fatally injured or killed it fostered an impression that hurling was a volatile and violent game. Certainly, this was the lesson that readers were encouraged to draw from the account of 'a furious and bloody battle' fought on Sunday 28 February 1725 'between the mob of the town', which had gathered on Oxmantown Green 'in order to divert themselves with hurling, playing cat, and jumping etc', and 'the standing army', in the course of which many on both sides were seriously injured.[25] In reality, this incident was a consequence first and foremost of the troubled state of the relationship between the army and the public in the metropolis rather than a consequence of the predisposition of hurlers to violent disorder, but observers were not invited to arrive at the latter conclusion by a single event in the capital. Seven years later, concern was properly voiced when a priest named Thomas White died from the injuries he received when he intervened on St James' day in 1732 'to appease the mob' which had incited 'many quarrels and riots' at a hurling match at Clonard Bridge in county Meath.[26] Moreover, before the memory of this 'odd proceeding' had time to fade, it was reported that a young woman was 'instantly' killed by a stray bullet fired in the course of a duel involving two local gentlemen who chose the occasion of a hurling match near Athy, county Kildare, to resolve an affair of honour.[27] This was a freakish event, and it might plausibly have been categorised as such. However, the same rationalisation could not be advanced nine years later

---

24 James Kelly, 'Disappointing the boundless ambitions of France': Irish Protestants and the fear of invasion, 1661–1815', *Studia Hibernica*, 37 (2011), pp 55–6; James Kelly and M.A. Lyons (eds), *The proclamations of the kingdom of Ireland, 1660–1820* (5 vols, Dublin, 2014), iii, George I: no. 68. 25 *A full and true account of a furious and bloody battle which was fought on Sunday the 28th day of February, 1724–5 in Oxmantown Green, between the mob of the town and the standing army* (Dublin, 1724–5). 26 *Dublin Evening Post*, 1 Aug. 1732; Brady (ed.), *Catholics in the eighteenth-century press*, p. 52. 27 *Dublin Evening Post*, 11 Sept. 1733.

when 'several persons were desperately hurt and wounded' in the course of a 'fray between the county and town parties' which was precipitated by a hurling match two miles outside Limerick.[28]

Though some were disposed, based on such incidents and the enduring association they created between hurling and violence, to equate a 'hurling match' with 'an unlawful assembly' – the implication being that the law with respect to the latter should always be applied to the former – this was to misrepresent the reality of the sport of hurling. This cannot easily be demonstrated for the early eighteenth century because of the paucity of reports of ordinary games, but they are not entirely absent. One such encounter, in which 'thirty men from each side of the Liffey' competed for a prize of 30s., took place at Tully fair, near the Curragh in county Kildare, on 15 July (St Swithin's day) 1708. The fact that 'a barrel of ale, tobacco and pipes' were provided the hurlers in return for the entertainment they supplied suggests that this was a convivial occasion.[29] This impression is reinforced by an examination of the larger sample of some fifty games that took place over five decades between the mid-1740s to the mid-1790s. This is not to suggest that these occasions were free of controversial incident; approximately 25 per cent of this sample gave rise to some riotous or violent activity, but the fact that they were exceeded, by a ratio of 3:1, by games in which nothing untoward occurred demonstrates that fatal or injurious violence, though prevalent, was not endemic to hurling. This ratio certainly sustains a palpably less negative impression of the sport than that advanced by a commentator writing in the *Freeman's Journal* in 1764, who was so appalled by what he observed on the playing field, and by the behaviour of those in attendance, that he deemed hurling a 'cursed exercise' that fostered 'drunkenness, blasphemy, and all manner of debauchery'.[30] Hurling was a physically competitive activity, as John Dunton had observed, and those unfamiliar with its grammar and physicality could easily be repelled by what it involved. Arthur Young was more ambivalent; his dismissive comparison with cricket apart, he commented admiringly on the 'feats of agility' hurling demanded of those who played the game.[31] The reality for those who enjoyed watching as well as for those who participated was that it brought a measure of excitement and animation to people's lives; it offered a release from the humdrum and a respite from the daily grind whatever that might be. It was no different in this respect than other sports in the late early modern era; indeed, it resembled them in that it was the sport of choice of a particular social interest and it was possessed of a regional footprint.

Despite the modest size of the available sample (see Table 8), hurling was clearly, as Kevin Whelan demonstrated in 1993, a regional and not a national activity.[32] There are a number of ways by which its regional footprint can be

---

28 *Dublin Gazette*, 19 June 1742. 29 *Dublin Gazette*, 28 June 1708; *Flying Post, or the Postmaster*, 29 June 1708; Robert Munster, *The history of the Irish newspaper, 1685–1760* (Cambridge, 1966), p. 114. 30 *FJ*, 25 Aug. 1764. 31 Young, *Tour of Ireland*, i, 447, ii, 147. 32 Whelan, 'The geography of hurling', passim.

Table 8: Hurling: identified representative appearances, by county, 1708–93					
			LEINSTER		
Dublin	*Kildare*	*Kilkenny*	*King's county*	*Queen's county*	*Wexford*
1	1	10	–	2	2
			MUNSTER		
Clare	*Cork*	*Kerry*	*Limerick*	*Tipperary*	*Waterford*
1	2	–	3	19	3
			CONNAUGHT		
	Galway			*Mayo*	
	7			1	

Source: *Dublin Gazette*, 1708; *Dublin Evening Post*, 1732–3; *Dublin Gazette*, 1742; *Pue's Occurrences*, 1746, 1752, 1755–9; *Universal Advertiser*, 1753–5, 1757; *Finn's Leinster Journal*, 1768–70; 1773–5, 1779; *Freeman's Journal*, 1773–5, 1779, 1761, 1784–5; *Cork Evening Post*, 1769; *Hoey's Publick Journal*, 1771, 1773; *Dublin Evening Post*, 1779; *Hibernian Journal*, 1773–5,1786, 1792; *Volunteer Journal (Cork)*, 1786; *Belfast News Letter*, 1786; *Dublin Chronicle*, 1788; *Clonmel Gazette*, 1792; *Cork Gazette*, 1793

Table 9: Hurling: location of matches by province and county, 1708–93						
			LEINSTER			
Dublin	*Kildare*	*Kilkenny*	*King's county*	*Meath*	*Queen's county*	*Wexford*
15	3	8	3	1	1	1
			MUNSTER			
Clare	*Cork*	*Kerry*	*Limerick*	*Tipperary*	*Waterford*	
1	1	–	3	6	3	
			CONNAUGHT			
	Galway			*Mayo*		
	4			1		

Source: as Table 8

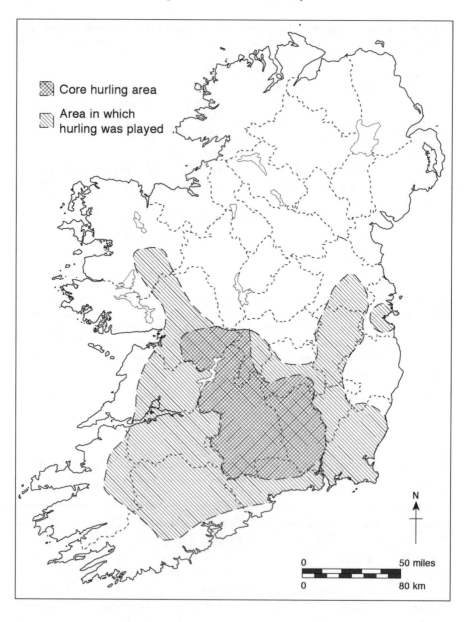

Map 7: The geography of hurling, 1700–1800: core and contiguous areas

measured, but the most reliable are the place of origin of the teams that took to the field, and the identifiable locations of reported matches. In provincial terms, this means Munster, Leinster and Connaught, but the fact that Connaught only featured once in a representative capacity (in 1792), and was then teamed up with Munster, in a match against Leinster,[33] reinforces the strong impression provided by the fact that Munster and Leinster engaged in representative matches in the late 1740s, late 1760s, early 1770s and early 1790s that, south Galway excepted, the country's hurling core was largely a Munster and Leinster phenomenon (Maps 7 and 8). However, as in Connaught, hurling was not pursued with equal enthusiasm across all of Leinster and Munster. Based on the number of identifiable teams – county, baronial and parish – and the locations in which games took place, it is apparent that within the province of Leinster, hurling had little or no foothold in the northern counties of Longford, Westmeath, Meath and Louth. This might be deemed unfair to county Meath, which provided the location for a match in 1732, but both the time and nature of this game,[34] and the fact that the other references to the playing of the sport in the county are separated by nearly half a century,[35] sustain the impression provided by the cartographic representation of the geography of known teams that hurling in Leinster was concentrated south of the line of latitude 53 degrees 30 minutes, or the present Dublin–Galway road (see Map 7). Moreover, hurling was not equally firmly anchored in central and south Leinster. Based on a reading of the cartographic representation of the locations at which games were reported (Map 8) and the broader absence of reference in the contemporary press, it is reasonable to conclude that the game was little played in counties Wicklow or Carlow, though popular memory recalled in the late nineteenth century that 'the famous hurling-match between the people of Wexford and Carlow' was played annually on the 'hurling green' to coincide with the pattern at Ballynaharna on the Wexford–Wicklow border.[36] However, this match barely registered with the public outside its immediate hinterland, and was not reported in the press. It may well be that there were other similar traditions, and locations where hurling was played in a still less structured manner that have not been recorded, which may qualify the accuracy of any attempt at its cartographic representation based on reported games. Allowance must also be made for the fact that those games that took place in the environs of Dublin city were predominantly played by visiting regional teams or by migrants. In addition, it is apparent that the sport was hardly played, if at all, over large areas much of King's county, Queen's county, county Kildare, and (possibly) county Wexford. This point needs to be made because tempting as it might be to conclude from the fact that county Kildare provided the venue for three games (in 1708, 1733 and 1755); King's county for three (1758, 1773

33 *Hibernian Journal*, 8 Oct. 1792. 34 *Dublin Evening Post*, 1 Aug. 1732. 35 There are two references dating from 1745 and 1790: see de Búrca, *The GAA: a history*, pp 3, 7. 36 G.H. Kinahan, 'Sepulchral and other prehistoric relics, counties Wexford and Wicklow', *PRIA*, 2nd series, 2 (1879–88), p. 154.

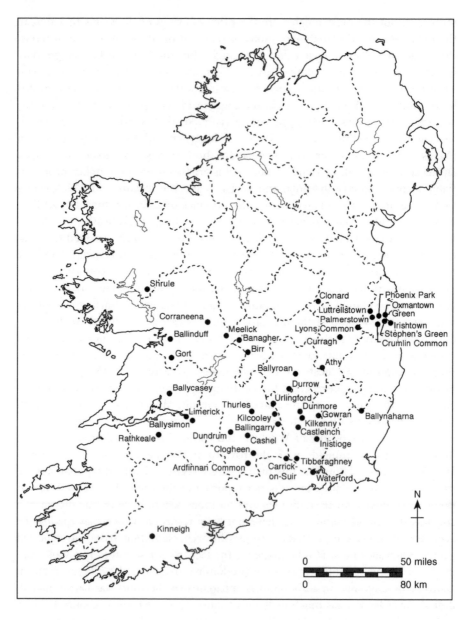

Map 8: The geography of hurling, 1708–93: location of games

and 1774), Queen's county for two (1768, 1788) and county Wexford for one (local) event (1781),[37] that hurling was strong in these counties, a contrary interpretation can also be offered. Significantly, county Kildare fielded a county team but once (the same as county Dublin) and that was in an exhibition match,[38] and no recorded team took to the field to represent King's county, Queen's county or county Wexford (the pattern at Ballynaharna apart). This may not constitute the full story, however, and it may be that other sources, which are less amenable to cartographic presentation, provide the necessary amplification. The cartographic representation of the newspaper evidence is certainly inconsistent with the impression provided by Robert Devereux, and others, of the enthusiasm for the sport manifest in county Wexford, which sustained a distinct identity – that of the 'yellow bellies' – constructed around the colour of the scarves teams from that county wore round their waist.[39] This important caveat entered, a case can still be made, based on the number of identifiable references, that in the eighteenth century the sport of hurling in Leinster was particularly strong in county Kilkenny, which (after Dublin) provided the location for the largest number of games, and (after county Tipperary) the second-largest number of teams. There are obvious risks associated with relying on newspaper reports of games played, but – the special case of Dublin apart – they sustain the impression that county Kilkenny was the heartland of hurling in Leinster. In addition, based on their capacity to field teams, and their cultural receptivity to the game, there were significant pockets of engagement in counties Wexford, Queen's and King's, deriving in the latter instance, not from its proximity to county Kilkenny, but from its geographical contiguity to localities in which the sport was played in counties Galway and Tipperary.

The situation was comparable in Munster, where county Tipperary was the county with the strongest hurling culture, and the greatest number of teams. These included representative teams for the baronies of Upper and Lower Ormond, Eliogarty, Kilnemanagh, Iffa and Offa East, and Iffa and Offa West,[40] but it is surely more significant that teams representing county Tipperary featured still more commonly, and, based on the fact that they played county Kilkenny (3 times), county Galway (2), county Waterford (1) and a barony of Lower Ormond team at Ballinderry Green in 1775, were possibly more outward-looking than counties Galway and Kilkenny.[41] Next to county Tipperary, the most identifiable centres of hurling in Munster were in counties Limerick and Waterford, but the absence of reference to county teams suggests that the

37 *Dublin Gazette*, 28 June 1708; *Dublin Evening Post*, 11 Sept. 1733; *PO*, 20 Sept. 1755 (Kildare); *PO*, 12 Aug. 1758; *FLJ*, 13 Oct. 1773, 28 Sept. 1774 (King's county); *FJ*, 23 Oct. 1781 (Wexford); *FLJ*, 3 Sept. 1768; *Dublin Chronicle*, 24 Oct. 1788 (Queen's county). 38 *Corke Journal*, 22 Sept. 1755. 39 Coleman, 'Hurling in the Co Wexford in 1779', pp 115–18; see also Kinahan, 'Sepulchral and other prehistoric relics', p. 154; Ó Caithnia, *Scéal na hIomána*, pp 35–40. 40 *PO*, 12 Aug. 1758; *Cork Evening Post*, 4 Sept. 1769; Fogarty, *Tipperary's GAA story*, p. 16. 41 *FLJ*, 3 Aug. 1768, 12 July 1769, 27 Oct. 1770 (Kilkenny); *FLJ*, 13 Oct. 1773, 28 Sept. 1774 (Galway); Ó Maolfabhail, *Camán*, p. 140 (Wexford); *Hibernian Journal*, 9 Aug. 1775 (Ormonde barony).

focus was local, and, by extension, that the sport was pursued in a less structured way than was the case in counties Kilkenny, Tipperary and Galway. In
county Waterford, for example, the sport was sufficiently firmly rooted to draw
large crowds to watch local teams compete.[42] The ability of county Clare to
present a representative team in 1759 suggests that hurling was played to an
advanced level in that shire, but the fact that it was against county Galway
supports the conclusion that it was part of a sporting axis orientated north–
south, whose epicentre was located in south county Galway, and which on
occasion extended northwards to include county Mayo, which played one representative game against county Galway in 1769.[43] The situation in county
Cork is still more opaque, but reports of a game at Kinneleagh indicate that
hurling was played in the county, while a similar case can be made for county
Kerry on the basis of the Halls' well-known description and 'hurling scene' in
that county in the 1830s, but here too its geographical and social extent remain
to be elucidated.[44]

This leaves Dublin, which, if one measured the engagement with the sport of
hurling based simply on the number of reported games, exceeded counties
Tipperary and Kilkenny combined. However, because Crumlin Common was the
location of six of the seven inter-provincial matches between Munster and
Leinster that took place between 1748 and 1773; and because games of an
exhibitory nature (which included matches between married men and bachelors)
also took place at Luttrellstown races (1748), on Irishtown Green (1757) and in
the Phoenix Park (1792), it is clear that Dublin was less a major centre of hurling than a primary centre of hurling watching.[45] This conclusion is supported
by the fact that Dublin only once fielded a representative team, and that was for
an exhibition match, which took place in front of a large crowd at Lyons
Common, county Kildare, in 1755.[46] One must not, of course, overlook the
games of hurling that were organised with increasing frequency from 1779 for
Sunday afternoon in the Phoenix Park. These were evidently of greater consequence than the random encounters that were a feature of many reported 'diversions', but since they were in all probability played by migrants they cannot be
equated with the representative or, even, with the exhibition matches, which are
a more reliable index of the strength of the sport.[47] In sum, the available evidence
supports the conclusion that counties Kilkenny, Tipperary and Galway were the
three primary hurling counties in the country in the second half of the eighteenth
century, and that the sport was sufficiently well developed in parts of the nearby

42 Piaras de Hindeberg, 'Seanchas as dúithche Paorach', *Béaloideas*, 13 (1940), pp 252–3.   43 *Public Gazetteer*, 13 Oct. 1769.   44 *Cork Gazette*, 3 July 1793; Mrs Hall, *Ireland, its scenery, character etc* (new edn, 3 vols, London, [1844]), i, 256–8. Identifying the location of Kinneleagh is problematic. It may correspond to Kinneigh, near Dunmanway.   45 *Dublin Courant*, 21 May, 4 June, 16 Aug. 1748; *FDJ*, 4, 11 June 1748; *Munster Journal*, 22 May 1749; *PO*, 25 Sept., 2 Oct. 1756; *UA*, 27 Sept. 1757; *Hibernian Journal*, 17 Oct. 1792.   46 *PO*, 20 Sept. 1755.   47 *FJ*, 20 July, 3 Aug. 1779; *Dublin Evening Post*, 12 Aug. 1779.

counties of Queen's, King's, Wexford in Leinster, and Waterford, Cork, Limerick, Kerry and Clare in Munster to constitute a region where hurling was the primary popular sporting activity.

Though strong reservations continued to be harboured, the attitudinal hostility towards hurling that one can identify in the public sphere eased palpably in the middle decades of the eighteenth century. One can only surmise why this was the case, but it is hardly coincidental that it overlaps with the modest but significant diminution in politico-religious suspicion that flowed from the failure of Ireland to rise in support of the Jacobite cause in 1745, since it meant that Irish Protestants could with less legitimacy thereafter ascribe ulterior, political, motives to sporting gatherings. It also had the effect of liberating those elements of the gentry, which were ethnically, religiously, and culturally more closely connected to the rural populace, and the expanding ranks of the rural bourgeoisie, which benefited from commercial and economic growth, to assume the critical organisational role that was required to bring the game into the public arena. This would hardly have happened, of course, without a parallel expansion of the public sphere, which was predicated in turn on improvements in the levels of literacy, and a growth in the use of English, which generated an enhanced audience for popular print and for local news.[48] The first manifestation of this with implications both for the conduct of hurling and how it was regarded was provided by the report in *Pue's Occurrences* in the summer of 1746 announcing that the 'famous match of hurling' between married men and bachelors that was an annual event in county Galway would take place in a new and more convenient location.[49] However, this was of only symbolic import by comparison with the sequence of four 'grand hurling matches' between the provinces of Munster and Leinster in the summers of 1748 and 1749 on Crumlin Common. It is not apparent if these games were conceived as a series, but the rivalry generated by Leinster's triumph in the first match, which was held on 19 May 1748, after three-quarters of an hour of intense competition, encouraged two further matches the same year. Munster's failure 'to retrieve their honour' ensured the rivalry was renewed in 1749, when a further match was played, and

---

48 Kelly, 'Disappointing the boundless ambitions of France', pp 67–70; C.D.A. Leighton, *Catholicism in a Protestant kingdom: a study of the Irish ancien régime* (Dublin, 1994); David Dickson, 'Jacobitism in eighteenth-century Ireland: a Munster perspective', *Éire-Ireland*, 39:3 and 4 (2004), pp 42–52; L.M. Cullen, 'Economic development, 1691–1750', idem, 'Economic development, 1750–1800' in W.E. Vaughan and T.W. Moody (eds), *A new history of Ireland*; iv, *Eighteenth-century Ireland* (Oxford, 1986), pp 148–50, 159–63; Munter, *The history of the newspaper in Ireland, 1685–1760*, pp 151–6, 186–8; James Kelly, 'Political publishing, 1700–1800' in Raymond Gillespie and Andrew Hadfield (eds), *The Oxford history of the book in Ireland iii: early modern Ireland* (Oxford, 2006), pp 225–31; Whelan, 'The geography of hurling', p. 28; idem, 'An underground gentry: Catholic middlemen in eighteenth-century Ireland', *Eighteenth-Century Ireland*, 10 (1995), pp 7–68; Toby Barnard, 'The gentrification of eighteenth-century Ireland', *Eighteenth-Century Ireland*, 12 (1997), pp 137–55; Kelly, 'Introduction: establishing the context' in Kelly and Mac Murchaidh (eds), *Irish and English*, pp 32–6. **49** *PO*, 5 Aug. 1746.

Fig. 23 William Cavendish, marquis of Hartington (1720–64), subsequently fourth duke of Devonshire, was lord lieutenant of Ireland between March 1755 and November 1756, in which capacity he was present at an exhibition hurling match on Lyons Common in 1755 (oil on canvas by William Hogarth, 1741, Yale Center for British Art, Paul Mellon Collection).

the series was brought to an indeterminate conclusion by the onset of darkness.[50] This ought, one might conclude, have provided the signal for the inauguration of a regular series, but this was not to be. Though the rivalry was belatedly renewed two decades later, the primary significance of the matches on Crumlin Common in 1748 and 1749 was to give hurling an enhanced profile by increasing public awareness of the game and how it was played. The positive consequences of this were revealed in July 1753 when an open invitation was extended to 'any 24 men' to participate in 'a hurling match for a silver laced hat' at the summer meeting of Crumlin races.[51] This was a quite transparent attempt to capitalise on the new-found interest in hurling, but the fact that the organisers of Rathkeale races promised 'a hurling match for 200 guineas' in their programme of events for the annual race week scheduled in 1754 for July, and that novelty bachelor versus married men matches were held on Michaelmas Day in 1756 on Crumlin Common and on Irishtown Green on the same day a year later suggests that there was an audience for such entertainments.[52] If there were any doubts on that score they were emphatically dispelled in September 1755 when

50 *Dublin Courant*, 21 May, 4 June 1748; *FDJ*, 4, 11 June 1748; *Munster Journal*, 22 May 1749; Ó Maolfabhail, *Camán*, pp 137–8. 51 *UA*, 17 July 1753; Ó Maolfabhail, *Camán*, p. 138. 52 *UA*, 11 May 1754, 27 Sept. 1757; *PO*, 25 Sept., 2 Oct. 1756.

'a match of hurling between the county of Kildare and the county of Dublin, for 18 caroline hats' held on Lyons Common, county Kildare, was watched by a crowd estimated at 10,000 among whom 'the marquis of Hartington, the lord lieutenant, and a most brilliant appearance of nobility and gentry' were conspicuous.[53] This was an exceptional event, and even if the lord lieutenant's presence owed more to his determination to defuse the political tensions animated by the money bill dispute than to his curiosity about the sport, it was significant nonetheless.[54] In a society as hierarchically pre-occupied as eighteenth-century Ireland, the lord lieutenant set the tone, and he could, by his presence alone, induce others among the elite to look more favourably upon the sport and to accept that it demanded skill and finesse as well as brawn and aggression to play well. A sympathetic response could not be assumed, however; the notice published in *Pue's Occurrences* in July 1753 to the effect that a match was 'shortly to be played by some gentlemen' at Ballycasey, county Clare, suggested that there was an openness to the game among gentlemen in certain quarters.[55] But the death, widely reported, of Pierce Clary in June 1755 when Robert Ridge, esq. responded by firing into the crowd when resistance was shown to his attempt to disperse 'a number of disorderly persons assembled at a hurling match' at Corrannaghrag in county Galway echoed the suspicion with which the assembly of sporting crowds continued to be regarded in some quarters, and the murderous violence it could easily precipitate.[56] Moreover, the conviction that hurling was a disagreeably violent sport was given little opportunity to dissipate. In September 1756 a woman had her leg broken and another lost an eye in the course of the annual Michaelmas day match, which took place on Crumlin Common that year, between teams of married men and bachelors.[57] The nervousness the sport promoted in certain circles was thus never entirely to be overcome. It was evidently a factor in the decision to 'quash ... such meetings in a great measure in the county Wexford' in the mid-1760s; and the death in 1769 of James Hingardile at Fethard from 'a stroke of a stone on the temple' received in the course of a match, prompted calls upon the gentlemen of county Tipperary to do likewise.[58] They did not respond as requested, but such incidents dovetailed with the reflexive tendency of many Protestants to ascribe a subversive intent to all manner of wrong doing, up to an including mass rural protest. It is both noteworthy, and indicative, that the same commentator perceived a connection between hurling and Whiteboyism: 'at these hurling meetings all associations and midnight revels are hatched; and positively hurling matches were the beginnings of the deluded unthinking people called

---

53 *PO*, 20 Sept. 1755; *Corke Journal*, 22 Sept. 1755; Ó Maolfabhail, *Camán*, p. 138; *HBC*, p. 165. **54** See J.C.D. Clark, 'Whig tactics and parliamentary precedent: the English management of Irish politics', *Historical Journal*, 21 (1978), pp 275–301; Eoin Magennis, *The Irish political system, 1740–1765: the golden age of the Undertakers* (Dublin, 2000), chapter 4. **55** *UA*, 28 July 1753. **56** *UA*, 17 June 1755; *PO*, 21 June 1755; Jack Burtchaell, 'British Irish news in the 1750s', *Decies*, 52 (1996), p. 20. **57** *PO*, 25 Sept., 2 Oct. 1756. **58** *FJ*, 19 Sept. 1769.

Whiteboys', he observed in 1769, alluding both to the Whiteboys movement of
the early 1760s, and the protest then simmering in county Kilkenny.[59]

In order that the strengths of what one admirer described as a 'manly, fine
diversion' might be better appreciated, and that spectators who came to view the
game did so at minimal personal risk, it was necessary that the game should
become more spectator-friendly, and less readily equated with violence on, as well
as off, the playing area.[60] The problem for hurling, as for virtually every other
sporting activity (horse racing partially excepted), was that it did not possess an
administrative or a ruling organisation, or any other mechanism whereby such
issues might be addressed.[61] It was recognised in certain quarters that the sport
would be well served if 'everything was conducted with the greatest order and regularity', and if games in which 'none of the hurlers were in the least hurt, the
greatest harmony having subsisted' were the norm rather than the exception. The
former observation was offered of the match, attended by the marquis of
Hartington at Lyons Common in September 1755, the latter of an equivalent occasion in county Galway four years later.[62] Perceiving the value of such events, the
organisers of two matches on Irishtown Green in 1757, including the annual
Michaelmas day match between bachelors and married men, which had resulted in
serious injuries in 1756, let in be known in advance that 'the green will be
corded'.[63] Their object was to allay the legitimate concerns of spectators for their
safety, and while this was not generally deemed a matter of compelling concern,
the fact that the 'grand match' between the 'boys' of the baronies of Upper and
Lower Ormond, and those of Thurles and Kilnamanagh that was played at Brittas,
county Tipperary in 1770 was played 'on a delightful green, properly corded and
cleared' indicates that the message was not lost on all in hurling's heartland.[64]
However, the absence of a mechanism to make this normative ensured that tradition remained dominant, and that the game continued to be prone to episodes of
discrediting violence, and that the hurley, in particular, was regarded with justifi-
able unease by society at large. This, inevitably, was the dimension of the game
that the press chose to highlight, and the fact that between the mid-1760s and
mid-1770s some ten deaths could be ascribed to events on the hurling field or to
the use of the hurley in an offensive fashion perpetuated this negative impression.[65]

The manner in which the game was, and continued to be conducted also provided plenty of grounds for unease. Played in the absence of a referee, or any

59 *FJ*, 19 Sept. 1769; J.S. Donnelly, 'The Whiteboys, 1761–65', *IHS*, 21(1978–9), pp 20–55; idem,
'Irish agrarian rebellion: the Whiteboys of 1769–76' in *PRIA*, 83C (1983), pp 293–331.   60 *PO*, 30
May 1752.   61 For the case of horse racing, see Kelly, 'The Turf Club', pp 417–23; above, pp 88,
94–5, 105–6; Vamplew, *A social and economic history of the turf*, pp 78–82.   62 *PO*, 20 Sept. 1755;
Public Gazetteer, 13 Oct. 1759.   63 *UA*, 9 Aug., 27 Sept. 1757.   64 *FLJ*, 29 Aug. 1770; Ó Caithnia,
Scéal na hIomána, pp 48–9; Fogarty, *Tipperary's GAA story*, p. 16.   65 For reported incidents involving deaths and serious injuries, see *Dublin Gazette*, 15 Oct. 1765 (death); *Public Gazetteer*, 12 July
1766 (death); *Dublin Mercury*, 15 July 1766 (death), 4 Oct. 1766 (injury); *FLJ*, 16 July 1768 (reputed
fatal and dangerous injuries); *FLJ*, 18 Sept. 1773 (fatal injury inflicted in a riot); *FJ*, 23 June 1774
(fatal injury); *Hibernian Journal*, 16 Sept. 1774 (death); *FLJ*, 10 Apr. 1776 (death and execution).

identifiable mediating authority, the sheer physicality of the game had the capacity to shock even sympathetic observers. The reaction of the French traveller, Coquebert de Montbret, is a case in point. Having observed two teams in county Galway in the summer of 1791, he commented in the notes he made of what he saw that it was 'terrifying to see the way they rush against each other to force the ball to pass under the goal'.[66] Given that this was the response of someone who was well disposed, it is unsurprising that hostile observers appealed routinely to superlatives to condemn a game that, they perceived, excused excess and partisanship in the 'supposed gentlemen' who organised and followed teams, and that encouraged

> the hurlers themselves ... [to] take away each others lives by jostling, or pretending to strike the ball when hovering in the air, and aiming at the same time with greatest force at the temple of one of the antagonists... I've heard of several persons being killed on the spot, and others never recover from the bruises etc. etc. received at this cursed exercise.[67]

At a lower social level, hurling was perceived to encourage social practices that the polite found distasteful, and were emblematical of the lack of refinement they equated with popular culture. These included the custom, observed by Arthur Young, whereby a particularly proficient hurler might have his choice of the local young women as his partner, or an unmarried young woman was the prize of a member of a winning team. The influential agronomist described the latter practice in his celebrated 'tour', the first edition of which was published in London in 1780:

> There is a very ancient custom here, for a number of country neighbours among the poor people, to fix upon some young woman that ought, as they think, to be married; they also agree upon a young fellow as a proper husband for her; this determined they send to the fair one's cabin to inform her, that on the Sunday following *she is to be horsed*, that is, carried on men's backs. She must then provide whisky and cider for a treat, as all will pay her a visit after mass for a hurling match. As soon as she is *horsed*, the hurling begins, in which the young fellow appointed for her husband has the eyes of all the company fixed on him; if he comes off conqueror, he is certainly married to the girl, but if another is victorious, he as certainly loses her; for she is the prize of the victor. These trials are not always finished in one Sunday, they take sometimes two or three; and the common expression when they are over is, *such a girl was goal'd*. Sometimes one barony hurls against another, but a marriageable girl is always the prize.[68]

66 Ní Chinnéide, 'Coquebert de Montbret's impressions', p. 11. 67 *FJ*, 25 Aug. 1764. 68 Young, *A tour in Ireland*, i, 446–7.

If the very idea of proffering a girl as a 'prize' to a member of a victorious team in a hurling match seems too stereotypically sexist to be true, it is important to note that the capacity to play hurling well was a source of admiration and respect not only among the male population, but also among women. Indicatively, John Dunton commented on the presence of women at games of hurling in the late seventeenth century, and the attitudes that informed their actions then had so little changed by the early nineteenth century that holly bushes borne by mummers on May day might have 'new hurling balls' attached. Significantly, they were given as presents by girls to young men, from which one may conclude not only that hurling was held in high regard in the communities in which it was played but also that proficiency in the sport was equated with virility.[69]

This notwithstanding, perhaps the most striking manifestation of the enduringly traditional character of the sport of hurling, and the way it was played, is provided by the fact that there was still no consensus on the number of players that defined a team. Hurling was not profoundly in arrear of cockfighting in that respect, but it is notable that though the latter embraced 21 as the preferred standard number in a long main, the *aficionados* of hurling were slow to acknowledge that standardisation was a still more compelling *desideratum* in a ball sport. It is not possible, certainly, to endorse Patrick Fagan's contention that 21 was 'the normal number', though this was the number invoked by James Devereux in 1779, since in addition to the teams of 12, 17, 20 and 25 that Fagan cites, teams of 18, 24, 27 and 30 have also been identified.[70] Moreover, the observation of Thomas Crofton Croker in 1825 that 'the number of hurlers may be twenty, or even a hundred' provided the teams were 'of nearly balanced powers, either as to numbers or dexterity' suggests that moves to establish a standard (or uniform) number progressed slowly, if at all.[71] Evidently, teams could be of any size provided they were of equal strength, though it may be significant that the prevailing trend was downwards.

There is some suggestion too that there was a tendency towards greater regularisation in the time when hurling matches were played if not in the duration of the game. Hurling was essentially a later summer game. An impressive 67 per cent (33 out 49) of our sample of datable matches were played in July, August and September, with September tipping easily the scale with 31 per cent compared with 18 per cent each for July and August (see Table 10). Matches were also scheduled in May, June and October, but less commonly, while playing ceased for the duration of the winter and spring; no matches were played between November and March. By comparison with the seasonal bunching that was a fea-

69 Dunton, *Teague land*, p. 92; Thomas Crofton Croker, *Fairy legends and traditions of the south of Ireland* (London, 1825), pp 305–6.   70 Patrick Fagan, *The second city: Dublin 1700–1800* (Dublin, 1986), pp 78–9; Coleman, 'Hurling in the Co. Wexford in 1779', p. 117; *Dublin Gazette*, 28 June 1708; *UA*, 17 July 1753; *PO*, 30 May 1752, 20 Sept. 1755; *Cork Evening Post*, 4 Sept. 1769; *Finns' Leinster Journal*, 29 Aug. 1770.   71 Crofton Croker, *Fairy legends and traditions of the south of Ireland*, pp 305–06.

Table 10: The timing of hurling games by month and day, 1740–93

MONTH

April	*May*	*June*	*July*	*August*	*Sept.*	*Oct.*	*Nov.–March*	*Total*
1	5	4	9	9	15	6	–	49

DAY

Mon.	*Tues.*	*Wed.*	*Thurs.*	*Fri.*	*Sat.*	*Sun.*	*Holidays*	*Total*
6	1	4	8	2	2	13	4	40

Source: *Dublin Gazette*, 1742; *Pue's Occurrences*, 1746, 1752, 1755–9; *Universal Advertiser*, 1753–5, 1757; *Finn's Leinster Journal*, 1768–70, 1773–5, 1779; *Freeman's Journal*, 1773–5, 1779, 1761, 1784–5; *Cork Evening Post*, 1769; *Hoey's Publick Journal*, 1771, 1773; *Dublin Evening Post*, 1779; *Hibernian Journal*, 1773–5, 1786, 1792; *Volunteer Journal (Cork)*, 1786; *Belfast News Letter*, 1786; *Dublin Chronicle*, 1788; *Clonmel Gazette*, 1792; *Cork Gazette*, 1793

ture of the monthly calendar, the hebdomadal calendar was appealed to more evenly. One might have anticipated that Sundays and holidays were by a large margin the days when most matches were played because they were days of rest, but while there was bunching (particularly in Dublin) on those days (Sundays, 31 per cent; holidays, 10 per cent), they did not eclipse the remainder of the week, and Thursdays (20 per cent) and Mondays (15 per cent) were also commonly resorted to; Tuesdays, Fridays and Saturdays were the least popular days (Table 10). Based on a handful of references, 4 p.m. was the preferred starting time, but 6 p.m. and later starts are also recorded.[72] A 4 p.m. throw-in[73] usually ensured there was enough light to allow a match to be played to completion, but because there was no defined duration, and most matches were deemed over when one team 'goaled', meaning that they forced the *sliotar* through their opponents goal area, their conclusion could not easily be forecast. Since the goal, 'loop' or 'bow', which was located at each end of the playing area, was constructed by sticking both ends of a sally stick or other flexible bough in the ground to form an arch, scoring was at a premium.[74] As a result, while it could happen, as was the case of the game between counties Waterford and Tipperary at Carrick-on-Suir in September 1788, that matches might last an unsatisfactory ten minutes,[75] it was still more likely that they would continue, scoreless, until the loss of light forced

72 *UA*, 27 Sept. 1757; *FLJ*, 12 July 1769, 19 July 1775. 73 Evidence that the game was started by a throw-in is provided by the reference in Robert Devereux's 1779 poem to the ball being thrown in by a 'veteran': Coleman, 'Hurling in the county Wexford in 1779', p. 117. 74 Young, *A tour in Ireland*, i, 447; McGrath (ed.), *Diary of Humphrey O'Sullivan*, iv, 91 and note 1, citing *Irish Press*, 24 July 1936; Fogarty, *Tipperary's GAA story*, p. 16. 75 Ó Maolfabhail, *Camán*, p. 140; Fagan, *The second city*, p. 78; Patrick Power, 'A Carrickman's diary, 1787–1809', *Journal of the*

their abandonment without a result. There is, as this suggests, scant information on the duration of matches, even those that were completed satisfactorily. The first two encounters in the inter-provincial series played in 1748 between Munster and Leinster lasted 45 minutes and one hour respectively; the third was pursued inconclusively until nightfall forced its abandonment, and the fourth, and final match, was called off without play when 'the Munster party thought proper to decline the combat'.[76] Some years later, at Clogheen, county Tipperary, a twenty-a-side game 'between' teams managed by Robert O'Callaghan (1710–61) of Shanbally, who represented Fethard in the Irish parliament for the five years 1755–60, and James Butler of Kilkenny commenced on the assumption that the team that scored 'the most goals in an hour and half' would 'determine the bets'.[77] The idea of a 'limited time' game, which was the choice taken on this occasion, was evidently sufficiently novel to be deemed worthy of notice, but it is also significant that it did not set the pattern for the future. The expectations of spectators were met once a game went over an hour, and a game of an hour-and-a-quarter or an hour-and-a-half was deemed a good show.[78]

The presence of crowds estimated at 10,000 at hurling games on Lyons Common in 1755, at Birr in 1773, and Thurles in 1775, attest to the putative drawing power of hurling. These are suspiciously rounded figures, to be sure. Moreover, it is not unreasonable to surmise that a substantial proportion of those present at Lyons Common in 1755, and at the Phoenix Park on 15 October 1792, when the presence of the countess of Westmorland, the wife of the then lord lieutenant, contributed in no small way to the 'vast concourse of spectators' that assembled, possessed little interest in hurling.[79] Yet, as the presence of 'the greatest concourse of company ever seen on any such occasion' at the match played at Clogheen, county Tipperary in 1752 'between [the teams of] Robert O'Callaghan and James Butler' illustrates, hurling generated allegiance at parish, baronial and county level sufficient to attract substantial attendances. This was not enough to sustain a national sport, or to release the organisers of matches, particularly those of a representative and exhibitory nature that were targeted at the genteel, of the responsibility of maximising the appeal of the sport and enhancing the spectator experience by expanding the menu of entertainments on offer. In so doing these organisers were emulating horse racing and cockfighting where ancillary entertainments were proffered in order to attract wives, families or others with merely a casual or passing interest in the sport, thereby increasing the revenue generating capacity of the event and the public profile of the venue. The first identifiable application of this approach in hurling dates from 1746 when, to coincide with the news that the location of the annual bachelors versus married-men match in county Galway was moving from Ballinduffe to the

Waterford and South-East of Ireland Archaeological Society, 14 (1911), p. 150.   **76** *FDJ*, 4, 11 June 1748; *Dublin Courant*, 21 May 1748.   **77** Johnston-Liik, *History of the Irish parliament*, v, 381; *PO*, 30 May 1752.   **78** *PO*, 12 Aug. 1758.   **79** *PO*, 20 Sept. 1755; *FLJ*, 13 Oct. 1773; *Hibernian Journal*, 17 Oct. 1792; *Clonmel Gazette*, 20 Oct. 1792.

turlough of Newtown, it was announced that those attending the hurling could partake of a variety of other diversions:

> There will be a bridle, saddle and sweep stakes run before the hurling, and a ball at night at Mr Edmund Ruberry's in Gort, for the entertainment of the ladies, where all possible care will be taken for their reception. Also a buck hunt next morning.[80]

It is not clear if this augmented menu of entertainment possessed the requisite appeal, but it is reasonable to assume that it achieved its purpose, as others followed suit. More than a decade later when the hurlers of county Clare and county Galway met in a representative match in October 1759, the organisers added to the drama of the occasion by having the Galway team

> march ... from Gort to the turlough, two miles distant, preceded by a band of music, a French horn, a running footman, and a fellow in an antic [*sic*] or harlequin dress. ... The above procession closed with many carriages and horsemen; the numerous company at the turlough made a fine appearance.[81]

This was contrived ceremony, consciously constructed to generate a festive atmosphere, and, as the hosting of an elegant entertainment for the Clare hurlers on the following evening attested, structured to demonstrate that a hurling match could be the centrepiece of a veritable local carnival. What this, and comparable events demonstrated, was that by the mid-eighteenth century hurling operated in a competitive sporting milieu in which those who best perceived the connection between sport, entertainment and money, endeavoured to exploit it for personal gain. It is not apparent precisely who was behind the events referred to above in county Galway, or who sought to organise a bachelors versus married-men match at Ardfinnan Green in south county Tipperary in 1769, but the fact that the latter was confined to 'gentlemen of the baronies of Iffa and Offa' and that the entertainment included 'a cold dinner, and a ball at night for the ladies' indicates that the priority was the attraction of paying clientele rather than the quality of the sport.[82] Tellingly, this was not the last such overture; the promise of an 'elegant assembly in Thurles, for which the best music is engaged and every material to render the entertainment pleasing to the ladies', was advertised in an attempt to attract spectators to a match in August 1770. It must not have had the desired effect, as it was not repeated. Evidently, hurling did not appeal to the same social interest as horse racing, for whom such entertainments enjoyed a longer innings.[83]

---

80 *PO*, 5 Aug. 1746. 81 *Public Gazetteer*, 13 Oct. 1759; *PO*, 16 Oct. 1759. 82 *Cork Evening Post*, 4 Sept. 1769, printed in Ó Caithnia, *Scéal na hIomána*, p. 48. 83 *FLJ*, 29 Aug. 1770, printed in Ó Caithnia, *Scéal na hIomána*, pp 48–9.

It is also the case that hurling was not as dependent as horse racing and cock-fighting on gambling to fuel public interest. Be that as it may, one cannot over-look the fact that money was integral to the sport, and that the prize money on offer was generally significantly in excess of the 30s. available to the victors of the game played at Tully fair in 1708.[84] In certain instances, the prize on offer was merely honorific. In keeping with the fact that they subscribed 6d. sterling apiece, the 48 players who participated in the exhibition match organised as part of Crumlin races in August 1753 played for a silver laced hat valued at £1 2d. 9d.[85] The eighteen 'gentlemen' assembled to represent Kildare and Dublin at Lyons Common in 1755 competed for more ordinary 'caroline hats' but since their audience included the lord lieutenant, this was first and foremost an exhi-bition rather than a competitive match.[86] The sums of money presented to the winners, and still less the sums bet by the patrons of teams and by spectators are not always identifiable, but the usual prize was of the order of 20 to 50 guineas. This is somewhat in arrear of the prizes offered at regional cockfights in Ulster, and was presumably in keeping with the resources to which the organisers of these teams had access.[87] However, as with cockfighting, when the gentry were involved the prizes on offer could (but did not necessarily always) rise in pro-portion. Indicatively, the winners of the hurling match added to the programme at Rathkeale races in July 1754 were promised £200, a sum that was not again publicly on offer until September 1768.[88] Sums of this order became more common thereafter, but even the prizes of 100, 200 and 300 guineas offered in the course of the following decade were dwarfed by the 1000 guineas that was at stake when teams representing counties Tipperary and Galway competed before a large crowd near Banagher in September 1773.[89]

This was an exceptional sum – so large indeed, that one may surmise it was one of those cases in which two passionate landed patrons, or more likely, a number of landed patrons were embroiled in an acute rivalry. The 'patronage of local gentry families, particularly those most closely embedded in the life of the local people', was, Kevin Whelan has argued, 'the most important factor' in determining where hurling was played in the eighteenth century.[90] This is hardly true in all cases (one may instance Crumlin Common and Irishtown as obvious exceptions), but there is convincing evidence certainly to attest to the involve-ment of individual members of families such as the Cosbys of Stradbally, Queen's county, the Cuffes of Desart, county Kilkenny, the Colcoughs of Duffry Hall, county Wexford, the O'Callaghans of Shanbally and the Matthews of Thomastown, county Tipperary, and impressive lists of gentry patrons have been assembled.[91] However, as the strong reliance on folkloric evidence to sustain this

84 Above, p. 246.   85 *UA*, 17 July 1753.   86 *PO*, 20 Sept. 1755.   87 Above, pp 180–1; see, for example, *PO*, 25 Sept. 1756, 1 Sept. 1759; *UA*, 9 Aug., 27 Sept. 1757; *FLJ*, 3 Aug., 3 Sept. 1768, 12 July 1769; *Hoey's Publick Journal*, 14 Aug. 1771; *Hibernian Journal*, 9 Aug. 1775, 8 Oct. 1792. 88 *UA*, 11 May 1754.   89 *FLJ*, 12 July 1769, 13 Oct. 1773; *Cork Evening Post*, 4 Sept. 1769; *Hibernian Journal*, 30 Sept. 1774.   90 Whelan, 'The geography of hurling', p. 28.   91 Whelan,

conclusion counsels, it is important neither to exaggerate nor to romanticise the intimacy of the relationship of gentry and people. Accounts of the involvement of 'gentlemen' in the game both in a playing capacity and organisational role are generally best interpreted to refer to esquires, strong farmers and middlemen than peers of the realm and eminent landed commoners.[92] The fact that more games took place on public commons and fair greens than on bespoke pitches in private ownership also cautions against exaggerating the support of the landed elite for the sport. Yet their involvement was immensely significant symbolically as a demonstration of the social respectability hurling achieved between the 1740s and 1790s, as well as a manifestation of the deferential respect that, it has been suggested, characterised the relationship of landlord and tenant in the eighteenth century.[93] The presence of the marquis of Hartington, and sundry peers and gents at Lyons Common in 1755 was a significant moment in the evolution of this relationship, but it must also be noted that it mirrored a process already under-way. Moreover, it was comparatively short-lived. It peaked between 1768 and 1775 when various entrepreneurs and impresarios in the hurling heartland of counties Kilkenny and Tipperary organised what were essentially exhibitions aimed at attracting the respectable, and their money.

The most revealing illustration of the intrinsically commercial impetus that drove this activity is provided by the fact that these games were advertised.[94] But it is indicative also that the prize money on offer was often greatly in excess of that previously available, and when the quintessential exhibition of the sport – the inter-provincial encounters of Munster and Leinster – was revived in 1768, that this, 'the grandest match that was ever hurled in Ireland', was played on Urlingford fair green in county Kilkenny.[95] It was followed on St James' day in 1769 by a match at Galbertstown, county Tipperary, involving 'three [Tipperary] baronies against all Ireland for 100 guineas a side, play or pay'.[96] Saliently, this was to be the last such game in the Kilkenny–Tipperary region, because, in keeping with the failure of the ancillary entertainments to pay their way, when the next inter-provincial match took place in 1771, it was played on Crumlin Common, and the prize money on offer was a modest 50 guineas.[97] The reduction in prize money did not signal the end of inter-county hurling, which continued to flourish for a number of years, but as the gentry withdrew, there were fewer 'grand' matches, and fewer inter-county games. The reversion of the sport to the localities demonstrated clearly once more that hurling was quintessentially

'The geography of hurling', p. 29; Ó Caithnia, *Scéal na hIomána*, pp 24–42; S.J. Connolly, '"Ag déanamh commanding": elite responses to popular culture, 1660–1850' in K.A. Miller and J.S. Donnelly (eds), *Irish popular culture, 1650–1850* (Dublin, 1998), p. 13. **92** Significantly, the number of matches involving gentlemen was small: *UA*, 28 July 1753; *PO*, 20 Sept. 1755; *FLJ*, 3 Aug. 1768, 19 July 1775. **93** See L.M. Cullen, *The emergence of modern Ireland 1600–1900* (London, 1981), chapter 3; Whelan, 'An underground gentry', pp 22–36; Connolly, '"Ag déanamh commanding": elite responses to popular culture, 1660–1850', pp 12–13. **94** *FLJ*, 3 Aug., 3, 7 Sept. 1768, 12 July 1769, 29 Aug. 1770. **95** *FLJ*, 7 Sept. 1768 **96** *FLJ*, 12 July 1769. **97** *Hoey's Publick Journal*, 14, 19 Aug. 1771. A further game followed in 1773, ibid., 30 July 1773.

a popular recreation, and that its practitioners were drawn primarily from the peasantry of a comparatively restricted, if essentially economically vigorous region, and in Dublin from a group of economic migrants who were co-equal with the artisans, apprentice and penny boys that sustained bull-baiting.

This was demonstrated particularly vividly in 1779 when, as part of the initiative that saw the controversial sport of bull-baiting move from the increasingly keenly contested streets of the capital to the Phoenix Park, hurling made a similar move from the only slightly less contested open spaces of Oxmantown Green, Irishtown Green and Crumlin Common. Though the authorities were disposed at the outset to turn a blind eye to this development, perceiving the Fifteen Acres of the Park as a less disagreeable location than any of the green areas previously employed, this was not a widely shared opinion. Specifically, there were those who objected on religious grounds to what they perceived as the profanation of the Sabbath, and their number was augmented by the burgeoning ranks of the respectable for whom demotic sports were simply objectionable.[98] Compelled by the weight of public comment, the sheriff William Worthington intervened on Sunday 1 August to prevent 'a disorderly, riotous and wicked set of persons from associating on the Sabbath day to the great scandal of religious, and evil example to the lower order of working people'.[99] The hurlers were not easily dissuaded, however, and they were back the following week. Indeed, the Park's place as the primary venue for popular recreation in the capital was strengthened for a time by the decision of the practitioners of bull-baiting to opt for this location and to enter into a wager with their sporting rivals in which the winner would be the sport which drew the 'greater number of spectators'.[100] Since the hurlers were capable of attracting an audience of several thousand, it can be concluded that the number of people present on a given Sunday was sizeable. This served both to encourage the authorities to proceed gingerly, and to increase the ire of the respectable who regarded all popular sport with unconcealed disapproval. The religiously inspired hostility of the powerful sabbatarian interest was one consideration,[101] but it was given a particular import in the case of hurling by the identification of the sport with violence, which tendency was underlined in 1779 and in 1781 by reports of fatal injuries inflicted during matches played in counties Kilkenny and Wexford. Significantly, in the county Wexford case, a troop of local Volunteers sought out those responsible and they were warmly applauded for pursuing three perpetrators, who sought to hide in the Wicklow mountains.[102]

The increasing disinclination to treat injuries incurred in the course of a hurling game as an inevitable consequence of manly sporting activity was not lost on players. This is the import certainly of the decision of the '15 or 16 persons' who were involved in 'a quarrel at a hurling match at Dunmore', county Kilkenny, 'in which one James Kenny was killed by the stroke of a hurl', to flee the locality.[103]

98 *FJ*, 20 July 1779. 99 *FJ*, 3 Aug. 1779. 100 *Dublin Evening Post*, 12 Aug. 1779; *FJ*, 14 Aug. 1779; above, pp 228–30. 101 *FJ*, 2 June 1785. 102 *FLJ*, 25 Sept. 1779; *FJ*, 23 Oct. 1781.

Yet this attitudinal shift did not dissuade those who loved hurling from playing the game. The Phoenix Park served as the primary public playing arena of the sport through the 1780s and early 1790s, but it was also played openly in counties Tipperary, Waterford, Limerick, Cork, Queen's county, Galway and Kilkenny.[104] However, whereas a majority of the references to hurling in the 1750s, 1760s and early 1770s that have been located in the press take the form of advertisements announcing impending games, or reporting on of games that were completed, they were now disproportionately of games in which fatalities ensued.[105] This pattern served inevitably further to reinforce the appreciating negative image that contributed to the sport's loss of popularity. It need not have been so. The presence of the countess of Westmorland, with 'several of the nobility and gentry' inevitably in tow, at a game in the Phoenix Park on 15 October 1792, a week after Leinster played a combined Connaught and Munster team, indicated that the sport still had the capacity to excite genuine interest among the country's social elite. But this event defied the by then prevailing trend. Moreover, the game did not proceed precisely as intended. 'Much agility and athletic contention took place, and great diversion was afforded' to the edification of the vicereine's party until the throng of spectators 'forced into the playground'. A number of gentlemen 'most obligingly used their endeavours to prevent any interruption to the players', but their efforts were in vain, and the match had to be abandoned 'without either side claiming triumph'.[106] Colonel Charles Lennox (1764–1819) (Fig. 31), the colourful and passionate sportsman, who subsequently served for six years, 1807–13, as lord lieutenant of Ireland, responded to this set-back by proposing 'to establish a prize of 100 guineas annually for superiority in hurling on the Fifteen Acres in the Phoenix', but he did not secure the required backing.[107] It was a lost opportunity, which did not surprise the more perceptive social observers who, commenting in advance of the game, referred critically to the changed social profile of those who were to take to the field: 'Formerly this manly exertion was exhibited by gentlemen of the country; it is now practised by a set of people little better than labourers', it was pointedly observed.[108] The inevitable conclusion, reinforced by the events of 15 October, that hurling was no longer an appropriate sport for respectable members of society, and that those who had not already done so were well advised to withdraw from active engagement was confirmed some months later. In April 1793, the lord mayor of the city, William James, and his brother 'were grossly assaulted' when they and some officers of the police sought 'to disperse a hurl-

103 *FJ*, 11 Sept. 1784. 104 *FJ*, 2 June 1785; *Volunteer Journal (Cork)*, 22 May 1786; *Hibernian Journal*, 22 May 1786; Ó Maolfabhail, *Camán*, p. 140; *Dublin Chronicle*, 27 Sept., 24 Oct. 1788; *Cork Gazette*, 3 July 1793; Ní Chinnéide, 'Coquebert de Montbret's impressions', p. 11; *Hibernian Journal*, 8 Oct. 1792. 105 *Volunteer Journal (Cork)*, 22 May 1786; *Hibernian Journal*, 22 May 1786; *Dublin Chronicle*, 27 Sept., 24 Oct. 1788; *Cork Gazette*, 3 July 1793. 106 *Hibernian Journal*, 17 Oct. 1792; *Clonmel Gazette*, 20 Oct. 1792. 107 *FJ*, 6 Nov. 1792; for Lennox see *ODNB sub nom*, and below, pp 326–7. 108 *FJ*, 13 Oct. 1792.

ing match in the inside of Stephen's Green'. Though the Green had been allowed decline to a point that it was deemed 'a disgrace to the city', the assault on 'the chief magistrate' and the profanation of the space, and of the Sabbath, 'with hurling and football matches' represented a new low, and it served to affirm the credibility of those who disapproved of all forms of popular recreation, with whom the tide of opinion was now running strongly.[109]

The perception, implicit in the manner that such events were reported, that Stephen's Green and the Phoenix Park were inappropriate places for games of hurling echoed, if it did not anticipate, a similar trend in England, which held that it was disruptive and undesirable to play games on public spaces, and, when it took place on Sunday, an infraction of the divine injunction to keep the Sabbath holy.[110] The augmented authority with which such sentiment was issued, and its increased purchase in the public sphere as the eighteenth century approached its end, did not bode well for the future of hurling. Its deteriorating fortunes were accentuated in the second half of the 1790s, and in the tense years following the 1798 rebellion particularly, by the reanimation of the suspicion, previously manifest in the 1690s and early 1700s, that linked hurling with sedition, since the authorities were not alone in suspecting that gatherings of young men, ostensibly to play hurling, was merely a cover for seditious activity.[111] Such suspicions, and the consequent interventions to disperse such assemblies, did not prevent the staging of hurling games in Galway, Cork, Dublin and other locations, but in common with cockfighting, it was no longer a socially respectable activity.[112] Ó Caithnia's understanding of historical causality is thus in error when he ascribes the decline that inevitably followed to the 1798 Rebellion and the Act of Union.[113] Political events rarely possess such direct social consequences, and they did not in this instance.

The decline of hurling bears comparison with cockfighting, because what was at issue in both instances was an attitudinal, cultural and religious shift, which meant it was no longer socially respectable to participate in these recreational activities. In common with cockfighting, the decline of hurling was prolonged (but less complete). It commenced in the 1770s with the withdrawal of advertising from the press, and was under way in earnest by the end of the decade when the authorities sought to prevent the playing of games in public spaces in and near the capital. The relaxation of this opposition during the 1780s allowed hurling to survive in Dublin into the 1790s when the combination of opposition to the profanation of the Sabbath and political fears that the sport was being used as a cover

109 *FJ*, 23 Apr. 1793; above, pp 192–9; Desmond McCabe, *St Stephen's Green, Dublin 1660–1875* (Dublin, 2011), pp 181–202.　110 Griffin, *England's revelry*, p. 104; Fourth commandment.　111 Thomas Bartlett (ed.), *Revolutionary Dublin, 1795–1801: the letters of Francis Higgins to Dublin Castle* (Dublin, 2004), p. 47; Diary of Judge Robert Day, 1802 (RIA, MS 12.W.11); Patrick Geoghegan, *Robert Emmet: a life* (Dublin, 2002), p. 136; Allan Blackstock, *An ascendancy army: the Irish yeomanry, 1796–1834* (Dublin, 1998), p. 252.　112 Ibid.; O'Leary, *Kileenadeema Aille*, p. 250.　113 Ó Caithnia, *Scéal na hIomána*, p. 13.

for sedition effectively ensured its complete marginalisation. It was less seriously affected in its rural heartlands, where it continued to be played. Humphrey O'Sullivan's passing references to 'a hurling match among the younger boys on the fair green' at Callan in the 1820s and 1830s, and to a game, presumably played by adults, for the prize of a May ball in 1829 suggests that the sport possessed a firm hold on the populace of county Kilkenny, but even this region was not free of opponents.[114] O'Sullivan records the intervention of a local priest, 'who scattered the hurlers', who had gathered at Goatsbridge, near Thomastown, on Easter Sunday in 1828 '… like a flock of sheep before a lion'. Other Catholic clergy perceived that they were entitled to do likewise; Thomas Crofton Croker observed how 'a number of shock-headed youths enjoying a game of goal' in county Kerry '… all scampered off' when they perceived a priest in the vicinity, before he 'could arrive at the field of action and recognise the transgressors'.[115] It is not easy to determine how seriously this affected the playing of the game, but it was evidently a matter of consequence because of the increasing deference shown the clergy by the Catholic population. Moreover, the landed elite was no longer regarded with sufficient respect to be in a position to serve as a counter-vailing force. Some landowners, in county Galway and elsewhere, sought either to sponsor or to facilitate the game well into the nineteenth century,[116] but their number declined because the expanding social chasm that was an enduring legacy of the politicisation and sectarianisation of Irish society that was a feature of the 1790s discouraged such involvement. Moreover, in keeping with the fact that hurling was increasingly deemed 'injurious to the morals and industry of the younger classes' by those committed to economic improvement intensified efforts were made to interdict its playing.[117] In a repeat of the attitudes observable during the second half of the 1790s, gatherings of young men in county Kilkenny to play hurling ('hurling meetings') were viewed with suspicion by the authorities during the tithe war of the 1830s, and discouraged.[118] Boys playing the sport on the streets of Dublin in the 1840s were fined, and their parents called upon to prevent what was now regarded as anti-social activity.[119] And there was the ongoing phenomenon of court cases in which individuals were arraigned or tried for murder in which the 'mortal wound' was inflicted with a hurley.[120] Despite this, hurling survived as a recreational activity in different parts of the country into the mid-nineteenth century; indeed, research on the playing of the game in county Tipperary between the end of the Great Famine and the founding of the

114 McGrath (ed.), *Diary of Humphrey O'Sullivan*, i, 79, 81, ii, 149–51, 153.   **115** Ibid., i, 245; Thomas Crofton Croker, *Legends and lakes of Killarney* (2 vols, London, 1829), ii, 63.   **116** *FJ*, 1 Jan. 1841; de Búrca, *The GAA: a history*, pp 3–4.   **117** James Kelly, *Sir Richard Musgrave, 1746–1818: ultra-Protestant ideologue* (Dublin, 2009), chapters 6 and 7; idem, 'The politics of Protestant ascendancy in county Longford, 1630–1840' in Martin Morris and Fergus O'Ferrall (eds), *Longford: history and society* (Dublin, 2010), pp 191–6: Hely Dutton, *Statistical survey of county Clare* (Dublin, 1801), pp 301–2.   **118** *FJ*, 13 June 1831; Patrick O'Donoghue, 'Causes of the opposition to tithes, 1830–38', *Studia Hibernica*, 5 (1965), pp 7–28.   **119** *FJ*, 28 Oct. 1843.   **120** *Tuam Herald*, 29 Mar. 1845; *FJ*, 24 Mar. 1847.

Gaelic Athletic Association in 1884 suggests it may not have experienced a decline quite so 'sharp' as once conceived,[121] but it would have been hazardous confidently to forecast a positive future for the sport in the early 1840s when its fortunes, and prospects, seemed at a low ebb.

COMMONS

By comparison even with hurling, where the contemporary record is weak, commons has left an especially thin evidential trail. Like hurling, it was played with a carved stick, the *camán*, from which the sport derived the name by which it was colloquially known in the eighteenth and early nineteenth centuries. Though the usage of the *camán* to strike a ball, known in this instance as the *cnag*,[122] bears obvious comparison with hurling, which has encouraged speculation that the two sports possess a common origin, this remains definitively to be proven, and though a relationship is assumed, the more pertinent point from a late early modern vantage point is that they constituted two distinct sports. Significantly, they possessed different geo-spatial distributions. The most complete historic map of the sport not only suggests that commons was exclusively practised in the northern half of the country, but also that the area of possible overlap with hurling was so minimal as to imply that the two sports existed independently of each other (see Maps 7, 8 and 9). This regional differentiation is all the more striking when it is noted that the evidence indicating that commons was played in a band of counties embracing north Connaught (Mayo, Sligo, Roscommon and Leitrim), south Ulster (Cavan and Monaghan), and north Leinster (counties Longford, Westmeath, Meath, Louth and Dublin) derives almost exclusively from folklore, is resistant to secure dating, and that in as many as five of these eleven counties there is only one reference. Moreover, only two corroborating documentary references have been identified (one for county Westmeath, and the other for southern Monaghan) and these are so far apart spatially as to beg more questions than they proffer useful answers. These reservations entered, the folkloric and documentary evidence together suggest that though commons may once have sustained a presence in the northern half of the island, and that its regional boundary was provided by the counties of north Leinster and north Connaught, it experienced a serious contraction, possibly in the second half of the eighteenth century. It continued to be played locally into the early nineteenth century across much of the province of Ulster,[123] but this could not be sustained, and based on

121 de Burca, *The GAA: a history*, pp 5–6; Patrick Bracken, *'Foreign and fantastic field sports': cricket in county Tipperary* (Thurles, 2004), pp 10, 17 note 43.   122 The term *cnag* in Scottish Gaelic has various meanings, one of which is a shinty ball (Dwelly's *Classical Gaelic dictionary*). In Irish it is defined as a 'hurley ball' or 'hard ball': O Duinnín's *Foclóir Gaedhilge agus Béarla*; O Donaill's *Foclóir Gaeilge-Béarla*).   123 William Shaw Mason, *A statistical account or parochial survey of Ireland* (3 vols, Dublin, 1814–19), ii, 160, iii, 207; Day and McWilliams (eds), *Ordnance survey*

the observations of the memoirists working on behalf of the Ordnance Survey, which date from 1821, and 1832–7, it only registered a multiple presence in the 1830s in counties Antrim (5 parishes) and Londonderry (9 parishes), and on the Inishowen peninsula, county Donegal (3 parishes), which were its final redoubts (Table 11, Map 9).

Table 11: Number of Ulster parishes in which commons was played, 1810–40				
		COUNTY		
Antrim	*Donegal*	*Down*	*L'Derry*	*Monaghan*
5	3	1	9	1

Source: *Ordnance survey memoirs of Ireland*, ed. Angelique Day and Patrick McWilliams (40 vols, Belfast, 1990–98); William Shaw Mason, *A statistical account or parochial survey of Ireland* (3 vols, Dublin, 1814–19)

It is apparent from these memoirs also that the sport of commons, as it was then universally called, in keeping with the linguistic penetration of English, differed significantly from that of hurling. Unlike hurling, which was played through the summer, peaking at the summer-autumn transition, commons was a high winter activity that was 'most generally' played at Christmas and New Year. This was possible because it was a ground game played with a 'stick bent at its lower extremity'. The *camán* has been compared to an 'inverted walking stick' and a 'reaping hook', which provide helpful clues to its size and form, but they do not accurately convey its effectiveness in striking the hard wooden ball, or *cnag*, which was the focus of the game. Cut not from ash, which was the favoured wood of the hurler, but from furze, whitethorn or blackthorn, the *camán* was suited to the task of grubbing the *cnag* from the earth or sand (when the game was played on the shoreline), wresting it from the control of an opponent, and striking it to keep it 'away from the opposing party'. This enabled one team to gain an advantage, but it also facilitated the physical contact that was integral to the game, and the demonstrations of manliness that it encouraged.[124] A clearer perspective is provided by Hugh Dorian, who recalled the game as it was played on the Inishowen seashore during his youth:

---

memoirs: county Londonderry, xxx, 11. **124** This reconstruction of the sport is based on the description of the manner in which the game was played in north Down in Shaw Mason, *Parochial survey*, iii, 207; Brian McGinn, 'A century before the GAA: hurling in eighteenth-century New York', *Journal of the New York Irish History Roundtable*, 1997, pp 53–4; and Day and McWilliams (eds), *Ordnance survey memoirs: county Antrim*, xxi, 109 (parish of Magheragall).

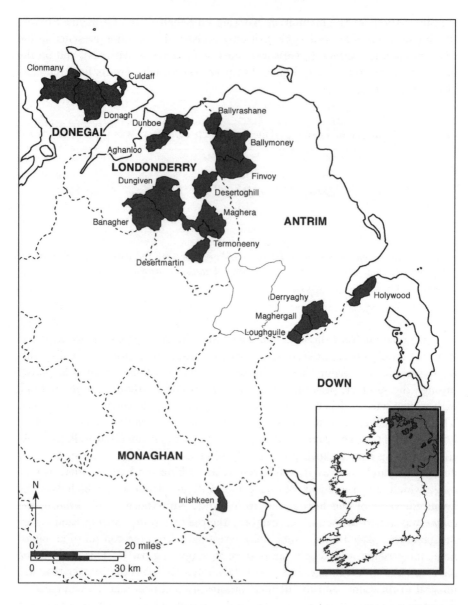

Map 9: The geography of commons: parishes in which the sport was played in
Ulster in the early nineteenth century

The best of the men picked from the opposite parts of the parish met here [the strand], and an equal number of men were set to face each other for the start; then each side commenced in earnest to take away the ball or 'bool'. This ball, made of hard wood, was sunk in the ground and two men, one on each side began to unearth it, pick it up, and try to have the first blow sent in his own direction. A good deal of sparring went on at this interval, during which time their abettors had their eyes strained, waiting for their turn. The ball at length got over ground and the game started with at first fair play and regularity; soon discipline was forgotten as the players got heated, order was broken up, and each side strove by every means, foul or fair, to win mastery.[125]

Commons was, as this, and allied descriptions suggest, not a sophisticated, and still less a refined, sport. It was, to be sure, little different in this respect than most of the traditional ball games, whether played with a stick or otherwise, that were pursued across the British Isles, whose origins, rules, and relationship, one to the other, is difficult to unpick.[126] However, unlike hurling, its closest Irish comparator, commons was doubly disadvantaged. In the first instance, like hurling and football, it was regarded suspiciously by the Protestant population in the late seventeenth and early eighteenth centuries arising from their political and religious insecurity, which encouraged them to perceive every popular gathering as a potential threat. As a result, commons was specifically mentioned in the 1695 legislation, which illegalised 'tumultuous and disorderly meetings' held on Sundays, and was subsequently interpreted as having a more general application when the kingdom experienced one of its periodic invasion scares.[127] Yet when concern on this score abated, commons continued to be regarded unfavourably, with the result that it did not secure patrons of appropriate social standing locally or of broader vision, who had the resources, ambition and capacity to organise representative matches, and to take the game into the public sphere. This may be ascribed in part to the attitudinal gulf that separated the largely Catholic peasantry that played the game, and the mainly Protestant (Church of Ireland and Presbyterian) strong farmers and gentry that filled the middle to upper orders of Ulster. It is significant that when this chasm did not obtain, as was the case with cockfighting, the sport flourished, and it only embarked on the long decline that transformed it into a minority pastime when it was no longer deemed respectable.[128] It was the misfortune of commons, however, to undergo the

125 Hugh Dorian, *The outer edge of Ulster: a memoir of social life in nineteenth-century Donegal*, ed. Breandán Mac Suibhne and David Dickson (Dublin, 2000), p. 71.   126 See F.P. Magoun, *History of football from the beginnings to 1877* (Koln, 1938); Brailsford, *Sport and society: Elizabeth to Anne*, pp 53–8; idem, *A taste for diversions*, pp 39–41, 213–16.   127 See above, pp 244–5; 7 William III, chap. 17; Kelly and Lyons (eds), *The proclamations of Ireland*, iii, George I: no. 68.   128 Above, pp 192–200.

decline that was the fate of so many sports that could not meet the exalted standards that the combination of religious observance and social respectability
demanded in the early nineteenth century, without having ever experienced the
respectability that hurling and cockfighting enjoyed for a time, and horse racing,
and hunting, were long to retain.

The decline of commons is difficult to track, but having already experienced
a major contraction in the course of the eighteenth century, it accelerated in the
interval between the brief (and not always insightful) descriptions of the sport
presented in the accounts of the parishes of Hollywood, county Down (1813),
and Culdaff, at the tip of the Inishowen peninsula (1816), included in William
Shaw Mason's *Parochial survey*, and the memoir compiled on behalf of the
Ordnance Survey for the parish of Banagher in county Londonderry in 1821.
Cockfighting, the memoirist observed, was still popular in the parish, whereas
commons, which 'used to be a favourite Christmas sport, ... is now almost forgotten'.[129] Banagher was not exceptional in forsaking commons. The sport was
also spoken of in the past tense, albeit more than a decade later, in the parishes
of Magheragall and Derryaghy, county Antrim, and Ballyrashane, county
Londonderry.[130] In these instances, as exemplified by Ballyrashane, commons
'gradually died away'. Moreover, the pattern was comparable in other locations,
as memoirists reporting on parishes in counties Antrim, Donegal, Monaghan and
Londonderry noted that commons was 'declining', 'diminishing from the gradual increase of seriousness in the general character of the parishioners', and was
now practised only once, or twice year, on Christmas and New Year's Day.[131] Yet
there were some parishes in which the commitment to 'ballplaying, hurling and
suchlike' remained robust, notably in county Down. These were the exceptions,
however. The fact that, as was observed of Loughguile, 'common playing ... is
still kept up here, chiefly among the Catholics', and that such parishes were now
outnumbered by those in which the sport was acknowledged to be in decline did
not bode well for the future. In this respect, the prospects for commons were
poorer than they were for hurling, which was encountering difficulty in its southern fastnesses.[132]

129 Shaw Mason, *Parochial survey*, ii, 160, iii, 207; Day and McWilliams (eds), *Ordnance survey
memoirs: county Londonderry*, xxx, 11 (parish of Banagher).   130 Day and McWilliams (eds),
Ordnance survey memoirs: county Antrim, xxi, 109 (Magheragall); viii, 113 (Derryaghy); Day and
McWilliams (eds), *Ordnance survey memoirs: Londonderry*, xxii, 52 (Ballyrashane).   131 Day and
McWilliams (eds), *Ordnance survey memoirs: county Antrim*, xxiii, 73 (Finvoy); xi, 10–11 (Aghanloo);
Day and McWilliams (eds), *Ordnance survey memoirs: Londonderry*, vi, 126 (Termoneery); xi, 11
(Aghanloo); xi, 54 (Drumboe); xv, 76 (Dungiven); xxvii, 18 (Desertoghill); Day and McWilliams
(eds), *Ordnance survey memoirs: county Donegal*, xxxviii, 32–3 (Donagh); xxxviii, 17 (Clonmany); Day
and McWilliams (eds), *Ordnance survey memoirs: county Monaghan*, xl, 128 (Iniskeen).   132 Knox,
A history of the county of Down, p. 56; Day and McWilliams (eds), *Ordnance survey memoirs: county
Antrim*, xvi, 18–9 (Ballymoney); xiii, 65 (Loughguile); Day and McWilliams (eds), *Ordnance survey
memoirs: Londonderry*, xviii, 100 (Maghera); xi, 10–11 (Aghanloo).

FOOTBALL

The challenges experienced by football were also a cause of concern for those who played that sport. Football was not an indigenous game, but a lowly-valued cultural offshoot of the English presence in the kingdom. As a result, its history is particularly difficult to reconstruct, as the disjointed and fragmentary character of Liam P. Ó Caithnia's brave effort to do so amply attests.[133] This important reservation entered, it may reasonably be surmised, based on the references to the game in a number of urban locations, that football took sufficiently firm root among the English (later Old English) communities of Galway, Cork and Dublin in the sixteenth century to merit specific mention in the decrees emanating from the patriciates of these conurbations. Signally, the Corporation of Galway in 1527 distinguished between games played with 'the litill balle', which it sought to discourage, and those with 'the great foote balle', which it favoured.[134] The Corporation of Cork was less positive a century later, but it too contrived to distinguish between the 'tossing of great balls', which it sought merely to discourage within the city walls, and 'hurling in the open street with the small ball', which it explicitly ordered must be 'given over'.[135] The implications of this cultural and sporting distinction notwithstanding, the political eclipse in the seventeenth century of the Old English in the towns and cities of the kingdom, and the loss of the land and influence that had provided the basis for their power had a seriously deleterious impact on the sport of football.[136] It is not possible at present (and it may never be) even to hazard an informed guess at the order of the decline it experienced, but the description of the sporting landscape prepared by John Dunton in 1698 suggests that not only was it not a national sport, but also that it was pursued over a smaller geographical area than hurling, encompassing north Leinster and south Ulster. Dunton's brief reference to the sport in north county Dublin suggests that it was, in so far as he was aware, confined to that particular area, that it was little played, and, by implication, that its future was far from assured: 'they doe not play often at football, only in a small territory called Fingall near Dublin the people use it much', he noted.[137]

If, as Dunton's fleeting reference suggests, the fortunes of football were at a low ebb in the late 1690s, the inauguration of a long era of peace, following the military defeat of the Jacobites by the army of William of Orange in 1690–1, brought a measure of social and political stability to the country that permitted re-engagement with football, which in time allowed it to consolidate, and slowly to expand. It did this initially against a hostile backdrop, as the suspicion with

133 Liam P. Ó Caithnia, *Báirí cos in Éirinn (roimh bhunú na gCumann Eagraithe)* (Baile Átha Cliath, 1984). 134 O'Sullivan, *Old Galway: the history of a Norman colony in Ireland*, pp 441–2. 135 Caulfield, *Council book of the corporation of Cork*, p. 157. 136 See, particularly, Hans Pawlisch, *Sir John Davies and the conquest of Ireland: a study in legal imperialism* (Cambridge, 1985); Aidan Clarke, *The Old English in Ireland, 1625–42* (London, 1966). 137 Dunton, *Teague land: or a merry ramble*, p. 92.

which the Protestant authorities regarded hurling was also directed at football. Indicatively, 'football' was specified (alongside hurling and commons) in the sabbatarian legislation enacted in 1695, which sought to proscribe large public gatherings on the grounds that they were 'tumultuous and disorderly', and subsequently included with the two other sports in the instruction to 'sheriffs, justices of the peace, magistrates and other officers' that was publicly proclaimed in 1719 when the authorities feared that these and allied events might be used as a cover to prepare for the reception of an invading Spanish army.[138] These concerns were exaggerated, but they reinforced, when they did not just inform, the attitudinal hostility that was directed at sport in general, and collective recreations in particular. As a consequence, most sporting activity (other than horse racing and hunting) was not only afforded little public notice but also regarded suspiciously by those in power.

In keeping with the fragmentary character of the evidence, the picture that one can recreate of the history of football in the early eighteenth century is fractured and incomplete. It does, however, sustain the impression already advanced that the area of greatest activity was northern Leinster – specifically counties Meath and Dublin – and that it also possessed a foothold in south Ulster. This northern Leinster focus is attested by the poem 'Iomáin na Bóinne' by Séamus Dall Mac Cuarta (1647–1733), which post-dates the Hanoverian succession. This poem purportedly refers to a match involving teams from communities bordering the rivers Boyne and Nanny in county Meath. As is to be anticipated of such verse, which is primarily devoted to celebrating the merits of the 'buachaillí béim-ghasta Bóinne' ('the strong fast boys of the Boyne', meaning the Irish) over 'lucht búta 'gus prácáis' ('the people of boots and hotch-potch', meaning the English), the text is short on actual details as to how the game was played but a reference to 'dháréag … a nguaine le cheile' (twelve … their shoulders together) suggests that each team comprised twelve players, who were drawn from south Ulster as well as county Meath, and that one goal was all that was required to prevail.[139]

A somewhat more detailed view of the sport, and how it was played can be gleaned from the 'mock heroick poem, in three cantos' penned by Matthew Concanen (1701–49), which appertained to a game between Lusk and Swords which was played on Oxmantown Green in Dublin. This was not the author's first literary venture, but it was his most successful work to date, and while his imitation of the style of Pope's *Rape of the lock* guaranteed a certain interest, it rarely rises above the mediocre artistically. Yet the poem, which was first published 'for the author' in Dublin in 1720, evidently struck a chord, since it was

---

138 See above, pp 244–5; 7 William III, chap. 17; Kelly and Lyons (eds), *The proclamations of Ireland*, iii, George I: no. 68. **139** Séamus Dall Mac Cuarta, 'Iomáin na Bóinne'. The poem is variously dated. De Búrca (*The GAA: a history*, p. 4) attributes it to 'the late 1600s'; it has elsewhere been ascribed a date of 1712, but the reference to King George suggests it must postdate the Hanoverian succession (1714). The poem is printed in Tom French (ed.), *A Meath anthology* (Navan, 2010), pp 50–1.

published in London in 1721, and again in 1722 when it was the focal point of Concanen's *Poems, upon several subjects*, which volume was printed by Aaron Rhames of Dublin.[140] In practice, though it is frequently appealed to, and has been subjected to a forensic analysis by Ó Caithnia for information on the game,[141] Concanen's 'match' is probably more significant as a pointer to the fact that the sport had expanded beyond its north county Dublin/north Leinster bastion, and that one of the means by which this was achieved was the migration of people from the countryside. Indeed, it is not improbable that economic migrants from that region, rather than organised teams (as implied by Concanen), were responsible for the addition of football to the menu of popular recreations that were played in the metropolis, on Sundays particularly, which were not only a source of disquiet, but also publicly identified as a cause of the disorder that the consolidating nexus of polite opinion and the civil authorities perceived as a nuisance. This flowed logically from the tendency, previously identified with reference to hurling, to highlight those games and gatherings that resulted in injury or death, and to ignore the significance of the fact that since football was reliably characterised as a 'usual diversion' by 1730, most games passed off without incident.[142]

Because of the low regard with which football was held, those mentions that one encounters in English language sources are characteristically short of specific detail on the manner in which the game was played, while Irish language authors (presumably) declined to offer details because their audience did not require such information. Yet such glimpses as one can catch from both offer more genuine insights than the fictional inter-county match described in the memoirs of Dudley Bradstreet (1711–63), a military adventurer from county Tipperary. Writing in the 1750s in an obviously sensationalist fashion, Bradstreet's account of 'a football match at a place called Aghamore, where the county of Longford challenged the county of Westmeath' would, if it could be shown to be credible, suggest that football was played at an advanced level as far west as the Shannon, when the most secure reference to the playing of the game in the second quarter of the eighteenth century appertains to an exhibition 'match between married men and bachelors' at an inaugural fair in Dangan, county Meath, on New Year's day in 1731.[143] More problematically, Bradstreet's account of the preparations for the game, of the manner in which he was chosen captain of the Longford team, of the way in which he contrived, using a sexworker he knew who happened to be present, to get the opposing captain drunk, and his militarised description of the game, with its stereotypical account of how 'the enemy, seeing the day lost at football, attempted to retrieve their honour by

---

140 Matthew Concanen, *A match at foot-ball: a poem in three cantos* (Dublin, 1720); idem, *A match at foot-ball, or the Irish champions: a mock heroick poem in three cantos* (London, 1721); idem, *Poems upon several occasions, by the author of the match at foot-ball* (Dublin, 1722); Frances Clarke, 'Matthew Concanen' in *DIB*. **141** Ó Caithnia, *Báirí cos in Éirinn*, pp 30–42; Fagan, *The second city*, pp 79–80, 175–6. The text of the 'poem' is printed on pp 186–201. **142** *Dublin Weekly Journal*, 23 May 1730. **143** *FLJ*, 2 Jan. 1731; Powell, *The politics of consumption*, p. 122.

strokes', is too egotistical and too clichéd to pass muster as a credible historical source.[144]

Bradstreet's hyperbole may have appealed to contemporaries unfamiliar with the sport because the occasional reports they encountered in the press were equally stereotyped. Indeed, even more so than was the case with hurling, the press fuelled the impression that football and disorder were indivisible. Football, as the newspapers presented it, and bodies like the vestry and parishioners of St Paul's parish in Dublin, and Dublin Corporation echoed, was a game played by 'disorderly, idle and wicked persons', who had no regarded for the lives or properties of others. The security of church property was the priority, certainly, of the minister, churchwarden and parishioners of St Paul's who petitioned Dublin Corporation in 1737 for authorisation to rail in the walks that linked the Church and Oxmantown Green, because of the damage done to the 'windows, trees and walls' of the church by those who gathered to play games on Oxmantown Green. Dublin Corporation acceded to the request. They shared the public perception that football was a disagreeably violent pursuit, but as much as they feigned concern about the violence footballers visited on each other, they were genuinely bothered by the injuries incurred by innocent members of the public.[145] Instances were not hard to find. For example, a passer-by was fatally injured by a stone thrown by one of a group of 'idle fellows, assembled to their usual diversion of foot-ball playing and throwing of stones' in 1730.[146] Ten years later, when the river Liffey was frozen over, officials apprehended and incarcerated footballers for creating a public nuisance by playing on the frost-bound river.[147] By then, the sport had expanded far beyond its onetime northern Leinster heartland, and had developed to such an extent that inter-county games were possible; a game involving 20 men from Maynooth against 20 men from county Meath in July 1745 was followed in August 1746 by an impressive exhibition at Birr, King's county, between a team of yeoman farmers and bachelors.[148] It seemed then that football would follow the example of hurling and embrace a pattern of play that included inter-county and other high profile games across the geographical expanse of the country where the game was played. But it was not to be.

Unlike cockfighting and hurling, both of which enjoyed the favour of the respectable at different points, and for different time periods during the eighteenth century, football never enjoyed the same good fortune. It is not that there were not moments, such as those just described in the mid-1740s, when respectability beckoned, but the association of the game with damage to property, idleness,[149] disorderly conduct, and, occasionally, with violence proved stronger. Moreover, the

144 *The life and uncommon adventures of Captain Dudley Bradstreet*, ed. G.S. Taylor (London, [1929]), pp 46–51; Ó Caithnia, *Báirí cos in Éirinn*, pp 43–6. The original text of Bradstreet's 'adventures' was 'printed and sold by Samuel Powell, for the author' in Dublin in 1755. 145 Gilbert (ed.), *Calendar of ancient records of Dublin*, viii, 241. 146 *Dublin Weekly Journal*, 23 May 1730. 147 Fogarty, *Tipperary's GAA story*, p. 13. 148 Ó Caithnia, *Scéal na hIomána*, pp 18–19. 149 Toby Barnard (ed.), 'A description of Gort in 1752 by Thomas Wetherall', *Journal of the Galway*

sport's negative image encouraged the authorities to corral the game at virtually every opportunity, though football did not intrude onto the streets of the capital, and was rarely to be encountered on the squares, green and commons of Dublin or other urban centres. Yet it was frequently pursued at locations within sufficient proximity of the country's main cities and towns to give a contrary impression, and to attract negative notice. This was the case on Sunday, 17 March 1754 when a group of young men broke down some 'fences and hedges' in order to play 'a match of football' 'in the fields adjoining' Baggot Street, Dublin. Responding to 'an application' requesting his intervention, the arrival of the lord mayor, Andrew Murray, 'a guard of soldiers, and a posse of constables' at the makeshift sports ground caused the assembled crowd to scatter, but not before the lord mayor apprehended three persons, who were conveyed to Newgate prison.[150] Six weeks later, the high constable 'dispersed a great number of idle disorderly people' who had assembled at Oxmantown Green for the same purpose, while in a still-more striking expression of official determination that football would simply not be tolerated within the expanding city footprint, sheriff Michael Sweeney and a guard apprehended eight individuals who had assembled for this purpose in July 1758, and made clear his conviction that they should be transported out of the jurisdiction by putting them 'on board the tender in the harbour'.[151]

Such interventions left their mark as football all but disappeared from the metropolitan sporting landscape for a number of years thereafter, though interest in playing the game persisted. Moreover, attitudes were not so unrelenting outside the city boundaries. There, following the precedent set by cockfighting and hurling, some members of the gentry contrived to facilitate the sport. In an illustration of how this could work to advantage, 'a grand match was played at Clonshaugh, [north county Dublin,] the lodge of James Massy Dawson' in the spring of 1763 between a team 'of twelve lads of that place and Santry, and the same number from Malahide'. It was a keenly contested game that lasted for three hours 'to the entire satisfaction of the spectators and combatants, who celebrated the evening with great mirth and jollity'.[152] This was a clear illustration of the pleasure the game could bring when played in the right spirit and in a congenial environment. It may also be significant, that the game was played on a Monday. The problem, in so far as the sport was concerned, was that it possessed too few well-connected patrons to induce a sufficiency of opinion formers, lawmakers, and law enforcers to reconsider their attitude to the game, and since matches were mostly played on a Sunday, in defiance of the fourth commandment and the efforts of those who took this injunction seriously, opposition to football remained firm. The clash of attitudes involved is well illustrated by the account of an incident on Oxmantown Green in September 1763:

Archaeological and Historical Society, 61 (2009), p. 111. **150** *UA*, 19 Mar. 1754; Ó Caithnia, *Scéal na hIomána*, p. 22. **151** *PO*, 29 Apr. 1755; *Cork Evening Post*, 3 July 1758; Ó Caithnia, *Scéal na hIomána*, p. 44. Sweeney (variously spelled Sweney, Sweny) was city sheriff 1757–8: Gilbert (ed.), *Calendar of ancient records of Dublin*, x, 472. **152** *The Public Gazetteer*, 9 Apr. 1763.

In the time of divine service, in the afternoon, the congregation at St
Paul's church were alarmed with a horrid noise made by a multitude of
the rabble who assembled in Oxmantown Green, and there amused themselves, some in the more robust exercise of football, whilst others were
playing at fives against the church wall, to the no small annoyance, as well
of the officiating clergymen and his audience, as of the neighbourhood,
who were under a necessity of closing their doors and windows, to secure
themselves against the insults of these mischievous vagrants.[153]

Such disagreeable intrusions upon the legitimate aspiration of those who sought
to worship in a calm and peaceful environment could, critics of popular recreations maintained, 'easily be prevented' by the strategic placement of a 'a small
party of soldiers'.[154] As a result, the calls of those who favoured enhanced official
intervention grew louder as the ranks of the respectability-seeking middling sort
expanded with the size of the city. Signally, this was an issue upon which the
voice of the conservative establishment, as expressed in the *Dublin Gazette*, was
at one in the 1760s with the reform-minded patriotism articulated by the newly
established *Freeman's Journal*.[155] There were dissentients, of course, but even
those who properly distinguished between 'the laudable purpose of playing at
football' and the boorish behaviour it generated – rioting, disorder, civil disturbance – acknowledged that the conduct of many footballers was 'an affront to the
laws, and deserves a rigorous chastisement'.[156]

Obliged by the weight of hostile opinion, and the resolution of the authorities to accept that the city did not possess the appropriate spaces on which to
play the game, footballers in the city anticipated the steps later taken by the practitioners of bull-beating, and retreated to the periphery, and away from the now
sharply contested space in the increasingly built-up area of Oxmantown Green.
Beginning in the mid-1760s, football was played at Kilmainham in the fields
belonging to the Royal Hospital, at Dolphin's Barn, in fields off the Drumcondra
road, on Merrion Fields, in the Phoenix Park, in fields off Eccles Street, and in
Rathfarnham.[157] The presence of a crowd 'some thousands' strong at Kilmainham
in April 1765 to watch a team of journeymen bakers take on the brewers' servants suggested initially that this was the way forward, but this would only be
the case if the shrill cries of criticism were muted, which never happened. In its
account of this match, the *Dublin Gazette* was as unforthcoming as ever, insisting that the game was pursued 'to the great detriment of the improvements
thereabouts and to the scandalous breach of the Lord's day'.[158] In order to prevent such disagreeable infractions, it was necessary, it was opined, that the civil
and military authorities combined their resources. Indicatively, when the authorities did not respond promptly to prevent games at Dolphin's Barn in 1771, and

153 *The Public Gazetteer*, 20 Sept. 1763. **154** Ibid. **155** See *Dublin Gazette*, 28 Apr. 1765; *FJ*, 4
May 1765. **156** *Hibernian Journal*, 29 Jan. 1772. **157** *Dublin Gazette*, 28 Apr. 1765. **158** *Dublin
Gazette*, 28 Apr. 1765; *FJ*, 4 May 1765.

at Merrion Fields in May 1774, the newspapers pointedly queried why this was so.[159] To be fair, the authorities had no hesitation in intervening when they perceived that there was cause; when 'a riotous mob' assembled in fields at Drumcondra 'to play football' in the spring of 1774 a large party of the 55th foot regiment was deployed successfully to 'disperse' the crowd.[160]

Though the recourse to the army was unusual, its involvement in this instance echoed the preparedness of respectable opinion by the mid-1770s to countenance whatever steps were necessary to discourage the assembly of 'riotous and disorderly' persons to play football. This mirrored the appreciating conviction that football lay at the root of a series of incidents in which 'lives have been lost, and many persons maimed and wounded, the laws openly violated, evil example suffered to grow, and private property much injured'.[161] So when it emerged in July 1779 that 'a mob of people have for several Sabbath days past assembled in the Phoenix Park to play at football', and that the authorities declined to intervene, there were loud calls that this 'mob of people' was not left 'unmolested, and in open defiance of the laws, divine and human, permitted to continue their Sunday gambols'. The authorities contrived for a number of weeks to wait it out, presumably calculating that the cries of outrage would soon dissipate, but this was not to be. The presence of hurlers as well as footballers at the same location was too challenging to be ignored; the authorities intervened, and the sportsmen were ordered to disperse.[162] As a result, instead of the *modus vivendi* between the municipality and the practitioners of popular sports that might otherwise have evolved with time, the incapacity of the nexus of polite opinion, sabbatarians and the forces of law and order, for whom popular sport was a point of concern, to accommodate football and allied sports ensured that relations remained strained. This led inevitably to more confrontation as well as to more violence and (unnecessary) death. One innocent victim was Richard Coleman, a baker's apprentice from Church Street, who was shot in fields off Eccles Street in April 1780 at a sporting event by a watchman named John Eagan. The fact that the coroner's inquest returned a verdict of 'wilful murder' against Eagan reinforced the belief in certain quarters that the campaign against football, and allied demotic recreational activities, should be pursued with greater circumspection, but the appeal for restraint did not register generally. The expanding ranks of respectability were more preoccupied with preventing the disorder they reflexively identified with demotic sports, and, in particular, with ensuring the proper observation of the Sabbath, and they were simply not appeased by the recourse of the practitioners of controversial team, blood and fighting sports to the 'the suburbs or outskirts of Dublin'. Indicatively, the fields near Merrion Square were the site of a significant confrontation between sportsmen and Alderman John Exshaw (Fig. 24) and 'a party of police, in May 1787.[163] The outlook of the respectable was echoed by the

159 *Hibernian Journal*, 8 July 1771, 23 May 1774; *FJ*, 24 May 1774. **160** *Hibernian Journal*, 20 Apr. 1774; *FJ*, 21 Apr. 1774. **161** *Hibernian Journal*, 23 May 1774. **162** Above, pp 229–30, 264; *FJ*, 20 July, 3 Aug. 1779. **163** *Hibernian Journal*, 10, 12 Apr. 1780, 16 May 1787; *FJ*, 9 June 1785,

Fig. 24. Alderman John Exshaw (1753–1827), lord mayor of Dublin, 1789–90, 1800, was the publisher of *Hue and Cry*, the police gazette, and divisional justice of police, 1786–8. Like many lords mayors, he sought actively to combat sporting activity that was pursued on the streets of the capital (miniature in private possession).

commentary that accompanied a report published later the same decade of the 'desperate quarrel' resulting in 'much bloodshed and battery', which followed a football match 'played at the foot of the mountain called the Three Rocks, a few miles above Rathfarnham between a party of Mountaineers, and the neighbours of the adjacent valley':

> The total disrespect of the Sabbath among the peasantry of this country is the constant theme of just reproach from our British neighbours. This fault, we are obliged to say, predominates chiefly amongst those of the Roman Catholic persuasion, who form very considerably the majority of the lower class of people, and when we reflect that their clergy hold over them such powerful sway, that scarcely even the most profligate of them will dare to be absent from divine worship on Sunday, we are inclined to think that a more general regard to the sanctity of the Lord's day, might with equal facility be impressed on their conduct; for of what effect can it be to inculcate a sense of indispensable duty in devoting a single hour to the worship of the deity, on that day, if the remainder is, without scruple, devoted to riot, drunkenness, sport, which are indeed the principal devotions of an Irish country Sabbath.[164]

Though this vision of a decorous Sabbath appealed, in spite of the sectarian clothing in which it was swathed, to respectable Catholics, and to the Catholic clergy, who were equally eager to encourage greater deportment among Catholics of all classes, it did not inhibit the playing of football.[165] The detailed report of a

17 May 1787; *Volunteer Evening Post*, 17 May 1787.   **164** Brady (ed.), *Catholics in the eighteenth-century press*, p. 265.   **165** For the now classic analysis of attitude of the Catholic clergy see S.J. Connolly, *Priests and people in pre-famine Ireland* (Dublin, 1982), pp 135–48.

fatal brawl that followed a match at Timolin, county Wicklow, in February 1792 suggests that the assertion that the playing of sport on Sundays was widespread across Ireland as the eighteenth century drew to a close may well be true.[166] It is not possible precisely to map those areas where football was played but there is evidence to suggest that as well as north Leinster, it was also popular in south and east Ulster, and north Connaught.[167] Source material is still far from plentiful, but popular songs in Irish celebrating the playing of the sport at Anagassan, county Louth, Omeath, county Louth, and Enniskeen, county Monaghan, in the second half of the eighteenth and early years of the nineteenth centuries complement the equally selective references in English language sources as to the sport's geospatial footprint.[168] There were, in addition, possible regional variations of which *caid* or *cad*, which was played in Munster (counties Kerry, Cork, Limerick, Tipperary and Waterford) is the best known, but nothing secure has been established as to the form these regional variants took for the time period with which this book engages.[169]

In any event, the deterioration in the civil environment that followed the politicisation of the population in the 1790s served to reinforce the conviction, already strongly held, that society would be bettered by the eradication of football. This perception was explicitly articulated by the Secret Committee of the House of Commons established to investigate the origins of the 1798 Rebellion. It observed with reference to the proclamation promulgated on 16 November 1796 applying the recently ratified Insurrection Act that it was 'issued for the prevention of large assemblies of people, who in the province of Ulster had made potato digging, reaping of corn, football matches etc. the ostensible pretexts for purposes of concealed treason'.[170] Similar sentiments were forthcoming three years later from Garadice, county Leitrim, *à propos* of 'large meetings under pretence of playing football', and they proved enduring.[171] In 1805, the under secretary at Dublin Castle, Alexander Marsden, responded nervously to reports from county Meath of a series of football matches that 'there is much reason to suspect there is some mischievous design at the bottom'.[172]

These were significant comments because, until this point, no observable reservation had been entered with respect to the playing of football outside of the

---

166 Ó Caithnia, *Báirí cos in Éirinn*, p. 52.   **167** See *FLJ*, 25 Aug. 1798; W.P. Percy to [Lord Clements], 19 July 1801 (NLI, Killadoon papers, MS 36061/33, printed in A.P.W. Malcomson (eds), *The Clements archive* (Dublin, 2010), p. 545.   **168** Énrí Ó Muireasa (eag.), *Céad de cheolta Uladh* (2nd edn, Newry, 1983), pp 34–7, 204–5; Énrí Ó Muirgheasa (eag.), *Dha chéad de cheoltaibh Uladh* (Baile Átha Cliath, 1934), pp 362–8; Denis Carolan Rushe, *Monaghan in the eighteenth century* (Dublin, 1916), p. 80; Peadar Livingstone, *The Monaghan story* (reprint, Enniskillen, 1980), pp 324, 326.   **169** Those references that this writer has located for *cad* date from the mid-, or later nineteenth century. As the alternative designation, *rough and tumble*, suggests this was an intensely physical game: see Ó Caithnia, *Báirí cos in Éirinn*, pp 60–1, 77–80.   **170** Report of the secret committee, presented to the House of Commons, Aug. 1798, cited in *FLJ*, 25 Aug. 1798.   **171** Percy to [Clements], 19 July 1801 (NLI, Kiladoon papers, MS 36061/33).   **172** Marsden to Irwine, 30 Mar. 1805 (NAI, State of the Country papers, 1031/52).

metropolitan area of Dublin, where it most obviously collided with the ideals of politeness in an urban space increasingly keenly felt by the respectable. Now in a reversion to the attitudes last officially proffered in 1719, the Protestant elite across the kingdom was encouraged to look suspiciously once more upon another standard plebeian recreational activity. It is difficult even to speculate as to the impact of this disposition, but by convincing the respectable that football, like most other popular recreations, was now doubly undesirable, it accentuated trends already in train. It certainly did not stop football being played. Based on scattered, passing references in the Ordnance Survey memoirs for the province and other contemporary accounts, football was played in several parts of Ulster away from the heartland of commons in the early nineteenth century on holidays and certain stated days.[173] However, like commons, it was vulnerable in the face of the twin challenges of the expanding aspiration to achieve social respectability and the allied campaign by the Catholic clergy to curb customs and practices they believed unedifying, improper, or 'demoralizing'.[174] As a result it was in visible contraction in the wealthier, eastern part of the province by the 1830s.[175]

CONCLUSION

By the 1830s the three main team sports played in Ireland were in decline. Their situations varied in important respects, however. Having been excluded from the urban world, hurling and football continued to be played, if not intensively, in rural areas. Commons was in a weaker situation; it had never penetrated the urban world, and now that it was being forsaken in its rural heartland, its very survival could not be assumed. Their potentially parlous situation notwithstanding, team sports were not without defenders who recognised the societal value of the manly virtues promoted by collective recreational activity, but there were few voices who recommended team activity as a source of community, social cohesion or, even, local or national identity. Ireland in this respect did not differ from England, where 'mass football games found few articulate friends'.[176] The perception that associated team sports with violence, disorder, disrespect for property and, in a country deeply divided religiously, with disrespecting the Sabbath, was deeply inculcated, and it would take time for an alternative, more positive discourse to emerge, and still longer for an alternative vision to gain sufficient currency and intellectual ascendancy to permit either their revitalisation, or their reinvention as vibrant recreational sports.

173 Day and McWilliams (eds), *Ordnance survey memoirs*, passim; McGrath (ed.), *Diary of Humphrey O'Sullivan*, ii, 373.   174 Day and McWilliams (eds), *Ordnance survey memoirs: county Down*, iii, 37 (Kilbroney); Day and McWilliams (eds), *Ordnance survey memoirs: county Monaghan*, xl, 133, 140, 148 (Killanny, Magheracloone, Magheross).   175 Day and McWilliams (eds), *Ordnance survey memoirs: county Down*, iii, 37 (Kilbroney).   176 Brailsford, *A taste for diversions*, pp 62–3.

6

Pugilism and wrestling

Addressing the subject of 'manly exercises, sports [and] recreations', the anonymous English visitor who recorded his impressions of Dublin in 1732 observed that 'the people of Ireland' were as disposed as their neighbours to pursue 'cudgels, boxing and wrestling'.[1] However, as previous chapters have shown, Ireland was not a passive receptor or imitator of English recreational pursuits in the late early-modern period. It possessed distinct cultural traditions, which influenced which recreations were pursued. Hurling is the most obvious case in point, but it can also be identified, as the particular history of cockfighting attests, in the manner in which essentially English sports were conducted. This is true to a lesser extent of pugilism.

It is apparent, from the extensive reportage it was accorded in the Irish press, that the *floruit* of pugilism in late Georgian and Regency England was keenly followed in Ireland. It is thus not coincidental that the highpoint of pugilism in England coincided with its most active phase in Ireland.[2] However, Irish pugilism differed in a variety of respects from its English equivalent, and it was not only a matter of scale. The former did not, to be sure, have access to anything like an equivalent pool of talented practitioners; it was also palpably more poorly organised, less well funded, and less well supported with the result, inevitably, that it was financially less advantageous to those who pursued the activity. Pugilism was also regarded with even less favour for most of the time during which it was pursued, because the cultural, social and religious chasm that divided the elite from the populace ran deeper in Ireland than it did in England. As a consequence, other than Dan Donnelly and Jack Langan, and then briefly, pugilists in Ireland did not enjoy the patronage the leading practitioners of the sport enjoyed in England. This ensured that it was more easily forced to the social margins when interest declined in the decades spanning the end of the Hanoverian era and beginning of the long reign of Queen Victoria.

As the account of recreational activity in Ireland in 1732 quoted above attests, pugilism was not the only fighting sport practised in Ireland. Wrestling and cudgelling were also pursued. However, because they were not practised in a structured or formal way, and were seldom reported or commented upon, they

1 'Description of Dublin, 1732' in Gilbert (ed.), *Calendar of ancient records of Dublin*, x, 527. 2 The comparative perspective on English pugilism provided here derives in the first instance from Dennis Brailsford's excellent *Bareknuckles: a social history of prize-fighting* (Cambridge, 1988), passim.

are exceptionally difficult to penetrate. There was certainly no regional equivalent in Ireland to Devon and Cornwall, or Cumberland and Westmoreland,
where wrestling rivalled prizefighting as a popular recreation.[3] Yet there are sufficient passing references to suggest that both were pursued locally, and, in the
case of cudgelling, in a socio-cultural realm that echoed, when it did not coincide with that of faction fighting. A reasonable case might be constructed in support of the argument that cudgelling was a quintessential example of controlled
recreational violence. The fact that it was mentioned alongside 'boxing and
wrestling' as a popular activity in 1732; that 'a lac'd hat' was 'cudgelled for' at
Dangan fair (county Meath) in 1731; and that it featured, alongside hurling, as a
demonstration sport at Luttrellstown races (Chapelizod, county Dublin) in 1748
certainly suggests that it was a popular diversion in parts of north Leinster
during the first half of the eighteenth century. It may, as in England, have been
'a common feature' at fairs, but we know little of the sports and recreations that
were conducted at such events. Moreover, it is surely significant that it is elusive
thereafter.[4] It might be argued that cudgelling belongs in the same category of
fighting sports as pugilism, since a properly conducted cudgelling contest was not
a physical free-for-all. However, since the boundary between fighting sports and
violence was unstable and cudgelling involved the use of weapons, a stronger case
can be made in support of the contention that it either straddled the permeable
line that separates the history of sport from the history of recreational (and
specifically factional) violence, or, because it was reliant on a weapon, that it
crossed that line and is better located with the history of factional violence. The
careful and deliberate manner in which members of Dublin premier factions –
the Ormond and Liberty Boys – fashioned their own particular cudgel – the fal-
chion – from the smoke-hardened staves of oak casks in order to maximise their
usefulness as weapons may thus have been a significant departure in the history
of the practice in Ireland,[5] and in the migration of cudgelling from the realm of
sport into that of collective recreational violence, of which the faction fight is the
most emblematic Irish manifestation.[6]

PUGILISM

The first identified reference to 'a boxing bout' in Ireland, in which the name of
the principals is known, dates from December 1749. The occasion was a court
case at the commission of Oyer and Terminer for the city of Dublin in which two
men, named Cavanagh and O'Brien, were tried for the murder of another, named

3 Brailsford, *Bareknuckles*, p. xii.   4 As note 1; *FDJ*, 2 Jan. 1731; *Dublin Courant*, 16 Aug. 1748;
Collins et al. (eds), *Encyclopedia of traditional British rural sports*, p. 88.   5 Kelly, *The Liberty and
Ormond Boys*, p. 37.   6 For some recent (incomplete) attempts to explore faction fighting in particular contexts see Kelly, *The Liberty and Ormond Boys*, passim; Gerard Curtin, *West Limerick:
crime, popular protest and society, 1820–1845* (Ballynahill, county Limerick, 2008), pp 69–89.

Cullen, who died as a result of injuries incurred 'in a boxing bout at Newcastle in the county of Dublin'. No details of the fatal 'bout' that precipitated Cullen's death have been located, but it is noteworthy that Cavanagh was found guilty of the lesser crime of manslaughter and O'Brien acquitted.[7] It is notable also that the fight post-dated the preparation by Jack Broughton of London in 1743 of the eponymous set of rules that guided prizefighting until they were superseded in 1867 by the still better-known marquess of Queensberry rules. In broad terms, Broughton's rules might be compared to those devised to regulate cockfighting, since they provided the sport with a basic set of guidelines that stipulated how a prizefight ought properly to be conducted. To this end, they directed, inter alia, that fights should take place within a square that was clearly 'chalked' on a raised stage or platform; that there should be a 'second', or assistant, whose role was to present fighters at the beginning of a bout, and at every 'fresh set-to after a fall'; that a fighter who failed to re-present within thirty seconds 'after a fall' was 'deemed a beaten man'; that 'only principals and seconds' could occupy the square; that the winner was entitled to two-thirds of the purse; that there should be two or, in cases of disagreement, three 'umpires' to 'prevent disputes in every main battle'; and that it was contrary to rule for a fighter 'to hit his adversary when down or seize him by the hair, the breeches, or any part below the waist'.[8] Though Broughton, who was a skilled and experienced exponent of the pugilist's craft, drafted these rules for use in his London amphitheatre, they epitomised best practice at the time, and they were generally embraced. Their adoption was facilitated by the fact that they made for a better and more regular spectacle, which was no less crucial in pugilism than it was in cockfighting, since substantial sums of money were often at issue, both as prize money and as bets. As a result, during the seven years that Broughton's amphitheatre enjoyed royal favour, it set the standard by which the sport was defined.[9]

There is no evidence to suggest either that Broughton's rules were adopted in Ireland, or that there was a venue (or venues), in the tradition of that established in London in 1720 by James Figg and improved upon by Jack Broughton in 1743, dedicated to the promotion of boxing either as a skill or a sport. Yet, developments in England did not leave Ireland untouched. The most compelling indication is provided by the exhibition match involving three London-based pugilists, which was staged at Dublin's Ormond market in January 1753:

> At an house in Ormond market, a combat was fought between the famous Martin Ochy, celebrated for boxing and vanquishing several London butchers, and Daniel Dugan, a famous jaw-bone breaker from the said city, who in 12 minutes was vanquished by his antagonist, who also discomfited the celebrated hero, Tom Smallwood, on the stage in four minutes.[10]

7 *Munster Journal*, 14 Dec. 1749.   8 The rules are printed in Brailsford, *Bareknuckles*, pp 8–9; Collins et al. (eds), *Encyclopaedia of traditional British rural sports*, pp 50, 217; see also Brailsford, *A taste for diversion*, p. 171.   9 Brailsford, *Bareknuckles*, pp 9–11.   10 *UA*, 30 Jan. 1753. Tom

The opinion, offered at the close of the report of this event, that 'it is hoped these champions will be either obliged to lay aside these proofs of their prowess, or prepare to travel back to the other side of the water', indicates that the interest in pugilism manifested by the butchers and allied trades of Ormond market was not reciprocated by the general public.[11] It may be, as in England, that respectable opinion in Ireland was influenced by the withdrawal of royal favour following Jack Broughton's unexpected defeat in the ring by Jack Slack in April 1750, which cost the duke of Cumberland a reputed £10,000.[12] But it is still more likely that the newspaper captured the genuine reservations of the respectable, who were disposed to view pugilism through the same critical lens as they did other plebeian sports. There were certain striking points of comparison, based on the accounts of the sport provided in the press, which served to sustain a negative impression. There was, for example, the 'dreadful accident' on George's Quay in June 1750 which resulted in an unspecified number of deaths and serious injuries when an 'anchor-smith's forge' gave way under the weight of those who had clambered on it to watch Maguire, who was a member of the Liberty Boys faction, fight Carpenter, from the rival Ormond Boys.[13] This incident prompted an outcry, and eager to discourage boxing, and allied practices, the managers and medical men in the main Dublin hospitals informed the public that they would refuse medical treatment to those who incurred injury in these, or allied, avoidable circumstances:

> The governors, physicians and surgeons of the several hospitals of this city are come to a resolution not to admit any persons whatever in these places, who shall receive any main or wound, by rioting, quarrelling, or boxing in any manner whatever; those useful places being intended only for the reception and cure of those, who come by their illness or wounds in an natural or accidental way.[14]

This was as unambiguous a statement as it was possible for the hospital authorities to make of their disapproval of pugilism, but if it was their expectation that their intervention would discourage the practice it was already too late. Pugilism was not by any means a major sport at this point, but the publication of a report in September 1751 of the defeat at Kilmainham of 'a noted buffer' from Chapelizod by one of the Liberty Boys reinforces the impression provided by the

---

Smallwood (1721–68) was a significant figure in mid-eighteenth-century pugilism, who was sketched by George, Lord Townshend (National Portrait Gallery, 4855 (31, 34)). He was described as 'of great pugilistic notoriety' by Pierce Egan (*Boxiana, or sketches of ancient and modern pugilism*, vol. 1 (London, 1830), p. 68); he is also mentioned in *Pancratia, or a history of pugilism, containing a full account of every battle of note from the times of Broughton and Slack, down to the present day* (London, 1812), p. 44. Neither Martin Ochy nor Daniel Dugan is mentioned in either of these compendious works. 11 *UA*, 30 Jan. 1753. 12 Brailsford, *Bareknuckles*, pp 10–11, 13–14. The fight was reported in the *BNL*, 24 Apr. 1750. 13 *BNL*, 5 June 1750. 14 *Munster Journal*, 4 June 1750.

exhibition match held in the vicinity of Ormond market that it was regarded favourably by the artisans and labourers that provided the members of the city's major factions.[15] It had certainly taken root in the plebeian culture of the city two years later when pugilistic encounters were reported as having taken place at Martin's Lane, Arbour Hill and Lazer's Hill. These events did not escape the notice of the municipal authorities, and they contrived, when circumstances permitted, to anticipate or to disrupt such events in order (it was maintained in 1753 when the lord mayor, Andrew Murray, sent the high constable with a party of soldiers to Lazer's Hill for this purpose) 'to prevent those riots and disorders, which are usual at such assemblies'.[16] The accidental death of a child, who was 'trod to death' at one such encounter on 2 March, and the report later the same year from Phillipstown, Queen's county, that William Boyd not only bit off the thumb of William Connor in an 'extraordinary boxing match' but also swallowed the severed digit,[17] strengthened the authorities, and larger swathes of the general public, in the conviction that boxing was an unedifying, dangerous and violent activity, and that they were justified in their efforts to discourage it.

Irish opinion mirrored that in England in this respect, but the reality, in both jurisdictions, was that there were plenty of men prepared to put their bodies on the line, and still more, stimulated by the endorphin surge generated by watching and betting on such tests of skill and strength, who were eager to participate after a more vicarious fashion. As a result, pugilism was soon enmeshed in a cat-and-mouse relationship with the authorities comparable to that pursued by the advocates of throwing at cocks and bull-baiting, in which those who deemed fighting a sporting activity, and those who anticipated financial gain (either from prize money or from betting) from so doing sought to keep one step ahead of the law. This notwithstanding, it can be argued, based on the recoverable record of prizefights, that pugilism in Ireland experienced significant fluctuations in fortune, and that the palpable surge in interest spanning the late 1740s and early 1750s referred to above was followed by a decade-and-a-half during which, based on the absence of reference in the press, the sport was in the doldrums. There is no obvious explanation for this, but it is hardly coincidental that it mirrors the fortunes of the sport in England, which has been attributed to the loss of public confidence as a result of a number of high-profile thrown fights. Pugilism, like cockfighting, had to be perceived to be credible if spectators and gamblers were to provide the prize money required to elevate the activity above mere brawling, and this evidently was not the case in the 1760s. It is not apparent why this intrinsically English problem should have a negative impact on the sport in Ireland, since pugilism was pursued at a palpably lower level there, but anglophone Ireland and England occupied a shared linguistic and public sphere, and while this did not presume uniformity across the sporting and recreational spectrum, the pattern was closer in some areas than in others.[18] It is certainly the case

15 *Dublin Courant*, 10 Sept. 1751. 16 *UA*, 3 Mar., 12, 16 June 1753. 17 *UA*, 3 Jan. 1754. 18 See

that the fortunes of pugilism in Ireland rose and fell in synch with those of the sport in England, and the 1760s and early 1770s were a low point in both kingdoms.[19] It is a measure of its lowly fortunes then that it was even speculated in 1771, in response to an otherwise inexplicable surge in interest in duelling outside of the social elite, 'that the lower order of Hibernians have dropped boxing, and taken to sword and pistol'.[20]

This was an overreaction. It can be shown that individuals from the so-called lower orders demonstrated a greater readiness, beginning in the late 1760s, to appeal to weapons to resolve differences and disputes, but they did not appeal to the rules of the code of honour to the exclusion of fisticuffs.[21] The arrest of eleven men who had gathered at Oxmantown Green on Sunday 11 June 1769 to view a boxing match, and an 'extra-ordinary battle … fought near Stoneybatter' in 1768 between 'two Amazonian women and two tailors for a guinea a head' (which, incidentally was won by 'the termagants') demonstrated that the pugilistic impulse was not dormant.[22] A more revealing illustration of the state of pugilism is provided by two reports from the early 1770s – the first of a match staged at Chequer Lane in Dublin, the second at Portarlington in Queen's county – because they appertain to planned events. These are unusual, but they are significant since they suggest that some, at least, among the champions of pugilism in Ireland recognised that the sport must be pursued in a structured and organised manner if it was to prosper, and to attract a loyal audience:

> Wednesday night [16 October 1771], a most remarkable concourse of people assembled at a house in Chequer Lane to the amount of upwards of two hundred, to see the decision of a bruising match between a noted slater and a butcher for 20 guineas, when after an obstinate and bloody engagement of 35 minutes the slater came off victorious. It were really droll to see with what order this motley crew conducted themselves, as there were benches fixed after the Broughtonian manner, and twelve of the antagonists' friends each had a large mould candle in his hand, and the least disturbance offered by the company was resented by the stuffing one of the burning candles in their faces. It is said there were 60 guineas depending on this battle.[23]

> Last Monday [12 September 1774] was fought at Portarlington, the long expected bruising-match between Timothy O'Dunn, coachmaker, and Matthew O'Connor, sawyer. The contest lasted about an hour and a quarter, in which time they fought nineteen bouts. O'Dunn's strength and har-

Kelly and Hayton, 'The Irish parliament in European context: a representative institution in a composite state', and 'conclusion' in idem and Bergin (eds), *The eighteenth-century composite state*, pp 3–20, 244–53. **19** Brailsford, *Bareknuckles*, pp 14–15. **20** *Hoey's Publick Journal*, 12 Aug. 1771. **21** Kelly, *'That damn'd thing called honour'*, pp 80, 118. **22** *Public Gazetteer*, 16 July 1768; *FLJ*, 10 June 1769; *BNL*, 16 June 1769. **23** *Hoey's Publick Journal*, 18 Oct. 1771.

diness, during the middle of the combat, seemed to promise him the victory; but O'Connor's judgement, coolness, spirit, and agility, at length prevailed, to the great satisfaction of great numbers of spectators (who assembled from all parts of the country) and the neighbourhood in general. Great betts were depending. O'Dunn was so emaciated as to be obliged to keep to his bed three days ...[24]

It is not apparent from these descriptions if the organisers of these events, and the principals followed Broughton's rules in their entirety, but it is clear that they were not pugilistic free-for-alls. However, the attempt to regularise the sport to which these reports bear witness was insufficient to win over the authorities.

The success of the authorities in interrupting matches on public spaces such as Oxmantown Green, Dublin (nine persons were arrested and consigned to jail in one swoop in June 1769) obliged those who fancied themselves as pugilists, those who sought to gain financially by betting on the outcome, and those who wanted simply to spectate, to seek out less familiar locations. This did nothing to diminish the resolution of the authorities to prevent such encounters taking place. Indeed, it may have heightened their resolve as these events were more prone to disturbance and disorder.[25] Certainly, the damage to property caused by 'a riotous mob assembled at Marrowbone Lane' to watch a fight in October 1772, and the death of one person and the injury of a number of others when the 'guard of soldiers' called to disperse a crowd gathered at the Blackpitts on a Sunday in September responded to a fusillade of stones with a volley of shots, served merely to intensify the antagonism that characterised the relationship between pugilists and the law. This was accented when Samuel Poole, the owner of the property at Blackpitts on which the incident occurred, was found not guilty when he was tried for murder because of his role in the affair.[26]

In any event, it did not prevent further pugilistic encounters. 'A great bruising match' at Athy, county Kildare in 1776 involving a recruiting officer, and a Munster man 'before a numerous deal of spectators', and a less public encounter in 1784 between two soldiers from different regiments stationed in the capital, which were interrupted by a local priest and regimental officers, indicated that the impulse to fight was stronger than the aspiration of the authorities to police it out of existence, not only because it was a product of cultural conditioning, but also because it was portrayed as instinctual behaviour.[27] The commitment to boxing was certainly in evidence in 1781 when an enterprising pugilist, who had lost an eye, offered 'to give instruction in the Broughtonian stile' to those who sought to acquire 'the necessary skills at the Adelphi Buildings in Paradise Row' in Dublin.[28] It is not apparent if this initiative attracted many paying customers,

24 *FJ*, 22 Sept. 1774; *Hibernian Journal*, 23 Sept. 1774. **25** *FLJ*, 10 June 1769. **26** *FJ*, 22 Sept., 8 Oct. 1772; *Hoey's Publick Journal*, 21 Sept., 9 Oct. 1772; BNL, 27 Oct. 1772. **27** *FLJ*, 9 Nov. 1776; *FJ*, 27 May 1784; *BNL*, 28 May 1784. **28** *FJ*, 9 Jan. 1781.

but since it was consistent with other trends, it suggests that interest in the sport appreciated in Ireland in the late 1770s and early 1780s. This elevated the profile of pugilism domestically, and laid the foundation for the visible intensification in pugilistic activity during the late 1780s and early 1790s, which coincided with the first phase of the thirty years during which pugilism flourished in regency England.[29]

By comparison with the highest levels of the sport in England, pugilism in Ireland was, and continued to be, pursued in an essentially unstructured way. There are many reasons for this, but perhaps the single most important was that, even more starkly than Bristol, Norwich and Birmingham, which played second fiddle to London in England, Dublin did not possess the necessary demographic, financial or infra-structural mass required to sustain an equivalent pugilistic culture.[30] In addition, there were no wealthy patrons prepared to champion talented individuals, to organise matches or, generally, to bankroll the sport. As a result, unlike England, where the patronage of royalty and members of the aristocracy was crucial in dissuading local officials from intervening to prevent encounters being pursued to a conclusion, and in identifying locations where fights could be staged free of the prospect of interruption, no such pressure was brought to bear on Irish sheriffs, mayors or magistrates.[31] Richard, the seventh earl of Barrymore in the Irish peerage, was an enthusiastic patron of the ring, but his involvement with the sport centred on London, and, in any event, he was so thoroughly anglicised he disposed of his Irish estates in order to meet his debts prior to his death in 1793.[32] There was no identifiable Ireland-based equivalent. Furthermore, the failure of Irish tavern owners and innkeepers to emulate their peers in London, and other English centres of pugilistic endeavour, to provide either the venue or the broader infrastructure that might have sustained the sport contributed to the failure of pugilism in Ireland to rise much above the level of a street activity in the late eighteenth century.[33] This certainly was where it stood in the mid-1780s, when, encouraged by accounts emanating from London, the number of reported pugilistic encounters increased sharply. In the words of one commentator, writing of Dublin in the spring of 1788:

> The populace of this city have begun to imitate the savage custom of the lower orders of the sister country, and scarce a day passes in consequence without a pitched battle being fought.[34]

This was to exaggerate. But the ease and frequency with which in the mid-1780s combatants, who might previously have been encouraged to disengage, 'in a few

29 For England see Brailsford, *Bareknuckles*, p. 23 ff; John Ford, *Prize fighting: the age of regency boximania* (Newtown Abbot, 1971).   30 Brailsford, *Bareknuckles*, pp 33–44.   31 Brailsford, *Bareknuckles*, pp 25–32, 67–8.   32 Brailsford, *Bareknuckles*, pp 26–9; GEC, *The complete peerage*, i, 446; J.R. Robinson, *The last earl of Barrymore* (London, 1894), pp 19–230 passim.   33 Brailsford, *Bareknuckles*, pp 18–19, 49, 67.   34 *Clonmel Gazette*, 4 Apr. 1788.

moments were surrounded by hundreds, who by huzzas, and thumps on the back, animated them to fight with more than savage rancour and fury' indicated not only that boxing was deemed a legitimate way to resolve differences but also that it possessed a strong attraction for those in search of spectacle. However, the impulsivity, and lack of structure that was the most compelling feature of the sport in Ireland ensured that much of the pugilistic activity was pursued in a less than regular manner.[35]

At its most basic, and sometimes most brutal, there were those cases in which individuals who 'agreed to decide' a 'dispute ... by a boxing match' took no notice of the fact that fighting was meant to be a demonstration of controlled aggression. An encounter at Dirty Lane in August 1788 in which one combatant, 'having knocked the other down, jumped on his stomach and killed him instantly' fits this description. Because the aggressor in this instance had clearly crossed the boundary of what was permissible, he was properly taken up and committed to Kilmainham jail.[36] The response was not always so decisive, even in instances in which individuals forfeited their lives, or lost the use of vital faculties. It is not apparent, for example, what sanctions, if any, were imposed on the inmate of Newgate prison, who delivered a mortal blow to a fellow inmate when 'having quarrelled, they agreed to settle the matter by a bruising match',[37] or on Grogan, a corn factor from Thomas Street, who in the space of 37 minutes in November 1785 so severely pummelled his antagonist, a skinner named Lumley from Watling Street, he had to be 'carried away senseless from the field'. Perhaps it was sufficient to keep the offending prisoner in custody, and to leave Grogan to contemplate the permanent physical injury he had incurred; Grogan may have come 'off victorious', but, according to the report of the fight, he suffered 'the ... loss of an eye and [had] the cartilage of an ear bit off'.[38] Since Grogan's injuries were not exceptional, and were consistent with what a pugilist might anticipate,[39] the authorities saw little reason to get involved after the event. Moreover, there is no evidence to suggest that the public was more than ordinarily animated by this outcome or by other instances in which named tradesmen squared up to each other at such locations as the Hospital Fields, and Marlborough Green when it did not lead to a breach of the peace, and the injuries received were delivered in manner consistent with the permissive rules of the sport.[40] This may account for the matter of fact way in which it was reported in 1789 that a man named Moran had died 'of the bruises he received' in 'a pitched battle' on Marlborough Green in May of that year. However, it is noteworthy that Moran was the second man to die 'within the space of ten months by boxing', and that this fact prompted some commentators to accuse the

35 *Saunders' Newsletter*, 10 Mar. 1785. 36 *FJ*, 7 Aug. 1788. 37 *Volunteer Evening Post*, 31 May 1787. 38 *FJ*, 24 Nov. 1785; *BNL*, 29 Nov. 1785. 39 Comparable injuries were inflicted in a fight between brothers-in-law in Dublin in 1789. Provoked by a quarrel to duke it out, they 'fought furiously for fifteen minutes' in the course of which one of the pugilists was deprived of his 'left eye': *FJ*, 10 Sept. 1789. 40 *FJ*, 24 Nov. 1785; *Hibernian Journal*, 18 May 1789.

magistrates of 'neglecting their duty' and, more seriously, of being 'accessories of murder' by not intervening to prevent such encounters taking place.[41] Hopes were also expressed in certain quarters that the legislature might take action. Four years earlier, *Saunders Newsletter* responded to a surge in the number of impromptu street fights by calling (in vain) upon parliament to approve legislation providing for 'a month's imprisonment and some severe lashes in Newgate' for those who engaged in this 'Gothic barbarity'.[42]

Legislation of the kind suggested would have been disproportionate given the scale of the increase in pugilistic activity. This is not to suggest that the concerns that were expressed about impromptu fights were not justified, since personal disputes could easily escalate into general affrays. In 1787, for instance, 'a row between two porters – one a timber porter on Rogerson's Quay, the other a corn porter on George's Quay [Dublin,] that they sought to settle by boxing' – flared out of control, when 'on the corn porter prevailing, some of [the timber porter's] companions attacked the victor, which led to an affray with the supporters of both principals getting involved'. As a result, two men were fatally injured.[43] The recently established Dublin police were not called upon in this instance, but their response two years later to a disturbance near to St Michael's Lane caused by a 'number of journeymen taylors' who took 'to decide' a quarrel that erupted 'at a customary annual entertainment given on Easter Monday ... by boxing in the street' provoked a serious incident. The immediate cause was not the boxing, which 'was attended with no other ill consequences than a few black eyes, bloody noses, and torn clothes', but the decision of the police to lay 'hold of two or three persons who appeared to be concerned in the affray'. This caused a mob to assemble, which sought to liberate the prisoners and disarm the police in the course of which 'two policemen were killed, and another dangerously wounded'.[44] Though this incident is more revealing of the antagonism that characterised the relationship of the Dublin populace and police, it also served vividly to demonstrate to the respectable citizenry the seriousness of the risk posed to public order by unregulated pugilism. It was a lesson that was not lost on the *aficionados* of the sport.

Fights between known or aspiring *bruisers*, which constitute the second, and most common, pugilistic category into which the reported encounters of the mid- and late 1780s can be assigned, rarely precipitated such significant breaches of public order. The identifiable principals, who derived in most instances from the same social groups as those just described, included a constable, a chairman, seasonal workers, porters of various hues, a shoemaker, a rope-maker, and one 'gentleman amateur of the Broughtonian art', who formally challenged and defeated his opponent, a 'runner to one of the Holyhead packets', in seven rounds.[45]

41 *Hibernian Journal*, 18 May 1789; *Ennis Chronicle*, 21 May 1789.   42 As note 35.   43 *Volunteer Evening Post*, 7, 10 July 1787.   44 *FJ*, 14 Apr. 1789; *Hibernian Journal*, 15 Apr. 1789; *BNL*, 17 Apr. 1789.   45 *FJ*, 11 Aug. 1785, 3 Oct., 12 Nov. 1789; *Clonmel Gazette*, 4 Aug. 1788; *Ennis Chronicle*, 5 Oct. 1789.

These were, as the latter contest exemplifies, usually structured trials of strength, fought according to rule, though they were as likely as the impromptu encounters considered above to take place in the open, and in Dublin on public spaces such as the Tenter Fields, the 'waste ground at the rere of Dirty Lane', and the Phoenix Park.[46] The phenomenon is well illustrated by an encounter at Ballymore Eustace, county Kildare:

> Thursday last [28 August 1788], a large mob of harvest men and other country people assembled on the Common of Broadlays, near Ballymore Eustace, to see a match of bruising between two stout reapers, one a Leinster, the other a Connaught man, who had mutually given and accepted a trial of skill in honour of their respective provinces. The contest, though not supported by much judgement on either side, was agreeable to the strictest rules of single combat, and the bravery and resolution of the parties would probably have continued the fight sometime longer, if a neighbouring gentleman had not proposed a cessation of arms on the principle that having already given the most convincing proofs of equal manhood, it would be scandalous for two brave fellows to maim each other through so mean a motive of malice. This remonstrance had its effect. The truly courageous universally disclaim all sentiments of revenge. The parties shook hands, and a handsome collection was made on the spot for their entertainment at a public house, where a few of the neighbouring gentlemen and farmers adjourned to preserve good order.[47]

The visible order, pugilistic discipline, and commitment to identify who was the best boxer manifest in this instance was also in evidence in the fight that took place in August 1785 in the Tenter Fields, Dublin, between Grogan, a constable, and Bryan, a chairman, in which the former was declared victor after 36 minutes. Significantly, because Bryan, the chairman, attributed his defeat to 'his being drunk the night before', the two men agreed to 'renew the combat' on the following Sunday.[48] Generally, fights between bruisers concluded with victory being awarded to one party before life-threatening injuries were incurred.[49] This could not be presumed, however, if the principals were equally matched and disposed to fight to exhaustion, as the report of an encounter involving a rope-maker and a porter in 1789 makes clear.

> Last week a desperate battle was fought in the Tenter Fields between one Fitzsimon, a rope-maker, and one Hamilton, a porter. They fought 44 rounds, [in] the first nine of which the rope-maker was knocked down

---

46 *FJ*, 11 Aug. 1785, 3 Oct. 1789; *Clonmel Gazette*, 4 Aug. 1788; *Ennis Chronicle*, 16 Nov. 1789. 47 *FJ*, 4 Sept. 1788. 48 *FJ*, 11 Aug. 1785. 49 As instanced by the 'desperate battle' between two 'noted bruisers', McDonough, a coal-porter, and Connor, a shoe maker, fought off Dirty Lane, which was won by the former: *Clonmel Gazette*, 4 Aug. 1788.

with nine blows before he could give his antagonist one, when the standers-by were for parting them, the contest seemed so unequal. But the rope-maker would not give in, declaring that he would fight until the other should say 'No', to which the porter replied 'he would not say no until the day of resurrection'. Upon which they continued boxing until the 44th round, when they became so weak, that the spectators parted them without being able to determine the victor.[50]

Trials of strength and skill such as these are not always distinguishable from the third, and most emblematical, type of pugilistic event that took place in Ireland in the late 1780s – those pursued for material gain. At their most basic, individuals might fight for something as ordinary as a 'gallon of whiskey', which was the prize on offer when a butcher and a blacksmith met 'in one of the fields between Rathmines and Milltown', county Dublin, in June 1789.[51] Money was a more familiar, and a more powerful inducement to most pugilists, though the sums on offer could be modest when set beside the sums that those who gambled on the outcome might win if they played the odds and judged the qualities of the protagonists correctly. A 'pitched battle' at Rathvilly, county Carlow, provides an example:

> Thursday last [25 May 1786], a pitched battle was fought at Rathvilly ... between a weaver and a shoe-maker for a sweepstake of ten guineas, subscribed by a number of persons, lovers of the ancient and noble Broughtonian science, and desirous of introducing it, among other improvements, into this kingdom. The contest lasted twenty minutes, when the shoe-maker was obliged to acknowledge the superior strength and agility of his antagonist, on receiving a blow in the stomach which almost brought him to ground, and he declared himself unable to proceed. The betts were six to four against the weaver; considerable sums were lost, and the knowing ones very much taken in.[52]

With so much potentially at stake, the organisation of boxing improved concomitantly. Prize money increased, greater effort was expended on identifying venues suited to pugilists as well as spectators, and organisers contrived to ensure more skilful displays of what was affectedly denominated the 'Broughtonian science'. Occasionally, this involved fighting indoors. The first identifiable instance of two pugilists squaring up in an indoor venue in the late 1780s occurred in 'a large malthouse', in an unnamed town 'not one hundred miles west of the metropolis', between a carpenter and a blacksmith who were incentivised to be aggressive by the offers of 'a purse of thirty guineas ... to the best bruiser who should disable his antagonist by the secret blows, or cross buttocks, within ... twenty minutes'. Drawn by the prospect of an exciting fight, a large audience of

50 *Ennis Chronicle*, 16 Nov. 1789.   51 *FJ*, 20 June 1789.   52 *Hibernian Journal*, 31 May 1786.

'ladies and gentlemen' assembled, and they were left in no doubt as to the potential brutality of the sport to which they were attracted when 'an unlucky stroke in the pit of the stomach, left the carpenter sprawling in convulsions, till death closed his eyes forever'.[53] Though the absence of corroborative evidence counsels against assuming that this report is true in all particulars, the incidental detail suggests not only that it was written by someone who was familiar with pugilism but also that it offers a genuine insight into the manner in which the sport was promoted. A still better sense of the way in which a prize match of this kind was conducted may be gleaned from the extended account published some fourteen months later of an encounter in the fields off Great Brunswick Street, Dublin:

> Monday, [15 October 1787] a vast concourse of people assembled in the fields behind St Mark's church to see a pitched battle that two noted bruisers had agreed to fight. Parties attended from the markets and the Earl of Meath's Liberty, to hold betts upon the occasion. The men did not seem by any means a proportionate match; one was a man rather advanced in years, the other in the vigour of his youth. ... Before they engaged they shook hands, which it seems is a necessary etiquette upon such occasions. The aged man was knocked down successively by the three first strokes, each of which was struck on the right temple; one of them closed his right eye, and the odds through the field were then seven to three against the *blinker*, as they called him. The battle loitered for about three minutes, during which time the combatants continued moving with much caution, without striking a blow; at length the young fellow received a stroke in the stomach, which caused him almost to double; a shout from the spectators augmented his embarrassment, and he was totally disabled in about a minute. The judges then declared in favour of the veteran, and remarked that all the money was won and lost ...[54]

The presence of 'judges' at this fight reinforces the conclusion, previously offered, that the advocates of the 'Broughtonian science' sought consciously to ensure that pugilism was conducted visibly and explicitly according to rule. This was emphasised on the same day when the acceptance by a butcher of a challenge issued by one of the seconds to fight 'any man ... for a guinea and a shilling', which the challenger assumed would be conducted there and then, was deferred for a week.[55]

The wish of its Irish *aficionados* to present pugilism as a disciplined and, by extension, fair and honourable sport was encouraged by the conviction that best practice was not just desirable, it was essential if the sport was to be liberated from the association with brutality that random brawling encouraged. The chasm between boxing (sport) and brawling (violence) was underlined by a surge in enthusiasm for the sport in the south-east of England in the second half of the

53 *Hibernian Journal*, 14 Aug. 1786.   54 *FJ*, 18 Oct. 1787.   55 Ibid.

Fig. 25 Peter Corcoran was one of the first Irish pugilists to make an impact on the London circuit (steel plate from a collection of engraved plates, *c.*1840, originally published in Pierce Egan, *Boxiana, or sketches of ancient and modern pugilism* (London, 1812–20): author's collection).

1780s, and the consequent increase in the volume of print devoted to reporting the deeds of the champions and challengers as pugilism embarked on its golden era.

It is difficult to pinpoint the impact of developments in England in the 1780s and afterwards on pugilism in Ireland, but it is not simply coincidental that the acceleration in interest in the sport in Ireland coincides with its increased popularity in England. This conclusion is strengthened by the recognition by a number of Irish newspapers that it was a subject of interest to their readers. The coverage of English pugilism in the Irish press did not commence with the decision of the *Hibernian Journal* in 1786 to inaugurate a column entitled 'boxing matches', but it did represent the beginnings of a new phase.[56] Previously, in the 1750s and 1760s, there was some reporting of the activities of both Jack Broughton and Jack Slack.[57] Coverage then was intermittent rather than regular, but interest in the sport was sufficiently developed to cause the *Freeman's Journal* and the *Belfast News Letter* to augment their reports during the 1770s, particularly (but not only) when the news item possessed an Irish angle. The *Freeman's Journal*, for example, accorded detailed coverage to the defeat in 1776 of Peter

56 *Hibernian Journal*, 19 June 1786.   57 *BNL*, 24 Apr. 1750, 13 June 1760, 12, 14 May 1765.

Corcoran (see Fig. 25), 'the noted Irish bruiser', by Henry Sellars at the Crown Inn in Staines-upon-Thames.[58]

His Irish background, notwithstanding, Corcoran's pugilistic endeavours in the 1770s were not sufficient to cause any Irish newspapers to embark on the regular and routine reporting of the English boxing scene. That did not commence until 1786 when Sam Martin prevailed over Richard Humphries in a celebrated encounter at Newmarket. Even then, most reports of the contest contrived to include an Irish angle – specifically the under-card, which featured a fight between an Irishman named Crawley and an Englishman named Hemmings.[59] Encouraged, or so one presumes, by the response, the *Hibernian Journal, Freeman's Journal, Belfast News Letter, Dublin Weekly Journal*, and other news-sheets, contrived thereafter to satisfy their readers appetite for information by routinely carrying boxing news from London. As a result, it was possible within a few years for the purchasers of Irish newspapers not only to read detailed accounts of the epic contests between Richard Humphries and Daniel Mendoza in 1788 and 1789 that raised the profile of pugilism to unprecedented heights, but also to be kept apprised of the deeds of John Jackson, Joe Ward, 'Big Ben' Bryan and the other pugilists and personalities that populated the sport.[60] Moreover, coverage was not exclusive to the main Dublin and Belfast titles that aspired to an island-wide readership. The *Ennis Chronicle* provided readers of the mid-west with equally detailed accounts, while the *Cork Gazette*'s more discrete columns kept its Munster readers informed of developments in Great Britain.[61] As a consequence of this reportage – unprecedented and unrivalled (horse racing possibly excepted) for an English sport in Ireland – Irish fans had the opportunity not only to engage directly with the major championship matches and individual rivalries that defined this early exciting phase in the history of pugilism, but also to learn its history, and, possibly more importantly, revealing details as to how it was conducted at the most advanced, and professional, level.[62] Indeed, with the support of the press, which also reported the palpably less sophisticated, less lucrative, and less structured world of domestic pugilism, it appeared during the early 1790s that the sport was well placed to take off and become a significant presence on the Irish recreational landscape.

---

58 *BNL*, 24 Sept. 1773, 21 Jan., 20 May 1774; *FJ*, 29 June 1776; Brailsford, *Bareknuckles*, p. 16. Significantly, Corcoran retained his legendary status in Ireland; the boxer who issued a challenge to all comers behind at St Mark's Church in 1787 declared that he was 'the first pupil ever the celebrated Corcoran had taught': ibid., 18 Oct. 1787. 59 *BNL*, 12 May 1786; *Hibernian Journal*, 19 June 1786. This Crawley is not to be confused with Peter Crawley who was briefly champion in 1827: Brailsford, op cit., p. 86. 60 *Hibernian Journal*, 21 July 1786, 16 Jan. 1788, 7 Jan. 1790, 20, 26 Jan. 1791; *FJ*, 14 June 1788, 16, 18 Aug. 1792; *Dublin Weekly Journal*, 29 Jan. 1791; *BNL*, 13 July, 13 Nov. 1787, 18 Jan., 8 Feb., 25 Apr., 20 June, 15, 22 Aug. 1788, 27 Feb., 19 May, 23, 30 Oct. 1789, 28 Jan. 1791, 25 May 1792. 61 *Ennis Chronicle*, 12 Jan., 23 Mar., 21 May 1789, 12 May, 4 July 1791; *Cork Gazette*, 1790. 62 *Hibernian Journal*, 16 Jan. 1788; 'Further particulars' [to Humphreys versus Mendoza], *Ennis Chronicle*, 21 May 1789.

The most important change to the way in which boxing was pursued in Ireland in the early 1790s, when compared with the 1780s, was the decline in the number of personal and impromptu altercations. It cannot be claimed definitively that fights of this ilk did not continue to take place, perhaps even with some frequency, but their absence from the pages of the press suggests that there was a greater awareness of, and perhaps even willingness to be guided by Broughton's rules and the evolving etiquette that defined organised pugilism. If so, it was not accompanied by an equivalent improvement in the venues in which most encounters took place. The decision by two butchers to meet at Clarendon market in April 1791 could be interpreted as evidence of the wish in some quarters, at least when the weather was not clement, to opt for sheltered (preferably indoor) locations, but this is the only such instance that has been identified.[63] Most fights took place, as had been the practice for several generations, outdoors, on fields or greens, within ready proximity of the nearest urban centre. Among the locations to which recourse was made near Dublin, which was still the main centre of Irish pugilism, a field off the south Circular road, a field adjoining the North Strand, Marlborough Green, a green space adjacent to Long Lane, which had been availed of by the city's factions for their trials of strength several decades earlier, and the fields towards the rear of St Mark's Church on New Brunswick Street were deemed particularly convenient.[64] The latter location was so popular it was described in 1792 'as a sort of Campus Martius for pugilistic exercises'.[65] This designation suggests that the New Brunswick Street fields were more commonly resorted to than the surviving reports indicate, but it was in keeping with the fact that it possessed the crucial attributes of proximity, accessibility and seclusion that characterised such venues. Moreover, it had the additional advantage that the authorities were willing to turn a blind eye to its use as long as the fights that were conducted there did not escalate into violent riotousness. Saliently, such attempts as were made to identify comparable locations elsewhere in the country proved less than wholly successful. A widely reported fight was held in fields beyond Glanmire in Cork in 1791, and another more impromptu affair involving two soldiers took place in Irishtown, Limerick in 1795, but these were unique occasions as the prompt intervention of the authorities prohibited regular resort to either location.[66]

Heartened by the preparedness of the authorities to show a measure of tolerance, pugilists, their seconds, and the substantial crowds that enjoyed attending pugilistic encounters, contrived increasingly to behave in a manner that did not encourage intervention. This permissive attitude may have facilitated a greater number of fights than might have been the case had the authorities clamped down severely, but it was also insufficient to pave the way for the emergence in Ireland of a cadre of specialist (professional) pugilists. A majority of principals were

---

63 *FJ*, 28 Apr. 1791. 64 *FJ*, 2 Sept. 1790, 12, 29 May 1792; *Dublin Weekly Journal*, 31 Dec. 1791; *Hibernian Journal*, 28 Dec. 1791, 9, 30 May 1792. 65 *Hibernian Journal*, 9 May 1792. 66 *Hibernian Journal*, 31 Aug. 1791, 28 Dec. 1795.

drawn in the early 1790s (as previously) from the artisanal, craft and commercial trades, which embraced the anticipated array of porters, chairmen, butchers, weavers, plasterers, slaters and the like, who generally fought for modest purses of no more than five, ten or twenty guineas.[67] An added dimension was provided by the organisation, on occasion, of fights between representatives of English and Irish trades, but though these usually proved worthy adversaries, they were less crowd pleasing in practice, and less attractive to the press, than those involving known local bruisers.[68] These were so popular in the 1790s that crowds ran into 'thousands', which was substantially in excess of the numbers previously reported. For example, a crowd of 'some thousands' turned up at Marlborough Green in May 1792 to watch 'two celebrated bruisers' – Power, a weaver, and Byrne, a plasterer – square off.[69] The meeting the same month of a slater and a weaver in the fields at the back of St Mark's Church, which was determined in favour of the former, attracted 'more than five thousand spectators', and this number was nearly equalled a year later when 'four or five thousand persons' assembled at 7 am on Sunday 25 August 1793 'in the fields adjoining the Long Lane', 'to watch Rowe, the noted bully of the port, and another pugilistic hero of established fame from the county Wicklow'.[70]

Significantly, the large crowd that gathered to witness Rowe and his opponent was obliged to disperse by the arrival, accompanied by a company of foot, of a justice of the peace, who read the riot act, and impressed on the assembled crowd 'the impropriety of such proceedings'. According to the positive spin put on this intervention by the press, the city was thereby saved from 'a very serious riot'.[71] This possibility cannot be ruled out, but even without it, the accidental death of a young weaver and the serious injury of a number of others when the branch of a tree upon which eager onlookers had clambered gave way, convinced the authorities that it was time to take a more interventionist approach in order to curb 'such barbarous pastimes' and 'savage customs'.[72] This was not an unexpected response. Calls upon officials to be pro-active multiplied during the early 1790s, and the high sheriffs were warmly applauded the previous May when they intervened to disperse 'the mob, from whom much riot and outrage was dreaded', which was drawn by the prospect of a fight to the fields off Great Brunswick Street.[73]

Based on the number of reported incidents, it would appear that this interventionist approach had a distinct and identifiable impact. Pugilism did not cease, of course; the sport was too popular, and too lucrative. If, as was widely reported, 'near a thousand pounds were lost and won' on the encounter involving Kidney and Sheehan at Glanmire in county Cork in 1791, it is manifest that

---

67 *FJ*, 2 Sept. 1790, 28 Apr. 1791, 10, 12, 29 May 1792; *Dublin Weekly Journal*, 31 Dec. 1791; *Hibernian Journal*, 28 Dec. 1791, 9, 30 May 1792. 68 *FJ*, 2 Sept. 1790; *Dublin Weekly Journal*, 31 Dec. 1791. 69 *Hibernian Journal*, 30 May 1792. Significantly, this fight did not proceed because 'Byrne declined the battle'. 70 *FJ*, 12, 29 May 1792, 27 Aug. 1793; *Hibernian Journal*, 26 Aug. 1793. 71 *Hibernian Journal*, 26 Aug. 1793. 72 *Hibernian Journal*, 28 Aug. 1793; *FJ*, 12 May 1792, 29 May 1793. 73 *Hibernian Journal*, 9, 30 May 1792; *FJ*, 10, 12, 29 May 1792.

pugilism, like cockfighting and horse racing, could be a lucrative activity for those who were clever enough to play the odds:

> They had twenty-three bouts [*lege* rounds], during the first five of which bets ran high, and were three to one in favour of Sheehan; after that they descended to par, then rose in favour of Kidney, until they gradually were so high in his favour as five to one, which continued until Sheehan gave in.[74]

This fight prompted an exceptionally lively betting ring, but it illustrates well how the combination of the drama of fighting and gambling gave pugilism a distinct allure, and ensured that keenly contested encounters, even those involving fighters of only moderate skill, maintained their appeal within the plebeian and artisanal circles that sustained the sport in Ireland.

Despite, or perhaps because of, its evident popularity with the urban lower classes, pugilism in Ireland did not possess much attraction for even the more raffish among the country's aristocracy and gentry. As a result, the sport was ill-positioned to respond when news emanating from England that it was no longer 'the most fashionable amusement of the *beaux esprits*', dovetailed with the striking deterioration in law and order in the mid- and late 1790s, to precipitate its disappearance from the press.[75] Because of the difficulty of penetrating the cultural world of the pugilists, it is a challenge to establish precisely what impact this had on the manner in which the sport was conducted during these years. It is clear, based on the case of 'a groom that met his death by a boxing match' in Dublin in May 1797 that pugilism did not simply cease, and it may be, like cockfighting, which reverted at this time to the localised sport it had once been, that such pugilistic encounters as took place were impromptu events fought for small sums, comparable to 'shake bag' cockfights.[76]

The pugilistic impulse faded but did not die during the decade spanning the 1790s and early years of the nineteenth century when the sport all but disappeared from the public realm, Significantly, it also encountered difficulties then in England though the establishment of the pugilist as a sporting hero may have been a factor in assisting the country to negotiate the challenge posed by Revolutionary and Napoleonic France.[77] This was not without wider implications, as the emergence in England in the early nineteenth century of a new generation of pugilists, a number of whom were Irish or possessed of Irish ancestry, assisted with the reanimation of the sport there. Neither Bill Ryan, whose father Michael twice fought Tom Johnson for the title of champion in the 1780s, nor the talented John (Jack) O'Donnell, whose unbeaten run excited such admiration until he was

74 *Cork Gazette*, 24 Aug. 1791.   75 *FJ*, 28 Nov. 1793.   76 Higgins to Cooke, 30 May 1797 in Bartlett (ed.), *Revolutionary Dublin*, p. 164.   77 See Richard Holt, 'Heroes of the north: sport and the shaping of regional identity' in Jeff Hill and Jack Williams (eds), *Sport and identity in the north of England* (Keele, 1996), p. 144; Brailsford, *Bareknuckles*, passim.

Fig. 26 Dan Donnelly (1788–1820), 'the late Irish champion', whose rise to eminence aroused major excitement in Ireland in the early nineteenth century (steel plate engraving by Percy Robert from a drawing by G. Sharples from a collection of the engraved plates, *c.*1840, originally published in Pierce Egan, *Boxiana, or sketches of ancient and modern pugilism* (London, 1812-20): author's collection).

comprehensively outfought by Caleb Baldwin in September 1803, secured (or deserved) near the number of column inches that were devoted to John Gully, Tom Cribb, Jem Belcher, Tom Belcher, or Tom Molyneux, but they excited sufficient interest to cause Irish newspapers to re-commence reporting the sport, and once they did so, coverage soon expanded.[78] A turning point of a kind was arrived at in the lead-up to the eagerly anticipated battle between Cribb and Molyneux in December 1810, when Bradbury, the manager of the Theatre Royal in Crow Street, announced his intention, 'at the request of several gentlemen of this city, to give instructions in the scientific knowledge of pugilism and sparring' in specially appointed premises in Temple Lane.[79] It is not apparent if Bradbury made any money on the venture as he may have misjudged the national mood. Be that as it may, the public's interest in boxing was sufficient to cause the editor of the

78 Brailsford, *Bareknuckles*, pp 24–5, 27, 42, 44 and passim; *Cork Advertiser*, 22 Oct. 1801; *FLJ*, 22 Dec. 1802, 29 Oct. 1803; *FJ*, 4 Dec. 1804, 16 Jan., 27 Nov., 21 Dec. 1807, 18 July 1808, 27 July 1809, 8 Jan., 26 Apr. 1810. 79 *FJ*, 4, 26 Dec. 1810.

Freeman's Journal to continue to provide regular 'boxing' reports, which kept readers informed of developments in London and elsewhere.[80]

There was, at the same time, no evidence of a willingness within the ranks of Irish opinion-makers, exemplified by newspaper editors, religious ministers, and legal and political officeholders, to facilitate the sport locally. Indeed, the prevailing official attitude was epitomised by Andrew Watson, the mayor of Limerick, who informed two young men who sought permission in 1813 to put on an exhibition of boxing in the city that he 'would prevent them as much as possible, and that if they presumed to exhibit, [he] would not only take them into custody, but also the company that might enjoy their savage exhibition'.[81] The rising interest that was the Catholic clergy evidently was of the same opinion. In Galway in 1816, Fr McDermott 'exhorted with very commendable zeal such persons amongst the congregations of the Augustinian chapel, as may happen to have any taste for pugilism, against any cultivation of it'.[82]

Though individuals such as Watson who believed pugilism was 'the greatest disgrace to Great Britain' presented a barrier to the emergence of the sport out of the shadows in which it then lay, the reservoir of public interest in pugilism in Ireland ran deep.[83] Indicatively, this was animated quite unexpectedly when Dan Donnelly (1788–1820) (Fig. 26) was persuaded to take on Tom Hall, an experienced English pugilist, at the country's premier sporting venue, the Curragh racecourse, in September 1814. Donnelly was an untutored pugilist (reputedly, he had only one previous fight), but he was an imposing six feet and 14 stone, and he carried the hopes of a populace that wanted a champion they could call their own.[84] Billed as 'a trial between bodily strength and science' (in the manner of the previous contests involving Tom Cribb and Tom Molyneux in 1810–11), Donnelly's victory, before a huge crowd estimated at 'upwards of fifty thousand persons, a greater assemblage than ever was known in this country on such an occasion', after 18 rounds, was not uncontroversial. (Hall was judged to have forfeited the fight by 'slipping out of the ring' at the end of the eighteenth round, but he accused Donnelly of 'foul play', and early reports suggested that Donnelly was disqualified for striking his opponent when 'down'.)[85] But it was greeted in Dublin with unqualified joy, because it dovetailed with embryonic nationalist sentiment fuelled by economic disappointment and resentment at the failure of the Union parliament to concede Catholic emancipation.[86]

---

80 *FJ*, 15 Jan., 22 Mar., 27 May 1811, 29 Feb., 7 July, 5 Nov. 1812.   81 *FJ*, 5 Oct. 1813. These sentiments, which are dated 25 Sept. 1815, were first published in the *Cork Mercantile Chronicle*. 82 *FJ*, 17 Dec. 1816.   83 Ibid.   84 Donnelly is the only Irish pugilist to have multiple biographers. The standard, uncritical, modern life is Patrick Myler, *Regency rogue: Dan Donnelly, his life and legends* (Dublin, 1976). For an excellent dissection of the life and myth of Donnelly, see Neal Garnham, '"To die with honour or gain the day": Dan Donnelly as an Irish sporting hero', *IHS*, 37 (2010–11), pp 535–49.   85 *FJ*, 15, 16 Sept. 1814. Other accounts suggest that the attendance may have been 20,000: Feehan, *Cuirrech Life: the Curragh of Kildare*, p. 62.   86 *FJ*, 16 Sept. 1814; J.R. Hill, *From patriots to unionists; Dublin civil politics and Irish Protestant patriotism, 1660–1840*

Donnelly became a popular hero, and his standing as a national icon was copper-fastened fourteen months later when, on 13 November 1815, he met and comprehensively defeated another Englishman, George Cooper – 'one of the most scienced and best pugilists of the present day' – at the same Curragh location in eleven rounds.[87] Now commonly denominated the champion of Ireland (though there was no such title), who would 'very soon take the palm from the champion of England', Donnelly's achievements elevated pugilism in Ireland from a faintly disreputable sport to an activity that for a time transcended the lowly social origins of its practitioners, and often brutal demeanour.[88]

Indicatively, the improved profile the sport enjoyed not only encouraged well-known English pugilists (most of whom were past their prime) to travel to Ireland with offers to take on all comers, but also ensured that Irish fights were afforded notice that they would not previously have received.[89] More significantly, it was possible for the first time to stage matches involving Irish fighters in properly appointed rings. One of the most notable, involving Ned Malone and Andy Toole, took place in April 1818 at Clontarf, county Dublin, before a 'vast concourse of people'. Though popularly labelled 'a grand display of pugilistic science', the fight was arguably more significant because the victorious Malone had Jack Langan, who was Ireland's most promising fighter, in his corner.[90] An equally persuasive index of the dramatically enhanced profile of the sport at the time was provided by the fact that when he failed in his attempt late in 1815 to get Dan Donnelly into the ring with him, the once-imposing Tom Molyneux, who was the best known black boxer of his era, opted to stay in the country, and to eke out a living sparring and putting on exhibitions. A pale shadow of the man who had taken the legendary Tom Cribb to the brink of defeat, because he had chosen the life of 'the dandy, the boozer and the lothario' over that of the athlete, Molyneux's contribution to (or ability to capitalize on) the popularity of the sport may be gauged by the fact that he was scheduled to take to the ring in Ennis in February 1818 to meet 'a young combmaker from Limerick' until the intervention of the magistrates 'saved this aspiring youth', the local *Ennis Chronicle* observed not altogether kindly, 'from a good *combing*, and protected our moral character from an indelible stain'.[91] It was perhaps as well that the authorities had intervened since Molyneux did not have long to live. He died on 2 August in the barracks' bandroom in Galway where he spent the final two months of his life, a guest of the 77th regiment.[92]

The death of Tom Molyneux, a mere 'eight years after his glorious battles with Cribb', provided a vivid illustration of the heavy toll a career in pugilism

(Oxford, 1997), pp 267–70; Thomas Bartlett, *The fall and rise of the Irish nation: the Catholic question, 1690–1830* (Dublin, 1992), p. 268ff.   **87** *FJ*, 14 Nov. 1815, 17 Mar. 1819; Garnham, 'Dan Donnelly', p. 536, where the fight is wrongly ascribed to December. It is also wrongly assigned in the *DIB*.   **88** *FJ*, 14 Nov. 1815.   **89** *FJ*, 1 Mar. 1815; 23 Jan. 1817.   **90** *FJ*, 11 Apr. 1818.   **91** Garnham, 'Dan Donnelly', p. 536; Brailsford, *Bareknuckles*, p. 63; *Ennis Chronicle*, 18 Feb. 1818. **92** Brailsford, *Bareknuckles*, p. 63; *Ennis Chronicle*, 12 Aug. 1818.

could take on those who pursued the sport. Yet pugilism also offered opportunities that were not otherwise available to tough young men, and it was the prospect of an escape from indebtedness that lured Dan Donnelly, still the unchallenged hero of Irish pugilism, to England in 1819. Donnelly travelled with Jack Carter, an experienced English pugilist who knew this world well, and once he had completed a 'sparring tour in Lancashire' travelled to London, where the excitement generated by his arrival temporarily boosted the profile of a sport evidently in decline. Having negotiated the critical scrutiny of the exacting English fancy, Donnelly was paired with Sam Oliver, an experienced and respected English fighter, at Crawley Down, west Sussex, on 21 July 1819. The match drew a large crowd, estimated at 10,000, attracted by the novelty of an England versus Ireland match-up, and Donnelly did not disappoint. He won the 200 guineas purse in 32 rounds.[93] Donnelly's performance on this occasion was not as fluent as his previous defeat of George Cooper, but this mattered little to his many admirers in Ireland who were euphoric because he had defeated an experienced English fighter on English soil. Moreover, they had the pleasure of welcoming Donnelly back into their own bosom, as, instead of staying in England and exploring other potentially lucrative offers to fight, he came back to Dublin where he and the sport were then at the peak of their popularity.[94] Indeed, in obvious contrast to England, where following the example of the nobility and gentry who had all but forsaken the sport, the respectable middling sort were gravitating towards cricket, rowing and archery, pugilism was more popular than it had ever been in Ireland at this point.[95] Indicatively, as well as printed ballads and other exemplary forms of cheap print applauding Dan Donnelly's achievements, there was much else.[96] Features in popular periodicals such as Blackwood's *Edinburgh Magazine*, *The Gleaner*, *The Annals of Sporting*, and Pierce Egan's *Boxiana* proffered a highly sanitised vision of the sport, but this appealed to the public. It is hardly a coincidence that these magazines advertised in the mainstream press, or that, combined with the on-going detailed coverage accorded the sport in England in the same outlets, and the presentation by the re-branded New Theatre Royal of a musical entertainment to pugilism, they collectively sustained the impression that this was a vibrant, lively and exciting activity.[97]

Pugilism might have become still more popular in Ireland if Donnelly had possessed the requisite skills, determination and drive to act as more than a (passive) figurehead for the sport. He did not possess the necessary self-discipline, however. His ambition, following in the tradition of many successful pugilists, was to own a pub, rather than to grow and develop the sport, or, to become a

---

93 *FJ*, 28, 29 July 1819; Garnham, 'Dan Donnelly', pp 536–7. **94** *FJ*, 28, 29 July 1819. **95** Brailsford, *Bareknuckles*, pp 83–4. **96** The ballads and broadsides published celebrating Donnelly are listed in Séamas Ó Casaide, 'Street ballads on Irish boxers', *Irish Book Lover*, 28 (1942), p. 91, and discussed by Garnham, 'Dan Donnelly', pp 541–3. **97** *FJ*, 26 Jan., 12 June, 25 Sept. 1815, 1 Mar., 19 June, 11 Sept. 1819, 16 Jan., 26 Sept., 24 Oct. 1820, 22, 24 Jan., 14, 17 Mar. 1821, 11 Jan., 31 Oct. 1822, 28 July, 6 Aug., 30 Sept. 1823. *Ennis Chronicle*, 2 Sept. 1818, 9 Jan. 1819.

champion of note. Indicatively, on his return to Dublin in August 1819, his first undertaking was 'to make arrangements for his tent at the approaching fair of Donnybrook' where Bob Gregson, George Cooper and he demonstrated their 'pugilistic skills' before an admiring, paying audience.[98] He subsequently offered a comparable demonstration in September at the Curragh, while he contemplated, and subsequently agreed to two fights with Jack Carter – the first was scheduled to take place at Fownes Street in Dublin on 5 October, and the second at an undisclosed destination not thirty miles from Dublin on 25 November. The public was primed to believe this was a grudge match, but the rivalry was contrived, and the fact that there is no record that either fight took place suggests that it was merely a money-making scheme.[99]

Be that as it may, Donnelly was good for pugilism in Ireland, and the outpouring of grief that followed his premature, and unexpected, death, on 17 February 1820 was genuine.[100] The sport contrived to exploit his memory for a time, notably at Donnybrook Fair, where 'a most spacious booth [wa]s commodiously erected in the same place our much lamented champion Donnelly, Gregson and Cooper had the honour of being so numerously and respectably attended' in 1819, but this had a limited life.[101] The staging of a number of well-publicised fights at Milltown Fields in Dublin in March 1821, at Kilkenny in May 1823, and Dalkey, county Dublin in July of the same year was evidence that there was an interested constituency for whom pugilism possessed genuine fascination. The presence of an estimated three thousand people at the latter fight was more impressive certainly than the 'several hundred spectators' who watched Malone, a slater, defeat Collins, a farrier, in eleven rounds or 28 minutes at Milltown, but the re-emergence of public criticism of the sport, and the intervention of the police at Dalkey in July indicated that the glow of Donnelly's achievement faded fast.[102] It was also apparent that the future of the sport in Ireland rested on the shoulders of John (Jack) Langan (1798–1846) (Fig. 27), a more determined and skilful boxer than Dan Donnelly, whose victory over Owen McGowan at the Curragh in May 1819 identified him as the leading fighter in Dublin. The popular ascendancy of Donnelly (and Langan's own restlessness) confined his prospects then, but Donnelly's early death, and Langan's return from South America, cleared the way, and the latter effectively assumed the mantle of champion of Ireland in 1822 when his challenge to fight anyone 'for any sum they shall think fit to deposit or secure' was not taken up.[103] A year later he was in England, where he demonstrated his prowess by defeating a local hard man in Lancashire. This paved the way for the challenge he served on Tom Spring, then the English champion, and when his challenge was accepted, the

98 E.D. Krzemienski, 'Fulcrum of change: boxing and society at a crossroads', *The International Journal of the History of Sport*, 21:2 (2004), pp 168–9; *FJ*, 13 Aug. 1819, 28 Aug. 1820. 99 *FJ*, 24 Aug., 14, 23 Sept. 1819. 100 Garnham, 'Dan Donnelly', p. 537 and passim; Myler, *Regency Rogue*, pp 126–33. 101 *FJ*, 28 Aug. 1820. 102 *FJ*, 14 Mar. 1821, 21 May, 16 July 1823. 103 *DIB*, *sub nomine*; *FJ*, 3 Apr. 1822.

Fig. 27 John Langan (1798–1846) was the finest Irish pugilist, and a worthy
challenger of Tom Spring, the 'champion of England' (steel plate engraving
plate from a collection of engraved plates, *c.*1840, originally published in Pierce
Egan, *Boxiana, or sketches of ancient and modern pugilism* (London, 1812–20):
author's collection).

two fights that followed to determine who was champion of England *and* Ireland, at Worcester on January 1824, and at Chichester in June 1824, were among the most brutal bare-knuckle fights of the pugilistic era. Langan lost both, after 78 and 74 rounds respectively, but his strength and determination demonstrated that though he was not fancied in certain quarters in England prior to the match-up, he was a worthy opponent, and that the 'intense interest' and the £500 staked by both sides was entirely justified.[104]

Langan was accorded a hero's welcome on his return to Ireland. Like Donnelly before him, he endeavoured to cash in on his popularity with exhibitions of his skills. He performed in a 'grand sparring match' on 22 April 1824 in the Fishamble Street Theatre, but the declining interest in staged performances of this ilk limited the sum he could glean in this way.[105] Langan's decision some time afterward to take up residence in Liverpool was evidence that the high watermark of Irish pugilism had passed. A significant moment was reached when, in the mid-1820s, the *Freeman's Journal*, which for more than a decade was content to proffer a positive perspective on the sport bowed to the appreciating weight of the broader currents of public opinion and began to carry commentary that was intrinsically critical. Much of this commentary was second hand – copied verbatim from respectable English publications such as the *Morning Chronicle*, and the *Weekly Globe*. This had the effect, inevitably and over time, of bringing Irish attitudes to pugilism into conformity with mainstream British opinion, which increasingly linked the sport with such discredited practices as duelling. Furthermore, by highlighting its links to the criminal underworld, and its brutality, it hastened the rapid marginalisation of a sport that had contrived in vain throughout its existence to shake off its disreputable image.[106]

Pugilism was not without its defenders; nor those who were willing to fight. Suggestions that it was a distinctively 'English' practice, and that it deserved to be supported for this reason alone registered strongly in certain quarters.[107] This claim possessed less purchase in Ireland than in England, for the simple reason that the smaller island's population was increasingly perceived to possess an unhealthy predilection for violence, but regardless of the broader perception, it was apparent before the end of the 1820s from the contracting lists of 'fights to come' and 'thin' audiences at those bouts that did take place that the sport's best days were behind it in its English (and Irish) heartlands.[108] However, as was the case with cockfighting and other blood sports, the impulse to fight persisted, and though there was to be no return in Ireland to the heyday of the Donnelly–Langan era, pugilism experienced occasional highpoints that interrupted the ostensibly relentless trajectory of decline that defined the sport in the mid-nineteenth century. The celebrated Heenan–Sayers match at Brighton in 1860 for the

---

104 *FJ*, 12 Jan. 1824; *DIB, sub nomine*; Brailsford, *Bareknuckles*, pp 73, 85, 87. 105 *FJ*, 22 Mar. 1824. 106 *FJ*, 30 Oct. 1824, 13 Jan., 9 Mar., 20 June, 28 Oct. 1825, 2 Aug. 1827, 5 June 1829. 107 *FJ*, 7 Jan. 1825, 24 Oct. 1829; Brailsford, *A taste for diversions*, pp 62–3. 108 *FJ*, 21 July, 1827, 10 Oct. 1829.

World Championship has been instanced as one such episode, but, if so, it provided only a brief respite. Indeed, it can reasonable be countered that this match's primary impact on Ireland was to cause the Royal Irish Constabulary to intensify its commitment to prevent 'illegal pugilistic encounters'. The fact that the formidable archbishop of Dublin, Cardinal Paul Cullen, called explicitly in 1865 on 'the clergy and faithful to discountenance [pugilism] by every means in their power' indicated that church as well as state were arrayed against it, and that the future for the sport was decidedly unpromising.[109] Like a number of other sporting activities, it only survived because it changed. The marquess of Queensberry, and his famous rules were crucial to this 'civilising process', and the transformation of pugilism into the modern sport of boxing in which incarnation it was to acquire a new lease of life that has allowed it to survive to the present day.[110]

WRESTLING

The observation in the report of the victory of Dan Donnelly over Sam Oliver at Crawley Down in 1819 that, in an otherwise undistinguished performance, 'his great superiority was in wrestling' might suggest that Donnelly had knowledge of that fighting discipline, but there is no evidence to support this.[111] Moreover, it is necessary to bear in mind that pugilism was not a pure sport; it allowed for a variety of moves and practices redolent of wrestling. It was permissible, under the Broughtonian rules, for example, to seize an opponent above the waist in order to secure them for a blow, or a throw. Moreover, the famous cross-buttocks move, which Donnelly deployed against George Cooper, and may have resorted to in the fight with Sam Oliver, allowed a fighter not only to throw an opponent with force to the floor, but also to drop upon him while he was on the ground (which was often made of board) in the hope of winding him sufficiently to ensure either that he did not get up within the allotted thirty to thirty-eight seconds, or that he would not be able to resume fighting after the thirty-second interval between rounds if an official break was called.[112]

It is not apparent what impact, if any, the regional traditions of wrestling practised in Cumberland–Westmoreland, Lancashire, and Devon–Cornwall had on English pugilistic practice.[113] The picture is still more opaque for Ireland. The

109 Garnham, 'Dan Donnelly', p. 547; *Catholic Directory*, 1865, p. 381. 110 K.G. Sheard, 'Aspects of boxing in the western "civilizing process"', *International Review for the Sociology of Sport*, 32 (1997), pp 31–57; idem, 'Boxing in the western civilizing process', E. Dunning. D. Malcolm and I. Waddington (eds), *Sports histories: figurational histories in the development of modern sports* (London, 2004), pp 15–30; Krzemienski, 'Fulcrum of change: boxing and society at a crossroads', pp 161–80; Boddy, '"Under Queensberry rules, so to speak"', pp 398–403. 111 *FJ*, 29 July 1819. 112 Brailsford, *Bareknuckles*, pp 8–10; *FJ*, 14 Nov. 1815, 29 July 1819; Boddy, '"Under Queensberry rules, so to speak"', p. 400. 113 Collins et al. (eds), *Encyclopedia of traditional British rural sports*, pp 283–9.

observation that wrestling was one of the fighting sports practised in Dublin in 1732 suggests that wrestling was pursued in the kingdom in the same informal manner as boxing prior to the adoption of the Broughton rules, and the transformative impact of the emergence of pugilism. The latter took a long time, as we have seen. Indeed, based on the number of matches that originated as personalised altercations and trials of strength in the 1780s, it can reasonably be suggested that it did not take place prior to the early 1790s, and only flourished with the emergence, some twenty years later, of Dan Donnelly and Jack Langan. Wrestling, meanwhile, continued to be conducted as it had always been – according, possibly, to a set of codes or rules that continue to resist excavation. Based on the passing observation by Philip Fogarty, *à propos* of the way in which hurling was played in county Tipperary, that 'if a player fouled another, he was in honour bound to wrestle him when the game was over', it might be surmised that wrestling was part of a traditional informal male culture, which invoked physical prowess both as the primary measures of masculinity and the adjudication of dispute.[114] If this is the case, it obviously meant that those who were physically stronger for genetic reasons were more likely to prevail in life as in sport, and that competition favoured the bigger, the stronger and the tougher. It may also have meant that, as in the animal kingdom, determining who was most proficient at a particular sport possessed more than a recreational function; it may also have been socially (and biologically) consequential within the group that valued that recreation.

If this is the case, it would suggest that the attachment of different communities of practitioners to the more physically demanding plebeian sports was more than a cultural statement informed by the conviction that a particular game, or games, was integral to their identity because it was part of the tradition they had inherited. It would suggest that there were forces at work, beyond an expression of cultural attachment, and a reluctance to change, that must be considered when one seeks to make sense of the unwillingness of the populace to observe the directions of duly appointed officials when instructed to desist from certain sporting activities. This can be illustrated by the response to the attempt by Sheriff Ambrose Leet in Dublin in 1785 to discourage football, wrestling and other physical recreations on the grounds that they constituted a profanation of the Sabbath. The *Freeman's Journal* reported the incident as follows:

> Through the indefatigable attention of Mr Sheriff Leet to support, on all occasions, the police of this city, that active magistrate, through his spirited conduct, has made a great step towards suppressing those outrageous and scandalous meetings, which for several weeks past, have been carried on in the suburbs or out-skirts of Dublin, on Sundays. These meetings are formed of multitudes of vagabonds and profligate people, for the purposes of playing at football, *wrestling*, quarrelling and fighting. Sunday afternoon last [5

114 Fogarty, *Tipperary GAA*, p. 16.

June], Mr Sheriff Leet repaired to the Canal, where multitudes of idle people were assembled, and coolly expostulated with them on the crime of Sabbath breaking, gambling, profane swearing, etc. and requested them peaceably to depart, without compelling him to call in the aid of the military, which were at hand. His expostulations were in vain, and they accordingly made two rings, one for *wrestling*, the other for fighting; but the Sheriff sent off quietly for the infirmary guard, who, on their arrival, obliged the mob to depart. The Sheriff assured them that he would pay a visit to that spot every Sunday while he remained in office, as also to all such disgraceful places, being determined to make examples of any person he should find there in future, violating the Sabbath, and committing outrage.[115]

It is not clear if Sheriff Leet's commitment to inhibit wrestling was as resolute as he promised, or as successful as he intended. It may be surmised, since his intervention coincided with the increase in pugilism discussed above, that his term as sheriff did not have the impact he desired. Wrestling certainly continued. It was one of the identified recreations pursued by the 'disorderly mob' that assembled in the early summer of 1787, until the much-praised intervention of John Exshaw (see Fig. 24) on 13 May put an end to the practice.[116] However, if wrestling secured a much-needed boost from the increased interest in pugilism at this time, it was ephemeral and is resistant to identification. Indeed, the contrary is more likely to be true. Wrestling was another casualty of the embrace of respectability that took a heavy toll on traditional demotic sports in the late eighteenth–early nineteenth centuries. It is notable, for example, that though wrestling featured alongside pugilism as the two fighting sports that *The Annals of Sport and Fancy Gazette* addressed in the early 1820s, its coverage was exclusively of regional English wrestling.[117] Still more indicatively, when Jack Langan staged his 'grand sparring match' at the Fishamble Street Theatre in April 1824, the demonstration of wrestling that was included on the programme was 'the system of wrestling, so necessarily connected with that of pugilism'. In other words, wrestling was no longer recognised and no longer functioned as a separate sport in Ireland by that time. This is not to imply that traditional wrestling disappeared without trace. It continued to be pursued in certain locations; it was identified by the memoirists working on behalf of the Ordnance Survey in parts of Ulster in the 1830s, and it makes a passing appearance in Humphrey O'Sullivan's diary of life in south Kilkenny at nearly the same time.[118] The fullest and most useful description of the manner in which the sport was conducted, and the ordinariness of the stakes that were competed for in this rural milieu, where wrestling *was* a recreational activity, relate to the parish of Inniskeen, county Monaghan:

115 *FJ*, 9 June 1785.   116 *Hibernian Journal*, 16 May 1787; *Volunteer Evening Post*, 17 May 1787; *FJ*, 17 May 1787; above, pp 279–80.   117 *FJ*, 6 Jan. 1823.   118 McGrath (ed.), *The diary of Humphrey O'Sullivan*, i, 159.

Hurling and wrestling [are] the principal amusements. There is a rude stone in the churchyard having a hole in its centre, for the purpose of receiving a stick on which used to be suspended articles of wearing apparel to be given as prizes to the best wrestlers. This amusement took place during the Christmas [season].[119]

Signally, by the 1830s when this memoir was prepared, wrestling was spoken of in the past tense. It may not have disappeared completely by that date, but in so far as it was pursued at all it was as an occasional rather than a regular activity.

CONCLUSION

By comparison with horse racing, hurling and cockfighting, the fighting sports of pugilism and wrestling appealed to a small and devoted social interest in Ireland. Like throwing at cocks and bull-baiting, both were distinctly plebeian sports, but unlike the latter, which appealed primarily to participants, pugilism was first and foremost a spectator activity. Moreover, again in contra-distinction to throwing at cocks and bull-baiting, it looked towards the future in the manner in which it was organised, and in its embrace of the concept of a 'national champion' it heralded the national rivalries that were to prove so crucial to the development of the sport once nationalism became such an all consuming signifier of identity in the second half of the nineteenth century. But this is to anticipate, and, perhaps, to presume. As it was pursued and practised in the eighteenth and early nineteenth centuries, pugilism was simply too brutal, too violent, and too plebeian to pass muster with the increasingly refined sensibilities that politeness and respectability encouraged and promoted, and that became the defining attributes of the middle and upper classes in the nineteenth century. Neither of these interests was opposed to violence *a priori*; they had little difficulty running a horse to exhaustion, tearing a fox to pieces, or hanging criminals. However, they were selective about the violence they could countenance, and pugilism, as it was pursued in the early nineteenth century, did not meet their exigent, if inconsistent, criteria. What saved pugilism from obliteration, and was not available to the practitioners of throwing at cocks, cockfighting and bull-baiting, was that it possessed the capacity to change. Jack Broughton's rules were the most obvious eighteenth-century demonstration of this; the marquess of Queensberry rules were to be its nineteenth-century salvation. In common with hurling and football, pugilism was not in an especially healthy place as the Hanoverian era drew to a close, but because it could, and did, change, like them it possessed a future.

---

119 Day and Williams, *Ordnance survey memoirs, county Monaghan*, xl, 128. Wrestling was also pursued in Dungiven, county Londonderry: Day and Williams, *Ordnance survey memoirs, county Londonderry*, xvi, 76.

7

Minority sports: bowling, tennis, cricket, pitch and toss, athletics, handball and long bullets

When Thomas Fairfax, the author of *The complete sportsman, or country gentle-men's recreation*, listed the sports that might occupy a person of respectability in the mid-eighteenth century, horse racing, cockfighting and hunting were given pride of place, but, as well as a variety of rural pursuits which do not qualify as sport (such as dog and pigeon breeding etc), he also cited bowling.[1] Similarly, when the author of the 'description of Dublin in 1732' listed the 'sports [and] recreations' pursued by 'the people of Ireland', as well as the popular, and highly visible, recreations considered in previous chapters, he cited 'cards, dice, billiards, tables, [and] draughts', among a variety of other recreational pursuits that included singing, dancing, music and drinking.[2] The point is that as well as the esteemed sports of the elite, such as horse racing and hunting; the tolerated recreations of the weaver and yeoman farmer – cockfighting and hurling; and the controversial sports of the populace – bull-baiting, throwing at cocks, football and pugilism, considered above, there was a variety of other distinguishable sporting recreations that were less visible, were in decline, were emerging, or were pursued by select interests. The purpose of this chapter is to engage with such minority sports, though many have left a less than obvious mark on the contemporary record. Even more so than is the case with the sports addressed in the preceding chapters, the shards of evidence that have been located sometimes fit poorly together and the resulting reconstructions can be more than ordinarily incomplete. It may be that an anthropological approach, and the application of ludic theory, would permit a more revealing interrogation of these sparse data, but it would be out of place here; this is essentially an empirical work of recovery; a more theoretically informed engagement is for another occasion.

The sports addressed below are categorised according to contemporary perceptions of respectability. In practice, this has resulted in their assignment to elite and popular categories. This binary distinction is unproblematic when traditional elite sports such as bowling and tennis, and modern elite sports such as cricket and rifle shooting are at issue; it is also self-evident that sports such as long bullets, and pitch and toss can safely be categorised as popular, but it is palpably less clear if this categorisation is fluid enough to accommodate either billiards or ath-

---

1 Thomas Fairfax, *The complete sportsman, or country gentlemen's recreation* … (Dublin, 1764). This text, first published in London in 1759, went to many editions.   2 Gilbert (ed.), *Calendar of ancient records of Dublin*, x, 527.

letics. And then there are activities that were manifestly recreational, which do not merit inclusion for a variety of reasons. Gambling is the most obvious; gambling was intrinsic to much sporting activity, but can one define gambling as a sport? Based on the definition of a sport as an activity requiring physical exertion and skill in which an individual or team competes against another or others, the answer must be no, but this cannot be applied inflexibly since many of the sports pursued in the late early modern period clearly do not satisfy this definition. In practice, gambling might be said to straddle the boundary between sport and recreation, but since that is a mutable and inherently unstable space, any attempt to draw a hard and fast distinction is bound to fail. As a result, the categorisation of sports as elite and popular pursued in this chapter is not without limitations. It is less than helpful, for example, when one seeks to identify underlying trends across time, and, specifically, to locate the forces that contributed to the decline in sports such as cockfighting, and the emergence of other organised activities such as cricket and rifle shooting. Moreover, the distinction between elite and popular sport becomes increasingly untenable the closer one gets to the point – touched upon in earlier chapters on cockfighting, hurling and hunting – where the populace and the elite not only gained common enjoyment from watching a particular activity, but also pursued it together. However, it offers a functional organisational principle, consistent with the approach employed in this book, which assists with the location of the minority sports that are the chapter's focus.

ELITE MINORITY SPORTS

There were at least three identifiable minority sports – bowling, tennis and cricket – that were exclusive to the elite in late early modern Ireland. Bowling and tennis possess a shared history in that they were introduced into the kingdom by the New English as part of the process of intensified linguistic and cultural anglicisation they pursued during the sixteenth and seventeenth centuries. Cricket, by contrast, comes at the end of the time period addressed in this study; it is essentially an early nineteenth-century phenomenon, having made a late, cameo entrance on the Irish sporting landscape towards the end of the eighteenth century. Long perceived as the quintessential garrison sport, its reliance on the military sustains this characterisation, but its early history is significant for the history of sport in Ireland because it heralds a more enduring sporting development – the emergence and triumph of organised team sports. Unlike England, where the origins of the modern game of cricket can be located in the synergistic interaction of a demotic game, rules, organisation and elite patronage, cricket came to Ireland in a fully developed form. It took time to take root, but it had established a sufficient club structure by the 1840s to demonstrate the viability of the organisational model that was crucial to the later success of the nationalist games that continue to define Ireland's sporting landscape.

Bowling

Among the various sports named in the regulatory decrees and ordinances issued by various municipal and national authorities in Ireland in the sixteenth and early seventeenth centuries, there is no reference to bowling.[3] It could be suggested that this reflected the fact that, in contrast to the other activities mentioned, its practitioners observed the injunction to honour the Sabbath and holy-days, which provided the primary impetus for the efforts of Dublin Corporation in 1612 and 1613 to forbid 'plaieing at stodball, coiting, tennes, cudgiells' or other 'like exercises' during the reign of James I. However, since these games were denominated 'unlawfull',[4] and bowling was not, there is more to it than that. Indicatively, attempts were made by statute to proscribe bowling in England during the Middle Ages, when its popularity was seen to compromise the favoured sport of archery, on the grounds that it was in the royal interest to discourage recreational activity that was not manifestly utilitarian. This was insufficient to stem the appeal of bowling, or the establishment of bowling alleys (the first known example was opened in London in 1455), but the attitudinal prejudice that informed such actions, and the enduring desire to promote useful skills such as archery, was still current in Galway in the 1520s.[5] In England, meanwhile, concern that the appeal of the sport, which had spread beyond the ranks of the elite, was an inducement to idleness prompted the enactment in 1541 of an 'unlawful games act' aimed at confining the playing of the game by artificers, labourers, apprentices and servants to the Christmas season, and then under supervision, but permitting those possessed of property valued at £100 p.a. to create private greens.[6] As a result, bowls was effectively recognised in law as the sport of the elite and, whether it is apocryphal or true, its status was affirmed by the legend of Sir Francis Drake's choosing to complete a game of bowls before embarking in July 1688 to intercept the Spanish Armada.[7] It is no surprise, therefore, that it was introduced into Ireland as part of the process that saw the New English elite take control and command of the levers of political, economic and social power during the Tudor era.

Though it may reasonably be surmised that it dates from the late sixteenth century, it is not clear when the first bowling green was constructed in Ireland. An 'inrayled bowling place' was certainly *in situ* in the second decade of the seventeenth century.[8] Located on Hoggen Green, between the newly established Trinity College and Dublin Castle, the green was laid out on public ground. This was appropriate for a public facility, but it also meant that it was vulnerable if, in accordance with the prevailing trend, which was to vest the administration of such

3 See O'Sullivan, *Old Galway*, pp 441–2; Gilbert (ed.), *Calendar of ancient records of Dublin*, iii, 20, 39–40. 4 The inclusion of tennis on the list of proscribed sports is puzzling, since it was an elite activity. 5 O'Sullivan, *Old Galway*, pp 441–2. 6 *An acte for mayntenance of artyllarie and debarringe of unlawful games*: 33 Henry VIII, chap 9 (Eng); Collins et al. (eds), *Encyclopedia of traditional British rural sports*, p. 47. 7 Harry Kelsey, *Sir Francis Drake: the queen's pirate* (London, 1998). 8 Gilbert (ed.), *Calendar of ancient records of Dublin*, iii, 133.

facilities in a named individual, that person was permitted to establish an interest in the space 'whereby in time they maie clayme propertie thereunto'. Apprehending precisely this prospect because 'certaine strangers' were at liberty to 'receive the benefit and profitt' of the bowling green 'without yielding any manner of rent chardge to this cittie', Robert Taylor, one of the Corporation auditors, and, from 1619, one of the 'agentes to prosecute the citty causes and suytes', appealed to the Corporation to take appropriate precautions.[9] While the intentions of some of the players in this drama remains opaque, it can reasonably be surmised that Taylor was not a disinterested party since the Corporation determined in January 1621 that 'Robert Taylor shalbe allowed to make what profit and benefitt he cann of the free use or exercise of bowling' contingent on his assuming 'the chardge and care of looking and overseeing the said inrayled bowling place during our pleasures'.[10] It is to be presumed that Taylor lived up to his part of the agreement, and that he profited from the arrangement because bowling was a fast-growing sport at this time. Greens, which can be assigned an early seventeenth-century date, were also established in Bandon (1610), Londonderry (1639), Athlone, and possibly, Armagh and Carlingford.[11]

However, the supportive environment of the reign of James I did not long survive the accession in 1625 of Charles I, and the fortunes of Hoggen Green bowling green took a palpable turn for the worse. The war-torn environment of the 1640s was certainly not conducive to recreational sport in the metropolis, or elsewhere on the island, and this was but a prelude to the still-more hostile atmosphere generated by the Commonwealth, which assumed control of Dublin in 1649. As a result, the 'Bowleinge Alley on Hoggen Greene' was allowed to fall into decay, and though it retained its name, and its 'rayles', it was already 'a wast peece of ground' when, in 1653, it was leased to Robert Hughes, 'gentleman', for twenty-one years for the yearly rental of 40s. It is not clear what Hughes planned for the site, which measured 'in length from north to south, one huyndred and fiftie and sixe foote, and in breadth, from east to west at the end thereof, towards Checker Lane, one hundred and eleven foot, and in breadth in the other end thereof towards Trinitie Colledge, one hundred and sixe foot', but it is noteworthy that he was not required by the terms of his lease to reserve it for the sport for which it had originally been enclosed.[12] If this suggests the expansion of the city that was already under-way had caused some to conclude by the early 1650s that Hoggen Green was ripe for development, this opinion was still more generally shared nine years later when in 1662 the Corporation determined 'that Henry Jones, lord bishopp of Meath, shall have a lease for the termes of ninetie and

9 Gilbert (ed.), *Calendar of ancient records of Dublin*, iii, 115, 127, 128, 132, 133.   10 Gilbert (ed.), *Calendar of ancient records of Dublin*, iii, 133.   11 O'Flanagan, *Irish historic towns atlas, Bandon*, section no. 21; Thomas, *Irish historic towns atlas, Derry/Londonderry*, section no. 21; Murtagh, *Irish historic towns atlas, Athlone*, section no. 21; *Irish historic towns atlas, Armagh*, section no. 21; Robinson, *Irish historic towns atlas, Carrickfergus*, section no. 21.   12 Gilbert (ed.), *Calendar of ancient records of Dublin*, iv, 58.

Fig. 28 Oxmantown bowling green, *c.*1760 (extract from John Rocque, 'Map of Dublin' (Dublin, 1756–70). Reproduced from a map in Trinity College Library, Dublin, with the permission of the Board of Trinity College).

nine yeares ... upon all ... the wast peece of ground, commonlie called the Bowleinge Alley'. Significantly, the site, which was now enclosed by a 'mudd wall', was leased to Jones (1605–82) on condition that he invested £500 within seven years 'in building on the said ground'. This was Jones' intention. He was acting on behalf of the Church of Ireland, which had identified the site as a suitable location for a church for the parish of St Andrew, and the commencement of construction in 1665 spelled the end for the city's first 'bowling alley'.[13]

Though the Hoggen Green bowling ground was not operational when the site was handed over for development, the patriciate that dominated Dublin Corporation clearly perceived that the city would benefit from the availability of such a facility.[14] This was not a pressing matter prior to this point because of the existence during the 1640s of a bowling alley, commonly called the *Yellow Lyon*, on Winetavern Street.[15] However, since this too was lost to development by the early 1660s, the Corporation felt obliged to intervene, and in 1664, a year before building commenced on St Andrew's church, they authorised the establishment of a bowling facility on a suburban site close to Oxmantown Green on the city's northside (see Fig. 28). The person charged with this task was Richard Tighe, 'of the city of Dublin, alderman', who was granted the 'fee farme of a parcel' of potentially prime development land between the Green and the river Liffey in February 1664 on condition that he also construct a bowling green in the area. Having identified an appropriate site contiguous to the Green to the west of the Blue Coat Hospital for boys, the Corporation authorised Tighe to turn this space into a functional bowling green. Specifically, he was instructed

> To build a wall of stone or brick round about the said bowling greene, to containe tenne foote in height and twentie inches in thicknesse; and also to build a convenient house on some parte of the said ground for the accommodation of gentlemen and others, which shall resort to the said Greene; and ... Richard Tighe shall at his owne charges levell the said ground for making the said bowling green, which is to containe in length twentie eight pearches, and to sod the same; and that the said twenty eight pearches of ground shall be disposed of to noe other use but for a bowling greene.[16]

Tighe did not delay complying with the terms of the agreement he had entered into to construct a bowling green and adjoining terrace walk, and the site was

13 Gilbert (ed.), *Calendar of ancient records of Dublin*, iv, 238, 529–30, v, 212; Gilbert, *History of the city of Dublin*, iii, 306. 14 Colm Lennon, *Society and religion in Dublin, 1548–1613: the urban patricians in the age of Reformation* (Dublin, 1989). 15 Gilbert, *History of the city of Dublin*, i, 377; Lennon, *Irish historic towns atlas, Dublin*, section no. 21. 16 Gilbert (ed.), *Calendar of ancient records of Dublin*, iv, 285–6.

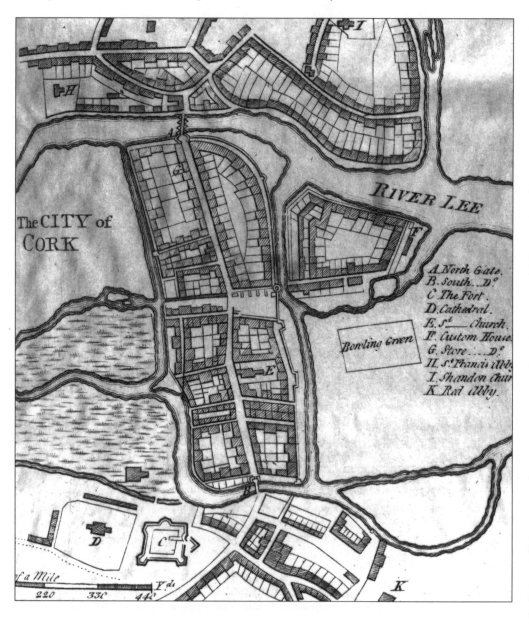

Fig. 29 Map of Cork city, *c.*1690, featuring a bowling green (courtesy of Cork
City Council Libraries).

evidently fully functional in the late 1670s when it was described by Robert Ware as 'one of the fairest [bowling greens] in Christendom, being nobly embellished with walkes and walls sett round with choice fruit bearing trees'.[17]

The attentiveness of the Corporation then, and in 1682, when William Ellis was specifically instructed 'not to build any houses or edifices between the Bowling Green and the river', without the express permission both of the Corporation and Tighe family, reflected the high regard in which the sport continued to be held during the final decades of the seventeenth, and early eighteenth centuries.[18] This is corroborated by the actions of landowners like Edward, Earl Conway, who established a bowling green at his residence, Portmore Castle, in south county Antrim; by the earl of Meath who did likewise at Kilruddery, county Wicklow; by the earl of Antrim at Dunluce, by Viscount Fitzwilliam at Mount Merrion, and by Thomas, twentieth Baron Kerry, Sir Thomas Crosbie and many others, who perceived a bowling green as an integral feature of a well-appointed demesne.[19] But it is still more manifest in the commitment of municipal officials to provide such a facility within their jurisdictions. Next to Dublin, Waterford provides the best-documented illustration of this. Here too the local corporation took it upon itself to ensure that the green (which was already a fixture in the city when it was afforded its first mention in the council book) was properly maintained, and when it was set to James Hickes at 10s. per annum in 1693, it was ordained that he keep 'the green in order for the recreation of the citizens etc'.[20] The situation in other municipalities is more resistant to elucidation, but it is notable that decisions were taken either to establish a bowling green for the first time or to replace a previous facility that had become run down at Bandon (1685), Londonderry (*ante* 1689), and Kilkenny (1695), and that the bowling green is clearly visible on a 1690 map of Cork (Fig 29). It was during these decades also that the foundations were laid for the surge in the creation of greens that was to take place in the first half of the eighteenth century when, based on the number of bespoke greens in towns and on demesnes across the country, the sport was at its most popular.[21]

Consistent with this trend, both Armagh and Downpatrick expanded the available urban network by inaugurating bowling greens in 1703 and

---

17 Robert Ware, 'The history and antiquities of Dublin, collected from authentic records and the manuscript collections of Sir James Ware', 1678 (Armagh Public Library, Lodge MSS), p. 19. In 1676, Corporation allocated a part of Oxmantown Green to the north of the bowling ground to be 'set apart for the use of the artilery yard': Gilbert (ed.), *Calendar of ancient records of Dublin*, v, 114–15. 18 Gilbert (ed.), *Calendar of ancient records of Dublin*, v, 237–8. 19 See Stringer, *The experienced huntsman*, p. 5 for Portmore; O'Kane, *William Ashford's Mount Merrion*, p. 11; eadem, *Ireland and the picturesque*, pp 39–41, 50; evidence for Kilruddery (earl of Meath), Lisburn castle (Earl Conway), Dunluce castle (earl of Antrim) and Crom Castle, the home of the earls of Erne, can conveniently be located on the websites of these historic monuments. 20 Seamus Pender (ed.), *Council books of the corporation of Waterford, 1662–1700* (Dublin, 1964), pp 135, 207, 304. 21 O'Flanagan, *Irish historic towns atlas, Bandon*, section no. 21; Thomas, *Irish historic towns atlas, Derry/Londonderry*, no. 21; Bradley, *Irish historic towns atlas, Kilkenny*, no. 21; Mullin, *Derry/Londonderry*, p. 67.

1708.[22] Paradoxically, the best evidence of the popularity of the sport is provided by the petition presented to Dublin Corporation in 1724 by Richard Tighe, the grandson of the man of the same name who had concluded an agreement with the Corporation in 1664 to develop the Oxmantown bowling green, seeking to be released from the more restrictive covenants of the original lease in order that he might embark, with others, on the development of the area. The Corporation agreed to the fundamental recasting of the terms of the original lease because they recognised that Oxmantown Green no longer possessed the appeal for elite players that made a bowling green a viable financial proposition for a private undertaker. Neither the petitioner nor the Corporation mentioned by name the 'other bowling greens which seem to be mostly resorted to' in the official documentation that informed the deliberations that prompted this decision, but it can plausibly be surmised that Oxmantown's diminishing appeal was linked to the failure of the urban development that had taken place in the interval to attract the wealthy residents that, it was once anticipated, would be drawn to the area.[23] Quite the opposite; they were increasingly attracted elsewhere as the allure of Oxmantown Green as a place of popular recreation, the proximity of the army barracks, and the ambitious modern streetscapes already taking shape further east on both the north and south sides of the river Liffey drew those for whom bowling was an engaging recreation away from Oxmantown.[24] Though the chronology remains to be calibrated, it is apparent that Marlborough bowling green, which was established in 1733 in the fields behind fashionable Drogheda Street (and directly off Marlborough Street), was one of the locations that usurped Oxmantown in the affections of bowlers. The *beau monde* was attracted by its greater accessibility, and by the fact that it was an altogether more regular, more commodious and better-appointed space (Fig. 30).[25] Marlborough green's geographical hinterland was the expanding residential streets developed north of the river Liffey by Charles Gardiner (*c.*1712–69) and by Luke, his son (1745–98).[26] To the south of the river, meanwhile, development was also pushing eastwards, which encouraged suggestions that the 'piece of ground on the east end of the lord mayor's house in Dawson Street', which had been secured on a 'fee farm lease' from Lord Molesworth, should be 'walled in and made a bowling green'. When this suggestion was first considered in 1733 at the request of a number of members of the common council, the Corporation agreed that the ground should

22 McCullough and Crawford, *Irish historic towns atlas, Armagh*, no. 21; Buchanan and Wilson, *Irish historic towns atlas, Downpatrick*, section no. 21.   23 Gilbert (ed.), *Calendar of ancient records of Dublin*, vii, 273–4.   24 See Brendan Twomey, *Smithfield and the parish of St Paul, Dublin, 1698–1750* (Dublin, 2005); Edward McParland, *Public architecture in Ireland, 1680–1760* (London, 2001). 25 See *The A–Z of Georgian Dublin: John Rocque's maps of the city in 1756 and the county in 1760* (Lympne Castle, 1998), pp 4, 6; Colm Lennon and John Monague, *John Rocque's Dublin: a guide to the Georgian city* (Dublin, 2009), pp 28–9.   26 Maurice Craig, *Dublin, 1660–1860: a social and architectural history* (Dublin, 1969), pp 101–4; Edel Sheridan, 'Designing the capital city, Dublin 1660–1810' in Joseph Brady and Anngret Simms (eds), *Dublin through space and time, c.900–1900* (Dublin, 2001), pp 91–100.

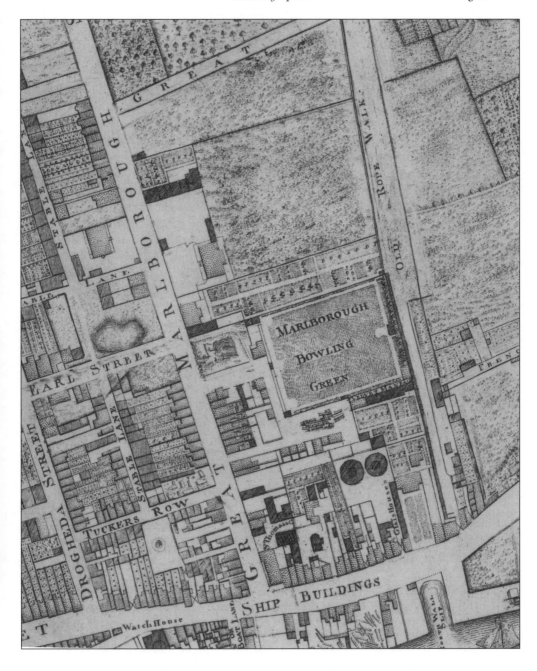

Fig. 30 Marlborough bowling green, *c.*1760 (extract from John Rocque, 'Map of Dublin' (Dublin, 1756–70). Reproduced from a map in Trinity College Library, Dublin, with the permission of the Board of Trinity College).

'be walled in and levelled'. This was not sufficient to create a bespoke bowling green, and the matter had to be revisited three years later, when an instruction was issued that the ground should be 'dug and sowed with hayseeds', which was done, with the result that the two most fashionable areas of the city each had a bowling green. Their careful delineation on John Rocque's landmark 1756 map of the city attests to their importance as recreational venues.[27]

By the mid-1750s when Rocque published his impressive cartographic essay, Dublin possessed three of the country's main bowling greens and a new facility in the gardens of the Lying-in hospital, which could be accessed for sixpence.[28] An incomplete survey has identified others in a playable condition in Carrickfergus, Kilkenny, Dundalk, Bandon, Londonderry and Limerick.[29] This was the high point of the sport, however. The proliferation of rival attractions thereafter, particularly horse racing, which drew on the same social constituency, encouraged the elite to forsake public facilities, and the willingness of some landowners to plant their private greens with trees suggests that this was the fate also of many private lawns This did not mean that public courts fell rapidly into decline. Soldiers based in the nearby Royal Barracks used Oxmantown bowling green as a place of recreation into the 1770s, when the threat of houghing inevitably induced a degree of wariness on their part.[31] Elsewhere, public greens became places of general congregation rather than sites specific to the sport of bowling. When John Tennent was an apprentice in Coleraine in the late 1780s, the bowling green in the town was no longer reserved for the practitioners of the sport; it was, in Tennent's words, 'the place where persons of every description goes in the time of Easter to divert themselves', and this was still the case nearly half a century later.[32] The rate at which this change occurred varied according to location; the green in Kilkenny was still in use in 1788, that at Dundalk in 1832, but others, like that at Carrickfergus, were indicatively known as 'the old bowling green' by the early nineteenth century, when the increasingly rare reference to their use provides the most eloquent testimony of the decline of bowling as a public recreation.[33] Bowling continued to be played during the nineteenth century, but it was largely confined to the bespoke greens of the demesnes of major aristocratic families, where it survived as a quintessential recreation of Ireland's landed elite.[34]

27 Gilbert (ed.), *Calendar of ancient records of Dublin*, viii, 115, 201–2; *John Rocque's maps of the city in 1756*, p. 12; *UA*, 29 Jan. 1757.   28 See Lennon and Monague, *John Rocque's Dublin: a guide to the Georgian city*, pp xi–xvi.   29 Robinson, *Irish historic towns atlas, Carrickfergus*, section no. 21; Bradley, *Irish historic towns atlas, Kilkenny*, section no. 21; O'Sullivan, *Irish historic towns atlas, Dundalk*, no. 21; O'Flanagan, *Irish historic towns atlas, Bandon*, no. 21; Thomas, *Irish historic towns atlas, Derry/Londonderry*, no. 21; O'Flaherty, *Irish historic towns atlas, Limerick*, no. 21.   30 O'Kane, *Ireland and the picturesque*, p. 146.   31 *FLJ*, 10 Sept. 1774.   32 Calvert (ed.), 'The Journal of John Tennent', p. 91; Day and McWilliams (eds), *Ordnance survey memoirs, county Londonderry*, xxxiii. 59.   33 Bradley, *Irish historic towns atlas, Kilkenny*, section no. 21; O'Sullivan, *Irish historic towns atlas, Dundalk*, no. 21; Robinson, *Irish historic towns atlas, Carrickfergus*, no. 21.   34 There was a bowling green at Hillsborough, for example: *FJ*, 12 Oct. 1809.

Tennis

Based on the evidence of indentures, tennis (by which one means the game known as royal or, more commonly, real tennis, which was played in a walled court with a cork ball) was a popular game with apprentices in Galway in the early sixteenth century.[35] Since this coincides with Henry VIII's well-chronicled enthusiasm for the sport, it may be that the appeal of the recreation evident in Galway was emulated in other urban centres. In any event, political and religious change arising out of the Tudor conquest and the Protestant Reformation fostered a more censorious attitude towards recreational activity, and the tolerance afforded the sport manifest in Galway in the 1520s withered in the course of the sixteenth century. As a result, it featured on the list of 'unlawful games' identified by the Corporation of Dublin in 1612 and 1613 when they sought to discourage apprentices, journeymen and others aged fourteen and above from idle pursuits, and, particularly, from infringing the injunction to observe the sabbatarian imperative.[36] This suggests, its royal associations notwithstanding, that tennis was not a popular recreation with the elite then, or a century earlier when the apprentices of Galway were 'exhorted not to gamble away their masters' goods or money on the game'.[37] The enduring concern of masters, and parents, that their charges should eschew idleness and develop habits of thrift and industry provided the primary incentives for such cautions, but they were augmented in the early seventeenth century by the perception of the authorities in the capital that tennis courts were foci of anti-social activity; the death in November 1609 of Simon Barnewall in a *rencontre* involving Christopher St Lawrence, the ninth Lord Howth, and Roger Jones and various retainers at a court in Dublin certainly served to foster this impression.[38]

The Thomas Street court, where the Howth–Jones dispute was pursued to its fatal resolution, was one of three (possibly four) tennis courts in Dublin in the early seventeenth century.[39] There were more tennis courts than bowling greens, though, like bowling greens, it is not always easy to establish which flourished, and when. Be that as it may, the location of courts on St John's Lane (off Thomas Street), Winetavern Street, and Cork Hill meant that tennis was a viable recreational option during the early decades of the seventeenth century.[40] This was satisfactory as long as the courts were viable and well maintained. However, interest was prone to fluctuate, with the result that, once established, the long-term survival of a ground could not be assumed. The St John's Lane ground, for example, was converted into a timber yard at some point late in the seventeenth century.[41] The longest lasting court was on Winetavern Street; it functioned as a tennis-playing venue for at least a century from the 1620s. It was clearly not in

35 O'Sullivan, *Old Galway*, p. 442.   36 Gilbert (ed.), *Calendar of ancient records of Dublin*, iii, 20, 39–40.   37 O'Sullivan, *Old Galway*, p. 442.   38 Kelly, *'That damn'd thing called honour'*, pp 27–8. 39 It is probable that the Thomas Street court and the John's Lane (which joins Thomas Street) court are one and the same.   40 Clarke, *Historic towns atlas, Dublin*, section no. 21; Lennon, *Historic towns atlas, Dublin*, section no. 21.   41 Gilbert, *History of the city of Dublin*, i, 53–4.

the best condition in 1721 when the collapse of one of the court walls (because of pressure exerted externally by a coal pile) resulted in the death of William Green, a jockey, who was playing when the wall gave way.[42] Despite Green's unfortunate death, the Winetavern Street court survived until the mid-1750s, when it was finally 'dug up'.[43]

Like bowling greens, tennis courts presented attractive development opportunities in expanding urban locations, but there was sufficient interest in the sport during the eighteenth century to ensure that new courts took the place of at least some of those that were lost. This meant that the sport was not entirely reliant on a creaking seventeenth-century infrastructure. It is notable, for instance, that a new tennis court was built in Limerick in the late 1760s.[44] The most ambitious initiative of this kind was undertaken in Dublin at mid-century when 'several noblemen and others ... entered into a subscription, in order to encourage the building of a tennis court for their amusement and exercise'. A fully closed court was duly constructed on Lazer's Hill, but the failure of the original subscribers to maintain their involvement meant that the undertaking was in acute financial difficulty by July 1755 when the 'proprietor' let it be publicly known that 'the income ... hath not been sufficient of late to pay the necessary servants attending', and that the court, which was then 'shut', would remain closed unless sufficient subscriptions were forthcoming 'to repair the court'.[45] It is not apparent if this ultimatum had the desired effect, or if there were enough people interested in tennis and in a position to pay the 40s. per quarter (£8 per annum) membership fee, exclusive of the expenditure on racquets and other playing paraphernalia required to play the game. Moreover, it was not as if those whose sole interest was playing did not have other options. There was also a (public) tennis facility, with three unroofed playing courts off Barrack Street, at the southern tip of Oxmantown Green, which is featured on Rocque's map of the city (1756). And there were one or two more on Dame Street (*c*.1754–72), though it is unlikely that the *habitués* of these courts, and still less those who frequented the court in Pyed-Horse Yard off Winetavern Street, which attracted 'some of the most nefarious characters in the city' following its opening in 1760, appealed to the socially eminent, who were drawn for a time to the Lazer's Hill club.[46]

If the availability of this range of playing facilities suggests that tennis possessed a strong and diverse support base in Dublin in the third quarter of the eighteenth century it flattered to deceive, as the sport experienced a serious reversal of fortune in the final decades of the century. Indicatively, the Lazer's Hill facility was lost to the sport, and converted to other uses.[47] Tennis was not

42 Gilbert, *History of the city of Dublin*, i, 157; *Whalley's Newsletter*, 26 June 1721. 43 *UA*, 2 Apr. 1755. 44 O'Flaherty, *Irish historic towns atlas: Limerick*, section no. 21. 45 *UA*, 26 July 1755. 46 *UA*, 2 Apr. 1754; Rocque, *Map of Dublin in 1756*, p 6Ab; Gilbert, *History of the city of Dublin*, i, 160; Lennon, *Historic towns atlas, Dublin*, section no. 21. 47 The venue became a private dining club of the King's Inns for a time in the 1790s: Colum Kenny, *King's Inns and the kingdom of*

without its champions, however, and eager to revive the sport, to provide a facility that would appeal to the right social set, and to avail of existing facilities, 'a
number of gentlemen of fortune and consequence' contrived in 1802 to form 'a
club, to be supported by annual subscription, to revive the game of tennis'. This,
they believed, could be achieved by refurbishing 'the old tennis court' on Lazer's
Hill (now Townsend Street), which lay idle now that it was no longer needed as
'the King's Inns dining hall'.[48] It was a mis-timed initiative. The recent abolition
of the Irish parliament combined with the preference manifested in the early
nineteenth century by the landed elite for life on their estates thinned the
wealthy constituency on which the restored club was reliant for members, with
the result that the court was soon in difficulty once more. The announcement by
the Commissioners of Wide Streets in 1811 that they would 'receive proposals
... for the purchase of the materials of the large building, formerly the tennis
court' signalled the end of this attempt to create a club that would serve as a
focus of the game in the capital.[49] A comparable situation obtained in Limerick,
where a tennis court, opened in the mid-1780s, was built over in 1827.[50]
Obviously, this was not a good omen, though it did not spell the end of royal
tennis on the island. The court in Kilkenny, plotted on Rocque's 1758 map of
the city, survived until at least the 1840s, but the sport itself was in terminal
decline in Ireland before then, so that when lawn tennis emerged later in the
century it did so as part of a new phase in the history of sport on the island
rather than as the continuation of a centuries-long tradition.[51]

Cricket
Unlike England, where it was 'uniquely developed' and 'the only large scale sport
with a substantial plebeian element to win any measure at all of positive
approval', cricket was the most iconic English sport that failed to take root in
Ireland during the eighteenth century.[52] There are a number of reasons. The
first, and perhaps most important, is that the rustic bat and ball games such as
stoolball and stowball that provided the cultural foundation for cricket in England
never flourished in Ireland.[53] 'Stoodball' (or stool-ball, in which an upturned
stool functioned as a primitive wicket) was included in the category of 'unlawfull
games' identified by Dublin Corporation in 1612–3 that it sought to interdict,
but the absence of complementary evidence indicating who played it, and when,
suggests it was the interest of only a tiny minority, and the failure of the English
visitor who dilated on Irish recreational sports in 1732 even to mention it indicates that it had not prospered in the interval.[54] As a result, there was no foun-

Ireland: the Irish 'Inn of Court', 1541–1800 (Dublin, 1992), pp 248–9. **48** *FLJ*, 12 Sept. 1802. **49**
FJ, 17 Apr. 1811. **50** O'Flaherty, *Irish historic towns atlas: Limerick*, section no. 21. **51** Bradley,
Historic towns atlas, Kilkenny, section no. 21; Ulick O'Connor, *The Fitzwilliam story* (Dublin, 1977).
52 Brailsford, *A taste for diversions*, pp 41, 44. **53** Strutt, *The sports and pastimes of the people of
England*, pp 84–102; Collins et al. (eds), *Encyclopedia of traditional British rural sports*, pp 251–3.
54 Gilbert (ed.), *Calendar of ancient records of Dublin*, iii, 20, 39–40, x, 527.

Fig. 31 Charles Lennox, fourth duke of Richmond (1764–1819), was not only the moving spirit behind one of Ireland's most celebrated cricket games, but also one of the organizers of a demonstration hurling match in the Phoenix Park (engraving by John Hoppner Meyer after a portrait by John Hoppner, London, *c*.1810 (private collection)).

dation, equivalent to that which existed in south-east England, on which to build when cricket, like pugilism, 'enjoyed an initial period of prosperity in the middle of the [eighteenth] century, but faded with the loss of its important early sponsors'.[55] The reliance of cricket upon the organisational and financial input of members of the landed elite bears comparison with the elite patronage afforded hurling in mid-eighteenth-century Ireland, but cricket sustained that engagement for longer, and at a higher level. Still more importantly, it evolved as a game with the assistance of a more sophisticated code of rules. As a result, the sport was particularly well placed when it embarked, in the 1760s, on a new phase of growth, and (as exemplified by the Hambledon Club) 'it rose rapidly to prominence' as 'gentlemen amateurs tapped both the skills of professional players and the interests of spectators over a wide area of southern England'.[56]

Unlike pugilism, which fed into an existing disposition to engage in such endeavour in Ireland,[57] the growth of English cricket left Ireland untouched through the 1770s and 1780s. Indeed, it might have continued to do so through the 1790s had not a number of skilled practitioners of the game, and a number

55 Brailsford, *A taste for diversions*, p. 43; Keith Andrew, *The handbook of cricket* (London, 1989), p. 5.   56 Brailsford, *A taste for diversions*, p. 42.   57 Above, pp 285–90.

of prominent office holders contrived in August 1792 to organise 'a grand cricket match' – essentially a rarefied exhibition – between a select military and civilian eleven. The prime movers were Lieutenant Colonel Charles Lennox (Fig. 31), a keen cricketer and founder member of the Marylebone Cricket Club (1787), who was an officer in the 35th regiment of foot, and Robert Hobart (1760–1816), the then chief secretary to the lord lieutenant, who succeeded to the peerage as the seventeenth earl of Buckinghamshire in 1804.[58] The match, 'which took rise from an expression thrown out ... in a convivial party' by Lennox that was taken up by Hobart, was for £1,000 (£500 a side) but, though a sizeable sum, the order of the wager was of less import historically than the fact that the game between eleven soldiers, which comprised the 'garrison' team, and eleven officials on the 'all Ireland team' was conducted according to the rules of the sport, and was officiated by two umpires and a scorekeeper. In truth, it was not much of a contest. The opening batsmen of the garrison eleven – Lieutenant Colonel Lennox (59) and Ensign J. Tufton (86 not out) – accounted for 145 of the 240 of their team's first innings total, which (depending on the report one chooses to believe) was either 105 or 94 runs in excess of the two innings total (76 and 59/70) of the 'all Ireland' team. The latter's best player, Edward Cooke, the under secretary (military department), produced impressive figures of 7 wickets and 39 runs. But his achievement served only to highlight the limitations of his team-mates, and the fact that the game was completed in an afternoon indicates how mis-matched were the two teams.[59] The magnitude of the defeat was not lost on those who reported the game, or indeed the game vice-reine, Sarah, the countess of Westmorland, who 'lost ten guineas by betting on Ireland', but such pecuniary losses were less significant than the occasion, which might, in other circumstances, have provided a perfect platform from which to launch the sport nationally, as the bespoke arrangements for the occasion made clear:

> Two handsome marquees were pitched, one in Mr Hobart's shrubbery, for the reception of a brilliant circle of ladies of distinction, who graced the simplicity of the manly scene with their presence; the second for the accommodation of the cricket players, on the other side of the Ha Ha, in the Fifteen Acres. The band of the 35th regiment attended, and played a variety of favourite airs during this pastime, which contrasted with the enervated amusement of the present taste, must be acknowledged, to be rational, salubrious, and deserving of encouragement.[60]

Despite the one-sided nature of the game, the occasion was deemed a success, which inevitably prompted calls for 'another' match. This was the intention, but in the absence of far-seeing patrons and of a domestic organisation equivalent to the Marylebone Cricket Club (MCC), which was in the process of establishing

---

58 See *DNB*, *sub nom.*; *HoP*, *sub nom.* 59 *Hibernian Journal*, 10 Aug. 1792; *FJ*, 4, 11 Aug. 1792; *FLJ*, 11 Aug. 1792. 60 *Hibernian Journal*, 10 Aug. 1792.

itself as the ruling body of cricket in England, the sport was rudderless in Ireland.[61] As a consequence, cricket remained firmly identified with those elements of the military, English overwhelmingly, who brought the game with them to their Irish posting, and gentlemen who had encountered, and played, the sport at English boarding school or university. It is thus no coincidence that though there were 'grand' games in the Phoenix Park in 1799, and in Cork in 1800, the participants in Dublin were 'gentlemen', and in Cork soldiers, and that in both instances the players' knowledge of the game was acquired while in England.[62] This was true also of the soldier from the Royal Barracks who, for a time in 1803, used the playing field of the King's Hospital as a cricket ground.[63]

In keeping with the fact that the game in England experienced 'something of a decline' at this point, the absence of further reference suggests that the sport was barely played in Ireland in the early nineteenth century. This trough spanned some two decades, and it took the reanimation in interest in the game in England that can be dated to the mid-1820s to spark a comparable renewal of interest in Ireland. The expanding coverage of English cricket in Irish newspapers from the mid-1820s is one index of the domestic following the sport elicited.[64] Saliently, it mirrored the accelerating integration of Protestant Ireland into the Anglophone cultural world that was a feature of the nineteenth century, and it was appropriate therefore that the avatars of this cultural melding were members of gentry families who had encountered the game while in public school in England.

The emergence of cricket as a visible sport may be said to have comprised a number of over-lapping phases. The first, manifest in the encounter on the Castle lawn in Kilkenny on 8 August 1829 between two teams constituted from the local gentry or the private match at Killinchy, county Down in 1828, comprised exhibition games.[65] The second involved the formation of cricket clubs. The first was founded by William Le Poer Trench, later second Viscount Clancarty, at Ballinasloe in 1825, but it was followed shortly afterwards by a student club at Trinity College (1827), by the Phoenix Club (1830) and by Garrison, Court and City of Dublin clubs (c.1828) in the capital, Belfast CC (1830), and county clubs in Kilkenny (1830), Carlow (1831) and Queen's county (*ante* 1834).[66] Because of the absence of alternatives, as well as each other, these clubs, and the various *ad hoc* teams that were also assembled to play the game,

61 Brailsford, *A taste for diversions*, pp 162–4. 62 *Dublin Evening Post*, 30 Mar. 1799; Neal Garnham, 'The role of cricket in Victorian and Edwardian Ireland', *Sporting Traditions*, 19:2 (2003), p. 28. 63 Bracken, *Foreign and fantastic field sports*, p. 10, citing Noel Mahony and Robert Whiteside, *Cricket at the King's Hospital, 1897–1997* (Dublin, 1997), p. 1. 64 Bracken, *Foreign and fantastic field sports*, pp 12–13; Peter Wynne-Thomas, *The history of cricket: from the Weald to the world* (London, 1997), pp 43–4; *FJ*, 16 Aug. 1811, 18, 19 July, 16 Aug. 1827, 24, 29 July 1828. 65 Michael O'Dwyer, *The history of cricket in county Kilkenny – the forgotten game* (Kilkenny, 2006), p. 17; Bracken, *Foreign and fantastic field sports*, pp 13–14. 66 Bracken, *Foreign and fantastic field sports*, p. 13; Garnham, 'The role of cricket in Victorian and Edwardian Ireland', p. 28; O'Dwyer, *The history of cricket in county Kilkenny*, pp 11–12.

were instinctively drawn during this embryonic phase towards the local military garrisons both for players, and teams to play. It is instructive, for example, that the first recorded game played by the County Kilkenny CC, which took place in September 1830, was against a team drawn from the officers of the 21st regiment of Fusiliers. Six years later, it engaged in a series of matches with a team comprising one known player and ten men drawn from the 82nd regiment. Meanwhile, in the summer of 1831 in 'the first cricket match[es] ever played in Ireland between two regularly established clubs of different counties', Kilkenny CC took on and defeated Ballinasloe CC, home, at the Norelands (its ground and the place of residence of William Bayley, its founder), and away at Garbally, county Galway.[67] In nearby county Wexford, a mixed team comprising members of the town garrison and a 'few' local 'amateurs' met in front of the jail ground in 1833.[68] These, and the games that followed during the mid-1830s involving teams from counties Kilkenny, Carlow, Queen's county, and county Tipperary, from Ballinasloe and Dublin (the Phoenix CC, Dublin CC and Garrison CC) may reasonably be described as exhibitions rather than competitive games, but they were played in a competitive spirit, and they were essential foundation-building exercises, as they encouraged further additions to the slowly burgeoning network of clubs – Carrick-on-Suir (1834), County Tipperary CC (1836), Lisburn (1836), Ulster CC (1836), Wexford (*ante* 1838), Huntington CC (*ante* 1837), Kilkenny Barracks CC – that permitted an expanded inter-club, and inter-county, competitive circuit before the decade was over. Thus in 1837, the Huntingdon and Carlow Cricket Clubs, both comprised of members of local gentry families, held 'a grand field day' at Mullamore, county Kilkenny. In 1838, the Carlow Club lost to Meath Cricket Club, which lost in turn to the gentlemen from Queen's county.[69] The strong presence cricket registered in south Leinster at this time was emulated in a number of other locations. The Phoenix Club of Dublin possessed a reasonable claim to the title of best club in the country, when it travelled in August 1839 to take on Kilkenny at the Norelands, by then acknowledged as the centre of cricket in county Kilkenny, where the sport was so firmly rooted it was twinned with hurling, as one of 'the two games of driving' played in the county. The situation was not altogether different in Ulster, where the Belfast Cricket Club hosted, and defeated, the Ulster Club in the summer of 1839.[70]

Though the standard of cricket played in Ireland was modest, by the late 1830s the sport was sufficiently confident, and ambitious for the future, to contemplate establishing a network of playing fields. The ostensible permanence of the cricket pitch created on the lawn at Kilkenny castle was acknowledged when

---

67 *FJ*, 30 Sept. 1830, 25 July 1836; O'Dwyer, *The history of cricket in county Kilkenny*, pp 12, 17–20; Bracken, *Foreign and fantastic field sports*, pp 14–15. 68 *FJ*, 22 May 1833. 69 O'Dwyer, *The history of cricket in county Kilkenny*, pp 20–1; Bracken, *Foreign and fantastic field sports*, pp 14–15, 20; *FJ*, 13 Sept. 1837, 4 Sept. 1838. 70 *FJ*, 12, 14 Aug. 1839; Garnham, 'The role of cricket in Victorian and Edwardian Ireland', p. 38; McGrath, *Diary of Humphrey O'Sullivan*, iv, 91.

it was included on the Ordnance Survey map.[71] Another significant milestone was reached when the board of Trinity College agreed in the early 1840s to meet the cost of laying down a pitch for staff and students. Previously, plans circulated in the mid-1830s to develop a 'Metropolitan cricket ground for the use of gentlemen and officers', off Baggot Street in Dublin (equivalent to Lord's in London), had come to naught. This combination of success and failure might reasonably be deemed an accurate measure of what had been achieved by the sport since the early 1790s, but, based on the number of clubs playing the game, it is apparent that by the early 1840s cricket had carved out a distinct space on the Irish sporting landscape in just over a decade, and that, as in the south of England, it flourished as the sport of the social elite.[72] Its minority status notwithstanding, the fact that cricket was embarked on a growth phase that was to continue for several decades as the Hanoverian dynasty drew to a close and the reign of Victoria began not only bucked the pattern of decline that was a feature of many sports, but also demonstrated (contrary to some claims) that the sporting impulse remained strong. It also pointed to the future, and to the fact that the sports most likely to prosper were those possessed of a clear set of rules, and an appropriate organisational structure.[73] This conclusion receives some reinforcement from the fact that it was during this period also that the organisational foundations of the sport of rifle shooting, hitherto pursued by individuals, were laid.[74] The crucial moment here occurred in 1829 when the island's first rifle club, the Ulster Rifle Association, was formed with James Stevenson (Blackwood), second Baron Dufferin as its first president. Like cricket, it was an elite recreation, but it is a measure of its appeal, and its impact, that it was able to put 'a very fine range' in place and to organise 'numerous prize meetings', which by the 1870s attracted 'rifle shots from all parts of the country'.[75]

Running and allied athletic activity
In addition to those already mentioned, there was a number of other sporting activities that are challenging to fix on the recreational landscape either because they possessed few devotees, or because they were inherently random. The urge to run competitively was one such activity. Running was not pursued in an organised way in late early modern Ireland, and when it was resorted to it was as likely as not to take the form of a novelty entertainment at a fair or festival, or to be prompted by a wager, which represents the clearest indication that the primary motivation to race was financial gain rather than sporting achievement. These tendencies can be illustrated by the inclusion on the menu of entertain-

---

71 O'Dwyer, *The history of cricket in county Kilkenny*, p. 22.   72 O'Dwyer, *The history of cricket in county Kilkenny*, pp 23–4; Bracken, *Foreign and fantastic field sports*, pp 16, 21.   73 Garnham, 'The role of cricket in Victorian and Edwardian Ireland', pp 38–9; Bracken, *Foreign and fantastic field sports*, pp 21–2.   74 The individualistic character of shooting to this point can be inferred from the manner in which it was reported: see, for example, *UA*, 18 Nov. 1755; *Hibernian Journal*, 24 Oct. 1791.   75 Knox, *A history of the county of Down*, p. 57.

ments offered at Dangan fair (county Meath) in 1731 of a race 'for a lac'd smock run for by virgins', or by the following wager entered into in 1763 at county Cork:

> A man undertook for a wager to run round the Lough (which is computed to be near an English mile) while another person should eat six ounces of queencakes, which he performed with the greatest of ease, having gone his course before the other has eat[en] five ounces.[76]

A more orthodox, but still quirky, test of physical prowess was called for sixteen years later at Ballsbridge, county Dublin, when 'an old gentleman and a young man' entered into a wager for 20 guineas that the former could hop two hundred yards faster than the latter could run the same distance. This, quite obviously, was not a test of equals, and it hardly qualifies as a sporting activity for this reason, but in a milieu in which there was no tradition of formal athletic engagement, but which was not short of the curiosity that is integral to competitive sport, it was of sufficient interest to attract 'several hundred spectators' who, like the newspaper editor who printed the story, were astounded when the gentleman won.[77] Other contests possessed greater credibility because they were more explicitly tests of athletic ability. These include the wagers laid by Captain Wesley and Mr Whaley in 1789 to determine whether the former could walk five miles in 55 minutes, and by Vere Hunt and Lieutenant Arkwright to establish if the latter could run 6 Irish miles within an hour.[78] More obviously than the 'pedestrian racer' who accepted wagers to walk round Stephen's Green within an ostensibly challenging time-limit in 1795, these competitive wagers were a step towards the normalisation of the idea that athletic competition was legitimate sporting activity.[79]

As was the case with a number of other sporting pursuits, the cause of athletics in Ireland was assisted by reports of athletic contests in England extracted from the English press for publication in Irish newspapers. Though a substantial proportion of these reports were akin to the idiosyncratic athletic competitions upon which bets were laid in Ireland, reports such as that carried in the *Freeman's Journal* in 1809, of 'a grand foot race' in Hampshire between two recognised endurance specialists to determine who could run 'the greater distance in 48 hours' clearly possessed athletic legitimacy.[80] Be that as it may, the athletic impulse was not sufficiently securely anchored in Ireland to sustain even random athletic competition during the eighteenth or early nineteenth centuries. Indicatively, there was no Irish equivalent to the Highland Games, which commenced in Scotland in 1819.[81] Moreover, such efforts as were made to replicate

76 *FDJ*, 2 Jan. 1731; *The Public Gazetteer*, 15 Mar. 1763. 77 *FLJ*, 13 Mar. 1779. For an equivalently quirky race between two gentlemen – one on horse-back and the other on foot – see *Hoey's Publick Journal*, 29 Oct. 1770. 78 *Ennis Chronicle*, 21 Sept. 1789; *Cork Courier*, 20 Dec. 1794. 79 *Hibernian Journal*, 12, 21 Oct. 1795. 80 *FJ*, 4 Oct. 1809. 81 Collins et al. (eds), *Encyclopedia of*

successful competitive athletic events, which were pursued successfully elsewhere, were rarely repeated. One may instance the 'rowing match between two eight-oar barges for a hundred guineas in the harbour of Cork' which was held during Cork races in 1755, and Edward Newenham's attempt in 1781 to organise a Liffey boat race, which were unique events.[82] Still more significantly, though there was an awareness of the Olympiad of Ancient Greece, it was not associated with sport, and the most significant step in the direction of placing competitive sport on firm foundations – *L'Olympiade de la République*, which was held annually in revolutionary France between 1796 and 1798 – was not even reported in the Irish press.[83] This is not to suggest that the desire to identify who was the faster or stronger did not exist, or that it did not prompt competition. However, there was no consensus as to the capacities and capabilities that might be measured or the means by which this might be done, only idiosyncratic and random events of the kind referred to above, and of the kind recorded by James Ryan of Carrick-on-Suir, who noted in his 'diary' a wager concluded in 1799 in which James Barron of Georgestown bet successfully he could walk four miles in an hour.[84] Be that as it may, attitudes towards athletic competition were not fixed, and there are indicators that such activity became progressively more structured in the early nineteenth century, with Ulster leading the way. According to the accounts of the recreational activity prepared by the memoirists employed by the Ordnance Survey in the 1830s, athletic competition was a staple recreational pursuit across much of the province, though the number of references to specific skills is small. Be that as it may, 'leaping', 'jumping', 'throwing the stone' and 'races between men' and 'between women' were variously pursued in parishes in counties Monaghan (1), Fermanagh (1), Londonderry (1) and Antrim (4).[85] 'Throwing the stone', which was described 'as the chief amusement' of 'country men' in the parish of Blaris, in south county Antrim, and was also recorded in Dungiven, county Londonderry, and Donaghmoyne, county Monaghan, involved throwing a stone from the shoulder, in a manner redolent of the modern shot putt, though it may be that it had its origins in Scotland, where 'putting the stone' was a staple feature of the Highland Games. Evidently, some practitioners of the sport were so proficient they could propel 'the shoulder stone ... an enormous distance'.[86] There is less information as to the form leaping and jumping took, but since they are invariably mentioned together it is reasonable to assume that they were separate activities, presumably equating with the modern long and

traditional British rural sports, p. 148.   82 *UA*, 3 May, 21 June 1755; 'Some attention to the naval line, 1781', *Irish Sword*, 9 (1969–71), p. 75; *FJ*, 6 Sept. 1781.   83 *FJ*, 1 Dec. 1809, 20 Nov. 1829, 18 Jan. 1841.   84 Patrick Power, 'A Carrickman's diary, 1787–1809', *Journal of the Waterford and South-East of Ireland Archaeological Society*, 14 (1911), p. 150.   85 Day and McWilliams (eds), *Ordnance survey memoirs, county Monaghan*, xl, 109; Day and McWilliams (eds), *Ordnance survey memoirs, county Fermanagh*, iv, 130; Day and McWilliams (eds), *Ordnance survey memoirs, county Londonderry*, xv, 14, 76; Day and McWilliams (eds), *Ordnance survey memoirs, county Antrim*, xxi, 109, viii, 15, 141–2, xxxvii, 77, 175–6.   86 Day and McWilliams (eds), *Ordnance survey memoirs, county Antrim*, viii, 15; see also Knox, *A history of the county of Down*, pp 61–2.

high jump. If this is so, the fact that most jumping sports (high jump, long jump, triple jump and pole vault) are believed to have German antecedents cautions against assuming that they were all a produce of cultural diffusion from Great Britain, or that they provide a seamless link with latter-day expressions of the athletic impulse.[87] Racing for 'wearing apparel and other prizes', as exemplified by the Christmas day assembly at Carrickfergus that came to an end in the early 1830s, or long distance walking 'for a heavy wager' in county Kilkenny in 1830 were born out of the instinctive competitiveness and the desire for gain that was at the heart of much sporting competition, though it hardly meets the definition of athletic competition.[88] Athletics may not have had to await the emergence of the Amateur Athletic Association in 1880 to evolve as a sport; its prior adoption by boarding schools was an import step forward, but, based on those accounts that one can locate of athletic activity in the eighteenth and early nineteenth centuries, it remained an essentially formless, serendipitous pursuit until the mid-nineteenth century.

POPULAR MINORITY SPORTS

As the histories of many sporting pursuits examined above have demonstrated, the distinction between popular and elite sports, while organisationally (and taxonomically) useful, can provide a misleading impression as to when a sport's appeal transcended a particular social interest. The cases of cricket in south-east England, and cockfighting and hurling in mid-eighteenth-century Ireland might reasonably be invoked in this context, but it is important also to note that the social profile of those who pursued a sport was neither fixed nor unchanging. Billiards is a case in point. A recreational staple in exclusive gentlemen's clubs by the late nineteenth century, it occupied an explicitly more ambivalent societal position in the mid-eighteenth century, when billiard tables were to be found in coffee houses and other places of entertainment and lumped in with other gaming media, which were deemed 'dangerous nuisances, too long tolerated, and too fatally felt in their effects'. As such it was the subject periodically of hostile attention from zealous officials who targeted the 'seminaries of vice and villainy' in which billiard and other gaming tables were located 'out of regard for the publick welfare'.[89] On one such occasion, in 1755, the lord mayor, Hans Bailie, and the high sheriff, Philip Crampton, 'attended by a party of the main guard, went to College Green and took down a billiard table, prior to burning it in the street'.[90] It might reasonably be suggested that Crampton's presence had more to do with his ambition (later realised) to become lord mayor, but this is less note-

---

87 Collins et al. (eds), *Encyclopedia of traditional British rural sports*, p. 35. 88 Day and McWilliams (eds), *Ordnance survey memoirs, county Antrim*, xxxvii, 175–6; McGrath, *Diary of Humphrey O'Sullivan*, ii, 287. 89 *Hoey's Public Journal*, 15 Oct. 1770; *UA*, 1 Mar. 1755. 90 *PO*, 19 Apr. 1755; see also *UA*, 1 Mar., 21 June 1755.

worthy than the fact that the appeal of billiards spanned the social spectrum. Indicatively, it was identified as a gentleman's sport a year earlier.[91] The problem for billiards was that it was also firmly identified with gambling, and the amoral and criminal conduct that the moralistic reflexively associated with this activity. Respectable opinion was not consistent on this point.[92] Indeed, it might reasonably be accused of being hypocritical. The respectable combined a remarkable capacity to tolerate, if not simply to countenance gambling by, and within, the elite, without which sports as diverse as horse racing, cockfighting, pugilism and cricket simply would not have survived, with an equally adamantine hostility to a variety of popular sporting recreations that were no less dependent on gambling for their existence. This disposition was highlighted by the *Freeman's Journal*, during its early crusading years, when it gave full backing to a succession of municipal officials, who targeted billiard tables for destruction on the grounds that they encouraged 'gaming ... among the lower class'.[93] The attitude was expressed particularly vividly in the commentary that accompanied an account of the actions in 1765 of James Taylor, the then lord mayor, in taking 'down several billiard tables':

> The activity and spirited behaviour of our chief magistrate encourages us to hope that every nuisance with which he is made acquainted will speedily be removed; and as there are not any more destructive to industry, and consequently dangerous to society, than the many public places of gaming, viz. billiard tables, ball courts, shuffle boards and skittle-grounds, where the most abandoned profligacy may be seen, and the greatest temptations thrown in the way of thoughtless youths by which they are led to rob their masters or employers, to support their idle extravagance, it is sincerely wished that he may be rightly informed of those enemies to the public, who in defiance of law, for their own vile ends, support such places. The practices of those daring offenders have of late been taken so little notice of, that some have been so audacious as to set up new species of gaming in Ram Alley, very near the hearing room just under the eyes of our magistrate, where, nothing is more true, than that the most horrid crew resort thither, to the great annoyance of many of the peaceable and well-disposed inhabitants, who are shocked at their abominable blasphemies, and riotous behaviour. ... We think we cannot be too early in advertising those real nuisances so dangerous to society; but the opportunity which every season affords the sharper to seize his prey at the billiard tables etc. ... will, we hope, stir up our worthy Lord Mayor, to do an act of justice to the public in pulling down those dangerous places of resort ...[94]

91 *UA*, 9 Feb. 1754. 92 *FDJ*, 21 Nov. 1747. 93 *FJ*, 12 Oct. 1765, 17, 20, 22 Aug. 1771, 7 Sept. 1774. The *Hibernian Journal* took a comparable attitude; see *HJ*, 30 June 1775. 94 *FJ*, 12 Oct. 1765.

Such attitudes, which echo the decrees issued by the corporation in the 1610s against a quite different menu of sports, was deemed equally applicable in the eighteenth century to a variety of popular sporting recreations, of which pitch and toss was probably the most widely practised.

Pitch and toss and other 'vagabond games'[95]

Pitch and toss was a game of skill and chance in which the player who pitches a coin nearest to a mark has the first chance to toss all the coins, winning those that land heads up.[96] Though it has been likened to quoits, which the authorities of early seventeenth-century Dublin targeted for proscription, pitch and toss was a still simpler sport, and of still greater appeal to the urban young and youthful.[97] As such, it was high on the radar of the respectable and the moralistic whose narrow perspective as to what was acceptable carried increasing authority as the permissive attitude of the restoration era ceded incrementally, if unevenly, during the eighteenth century to the censoriousness respectability that came to prevail in the nineteenth. Described routinely as a 'great annoyance' by the residents of the built-up areas in which it was played, those who engaged in 'pitch and toss and other idle vagabond games' (skittle playing, nine holes, six penny hazard, etc.)[98] were unreservedly caricatured as wanton miscreants 'whose horrid blasphemous oaths and imprecations are shocking to the ears of every hearer who has the least sense of religion or common decency'. The genuine antipathy to which such commentaries gave expression was intensified by the frequency with which such 'execrations and blasphemies' were to be heard on a Sunday, and by the apprehension generated by 'the crowds of blackguard boys' that assembled either to play the game or to gamble on the outcome.[99] For the apprentices, labourers and others who comprised these gatherings, by contrast, these occasions served not only to fill in the time, which could hang heavily on such days, but also to generate the possibility of a financial windfall. Encouraged by similar calculations to play at dice, the working denizens of the urban spaces where such practices were ubiquitous were soon enmeshed in a struggle comparable to that pursued by the devotees of bull-baiting, throwing at cocks, football and other demotic recreations to which the champions of respectability took exception. Indicatively, when the minister, churchwardens and parishioners of the parish of St Paul appealed to Dublin Corporation in 1737 for permission to be allowed 'rail in the two walks that join the said church' on Oxmantown Green, they specified 'dice [and] long bullets', as well as football among the 'mischiefs' that were damaging 'the walks, windows, trees and walls' of the church.[100] Moreover, respectable

95 *FJ*, 14 Feb. 1791. **96** Collins et al. (eds), *Encyclopedia of traditional British rural sports*, p. 208; McGrath, *The diary of Humphrey O'Sullivan*, iii, 19. **97** Collins et al. (eds), *Encyclopedia of traditional British rural sports*, pp 208, 225; Gilbert (ed.), *Calendar of ancient records of Dublin*, iii, 20. **98** *Hibernian Journal*, 12 July 1771, 28 July 1786; *FJ*, 12 Oct. 1775. **99** *FJ*, 8 Sept. 1770, 25 Aug. 1771, 14 Feb. 1791; *Hibernian Journal*, 27 Apr. 1774. **100** Gilbert (ed.), *Calendar of ancient records of Dublin*, viii, 241.

opinion was encouraged by the ostensible receptivity of MPs to their complaints. The enactment by the Irish parliament in 1739 of legislation deeming 'publick gaming tables ... public nuisances', which was targeted at eliminating card-playing, billiards and allied games, prompted the lord mayor of Dublin Andrew Murray in 1754 to announce his intention 'rigorously to execute' this and other laws to eliminate all gaming on the grounds that it tended 'to the corruption of youth, the utter ruin and impoverishment of many families, and to the reproach of the laws and government of this realm'.[101]

Commentaries criticising 'the fatal spirit of gaming', and authors like Edmond Hoyle (1772–69), several of whose titles indicating how to play backgammon, brag, quadrille and whist were published in Dublin in the 1750s, were as ineffectual as the efforts by successive lords mayor to proscribe 'unlawful games' and to close down gaming houses.[102] The predilection for gambling whether it took the form of playing for pennies on the streets or for sizeable sums on the gaming, card or billiard tables in backstreet establishments, remained undiminished.[103] This prompted an intensified effort by successive lords mayor in the early 1770s, in response to a perceived increase in gambling, to disrupt such activities by seizing dice, interrupting games, and lodging those encountered in such establishments in jail.[104] In addition, the corporation vowed in 1777 to 'support the sheriffs in the most effectual manner' in prosecuting 'the owners or occupiers of such houses', but it was without tangible result. A further effort was made in the early 1780s but it is a measure of the appeal of such recreations that the problems ascribed to gaming remained as pressing as ever in the early 1790s when billiards, dice, and pitch and toss were once again the target of critical public comment.[105] However, gaming in all its manifestations was not immune to the changing mood of the country, and the more censorious attitude that gradually took hold in the late eighteenth and early nineteenth centuries hastened the eclipse of many traditional games, including pitch and toss, of which Humphrey O'Sullivan of Callan, county Kilkenny, observed in 1831 that it had 'gone much out of use'.[106] O'Sullivan's reference to the sport reminds us that though the slivers of evidence appertaining to games such as pitch and toss derive primarily from urban spaces, Dublin particularly, it was not exclusively an urban sport.

---

101 *An act for the more effectual preventing of excessive and deceitful gaming*: 13 George 11, chap 8; *UA*, 23 Feb. 1754. 102 Edmond Hoyle, *A short treatise of the game of brag, containing the laws of the game* (Dublin, 1751); *A short treatise of the game of back-gammon ...* (Dublin, 1753); *A short treatise of the game of quadrille, shewing the odds of winning or losing most games that are commonly played* (Dublin, 1754); *A short treatise of the game of whist, containing the laws of the game* (Dublin, 1762); *Public Gazetteer*, 3 Feb. 1759; *Hoey's Publick Journal*, 21 Aug. 1771. 103 *Public Gazetteer*, 12 July 1760, 2 Oct. 1762, 16, 30 May 1767; *PO*, 25 Dec. 1759. 104 *Hoey's Publick Journal*, 30 Jan., 21 Aug. 1771, 7 Apr., 8 Oct., 27 Dec. 1773; *Hibernian Journal*, 2 June 1773, 14 Sept. 1774; *FJ*, 12 Oct. 1775, 20 Jan. 1777. 105 Gilbert (ed.), *Calendar of ancient records of Dublin*, xii, 522; *Hibernian Journal*, 11 Jan., 16 Oct. 1782, 10 May 1784, 7, 11, 25 Sept. 1789; *Clonmel Gazette*, 8 May 1788; *FJ*, 26, 31 Aug., 2 Sept. 1790, 14 Feb., 29 Nov., 3 Dec. 1791, 18 May 1793; Powell, *The politics of consumption*, p. 118.

Evidence from early nineteenth-century north Ulster indicates not only that pitch and toss (or 'skying' as it was called in county Londonderry) continued to be practised, but also that it was one of a number of recreations, of which card-playing was by far the most common, to which elements of the population continued to have resort, perhaps with greater frequency than to such one-time staple recreations as cockfighting, which continued to be pursued in Ulster on such red-letter holidays as Easter Monday.[107]

Handball

As the examples of pitch and toss, and card-playing, exemplify, many minority recreational practices acknowledged no urban-rural divide. This was a feature, of course, of horse racing, cockfighting, bull-baiting, pugilism and other sports, though it is evident also that the larger demographic concentrations in urban areas was more conducive to the provision of the facilities that certain sports demanded. Handball is a case in point. Ostensibly an uncomplicated sport, handball optimally required a court, or alley, if it was to be played properly. In the absence of these facilities, disused real tennis courts were an alternative, and several such sites seem to have been colonised for that purpose. The most notable was on Winetavern Street, which, following its decommissioning as a tennis course, functioned for nearly a decade as a 'ball yard' until the intervention, once more, of the authorities prompted its demolition.[108] As the fortunes of this alley suggests, handball was regarded with unease by those in authority. It was not perceived with quite the same disfavour as bull-baiting and throwing at cocks, but, like football and pitch and toss, it was warmly disapproved of by the guardians of morality and the apostles of public decorum, as an invitation to raucous, raffish and disorderly behaviour, which, when it was conducted in urban areas, posed a direct challenge to the vision of an orderly community that the respectable championed. It is thus not coincidental that one of the earliest references to the sport, dating from 1714, is contained in an instruction issued by the corporation of Londonderry forbidding the playing of ball in the market house of that city.[109] Significantly, municipal officials in Dublin were no less anxious to curb the playing of the sport.

It is not possible securely to establish how many ball alleys there were in Dublin, or any other city at a given time, or indeed, confidently to construct its historical trajectory. The reference in the town statutes of Galway for 1527 to handball would suggest that it was a long established sport. Be that as it may, the earliest evidence for ball alleys in the capital dates from the mid-eighteenth century. It was evidently a popular recreation with certain groups of young men at that time, which may account for the tendency of municipal offi-

---

106 McGrath (ed.), *The diary of Humphrey O'Sullivan*, iii, 19–20. **107** Day and McWilliams (eds), *Ordnance survey memoirs, county Londonderry*, xviii, 73, xxxi, 60, xxv, 54; Day and McWilliams (eds), *Ordnance survey memoirs, county Antrim*, xxi, 70. **108** Above, pp 323–4; *Public Gazetteer*, 25 Feb. 1764. **109** Mullin, *Derry/Londonderry*, p. 67.

cials to deem ball alleys (or 'ball-yards' as they were termed) objectionable
'receptacles of idle and disorderly persons' and 'nurseries of vice and idleness'.
In keeping with this perception, the lord mayor, Hans Bailie, issued 'directions
for demolishing several ball yards' in 1755, while nine years later, in 1764, the
then lord mayor William Forbes instructed that the 'ball-yards in York Street,
Aungier Street, Dame Street, John's Lane and Winetavern Street ... be dug up
and demolished'.[110] Forbes' action prompted much animated comment, and a
lawsuit seeking compensation for the destruction of property. Since it was
common procedure, prior to the implementation of such an order, to secure a
grand jury presentment, Forbes had clearly acted hastily, but the Corporation
was unapologetic. When the matter came before them on 11 April 1766, they
undertook to assume the costs of defending the suit, and signalled their strong
support for their lord mayor's actions. Forbes was, they pronounced, entirely
justified in:

> pulling down and suppressing ... a notorious disorderly ball yard at the
> corner of Aungier Street and York Street, which was represented to him
> by the principal inhabitants, as a great nuisance to the neighbourhood, by
> breaking their windows, cursing, swearing, and all manner of vice that a
> place frequented by profligate vagabonds was capable of.[111]

Forbes' decision to order the destruction of four, possibly five, ball alleys was an
unusually direct response to the perennial problem of disorderliness that the
respectable identified with demotic sports. It might be suggested, in an attempt
to account for his decision, that the lord mayor was guided in his actions by his
own class prejudices, but while this would be legitimate if the substantive matter
was the verbal boisterousness of the gangs of lower socio–economic males that
congregated at the city's ball alleys, the reality was he was still more animated by
the damage that was being done to property, specifically windows, because of ball
play. Moreover, there was the allied fact that ball alleys were used for purposes
other than handball, as evidenced by an incident on 30 May 1753, when Thomas
Davis, a shoemaker, was brought to the Inns Quay Infirmary having 'broke[n] his
leg by a fall in a ball-yard in James Street'.[112]

Draconian though his intervention was, the actions of William Forbes served
only to disrupt, and not to terminate ball playing in the capital. There were other
ball alleys, possibly makeshift in many instances, at which individuals continued
to gather. This served only to cause the authorities to invoke still-more severe
sanctions, as exemplified by Sir Thomas Blackhall, the lord mayor, who took up
'not only the players, but [also] lookers on' when he moved against 'those seminaries of vice and destruction of youth' in 1769.[113] Blackhall's approach was not
sustained, but the interventionist inclination of the authorities in Dublin may

110 *UA*, 21 June 1755; *Public Gazetteer*, 25 Feb. 1764.   111 Gilbert (ed.), *Calendar of ancient records of Dublin*, xi, 328–9.   112 *UA*, 2 June 1753.   113 *FJ*, 12 Aug. 1769.

have had the effect over time of consigning ball playing in the city towards the same marginal space to which they sought to assign gaming.[114] There was no identifiable debate as to whether this was a wise course of action, but one may reasonably conclude from the greater receptivity of the authorities in Limerick to the establishment of ball alleys in their city that opinion was far from unanimous on the subject. Limerick city possessed at least five alleys in the late 1760s, and while interest in the sport may have contracted thereafter, the decline was not permanent, and it was well and truly in retreat by the turn of the century when, as well as those that had survived, new ball alleys were in place in Maynooth, Kildare and Athlone.[115]

Moreover, this was the prelude to a virtual nationwide surge in ball alley construction that was to transform the fortunes of the sport, as new ball courts were built between 1815 and 1845 in Kildare, Maynooth, Kilkenny, Armagh, Fethard, Mullingar, Bandon and other locations.[116] The sport certainly took firm root in Ulster in the early nineteenth century, encouraged by various local entrepreneurs who conceived that they could make a ball alley profitable, and by the decline in interest in cockfighting. Some of the facilities that resulted were impressive. The alley erected at the rear of a public house in the 'Scotch quarter' of Carrickfergus was '64 by 24 feet. Walls are all of brick and is 24 feet all round; floor is flagged'. Others were manifestly less well appointed; it was observed of the parish of Drumachose in north county Londonderry in 1835 that 'several ball courts have been built, but they have invariably fallen down'.[117] Some alleys, generally the more impressive, were built as commercial concerns, and a charge applied. The admission price to the bespoke alley to the rear of Percival Ingram's public house in Carrickfergus was 2*d*. in 1839–40. It cannot be assumed that such courts were profitable, or even paid their way, for though the Ordnance Survey memoirists reported from the parishes of Carnteel and Killyman, in county Tyrone, in the mid-1830s that handball was 'the chief amusement', the reports from Derryaghy, in south county Antrim, and Drumachose in county Londonderry were palpably less positive.[118]

The mixed picture provided by the Ordnance Survey memoirs, notwithstanding, the construction of ball alleys indicates that handball had not just overcome the serious challenge it encountered from officialdom in the Dublin

114 *FJ*, 26 Aug. 1790.   115 Andrew, *Irish historic towns atlas: Kildare*, section no. 21; Horner, *Irish historic towns atlas: Maynooth*, section no. 21; Murtagh, *Irish historic towns atlas: Athlone*, section no. 21.   116 Bradley, *Irish historic towns atlas: Kilkenny*, section no. 21; McCullough and Crawford, *Irish historic towns atlas: Armagh*, section no. 21; O'Keeffe, *Irish historic towns atlas: Fethard*, section no. 21; Andrews and Davies, *Irish historic towns atlas: Mullingar*, section no. 21; O'Flanagan, *Irish historic towns atlas: Bandon*, section no. 21.   117 Day and McWilliams (eds), *Ordnance survey memoirs, county Antrim*, xxxvii, 149; Day and McWilliams (eds), *Ordnance survey memoirs, county Londonderry*, ix, 82.   118 Day and McWilliams (eds), *Ordnance survey memoirs, county Antrim*, xxxvii, 149; Day and McWilliams (eds), *Ordnance survey memoirs, county Tyrone*, xx, 22, 68; Day and McWilliams (eds), *Ordnance survey memoirs, county Antrim*, viii, 113; Day and McWilliams (eds), *Ordnance survey memoirs, county Londonderry*, ix, 82.

metropolitan area in the eighteenth century, but survived to establish a distinct presence on the non-metropolitan sporting landscape in the early nineteenth century. More generally, it was part of a broader rural engagement in 'ball playing' that embraced commons, hurling and football.[119] In so far as one can establish, during the pre-Famine era handball largely functioned as a local sport that served the recreational needs of the boys and young men within a distinct locality, for whom the aim of becoming the local champion sufficed. In this, it bore comparison with many traditional sports, which served the needs of communities whose quotidian horizon was inward, and for whom travel was a utilitarian activity. However, handball survived the collapse in traditional sports that was a feature of the early nineteenth century, and the trauma of the Great Famine, which did for many traditional religious practices.[120] Indeed, it was able for a time to sustain the 'first professional tour … in 1850 when players such as Martin Butler of Kilkenny travelled across Ireland playing for money against local champions'. The fact that it was deemed 'a favourite pastime' in Ulster in the 1870s was evidence of its adaptability, and of the fact that this was the key to the capacity of individual sports to survive the changes in attitudinal disposition that was so influential in determining which sports flourished in, and which survived the transition from early modernity to modernity.[121]

Long bullets
One of the quintessential local sports, which enjoyed a regional distribution still more confined than that of handball, was long bullets. Better known today as 'road bowls', this plebeian sport may share a common ancestry with lawn bowls. Be that as it may, it had put down sufficiently firm-roots in Ulster by 1714 to cause the corporation of Londonderry to proscribe the playing of the sport on the city walls, 'on paine of paying five shillings for each offence'.[122] It is not clear how popular the sport was in the country at that time. The balance of opinion has it that the sport was introduced into Ulster by weavers from Britain, and that, once established, 'it spread quickly through Antrim, Armagh, and parts of Derry, Down and Tyrone'.[123] The premier historian of the sport has advanced a plausible argument in support of his contention that the sport was subsequently brought from Ulster to Cork 'with weavers and migrant textile workers' who 'formed a majority of the industrial households in the landlord-sponsored enterprises at Dunmanway, Inishannon and Killarney'.[124] Yet it should be noted that the inclusion of a reference to long bullets on the list of objectionable recreations

---

119 Day and McWilliams (eds), *Ordnance survey memoirs, county Antrim*, xvi, 18–19; Day and McWilliams (eds), *Ordnance survey memoirs, county Londonderry*, xi, 10–11.   120 Eugene Hynes, 'The great hunger and Irish Catholicism', *Societas*, 8 (1978), pp 137–55.   121 Collins et al. (eds), *Encyclopedia of traditional British rural sports*, p. 143; Knox, *A history of the county of Down*, p. 56.   122 Collins et al. (eds), *Encyclopedia of traditional British rural sports*, pp 47, 229–31; Fintan Lane, *Long bullets: a history of road bowling in Ireland* (Cork, 2005), p. 16; Mullin, *Derry/Londonderry*, p. 67.   123 Lane, *Long bullets*, pp 11–12, 16.   124 Lane, *Long bullets*, pp 20–1; David Dickson, *Old world colony: Cork and south Munster, 1630–1830* (Cork, 2005), p. 204.

to which the minister, churchwardens and parishioners of St Paul's church took exception in 1737 suggests that it may also have been played in Dublin at that time.[125] If so, the absence of further mention would indicate that the metropolis was not a conducive environment. A subsequent reference to a form of street bowling played in Dublin in the 1780s might suggest otherwise, but the fact that it was played with a 'leaden ball' implies that this game of 'long bullets' was the eighteenth-century form of skittles, which involved throwing a lead ball at nine pins, rather than road bowls, though one cannot entirely rule out the possibility that a variant form persisted in the metropolis.[126]

The implication that the game of long bullets, whose object is to cover a course, generally a two- or three-mile stretch of road, with a lead ball (or bullet) weighing between 28 and 32 ounces, in the least number of throws, for 'a wager of either money or whiskey',[127] was once played over more of the country than is currently acknowledged or took different forms in different parts of the country is unproven, but it is a possibility. What is demonstrable is that reliable evidence exists to indicate that long bullets was played on the outskirts of Cork in the late 1780s, that it was disapproved of by respectable society, and that it seldom, if ever, featured in the public sphere other than when it was the cause of an accident such as happened during a score in 1789 when an eight-year-old boy died as a result of a blow received to the head from a misdirected bullet.[128] Prompted by a number of other deaths in the course of the next decade, the sheriffs of Cork followed the by now well worn path when it came to controversial demotic diversions of attempting to prosecute long bullets out of existence by detaining those who engaged in the sport. This policy was initiated in 1803, but it was quickly apparent that it was unlikely to succeed so long as the devotees of the sport continued to take to the roads, and the community accepted the resulting inconvenience as of insufficient consequence to turn against those who were committed to the game. This is not to suggest that the sport did not endure testing times during the early nineteenth century, but it survived as a minority activity because those who carried the standard for the sport were determined it should continue and were regarded with sufficient respect within the county Cork community to negotiate the key inter-generational transition.[129]

The situation was different in Ulster because the combination of economic and social change experienced across the province, and the sharp shifts in attitude that resulted in the abandonment at different moments of a number of sports, was more decisive there than in the smaller bastion of long bullets in county Cork. The dramatic attitudinal shift that transformed cockfighting from a respected, and possibly widely practised, sporting activity into a marginalised local recreation took no more than a few decades, and based upon the evidence

125 Gilbert (ed.), *Calendar of ancient records of Dublin*, viii, 241. **126** *Hibernian Journal*, 28 July 1786; Collins et al. (eds), *Encyclopedia of traditional British rural sports*, p. 181. **127** Day and McWilliams (eds), *Ordnance survey memoirs, county Londonderry*, xviii, 18, 73. **128** Lane, *Long bullets*, pp 21–2. **129** Ibid., pp 23–5.

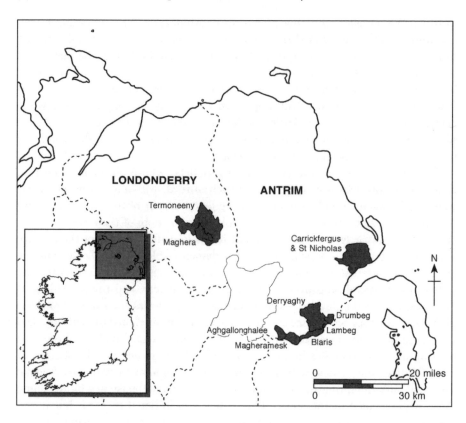

Map 10: The geography of long bullets: parishes in which the sport was played
in counties Antrim and Londonderry in the early nineteenth century

gathered by the memoirists of the Ordnance Survey in the 1830s long bullets had
so far retreated in counties Antrim and Londonderry that it was confined in the
former to six contiguous parishes on the county's southern boundary, and to two
rural parishes in the south east of county Londonderry (see Map 10). Moreover,
it was in rapid retreat, having 'ceased almost altogether' in Carrickfergus and
Magheragall, and survived in a diminished capacity in Blaris and nearby
Derryaghy.[130] Previously, a dynamic sport, albeit on a smaller scale than cockfighting, it was no longer able to sustain the healthy competitive dimension
between neighbouring parishes that was once a crucial measure of its popularity.
Commenting in 1837 on the game in the parish of Magheragall, county Antrim,
the Ordnance Survey memoirist observed:

130 Day and McWilliams (eds), *Ordnance survey memoirs, county Antrim*, viii, 113, 141–2, xxi, 37,
128; xxxvii, 76–7, 175; Day and McWilliams (eds), *Ordnance survey memoirs, county Londonderry*,
xviii, 18, 73; Lane, *Long bullets*, pp 17–18.

Bullet playing, which consists in rolling a heavy iron ball along the surface, was so extensive in this and Blaris parish at a former period that the 2 parishes often contested for bets of 10 guineas a side, to be decided by the above play.[131]

The game was in an equally unhealthy state in the parish of Termoneeny, county Londonderry. It was observed there in 1836:

They have a game which consists of a trial of strength; 2 parties assemble and try which will send an iron ball the longest distance on some level part of the public road, which is hard and therefore better suited to the purpose.[132]

The situation was comparable in county Down, where long bullets was previously 'in high favour among the labouring population'. Moreover, once it was deemed 'dangerous' to play the game 'on the public roads' the weight of respectable opinion synergised with the disapproval of the law authorities. This was a powerful combination in nineteenth-century Ireland, and it was sufficient to prevent the playing of the game with the result that long bullets was described as 'almost entirely suppressed' in the county by the 1870s.[133] There is no equivalent information on the state of the sport in county Armagh, which is greatly to be regretted, since this is the Ulster county where it has survived into the present, but while such information would permit an amplified picture to be drawn, it is unlikely if it would dramatically alter the picture of a traditional pursuit that was in rapid retreat in the early nineteenth century.[134]

CONCLUSION

Long bullets was not the only rural sport with an ostensibly bleak future at this moment. But whereas it defied the odds and survived, and was to grow again in the twentieth century because it adopted modern organisational methods, others succumbed completely. The fighting sports were the most vulnerable because they most directly contravened the appreciating societal conviction that such violent and bloody sports deserved to be extirpated because they were rude and unsophisticated. If, as this suggests, the early nineteenth century was a transi-

131 Lane, *Long bullets*, p. 18; Day and McWilliams (eds), *Ordnance survey memoirs, county Antrim*, xxi, 109.   132 Day and McWilliams (eds), *Ordnance survey memoirs, county Londonderry*, vi, 126. 133 Knox, *A history of the county of Down*, p. 57.   134 Lane, *Long bullets*, pp 17–18; Raymond Murray (ed.), *The Armagh bullet thrower* (Armagh, 1976); T.G.F. Paterson, 'Long bullets in county Armagh', *UJA*, 9 (1946), pp 58–68; idem, 'The game of long bullets in county Armagh', *County Louth Archaeological Journal*, 11:2 (1946), pp 90–5.

tional moment in the history of sport in Ireland because many once firmly established diversions were either in decline or being forced underground, it has also
to be recognised that there was a number of emerging minority, or niche, sports
for whom the future seemed more promising.

Though it is apparent from what has gone before that late early modern
Ireland sustained a diverse array of recreational sports, sport was but one
dimension of a densely populated recreational landscape. This is not the place
to explore that landscape other than in so far as it appertains to the world of
recreational sport, but it is pertinent to observe that the decline in the participation in sport that took place in the early nineteenth century was compensated
for, at least in part, by the resort to fairs and markets 'as much for amusement
as business'.[135] Indeed, it is likely that for the majority of the population who
did not engage in sport that 'going to fairs' may have rivalled drinking and
dancing as their main diversion.[136] The variety of recreational opportunities and
ancillary activities associated with, and integral to the pleasure provided by
major regional fairs and patterns has as yet to be fully reconstructed.[137] But it
is noteworthy, based on the presence of boxing exhibitions at Donnybrook Fair
in the early 1820s and horse racing, chasing a soaped pig, 'races between men,
and between women, jumping in sacks and a variety of similar sports' at
Carrickfergus a decade later, that sport sustained a significant presence at such
occasions.[138] Be that as it may, it was clearly secondary to 'dram drinking' in
the tents and booths that were a familiar feature on fair greens, and at the gathering points for major national and regional patterns, to which Catholics flocked
in large numbers. It was not necessary, of course, to visit a fair to drink.
Alcohol was readily available, and the volume in which it was consumed indicates that drinking was a common and popular recreational activity.[139] Like
most sporting activity, it was acutely gender bound. The most important recreational exception to this was dancing. Dancing was the most common recreational practice pursued in late early modern Ireland. It features as prominently
in the 'accounts of the manners ... of the native Irish peasantry' penned by
tourists and travel writers, as it does in the recollections by authors of their
childhood and in the dispassionate descriptions of 'the habits of the people'

135 Day and McWilliams (eds), *Ordnance survey memoirs, county Antrim*, xiii, 46–7.   136 Day and
McWilliams (eds), *Ordnance survey memoirs, county Antrim*, x, 40, xiii, 46–7, 50, 113, xvi, 112, xix,
31, xxi, 70; xxxvii, 77; Day and McWilliams (eds), *Ordnance survey memoirs, county Monaghan*, xl,
66, 93, 121; Day and McWilliams (eds), *Ordnance survey memoirs, county Cavan*, xl, 9, 36.   137 S.J.
Connolly, *Priest and people in pre-Famine Ireland, 1780–1845* (Dublin, 1982), pp 135–48; Diarmuid
Ó Giolláin, 'The pattern' in J.S. Donnolly and Kerby Miller (eds), *Irish popular culture, 1650–1850*
(Dublin, 1998), pp 203–4, 205–6.   138 Above, p. 305; Day and McWilliams (eds), *Ordnance survey
memoirs, county Antrim*, xxxvii, 77.   139 See Elizabeth Malcolm, '*Ireland sober, Ireland free': drink
and temperance in nineteenth-century Ireland* (Dublin, 1986); Day and McWilliams (eds), *Ordnance
survey memoirs, county Tyrone*, xx, 27–8; Day and McWilliams (eds), *Ordnance survey memoirs, county
Londonderry*, xxv, 54, xxvii, 110, xxxiii, 14; Day and McWilliams (eds), *Ordnance survey memoirs,
county Antrim*, x, 13; Day and McWilliams (eds), *Ordnance survey memoirs, county Monaghan*, xl,

prepared on behalf of the Ordnance Survey.[140] Indicatively, it was also singled out for criticism by reform-minded clerics of all denominations, for much the same reason that they targeted sport.[141] Card-playing was another recreational activity that was likewise not bound by season, weather or gender. However, while commonplace, particularly among the elite in the eighteenth century, and the generality of the population in Ulster in the early nineteenth century, cards bring the story of recreation into another realm, beyond that of sport.[142]

This chapter has not engaged with all of the minority and niche sports that were pursued in late early modern Ireland. (It has not, for example, engaged with fishing and shooting, which, influenced by and following the example of England, and Englishmen who sang the praise of Irish rivers and lakes, gave the sport of hunting another dimension in the early nineteenth century.)[143] Yet it has demonstrated that a niche sport can function if a small band of committed enthusiasts leverage the resources required to allow it to be played, and that it can survive if they are able successfully to transmit the knowledge, conviction, and commitment from generation to generation. However, the sporting land-scape is inherently fluid, and no matter how committed an individual, or corpus of individuals may be to a sport's practice and perpetuation, they will be hard pressed to sustain a sporting endeavour, be it a mass or elite activity, if it is rejected by society at large. It can be done of course, as some of the minority sports addressed in this chapter attest, but the rise and decline of sports, both individually and collectively, mass and minority, tends to mirror larger social, economic and political forces. By assisting with the identification of the under-lying trends that shape the broader milieu in which sport was conducted in late

109. **140** Dunton, *Teague land*, pp 82–3; *The Public Gazetteer*, 1 July 1760; Barnard (ed.), 'A description of Gort in 1752 by Thomas Wetherall', pp 111, 112; Young, *A tour in Ireland*, i, 44; W.R. Wilde, 'Memoir of Gabriel Berenger and his labours in the cause of Irish art', *Journal of the Royal Historical and Archaeological Associations of Ireland*, 1 (1870–1), p. 128; *The life of Patrick Cunningham*, pp 4–5; Shaw Mason, *Statistical account*, iii, 207; Day and McWilliams (eds), *Ordnance survey memoirs, county Antrim*, ii, 23, x, 5, 13, 40, xiii, 15, 33, 56–7, xvi, 86, 99, xxi, 138, xxiv, 47, 132, xxvi, 28, xxix, 94, 113, xxxii, 37, xxxv, 23, 93–4; Day and McWilliams (eds), *Ordnance survey memoirs, county Londonderry*, vi, 10, 55–6,126, xxxi, 60, xxxiii, 37; Day and McWilliams (eds), *Ordnance survey memoirs, county Armagh*, i, 90; Day and McWilliams (eds), *Ordnance survey memoirs, county Down*, iii, 37, vii, 72, xii, 60; Day and McWilliams (eds), *Ordnance survey memoirs, county Fermanagh*, xiv, 107. **141** Holmes, *The shaping of Ulster Presbyterian belief and practice*, pp 111, 173; Connolly, *Priests and people in pre-Famine Ireland*, pp 123–4, 168–9, 176. **142** Dunton, *Teague land*, p. 93; Day and McWilliams (eds), *Ordnance survey memoirs, county Antrim*, xix, 61, xxi, 22, xxiii, 133, xxvi, 87, 106; Day and McWilliams (eds), *Ordnance survey memoirs, county Londonderry*, xxxi, 60. **143** For evidence of the growing appeal of fishing and shooting, see *The angling excursions of Gregory Greendrake in the counties of Wicklow, Meath, Westmeath, Longford and Cavan* (Dublin, 1832); O'Gorman, *The practice of angling, particularly as regards Ireland* (Dublin, 1845); *The Angler in Ireland, or an Englishman's ramble through Connaught and Munster, during the summer of 1833* (2 vols, London, 1834); Henry Newland, *The Erne: its legends and its fly-fishing* (London, 1851); W.H. Maxwell, *Wild sports of the west* (2 vols, London, 1832); *Hints to young sportsmen on the art of shooting* (London, 1829).

early modern Ireland, the fortunes of individual minority sports serve not only to demonstrate the inherently mutable and contingent character of the history of individual sports, but also to highlight the larger social forces that shaped the history of sport.

Conclusion

Sport sustained a prominent presence on the Irish landscape during the period 1600–1840, yet it is not always easy to identify how a particular sport was played, organised, and still less to establish with certitude the social background of those who participated as organisers, players, spectators and, in the case of gambling sports, as punters. There are many reasons why this is the case. The evidential deficit has been referred to frequently in the course of this volume. This may be ascribed, in part at least, to the fact that since most sports did not require an elaborate paper-based bureaucracy to flourish, there was no archive to preserve, but it is hardly coincidental that this echoes the shared perception of ministers, law-makers and opinion formers that sport was of minor consequence when set beside those things that obviously did matter – religion, politics, war, literature, commerce, philosophy, science and so on – which have left a palpably more substantial documentary footprint. Given this attitude, it might be suggested that neglect was a benign outcome, since it might have been far worse. A large, possibly a majority of decision makers, law officers, administrators and opinion-formers – clergy, social improvers, humanists, the champions of order and conformity – were fully convinced that demotic sports were 'barbarous customs' and 'vulgar dissipations' that those who aspired to lead a Godly life, or to satisfy the advanced ideals of civility and politeness must oppose.[1] This is why when one quarries the more promising evidential seams in search of information with which to reconstruct the world of recreational sport one has first to take cognizance of the fact that much of the evidence upon which one draws derives from an attitudinal spectrum that was reflexively disposed to view non-elite sports in negative terms. It is particularly difficult, for this reason, to divine the motives of those who pursued other than respectable diversions, which accounts for a majority of the sports considered in this volume. It is easier, because it assumes a larger place in the evidential record, to explain what informed those who dismissed sport as frivolous and uncouth. For those for whom life was a mere ephemeral rehearsal for an eternal, more purposeful, spiritual existence, as well as for those who were materialists, recreation was variously regarded as an incentive to engage in behaviour that was not only offensive to God, good sense and decorum, but also contrary to economic self-interest and a misuse of time, effort and energy. Of course, the fact so many of the activities that constituted

---

1 These terms were used with reference to throwing at cocks: see Griffin, *England's revelry*, pp 128, 130.

sport, as it was then defined, either involved the spilling of blood (human as well as animal), or blood-letting was a contingent outcome of the way in which they were played, encouraged those who were repulsed by such endeavour in the rectitude of their conclusion that society would be improved if most sports were regulated or legislated out of existence. This is not to suggest – the frequent allegations of barbarity notwithstanding – that this negative perception of sport was unanimous. Many commentators clearly perceived little that was life affirming in sporting activity, but there were some who shared the more positive, and modern, perspective of the memoirist, writing in the 1830s, who opined that participation in 'manly sports ... would be of great advantage to the population generally'.[2] Yet the primary societal preoccupation then, and earlier, was less with encouraging participation than with interdicting the misbehaviour, and anti-social conduct that sport was perceived to foster.

While it is self-evident that the definition of what constituted misbehaviour or anti-social conduct is determined by perspective, few, or any, of those who articulated such sentiment in the early modern era were disposed to interrogate their own opinions. Indeed, regardless as to whether their *Weltanschauung* was anchored in scripture, sentiment or social prejudice, their opinions were advanced with conviction and certitude, and their authors seemed blithely unconcerned by, or simply oblivious to the fact that the arguments they advanced against sport, and demotic sports particularly, were incomplete and/or inconsistent. It is striking, for example, that most of those who denominated bull-baiting and throwing at cocks 'barbarous' in the mid-eighteenth century articulated few objections about cockfighting, and when the public did commence, several decades later, to look unfavourably upon that sport, they expressed no reservations with fox-hunting and hare-coursing. It is equally striking that concern was rarely expressed openly about the physical demand of frequent, long races upon horses, or with the fact that it was deemed legitimate both to use spurs and whips in order to eke out the last ounce of pace for the personal and financial gratification of their owners and punters.

One must not, of course, judge the behaviour of people in the past by standards they did not recognise. This can present problems when, as is the case with many of the sports pursued in the late early-modern era, legitimate humanitarian sensitivities are aroused by the violence that was visited, whether consciously or insouciantly, upon the animal and human participants in such activities. The purpose of this work has been to describe rather than to judge, on the grounds that this is more likely to assist with the recovery of a sporting *milieu* that was variegated as well as volatile. Horse racing emerges from this narrative as the best organised, the best funded, and the only major sport pursued in every region of the island. In so doing, it mirrors the *ancien régime* character of Irish society. Horse racing was the sport of the aristocratic elite, and its privileged position on the Irish sporting landscape echoed that of the landed ascendancy,

2 Day and McWilliams (eds), *Ordnance Survey memoirs, county Londonderry*, xi, 109.

which organised, and, with a modicum of state and municipal assistance, financed the sport. Indeed, the primary conclusion of this inquiry is also one of the most obvious: the sports that are played in a society reflect the balance of social and political power, attitude and influence, and, as a consequence, the sports that are in the ascendant at any given time not only echo the prevailing social order but also its values. By extension, the changing fortunes of individual sports are invariably revealing of the attitudinal changes at work in a society and of the shifting fortunes of the social interests of which it is composed.

This conclusion presumes, of course, that people are at liberty to play the sports they wish, and are not required, either by legal or other pressures, to pursue games that others judge appropriate. Since those in positions of power in late early modern Ireland did not use the levers of state *actively* to promote individual sports (horse racing possibly excepted), and only fitfully opposed those games of which the respectable strongly disapproved, it cannot be said the still embryonic Irish state was even neutral in its attitude. Indeed, one might plausibly argue that sport *per se* was just about tolerated, and that certain sports were actively discouraged during the sixteenth and early seventeenth centuries, which provides the backdrop against which the individual sports' histories elaborated in this work are delineated. Were the authorities in a position then to enforce their will, it is improbable – taking the deliberations of Dublin Corporation in the 1610s as a guide, – a few utilitarian and decorous recreational activities excepted – that sport would have been permitted to achieve the prominent place it came to occupy in the eighteenth century. These decisions were consistent with the prevailing religious and utilitarian convictions that sport *per se* was an intrinsic waste of time, resources, and human capacities. However, the ludic impulse of the population was stronger than the instrumentalist instinct of officials to achieve control, with the net result that a number of emblematical new recreations – bowling and horse racing notably – introduced by and acceptable to the New English elite joined the small number of already established Gaelic Irish[3] and Old English sports[4] on the then sparsely populated sporting landscape. Sixteenth- and early seventeenth-century Ireland was not, as this suggests a rich or especially supportive sporting environment, and, by comparison with England, Ireland sustained a narrow range of sporting activities.[5] Moreover, though indicative steps were taken to establish horse racing in the 1630s, the militarised landscape of the 1640s and the ascendancy of the Puritans, which followed, extended this essentially uncongenial environment into the middle decades of the seventeenth century. The Commonwealth was not as proscriptive when it came to sport as legend suggests,[6] but the 1650s were far from favourable, with the result that though the ascension to the throne in 1660 of the fun-loving Charles II has-

---

3 Hurling, notably.   4 Real tennis, handball, quoits, bull-baiting, for example.   5 Brailsford, *Sport and society; Elizabeth to Anne*, chapters 1 and 2; Strutt, *The sports and pastimes of the people of England*, passim.   6 Brailsford, op. cit., pp 122–57; Toby Barnard, *Cromwellian Ireland: English government and reform in Ireland 1649–1660* (Oxford, 1975).

tened a dramatic change of mood, it took the full span of the Restoration for sporting activity to achieve a visible presence on the Irish landscape. Horse racing, inevitably, paved the way, not least because it was favoured at the highest level, but the generally permissive atmosphere, exemplified by Charles II, registered across the three Stuart kingdoms.[7]

Meanwhile, the transformative effect, identifiable in so many walks of life, of the migration to Ireland of English and Scottish settlers, who arrived in sufficient numbers in the seventeenth century to transform the demographic balance of the island, can also be detected in the expanding menu of sporting possibilities that gradually became available.[8] The attenuated evidential record means that this process is often opaque, but a persuasive case can be advanced that it was during this century that sports as diverse as cockfighting, throwing at cocks, bowling and long bullets took root and emerged as popular activities.[9] The demographic and cultural transformation then taking place had the effect also of binding Ireland closer to Britain, which meant the kingdom was receptive to further cultural transfers that facilitated the adoption in the eighteenth century of organisational innovations made in England (in horse racing and cockfighting, notably), and the embrace of emerging forms of sporting activity such as pugilism.[10] As a result, there was a palpable surge in the number of individual diversions in Ireland; sport became more visible, more pervasive and more diverse. Encouraged by an unusual degree of political and social stability, economic and demographic growth, the emergence from the 1720s of a press that served as a conduit of information about sport as well as other events, a greater receptivity to new ideas, and the permeation of the English language, sport enjoyed an unprecedented efflorescence.[11] The most visible manifestation of this was the amount of space allocated to advertising and reporting horse racing in the press, but this was a manifestation in turn of the fact that the number of regional and local meetings organised in the 1720s and 1730s threatened to eclipse the iconic national meetings, at the Curragh and the Maze, that had established a firm foothold in the late seventeenth century.

---

7 Brailsford, *Sport and society; Elizabeth to Anne*, chapter 6. 8 For settlement in seventeenth century, see Raymond Gillespie, *Seventeenth-century Ireland: making Ireland modern* (Dublin, 2006), passim. 9 Patrick Fagan, 'The demography of Dublin in the eighteenth century', *Eighteenth-century Ireland*, 6 (1991), pp 121–56; David Dickson, 'The demographic implications of the growth of Dublin, 1650–1850' in Richard Lawton and Robert Lee (eds), *Urban population development in western Europe from the late-eighteenth to the early-twentieth century* (Liverpool, 1989), pp 178–89. 10 For the broader context in which these shifts occurred see, especially, Toby Barnard, *A new anatomy of Ireland: the Irish Protestants, 1649–1770* (London, 2003); idem, *Making the grand figure: lives and possessions in Ireland, 1641–1770* (London, 2004). 11 See S.J. Connolly, *Divided kingdom: Ireland 1630–1800* (Oxford, 2008), chapter 6 and ff; L.M. Cullen, *An economic history of Ireland since 1660* (London, 1972), chapters 3 and 4; David Dickson, Cormac Ó Grada and Stuart Daultrey, 'Hearth tax, household size, and Irish population change, 1672– 1821', *PRIA* 82C (1982), pp 125–81; Munter, *History of the newspaper*, pp 131–56; James Kelly and Ciarán Mac Murchaidh, 'Introduction' in idem (eds), *Irish and English: essays on the Irish linguistic and cultural frontier*, pp 25–42 passim; Michael Brown, *The Enlightenment in Ireland* (forthcoming).

There was a further surge in regional and local meetings from the late 1740s, which must be linked into the synchronous acceleration in the emergence of a civil society, which Kelly, Powell and others have identified in the surge in the number of clubs and societies.[12]

With a firm foundation in place, horse racing remained Ireland's premier sport through the eighteenth century and beyond. Its success sustained a number of allied recreational activities of which hunting was the most popular, but it is perhaps more significant that, in the world of eighteenth-century Ireland, it was emblematical of the social inclusivity of sport; in the words of Dennis Brailsford, there were few sporting pursuits where 'the barriers of rank [were] insurmountable', but the extent to which inclusion was pursued could, and did, vary. Be that as it may, horse racing was one of the more all-embracing, and the ease with which race organisers incorporated cockfighting, hurling, or even pugilism onto the menu of entertainments presented racegoers was emblematical of the permeability of the boundaries that separated sports, and of the capacity of social classes to mix on the sports ground.[13]

This is not to suggest that sport transcended social distinction; the hierarchical order that defined Ireland's *ancien régime* was too deeply entrenched for that. However, it did sustain a range of activities and milieus in which classes mixed, and in which social co-operation and interaction was required to achieve success. This was most manifest in the involvement of members of the gentry (not all of whom were of Gaelic Irish or Old English descent) in promoting the game of hurling, but it was visible also at the racecourse, in the cockpit, and on the hunting ground. In this way, sport both contributed to and mirrored the capacity of all interests in the eighteenth century to compartmentalise the deep-lain suspicions that were an enduring legacy of conquest and expropriation in the sixteenth and seventeenth centuries, and, thereby, to foster the concord and co-operation that characterised the landlord–tenant relationship on many estates and in many parts of the country.[14] This disposition was obviously integral to the success of demotic sports such as hurling, and to a lesser extent cockfighting, which were embraced, however briefly, or conditionally in some instances, by the elite. There were other, primarily traditional, sports that populated the eighteenth-century

---

12 Kelly and Powell (eds), *Clubs and societies in eighteenth-century Ireland*, passim; see also Jim Livesey, *Civil society and empire: Ireland and Scotland in the eighteenth century Atlantic world* (New Haven, 2009).   13 Brailsford, 'A taste for diversions', pp 50, 88.   14 See, inter alia, Toby Barnard, 'The uses of 23 October 1641 and Irish Protestant celebrations', *English Historical Review*, 106 (1991), pp 889–920; James Kelly, 'The glorious and immortal memory: commemoration and Protestant identity in Ireland, 1660–1800', *PRIA*, 94C (1994), pp 25–52; S.J. Connolly, '"Ag déanamh commanding": elite responses to popular culture, 1660–1850' in K.A. Miller and J.S. Donnelly (eds), *Irish popular culture, 1650–1850* (Dublin, 1998), pp 1–31; idem, 'Albion's fatal twigs: justice and law in the eighteenth century' in Rosalind Mitchison and Peter Roebuck (eds), *Economy and society in Scotland and Ireland, 1500–1939* (Edinburgh, 1988), pp 117–25; Thomas Bartlett, 'The end of moral economy: the Irish militia disturbances of 1793', *Past and Present*, 91 (1983), pp 41–64.

sporting landscape that failed to achieve even that limited measure of acceptance, and were palpably more confined socially as a result. Bull-baiting and throwing at cocks fit this category; so too do football, long bullets and wrestling. These were demotic recreations that the elite shunned, and the respectable, which embraced the rising middling sort, were disposed increasingly to despise. For some of these sports, the eighteenth century was both their highpoint and their swansong, since they were all but totally discredited in respectable and intellectual circles by the beginning of the nineteenth century, when some (but not all) disappeared from view.[15]

For all the ostensible variety of the sports that were played, the eighteenth-century landscape was by no means fully populated by sporting activity; there were regions where sport was seemingly little practised, and whole social layers (indeed, one gender) which did not pursue any sporting activity. Moreover, other than horse racing and hunting, no sport can reasonably be defined as national. Cockfighting did, to be sure, forge a regional competitive structure that persisted for more than half a century; so too did hurling for a slightly shorter period, but neither can be regarded as a national sport and neither negotiated the profound attitudinal shift that took a firm hold before the end of the eighteenth century. The adoption by these sports of the barony, town and county as competitive units set a potentially important precedent that may well have served as a source of identification, and perhaps as a focus of identity, but it was not sufficiently sharply defined to sustain the sport, as both had contracted by the early nineteenth century, when they functioned within a local (intra-county) milieu. It may be, those headline provincial and inter-county encounters apart, that more activity during sport's eighteenth-century peak was pursued locally than can presently by identified. If so, the organisational effort required has left no readily recoverable evidential trace, and its importance as a force for communal and local identity, and sectional expression, remains to be captured. It is certainly problematic that we are so dependent on information mediated through the prism of those who not only did not fully understand demotic sport, but also often made absolutely no effort to do so, but this is one of the methodological challenges that the early modern era habitually throws up.

While it is apparent, based on the corpus of reported activity, that sport expanded in the mid-Hanoverian era, it is also the case that it generated more negative comment than positive applause. Guided by a religious sensibility, which was predisposed to regard enjoyment suspiciously, and energised by the commitment to personal self-discipline and self-denial,[16] and to societal betterment that the embrace of an ethic of improvement encouraged, an influential strand of commentary emerged that was predisposed to eye sport negatively.[17] Repelled by

---

15 Above, chapters 4, 6 and 7; Griffin, *England's revelry*, p. 130.   16 See *FJ*, 3 July 1759 where 'self denial' is deemed 'the highest exaltation of human virtue'.   17 Barnard, *Improving Ireland?: projectors, prophets and profiteers*, passim; D.W. Hayton, 'A question of upbringing: Thomas Prior, Sir John Rawdon, 3rd bt., and the mentality and ideology of "improvement"' in idem (ed.), *The*

the social disruption, verbal and physical violence, and by the sense of entitle-ment with which the devotees of some of the most controversial traditional sports appropriated public space, the increasingly self-assured 'middling sort' evolved an ideology of respectability, and appealed unhesitatingly to officialdom, locally and nationally, to give it legislative and regulatory effect.[18] They were assisted by the greater interventionism of the eighteenth-century state (particularly manifest in the realms of law and order, incarceration, education and poor relief), which laid the foundations for the surge in state power that was a feature of the nine-teenth century, and which received its most visible, and pertinent, expression in the inauguration of a national police. It was reinforced in its Irish context by the 'sharpening class segregation' identified in early-nineteenth-century Britain, which fostered a deepening sectarian as well as social chasm.[19]

For the practitioners of the most sharply criticised demotic sports, such as bull-baiting and throwing at cocks, these sports were possessed of legitimacy by reason of the fact that they had been transmitted across generations. They were also intrinsic to their identity, and integral to their entitlement to access public space on their own terms, by which they were enabled both to express and to perpetuate these symbols of their cultural distinctiveness. However, for those for whom the model of the public arena was not forged in the crucible of tradition but in the vision of a modern space in which the individual was at liberty to go about his or her business free from the threat of (verbal or physical) interruption and the prospect of an encounter with disturbing violence (be that to a human being or to an animal), this was an antique, and increasingly disagreeable prospect. They sought order, tidiness, and an opportunity to lead a decorous life, in order that they might better prepare on earth for the paradise to which they aspired *post mortem*. As a consequence, they were genuinely discommoded when they were obliged to negotiate a way through a thronging crowd that had gath-ered in a public space to participate in a bull beat, or other objectionable recre-ational activity, and increasingly scandalised when, instead of observing the third commandment to keep the Sabbath holy, elements of the populace routinely and cavalierly engaged in such or other equally objectionable practices on the Lord's Day.[20] Having in the 1690s, with limited effect, followed the example of Westminster and aspired to proscribe those sports that were the occasion of large gatherings, the Irish establishment declined to imitate the British legislature by

Anglo-Irish experience, 1680–1730 (Woodbridge, 2012), pp 174–98.   **18** Barnard, *A new anatomy*, chapter 9; Kelly, 'Duelling and the emergence of an Irish middle class', pp 89–107.   **19** Oliver MacDonagh, *The inspector general: Sir Jeremiah Fitzpatrick and the politics of social reform, 1783–1802* (London, 1981); idem, *A pattern of government growth, 1800–60: the Passenger Acts and their enforcement* (London, 1961); Palmer, *Police and protest in England and Ireland, 1780–1850*, passim; David Dickson, 'In search of the old Irish poor law' in Mitchison and Roebuck (eds), *Economy and society in Scotland and Ireland, 1500–1939*, pp 149–59; D.H. Akenson, *The Irish education experi-ment: the national system of education in the nineteenth century* (London, 1970); Paul Bew, *Ireland: the politics of enmity, 1789–2006* (Oxford, 2006), part 1; Brailsford, *A taste for diversions*, p. 181.   **20** Public letter censuring the playing of games and sports on Sundays, *FJ*, 28 Mar. 1767.

enacting a Sunday Observance Act (1781), or by promulgating a proclamation for 'the preventing and punishing of vice, profaneness and immorality' (1787) on the Sabbath day.[21] Yet by the 1780s the expanding ranks of Irish respectability were as convinced as their more numerous English equivalent that games ought not to be played on Sundays, and that 'barbarous' sports such as bull-baiting, throwing at cocks and cockfighting ought to be prohibited.[22] It is a measure of their influence, moreover, that they were more successful than their English peers in bringing the national and local press round to their point of view, since this was a critical step in the marginalisation of the sports to which they objected.[23] They aspired with equal conviction to promote a reformation in manners that would encourage those of the *hoi polloi* who gambled their hard-earned pennies on a sweated cockerel or risked all on the toss of a coin to forswear the evil habit of gambling, their predilection for expletives and imprecations, and their willingness to risk limb (if not life) in violent physical sporting activity because, they earnestly believed, these practices possessed no intrinsic cultural or aesthetic merit or personal benefit, and were probably offensive in the eyes of God. Impelled in Ireland, as in England, by the conviction that it was to society's betterment that municipal officials controlled urban greens, commons, squares and roads, so that these were no longer contested spaces where virtually anything went, but public places of easeful congregation and movement, their aspiration was vividly articulated by a gentleman of property who expostulated angrily in 1770, that he wished simply to be allowed go about his business free from the prospect of inconvenient and unscheduled interruption caused by 'wanton, idle vagabonds, worrying a poor bull to madness ... miscreants playing pitch and toss', and the like.[24]

Besides the press, which provided those who embraced such opinions with an expanding and increasingly influential platform from which to articulate and to advance their campaign, and which gave them a tangible advantage in the all-important public sphere,[25] the ranks of respectability possessed a dependable ally in the officers of municipal government, who shared this vision of a tamed public arena. Moreover, local officials were crucial to the capacity to progress towards this goal. A significant step in this direction was taken when a number of contentious traditional sports were consigned to the urban margins, since it served to push these objectionable activities largely out of sight. This sufficed for a time, but it was seldom enough. As a result, when marginalisation had been achieved, the serried ranks of the respectable did not let up; once they had arrived at the

21 Barnard, 'Reforming Irish manners: the religious societies in Dublin during the 1690s', pp 805–38; D.W. Hayton, 'Moral reform and country politics in the late seventeenth-century House of Commons', *Past and Present*, 128 (1990), pp 48–91; 21 Geo. III, chap. 39; Brailsford, *A taste for diversions*, p. 82. 22 *FJ*, 28 Mar. 1767; above, pp 192–200, 215–18, 229–30, 279, 323. 23 Brailsford, *A taste for diversions*, pp 61–2; Griffin, *England's revelry*, pp 111, 122–5; above, pp 200–1. 24 Griffin, *England's revelry*, chapters 3 and 4 passim; *FJ*, 8 Sept. 1770. 25 Munter, *History of the newspaper*, passim; James Kelly, 'Political publishing, 1700–1800' in Gillespie and Hadfield (eds), *The history of the book iii, early modern Ireland*, pp 218–31.

conclusion that a sport was 'barbarous', they were not disposed to rest until it was banned and suppressed. Beginning with the throwing at cocks, a number of venerable blood sports (bull-baiting and cockfighting, most notably) were forced out of the public arena and then made illegal. The die was already cast by the time a ban on abusing animals negotiated entry onto the statute book in 1835, but whereas previous interventions had largely failed for want of policing capacity, the fact that the state now possessed, in the form of a constabulary, the means of enforcing the law meant that the opportunities for evasion, and for survival were diminished accordingly, and most blood sports were soon so reduced that they survived in an attenuated form, if at all, and then largely underground. This was not the case, of course, with each and every sport with which respectable opinion entertained reservations. Hurling, football, long bullets, to name only three, survived to embrace the rules and organisational changes in the late nineteenth century that would permit them to flourish in the modern era, either because they possessed a more loyal constituency, or more usually because they did not excite the same degree of antipathy.

Still others changed profoundly. Indeed, this was the price of survival in certain instances, though it was not always sufficient, and, as exemplified by the case of bull-baiting, could be both too little and too late.[26] Organisation was another crucial consideration. Horse racing was the first sport to demonstrate the value of organisation, though in Ireland, as in England, it took a long time for the sport at large to acknowledge that it was in its interest to have a body (the Jockey Club) that both set and applied the rules and standards by which the sport was conducted, and served as an arbitrator when, as inevitably happened, differences defied swift resolution.[27] Their prolonged gestation notwithstanding, horse racing highlighted just how important it was to the development of a sport to have an agreed code of rules; it effectively defined what was a modern (as opposed to a traditional) sport, and established a precedent that others were obliged to follow if they were to survive and prosper. Yet organisation alone, as the example of cockfighting attests, did not guarantee survival. It required a complex of factors that were either not available or not availed of in all instances, with the result that it was quite apparent before the end of the eighteenth century that the varied menu of sporting options available in Ireland was contracting. Like the rise in interest that extended across the half-century which spanned the final decades of the seventeenth and the early decades of the eighteenth centuries, the attenuation that hastened the end of an era was extended over a number of generations, but it had reached a critical point by the 1830s when a number of the sports that had decorated the eighteenth-century sporting landscape had either already disappeared or were in terminal decline. The situation was observed by James Boyle, the Ordnance Survey memoirist for Carrickfergus, county Antrim. Reporting on the town and its vicinity in 1839, he noted:

26 Above, pp 228–33.   27 Kelly, 'The pastime of the elite', pp 417–23; Huggins, *Flat racing and British society*, pp 174–80.

> The taste for amusement has among all classes within a few years greatly declined, and many of their ancient and favourite games have fallen into disuse ... Horse racing, bull-baiting and bullet-playing etc.,[28] which were annually practised within the ... district or parish, time immemorial, ceased almost altogether 20 years ago ... The only amusements at present prevailing are cockfighting at Loughmourne on May Eve, ball-playing at a certain ball court in the Scotch Quarter. Dancing and other trivial practices among the youth of both sexes are held Easter Monday and May Eve ... about half a mile north east of the town.[29]

The change was so complete in north-east Ulster that memoirs for different parts of county Antrim echoed to the refrain that 'the taste for amusement and recreation has here, as everywhere else, declined within the last dozen years'.[30] And, as if to corroborate these observations, it was commonly remarked not only that specific sports (horse racing, bull-baiting, long bullets, cockfighting, commons, football) were in decline, but also, as evidenced by the parish of Kilbrony, county Down, that 'there are no public places of amusement'.[31] The reasons given for the diminished recourse to recreational pursuits differed. It was observed *à propos* of the parishes of Billy and Kilraghts in north county Antrim that 'cards and cock-fighting are held as disgraceful'. This sentiment had yet to achieve attitudinal ascendancy, but it had already made such a deep impression on those Presbyterian communities that had embraced a more conservative theology,[32] that there were locations where it was simply socially unacceptable for members of that communion to pursue such recreations. Saliently, it was observed in 1833 of the parish of Tullrusk, south Antrim, that the 'little cock-fighting' that was engaged in was 'confined to the Roman Catholics', and of the mid-county Antrim of parish of Kirkinriola that it was 'only resorted to by the more profligate'.[33]

If the identification of cockfighting as a sport that was pursued by Catholics and the morally challenged hastened its decline in those areas of Ulster where Protestants and Presbyterians perceived of themselves as not only religiously different, but also socially and morally superior to Catholics, sport more generally

---

28 Elsewhere he mentions 'the game of common ...', which was formerly very energetically kept up among the men at Christmas': Day and McWilliams (eds), *Ordnance survey memoirs, county Antrim*, xxxvii, 77.   29 Day and McWilliams (eds), *Ordnance survey memoirs, county Antrim*, xxxvii, 54, 175.
30 These, or comparable, sentiments were articulated with reference to the parishes of Carnmoney, Mallusk, and Templecorran: Day and McWilliams (eds), *Ordnance survey memoirs, county Antrim*, ii, 62, 113, xxxvi, 106.   31 As notes 18, 19; Day and McWilliams (eds), *Ordnance survey memoirs, county Antrim*, ii, 9, 63; Day and McWilliams (eds), *Ordnance survey memoirs, county Down*, iii, 37.
32 Ian MacBride, 'Memory and forgetting: Ulster Presbyterians and 1798' in Thomas Bartlett et al. (eds), *1798: a bicentenary* (Dublin, 2003), pp 478–96; Peter Brooke, *Ulster Presbyterianism: the historical perspective* (Dublin, 1987), pp 145–53; Holmes, *The shaping of Ulster Presbyterianism*, passim.   33 Day and McWilliams (eds), *Ordnance survey memoirs, county Antrim*, xvi, 48, 129, xxi, 138, xxiii, 107.

was dealt a serious blow across the province and beyond by the clergy of all denominations who frowned equally upon cockfighting, card-playing, football, dancing and other recreations 'from the supposition that they have a de-moralizing tendency'.[34] It is improbable that the clergy of any denomination could have compelled a congregation or community to forsake a recreation or recreations if other societal forces were not also at play, though it may be that it was decisive in those instances in which the interventions of priests or clergy were singled out for particular mention.[35] But there were powerful economic forces also at work. By the 1830s, the once-buoyant Ulster rural economy was suffering as the impact of mechanization and re-organization obliged the once-sturdily independent linen weavers of the eastern parts of the province and the more vulnerable spinners of the south and west to work longer hours for less financial reward.[36] Writing of the grange of Mallusk in south county Antrim in the late 1830s, James Boyle glossed his by now familiar observation about the decline in 'the taste for amusement' with a reference to the fact that people no longer had the time to play: 'all their industrious exertions and energies are called forth to meet the pressure of the times and to cope with the decline in prices'.[37] The 'pressure of the times', the 'want of the means of enjoying themselves', the lack of 'time' and the diminished 'observance of festivals and holy days', which had long facilitated recreational and sporting activity, had a tangibly dampening impact on social life in rural Ulster and elsewhere in the early nineteenth century, but it served to accent change that was already under way rather than to initiate it.[38] Moreover, it was warmly embraced by those who were of the opinion that traditional habits, of which the pattern and wake games were singled out for especial attention, and sport were equally 'inimical to industry in the southern part of Ireland'.[39] The transformation that was taking place certainly diminished the disposition to pursue recreational activity, but because it was not matched by an equivalent increase in industrial employment, its impact on economic activity was negligible.[40]

There were, to be sure other, more perspicacious individuals who recognised the 'great advantage to the population generally' that would accrue if it was in a

34 Day and McWilliams (eds), *Ordnance survey memoirs, county Down*, iii, 37.   **35** Day and McWilliams (eds), *Ordnance survey memoirs, county Antrim*, xiii, 8, xxiii, 16, xix, 104.   **36** See Liam Kennedy, 'The rural economy, 1820–1914' in idem and Philip Ollerenshaw (eds), *An economic history of Ulster, 1820–1940* (Manchester, 1985), pp 1–61; Brenda Collins, 'Proto-industrialization and pre-Famine emigration', *Social History*, 7 (1982), pp 127–46; K.J. James, *Handloom weavers in Ulster's linen industry, 1815–1914* (Dublin, 2006).   **37** Day and McWilliams (eds), *Ordnance survey memoirs, county Antrim*, ii, 113.   **38** Day and McWilliams (eds), *Ordnance survey memoirs, county Antrim*, ii, 9, 62, xxvi, 106; Day and McWilliams (eds), *Ordnance survey memoirs, county Londonderry*, xi, 10–11.   **39** Day and McWilliams (eds), *Ordnance survey memoirs, county Down*, xii, 126.   **40** See Cormac Ó Gráda, *Ireland before and after the famine: explorations in economic history, 1800–1925* (Manchester, 1988); idem, *Ireland before and after the famine: explorations in economic history, 1800–1925* (Oxford, 1994), part 1; E.L. Almquist, 'Labour specialization and the Irish economy in 1841: an aggregate occupational analysis', *Economic History Review*, 2nd series, 36 (1983), pp 506–17.

position to engage in appropriate 'manly sports by daylight under the direction of moral and respected persons'.[41] This was not a practical possibility then but the ingredients were already there. The island supported a number of organised sports (horse racing and hunting), unstructured demotic sports (hurling, football), while the growth of cricket demonstrated the potential of team activity if it was organised on modern principles. Furthermore, based on the evidence of the early modern era, it also harboured a strongly beating sporting pulse. There was no reason, if these forces were properly harnessed, why recreational sport could not extricate itself from the essentially depressed state in which it stood as Victoria ascended the throne.

Recovery could not be assumed, of course, and when it came it was to be heavily reliant on the organisational model pioneered in the global Anglo-Saxon world. Be that as it may, the varying fortunes of the many diversions pursued during the Stuart and Hanoverian eras demonstrate that sports, like nations, rise and decline, and that as some die and others change to survive, still others are born. Late early modern Ireland witnessed the eclipse of a number of essentially elite pastimes that were a legacy of the medieval era, the rise, *floruit*, and decline of a number of (mainly blood) sports, the see-saw fortunes of a number of team and fighting sports, and the emergence of one truly modern sporting phenomenon – horse racing. It also demonstrated that the sporting impulse, if not irrepressible, was certainly resilient, which was critical as the 'long transmutation of play from forms rooted in medieval chivalry and Renaissance manner on the one hand and rustic ritual on the other into sport that was organised, regulated, largely self-contained and often commercialised' was serpentine, and, in Ireland at least, still incomplete.[42] It was not clear *c.*1840 what the sporting landscape would look like in Ireland when that journey's end was reached, since other than horse racing and, perhaps cricket (on which the jury was still out), no sport had taken the organisational steps required to prosper in the era of mass recreational activity that was on the horizon. Yet the desire to play sport was engrained, and the population had amply demonstrated its receptivity to ideas from abroad. Moreover, there were a number of sports, which were potentially ideally suited to the era of team sport that the impending sporting revolution prioritised. In any event, if the experience of the seventeenth, eighteenth and early nineteenth centuries was any guide, it demonstrated that the sporting landscape would continue to evolve in a manner that reflected the values of the ascendant and other interests in society, the economy, social mores, and the prevailing *zeitgeist*. This was the case then, and it remains the case today.

41 Day and McWilliams (eds), *Ordnance survey memoirs, county Londonderry*, xi, 109.   42 Brailsford, *A taste for diversions*, p. 50.

Bibliography

PRIMARY SOURCES

I: MANUSCRIPTS

Armagh Public Library
Lodge collection: Survey of county Wicklow, *c.*1760 (MS KI, II, 14)
Lodge collection: Robert Ware, 'The history and antiquities of Dublin, collected from authentic records and the manuscript collections of Sir James Ware', *c.*1678 (MS H II)

Boston Public Library
Townshend papers, MS Eng.180

National Archives of Ireland
Blathwayt-May correspondence, 1697–9 (MS 3070)
Calendar of miscellaneous letters and papers prior to 1760
State of the Country papers, 1031/52

National Library of Ireland
Agreement to establish four plate races at Dunmore, county Kilkenny, 8 Oct. 1731 (MS 22427)
Killadoon papers (MS 36030)
Reports on private collections, no. 351: Baker papers
Walsh news-cuttings (MS 14026)

National Library of Scotland
Murray archive: John Murray's memorandum book, 1775 (MS 43018C)

National Library of Wales
Puleston papers (MSS 3579, 3584)

New York Public Library
Trumbull papers (MSS Col 3039)

Public Record Office of Northern Ireland
Ker papers (D2651)
Villiers-Stuart papers (T3131/C/5/47)

Royal Irish Academy
Diary of Judge Robert day, 1802 (MS 12.W.11)

The National Archives, Kew
Minutes of revenue commissioners, 1722 (CUST1/16)

Trinity College Dublin
Barker–Ponsonby papers (P3)
Conolly papers (MSS 3974–84)

2. PRINTED PRIMARY MATERIAL: MEMOIRS, MINUTE BOOKS, JOURNALS,
LETTERS, DESCRIPTIONS AND DOCUMENTS

Barrington, Jonah, *Personal sketches of his own time* (3 vols, London, 1827–32).

Berenger: 'Memoir of Gabriel Berenger and his labours in the cause of Irish art', ed. W.R. Wilde, *Journal of the Royal Historical and Archaeological Association of Ireland [JRSAI]* 4th series, 1(1870–1), pp 33–64, 121–52, 236–60.

Bradstreet: *The life and uncommon adventures of Captain Dudley Bradstreet*, ed. G.S. Taylor (London, [1929]).

Carrick-on-Suir: 'A Carrickman's [James Ryan] diary, 1787–1809', ed. Patrick Power, *Journal of the Waterford and South-East of Ireland Archaeological Society*, 14 (1911), pp 97–102, 145–50; 15 (1912), pp 39–7, 62–70, 124–37; 16 (1913), pp 18–27, 74–85, 176–82; 17 (1914), pp 4–16, 120–7.

Catholics: *Catholics in the eighteenth-century press*, ed. John Brady (Maynooth, 1966).

Cork: *Council book of the corporation of Cork from 1609 to 1643 and from 1690 to 1800*, ed. Richard Caulfield (Guilford, 1876).

Cumberland: *Memoirs of Richard Cumberland* (2 vols, London, 1807).

Cunningham: *The life of Patrick Cunningham* (Belfast, 1806).

Delany: *Autobiography and correspondence of Mrs Delany*, ed. Lady Llanover (6 vols, London, 1861–2).

De Montbret: 'Coquebert de Montbret's impressions of Galway city and county in the year 1791', ed. Síle Ní Chinnéide, *Journal of the Galway Archaeological and Historical Society*, 25 (1952), pp 1–14.

Dineley: 'Extracts from the journal of Thomas Dineley', ed. E.P. Shirley, *Journal of the Kilkenny and South East of Ireland Archaeological Society*, new series 1 (1856–7), pp 143–6, 170–88; 2 (1858), pp 22–32, 55–6.

Donegal: Dorian, Hugh, *The outer edge of Ulster: a memoir of social life in nineteenth-century Donegal*, eds Breandán MacSuibhne and David Dickson (Dublin, 2000).

Drogheda: *Council book of the Corporation of Drogheda*, ed. T. Gogarty (Drogheda, 1915).

Duhallow Hunt: 'Extracts from old minute book of Duhallow Hunt, 1800 to 1808', ed. James Grove-White, *Journal of the Cork Historical and Archaeological Society*, second series, 2 (1896), pp 1–8.

Dunton: John Dunton, *Teague land: or a merry ramble to the wild Irish: letters from Ireland, 1698*, ed. Edward McLysaght (Dublin, 1982).

Dunton: John Dunton, *Teague land, or a merry ramble (1698)*, ed. Andrew Carpenter (Dublin, 2003).

Farrell: *Carlow in 1798: an autobiography of William Farrell of Carlow*, ed. R.J. McHugh (Dublin, 1949).

Gort: 'A description of Gort in 1752 by Thomas Wetherall', ed. Toby Barnard, *Journal of the Galway Archaeological and Historical* Society, 61 (2009), pp 107–14.

Higgins: *Revolutionary Dublin 1795–1801: the letters of Francis Higgins to Dublin Castle*, ed. Thomas Bartlett (Dublin, 2004).

Horse racing: 'Horse racing in Antrim in 1710', *UJA*, second series, 7 (1901), p. 158.

Hunting: 'Miscellanea', *Journal of the Kildare Archaeological and Historical Society*, 10 (1922–8), pp 154–5.

Longford: 'Survey of documents in private keeping: Longford papers', ed. Edward McLysaght, *Analecta Hibernica*, 15 (1944), pp 109–27.

Meath: Tom French (ed.), *Meath Anthology* (Navan, 2010).

Neville: *The diary of Sylas Neville, 1767–88*, ed. Basil Cozens-Hardy (Oxford, 1950).

Newsmen: *The newsmen of Queen Anne*, ed. W.B. Ewald (Oxford, 1956).

Northern Rangers Hunt: 'Records of the Northern Rangers Hunt Club, Dundalk, 1774', ed. J.R. Garstin, *Journal of the county Louth Archaeological Society*, 5 (1924), pp 233–7.

O'Sullivan: *Cinnlae Amhlaoibh Uí Súilleabháin: the diary of Humphrey O'Sullivan …1827–36*, ed. Michael McGrath (Irish Texts Society: 4 vols, London, 1928–31).

Pepys: *The diary of Samuel Pepys*, eds Robert Latham and William Matthews (10 vols, London, 1970–83).

Rowan: *The autobiography of Archibald Hamilton Rowan*, ed. William H. Drummond, introduction R.B. McDowell (repr., Shannon, 1972).

Tennent: 'The journal of John Tennent, 1786–90', ed. Leanne Calvert, *Analecta Hibernica*, 43 (2012), pp 69–128.

Tone: *The writings of Wolfe Tone, 1763–98*, eds T.W. Moody, R.B. McDowell and C.J. Woods (3 vols, Oxford, 1998–2007).

Ulster songs: Énri Ó Muireasa, eag. *Céad de Cheolta Uladh* (2nd ed., Newry, 1983).

Ulster songs: Énri Ó Muireasa, eag., *Dha chéad de Cheoltaibh Uladh* (Baile Átha Cliath, 1934).

Young: *Arthur Young's tour in Ireland*, ed. A.W. Hutton (2 vols, London, 1892).

3. PAMPHLETS AND OTHER CONTEMPORARY PUBLICATIONS

A full and true account of a furious and bloody battle which was fought on Sunday the 28th day of February, 1724–5 in Oxmantown Green, between the mob of the town and the standing army (Dublin, 1724–5).

An ordinance prohibiting cock-matches (London, 1654).

Brookes, Richard, *The art of angling … in two parts … illustrated …* (Dublin, 1778).

Bullingbrooke, Edward and Jonathan Belcher, *An abridgement of the statutes of Ireland … to the end of the 25 years of the reign of …King George II* (Dublin, 1754).

Clemency to brutes: the substance of two sermons preached on a Shrove-Tuesday, with a particular view to dissuade from that species of cruelty annually practised, the throwing of cocks (London, 1761; Dublin, 1769).

Concanen, Matthew, *A match at foot-ball: a poem in three cantos* (Dublin, 1720).

Concanen, Matthew, *A match at foot-ball, or the Irish champions: a mock heroick poem in three cantos* (London, 1721).

Concanen, Matthew, *Poems upon several occasions, by the author of the match at foot-ball* (Dublin, 1722).

Cotton, Charles, *The compleat gamester: or, instructions how to play at billiards, trucks, bowls, and chess, together with all manner of usual and most gentile games either on cards or dice, to which is added, the arts and mysteries of riding, racing, archery, and cock-fighting* (London, 1674).

Crofton Croker, Thomas, *Fairy legends and traditions of the south of Ireland* (London, 1825).

Crofton Croker, Thomas, *Legends and lakes of Killarney* (2 vols, London, 1829).

Crofton Croker, Thomas, ed., *Killarney legends* (London, 1831).

Delany, Patrick, *The Tribune* (Dublin, 1729).

Dutton, Hely, *Statistical survey of county Clare* (Dublin, 1801).

Egan, Pierce, *Boxiana, or sketches of ancient and modern pugilism*, vol. 1 (London, 1830).

Fairfax, Thomas, *The complete sportsman: or country gentleman's recreation, containing the very best instructions under the following head, viz., of breeding and the management of game cocks …* (Dublin, 1764).

Falkland [J.R. Scott], *A review of the principal characters of the Irish House of Commons* (Dublin, 1789).

Goldsmith, Oliver, *History of the earth and animated nature* (6 vols, London, 1774).

Gibson, William, *A new treatise on the diseases of horses …* (3rd ed., Dublin, 1755).

Hall, A.M and S.C., *Ireland, its scenery, character etc* (new ed., 3 vols, London, [1845]).

Harris, Walter and Charles Smith, *The ancient and present state of county Down* (Dublin, 1744).

Heber, Reginald, *An historical list of horse matches run, and of plates and prizes run in Great Britain and Ireland in 1751* (London, 1752).

Herbert, William, *Irish varieties* (Dublin, 1836).

Hints to young sportsmen on the art of shooting (London, 1829).

H[owlett], R[obert], *The royal pastime of cock-fighting ... to which is prefixed a short treatise, wherein cocking is proved not only ancient and honourable, but also useful, and profitable* (London, 1709; reprint ed., Liss, 1973).

Hoyle, Edmond, *A short treatise of the game of brag, containing the laws of the game* (Dublin, 1751).

Hoyle, Edmond, *A short treatise of the game of back-gammon ...* (Dublin, 1753).

Hoyle, Edmond, *A short treatise of the game of quadrille, shewing the odds of winning or losing most games that are commonly played* (Dublin, 1754).

Hoyle, Edmond, *A short treatise of the game of whist, containing the laws of the game* (Dublin, 1762).

James, Robert, *The sportsman's pocket companion: being a striking likeness or portraiture of the most eminent race horses and stallions, that ever were in this kingdom ...* (London, [1760]).

Madden, Samuel, *Reflections and resolutions proper for the gentlemen of Ireland, as to their conduct for the service of their country, as landlords, as masters of families ...* (Dublin, 1738).

Markham, Gervase, *Country contentments, or, the husbandman's recreations: containing the wholesome experience, in which any ought to recreate himself, after the toyl of more serious business ...* (4th ed., London, 1631).

Maxwell, W.H., *Wild sports of the west* (2 vols, London, 1832).

Mozeen, Thomas, *A collection of miscellaneous essays* (London, 1762).

Newland, Henry, *The Erne: its legends and its fly-fishing* (London, 1851).

O'Gorman, *The practice of angling, particularly as regards Ireland* (Dublin, 1845).

Pancratia, or a history of pugilism, containing a full account of every battle of note from the times of Broughton and Slack, down to the present day (London, 1812).

Proctor, Henry, *The sportsman's sure guide, or gamester's vade-mecum, shewing the exact odds at horse-racing ...the whole forming a complete guide to the turf, the cock-pit, the card table* (Dublin, 1774).

Sharkey, Pat, *Irish racing calendar; containing an account of the plates, matches, and sweepstakes, run for in Ireland, in the year* (Dublin, 1790).

Shaw Mason, William, *A statistical account or parochial survey of Ireland* (3 vols, Dublin, 1814–19).

Stringer, Arthur, *The experience'd huntsman, or, a collection of observations upon the nature and chace of the stagg, buck, hare, fox, martern [sic] and otter. With ... directions concerning the breeding and entring of hounds: also the qualifications and conduct of an huntsman, and instructions to a park-keeper, all gathered from the experience of thirty years practice* (Belfast, 1714, 2nd ed., Dublin 1780).

Stringer, Arthur, *The experience'd huntsman*, ed. James Fairley (Belfast, 1977).

Strutt, Joseph, *The sports and pastimes of the people of England* (2nd edn, London, 1810).

Temple, William, 'Essay upon the advancement of trade in Ireland', in *The works of Sir William Temple in two volumes, to which is prefixed the life and character of Sir William Temple ...* (2 vols, London, 1740), i, 109–21.

The articles and orders agreed upon by the Corporation of horse-breeders in the county of Down, the 21 day of February 1703, to be kept and observed by all persons who shall bring a horse, mare or gelding of what size so ever, to run for the great and less plates given by the said Corporation; and also by all persons who shall be present at such horse-race (Dublin, 1703/4]. There is a copy of this title in the Beinecke Library, Yale University.

The angler in Ireland, or an Englishman's ramble through Connaught and Munster, during the summer of 1833 (2 vols, London, 1834).

The angling excursions of Gregory Greendrake in the counties of Wicklow, Meath, Westmeath, Longford and Cavan (Dublin, 1832).

The pack of bear dogs (Dublin, 1713).

The present state of Ireland (London, 1676).

The sportsman's dictionary, or the gentlemen's companion, for town and country, containing full and particular instructions for riding, hunting, fowling, setting, fishing, racing, farriery, cocking hawking etc, with the various methods to be observed in bleeding and dieting of horses, both for the road and turf ... (Dublin, 1780, 1786, 1792).

The trial of James Vance, esquire, one of the high sheriffs of the city of Dublin, on Thursday, the 25th February 1790, at the commissioner of oyer and terminer ... (Dublin, 1790).

Tuckey, Francis H., *The county and city of Cork remembrancer, or annals of the county and city of Cork* (Cork, 1837).

The universal sportsman or, nobleman, gentleman, and farmer's dictionary of recreation and amusement ... (Dublin, [1795]).

Wakefield, Edward, *An account of Ireland, statistical and political* (2 vols, London, 1812).

[Walsh, John Edward], *Sketches of Ireland sixty years ago* (Dublin, 1847).

Wilson, George, *The commendation of cockes, and cock-fighting, wherein is shewed, that cocke-fighting was before the comming of Christ* (London, 1607).

4: RECORD PUBLICATIONS AND SERIES

Calendar of ancient records of Dublin, eds Sir John and Lady Gilbert (19 vols, Dublin, 1889–1944).

Calendar of the Rosse papers, ed. A.P.W. Malcomson (Irish Manuscripts Commission: Dublin, 2008).

Council books of the corporation of Waterford, 1662–1700, ed. Seamus Pender (Irish Manuscripts Commission: Dublin, 1964).

Inchiquin manuscripts, ed. Sir John Ainsworth (Irish Manuscripts Commission: Dublin, 1961).

Ordnance survey memoirs of Ireland, eds Angelique Day and Patrick McWilliams (40 vols, Institute of Irish Studies: Belfast, 1990–8).

The Clements archive, ed. A.P.W. Malcomson (Irish Manuscripts Commission: Dublin, 2008).

The Conolly archive, eds Patrick Walsh and A.P.W. Malcomson (Irish Manuscripts Commission, Dublin, 2010).

The proclamations of Ireland, 1660–1820, eds James Kelly with Mary-Ann Lyons (5 vols, Irish Manuscripts Commission: Dublin, 2014).

5. NEWSPAPERS AND PERIODICALS

Anthologia Hibernica, 1793–4

Belfast News Letter, 1739–92

Catholic Directory, 1865

Clonmel Gazette, 1788–94

Cork Advertiser, 1801, 1812, 1818

Cork Courir, 1794

Cork Evening Post, 1758, 1769

Cork Gazette, 1790–1, 1793, 1796

Corke Journal, 1755

Dublin Chronicle, 1770

Dublin Chronicle, 1787–90, 1792

Dublin Courant, 1747–9, 1751

Dublin Daily Advertizer, 1737

Dublin Evening Post, 1732–5

Dublin Evening Post, 1779, 1786, 1799

Dublin Gazette, 1708, 1710, 1726–7, 1732–3, 1739, 1741–3, 1760, 1763, 1765, 1775

Dublin Gazette or Weekly Courant, 1727

Dublin Intelligence, 1710, 1719, 1731
Dublin Morning Post, 1785
Dublin Mercury, 1766
Dublin Newsletter, 1738, 1743
Dublin Weekly Journal, 1730, 1748, 1790–1
Ennis Chronicle, 1789–94, 1818–9
Faulkner's Dublin Journal, 1729–44, 1747–9, 1778
Finn's Leinster Journal, 1767–81, 1783, 1786–95, 1797–9, 1801–33
Flying Post, or the Postmaster, 1708
Freeman's Journal, 1763–77, 1779–93, 1799–1825, 1827–30, 1833, 1836–9, 1841, 1847
Hibernian Journal, 1771–82, 1784, 1786–95
Hoey's Publick Journal, 1770–76
Hume's Dublin Courant, 1719

Munster Journal, 1749–54, 1759, 1789
Public Gazetteer, 1759–69
Pue's Occurrences, 1718, 1729–59
Saunders Newsletter, 1785–6
The Anglo-Celt, 1851
The Constitution, or the anti-Union, 1799–1800
The Sporting Magazine, Aug. 1792
Tuam Herald, 1845
United Ireland, 1884
Universal Advertiser, 1753–63
Volunteer Evening Post, 1784, 1787
Volunteer Journal (Cork), 1783, 1785–6
Whalley's Newsletter, 1719–22
Whitehall Gazette, 1727

6. PARLIAMENTARY PROCEEDINGS, STATUTES

A collection of acts for the preservation of the game (Dublin, 1785).
A collection of acts for the preservation of the game (Dublin, 1794).
The parliamentary register or history of the proceedings and debates of the Irish parliament (17 vols, Dublin, 1782–1801).
Proceedings of the Irish House of Lords, 1771–1800, ed. James Kelly (3 vols, Dublin, 2008).
Statutes of the realm ed. A. Luders (11 vols in 12, London, 1810–28).
The statutes at large passed in the parliaments held in Ireland 1310–1800 (20 vols, Dublin, 1789–1800).

7. IRISH HISTORIC TOWN ATLAS

Clarke, H.B., *Irish historic towns atlas no. 11: Dublin, part 1, to 1610* (Dublin, 2002).
Gearty, Sarah, Martin Morris and Fergus O'Ferrall, *Irish historic towns atlas no. 22: Longford* (Dublin, 2010).
Gillespie, Raymond and Harold O'Sullivan, *Irish historic towns atlas no. 23: Carlingford* (Dublin, 2011).*Irish historic town atlas, volume I: Kildare, Carrickfergus, Bandon, Kells, Mullingar, Athlone* (Dublin, 1996).
Irish historic town atlas, volume II: Maynooth, Downpatrick, Bray, Kilkenny, Fethard, Trim (Dublin, 2005).
Irish historic town atlas, volume III: Derry-Londonderry, Dundalk, Armagh, Tuam, Limerick (Dublin, 2012).
Lennon, Colm, *Irish historic towns atlas no. 19: Dublin, part 2, 1610 to 1756* (Dublin, 2008).
O'Flaherty, Eamon, *Irish historic towns atlas no. 21: Limerick* (Dublin, 2010).

SECONDARY SOURCES

PUBLISHED WORKS

Anon., 'Answer to queries: bullbaiting', *UJA*, 8 (1860), pp 236–7.
Anon., 'Answer to queries: bullbaiting', *UJA*, 9 (1861–2), p. 148.

Anon., 'Dr Caulfield's notes on Cork events in 1769 and 1781', *Journal of the Cork Archaeological and Historical Society*, 11 (1905), pp 138–47.

Anon., 'Local historic scraps', *UJA*, 2nd series, 14 (1908), p. 135.

Anon., 'Proceedings and papers', *Journal of the Royal Historical and Archaeological Association of Ireland [JRSAI]*, 4th series, iii (1874–5), p. 154.

Anon., 'Some attention to the naval line, 1781', *Irish Sword*, 9 (1969–71), pp 75–6.

Akenson, D.H., *The Irish education experiment: the national system of education in the nineteenth century* (London, 1970).

Almquist, E.L., 'Labour specialization and the Irish economy in 1841: an aggregate occupational analysis', *Economic History Review*, 2nd series, 36 (1983), pp 506–17.

Andrew, Keith, *The handbook of cricket* (London, 1989).

Ashton, J., *The history of gambling in England* (London, 1898).

Ball, F.E., *A history of the county of Dublin, part 4* (Dublin, 1906).

Barker-Benfield, C.J., *The culture of sensibility: sex and society in eighteenth-century Britain* (Chicago, 2002).

Barnard, T.C., *Cromwellian Ireland: English government and reform in Ireland 1649–1660* (Oxford, 1975).

—, 'Planters and policies in Cromwellian Ireland', *Past and Present*, 61 (1973), pp 31–69.

—, 'The uses of 23 October 1641 and Irish Protestant celebrations', *English Historical Review*, 106 (1991), pp 889–920.

—, 'Reforming Irish manners: the religious societies in Dublin during the 1690s', *Historical Journal*, 35:4 (1992), pp 805–38.

—, 'The political, material and mental culture of the Cork settlers' in C.G. Buttimer et al. (eds), *Cork: history and society* (Dublin, 1993), pp 309–66.

—, 'The gentrification of eighteenth-century Ireland', *Eighteenth-century Ireland*, 12 (1997), pp 137–55.

—, *A new anatomy of Ireland: the Irish Protestants, 1649–1770* (London, 2003).

—, *A guide to sources for the history of material culture in Ireland, 1500–2000* (Dublin, 2004).

—, *Making the grand figure: lives and possessions in Ireland, 1641–1770* (London, 2004).

—, *Improving Ireland?: projectors, prophets and profiteers, 1641–1786* (Dublin, 2008).

—, 'The Dublin Society and other improving societies, 1731–85' in James Kelly and M.J. Powell (eds), *Clubs and societies in eighteenth-century Ireland* (Dublin, 2010), pp 53–88.

Bartlett, Thomas, 'The end of moral economy: the Irish militia disturbances of 1793', *Past and Present*, 91 (1983), pp 41–64.

—, *The fall and rise of the Irish nation: the Catholic question, 1690–1830* (Dublin, 1992).

Batty, Joseph, *Cock-fighting ban of Oliver Cromwell* (2nd edn., Midhurst, West Sussex, 2005).

Beacey, P., 'Prelude to a cockfight', *The Bell*, 11:1 (Oct. 1945), pp 574–6.

Beaver, Dan, 'The great deer massacre: animals, honor, and communication in early modern England', *Journal of British Studies*, 38 (1999), pp 187–216.

Benn, George, *History of Belfast* (Belfast, 1877).

Benson, Charles, 'The Dublin book trade' in J.H. Murphy (ed.), *History of the Irish book, volume 4: the nineteenth century* (Oxford, 2011), pp 27–46.

Bew, Paul, *Ireland: the politics of enmity, 1789–2006* (Oxford, 2006).

Blackstock, Allan, *An ascendancy army: the Irish yeomanry, 1796–1834* (Dublin, 1998).

Boddy, Kasia, '"Under Queensberry Rules, so to speak": some versions of a metaphor', *Sport in History*, 31:4 (2011), pp 398–422.

Bolton, G.C., *The passing of the Irish Act of Union* (Oxford, 1966).

Borsay, Peter, *A history of leisure: the British experience since 1500* (London, 2006).

Bowen, Desmond, *The Protestant crusade, 1800–70: a study of Protestant-Catholic relations between the Act of Union and disestablishment* (Dublin, 1978).

Bracken, Patrick, *'Foreign and fantastic field sports': cricket in county Tipperary* (Thurles, 2004).

Brailsford, Dennis, *Sport and society: Elizabeth to Anne* (London, 1969).

—, *Bareknuckles: a social history of prize fighting* (Cambridge, 1988).

—, *British sport: a social history* (Cambridge, 1992).

—, *A taste for diversions: sport in Georgian England* (Cambridge, 1999).

Broeker, Galen, *Rural disorder and police reform in Ireland, 1812–36* (London, 1970).

Brooke, Peter, *Ulster presbyterianism: the historical perspective* (Dublin, 1987).

Burke, Nuala T., 'An early modern Dublin suburb: the estate of Francis Aungier, earl of Longford', *Irish Geography*, 6:4 (1972), pp 365–85.

Burtchaell, Jack, 'British Irish news in the 1750s', *Decies*, 52 (1996), pp 13–38.

Canny, Nicholas, *Making Ireland British, 1580–1650* (Oxford, 2001).

Capp, Bernard, *England's culture wars: Puritan reformation and its enemies in the Interregnum, 1649–1660* (Oxford, 2012).

Chaloner, Desmond, 'County life in Meath, 1810–17: extracts from the Kingscourt journals', *Ríocht na Midhe*, 8 (1987), pp 16–31.

Clapson, Mark, *A bit of a flutter: popular gambling and English society, 1823–61* (Manchester, 1992).

Clark, J.C.D., *English society, 1688–1832: ideology, social structure, and political practice during the ancien regime* (Cambridge, 1985).

—, 'Whig tactics and parliamentary precedent: the English management of Irish politics', *Historical Journal*, 21 (1978), pp 275–301.

Clarke, Aidan, *The Old English in Ireland, 1625–42* (London, 1966).

Clarke, Frances, 'Matthew Concanen' in *DIB*, *sub nomine*.

Coleman, J., 'Hurling in the Co. Wexford in 1779', *Journal of the Waterford and South-East of Ireland Archaeological Society*, 12 (1909), pp 115–18.

Collins, Brenda, 'Proto-industrialization and pre-Famine emigration', *Social History*, 7 (1982), pp 127–46.

Connell, K.H., 'Illicit distillation' in idem, *Irish peasant society: four historical essays* (Oxford, 1968).

Connolly, S.J., 'Popular culture in pre-Famine Ireland' in C.J. Byrne and M. Henry (eds), *Talaimh an Eisc: Canadian and Irish essays* (Halifax, Nova Scotia, 1986), pp 12–28.

—, *Priests and people in pre-Famine Ireland* (Dublin, 1982),

—, 'Violence and order in the eighteenth century' in Paul Ferguson, Patrick O'Flanagan and Kevin Whelan (eds), *Rural Ireland 1600–1900: modernisation and change* (Cork, 1987), pp 42–61.

—, *Religion, law and power: the making of Protestant Ireland, 1660–1760* (Oxford, 1992).

—, '"Ag deanamh commanding": elite responses to popular culture, 1660–1850' in K.A. Miller and J.S. Donnelly (eds), *Irish popular culture, 1650–1850* (Dublin, 1998), pp 1–31.

—, 'Albion's fatal twigs: justice and law in the eighteenth century' in Rosalind Mitchison and Peter Roebuck (eds), *Economy and society in Scotland and Ireland, 1500–1939* (Edinburgh, 1988), pp 117–25.

—, *Divided kingdom: Ireland 1630–1800* (Oxford, 2008).

Costello, Con, *Kildare: saints, soldiers and horses* (Naas, 1991).

Craig, Maurice, *Dublin, 1660–1860: a social and architectural history* (Dublin, 1969).

Crawford, W.H., 'The political economy of linen: Ulster in the eighteenth century' in idem, *The impact of the domestic linen industry in Ulster* (Belfast, 2005), pp 86–104.

Cronin, Mike, William Murphy and Paul Rouse (eds), *The Gaelic Athletic Association 1884–2009* (Dublin, 2009).

Cullen, L.M., *An economic history of Ireland since 1660* (London, 1972).

—, *The emergence of modern Ireland 1600–1900* (London, 1981).

—, 'Economic development, 1690–1750', 'Economic development, 1750–1800' both in W.E. Vaughan and T.W. Moody (eds), *A new history of Ireland*, iv, *Eighteenth-century Ireland* (Oxford, 1986), pp 123–58, 159–95.

Curtin, Gerard, *West Limerick: crime, popular protest and society, 1820–1845* (Ballynahill, Co. Limerick, 2008).

Curtin, Winifred, 'The Saundersons of Castle Saunderson', *Breifne*, no. 39, 10 (2003), pp 94–108.

D'Arcy, Fergus, *Horses, lords and racing men: the Turf Club 1790–1990* (Kildare, 1991).

Davidoff, Leonore and Catherine Hall, *Family fortunes: men and women of the English middle class, 1780–1850* (London, 2002).

Davies, Mary, *That favourite resort: the story of Bray, county Wicklow* (Dublin, 2007).

de Burca, Marcus, *The GAA: a history* (Dublin, 1980).

de Hindeberg, Piaras, 'Seanchas as dúithche Paorach', *Bealoideas*, 13 (1940), pp 252–3.

Dickson, David, Cormac Ó Grada, and Stuart Daultrey, 'Hearth tax, household size and Irish population change, 1672–1821', *PRIA*, 82C (1982), pp 125–81.

—, 'In search of the old Irish poor law' in Peter Roebuck and Rosalind Mitchison (eds), *Economy and society in Scotland and Ireland, 1500–1939* (Edinburgh, 1988), pp 149–59.

—, 'The demographic implications of the growth of Dublin, 1650–1850' in Richard Lawton and Robert Lee (eds), *Urban population development in western Europe from the late-eighteenth to the early-twentieth century* (Liverpool, 1989), pp 178–89.

—, *Old world colony: Cork and south Munster, 1630–1830* (Cork, 2005).

—, 'Jacobitism in eighteenth-century Ireland: a Munster perspective', *Eire-Ireland*, 39:3 and 4 (2004), pp 38–99.

Donald, Diana, *Picturing animals in Britain, 1750–1850* (London, 2008).

Donnelly, J.S., 'The Whiteboys, 1761–65', *IHS*, 21 (1978–9), pp 20–55.

—, 'Irish agrarian rebellion: the Whiteboys of 1769–76', *PRIA*, 83C (1983), pp 293–331.

Ekirch, A. Roger, *Birthright: the true story that inspired* Kidnapped (London, 2012).

Fagan, Patrick, *The second city: Dublin 1700–1800* (Dublin, 1986).

—, 'The demography of Dublin in the eighteenth century', *Eighteenth-century Ireland*, 6 (1991), pp 121–56.

Falkiner, Caesar Litton, *Illustrations of Irish history and topography: mainly of the seventeenth century* (London, 1904).

Feehan, John, *Cuirrech life: the Curragh of Kildare* (Dublin, [2007]).

Finn, Tom, 'A race ball at Dingle in 1746', *The Kerry Magazine*, 12 (2001), pp 43–4.

Fleming, D.A., 'Diversions of the people: sociability among the orders of early eighteenth-century Ireland', *Eighteenth-Century Ireland*, 17 (2002), pp 99–111.

—, 'Clubs and societies in eighteenth-century Munster' in Kelly and Powell (eds), *Clubs and societies in eighteenth-century Ireland*, pp 427–46.

Fogarty, Philip, *Tipperary's GAA story* (Thurles, 1960).

Ford, John, *Prize fighting: the age of regency boximania* (Newtown Abbot, 1971).

Gantz, Ida, *Signpost to Eyrecourt: portrait of the Eyre family* (Bath, 1975).

Gattrell, Vic, *City of laughter: sex and society in eighteenth-century London* (London, 2006).

Garnham, Neal, 'The trials of James Cotter and Henry, Baron Barry of Santry: two case studies in the administration of criminal justice in early eighteenth-century Ireland', *IHS*, 31 (1999), 328–52.

—, 'The role of cricket in Victorian and Edwardian Ireland', *Sporting Traditions*, 19:2 (2003), pp 27–48.

—, 'Sport history: the cases of Britain and Ireland stated', *Journal of Sport History*, 3:2 (2004), pp 139–44

—, 'The survival of popular blood sports in Victorian Ulster', *PRIA*, 107C (2007), pp 107–26.

—, '"To die with honour or gain the day": Dan Donnelly as an Irish sporting hero', *IHS*, 37 (2010–11), pp 535–49.

Geoghegan, Patrick, *Robert Emmet: a life* (Dublin, 2002).

—, *The Irish Act of Union: a study in high politics, 1798–1801* (Dublin, 1999).

Gibson, C.B., *The history of the county and city of Cork* (2 vols, Cork, 1861).

Gilbert, Sir John, *History of the city of Dublin* (3 vols, Dublin, 1859–61).

Gilbey, Walter, *Sport in the olden time* (reprint, Liss, Hampshire, 1975).

Gillespie, Raymond, *Seventeenth-century Ireland; making Ireland modern* (Dublin, 2005).

—, *The transformation of the Irish economy, 1550–1700* (Dundalk, 1991).

—, *Reading Ireland: print, reading and social change in early modern Ireland* (Manchester, 2005).

— and Andrew Hadfield (eds), *The Oxford history of the Irish book, vol. 3: the Irish book in English, 1550–1800* (Oxford, 2006).

Gray, W. Russel, 'For whom the bell tolled: the decline of British prize fighting in the Victorian era', *Journal of Popular Culture*, 21:2 (1987), pp 53–64.

Griffin, Emma, 'Popular culture in industrializing England', *Historical Journal*, 45 (2002), 619–35.

—, *England's revelry: a history of popular sports and pastimes, 1660–1830* (Oxford, 2005).

—, *Bloodsport: hunting in Britain since 1066* (London, 2007).

Guinness, Desmond, 'Robert Healy: an eighteenth-century Irish sporting artist', *Apollo*, 115:240 (Feb. 1982), pp 80–5.

Hayton, D.W., 'Moral reform and country politics in the late seventeenth-century House of Commons', *Past and Present*, 128 (1990), pp 48–91.

—, 'A presence in the country: the Brodricks and their "interest"' in idem, *The Anglo-Irish experience, 1680–1730: religion, identity and patriotism* (Woodbridge, 2012), pp 76–103.

—, 'A question of upbringing: Thomas Prior, Sir John Rawdon, 3rd bt., and the mentality and ideology of "improvement"' in idem (ed.), *The Anglo-Irish experience, 1680–1730: religion, identity and patriotism* (Woodbridge, 2012), pp 174–98.

—, 'Irish tories and victims of Whig persecution: Sacheverell fever by proxy', *Parliamentary History*, 31:1 (2012), pp 80–98.

Hennessey, W.M., 'On the Curragh of Kildare', *PRIA*, 9 (1864–6), pp 343–55.

Henry, Brian, *Dublin hanged: crime, law enforcement and punishment in late eighteenth-century Dublin* (Dublin, 1994).

H.G.H.C., *Amateur Boxing Association: its history* (London, 1965).

Hickey, Kieran, *Wolves in Ireland: a natural and cultural history* (Dublin, 2011).

Hill, J.R., *From patriots to unionists: Dublin civil politics and Irish Protestant patriotism 1660–1840* (Oxford, 1997).

Holt, Richard, 'Heroes of the north: sport and the shaping of regional identity' in Jeff Hill and Jack Williams (eds), *Sport and identity in the north of England* (Keele, 1996), pp 137–64.

Hore, John Philip, *The history of Newmarket and the annals of the turf* (2 vols, London, 1886).

Hore, P.H., *History of the town and county of Wexford* (London, 1906).

Huggins, Mike, *Flat-racing and British society, 1790–1914: a social and economic history* (London, 1999).

Hunt, Tom, *Sport and society in Victorian Ireland: the case of Westmeath* (Cork, 2007).

Hutton, Ronald, *Charles the second, king of England, Scotland, and Ireland* (Oxford, 1989).

—, *The Stations of the sun: a history of the ritual year in Britain* (Oxford, 1996).

Hynes, Eugene, 'The great hunger and Irish Catholicism', *Societas*, 8 (1978), pp 137–55.

James, K.J., *Handloom weavers in Ulster's linen industry, 1815–1914* (Dublin, 2006).

Jobey, George, 'Cock-fighting in Northumberland and Durham during the eighteenth and nineteenth centuries', *Archaeologia Aeliana*, 5th series, 20 (1992), pp 1–25.

Kelly, James, *Prelude to Union: Anglo-Irish politics in the 1780s* (Cork, 1992).

—, 'Jonathan Swift and the Irish economy in the 1720s', *Eighteenth-Century Ireland*, 6 (1991), pp 7–36.

—, 'Harvests and hardship: famine and scarcity in Ireland in the late 1720s', *Studia Hibernica*, 26 (1991–2), pp 65–106.

—, *'That damn'd thing called honour': duelling in Ireland, 1580–1860* (Cork, 1995).

—, 'The glorious and immortal memory: commemoration and Protestant identity in Ireland, 1660–1800', *PRIA*, 94C (1994), pp 25–52.

—, 'Conservative political thought in late eighteenth-century Ireland' in S.J. Connolly (ed.), *Political ideas in eighteenth century Ireland* (Dublin, 2000), pp 195–221.

—, *Sir Edward Newenham, MP, 1734–1814: defender of the Protestant constitution* (Dublin, 2002).

—, *The Liberty and Ormond boys: factional riot in eighteenth-century Dublin* (Dublin, 2006).

—, 'Political publishing, 1700–1800' in Raymond Gillespie and Andrew Hadfield (eds), *The Oxford history of the book in Ireland, iii: early modern Ireland* (Oxford, 2006), pp 215–33.

—, 'Health for sale: mountebanks, doctors, printers and the supply of medication in eighteenth-century Ireland', *PRIA* 108C (2008), pp 75–113.

—, *Sir Richard Musgrave, 1746–1818: ultra-Protestant ideologue* (Dublin, 2009).

—, 'Drinking the waters: balneotherapeutic medicine in Ireland, 1660–1850', *Studia Hibernica*, 35 (2008–9), pp 117–18.

—, 'The emergence of the middle class and the decline of duelling' in Maria Luddy and Fintan Lane (eds), *Politics, society and the middle classes in modern Ireland* (Basingstoke, 2009), pp 89–106.

— and M.J. Powell (eds), *Clubs and societies in eighteenth-century Ireland* (Dublin, 2010).

—, 'The politics of Protestant ascendancy in county Longford' in Martin Morris and Fergus O'Ferrall (eds), *Longford: history and society* (Dublin, 2010), pp 179–202.

— and Martyn J. Powell, 'Introduction' in idem (eds), *Clubs and societies in eighteenth-century Ireland* (London, 2010).

—, 'The pastime of the elite: clubs and societies and the promotion of horse-racing' in James Kelly and M.J. Powell (eds), *Clubs and societies in eighteenth-century Ireland* (Dublin, 2010), pp 409–24.

—, 'The Bar Club, 1787–93: a dining club case study' in idem and M.J. Powell (eds), *Clubs and societies in eighteenth-century Ireland* (Dublin, 2010), pp 373–91.

—, 'Sustaining a confessional state: the Irish parliament and Catholicism' in idem, David Hayton and John Bergin (eds), *The eighteenth-century composite state: representative institutions in Ireland and Europe, 1689–1800* (Basingstoke, 2010), pp 44–77.

— and D.W. Hayton, 'The Irish parliament in European context: a representative institution in a composite state', and 'Conclusion' in Kelly, James, D.W. Hayton, and John Bergin (eds), *The eighteenth-century composite state in Ireland and Europe, 1689–1800* (Basingstoke, 2010), pp 3–20, 244–53.

—, 'The historiography of the penal laws' in John Bergin et al. (eds), *New perspectives on the penal laws* Eighteenth-Century Ireland: special issue no. 1 (Dublin, 2011), pp 27–52.

—, 'Elite political clubs, 1770–1800' in idem and M.P. Powell (eds), *Clubs and societies in eighteenth-century Ireland* (Dublin, 2010), pp 264–89.

—, '"Disappointing the boundless ambitions of France": Irish Protestants and the fear of invasion, 1661–1815', *Studia Hibernica*, 37 (2011), pp 27–105.

—, 'Introduction: establishing the context' in idem and Ciaran MacMurchaidh (eds), *Irish and English: essays on the linguistic and cultural frontier 1600–1900* (Dublin, 2012), pp 15–42.

—, 'Protestants and the Irish language' in idem and Ciaran MacMurchaidh (eds), *Irish and English: essays on the linguistic and cultural frontier 1600–1900* (Dublin, 2012), pp 189–217.

Kelsey, Harry, *Sir Francis Drake: the queen's pirate* (London, 1998).

Kennedy, Liam, 'The rural economy, 1820–1914' in idem and Philip Ollerenshaw (eds), *An economic history of Ulster, 1820–1940* (Manchester, 1985), pp 1–61.

King, S.J., *A history of hurling* (Dublin, 1996).

Kinahan, G.H., 'Sepulchral and other prehistoric relics, counties Wexford and Wicklow', *PRIA,* 2nd series, 2 (1879–88), pp 152–60.

Knox, Alexander, *A history of the county of Down from the most remote period to the present day* ... (Dublin, 1875).

Krzemienski, E.D.,'Fulcrum of change: boxing and society at a crossroads', *International Journal of the History of Sport,* 21:2 (2004), pp 161–80.

Lane, Fintan, *Long bullets: a history of road bowling in Ireland* (Cork, 2005).

Leighton, C.D.A., *Catholicism in a Protestant kingdom: a study of the Irish ancien regime* (Dublin, 1994).

Lennon, Colm, *Society and religion in Dublin, 1548–1613: the urban patricians in the age of Reformation* (Dublin, 1989).

— and John Monague, *John Rocque's Dublin: a guide to the Georgian city* (Dublin, 2009).

Little, Patrick, *Lord Broghill and the Cromwellian union with Ireland and Scotland* (Woodbridge, 2004).

Livesey, Jim, *Civil society and empire: Ireland and Scotland in the eighteenth-century Atlantic world* (New Haven, 2009).

Livingstone, Peadar, *The Monaghan story* (reprint, Enniskillen, 1980).

Lowry-Corry, S.R., *The history of two Ulster manors* (London and Dublin, 1881).

Lucas, A.T., 'Hair hurling balls', *Journal of the Cork Archaeological and Historical Society,* second series, 57 (1952), pp 99–104.

—, 'Two recent finds: hair hurling ball from county Limerick', *Journal of the Cork Archaeological and Historical Society,* second series, 58 (1954), pp 78–9.

—, 'Hair hurling balls from county Limerick and county Tipperary', *Journal of the Cork Archaeological and Historical Society,* second series, 76 (1971), pp 79–80.

—, 'Hair hurling ball from Aughrim, county Kerry', *Journal of the Cork Archaeological and Historical Society,* second series, 82 (1977), pp 30–2.

Lynam, Shevawn, *Humanity Dick: a biography of Richard Martin, MP, 1754–1834* (London, 1975).

Lynch, Kathleen, *Roger Boyle, first earl of Orrery* (Tennessee, 1965).

Lynch, Ronan, *The Kirwans of Castlehacket, co. Galway: history, folklore and mythology in an Irish horse-racing family* (Dublin, 2006).

Magennis, Eoin, *The Irish political system, 1740–1765: the golden age of the Undertakers* (Dublin, 2000).

Mandle, W.F., *The Gaelic Athletic Association and Irish nationalist politics, 1884–1924* (London, 1987).

MacBride, Ian, 'Memory and forgetting: Ulster Presbyterians and 1798' in Thomas Bartlett et al. (eds), *1798: a bicentenary* (Dublin, 2003), pp 478–96.

MacDonagh, Oliver, *The inspector general: Sir Jeremiah Fitzpatrick and the politics of social reform, 1783–1802* (London, 1981).

—, *A pattern of government growth, 1800–60: the Passenger Acts and their enforcement* (London, 1961).

McCabe, Desmond, *St Stephen's Green, Dublin, 1660–1875* (Dublin, 2011).

McEvoy, Michael, *Return to the bull ring* (Drogheda, 1997).

McDowell, R.B., 'Introduction' in *The autobiography of Archibald Hamilton Rowan,* ed., William H. Drummond, introduction R.B. McDowell (repr., Shannon, 1972), pp v–xi.

McGinn, Brian 'A century before the GAA: hurling in eighteenth-century New York', *Journal of the New York Irish History Roundtable* 11 (1997), pp 51–9.

McGonigle, Martin, 'Hurling in Donegal before the GAA', *Donegal Annual*, no 64, 2012, pp 39–51.

McGrath, C.I., 'Securing the Protestant interest: the origins and purpose of the penal laws of 1695', *IHS*, 30 (1996), pp 25–46.

MacGregor, Arthur, *Animal encounters and animal interaction in Britain from the Norman conquest to World War One* (London, 2012).

Macintyre, Angus, *The Liberator: Daniel O'Connell and the Irish party, 1830–47* (London, 1965).

McLysaght, Edward, *Irish life in the seventeenth century* (2nd ed., Shannon, 1969).

McNamara, L.F., 'Some matters touching Dromoland: letters of father and son, 1758–59', *North Munster Antiquarian Journal*, 28 (1986), pp 62–70.

McParland, Edward, 'The Wide Streets Commissioners: their importance for Dublin architecture in the late eighteenth-early nineteenth century', *Bulletin of the Irish Georgian Society*, 15 (1972), pp 1–32.

—, *Public architecture in Ireland, 1680–1760* (London, 2001).

McSkimmin, Samuel, *The history and antiquities of the county of the town of Carrickfergus, from the earliest records till 1839: also a statistical survey of said county* (Belfast, 1909).

McTear, Thomas, 'Personal recollections of the beginning of the century', *UJA*, 2nd series, 5 (1899), pp 67–80.

Malcolm, Elizabeth, *'Ireland sober, Ireland free': drink and temperance in nineteenth-century Ireland* (Dublin, 1986).

Malcomson, A.P.W., *Nathaniel Clements: government and the governing elite in Ireland, 1725–75* (Dublin, 2005).

—, 'The fall of the house of Conolly, 1758–1803' in Eoin Magennis and Allan Blackstock (eds), *Politics and political culture in Britain and Ireland, 1750–1850* (Belfast, 2007), pp 107–56.

Malcolmson, R.W., *Popular recreation in English society 1700–1850* (Cambridge, 1973).

Magoun, F.P., *History of football from the beginnings to 1877* (Köln, 1938).

Mahony, Noel and Robert Whiteside, *Cricket at the King's Hospital, 1897–1997* (Dublin, 1997).

Maxwell, Constantia, *Dublin under the Georges, 1714–1830* (London, 1937).

Mayes, Elizabeth (ed.), *Aras an Uachtaráin* (2nd edn., Dublin, 2013).

Mayo, Earl of and W.B. Boulton, *A history of the Kildare Hunt* (London, 1913).

Middleton, Iris M., 'Cock-fighting in Yorkshire during the early eighteenth century', *Northern History*, 40 (2003), pp 139–46.

—, 'The origins of English fox hunting and the myth of Hugo Meynell and the Quorn', *Sport in History*, 25 (2005), pp 1–16.

— and Wray Vamplew, 'Horse-racing and the Yorkshire leisure calendar in the early eighteenth century', *Northern History*, 40:2 (2003), pp 259–76.

Mirala, Petri, *Freemasonry in Ulster, 1733–1813: a social and political history of the masonic brotherhood in the north of Ireland* (Dublin, 2007).

Mulcahy, John, 'Lost to Castletown', *Irish Arts Review*, Summer 2012, pp 98–103

Mullin, T.H., *Ulster's historic city: Derry/Londonderry* (Coleraine, 1986).

Munter, Robert, *The history of the newspaper in Ireland, 1685–1760* (Cambridge, 1966).

Murray, Raymond (ed.), *The Armagh bullet thrower* (Armagh, 1976).

Myler, Patrick, *Regency rogue: Dan Donnelly, his life and legends* (Dublin, 1976).

Neely, W.G., *Kilcooley: land and people in Tipperary* (Dublin, 1983).

Ó Caithnia, Liam P., *Scéal na hiomána: ó thosach ama go 1884* (Baile Átha Cliath, 1980).

—, *Báirí cos in Éirinn (roimh bhunú na gCumann Eagraithe)* (Baile Átha Cliath, 1984).

Ó Casaide, Séamas, 'Street ballads on Irish boxers', *The Irish Book Lover*, 28 (1942), p. 91.

O'Connor, Ulick, *The Fitzwilliam storey* (Dublin, 1977).

Ó Crannlaighe, P., 'Cock-fighting', *The Bell*, 9:6 (Mar. 1945), pp 510–13.

O'Donoghue, Patrick, 'Causes of the opposition to tithes, 1830–38', *Studia Hibernica*, 5 (1965), pp 7–28.

O'Dowd, Mary, *A history of women in Ireland, 1500–1800* (London, 2005).

O'Dwyer, Michael, *The history of cricket in county Kilkenny – the forgotten game* (Kilkenny, 2006).

O'Farrell, Fergus, *Catholic Emancipation: Daniel O'Connell and the birth of Irish democracy* (Dublin, 1985).

Ó Gráda, Cormac, *Ireland before and after the famine: explorations in economic history, 1800–1925* (Manchester, 1988).

—, *Ireland: a new economic history, 1780–1939* (Oxford, 1994).

O'Kane, Finola, *William Ashford's Mount Merrion: the absent point of view* (Tralee, 2012).

—, *Ireland and the picturesque: design, landscape painting and tourism in Ireland, 1700–1830* (London, 2013).

O'Leary, Pat, (ed.), *Killeenadeema Aille: history and heritage* (Loughrea, 2009).

Ó Maolfabhail, Art, *Camán: two thousands years of hurling in Ireland* (Dundalk, 1973).

O'Sullivan, M.D., *Old Galway: the history of a Norman colony in Ireland* (Cambridge, 1942).

Ohlmeyer, Jane H., (ed.), *Ireland from independence to occupation, 1641–1660* (Cambridge, 1994).

—, *Making Ireland English: the Irish aristocracy of the seventeenth century* (London, 2012).

Palmer, Stanley H., *Police and protest in England and Ireland, 1780–1850* (Cambridge, 1988).

Paterson, T.G.F., 'Long bullets in county Armagh', *UJA*, 9 (1946), pp 58–68.

—, 'The game of long bullets in county Armagh', *County Louth Archaeological Journal*, 11:2 (1946), pp 90–5.

Patterson, James G., *In the wake of the Great Rebellion: republicanism, agrarianism and banditry in Ireland after 1798* (Manchester, 2008).

Pawlisch, Hans, *Sir John Davies and the conquest of Ireland: a study in legal imperialism* (Cambridge, 1985).

Peate, I.C., *The Denbigh cockpit and cock-fighting in Wales* (Cardiff, 1970).

Ponsonby, Gerald, 'Bishopscourt and its owners', *Journal of the County Kildare Archaeological Society*, 8 (1915–17), pp 3–29.

Porter, J.H., 'Cock-fighting in the eighteenth and nineteenth centuries: from popularity to suppression', *Reported Transactions of the Devonshire Association for the advancement of science*, 118 (1986), pp 63–71.

Powell, M.J., *The politics of consumption in eighteenth-century Ireland* (Basingstoke, 2003).

—, 'Hunting clubs and societies' in James Kelly and M.J. Powell (eds), *Clubs and societies in eighteenth-century Ireland* (Dublin, 2010), pp 392–408.

—, 'Moral economy and popular protest in the late eighteenth century' in Michael Brown and Sean Patrick Donlan (eds), *Law and other legalities of Ireland, 1689–1850* (Aldershot, 2010), pp 231–53.

Power, Sir John, *Memoir of the Kilkenny hunt* (2nd ed., Dublin. 1911).

Prim, J.G.A., 'Olden popular pastimes in Kilkenny', *Transactions of the Kilkenny Archaeological Society*, first series, 2 (1852–3), pp 319–35.

Robinson, J.R., *The last earls of Barrymore* (London, 1894).

Rogers, Mary, *Prospect of Fermanagh* (Enniskillen, 1982).

Rogers, Pat, 'The Waltham blacks and the Black Act', *The Historical Journal*, 17 (1974), pp 465–86.

Rushe, Denis Carolan, *Monaghan in the eighteenth century* (Dublin, 1916).

Ryan, David, *Blasphemers and blackguards: Ireland's hellfire clubs* (Dublin, 2012).

George Ryley Scott, *The history of cock-fighting* (London, [1957]).

Sheard, K.G., 'Aspects of boxing in the western "civilizing process"', *International Review for the Sociology of Sport*, 32 (1997), pp 31–57.

—, 'Boxing in the western civilizing process' in E. Dunning. D. Malcolm and I. Waddington (eds), *Sports histories: figurational histories in the development of modern sports* (London, 2004), pp 15–30.

Sheridan, Edel, 'Designing the capital city, Dublin 1660–1810' in Joseph Brady and Anngret Simms (eds), *Dublin through space and time, c.900–1900* (Dublin, 2001), pp 66–135.

Simms, J.G., *Jacobite Ireland, 1685–90* (London, 1966).

Simpson, Linzi, *Smock Alley Theatre: evolution of a building* (Dublin, 1996).

Sneddon, Andrew, 'Legislating for economic development: Irish fisheries as a case study in the limitations of "improvement"' in D.W. Hayton, James Kelly and John Bergin (eds), *The eighteenth-century composite state: representative institutions in Ireland and Europe, 1689–1800* (Basingstoke, 2010), pp 136–59.

Sweeney, Tony, Annie Sweeney, Francis Hyland, *The Sweeney guide to the Irish turf from 1501 to 2001* (Dublin, 2002).

Thomas, Keith, *Man and the natural world: a history of the modern sensibility* (Oxford, 1983).

Thompson, E.P., *Whigs and hunters: the origin of the Black Act* (London, 1975).

Twomey, Brendan, *Smithfield and the parish of St Paul, Dublin, 1698–1750* (Dublin, 2005).

—, 'Financing speculative property development in early eighteenth-century Dublin' in Christine Casey (ed.), *The eighteenth-century Dublin townhouse* (Dublin, 2010), pp 29–45.

Vamplew, Wray, *The turf: social and economic history of horse racing* (London, 1976).

Walsh, M.W., 'November bull-running in Stamford, Lincolnshire', *Journal of Popular Culture*, 30 (2004), pp 233–47.

Walsh, P. 'Eighteenth-century Kilkenny', *Old Kilkenny Review*, 17 (1965), pp 42–3.

Welcome, John, *Irish horse racing: an illustrated history* (London, 1982).

Whelan, Kevin, 'The geography of hurling', *History Ireland*, 1:1 (1993), pp 27–31.

—, 'An underground gentry? Catholic middlemen in eighteenth-century Ireland', *Eighteenth-Century Ireland*, 10 (1995), pp 7–68.

Wilson, Ben, *Decency and disorder: the age of cant, 1789–1837* (London, 2007).

Wynne-Thomas, Peter, *The history of cricket: from the Weald to the world* (London, 1997).

UNPUBLISHED THESES

Burke, Nuala T., 'Dublin 1600–1800: a study in urban morphogenesis' (TCD, PhD, 1972).

Fleming, D.A., 'The government and politics of provincial Ireland, 1691–1781' (Oxford University, DPhil, 2005).

Joseph Liechty, 'Irish evangelicalism, Trinity College Dublin, and the mission of the Church of Ireland at the end of the eighteenth century' (NUIM, PhD, 1987).

Richey, R.A., 'Landed society in mid-eighteenth century county Down' (QUB, PhD, 2000).

WORKS OF REFERENCE

Alumni Dublinenses, ed., G.D. Burtchaell and T.U. Sadleir (London, 1924).

Burke, Sir Bernard, *A genealogical and heraldic history of the landed gentry of Ireland* (London, 1912).

Burke's Irish family records (London, 1976).

Cokayne, G.E., *The complete peerage*, edited by Vicary Gibbs et al. (13 vols in 14, London, 1910–59).

Cokayne, G.E., *The complete baronetage* (5 vols, Exeter, 1900–6).

Collins English dictionary (Glasgow, 1993).

Dictionary of Irish biography, eds James McGuire and James Quinn (9 vols, Cambridge, 2009).

Dictionary of national biography (22 vols, Oxford, 1908–9).

Dublin directory, 1783

Encyclopedia of traditional British rural sports, eds Tony Collins, John Martin and Wray Vamplew (Abingdon and New York, 2005).

English short title catalogue (3rd ed., London, 2003).

Handbook of British chronology, eds F.M. Powicke and E.B. Fryde (London, 1961).

Johnston-Liik, Edith, *History of the Irish parliament, 1692–1800* (6 vols, Belfast, 2002).

Moody, T.W. et al. (eds), *A new history of Ireland*, ix (Oxford, 1984).

O'Higgins, Paul, *A bibliography of Irish trials and other legal proceedings* (Abingdon, 1986).

Oxford Classical dictionary (Oxford, 1949).

Oxford dictionary of national biography (60 vols, Oxford, 2004).

Oxford English dictionary (2nd, ed., 20 vols, Oxford, 1989).

Pollard, M., *A dictionary of members of the Dublin book trade, 1550–1800* (London, 2000).

Strickland, W.G., *A dictionary of Irish artists* (2 vols, Shannon, 1969).

The A–Z of Georgian Dublin: John Rocque's maps of the city in 1756 and the county in 1760 (Lympne Castle, 1998).

Toole, James, *Newsplan: report of the Newsplan project in Ireland* (London, 1992).

Webb, A.J., *Compendium of Irish biography* (Dublin, 1878).

Index